LUTZEN & BAUTZEN

Napoleon's Spring Campaign of 1813

by

George Nafziger

EMPEROR'S PRESS
Chicago, Illinois
"Simply the Finest!"

LUTZEN & BAUTZEN

©Emperor's Press

Original Edition; Published in 1992

Printed and Bound in the United States of America

ISBN 0-9626655-6-8

THE EMPEROR'S PRESS
5744 West Irving Park Road
Chicago, Il. 60634 U.S.A.
Toll Free, if calling in U.S.A: 1.800.59.EAGLE
Calling from outside U.S.A: 312.777.7307
"Simply the Finest!"

• •

BOOKS BY GEORGE NAFZIGER
Poles and Saxons of the Napoleonic Wars, with Mariusz T. Wesolowski and
Tom Devoe, Emperor's Press, 1991
Napoleon's Invasion of Russia, Presidio Press, 1988
The British Military, 1803–1815, with S.J.Park, RAFM Company, 1983
Russian Army, RAFM Company, 1983

PRIVATELY PUBLISHED
The Armies of Spain and Portugal, 1992
The Wurttemburg Army, 1992
The Armies of Westphalia and Cleves-Berg, 1991
The Armies of the Kingdom of Bavaria and the Grand Duchy of Wurzburg, 1991
The Armies of Germany and the Confederation of the Rhine, Volume I, 1991
Napoleon's German Enemies: The Armies of Hanover, Brunswick, Hesse-Cassel,
and the Hanseatic Cities, 1990

For more information on books by George Nafziger, please write to the
EMPEROR'S PRESS.

TABLE OF CONTENTS

Introduction

This work follows on my study of 1812 campaign. The campaign is best seen as a continuation of Napoleon's greatest campaign—1812–1814. Though the 1812 campaign was an unprecedented disaster in the annals of military history, it was the 1813 campaign that broke the back of the French empire and truly turned the tide of French victories that had begun during the Revolution.

The campaign started with two weakened and struggling protagonists, France and Russia. The French Grande Armée staggered out of Russia with the Russian armies stumbling along, victorious, but suffering, after it. Then Napoleon's empire began to crumble. Bitter enemies sprang forward where there had been defeated and servile allies. They were enemies who had learned the art of war at Napoleon's knee. What was about to unfold was yet another bloody year of what history should truly have called the First World War.

The year 1813 saw armies of over a million men struggling over the fate of Europe. The winners were to set the stage for a century to come. Antagonism led to insult and insult to injury. Each side committed acts against the other that were to fester for generations again. The seeds of German nationalism were to sprout out of this campaign and, in 1870, lead to a unified Germany.

Territories seized and the distribution of power established during this period, coupled with agreements made at the Congress of Vienna after Napoleon was finally sent to St. Helena contributed directly to future European wars in 1866, 1870, 1914, and 1939.

Because of this, the year 1813 takes a significance in the history of western man like few other years. It was the turning point of many events. It seemed to be the end of Revolutionary France, it was the end of one of Europe's last great empires, it was a brief return to the way things were. Seemingly it put the European monarchies securely back on their thrones, but those thrones were gravely undermined and the year 1848 would shake them again.

1813 was a year of change, a year of struggle, and a year of destiny. Napoleon's ongoing, festering fight with England had kept him from total control of Europe. The Russian campaign had occurred as his economic war with England had begun to hemorrhage through Russian ports. His military campaign against Russia was an unmitigated disaster and the 1813 spring campaign was truly Napoleon's last military opportunity to reestablish his hegemony over continental Europe. His failure to achieve a decision in the Spring faced him with the prospect of a growing number of nations arrayed against him. Failure to reach a decision in the spring led to a desperate arms race during the summer of 1813 and two more years of warfare. The 1813 Spring campaign was pivotal. Decisions were made, opportunities missed and seized, troops pushed to the limits of endurance as Napoleon faced his old enemies once again on the battlefields of Germany. The old Napoleonic genius reappeared as he outmaneuvered and outfought his enemies, yet rather than grasping victory, the elusive crushing victory and his enemies slipped through his fingers as the sands of time slipped from January to June.

Because of the magnitude of events in 1813 this work is limited to the spring campaign. It covers the period from 1 January 1813 to early June 1813, when the famous summer armistice was signed and put into effect. A single volume could not hope to cover all of the events of 1813 and in order to keep the history in workable portions this study was limited to what can reasonably be covered in a single tome.

NOTES ON THE TEXT

To minimize the difficulty in keeping track of the various French and allied corps, French corps are always cited in Roman numerals, i.e. XVII Corps, and allied corps are always cited in Arabic numerals, i.e. 1st Corps.

The notation 1/,2/,Fus/1st Pomeranian Infantry Regiment indicates that the 1st, 2nd and Fusilier Battalions of the regiment are present. If used before a cavalry regiment, it means the 1st, 2nd, etc., Squadrons are present. This abbreviation is used extensively throughout this work.

ACKNOWLEDGEMENTS

I would like to acknowledge the assistance of a few people, without whom this work could not have been what it is. The first is the staff of the Anne S.K.Brown Military Collection, Brown University. They most graciously received me on numerous occassions, opening the collection to me, and giving me access to anything that they could to assist my researches.

The second is Mr. J.J.Slonaker of the U.S. Army Military History Institute who opened the doors to the Army's historical library to me, allowing me to have copies made of numerous rare and obscure works that have contributed significantly to this work.

Thanks must also be extended to the staff of the Cincinnati Public Library I buried with inter-library loan requests, sending them off seeking obscure works that haven't seen the light of day for years.

A special acknowledgement and most humble thanks goes to Mr. Warren Worley, who acted as a technical editor, catching various discrepancies, helping to flesh out the text with technical details and, most important of all, helping me to see the forest through the trees when I was up to my eyes in computer printouts, floppy disks, microfilms, and mountains of old tomes.

DEDICATION

This work is dedicated to the memory of
Richard B. Harrington
1926-1989
Curator
Anne S.K. Military Collection
1951-1989

Out of the Snows of Russia
The Military Situation
January-February 1813

Napoleon was in Paris on 19 December when Murat, King of Naples and the acting commander of the Grande Armée, arrived in Königsberg with a small cavalry escort. He had been preceded all week by swarms of fugitives fleeing the Russian winter. He expected an army corps of 25,000 men to arrive shortly but he was to be sadly disappointed, for two days later only a small force of 400 to 500 infantry and 200 to 300 cavalry arrived. All were in miserable condition and lacking order.

Exhausted and eviscerated, the French army had stumbled out of Russia. Of the 680,500 men that Napoleon had organized for the campaign against Russia, barely 93,000 remained. The main army, once boasting 450,000 men, now had a mere 25,000 men. Of the 66,345 men that had belonged to Davout's I Corps in June 1812, there remained only 2,281 standing to the colors. The 50,000 man Imperial Guard had been reduced to 500 men under arms and a further 800 sick, of whom 200 would never return to arms. The other corps under Schwarzenberg, Reynier, Macdonald and Augereau had returned with a total of 68,000 men. They had not been as heavily engaged as the main army. On 11 January the VII Corps of General Reynier contained 6,000 Saxons, 2,000 Poles, and 1,500 French. It was on the left bank of the Bug river, where it formed the left wing of the Austrian Hilfkorps under Feldmarschal Schwarzenberg.

Napoleon had left the army on 5 December 1812, before it had reached the comparative safety of Germany, for many reasons. He was concerned about the political situation in France and with his allies. When he left, Napoleon had transferred command to Maréchal Murat, King of Naples and his brother-in-law.

Murat began sending the wounded officers to Stettin and Cüstrin and declared that every soldier found on the right bank of the Vistula without authorization was to be considered an enemy. On 20 December the Imperial Guard was directed to Königsberg. The I and VI Corps went to Thorn to reorganize and recover from the campaign. The II and III corps were in Marienburg, the IV and IX Corps were in Marienwerder, the V Corps was in Warsaw, the VI Corps was in Plock, the artillery and engineers were in Danzig, the dismounted line cavalry was in Königsberg, and the Imperial Guard Cavalry was in Elbing. Despite the return to Germany, the French losses continued to mount. In Königsberg alone 50 to 60 soldiers died daily from the cumulative effects of the campaign and the frozen bivouacs.

Murat's order of the day of 31 December listed the positions of the French army as follows: The Imperial Guard was in Königsberg, covered by Heudelet's division (XI Corps) in Labiau. The I Corps was in Thorn, II Corps was in Marienburg, III Corps was in Elbing, IV Corps in Marienwerder, V Corps in Warsaw, VI Corps in Plock, VII Corps in Wengrod, on the road from Byalistok to Warsaw, VIII Corps was withdrawing into Westphalia, IX Corps was in Danzig, the X Corps was in Tilsit, moving on Königsberg and the XI Corps (2,000 men) was in Berlin.[1]

On 31 December Murat learned that there were 20,000 men around Königsberg who were capable of bearing arms and that 6,000 to 7,000 more could be rounded up from various posts in Prussia and the Grand Duchy of Warsaw. The bulk of the French were, however, totally without arms and equipment. It would take time to arm, provision and organize the survivors from the substantial magazines Napoleon had organized before he invaded Russia. Among his forces Murat had 7 to 8,000 officers and cadres who were useless when the reorganizations

THE FRENCH ARMY STUMBLED OUT OF RUSSIA

began. They were sent back to the depots in France so that they could be fleshed out and reformed into operational units.

Murat felt it was possible to hold the Vistula with his forces. He knew that it would be months before Napoleon could organize and send him a new army. If the Russians were to advance he would have to hold them with the forces at hand. However, Murat was certain that the Russians were not in a state to continue the winter campaign and that there would be some respite.

After a few days Murat was joined by Heudelet's Division of Augereau's XI Corps. It came from Hanover and had 10,000 infantry, 24 cannon, and Cavaignac's cavalry brigade (eight squadrons - 1,500 men). In addition, around Thorn and Plock there were 2,000 French, 4,500 Bavarians, and 1,500 Westphalians formed into batallions de marche,[2] who had just arrived from their homelands.

Despite the positive side to the reorganization, bad news came quickly. Yorck's Prussian division of Macdonald's X Corps, defected to the Russians on 30 December, as a result of the Convention of Tauroggen. This was too much for Murat, who hastily turned command of the Grande Armée over to Prince Eugène, Napoleon's adoptive son. As Murat fled to the warmth of Naples, Eugène shouldered the greatest burden of his life.[3]

At the end of December, before he retired to Naples, Murat had found himself commanding 22,000 men on his right, towards Tilsit, 22,000 men moving on Pregel, and a further 45,000 perfectly organized and equipped men on his far right. In addition, he had 25,000 men organizing in Königsberg. This gave him a total of 90,000 men to oppose the Russian army, if it chose to cross the Niemen.

Murat calculated that in two months he would have a reserve of fresh men join him. This included 20,000 men he had sent to rearm and equip themselves in the villages of the Vistula; a further 15,000 new drafts being raised in the Grand Duchy of Warsaw; Grenier's 20,000 man 35th Division, then in Franconia, enroute from Italy; 2,000 Young Guards then on the Oder; 1,200

Baden troops then in Karlsruhe; and 10,000 Prussians Napoleon had demanded from the King of Prussia as he passed through Germany on his way to France.

Despite the French propaganda, the Russian armies were not reduced to total impotence. They had not fallen apart as had the Grande Armée. Their continuing advance forced Murat to withdraw from Königsberg and reestablish the French position in Posen. The Russian army was still advancing westwards in late December. On 17 December Wittgenstein's forces were four miles north of Vilna and consisted of 1,207 officers, 33,236 men and 191 guns. Colonel von Tettenborn was in Tilsit on 21 December with 600 cossacks. General Paulucci, commander of the Riga garrison, had 2,213 men and six guns in Memel on 27 December. On 29 December Admiral Tchichagov's army, consisting of 15,500 men and 130 guns, and Platov's 6,600 cossacks and 16 guns were in Kovno. Tormassov's 17,000 men and 112 guns were in Vilna with the army's advanced guard, General Winzingerode had 16,000 men and 96 guns, and Vasil'chikov had another 11,800 men and 96 guns. The Russian left was on the Bug under General Osten-Sacken. Under him was General Mussin-Puschkin's corps with 19,345 men and 92 guns and General Essen III's corps with 9,139 men and 45 guns.[4]

On 31 December the Russian army stood posed on the eastern borders of Prussia. A corps of 6,000 to 8,000 men commanded by Generallieutenant Count Paulucci stood near Memel. The 1st Corps of General Wittgenstein stood with its first division, commanded by Generalmajor Diebitsch, in Lumpöhnen. Its second division, commanded by Generalmajor Schepelev, was in Tilsit shadowing the Polish-German division of French General Grandjean. Wittgenstein's third division was in quarters at Ragnit. To Wittgenstein's left was the cossack advanced guard of Generalmajor Czernichev, which was detached from Platov's cossack corps. The advanced guard of Admiral Tchichagov's Army of the Danube, commanded by Generallieutenant Tschlapitz, was in Raukischken. After a short pause, the Russian army was reorganized into the four main columns that were to form the heart of Russian army for the early period of the campaign. The main column consisted of Wittgenstein's command. The second column was commanded by General of Cavalry Platov and contained 6,000 to 7,000 cossacks. The third column was the Army of the Danube under Admiral Tchichagov and the fourth column was the main army, under General of Cavalry Tormassov. The Czar, Grand Duke Constantine and the supreme commander of the Russian armies, Field Marshal Kutusov, marched with Tormassov's column.[5]

FRENCH MANEUVERS

It was on 17 January that Murat abandoned the Grande Armée and passed command of it to Eugène. Eugène inventoried his battle worthy forces, not including what was moving to joint him, and found he had about 11,500.

While the shattered fragments were falling back to the west, they were being met by the beginning trickle of reinforcements that was to become a flood in a few short months. The 3/3rd, 3/105th, and 3/127th Line Regiments appeared and were assigned to Davout's I Corps to form the cadre of a new division. These three battalions, under the command of General Gérard, were in their turn directed to Bromberg. On 21 January Maréchal Davout moved the remains of the I and VIII Corps into Weichsel and the fortress of Thorn. He detached Gérard's division and passed control of it to Eugène.

On 11 January Murat ordered the 4th Bavarian Light Battalion, 281 men strong under the command of Oberstleutnant Theobald, into the fortress of Thorn.[6] On 17 January the Bavarian brigade of Generalmajor Zoller was dispatched to Thorn, bringing the Bavarian garrison to 130 officers and 2,597 men.[7] There it joined a 1,500 man French infantry garrison. Generallieutenant Wrede retained the rest of the Bavarian regiments of the 1st Division with him and moved into Polzk on 27 January. Later Davout decided to reduce the Bavarian forces in Thorn and to withdraw about 2,000 men. Instead the order was changed and French troops were withdrawn instead.[8]

Eugène directed the formation of a mobile corps to operate on the left bank of the Vistula, near Bromberg, in an effort to calm Schwarzenberg's fears and at the same time directed all remaining forces to Posen in an effort to organize what he called a "corps d'observation."[9]

The force he drew together consisted of the two battalions of the Velites of Turin and Florence, two cavalry companies of the Gardes d'Honneur of Turin and Florence, the three line battalions under General Gérard (30 officers & 1,662 men total); twelve elite Neapolitan infantry companies (drawn from the 5th, 6th, and 7th Infantry Regiments and formed into two battalions), the company of Neapolitan marines and a company of Neapolitan horse artillery (totaling 1,200 men); and the Imperial Guard under Maréchal Mortier (1,500 men and 300 horse) plus two battalions of voltigeurs and tirailleurs (37 officers and 1,584 men).

In addition, the Bavarian VI Corps, based on a report dating 10 January, consisted of 4,000 infantry and 300 cavalry. The Westphalian VIII Corps consisted principally of a column of recruits, 1,200 men, organized into two regiments de march.[10] Each of these regiments had two battalions formed with two companies.

There was still a fairly large number of Polish soldiers available. Of the five Lithuanian infantry regiments raised only three remained, but there were still four Vistula Regiments, and the 4th, 7th, and 9th Polish regiments assigned to the IX Corps. The 4th Vistula Regiment had about 1,500 men, but the 1st, 2nd and 3rd numbered about 150 men each. The 4th, 7th and 9th Polish Regiments had between them a total of about 700 men.

Only the 17th and 19th Lithuanian Uhlan Regiments under the command of by Prince de Gedroitze remained.[11] The others had been destroyed or simply vanished. Unfortunately, these two regiments were stripped of their horses in an effort to remount the Guard cavalry.

It was with these forces that the "Corps d'Observation" was formed. It consisted of four divisions. The French division under Gérard contained one battalion each of the 3/3rd, 3/105th and 3/127th Regiments, the twelve Neapolitan elite companies, the Neapolitan marine company and a Neapolitan horse battery equipped with eight guns. The force contained about 3,000 men. Gérard was ordered to move this force before Posen, half way to Gnesen.

A Polish division under General Girard was formed with the remnants of the 4th, 7th, and 9th Polish Infantry Regiments, the remnants of the 1st, 2nd, and 3rd Vistula Regiments, the entire 4th Vistula Regiment, and the 17th and 19th Lithuanian Uhlan Regiments, though the latter were not available until mid-February. The division had a total of about 3,500 men.[12] Girard was directed to establish his forces in Samter or Obernick

The Bavarian VI Corps was designated as the third division. Maréchal St. Cyr passed command on to General von Wrede. Wrede's division had, on 1 January, two infantry brigades, 3 squadrons, three 6pdr batteries, and four 12pdrs guns in a single battery. The total strength of this force was 296 officers, 4,574 men, 350 horses, and 145 train soldiers.[13] Wrede, in turn passed command of the corps to General Rechberg on 8 February.

By 1 February Rechberg's Bavarian division had badly declined in strength and contained only 120 officers, 2,892 infantry, 350 cavalry, 471 horses, and six guns. This force was directed to move on Gnesen.

The fourth division was the Guard division under General Roguet. On 23 January Eugène organized this reserve division in Posen. It consisted of two battalions of newly reformed Young Guard (one from 2nd Voltigeur Regiment and one from the 2nd Tirailleur Regiment), coming from Stettin, two battalions of Middle Guard (Velites of Turin and Velites of Florence), that had formed the headquarters guard, a small Hessian battalion, and small artillery train. This force had a total of about 2,000 men.[14] By 1 February this force raised its strength to 242 officers, 5,151 men, 1,365 horses, and 9 guns.[15]

The cavalry consisted of 650 Guard cavalry under the command of Major Lion, 124 Gardes d'Honneur from Florence and Turin, and about 300 Italian cavalry under the command of Major Palombini. This force of about 1,300 cavalry was placed under the command of Maréchal Bessières. The other force of cavalry available to the French was the 350 Bavarian cavalry under Rechberg.[16]

The artillery available to Eugène was very limited. He had a total of 27 guns available to him and a further 7 with I Corps distributed as follows:

	12pdrs	6pdrs	3pdrs	Howitzers
Imperial Guard	—	6	—	2
Hessians	—	1	—	—
Bavarians	—	4	—	2
Gérard	—	7	—	1
Girard	—	4	—	—
I Corps	1	1	3	2

THE RUSSIAN PURSUIT

As the other Russian columns had advanced, Sacken had pursued Reynier at a rather leisurely rate. The only actions were minor skirmishes between advanced posts. On 25 January Sacken was facing Reynier near Dobre, only three days march from Warsaw.

Four days earlier a force under Voronzov's consisting of about 500 to 600 infantry and a number of cossacks entered Bromberg where they encountered 800 infantry and four guns of Gérard's division. The Russians were driven out of the city and pursued about 3 miles from the city. Though a minor skirmish, it allowed Gérard to learn that the Russians had small forces supported by one or two batteries each in the towns of Culm and Culmsee, with another 200 horse and a half battery in Schweiz. His position was slowly being infiltrated by an enemy who was both more powerful and more mobile. It would soon be time for him also to move to stronger positions.[17]

THE RUSSIAN STRATEGY AGAINST SCHWARZENBERG

The goal of this maneuver was simple. The first four Russian columns would move to turn and envelope the French, then by a simple change of direction to the right, they would turn Schwarzenberg's right wing. Sacken's corps, seconded by the fifth column, was positioned to turn Reynier's flank, Schwarzenberg's right, if Schwarzenberg was to advance against the main Russian army.

Schwarzenberg had his headquarters and the advanced posts of the Austrian Hilfkorps in Pultusk. On his right, near Prassnitz, stood Reynier's Saxon corps. Schwarzenberg wrote to Eugène of this maneuver in an effort to justify his withdrawal south, but he neglected to advise Eugène, that he had deliberately allowed this enveloping maneuver to develop.

Schwarzenberg's forces consisted of 24,000 Austrians, 12,000 Saxons and French (on 16 January the Saxons had 246 officers, 7,121 men, and 2,507 horses), and a Polish division under Poniatowski consisting of 10,000 to 12,000 men. Sacken's forces and the main Russian army contained only about 60,000 to 62,000 men. Schwarzenberg had sufficient forces to maintain his position before the Vistula until Eugène could send him reinforcements, but he had no desire to engage the Russians.

During the Russian campaign, Schwarzenberg's corps had not been heavily engaged by the Russians. Indeed, he had been as passive as he could be, without obviously betraying the French main armies. This subtle betrayal continued and, during the last days of December, Schwarzenberg had concluded a "tacit and non-written" armistice with General Vasil'chikov.

The Austrian government was aware of this but, until it was certain that the French army was destroyed, determined to do little more than maintain its contingent in the theater of war. It chose to withdraw its forces to the frontier of Austrian Galicia, while at the same time entering into low level secret negotiations with the Russians.

A Russian Emissary To Schwarzenberg

The Czar, however, was unwilling to wait for this and sent a French emigre, Baron d'Anstett, to Schwarzenberg in an effort to persuade him to emulate Yorck's defection. However, Schwarzenberg lacked the strength of will and the hatred of the French of General Yorck. He formally refused d'Anstett's proposals. D'Anstett then pressed Schwarzenberg for a three month, written armistice, which stipulated solely that Schwarzenberg would withdraw towards the frontier of his country sufficiently to allow the Russians easy movement in the southern theater of war. Schwarzenberg refused to sign anything, and when he asked if this armistice was to extend to Reynier's corps, was told that the Czar would absolutely not enter into an accommodation with a French general. When d'Anstett departed no further agreement had been reached, but the understanding between Vasil'chikov and Schwarzenberg remained in effect.

Shortly after Schwarzenberg received an order from Vienna to withdraw into Austrian Galicia, but in a manner so as to not excite the suspicions of the French. Schwarzenberg quickly re-entered negotiations with Baron d'Anstett and renounced his earlier stipulations relating to Reynier's corps. However, nothing was signed and the entire agreement remained a verbal agreement between Schwarzenberg and Baron d'Anstett. The agreement was for an indeterminate time. The Austrians were to withdraw towards Austrian Galicia and occupy the Galician province of the Grand Duchy of Warsaw.[18]

The approach of the five Russian columns provided the pretext for this withdrawal and Schwarzenberg slowly moved south. He reported to Eugène that the Russians had enormous numbers and that they were maneuvering to attack him frontally, on the flanks and in the rear, that his position was untenable. Schwarzenberg directed the withdrawal of his forces behind the Vistula.

Eugène attempted to dissuade Schwarzenberg from this maneuver, stating that it was important that he remain firm before Warsaw. He further stated that it was impossible for the Russians to act so aggressively, because of the advanced season, the fatigue of their troops, and the logistical problems of interposing their army in the midst of so many French held fortresses.

Eugène did not leave the situation there, but chose to dispatch an aide, Commandant de Labédoyère, to the Austrian headquarters, to determine the truth of the matter. Labédoyère departed Posen on 26 January and returned on 1 February. He had seen enough to understand what was happening. He told Eugène that Schwarzenberg's advanced posts regularly communicated with the Russians, and did so in a non-hostile manner. He stated that Schwarzenberg was acting so as to in no way compromise his troops, and that everyone was imbued with one thought: to get to Galicia as quickly as possible.[19] Reynier's forces continued to withdraw on Schwarzenberg's right. His rearguard continually skirmished with Sacken's forces, clearly demonstrating the difference in attitude of the Russians towards the French and Saxons, vice their attitude towards the Austrians. However, soon after de Labédoyère's departure, Schwarzenberg brought the skirmishing to an end by covering Reynier's corps with a few Austrian cavalry squadrons.

Eugène soon received further confirmation of de Labédoyère's report, when Napoleon sent Schwarzenberg an order directing that under no conditions was he to withdraw behind Warsaw, but to move to Kalisch and Posen with Reynier's corps. The first order was issued on 30 January, and it was repeated on 3 February, when he announced the pending arrival in Posen of the divisions of Grenier and Lagrange and the support of 40,000 men in Kalisch. Lagrange's 31st Division was to be Eugène's second most powerful single division. It was formed with two brigades. Each brigade had two provisional demi-brigades formed with independent battalions of twelve line regiments. It had a total of 219 officers and 7,125 men on 5 January 1813.[20] Despite this, Schwarzenberg evaded these orders, reporting to Eugène that he was withdrawing towards Galicia.

As an excuse he pleaded that he could not stretch his communications with Cracow any further, because his reserve artillery, his supplies, reinforcements, and lines of evacuation for the hospitals lay in that direction. Furthermore, he stated, that once he was reorganized and reequipped he could, in the upcoming spring campaign, easily push the Russians out of the territory they occupied. Eugène became aware that Schwarzenberg's goal was, in fact, to abandon the French and was making every effort to enlarge the theater of war as much as possible.

Austrian Betrayal

On 24 January Schwarzenberg once again met with d'Anstett in the village of Wyzkof, on the Bug River, near Pultusk. Here they concluded an armistice that was of indefinite length. It required 15 days notice before the resumption of hostilities and that Warsaw would be evacuated as soon as possible, allowing the Russians to enter by 6 or 7 February. In eight days the Austrian corps was to have moved behind Pilicza, where it would remain for six days. From there it would move to Kamienna by 27 February where it would take up cantonments. Thus, Schwarzenberg would have successively evacuated the Grand Duchy of Warsaw and allow the Russians to safely fill the vacuum behind him without threat of aggressive action by the French.

In addition to allowing the Russians to safely occupy much of the Grand Duchy of Warsaw, it in essence handcuffed Reynier's corps. The Austrian corps supported his left flank. If he were aware of the armistice between the Austrians and Russians, he had two choices. He could remain where he was in relative safety, or he could attempt to rejoin the rest of the French army. If he were to attempt to rejoin the French forces in the Grand Duchy of Warsaw or Prussia, he would either have to pass in front of or behind Schwarzenberg's corps. Either maneuver would have been very difficult and the former could allow the Russians to crush his tiny force. However, Reynier was ignorant of the truth, and continued to obey his orders, following Schwarzenberg's withdrawal.

In Warsaw, Reynier, Poniatowski, and the French minister Bignon, argued with Schwarzenberg to defend Warsaw, but with no success. Only the appearance of Eugène at the Austrian headquarters could have prevented his further withdrawal. Unfortunately, Eugène remained in Posen.

On 1 February Schwarzenberg began the withdrawal behind Warsaw and officially announced to Poniatowski and the Polish government, that he was about to move behind Warsaw on the main road to Kalisch with Reynier. The Russians, true to their agreement with Schwarzenberg, continued to advance according to the stipulated timetable. Poniatowski's corps found itself obliged to withdraw and left Warsaw on 6 February, moving on Petrikau.[21] Reynier's corps, when it left Warsaw, took with it 6,356 sick. Only 3,000 men remained in the ranks. The corps had 30 guns in addition to twelve 4pdr regimental guns.[22] On 6 February Schwarzenberg abandoned Warsaw. Warsaw was abandoned and 1,500 Saxon, 1,000 French, 1,000 Austrian, and numerous Polish wounded, who could not be transported, were left to the mercy of the advancing Russians. An even larger number of wounded had been withdrawn during the days preceding the evacuation. The fortress of Modlin, which was well provisioned, was left with a garrison of 4,000 Poles, 600 French, and 600 Saxons.

Sadly, on 5 February Eugène wrote to Napoleon, stating that Schwarzenberg had announced to the Warsaw authorities that he would be unable to defend them. He stated that all of the Polish troops were to move on Kalisch to concentrate with the Austrians, "or General Reynier, if the Austrians abandon us." Eugène apparently suspected the defection would happen and had taken steps to minimize the damage when it came.[23]

PRINCE EUGENE BEAUHARNAIS

The government of the Grand Duchy attempted to rally the country to itself, but failed. Despite the declaration of a levée en mass[24] and various other efforts, not a single village or town resisted the Russian advance. Poniatowski lacked both the time and the money to reorganize his corps. The most that could be accomplished was the raising of a few hundred Polish cossacks. Behind Poniatowski's small force marched Schwarzenberg's corps. As the Austrians approached Galicia, their joy noticeably increased and they gave voice to their displeasure with Napoleon's policies and the French.

WARSAW FALLS

On the heels of the departing Poniatowski, the forces of Sacken, Docturov and Miloradovich arrived at the gates of Praga, the suburb of Warsaw on the right bank of the Vistula. At the same time the Czar entered Plock with Tormassov's column. To his right was Winzingerode's column, which had crossed the frozen Vistula three days earlier. These two columns were positioned as if to throw themselves on the rear of Schwarzenberg's forces if they did not withdraw promptly.[25]

As Miloradovich entered Warsaw, he directed Docturov to position his corps so as to isolate the garrison at Modlin, in conformance with instructions of Kutusov. He also dispatched Sacken with a small force of light cavalry, to continue the show of pressure against the Austrians. Radt's forces then blockaded Zamosc, where the Polish government had left a small garrison. Miloradovich's main forces then occupied Warsaw.

Winzingerode's forces were directed on Konin, five or six days march east of Posen. The forces of Tchichagov and Wittgenstein moved parallel to him, while Tormassov's forces prepared to depart Plock and follow him.

THE RUSSIAN ARMY OF THE WEST

On 30 January Tchichagov had begun marching towards Thorn. He positioned himself around it in blockade and summoned it to surrender. As it refused to surrender and he had no siege artillery, he left a blockading force of about 6,000 men. He continued on to cross the frozen Vistula and to establish himself around Bromberg. His forces were then diminished by a directive to detach 2,000 cavalry under General Tschlapitz towards Gnesen, where the Bavarian division of von Rechberg had long been posted.

Once in Bromberg, Tchichagov found part of Voronzov's flying corps, which he had detached three weeks earlier. Voronzov reported that the canal of Bromberg had numerous barges frozen in the ice that contained a considerable quantity of military cargo.[26] Voronzov had left a number of his men to guard this material and to direct it towards Posen.[27]

Wittgenstein continued to advance. He soon arrived in Dirschau and Preussisch-Stargard on the heights above Bromberg. The cossacks of Czernichev, Benkendorf and Tettenborn were ahead of him, clearing the path of any stray French and finding themselves received with joy by the Prussian population. When the cossacks arrived in the cantonments of the Prussian corps of General Bülow around Neu-Stettin, they found themselves cordially received. They continued their sweep westwards, with the forces of Benkendorf and Tettenborn touching the coast and those of Czernichev the vicinity of Posen. On 1 February Davout with a force of 1,500 men and six cannons arrived in Landsberg. On 5 February they encountered the cossack advanced guard of Wittgenstein's corps as they withdrew towards Stettin.

EUGÈNE'S MORALE FALLS

Schwarzenberg's retreat had begun the demoralization of Eugène. The arrival of Tschlapitz's cavalry and the flying column under Voronzov, further eroded his confidence. The news that Winzingerode's corps was approaching Konin caused him to believe that he was about to be attacked by a huge Russian army. After a few insignificant clashes, he decided to withdraw behind the Oder River and make it his line of defense.

With this decision made, Eugène wrote Grenier and directed him to stop the 35th Division at the Oder. On 6 February, Grenier's division had 19,341 men and 1,870 cavalry.[28] Grenier deployed his division such that the 1st Brigade was in Liebenwald, Riesenthal, Strasbourg, and Alt-Landsberg. The 2nd Brigade and the divisional artillery were in Berlin, the 3rd Brigade was in Cremen and Nauen, while the 4th Brigade was in Wittenwald, Jossen, Coepenick, Lettow, Saarmünd and Belietz. The 4th Italian Chasseur à Cheval Regiment was posted in Fürstemberg.[29]

Eugène ordered Lagrange to move his division to Berlin, but the 10th Demi-brigade provisoire (4/27th, 4/63rd, 4/76th, and 4/96th Line), the 12th Demi-brigade provisoire (3/123rd, 4/124th, and 4/125th Line) and 5 guns remained in Stettin, so only the four battalions of the 11th and 13th Demi-brigades provisoire (11th - 4/27th Légère, 4/50th Line and 13th - 4/5th, 4/11th 4/79th Line) and 5 guns, 3,442 men in all, went to Berlin. Poniatowski and Reynier were to continue their march on Kalisch. From there they were to move on Glogau, not Posen. Though an ill considered move, the evacuation of Posen and the Grand Duchy of Warsaw was now fact.

It is true that Eugène's position was weak with the withdrawal of Schwarzenberg into Galicia, but it was vital to hold that ground, because it allowed the French to cover both Dresden and Berlin. By holding that ground, France retained control over Germany and the region around Posen, where it could draft men and horses to rebuild its military machine. Eugène would have better served Napoleon, if he had allowed himself to be engaged by the Russians and fought a losing battle, instead of merely surrendering valuable territory without a fight.

As an afterthought, Eugène also advised the Prussian General Bülow to withdraw, but the response to the advice showed that it had little chance of being taken. Early on 11 February Eugène wrote to Napoleon announcing his decision to withdraw the following day. The Bavarians were to withdraw that evening for Powicz. The Poles and Westphalians, who were retiring on Obernick, were to march parallel to Eugène's main column. The force under Gérard (3 French battalions & the elite companies of Neapolitans) were posted before Posen and were to follow the Imperial Guard as a rear guard.[30]

Eugène departed Posen during the night of 11 February, leaving behind him about 1,000 non-transportable wounded. Rechberg's Bavarian division departed Gnesen on 13 February. They had been under continuous attack by Tschlapitz's light cavalry since 5 February.

On 7 February Rechberg's forces had engaged Tschaplitz's cavalry in a rather brisk exchange as the cossacks, supported by 3 guns, forced their way into the Bavarian positions. Though they were forced to withdraw, the shock to the Bavarians was significant.[31]

Rechberg received orders to move to Crossen and to establish a bridgehead on the Oder. His orders required that he move first through Prudewitz and join Gérard's division. The 1st Line Regiment formed the rearguard and Gérard's division led the way. Rechberg's division arrived in Crossen on 16 February after three days of forced marches with only 113 officers, 2,253 men,

TETTENBORN'S RAID ON BERLIN

and 384 horses. A further 54 officers and 1,244 men were in hospital. The rest of his sick and wounded were strewn behind him on the roads to Crossen.

On 11 February a Russian detachment of 3,000 infantry, 2,000 cossacks, and six guns attacked the 4th Vistula Regiment in the village of Rogösno. The assault was sufficient to dislodge the Poles of the Vistula Regiment and drove them back in good order on Obernick. Both sides reportedly lost about 90 men.[32]

On the same day a Polish battalion was captured in Obrzycko by General Zekinskov's force of 4,000 infantry, 2,000 cavalry, and 12 guns. At the same time General Voronzov's division moved before Obernick in an effort to pass through the village. Admiral Tschitakov's forces were in Bromberg. He detached a force of 2,000 cossacks and 2 guns who attacked the 17th Lithuanian Lancer Regiment on 10 February at Zirke driving them westwards as well.

Russian activity continued to press hard against Eugène and on 16 February a column of 800 cossacks passed Wriezen and surprised a battalion of 400 Westphalians in the village. The Westphalians were forced to capitulate.[33]

ODER RIVER LINE ABANDONED

Eugène and the main army moved along the main route from Posen to Berlin by Frankfurt-am-Oder. Czernichev clung to Eugène's flanks and rear, with his cossacks constantly harassing the French army. On 12 February a cossack detachment under Colonel Yesremov and Major Count Puschkin, moved between Posen and Landsberg. They crossed the frozen Warthe into Zirke, where a Polish and Lithuanian cavalry force was posted. In a violent attack which surprised the Poles, the Polish commander Prince Gedroitze, 30 officers, 900 men and 1,000 horses were reportedly killed, wounded, or captured for the loss of 12 cossacks.[34]

On 10 February the VIII Corps, which was being broken up by Eugène's needs, found Gérard's division reduced to the Neapolitan elites and three battalions of French infantry from the 3/3rd, 3/105th, and 3/127th Line Regiments. Gérard command a force of 95 officers, 2,790 men, 348 horses, and 8 guns. At the same time, Eugène formed a small division under Girard. It consisted of two battalions of the 4th Vistula Regiment, the rest of the Vistula Legion and the remains of the 4th, 7th and 9th Polish Line Regiments. This force had about 2,000 men and four guns. Various sources indicate that this division added 3,500 Polish recruits and may have had two small Westphalian infantry battalions attached to it.[35]

Grenier's force arrived in Berlin on 13 February. His division was divided into the two divisions of Generals Fressinet and Charpentier. They had about 18,000 infantry and 1,000 cavalry in the form of the 4th Italian Chasseur à Cheval Regiment. In addition to this force, Maréchal Augereau had a small force in Berlin that consisted of two infantry battalions and a squadron of the Würzburg Jäger zu Pferd.[36] Fressinet's division remained in Berlin, but Grenier lead Charpentier's division and the cavalry to Frankfurt-am-Oder where they were joined by Eugène.[37]

These forces arrived in Frankfurt on 18 February. Eugène was badly informed of the Russian movements and erroneously perceived that they were making a major movement on his right. This, coupled with news that the cossacks had crossed the frozen Oder at Zellin and captured the battalion of fresh Westphalian troops, shook his confidence.[38] He was told that a column of Russian infantry had crossed at Königsberg and that the bridge over the Oder at Schwedt, guarded by a detachment of the Stettin garrison, had been taken. As if that weren't enough he received a letter from Maréchal Augereau advising him of the great emotion created in Berlin by the news that Russian cossacks had been seen not far from the capital.

It was indeed true that the cossacks had penetrated to a few leagues from Berlin and that a Westphalian battalion had been captured at Wriezen. However, those Westphalian levies were more motivated by Yorck's defection than they were by a will to fight those they perceived as the liberators of Germany. Eugène did not see that. What he saw was the alarm spreading through eastern Germany by the forces of Tettenborn, Czernichev and Benkendorf, as well as a few weak squadrons of Russian hussars and dragoons. A total of 5,500 cavaliers were wreaking psychological havoc on him.

COSSACK STREIFKORPS

The first of these forces, under Czernichev, consisted of six cossack regiments, four squadrons of the Isoum Hussar Regiment, two squadrons of the Finland Dragoon Regiment and two Don Cossack horse guns. This force crossed the Oder at Zellin. Benkendorf's forces (five cossack regiments, 1 bashkir regiment, 1 combined hussar regiment, 2 squadrons of the Finland Dragoons, and 2 Don Cossack horse guns) crossed near Frankfurt. The last group, Tettenborn's forces had crossed below Schwedt. Tettenborn commanded four cossack regiments, 4 squadrons of the Isoum Hussar Regiment, and two squadrons of the Kazan Dragoon Regiment.[39] These three groups spread across the countryside in small detachments without support of any sort. There were two other raiding groups, Voronzov and Tschaplitz. However, Voronzov's cossacks remained in Posen and Tschlapitz's light cavalry had returned to the Army of the Danube, which was still before Bromberg and Thorn. Wittgenstein's forces stood in East Prussia.

Eugène's forces were preceded by Maréchal St. Cyr, whose newly formed corps consisted of the divisions of Lagrange (31st Division), Charpentier (36th Division) and Grenier (35th Division). When Eugène arrived in Frankfurt, Grenier's was there and Charpentier's division was near Cüstrin, and Lagrange's was in Berlin with seven battalions detached to Stettin.

As Eugène watched the Russian maneuver on his right unfold he determined that Berlin was the immediate goal of the Russian forces. He reacted immediately to cover Berlin and sent St.-Cyr to deploy Charpentier's division down the length of the Oder from Cüstrin to Wriezen and Freinwald. He then sent Grenier's division behind Charpentier and had him deploy from Frankfurt to Wernenchen and Strasbourg. Eugène quickly saw that these dispositions were inadequate and sent Girard's division to Cüstrin and left Gérard's division in Frankfurt. Roguet's Guard Division and the Guard Cavalry moved behind Frankfurt, so as to be closer to Berlin. Eugène's reserve consisted of the two battalions of Old Guard, two battalions of Young Guard, and a detachment of Italian Guard infantry, about 2,400 men, commanded by Général Roguet. His cavalry consisted of 500 Imperial Guard Cavalry, about 300 survivors of the 4th Italian Chasseur à Cheval Regiment, and 200 Würzburg Jäger zu Pferd.[40]

By 20 February Eugène's forces had completed two marches, and a message from Maréchal Augereau announced that Colonel Tettenborn, at the head of his cossacks, had penetrated into Berlin. Though quickly expelled by the French garrison and the Berlin Burgergarde quickly reestablished order, it was obvious from the Berliner's reception of the cossacks, that they were not destined to remain French allies long.[41]

Despite the quick departure of the cossacks, Augereau's headquarters was alarmed and demanded reinforcements from Eugène. He especially demanded a cavalry reinforcement, as all he had were two squadrons of Würzburg jäger zu pferd. Upon receipt of Augereau's message, Eugène immediately set out for Berlin and arrived there on 22 February, with the about 1,000 Imperial Guard cavalry. His reconnaissance sweeps were enough to push Tettenborn and Czernichev far enough away to no longer be a threat.

However, as the cossacks were pushed back, those of General Benkendorf moved to the north and attacked Müchenberg, where he defeated and destroyed the 4th Italian Chasseur à Cheval Regiment. The Italians lost heavily in this battle.[42] In addition, General Benkendorf seized the village of Fürstenwalde and its bridge over the Spree River from the Piedmontese Velites of Turin under Commandant Cicéron, without the Piedmontese firing a single shot. The lack of French cavalry was already beginning to have a negative impact on the campaign.

EUGÈNE CONCENTRATES HIS ARMY

In reaction to this series of small military defeats, Eugène decided to concentrate his forces around Berlin. Lagrange remained in Berlin, while Grenier, Charpentier, and Roguet were deployed around Kopenick, some distance to the east of Berlin. Girard was recalled from Cüstrin in which he left an adequate garrison. The Westphalian 4th and 5th Regiments, which he had recently received, were dispatched to Gérard, who he directed to evacuate Frankfort, after burning the bridge over the Oder. Gérard was to withdraw to Müllrose, on the canal which ran from the Spree to the Oder. Rechberg's Bavarian division was directed to leave Crossen, destroy its bridge over the Oder and move on Guben, where they were to await orders from Reynier. Reynier was at that time withdrawing towards Saxony.[43]

By executing these maneuvers, Eugène completely abandoned the Oder as his line of defense, even though it was not frozen over and still presented a major military obstacle to the Russians. Before this maneuver, he held three powerfully fortified bridgeheads on the Oder and controlled all the bridges over it. However, because of the audacious action of about 1,000 cossacks, he was bluffed into throwing all the advantages of his position away.

Without a doubt, the attitude of the Prussian population and their King contributed to his decision, but they are not sufficient to justify his evacuation of the Oder line. Indeed, the Prussians were being roused by the withdrawal. They knew of the advancing Russian armies and their increasing proximity fanned the Prussian nationalist fervor.

WINZINGERODE

The news of the occupation of the Grand Duchy of Warsaw, the passage of the Russian army over the Vistula and Yorck's defection electrified them. As the Russians occupied more and more Prussian territory the Prussian people became more aware of the chances of throwing off the yoke of "Napoleonic oppression." So, indeed, if Eugène had remained on the Oder, he probably could have held the Russians further from the Prussians and reduced their reaction to the presence of the Russian armies. As it evolved, each step backwards that Eugène took, had the opposite effect he desired and directly increased the threat to his army by an increasingly hostile Prussian population. On 27 February Eugène abandoned Kopenick and moved to Schönberg, slightly behind Berlin. He had only a small advanced guard posted before Berlin.

RUSSIAN ADVANCE SLOWS

The Russian forces were relatively immobile. Wittgenstein was reduced to 11,000 to 12,000 men and had remained in Preussisch-Stargard until 14 February, when he once again began slowly moving forward. He stopped his movement in Driesen on 27 February, but sent General Repnin forward with a force of 4,000 composed mostly of light cavalry to support Tettenborn, Benkendorf, and Czernichev. Wittgenstein was still 25 leagues from the Oder and over 50 leagues from Berlin. At that distance and with his diminished strength, he represented no military threat whatsoever to Eugène's substantially larger forces. The Army of the West, formerly the Army of the Danube, now commanded Barclay de Tolly, continued the sieges of Bromberg and Thorn, while Posen was occupied by Voronzov's flying column. This force provided no threat to Eugène either.

With the Russian southern flank covered by the convention with Schwarzenberg that neutralized his corps, as well as those of Reynier and Poniatowski, the Czar moved his forces towards Kalisch. Winzingerode led, with Miloradovich following close behind him. Though the Czar's maneuvers were more political in nature, no doubt the concentration of these three columns, were what provided Eugène with the justification to abandon Posen. Winzingerode force marched his column on Kalisch, in an effort to harass the withdrawal of Reynier and Poniatowski. He moved towards Konin, passed to the right of Posen and on towards Kalisch.

THE SAXON WITHDRAWAL

On 8 February the Saxon column under General von Gablenz was struck by Russian cavalry. A fighting withdrawal occurred and the Saxons reached Turck, where the 1st Saxon Light Infantry Regiment and a horse battery were posted. General von Gablenz attached them to his column and withdrew, losing about 100 men from his light cavalry.

On 10 February Gablenz's flank guard was struck by a force of Russians near Uniejow and at Brudzeow. He was driven back with some losses. He was attacked more vigorously on 11 February near Kolinowo and thrown back to Sadow, leaving a number of hussars as prisoners to the Russians. He continued his withdrawal and established the Polenz Chevauxlegers in Grzymiszew, the Saxon Hussars in Wronce, the Saxon light infantry and a battery in Turck, his force of Polish lancers in Sadow, and a detachment in Uniejow.

That evening his forces in Turek were struck three times by Russian cavalry, but the Saxons succeeded in holding their positions. Because of these uninterrupted attacks, Gablenz anticipated further attacks and concentrated his forces in the villages of Malanow, Dziadowice, Dzerbin, and Grombow. Here he hoped to receive support from the 21st Division. The attacks, however, were not renewed and Gablenz renewed his movement.

On 13 February Reynier arrived in Kalisch. Poniatowski, under Reynier's command, had delayed his withdrawal from the Grand Duchy of Warsaw in an effort to gather in detachments and recruits. His slow pace soon lead to a gap of five or six days marches between himself and Reynier. The Saxon division under Reynier was reduced to about 6,000 men, but Reynier's Corps was soon reinforced by Durutte's French 32nd Division. This division was formed from sixteen battalions of the penal regiments Belle-Isle[44] (later 36th Légère), Ile de Ré (later 132nd Line), Ile de Walcheren (later 131st Line), and the 1er and 2e Régiments de la Mediterranée (later 35th Légère and 133rd Line respectively). In addition, its most reliable infantry were the two battalions of infantry from the Grand Duchy of Würzburg. The division also had five foot batteries. Earlier it would have been a powerful force, except that it too was reduced in strength by the Russian campaign. In addition, Reynier had 3,000 Polish infantry and cavalry, most of which were new conscripts and lacked training and equipment.

THE BATTLE OF KALISCH

After five or six days of harassing attacks by cossacks and light cavalry on his right column, Reynier should have taken precautions against surprise. However, he neglected to do so and on 13 February bivouacked his forces too widely. Reynier's forces were posted as follows: Generalmajor von Gablenz formed the rear guard and was in Zelaskow and Zborow, three hours from Kalisch. Gablenz commanded 174 men of the Polenz Chevauxleger Regiment, 134 men of the Hussar Regiment, 400 men of the 1st Light Infantry Regiment and a horse battery with 83 men. Attached to him was the a battalion of the French 2e Régiment de la Mediterranée (133rd Line), which was posted in Nakwarizyn. Generalmajor Nostitz and six companies of the Saxon Prinz Anton Infantry Regiment and two regimental guns was in Borkow, 1 1/2 hours march from Kalisch. This force consisted of 19 officers and 300 men.

Jarry's brigade of Durutte's division occupied the right bank of the river, as well as the suburbs of Kalisch. Maury's brigade of Durutte's division was positioned slightly to the north on the road to Skarzew, and was designed to serve as a rallying point and reserve for Gablenz.[45]

Generallieutenant Lecoq with two companies of Prinz Anton, the von Liebenau Grenadier Battalion, and the two regimental guns of the Prinz Anton Regiment was in Kokanin, one hour from Kalisch. General Lecoq posted his forces in Kokunin, so that the two companies of the Prinz Anton Regiment blocked the road to Stawisczyn, a grenadier company blocked the road to

Kirchhof, and the remaining three grenadier companies formed a reserve and were posted on the road to Kalisch. Part of the von Polenz Chevauxleger Regiment was also posted in the village.

General von Steindel commanded the Prinz Clemens Infantry Regiment, with four regimental guns and the von Brause 6pdr Foot Battery. This force was posted between Kokanin and Kalisch in Pawloweck and Pruszkowo. It served the troops in Kokunin as a reserve.

General von Sahr's brigade was around Winiary, next to Kalisch. Von Sahr's brigade consisted of the von Anger, von Spiegel, and von Eichelberg Grenadier Battalions as well as the 2nd Light Infantry Regiment and Bonniot's 6pdr Foot Battery.[46]

At 3:00 a.m., Winzingerode's 6,000 cavalry, (several Cossack regiments, the Alexandria Hussar Regiment, and accompanying artillery under General Lanskoi), appeared suddenly and pierced the Saxon lines. They quickly seized Russow, which was garrisoned with an insignificant force. Lanskoi was followed quickly by Winzingerode's infantry, commanded by Prince Eugene of Wurttemberg, which assaulted the Saxons. After a three hour fire fight in the dark, the Russians forced the Prinz Clemens Regiment and the von Brause's battery to withdraw to Prosna.

A portion of the Polenz Chevauxleger Regiment attempted to retake Russow without success. This is hardly surprising, in as much as the Russian cavalry numbered several thousand men. At the same time, a large Russian cavalry force struck Borkow, which was garrisoned by the 200 man strong Polenz Chevauxlegers. The two companies of the Prinz Anton Infantry Regiment and three companies of the von Liebenau Grenadier Battalion in Kokanin were dispatched to assist the Polenz Regiment, but did not succeed in reaching the beleaguered regiment. In their own turn, the infantry was surrounded by cavalry and forced to withdraw into the town. There they took up positions in the buildings. The Russian attack was such that one of the companies of the Prinz Anton Regiment was eventually forced to surrender.

Two Saxon guns opened fire on the Russian cavalry, standing on the road to Stawisczyn. Two grenadier companies, placed behind Stawisczyn, advanced as skirmishers under the support of the von Polenz Chevauxlegers. Unfortunately, the distances were too great and the grenadiers were forced to fall back on the chevauxlegers. The Saxon cavalry advanced bravely to defend the grenadiers, but their cause was hopeless. They left their colonel and 166 men as prisoners in the hands of the Russians.[47]

The cavalry that drove back the von Polenz Chevauxlegers was followed quickly by more Russian cavalry under General Knorring. They struck the three companies of the Saxon Liebenau Grenadier Battalion, that were isolated in the plain. Some of the Saxons were dispersed as skirmishers into a small woods, each man fighting for himself. This force held the cossacks at bay, while the remainder formed themselves into two unequal squares. This force then began to march across the plain, fighting the Russian cavalry as they marched. Despite the heavy and repeated cavalry attacks, the fire of Russian artillery and 57 casualties left lying on the field, the brave little battalion marched towards safety. After an hour and a half of marching and combat they arrived on the heights to the north of Kalisch, where they were sheltered by Jarry's brigade.

At the same time, Winzingerode directed Lanskoi to send three regiments (White Russian Hussars, Lithuania Chasseurs, and a cossack regiment) to turn Kokanin by the west, in an effort to cut a force of Saxons off from retreat to Kalisch. At the same time, two jager battalions were sent forward in an assault on the Saxon positions. They were held at bay by the three companies of Saxons that held the north of Kokanin, as well as the Saxon regimental artillery.

In the battle before Borkow Generalmajor von Nostitz directed six companies of the Prinz Anton Regiment. This force totaled 19 officers, 300 men and had two 4pdr regimental guns. They bravely defended their position, but were eventually pounded into submission and surrendered to the Russians.

General Gablenz learned of the battle and took his brigade towards Kalisch, in an effort to relieve the situation. His brigade was joined by the von Gablenz Cavalry Regiment. As they moved to Kalisch, the Saxons were struck in the flank by six Russian squadrons, but quickly drove them back.

By the time he could see Kalisch, it had been taken by the Russians and he could not advance against it. He moved to Tolkinia, where he joined Maury's brigade (131st Line and Würzburg Infantry Regiment). Eventually he joined Zawadsky's Polish rearguard. This force, cut off from the rest of Reynier's forces, moved around the Russians, executing a 14 hour march, rejoining Reynier only after the battle was complete.

While Winzingerode's forces pushed between Kokanin and Borkow, other elements (White Russian Hussars, Lithuania Chasseurs, and a cossack regiment under Colonel Paradowski) moved down the main road to Kalisch and Prosna in a wide front. They moved directly on Pawloweck and Pruszkowo.

Oberst von Mellentin was the commanding officer of the Prinz Clemens Infantry Regiment, which was in Pawloweck. He ordered his infantry into square and defended his position during attack after attack by the Russian cavalry, greeting each charge with cannister from the von Brause foot battery. To counter this, the Russians brought up a battery of licornes, and three hours of counter battery fire began. The two Saxon 4pdrs and four munition wagons were destroyed. Finally the Saxons were driven out and obliged to cross over the Prosna stream. They moved quickly under the cover of darkness and the cover of skirmishers. They found the ice on the river sufficient to bear their weight and successfully executed their withdrawal, falling back on Durutte's division.[48]

Devaux's Brigade (35th and 36th Légère) was established on the right bank of the Prosna River after its night march. Jarry's brigade (132nd & 133rd Line) had arrived in Kalisch at about 2:00 a.m. and had taken up positions before the village, occupying the heights on the right bank (their right) with the 133rd Regiment and placing the 132nd Regiment on the left near Chocz.

The Russians did not delay long their assault on this force. They moved several columns of cavalry, supported by ten guns, which fired cannister at the French infantry. The French responded by sending forward a force of skirmishers to engage the artillery. This effort ceased when the Russians began to deploy their own infantry for an assault.

A fire fight began between the Russians and the 132nd Regiment. In holding their position the 132nd repeatedly made savage use of the bayonet, driving the Russians back from their position. The desperate situation was finally resolved when Durutte dispatched two guns that tipped the balance to the French and broke off the Russian attack.

At the same time the Russians began to advance along another line of attack, directly against Kalisch. Prince Eugene von Wurttemberg had been ordered to seize the city. He formed his corps into two lines, the first being Schakowski's and Sorhend's divisions and the second being the division under Bachmetiev. The Russian infantry was formed in attack columns and preceded by a strong line of skirmishers, drawn from all the regiments and placed under the command of Colonel Rebnitz. This attack was supported by two strong batteries placed in the first line.

The Russian attack threatened the French center along the route to Stawisczyn. General Jarry directed a heavy cannonade against the Russian columns advancing in that direction and advanced three companies of the 132nd Regiment into the suburb, where they manned the rim of a ravine. Two companies of the 35th Légère moved up to support them. A battalion was then established as a reserve by Devaux's brigade. Jarry also took pains to parade his forces back and forth before the enemy, so as to give them a distorted idea of his strength.

The Russians continued their advance in column, preceded by heavy screen of skirmishers. On the right Colonel Menu was forced back and the Russians penetrated into the suburb of Tyniec, where they occupied a few houses. General Jarry reported the gravity of his situation

21

to Durutte, whose only response was to hold to the last man. Jarry's response was to order a bayonet attack which, as a result of the efforts of the companies of the 133rd Regiment, drove the Russians back out of the suburb and along the route to Dobre. The Russian élan began to fail. On their right, two jager regiments which had advanced hard against the French, found themselves stopped by a ditch filled with water, but whose ice was too thin to support their weight. Their advance stopped and they found themselves smothered with fire from the French skirmishers on the far side of the ditch.

Jarry's action stalling the Russian left and holding to the last was critical. The order to hold to the last man was not a cynical move of desperation, but a calculated military necessity. Jarry had to hold as long as possible, so as to permit Sahr's Brigade, Maury's brigade and Gablenz's detachment to reach Kalisch. With the arrival of Sahr's brigade, Jarry found he was sufficiently strong to assume the offensive against the Russians.[49]

Generalmajor von Sahr's brigade had moved to Winiary in the afternoon. When the battle began, the von Anger Grenadier Battalion moved up the road towards Kalisch, in an effort to re-establish contact with the VII Corps. It quickly found that the Russians had occupied the Tyniec suburb with a combined force of cavalry, a horse battery, and some infantry. The Saxon grenadiers continued their advance, supported by the von Spiegel Grenadier Battalion and Captain Bonniot's 6pdr Foot Battery. This force established itself near the windmills and deployed its battery, while it waited for the arrival of the rest of the brigade. The Saxon artillery found the milling Russian cavalry an ideal target and inflicted many casualties upon it. When the brigade arrived the von Anger grenadiers moved forward and two companies occupied several of the houses, while the other two seized the bridge over the Prosna.

At the same time, the von Sahr Infantry Regiment and the von Eichelberg Grenadier Battalion advanced to attack the suburb. It was then that Jarry's brigade struck the other side of Kalisch, trapping the Russians in between. The Russian brigade in the suburb was engaged in a skirmish firefight that lasted eight hours. Eventually the entire Saxon brigade was sent by General Reynier into Kalisch. The Russians were forced to withdraw and, as Reynier lacked fresh troops to pursue the Russians, the battle ended at about 9:00 p.m.

The Saxon losses were General Nostitz, 3 colonels, 36 officers, 1,500 killed and wounded, 2,000 prisoners, 2 flags, and 8 cannon. The Russian infantry withdrew at dusk reporting the loss of 400 or 500 casualties. Lanskoi's cavalry reported a similar loss. General Zapolsky was wounded and died later.[50] The reports of Russian figures are probably understated, as they surrendered the field to the Saxons.

At midnight, Reynier evacuated Kalisch and forced marched his troops, leaving baggage and the enfeebled in his wake. He reached Glogau on 18 February without further contact with Winzingerode. However, once in Glogau he found no trace of a Saxon corps which was to have been organized there by the King of Saxony. It had moved, on orders from Eugène, to Bautzen, where it established itself on 1 March.

As a result of his victory over Reynier, Winzingerode had succeeded in separating him from Poniatowski. When he learned of Reynier's defeat, Poniatowski realized he could not hope to make Glogau and instead chose to move on Czentoschau[51] where he joined his force (60 officers, 996 men and 431 horses) to another small column (French: 12 officers and 205 men detached from Durutte's division—133 Saxons), that the Russian advance had cut off from Reynier's corps. He was joined by a mobile column under the command of Adjutant Commandant Wierzbicki and detached a garrison of 1,600 Polish infantry (300 veterans and 1,300 recruits) under the Polish General Zotowski which moved to Glogau. There it was joined by 2,000 newly raised men from the depots forming the 2nd and 14th Infantry Regiments and detachments of several Polish cavalry regiments (4th, 15th and 15th) with 1,900 horses under General Laczynski.[52] From here, Poniatowski deployed three infantry brigades, one to Bendzin and Czeladz, one to Niwka and Chrzanow, and one to Nowagoro, Slawkow and Olkusz.

RUSSIAN FORCES
BATTLE OF KALISCH
13 FEBRUARY 1813

COMMANDING OFFICER: GENERALLIEUTENANT WINZINGERODE

Advanced Guard: Generalmajor Lanskoi
- Grekov #3 Don Cossack Regt. (3)
- Alexandria Hussar Regt. (3)
- White Russia Hussar Regt. (3)
- Lithuanian Chasseur a Cheval Regt. (3)
- 39th Jager Regt. (1)
- Horse Battery No. 7
- Grekov #9 Don Cossack Regt. (3)
- Kutainikov #4 Cossack Regt. (3)
- Grekov #21 Cossack Regt. (3)
- Sutsherinov Cossack Regt. (3)
- Ural Cossack Regt. (3)

2nd Infantry Corps: Generallieutenant Prince Eugene of Wurttemberg
1st Brigade (3rd Division): Generalmajor Count Schachafskoy
- Mourmansk Infantry Regt. (1)
- Reval Infantry Regt. (1)
- Tchernigov Infantry Regt. (1)
- Reserve Battalion 7th Jager Regt. (1)
- Schusselburg Infantry Regt. (1)
- Reserve Battalion Ukranian Infantry Regt. (1)
- Position Battery #1
2nd Brigade (4th Division): Generalmajor Pischnitzsky
- Light Artillery Battery #6
- Tobolsk Infantry Regt. (1)
- Volhynie Infantry Regt. (1)
- Riajsk Infantry Regt. (1)
- 4th Jager Regt. (1)
- Reserve Battalion Archangel Infantry Regt. (1)
- Reserve Battalion Jaroslav Infantry Regt. (1)
- Reserve Battalion 8th Jager Regt. (1)

Corps: Generalmajor Bachmeiev (from 34th and 35th

Reserve Divisions)
1st Brigade: Generalmajor Tallisin
- Reserve Battalion 5th Jager Regt. (1)
- Reserve Battalion 4th Jager Regt. (1)
- Reserve Battalion Vitebsk Infantry Regt. (1)
- Reserve Battalion Kourin Infantry Regt. (1)
- Reserve Battalion Kolyvan Infantry Regt. (1)
- Reserve Battalion Kozlov Infantry Regt. (1)
- Reserve Battalion Narva Infantry Regt. (1)
- Heavy Battery #33
2nd Brigade: Generalmajor Zapolski
- Light Artillery Battery #7
- Reserve Battalion Vladimir Infantry Regt. (1)
- Reserve Battalion Tambov Infantry Regt. (1)
- Reserve Battalion Dnieper Infantry Regt. (1)
- Reserve Battalion Kostroma Infantry Regt. (1)
- Reserve Battalion 13th Jager Regt. (1)
- Reserve Battalion 14th Jager Regt. (1)
- Naval Equipage Battalion (1)

Cavalry Corps: Generalmajor Count Trubezsoi
1st Brigade: Generalmajor Count Witte
- 1st Ukranian Cossack Regt. (3)
- 3rd Ukranian Cossack Regt. (3)
2nd Brigade: Generalmajor Allenine
- Reserve Sqn/Kiev Dragoon Regt. (1)
- Reserve Sqn/New Russia Dragoon Regt. (1)
- Reserve Sqn/Karkov Dragoon Regt. (1)
- Reserve Sqn/Tchernigov Dragoon Regt. (1)
- Horse Battery #8
- Reserve Sqn/Moscow Dragoon Regt. (1)
- Reserve Sqn/Orenburg Dragoon Regt. (1)
- Reserve Sqn/Siberia Dragoon Regt. (1)
3rd Brigade: Generalmajor Knorring
- Soum Hussar Regt. (2)
- Lithuania Uhlan Regt. (2)
- Tartar Uhlan Regt. (3)
Striefkorps: Oberst Davydov
- Akhtyrsk Hussar Regt. (30)
- 1st Bug Cossack Regt.
- Popov #13 Cossack Regt.
- 100 Cavalry troopers from various Regt.s

Winzingerode chose not to pursue Reynier after his success. He remained in Kalisch several days. Later, when directed by Kutusov, he moved towards the frontier of Silesia and, on 27 February, arrived at Rawitsch. The cavalry division of Sulkowski moved between Warta and the Silesian frontier. Tolinski's brigade moved into Olsztyn, Zarki, and Woldowice where it linked with the Austrian forces of Schwarzenberg.[52]

Miloradovich departed Warsaw on 12 February and by the end of the month was on Winzingerode's right, around Gostyn. The Czar and Tormassov's column were in Kalisch on 24 February. From there they moved into quarters between Rawitsch and Gostyn. The end of February found Eugène's forces as follows:[54]

	Men	Guns
Division: Lagrange	3,442	5
Division: Grenier	10,300	22
Division: Charpentier	8,810	14
Guard: Roguet	5,151	9
Division: Girard	2,000	4
Division: Rechberg		(near Berlin)
Division: Gérard	2,500	8 (in Frankfurt)
Detachment: Carra St.-Cyr	3 coys	(in Hamburg)
Division: J.Morand	2,000	(in Swedish Pomerania)
7th Corps: Reynier		(west of Rothenburg)

SIEGES IN POLAND

As the allies advanced a number of French garrisoned fortresses were trapped in their rear. Modlin had a garrison of 1,000 Saxons (2/Niesmeuschal & 1/Prinz Frederich Regiments),[55] 1,000 French (1/133rd Line), and 3,000 Poles (3rd, 17th, 18th, 19th, 20th, and 21st Infantry Regiments) commanded by Général de division Daendels. It was blockaded on 27 December by Generalmajor Kleinmichel.

Thorn had been blockaded by Generallieutenant Tschaplitz, the commander of the advanced guard of the Army of the West. The command of the blockading force was transferred on 8 February to General of Infantry Count Langeron, who began the formal siege on 27 March. The fortress surrendered on 3 April. The fortress of Thorn was commanded by Général de brigade Poitevin de Maureilhou who commanded 4,000 Bavarians (6 ½ battalions) under Generalmajor von Zoller and a force of 1,500 French infantry (a regiment de marche and miscellaneous remnants).

The cossacks of Generallieutenant Radt surrounded the fortress of Zamosc on 9 February. The garrison consisted of about 4,000 Poles (1/,2/,3/13th Infantry Regiment, depots, and new levies) commanded by Général de division Hauke.

The fortress of Czentochau was taken under siege by Generallieutenant von Sacken and his Warsaw Corps. The siege was broken and on 25 March resumed by Generallieutenant Count Pahlen III. On 3 April a chance shot by a Russian battery detonated the main magazine and two days later the fortress capitulated.

---

[1] Vaudoncourt, Prince Eugène, Vol II, pg 122.

[2] A bataillon de marche was an ad hoc formation organized for the purpose of transporting newly trained recruits to formations in the battle zone.

[3] Charras, La Guerre de 1813, pg 36.

[4] Holleben, Frühjahrsfeldzuges, pg 28.

[5] The details of this reorganization can be found in the appendices.

[6] Bayerischen Kriegsarchiv, Darstellungen, pg 59.

[7] Holleben, Frühjahrsfeldzuges, pg 37.

[8] Bayerischen Kriegsarchiv, Darstellungen, pg 60.

[9] Revue d'Histoire, Vol 39, #115, pg 84.

[10] A regiment de marche was formed of several bataillons de marche. Though not intended as a combat formation, it did occassionally find itself thrown into that situation.

[11] Vaudoncourt, Prince Eugène, pg 128.

[12] This figure probably does not include the 17th and 19th Lithuanian Uhlan Regiments.

[13] Holleben, Frühjahrsfeldzuges, pg 37.

[14] Vaudoncourt, Prince Eugène, pg 131.

[15] Holleben, Frühjahrsfeldzuges, pg 37.

[16] Revue d'Histoire, Vol 39, #115, pg 89–90.

[17] du Cassé, Prince Eugène, Vol 8, pg 220.

[18] Charras, La Guerre de 1813, pg 111.

19 Charras, La Guerre de 1813, pg 113.

20 Revue d'Histoire, Vol 39, #115, pg 97.

21 Vaudoncourt, Prince Eugène, pg 132.

22 Holleben, Frühjahrsfeldzuges, pg 51.

23 du Cassé, Prince Eugène, Vol 8, pg 328.

24 A draft of all able bodied males, though this often had many loopholes for the wealthy or well connected.

25 Charras, La Guerre de 1813, pg 117.

26 The complete story of these barges can be found in The Memoirs of Baron Marbot, by Lt. Gen. the Baron de Marbot.

27 Charras, La Guerre de 1813, pg 121.

28 Holleben, Frühjahrsfeldzuges, pg 49.

29 Revue d'Histoire, Vol 9, #115, pg 103

30 du Cassé, Prince Eugène, Vol 8, pg 345–46.

31 Bayerischen Kriegsarchiv, Darstellungen, pg 65.

32 du Cassé, Prince Eugène, Vol 8, pg 345.

33 du Cassé, Prince Eugène, Vol 8, pg 364.

34 Weil, M.H, Campagne de 1813, La Cavalerie des armées alliés, pg 8.

35 Holleben, Frühjahrsfeldzuges, pg 38.

36 "Jäger zu pferd" is the German equivelant of the French term, "Chasseur à cheval." Literally, both are translated as, "mounted hunter," but the intent of the term is more one of, "a mounted light trooper intended for skirmish fighting."

37 Vaudoncourt, Prince Eugène, pg 135.

38 Weil, La Cavalerie des armées alliés, pg 9.

39 Weil, La Cavalerie des armées alliés, pg 9–10.

40 Vaudoncourt, Prince Eugène, pg 137.

41 du Cassé, Prince Eugène, Vol 8, pg 369.

42 de Vaudoncourt, Prince Eugène, pg 137.

43 Bayerischen Kriegsarchiv, Darstellungen, pgs 72–73.

44 The penal regiments were formed in 1810–1811 from draft evaders who were given an amnesty from the normal penalties providing they surrendered to the authorities. They were then reeducated, trained, and formed into operational military formations.

45 Revue d'Histoire, Vol 39, #128, pg 242.

46 Sporschil, Grosse Chronik, Vol I, pg 71–72

47 Revue d'Histoire, Vol 39, #128, pg 248.

48 Revue d'Histoire, Vol 39, #128, pg 251–252.

49 Revue d'Histoire, Vol 39, #128, pg 255.

50 Sporschil, Grosse Chronik, Vol I, pg 76, & Charras, La Guerre de 1813, pg 132–133. & Vaudoncourt, Prince Eugène, pg 135.

51 Poniatowski, Correspondance, #792.

52 Poniatowski, Correspondance, #795.

53 Poniatowski, Correspondance, #799.

54 Holleben, Frühjahrsfeldzuges, pg 55.

55 Poniatowski, Correspondance, #777.

The Politics of Early 1813

The Political Environment

The invincible was no longer invincible! Napoleon, successor to Friederich the Great, had been beaten. His omnipotent armies lay broken and scattered across the frozen swamps and forests of Russia.

On 5 December 1812 Napoleon had left the Grande Armée under the command of Murat, King of Naples, and returned to France. He traveled quickly, without escort, and felt obliged to conceal his identity as he traveled through Germany. He stopped in Dresden on 19 December to reassure the King of Saxony that all was not lost. While there he wrote to the Austrian Emperor, demanding that the Austrian Emperor provide fresh contingents to his army. He also wrote to the King of Prussia, calling on him to raise another 30,000 men, an order with which the King of Prussia seemed most willing to comply.

He resumed his travels and arrived in Paris on 19 December. The task that lay before him was immense. He had lost over 500,000 men, all their equipment, an army's complete artillery train, as well as four corps of cavalry and their horses. France was not completely secure. It too needed reassurance that the master had returned. On 23 October 1812, there had been an attempted coup d'etat by Malet, and Napoleon needed to take the reins of power firmly in his hands to prevent further such attempts at his throne.

Napoleon's Stance On Peace Negotiations

As news of the disaster spread the major powers of Europe began to act, all of them acting in their own interests. Austria was tied to Napoleon by the marriage of the Austrian Emperor's daughter to Napoleon. This complicated their situation and initially they attempted to mediate the situation. When the Austrians learned of the disaster in Russia in mid-December, they secretly dispatched an envoy to the Czar. A second envoy went to Schwarzenberg directing that he withdraw, avoid any serious conflict with the Russians, and, if possible, negotiate a secret, verbal armistice with the Russian generals.

While doing this Metternich and the other Austrian ministers professed their loyalty to France. In the same vein, the French ambassador to Vienna insinuated that in return for Austrian support, France would return former Austrian provinces in Illyria and Italy as well as restore Austrian hegemony over Germany.

However, Otto, the French Ambassador, was aware that Vienna was filled with secret agents from Russia and England, who actively agitated against the Austro-French alliance. His dispatches reporting on the agitation in Austria arrived in Paris at about the same time as Napoleon returned from Russia. In those dispatches he further stated he was not in accord with Napoleon's demand from Dresden that the Austrians provide a further 60,000 man contingent.[1] The Austrian Emperor was to eventually oblige Napoleon and order the raising of a corps of 60,000 men in Galicia and Buckowine, but Napoleon was not to see it fight by his side.[2]

Marshal Bubna, a seeming francophile, was selected to act as the Austrian agent in Paris. He was directed not to engage in any serious negotiation for an augmentation to the Austrian contingent or to engage in any other serious negotiations, but instead to offer the Austrian court as an appropriate intermediary for negotiations between the belligerents. He was to ask Napoleon what were his conditions for such a negotiation.

When Bubna made these overtures for an Austrian mediated peace to Napoleon, Napoleon laid down the following conditions under which he would accept a mediated peace. He offered to return Portugal to the house of Braganca, but Naples was to remain under Murat. Spain was still to be ruled by Joseph Bonaparte, his brother. He did, however offer to remove his army from Spain, while the British were to withdraw theirs to Sicily. In addition, the Russians were to return to their frontiers. He had no objection to their retaining the Polish provinces that they had held prior to 1812, but he would not allow one village of the Grand Duchy of Warsaw to pass to the Russians. The terms and conditions of the Treaty of Tilsit were to remain unaltered.

Napoleon added that he expected Austria to adhere to its treaty obligations to provide 60,000 in case the Russians should not accept these conditions. He went on to say that if the Austrian honor would not allow them to comply with this, they were free to withdraw their present corps under Schwarzenberg and to remain as a spectator to the French war with Russia.

Napoleon asked that the Austrian court dispatch to England a minister with his proposition and offered Austria the return of its Illyrian provinces in return for its cooperation and assistance after England agreed to a peace.

Ministers from Austria were also sent to the principal states of the Confederation of the Rhine; Bavaria, Saxony, Baden, and Wurttemberg, in an effort to provoke their active support and agitation for a negotiated peace. It was hoped that if these allies were persuaded to break their solid support of Napoleon, Napoleon might be forced to accept a mediated peace.

However, the Grand Duke of Baden, whose territories bordered France, refused to hear the proposals. The King of Württemberg listened, but promptly denounced the overture to Napoleon. The King of Bavaria listened and hesitated. He desired peace, but he had been given Austrian territories for his support of Napoleon in the 1805 and 1809 campaigns. He too denounced this activity to Napoleon.[3]

The King of Saxony knew that it meant he would have to renounce the crown of the Grand Duchy of Warsaw and that there would be other sacrifices he might have to make. However he weighed them against what he might gain from an alliance with Austria. In the end, at the sounds of Napoleon's first victories of 1813, he quickly heeled to Napoleon's side.

The kingdoms of all four monarchs suffered from the effects of the Continental System, agitation by German nationalists, and the "humiliation of servitude to France." However, their rulers had enlarged their territories and been raised to kings and grand dukes by Napoleon. In addition, France was much closer to their borders than were the Russian armies. The memories of conquering French armies marching through their provinces lingered on.

Austria was, at this time, remaining reasonably faithful to its alliance with France and Metternich had turned down a £10,000,000 sterling offer for an alliance with England, despite the miserable condition of the Austrian treasury.

Despite this fidelity, Austria was rearming. Her arsenals were filled with working artisans, major provision magazines were established, all military personnel on leave were recalled to the colors, volunteers were enrolled, preparations were made for major recruitment, procurement of horses was escalated, and an imperial order was issued directing the formation of an army destined to occupy Galicia and Buckowine.[4]

When word of these preparations reached France and the Austrians were once again pressed for a supplement to Schwarzenberg's corps. In response Metternich stated that this was an "interior" mobilization intended to put Austrian on a footing to act against France's enemies. Metternich told Otto that the Austrian court did not wish to alarm the Russians by enlarging their contingent under Schwarzenberg and provoke an attack before the Austrian army was ready.

Though this answer was given only limited credence by Otto, he was delighted by the apparent discomfort it caused the Czar. He continued to ply the Emperor with reasons why he should continue his alliance with France. He pointed out that should Russia succeed in swallowing all of the Grand Duchy of Warsaw Russia would then present a major threat to Austrian interests on her northern borders. Similarly he pointed out the potential danger of Germany falling into the Russian sphere of influence.

He did not know that the Austrians feared French victories more than they feared Russian victories. Metternich perceived the Russian resources as being limited, but those of France did not appear to be so limited. There also lurked a continued resentment for the years of humiliating defeats at French hands and a yearning to regain the provinces stripped away as a result of those defeats.

THE RUSSIAN POLITICAL SITUATION

The Russian armies, under Marshal Kutusov, stood on the borders of western Europe poised to strike. Russia stood at the brink of achieving geo-political goals established by Peter the Great. Russia sought to expand her borders north and westward, to disrupt and destroy Poland and to expand her influence into Germany by careful marriage alliances. Furthermore Russia attempted to expand her influence, either by direct force or by ruse, in the quarrels of the Germans.

Peter had also advocated alliances with Austria for the purpose of weakening the Ottoman Empire as well as to weaken Austrian control over Germany, both by keeping her involved in ruinous wars as well as by exciting the jealousy of the German princes against Austria. Russia actively sought to subject Germany and Poland to her hegemony.[5]

Russia stood at the crossroads of history. Her goals were so close, that she had only to reach out and seize them. The Grand Duchy of Warsaw, all that remained of Poland, would soon be overrun by her advancing armies. Those same armies were slowly flowing towards eastern Prussia; once there they would begin to give the Czar direct and immediate influence on the policies of the Prussia court. Once that was accomplished Prussia would quickly fall into the Russian camp.

The Convention of Tauroggen had neutralized a Prussian army and secret negotiations had accomplished the same with Schwarzenberg's corps to the south. Though the Austrian Emperor was not yet his ally, the Czar knew it was only a matter of time before his diplomats would once again excite the same nationalist ardor in the Austrian court that had driven them to launch their abortive 1809 campaign.

Kutusov's actions, however, did not coincide with these goals and he showed no inclination to launch the attack into western Europe. Czar Alexander, in contrast, was ready to fight the French until they submitted, Germany was liberated, and Russia had achieved her goals. The Czar was to prevail over Kutusov early in the campaign. Death too, was to intervene, for it removed Kutusov from the field in mid-April.

Yet various considerations conspired to hold Russia's goals just outside of her reach. The Russian treasury was drained and her armies were in a miserable state. Only the financial support of England kept the Russian military functioning. Russia desperately needed money, reinforcements, allies, and more money. Pursuing the war with Napoleon by herself would soon leave her exhausted at the end of her supply lines. In contrast, Napoleon was closer and closer to his sources of supplies and men. His ability to make war would grow faster than that of the Russians. Russia would soon find herself unable to survive the war if she continued to face Napoleon alone.

THE PRUSSIAN DILEMMA

Only Russia was at war with France, but Prussia and Austria were threats that needed to be watched. Both countries hated Napoleon for having stripped them of numerous territories, and for having repeatedly humiliated them on the field of battle. The Prussian nobility and townsfolk were more than willing to abandon their alliance with France, and plunge into open

YORCK MEETS DIEBITSCH TO ORGANIZE THE DEFECTION

warfare with France. In contrast their king, Frederich-Wilhelm, appeared to be a weak and insipid man who lived in absolute terror of Napoleon. He feared that Napoleon's armies would devastate Prussia, eradicate it as a state, and reform the Kingdom of Poland completely from Prussia's eastern provinces.

The truth of Frederich-Wilhelm's policies and personality is not clear. Superficially, he played the role of a weak and indecisive king. His wife reputedly drove him to act, while he vacillated and wavered. History has often portrayed his actions in early 1813 as being thrust on him, rather than the result careful planning.[6]

Others give him credit for being the ultimate Machiavelli. He came from the Brandenburg line of monarchs, who had a reputation for living by their wits. How else could a king and his kingdom survive? His armies, once the most feared in Europe, had been smashed by the French in one day at Jena-Auerstädt. His diminutive army could not hope to cross swords with the huge

French army. He had little choice but to play Napoleon's fool until the time came when he could strike back and hope to win.

Now, with the disintegration of the Grande Armée in Russia, Napoleon's reputation of invincibility broken, and fragments of the once powerful French army reeling backwards through his territories, Frederich-Wilhelm found himself faced with decisions to be made and chances to be seized. The decision to act was made, but did he seize them, or was he pushed into them? Did he carefully plot each move, or did circumstances conspire to force his hand? The truth will probably never be known.

The series of events began at 3:00 p.m. on 4 January 1813, a courier arrived at Marshal Augereau's headquarters with a dispatch announcing the defection of General Yorck. When news of this was transmitted to the King of Prussia he "suffered an attack of apoplexy". He was faced with the choice of disavowing Yorck's actions and presenting Napoleon with excuses for this action, or accepting the new political reality forced on him by Yorck's actions.

The Kingdom of Prussia was still heavily occupied by French garrisons, drawn from Augereau's XI Corps, in Pillau, Danzig, Thorn, Zamosc, Spandau, Stettin, Magdeburg, Berlin, Cüstrin, and Glogau. Murat, then commanding the Grande Armée, had 22,000 men and 33 cannon on the Vistula. The combined contingents of the Austrians, Polish, Saxons, and French under Schwarzenberg, Reynier, and Durutte contained a further 43,000 men and 127 cannons and a further 10,000 men were in various posts on the Oder River. In addition, Augereau had 19,300 men and 30 guns from Grenier's division in Berlin. This gave the French a total force in Prussia of approximately 158,000 men. Facing this force, only the Prussian forces of General Bülow were in a condition to undertake a campaign. In addition there were no provisions for financing a campaign nor were the magazines in a state to support one.

On the other hand, the King of Prussia was faced with extreme internal pressure to join the Russians. He faced a large faction, led by his wife, Queen Louisa, who pressed for revenge against the French for their humiliation of Prussia in 1806. He also was faced with the pending occupation of his eastern provinces by the Russian army. It was highly possible that the Russians would seize territory from Prussia as well.

Initially the King of Prussia denounced Yorck's actions as an act of insubordination and sent Prinz von Hatzfeld to Paris on 4 January 1813. He was to act as an envoy extraordinaire.[7]

Hatzfeld's mission was to advise Napoleon of the king's sentiments, his loyalty, and his intentions to adhere to the alliance between the two states.[8]

The King of Prussia dispatched an aide de camp, Major von Natzmer, to the general headquarters of Yorck. Here he was to pass command of the corps to General Kleist and take General Yorck under arrest. Yorck was then to be taken to Berlin and have his actions reviewed by a military council. His court-martial was then to be announced publicly and posted in the army's orders of the day.[9]

In addition, the King of Prussia dispatched his aide Natzmer on a secret mission. He was to approach the Czar Alexander and to sound him out on the possibility of a Russo-Prussian alliance. Natzmer was to determine the Russian position on Poland. He was to ensure that the Czar knew that Austria would not tolerate his annexation of all of Poland and that Prussia would not tolerate the continued existence of the Grand Duchy of Warsaw. The King of Prussia sought an alliance with Russia while not breaking the alliance with France.[10]

As yet a further contortion to the political situation, the King of Prussia secretly one of his aide de camps, Schack, to Yorck and Massenbach to advise them of Natzmer's pending arrival and his orders. He counseled them to abandon their commands and to place themselves under the protection of the Russians. Despite the protestations of the King of Prussia, Napoleon was painfully aware that Yorck's defection had forced a reorientation of the King of Prussia's political position. However, Napoleon rather naively felt that the King of Prussia's best interests lay in maintaining his alliance with France. He perceived Russia as being the greater threat to Prussian existence.

Hartzfeld, in the execution of his mission to Paris, fed Napoleon's illusions and stated that Prussia could raise a corps of 50,000 to 60,000 men for his service. It was also reported that Hartzfeld carried instructions to offer a family alliance, a marriage, between the Prussian royal family and the Imperial family. In response to Hartzfeld's mission Napoleon sent the King of Prussia his assurances of his attachments to the king and of his indignation at the actions of General Yorck.[11]

AUSTRIAN POLITICS

The news of Yorck's defection was no less embarrassing to the Austrians than it was to the Prussians. Napoleon was married to an Austrian archduchess. Metternich, fearing that he might not be able to control the pending political events, actively moved to contract a peace between the warring parties. Austria actively feared the intrusion into and the control of German politics by the Russians. To this end the Austrians felt an alliance with Prussia was their best recourse.

Metternich communicated his plans for peace to Hardenberg, knowing that Hardenberg was little more than an intermediary for the English. The terms for peace were the return of France to its natural boundaries, the Rhine, Alps and Pyrenees. Germany was to return to a collection of autonomous states whose independence was guaranteed by Austria and Prussia. Prussia was to be returned to the ranks of great powers. Italy was to be divided into two states, in which Austria was to receive its former territory up to the Mincio. The Ottoman Empire was to return to its boundaries established by the Treaty of Bucharest and Russia was to return to the boundaries established by the Treaty of Tilsit.

Metternich sought to push Napoleon to accept Austrian mediation, both to bring peace to Europe as well as to return lost Austrian provinces without resort to force of arms. In the hopes of pushing Napoleon to the negotiation table, he actively sought to destroy Napoleon's morale. He attempted to convince Napoleon that, despite the professed loyalty of his allies, they were planning to abandon him because of public pressure.

The Austrians remained superficially loyal, but they were hedging their bets. The corps of Schwarzenberg moved south, towards the Austrian frontier, where it could operate on lines of communication from the Austrian heartland. Once there, however, it could also disassociate itself from the French, if it became expedient.

Schwarzenberg, though less bold than Yorck, was also in contact with the Russians. Though nothing was put in writing, he had a verbal agreement with Miloradovich, the Russian general directly facing him, that the Austrian Hilfkorps would remain non-aggressive and would retire on Cracow, rather than Kalisch as ordered. This armistice, signed with the knowledge and consent of Metternich, was formally signed on 30 January 1813 in Zeycs. The Austrians agreed to slowly withdraw towards their borders and to take no offensive action against the Russians. This secret agreement allowed Metternich the freedom to negotiate while he appeared to adhere to Austria's agreements with France.[12]

Schwarzenberg's maneuvers obliged Reynier to act for himself and retire on Kalisch. In addition to this, Schwarzenberg's maneuvers were to oblige Poniatowski and his 8,500 Poles to withdraw into Galicia with him as well or be destroyed. This act effectively neutralized Poniatowski's force and it was not until the summer armistice that he was allowed to march through Austria and rejoin Napoleon in Germany.

By April, Austria planned to have 100,000 men under arms. This force, supported by an eventual further mobilization, was to assure the armed neutrality that Austria was to maintain until it was opportune to act otherwise.

Another adversary lurked in the far north in the person of Bernadotte, now Crown Prince and Regent of Sweden. He and Napoleon had a long standing animosity that traces its roots back to their courtship of the Clary sisters. It reached the breaking point during the 1809 campaign and both were glad to see Bernadotte's departure for Stockholm.

Bernadotte had shown himself to have less than the best of motives vis-a-vis France and its allies. In 1812 he secretly intrigued with the Czar of Russia to snatch Norway away from Denmark, nominally to compensate for Napoleon's occupation of Swedish Pomerania and the Russian occupation of Finland in 1809. He signed a treaty with Russia on 5 April 1812, agreeing to this transfer in return for his support of the Russian cause.[13]

In July Bernadotte signed a peace treaty with England, when the fortunes of war appeared to be turning against Russia. Despite this and the treaty with Russia, both of which remained secret, Sweden continued diplomatic relations with France. Once the news of Napoleon's disaster in Russia became known, all pretense of normalcy vanished from the Franco-Swedish relations. Bernadotte decried the invasion of Pomerania, broke diplomatic relations and on 7 January 1813, declared war against France.

Bernadotte believed that a Russian auxiliary corps of 10,000 was due to join with a similar number of Swedes under his command and begin amphibious operations against the French held coasts of Germany, but the Russians were too weak to provide the men necessary for this operation. As a result, Bernadotte remained in Sweden and watched the events on the Continent, while he negotiated further with England.

He sought to gain English acceptance of the convention signed with Russia that ceded Norway to Sweden. In addition, he sought a subsidy of 25,000,000 francs to support the operations of 30,000 Swedish soldiers in active operations in Germany against Napoleon. England acceded to these requests and also ceded to Sweden the island of Guadeloupe. The convention was signed on 3 March 1813.[14]

Bernadotte feared the might of the French armies and knew that any serious military reverse could break his precarious grasp on the Swedish crown. Despite this, he sent a division of Swedish troops into Swedish Pomerania on 18 March, where it quickly encountered the French division of J. Morand.

Bernadotte's force in Swedish Pomerania quickly grew to 30,000 Swedes. Once an alliance was forged with Prussia on 28 April 1813, it was agreed that a contingent of 27,000 Prussians and 30,000 Russians was to be joined to Bernadotte's command. This was eventually to become known as the Army of the North.[15]

Bernadotte proposed to his allies that he take his Swedish forces in Pomerania and liberate the Hanseatic cities, parts of Mecklenburg, and the neighboring lands not included in the former Electorate of Hanover. The prospects of this type of action by the Swedes greatly distressed the Danish court. They sought to ensure their territorial sovereignty. Their grievances over the British bombardment of Copenhagen, the burning of the Danish fleet, and the seizure of Danish merchants had forced them into an alliance with France. In reaction to the Swedish presence in Pomerania, the Danish mobilized their army and sent it to the border of Holstein.

On 22 March the Russian emissary Prince Dolgorouki arrived in Copenhagen to speak with Friedrich VI, King of Denmark. He pressed Friedrich to join the coalition against France. If the Danish King joined his forces to those of Russia and Prussia, Dolgorouki advised the king, the integrity of the Danish kingdom would be assured. In return for Danish cooperation, the king was offered the sovereignty of Holland, which had been offered to him in return for Norway earlier. The Danish sovereign saw he had no alternative and accepted the Russian offer to join the coalition.[16]

The Swedish Ambassador to Copenhagen learned of Dolgorouki's offers and advised the Swedish government of these developments. Bernadotte confronted the Czar with this, because

CONVENTION BETWEEN RUSSIA AND SWEDEN ST. PETERSBURG, 24 MARCH (5 APRIL) 1812

Article I, II & III. The powers of Sweden and Russia guarantee to each other their respective possessions.

Article IV. The Emperor Napoleon through his invasion of Swedish

Pommerania has demonstrated a hostile attitude towards Sweden and threatened to disturb Russian tranquillity, these two powers agree to make a diversion on the German coast to threaten the French army and allocate for that purpose 25,000 to 30,000 Swedes and 15,000 to 20,000 Russians.

Article V. In as much as the King of Sweden cannot take pArticle in this diversion, so long as Norway, which sits on his western border, is seen as an enemy power and, moreover, as Norway's geographical position, which by its nature should be a pArticle of the Kingdom of Sweden, the Czar of Russia under takes and obliges himself to join Norway to the Crown of Sweden, be it by means of negotiation or through the provision of a military corps of 35,000 men. The Czar

further obliges himself to assure Sweden possession of these lands by the conclusion of peace and not to lay down his arms until these lands are joined to Sweden.

Article VI.. In order that Sweden should obtain Norway, before it undertakes the agreed upon diversion, the Czar shall place the Russian Army Corps of Sweden at the disposal of the Swedish army for the purpose of the aforementioned undertaking.

Article VII. Both courts shall recommend to the cabinet of Copenhagen that the joining in alliance of Norway to Sweden be compensated in full to Denmark by means of provinces on its German borders. Both powers in this case do bind themselves to procure this compensation. That, however, these proposals essentially must be supported through force of arms, so shall they not honorably be made, until one the exchange is prepared.

Article VIII. .If in the case of Denmark's refusal, Sweden is obliged to attack Seeland, so shall the Russian corps described in Article VI shall be at the disposal of the King of Sweden.

Article IX. The Russian forces which shall be joined to the Swedish Army shall be ready to march out on 13 May 1812. When joined to the Swedish Forces the King of Sweden shall be the commander-in-chief of the combined force.

CONVENTION BETWEEN RUSSIA AND SWEDEN ABO, 18 (30) AUGUST 1812

Article I. With regards to the date of the Swedish diversion in Northern Germany committed to by the Czar of Russia, the promised corps of 25,000 shall be increased to 35,000 men and shall arrive in Schonen by the end of September. The remaining 10,000 men shall arrive by the end of November, weather permitting.

Article III. .As soon as the 25,000 Russians have landed in Schonen the King of Sweden sha!l begin the undertaking against the Danish islands.

Article IV. If the King of Denmark has not voluntarily agreed to the transfer of Norway and his troops have not joined the combined Russo-Swedish Army, it shall be necessary to attack Seeland. The Czar contracts (acknowledging the wishes expressed by the British Crown, that the island of Seeland shall be ruled by joint agreement

between the three powers) by the right of conquest diligently claim these islands for the King of Sweden under the condition that the King settles with England the English interests.

Article V.. As compensation for the support, which the Czar of Russia shall provide to the King of Sweden, the King of Sweden shall if the Czar has by the outbreak of war, expanded the Russian borders to the the Weichsel, the addition of these provinces as a lawful compensation for the efforts by the Czar against the universal enemy and will guarantee to him these possessions. The King of England shall be requested to provide a similar assurance and guarantee to Russian.

Article VII. As a show of the Czar's personal friendship for the King of Sweden and of his honorable wishes, in the interests of assuring their union, the Czar obliges himself to provide Sweden with a loan of 1,500,000 rubles to assist in this endeavor. The King of Sweden obliges himself to repay this loan 16 months after the union of Norway and Sweden is completed.

Article IX.. Both subscribing parties shall be endeavor bring the British Crown into this alliance and to formally agree to the union of Norway with Sweden.

it violated the terms of their treaty of alliance. The Czar, fearing that Sweden might back out of the alliance and begin operations against Russia in order to reclaim Finland, denounced Dolgorouki's actions vis-a-vis Norway, as having been beyond what he was authorized to offer.

At the same time, the Danish newspapers received word of the promise of indemnities to Denmark in the form of German territory, and published articles to the effect. In response, the Duchies of Mecklenburg and the Hanseatic cities of Hamburg and Lübeck began viciously denouncing these proposals. The politics of buying Danish cooperation with German territories became too hot, and under pressure from various Prussian politicians and other German patriots, Alexander renounced the idea of giving Denmark German territory under any conditions.

On 3 May Dolgorouki received an imperial letter denouncing his actions and directing his immediate return to Russia. As a result Denmark lost its chance to enter the coalition easily. Now it faced the prospect of joining the coalition that had already decided to strip it of Norway

Treaty on Subsidies Between Great Britain and Sweden Stockholm, 3 March 1813

Article I. His Majesty the King of Sweden engages himself to employ a corps of at least 30,000 men in direct operations on the continent against the communal enemy of the contracting parties. This army shall act in concert with the troops of Russia placed under the command of His Majesty the Royal Prince of Sweden, conforming with the stipulations that are currently in effect between Stockholm and St. Petersburg.

Article II. The aforementioned courts having communicated to His Britannic Majesty the existing engagements between themselves and, having formally demanded that His Majesty accede to them, His Majesty the King of Sweden having according to the stipulations contained in the preceding article, given a token of the desire which animates him, to contribute as much as possible on his part to the communal cause. His Britannic Majesty, in desiring return to give an immediate and non-equivocal proof of his resolution to join his interests with those of Sweden and Russia, promises and engages himself by the present treaty to accede to the existing conventions between the two powers, and such that His Britannic Majesty not only opposes any obstacle to the annexation and union in perpetuity of the Kingdom of Norway as an integral part of the Kingdom of Sweden, but further that he shall act, as in the eyes of the King of Sweden, serves to facilitate the execution of this, be it by the provision of good offices, and if necessary naval cooperation acting on concert with the forces of Sweden and Russia. It is, however, understood that there will be no recourse to force to effect the union of Norway to Sweden, unless the King of Denmark refuses to join in the Northern Alliance under the conditions stipulated by the existing agreements between the courts of Stockholm and St. Petersburg. His Majesty, the King of Sweden, engages himself to assure that this union occurs in such a manner so as to assure as much as possible the happiness and the liberty of the Norwegian people.

Article III. In order to give the greatest effect to the engagements contracted by His Majesty the King of Sweden in the first article of this treaty, which are for the purpose of the direct operations and against the communal enemy of the two powers, and finally to place His Majesty the King of Sweden in a state so as to be able to commence the aforementioned operations with out the loss of time and as soon as the season shall permit, His Majesty engages himself to provide to His Majesty the King of Sweden (independent of the other assistances which general circumstances may place at his disposition) for the service in the field during the present year as well as the equipment, transport and support of his troops the sum of one million pounds sterling payable month by month in London to the agent authorized by His Majesty, in a manner such that each monthly payment shall not exceed £200,000 sterling until the entire sum has been paid.

Article IV. It is agreed between the two contracting parties that an advance, whose sum and date of payment shall be determined between them, and which shall be deducted from the previously stipulated £1,000,000, shall be made to His Majesty the King of Sweden for placing in the field and paying for the movement of his troops. The remainder of the aforementioned subsidies, shall begin to run from the day of the debarkation of the Swedish army, as stipulated in the first article of the present treaty.

Article V. The two contracting powers desire a solid and durable guarantee of their political and commercial relations. His Britannic Majesty, animated by the desire to give his ally proofs of his sincerity, consents to cede to His Majesty and to his successors of the crown of Sweden, in the order of succession established by His Majesty and by the parliament of his kingdom, effective from the date of 26 September 1810, the island of Guadeloupe in the West Indies, and to transfer to His Majesty all the rights of His Britannic Majesty on this island, until such time as His Majesty may take actual possession. This colony shall be turned over to the commissioners designated by His Majesty the King of Sweden in the course of the month of August, of the present year, or three months after the debarkation of the Swedish troops on the continent. All shall be in accordance with the conditions agreed upon by the two powers in a separate article annexed to the present treaty.

Article VI. In a recriprocal consequence of what was stipulated in the previous article, His Majesty the King of Sweden engages himself to to accord, for the period of 20 years after the signing of this treaty, to the subjects of His Britannic Majesty the rights of warehousing in the ports of Gothenburg, Carlham and Stralsund, should this latter place return to Swedish domination, for all products and merchandise, be it from Great Britain, or its colonies, loaded aboard English or Swedish merchant vessels. The said objects, for whatever purpose introduced into Sweden, shall pay a 1% tariff on their entry and upon their exit. On all other objects relative to this article they shall conform to the general laws of Sweden, always treating the subjects of his Britannic Majesty on the same footing as the most favored nations.

Article VII. Dating from the day of signing of the present treaty, His Majesty the King of the United Kingdom of Great Britain and Ireland and His Majesty the King of Sweden reciprocally promise to not separate their interests and particularly those of Sweden to which are referred by the present treaty in any negotiation whatsoever with their communal enemy.

Article VIII. The ratification of the present treaty shall be exchanged in Stockholm in the space of four weeks or sooner if possible.

without compensation or remaining loyal to Napoleon. Though he chose the latter, Friedrich VI's actions were based primarily on self preservation, and his army never took an active part in the upcoming campaign. Instead it chose to remain on its own borders in an effort to prevent the further loss of territory.

The Rhinbund

Napoleon still held sway in the rest of Germany, formed into the Confederation of the Rhine. This control was not one of willing compliance in many states, such as Westphalia, where

FRIEDRICH WILHELM ESCAPING TO BRESLAU

German nationalism was beginning to burn in the hearts of those whose states had been broken apart to form a kingdom for Napoleon's brother Jérôme. Despite the faint cracks in the alliances with some of the Confederation of the Rhine countries, Napoleon's faith in his other German allies remained unshakable. They remained firmly yoked to the French wagon.

CONTINUING DEVELOPMENTS IN PRUSSIAN POLITICS

On 19 January the French learned that the King of Prussia planned to move the Prussian royal family to Breslau. A regency was to remain in Berlin, while the diplomatic corps was free to remain in Berlin or follow the king to Breslau.[17]

Natzmer had returned from his interview with the Czar and reassured Friedrich-Wilhelm of the Russian motives. He urged Friedrich-Wilhelm to escape the French and move the seat of the Prussian government to Silesia, which would then neutralized. Then the King of Prussia could escape French control and act as he choose. It was at this time that a division of Grenier's corps arrived in Berlin and cantoned itself around Potsdam, disregarding the formal terms of the Treaty of 24 February 1812. Though it is unclear if this move was motivated by a desire to intimidate and control Friedrich-Wilhelm, it did serve to stir up the Prussian population and gave rise to fears the French were there to seize the Prussian king if he acted against them.

The arrival of Grenier served to hasten the king's move to Breslau, and on 22 January the move began in an effort to present Napoleon with a fait accompli. Upon his arrival in Breslau on the 25th, the Berlin newspapers announced the move and recommended to their readers that they treat the French as allies.[18]

In an effort to mask Prussia's true intentions, vague assurances were made to Napoleon, indicating that if the Grand Duchy of Warsaw was invaded, it was natural that the 12,000 man Prussian Army then in Prussia would form the cadre of a new contingent that would move east

35

PRUSSIAN LANDWEHR ON THE MARCH

into Silesia. The French response to the King of Prussia's move came on 26 January and, in essence, accepted the move. However, Napoleon directed that the King of Prussia was in no manner to open negotiations with the Russians for the neutralization of Silesia.

Maréchal Lefebvre, then the French Embassy's First Secretary to Berlin, learned that the Prussian recruits from Brandenburg were being directed to Silesia and not towards Neu-Stettin. The maneuver's obviously hostile actions were not lost on the aging marshal. Indeed, most of the French stationed in Prussia were acutely aware of the Prussian hostility towards them. They also noted that the two Prussian armies, the one at Colberg and the other in Silesia, made no move to threaten the advancing Russians.

On 3 February Scharnhorst proposed to the king that he issue an edict directing the creation of "Freiwilliger jägers" or volunteer light infantry detachments every infantry battalion and cavalry regiment in the army. These volunteers were to arm and equip themselves at their own expense. At first the jägers were to be commanded by officers and non-commissioned officers of the regular army, but after a period of time they were to form their own cadres by election.

The jägers were to be volunteers, aged 17 to 24, capable of service for at least one year. They were to serve without pay, dignities nor distinctions. It was the Prussian equivalent of the French cry of 1792 - "la patrie en danger." Initially the king was uncertain of this and feared it would damage the class structure of the country by opening the officer corps up to bourgeois. However, the realities of the situation led the king to relent and the edict was issued on 9 February. Eventually most regular infantry battalions had a jäger detachment of 60 to 80 men.

On the same day, the King signed an edict that made all citizens of the Prussian provinces, despite their birth, rank in society or fortune, liable for the defense of the fatherland. This edict and another issued on 13 February, began the recall of the Prussian reserves and soldiers on leave, as well as the requisitions of horses and the drafting of men for the regular army.[19] On 7

February the Prussian Assembly considered an ordinance presented to it by its president, Graf Dohna. Its title was "Ordonnance on the landwehr and landsturm." This ordonnance was passed into law.

It established that the landwehr should consist of citizens 18 to 45 years of age, and capable of bearing arms, excepting various ministers, teachers and others. It was to be formed from volunteers, but if insufficient volunteers were found, it was to be supported by a draft. Its uniform was to be simple and its exercises reduced to the bare minimum. This militiamen was to receive his arms from the state, but his equipment came from his community.

The landwehr was to consist solely of infantry, formed into companies, battalions and brigades according to the province in which it was raised. Each brigade was to have four battalions. Their officers were to be drawn from the ranks by nomination and their nomination was not dependent upon the king or upon his agents. Only the brigade commanders were to be named by the king. The landwehr was to be paid only when in the presence of the enemy and was not to be employed outside of its province.

The landsturm was a call of all able-bodied men, below the age of 60, who were not members of the landwehr or the regular army. It was to receive the bare minimum of military training and was not to be called out until the enemy was in, or approaching their home province. Their armament was to consist of hunting rifles, pikes, farm tools, or anything else available. Their objective was to attack convoys, small detachments, stragglers, and marauders. They were not intended for use in major battles.[20]

About the same time, the Prussian Krümper system[21] began producing reserves and new recruits for Bülow and the other Prussian forces. In a period of six weeks, a total of 30,000 men were called to arms. The royal ordinance called for the organization of a further 30,000 landwehr. The execution of all this was to be handled by a general committee of seven members of the government, who would operate in concert with Yorck.

According to the ordinance, the Prussian countryside was to be divided into districts which were to raise landwehr brigades. In each of these districts the nobles, bourgeois, and property owning peasants organized a sub-committee, which received funding from the General Committee. Each sub-committee named the officers of the brigade for its district, subject to ratification by the General Committee. The General Committee nominated the brigade commanders, subject to approval by the king or his representative. The only modification to the ordinance was the direction that a volunteer cavalry regiment also be raised in each province, at the expense of that province.

At the same time as the King of Prussia moved to Breslau, the Estates of East Prussia met on their own initiative in Königsberg. They were cut off from communication with their king, who was still officially an ally of the French. They acted with great resolve and passed a resolution in favor of Yorck's defection. They made all the resources of their province available to Yorck, Bülow and Borstell, who were the principal military representatives available. They began to call up quotas of men due under this ordinance for Landwehr and Landsturm. The national pride of the townsmen of East Prussia brought out more than were called. In contrast, the peasants in the countryside showed no enthusiasm and had to be rounded up by dragoons.

On 9 February Pillau capitulated to the Russians, and Prussia found itself once more linked by sea communications with England. Its commander, Castella, had capitulated without firing a shot, to the first summons of the Russian General Sievers. Though Sievers did not have sufficient forces to prosecute a siege, much of the garrison was Prussian and, supported by the Prussian citizenry, they declared they would not fire on the Russians. Castella had little choice but to capitulate.[22]

As the campaign developed, the King of Prussia came more and more under the influence of the Russians. He sent his aide Natzmer to consult with the Czar. On his return, he reported to the King of Prussia that the Czar had offered an alliance with Prussia on the Prussian conditions. However, the king's indecisiveness prevented any serious negotiating at this time.

The King of Prussia departed Berlin on 22 January and arrived in Breslau, the capital of Silesia, on 25 January. This move brought great delight to his citizens for it signaled much. Despite that, he issued a proclamation exhorting his subjects, in particular the Berliners, to act with the French, as if they were allies and to act in an amicable manner towards Napoleon. He also announced a superior governmental commission established in Berlin, which was charged with maintaining the essential governmental services for the state during the king's absence.

Though his subjects viewed the move to Breslau as the prelude to a sudden breaking of alliances with France, they were soon disappointed. Friedrich-Wilhelm was stricken with fears and was still not able to bring himself to fight Napoleon again. He feared that Napoleon had massive resources from which to draw and that the French armies would once again overwhelm Prussia. Despite his fears and his inability to act decisively at this time, Friedrich-Wilhelm made every effort to continue the mobilization of Prussia's forces at the greatest speed possible. This was done under the guise of raising forces to support Napoleon's demands for a further contingent of forces to fight against the Russians.

As a follow up to Natzmer's contact with the Czar, the King of Prussia dispatched Oberst von Knesebeck to negotiate with the Czar, for terms of a potential military alliance. Knesebeck located the Czar on 15 February in Klodawa and presented his credentials.[23] The Czar moved to Kalisch in an effort to close with Breslau and improve communications. He also massed 40,000 Russian soldiers on the Silesian border, in an effort to increase the agitation of the Prussian citizenry and increase the pressure he could bring to bear on Friedrich-Wilhelm.

The Russian victory at Kalisch, the blockades of Thorn, Modlin, Czentoschau and Zamosc, the Russian occupation of the Grand Duchy of Warsaw, and the retreating French forces, provided the King of Prussia with powerful reasons to act. The Czar now occupied the greatest part of old Poland. During the Russian occupation of Poland, the Czar ordered his generals and troops to treat the Polish as "friends and brothers." He was actively politicking to be elected the constitutional king of a free and independent Poland. To do this, the Czar needed German support. The Czar saw that support would be best provided by Prussia. However, the Russian control of Poland was contrary to Prussian goals in this area and also provided motivation for Friedrich-Wilhelm to reach a condominium with the Czar, whereby Russian expansion could be controlled to Prussia's benefit.

When Knesebeck arrived at the Czar's headquarters, he had some suspicion of the Czar's intentions vis-a-vis the Grand Duchy of Warsaw. As both negotiators were aware of this, the Czar was willing to make concessions on this point, rather than drive Prussia firmly into Napoleon's arms because of his dream. Knesebeck played the negotiations slowly and stated that he was not fully empowered to come to terms, but must consult with Friedrich-Wilhelm.

To a degree the Prussians were playing both ends of the game. Napoleon had offered the Prussians, in return for a negotiated peace with Russia, compensations from the Grand Duchy of Warsaw and the Kingdom of Westphalia. A negotiated settlement of this sort would certainly have been preferable to the chances incurred in breaking from Napoleon and risking losing everything. In an effort to allow time to fully sound out Napoleon's proposal, Knesebeck delayed the negotiations with Czar Alexander as long as he could.

This plan was overturned by the return of Baron von Stein from Königsberg to the Czar's headquarters. He asked that he be sent to "negotiate directly with the King of Prussia," and that he would, "quickly form the alliance" that Knesebeck had not negotiated.

On 24 February Stein, despite an attack of gout, was stuffed into a miserable carriage and secretly dispatched to Breslau to negotiate with Friedrich-Wilhelm. Within minutes after his arrival in Breslau, he was in the presence of the King of Prussia.

He assured Friedrich-Wilhelm of Russia's good intentions towards Prussia, of its willingness to see Prussia restored all that it had lost after 1806, and of his desire to make Prussia greater than it had ever been before.

Von Stein then threatened Friedrich-Wilhelm with the Russian annexation of occupied eastern Prussia as far as the Vistula. In addition to this threat, his eastern provinces were detached from his authority, and his generals, notably Yorck, were breaking away from his control. The King of Prussia had little choice. The final straw came, when Napoleon renounced his earlier promise of territorial compensation from the Grand Duchy and Westphalia.

On February 26, the King of Prussia decided to move Prussia into the Russian camp and declare war on France. The actual treaty was signed on 27 February by the Prussians and on 28 February by the Czar. The treaty was an offensive and defensive alliance with the goal of the independence of Europe from Napoleon as well as the reconstruction of Prussia in conditions which guaranteed it peace and security. Neither country was to negotiate a separate peace with France, and both would act in concert to bring Austria into the alliance. The Russian military contingent was set at 150,000 men, and that to be provided by Prussia was 48,000 men, not including fortress garrisons. Russia further guaranteed to negotiate with England for subsidies for the Prussians. The Grand Duchy of Warsaw was to be divided, such that Prussia received what it had held prior to the Treaty of Tilsit, and Russia received the rest. The King of Prussia called on the whole Prussian nation to rise up against their oppressors, but because of his timidity, this proclamation was not published until 16 March. His declaration of war did not reach Paris until 27 March.

Prior to his formal declaration, the king began a process of decentralizing his kingdom, something most unusual for a monarchy in this period. He established four military governments. The government between the Elbe and the Oder was under General l'Estocq, that between the Oder and the Vistula was under Generallieutenant von Tauentzien, that between the Vistula and the Russian frontier was under Generallieutenant von Massenbach and the last, in Silesia, was under Generallieutenant Graf Götzen. The civil authorities of these four governments were completely self contained, and made responsible for the supply of recruits, equipment, etc., while the military authorities converted these raw materials into an army ready to fight the French.[24]

Clearly time was Prussia's greatest need at this moment, but events forced their hands. Napoleon began increasing his demands for military support on Prussia, and required that the Prussian military be placed at the disposal of his marshals. Further impetus to his demands arose, when the advancing cossacks pushed the French out of Berlin on 4 March 1813.

On 15 March Scharnhorst submitted to the King of Prussia his proposal for the total mobilization of the Prussian state, by means of the organization of a "landwehr" and a "landsturm." This program was an expansion of the earlier ordinance passed by the Prussian assembly. The king approved Scharnhorst's program on 17 March, but because of the lack of arms, supplies, and the requirement for training, no large formed bodies of landwehr took to the field until after the Armistice of 4 June 1813.

The king also authorized the formation of several "freikorps," which were to act in concert with the Prussian army. They were the "von Lützow Freikorps," which was raised on 21 March; the "von Reuss" foreign battalion and the "von Reiche freiwilliger jägers," both of which were formed of German deserters from the Grande Armée; "von Hellwig's Streifkorps," "von Schill's Hussars," and a number of other, smaller units.[25]

Much is said about the influence of German nationalism at this time. Secret organizations such as the Tugendbund, the nationalistic literature of Göethe, and the "Volkslieder" appear to have had very little significant influence at this time.[26] This is most eloquently demonstrated by the small numbers of men who came forward to "throw off the French yoke." Nearly all of these

Convention Between Russia and Prussia Breslau, 27 February and Kalish, 28 February 1813

Article I. There shall be, from the date of the signing of the current treaty, peace, friendship and alliance between His Majesty the Czar of all the Russias and His Majesty, the King of Prussia, their heirs and successors, their states and respective subjects in perpetuity.

Article II. The alliance between Russia and Prussia is offensive and defensive for actual war. Its immediate goal is the reconstruction of Prussia in the proportions which will assure the tranquillity of the two states and to establish guarantees. As this double objective cannot be obtained so long the French army occupies positions or strong points in Northern Germany, so long as this power exerts an influence in this area the principal military operations shall be directed towards this essential point.

Article III. As a result of the aforementioned article, the two contractual parties are agreed that they will assist with all means placed by Providence at their disposition; but, to precisely define the forces which will immediately be employed, His Majesty, the Czar of all the Russias engages himself to place in the field 150,000 men and His Majesty the King of Prussia no less than 80,000 men, without counting the garrisons of various fortresses. It is understood that His Prussian Majesty promises, with the good faith that is his character, to augment the number of his forces of all kinds, according to circumstances, and this augmentation shall consist of a national militia, whose raising shall be the result of communal efforts.

Article IV. The two powers shall constantly consult on the basis for a plan of operations and constantly act in concert on war operations. His Majesty the King of Prussia shall designate, for this purpose, a senior officer who shall be attached to the headquarters of His Majesty the Czar of all Russias, and who shall be empowered with all the powers necessary to act, without loss of time, upon all decisions which shall be made.

Article V. All who are available to the Prussian army shall commence to cooperate with those of His Majesty the Czar of all Russias, from the date of the ratification of the present treaty.

Article VI. The principals which unite the two contractual parties have for a unity of actions and intentions, His Majesty the Czar of all the Russias, and His Majesty the King of Prussia reciprocally engage themselves to at no point negotiate with the enemy, at no point to sign a peace, nor truce, nor convention which is kept secret from the other party.

Article VII. His Majesty the Czar of all the Russias and His Majesty the King of Prussia, shall communicate reciprocally and confidentially all accounts of their political acts and shall promptly put all their efforts to bring the Court of Vienna to unite itself as soon as possible to their cause.

Article VIII. His Majesty the Czar of all the Russias promises to support in the most efficient manner, all the measures taken by His Majesty the King of Prussia in England to obtain arms, munitions and subsidies from that power.

Article IX. It is determined that, in continuation of the present treaty, a separate convention on the commercial relations between the two powers shall be concluded. It shall be based on the principals of alliance which have been established by the contracting parties.

Article X. There shall be equally concluded a parallel convention to regulate all that should be necessary for the marches and provisioning of the armies of His Majesty of all the Russias while they are in the states of His Majesty the King of Prussia.

Article XI. The above articles shall be kept secret for a period of two months, but may be communicated immediately to Austria, England and Sweden.

Article XII. The present treaty shall be ratified in the shortest possible time, without which these preparations or military measures may be suspended.

Article 1 - Separate and Secret

The total security and independence of Prussia cannot be solidly established except by returning to him the force he had before the war of 1806. His Majesty Czar of all the Russias, who has, in this regard, in his official declarations, been heretofore been the voice of His Majesty the King of Prussia, by these secret and separate articles, hereby declares that it will not set down its arms so long as Prussia is not reconstituted in the statistical, geographical and financial proportions conforming to what it had prior to the preceding epoch. To this end, His Majesty the Czar of all the Russias promises, in the most like manner, he will apply for equivalent restitution, which according to circumstances meet the interests of the two states, to aggrandize Prussia from all the acquisitions which may be made by force of arms and negotiations in the northern part of Germany except the ancient possessions of the house of Hanover. In all these arrangements there shall be conserved in the different provinces which pass under Prussian domination the assembly and districts necessary to constitute an independent state body.

Article 2. To give the preceding article a precision conforming to the perfect understanding which exists between the two contracting parties, His Majesty the Czar of all the Russias guarantees to His Majesty the King of Prussia all his actual provinces, including Old Prussia, to which shall be joined a territory which, according to all the reports, military and geographical, bind that province to Silesia.

Article 3. The two contracting parties shall make every effort to bring the Austrian court into this alliance as soon as possible.

men were incorporated into the two small battalions of German volunteers: "von Reuss" and "von Reiche".

On 27 March the Prussian ambassador arrived in the Tuileries with the Prussian declaration of war against France. Napoleon's initial reaction was to distill the impact of this into numbers. He was told that there were 4,500,000 Prussian citizens and that they could present a field force of 40,000 men in two months. He further conjectured that they could never field more than 60,000 men. He gave no thought to the lessons of the French Revolution and the rush to arms of the French citizenry.[27]

Shortly after this, he learned that Lübeck, Hamburg, and the three departments forming the 32nd Military Division had revolted. He also learned that Mecklenburg-Schwerin and Mecklenburg-Strelitz had abandoned the Confederation of the Rhine to join Prussia and Russia. The impact of these defections was very small in terms of new combatants for Napoleon's enemies, but the morale effect was not so insignificant.

The Austrian position was significantly complicated by the defection of Prussia and the smaller states from the Confederation of the Rhine. There was a level of humiliation in Vienna, when a small state like Prussia showed the resolution and bravery to champion the independence of Germany, while Austria with 20,000,000 inhabitants, continued to act as a vassal of France. At this point Austrian support of France began to fade rapidly.

The Convention of Kalisch was signed in late February. It established a formal armistice between the Prussian and Russian armies, and the Austrian Emperor was advised of this convention. The Austrian mobilization continued and a corps of 30,000 men was ready to move if necessary.

Metternich continued negotiations with France and advised them, that the only solution for the present situation was the abandoning of the Grand Duchy of Warsaw to the Prussians and the return of the Illyrian provinces to Austria. Furthermore, the Hanseatic states and Holland were to be given their independence. Needless to say Otto remained bound by Napoleon's instructions which were as intransigent as ever and negotiations ceased to be a viable solution. Napoleon felt that he was being ill served by Otto and replaced him by the Comte de Narbonne, one of his aides de camp and an experienced diplomat. Narbonne arrived in Vienna on 17 March, and almost immediately was received by Metternich. When they met, Metternich found Narbonne bound by the same instructions that had bound Otto.[28]

Narbonne quickly evaluated the sentiments of the Austrian court and reported them to Napoleon. On 1 April he wrote Maret, Duke of Bassano, and the French Minister of Foreign Affair, stating that Metternich's support of the French system was valid, only so long as there was progress towards peace. He regarded it probable that Austria would take an active part in the war, if it was against France.

About the same time, he received a dispatch from Napoleon asking about the situation in Vienna vis-a-vis the defection of Prussia. Napoleon, furthermore, directed Narbonne to offer Austria a rich reward, in an effort to have them support his intended destruction of Prussia. Napoleon felt that, as Austria wished peace, they could request to open negotiations with Russia and that the Czar would accept them. An armistice was to be established during which insincere negotiations were to be conducted.

During this armistice, Napoleon would deal with Prussia. Narbonne was to offer to Austria the dismemberment of Prussia. 1,000,000 Prussians were to be left on the left bank of the Vistula, 2,000,000 were to go to Austria, and 2,000,000 more were to be divided between Saxony and Westphalia. Austria's share was to be the rich province of Silesia, stripped from Austria by Friedrich the Great barely 50 years before. In return the Austrians were to provide Napoleon with 100,000 men in early May.

This proposition clearly shows Napoleon's lack of understanding of Austrian concerns and desires. This was reflected by Metternich's cold reception of Narbonne's reading of Napoleon's letter of instruction. In response, Metternich demanded to know if Napoleon had decided to dissolve the Confederation of the Rhine and restore independence to the states he had dissolved, notably the Hanseatic cities and Holland. The response, which came weeks later was negative.

On 18 April, obeying his instructions from Paris, Narbonne asked if the Austrian auxiliary force of 30,000 men was ready act in co-operation with the French armies when Napoleon returned to the campaign. He once again became convinced that Austria would remain neutral, unless it could act militarily against the French. The auxiliary corps was not to be placed at Napoleon's disposition.

At the same time, Metternich actively intrigued to prevent the escape to Saxony of Poniatowski's small force, and the enfeebled Saxon VII Corps, that had been trapped by the withdrawal of Schwarzenberg. Metternich's policies and negotiations drew Austria into a situation where, though allied with France, she was actively arming and plotting against France. Though the Austrian court continued its intrigues, it was not to take an active military role in the upcoming campaign until much later in the year.

[1] Charras, La Guerre de 1813, pg 336.

[2] Thiry, Lutzen et Bautzen, pg 39.

[3] Charras, La Guerre de 1813, pg 334.

[4] Thiry, Lutzen et Bautzen, pg 39.

[5] Ragsdale, Détente, pgs 14–15.

[6] Chandler, The Campaigns of Napoleon, pgs 505–506 and 872.

[7] Charras, La Guerre de 1813, pg 144.

[8] d'Ussel, Defection de la Prusse, pg 172.

[9] d'Ussel, Defection de la Prusse, pg 156.

[10] Charras, La Guerre de 1813, pg 179–180.

[11] d'Ussel, Defection de la Prusse, pg 180.

[12] Thiry, Baron J., Lutzen et Bautzen, pg 40.

[13] von Quisthorp, Nord-Armee, Vol II, pg 219.

[14] von Quisthorp, Nord-Armee, Vol II, pg 223.

[15] von Quisthorp, Nord-Armee, Vol II, pg 225.

[16] Charras, La Guerre de 1813, pg 383.

[17] d'Ussel, Defection de la Prusse, pg 211–212.

[18] d'Ussel, Defection de la Prusse, pg 213.

[19] d'Ussel, Defection de la Prusse, pg 252.

[20] Charras, La Guerre de 1813, pg 173–175.

[21] The "krümper" system was the method the Prussians used to evade the restrictions on the size of the Prussian army established in the Treaty of Tilsit. It was a process by which recruits were brought into the Prussian army, trained and exercised, then discharged to a civilian status, and replaced by new recruits, who underwent the same process. This provided the Prussians with a large, ready reserve to be called back to the colors if and when war erupted.

[22] Vaudoncourt, Prince Eugene, pg 132.

[23] Charras, La Guerre de 1813, pg 192.

[24] Holleben, Frühjahrsfeldzuges, pg 109.

[25] Holleben, Frühjahrsfeldzuges, pg 167–169.

[26] The Tugendbund or "League of Virtue" was Prussian patriotic organization founded to promote Prussian morale and to achieve independence from the humiliations of the Treaty of Tilsit. It engaged in extensive anti-Napoleonic propaganda. The volkslieder or "people's songs" were popular nationalistic songs aimed at German nationalism and pride.

[27] Charras, La Guerre de 1813, pg 310.

[28] Charras, La Guerre de 1813, pg 360.

The Race to Rearm

THE ARMIES REBUILD

Once out of Russia, the French army quickly set about rebuilding itself around the cadres of veterans that survived the invasion, Augereau's XI Corps, Grenier's two divisions from Italy, and the garrisons of various German cities. The once powerful French I Corps had dwindled from 66,345 men to 3,019 by 8 January 1812. Of those only 674 officers and 1,607 enlisted, or a total of 2,281 men, were still capable of bearing arms.[1] On 1 February Eugéne wrote Napoleon from Posen and stated that the various army corps, which had only a year earlier contained over 125,000 French infantry, now contained:

I Corps	1,600
II Corps	1,900
III Corps	1,000
IV Corps	1,900
Total	*6,400*

Regiments now existed only in the form of small bodies of men equal to one or two companies.

The losses were not one sided. The Russians were equally exhausted, having suffered 150,000 dead from all causes and probably suffered a further 300,000 more crippled and maimed from wounds and frostbite. Despite these heavy losses they were probably in better condition to continue the fight than the French.

REFORMING THE INFANTRY

Even before the disaster of the retreat struck, Napoleon had begun rebuilding his army. In October, he'd written to his Minister of War to review the hospitals, depots, and other sources for every man that could be found who belonged to any regiment which had gone in part or in total into Russia. Out of a total of 26,505 men located, only 4,547 men fit for duty were identified, and of them only 1,822 were in a state ready for dispatch to the army.[2]

France and her allies frantically began reorganizing and rebuilding their armies. Napoleon drew troops from Italy and Spain, transferred the National Guard to the active army, and scraped the depots in France as well as the garrisons of Germany for every soldier who could carry a musket.[3]

The National Guard, whose legislative foundations forbade forced incorporation into the line army, found itself dragged, without a second thought, off to the frontiers by the Senatus Consultum of 11 January 1813.[4] The National Guard consisted of a total of 84,000 infantry and 9,000 artillerists trained and organized in 1812. These 88 cohorts of infantry were reorganized into the 135th through 156th Infantry Regiments.[5] The artillerists were used to reform and flesh out existing artillery units to full strength. These regiments were quickly sent to the front. Eleven went to the Armée de l'Elbe. The remaining regiments were sent to form the I and II Corps d'Observation du Rhin, with the exception of the 143rd Line Regiment which became the garrison of Puycerda.[6]

The men drawn from the depots were quickly organized into provisional companies of approximately 100 men. These companies were marched to the frontiers and, en route, they were issued arms and uniforms. Their training was completed on their way to the frontier. Once there they were organized into provisional battalions and the provisional battalions were organized into provisional regiments.

In addition, there were 98 companies of men detached from the depots of the infantry regiments that served as garrisons aboard the blockaded French naval vessels. These men were also formed into provisional battalions that served as garrisons along the Oder and elsewhere in Germany. This provided about 4,500 infantry.

Napoleon also turned to the Departmental Reserve Companies, a sort of auxiliary police force that was generally composed of veteran soldiers. Using the Decree of 7 February 1813, Napoleon drew from this force 3,307 men, who were sent to Mainz. Once they were in Mainz, they received officers and were formed into the 37th Légère Regiment of four battalions.[7] Two battalions of the Municipal Guard of Paris, the 3rd Battalion being in Spain, was bodily transferred to the army, sent to Erfurt and used to form the cadre for the newly forming 134th Line Regiment.[8]

Still further veteran soldiers were drawn from the naval artillery. The Naval Artillery was formed in 1792 and trained to serve as gunners aboard ship and as infantry ashore. A total of 18,000 men were tied up in this organization that had little or no function since the British had blockaded them into their ports. Napoleon gathered together the 13 to 14,000 dispersed marines for his new army, forming them into four Marine Infantry Regiments with a total of 26 battalions. These regiments was also directed to Mainz. According to some sources they were not to be among the better formations that were raised in this effort. However, they served in Marmont's army corps and in his memoirs he said, "The regiments of marine artillery formed the depth of my army corps, meriting many eulogies for their bravery and good spirit."[9] The quality of the marine infantry is, at best, subject to some debate. The marine regiments were reorganized and expanded as follows:

1st Marine Regiment
    1st Battalion through 4th Battalion   Brought to strength
    5th Battalion through 8th Battalion   Newly formed
2nd Marine Regiment
    1st Battalion through 5th Battalion   Brought to strength
    6th Battalion through 10th Battalion   Newly formed
3rd Marine Regiment
    1st Battalion through 2nd Battalion   Brought to strength
    3rd Battalion through 4th Battalion   Newly formed
4th Marine Regiment
    1st Battalion through 2nd Battalion   Brought to strength
    3rd Battalion through 4th Battalion   Newly formed[10]

Napoleon had called up the draft class of 1813 before he invaded Russia. It was in the depots at the end of November 1812, and consisted of 120,000 men. They would yield about 90,000 trained soldiers, who would have about enough time to receive a hat, a musket, and some training in the manual of arms before they would march into Germany. They were 19 years old.

These efforts at raising men were not sufficient for Napoleon, and he began a new levy against the draft classes of 1812, 1811, 1810, and 1809 in an effort to raise another 100,000 men. A further 150,000 men were drawn early from the class of 1814. Napoleon was reduced to drafting 18 year olds, something that had not normally been done by the French military. However, the men of the class of 1814 were not to arrive in the depots until April, because of the problems associated with clothing and feeding them.[11]

On 3 April, another Senatus-Consulte authorized a supplementary levy of 180,000 men. From the classes of 1807 through 1812 a further 80,000 men were to be drawn. The class of 1814 was to furnish 90,000 men, who were to be replaced by the Sedentary National Guard. This also included the raising of 10,000 Gardes d'Honneur.[12]

Gathering men together and training them was the first step. The second process was to form them together into new battalions and then to draw the battalions together to form divisions and corps.

On 23 January 1813 Napoleon directed that the 28 regiments being reorganized in the Grande Armée's I, II, and III Corps be rebuilt as follows:

> 1st Battalion Cadre to remain with the Army
> 2nd Battalion Cadre to reform at Erfurt
> 3rd Battalion Cadre to reform at Depot
> 4th Battalion Cadre disbanded
> 5th Battalion was the depot battalion and remained unchanged
> 6th Battalion Cadre to reform at depot
> 6th (bis) Battalion Cadre to organize in the interior of France[13]

Shortly later Napoleon changed his mind on this and issued directions that they be reorganized in the following manner:

> 1st Battalion Cadre 2 Cos to reform Garrisons on the Oder River
> 4 Cos to reform at Erfurt
> 2nd Battalion Cadre to reform at Erfurt
> 3rd Battalion Cadre to reform at Depot as 3rd Battalion and to
> be used to form Provisional Demi-brigades with the Class of 1814
> 4th Battalion Cadre merged into 3rd Battalion
> 5th Battalion was the depot battalion
> 6th Battalion Cadre merged into the 3rd Battalion
> 6th (bis) Battalion Cadre renamed 4th Battalion[14]

THE LACK OF HORSES

Because of the approaching Russians, the French citizenry began to act in an effort to save themselves from invasion. Many cities began voluntarily offering to raise and equip cavalry forces. Eventually 16,000 men were raised in this manner. The principal problem, however, was horses. In January 1813, the French cavalry depots had only 3,000 horses and barely 1,500 had returned from Russia. Napoleon's representatives began an immediate effort to gather up all the horses they could from the Grand Duchy of Warsaw, Prussia, Mecklenburg, and the other German states. However, the advancing Russian armies made this a difficult operation. On 4 January a requisition for 15,000 horses was made in France. The French government found itself forced to resort to taking horses without payment, as it had 20 years before during the early days of the French Revolution.

As a further step, Napoleon made purchases on the markets which produced 7,000 to 8,000 saddle horses, and stripped 3,000 to 4,000 horses out of the gendarmerie. Bourcier made arrangements for 5,200 horses for the cuirassiers, 2,400 for the dragoons and 14,000 for light cavalry. Arrangements were made for 6,000 in Warsaw, 2,700 in Posen, 3,000 in Glogau, 3,500 in Berlin, 3,200 in Hamburg, and 3,200 in Hanover.[15]

However, Eugène's withdrawal from the Grand Duchy and Prussia ruined Napoleon's arrangements for the procurement of 20,000 horses. With the loss of Poland, there remained only the German states, which could provide no more than 12,000 to 13,000 saddle horses. As a result of all of these efforts, a total of 60,000 were within Napoleon's grasp for the reformation of his cavalry. Unfortunately, these horses would arrive at the various depots at a very slow rate, without any regard to the urgency of the need.[16] This problem was to last throughout the campaign, but significant shortages existed into late May and many regiments were almost completely without mounts.[17]

The means of providing equipment for this mass of new cavalry was also lacking. In an effort to increase production, the various manufacturers increased the quantity, but reduced the quality of the equipment. This was to have a negative impact later.

Draft horses were in a similar situation. It was necessary to raise 30,000 draft horses for the 600 guns of the Grande Armée, and a further 15,000 for its military train. To fill this need Napoleon requisitioned 12,500, bought a further 10,000 in the French markets, and directed General Bourcier to buy 5,000 to 6,000 more in Germany.

THE REPLACEMENT OF THE CAVALRY

The first problem for the French army was the destruction of the trained cavaliers lost with the cavalry in Russia. There remained about 9,000 or 10,000 dismounted cavalry which had survived Russia. Napoleon supplemented them by drawing 3,000 officers and non-commissioned officers from the gendarmerie, and further increased the numbers with drafts. All of the surviving cavalry from Russia was sent to Brunswick and Hanover to be reorganized. The army retained five squadrons of Guard cavalry and sent the dismounted Guard cavalry to Fulda, where it formed the cadres for five more squadrons.[18]

Another new force of cavalry was organized by Napoleon. This was the Gardes d'Honneur. One major source of manpower that had escaped much of the impact of the wars was the upper and middle classes. Their sons had many of the prerequisite skills necessary for cavalry, as most already knew how to ride. They were often familiar with fire arms and would require little additional training. Also, by drafting them into the army, they provided Napoleon with the sons of many significant families to hold as hostage.[19] A total of four regiments of the Gardes d'Honneur, 10,000 men, were raised.[20] In addition to the native French forces, there were several Polish cavalry regiments that passed into French service. General Dombrowski was charged with their organization.

Once the dismounted cavalry was at Fulda, each line cavalry regiment grouped its survivors by companies of 100 men. All excess was sent to the depots, leaving about 10,000 to 11,000 dismounted cavalry in Hanover and Brunswick.

RAISING NEW CAVALRY CORPS

Napoleon disbanded the old cavalry corps and divisional organizations and ordered the formation of two new corps. The I Cavalry Corps was to have four divisions and the II Cavalry Corps was to have three. Each of the divisions was to have eight regiments of at least one squadron organized into four provisional regiments.[21]

The German magazines provided sufficient arms to reequip this force, but they lacked sufficient clothing and other equipment. General Belliard and General Bourcier were charged with procuring mounts for this force and by mid-March they had received 10,000 mounts for the army. But at the same time, the two cavalry corps had between them only 3,000 horses.

If Napoleon had had full magazines when he started reorganizing his forces in 1813, by the middle of March he would have been able to send 10,000 fully equipped cavalry to Eugène, who was in desperate need of cavalry to face the tremendous Russian superiority in this arm. Unfortunately, he did not.

In mid-March, when he learned that Bourcier had acquired 2,000 to 3,000 more horses, Napoleon dispatched from the French depots, 2,600 equipped, but dismounted cavaliers. This brought the French cavalry force to about 12,000 to 13,000 men, but many of them were still unequipped and many were new drafts.

After the organization of the first two cavalry corps was under way, Napoleon decided to organize a third cavalry corps. To do this, he swept up the remains of the cadres still in Hanover and Brunswick, called several cadres drawn from Spain, drew more officers and non-commissioned officers from the gendarmerie, graduated students from the cavalry school earlier than normal, and began to flesh this force out with conscripts from the class of 1812 who were familiar with horses. These men were was then sent to Mainz where they were to be mounted.

They were was placed under General Lebrun, and organized into two divisions, each with four régiments de marche. The first division contained the companies furnished by the depots of the regiments of the I Cavalry Corps and the second division contained the companies formed from the depots of the II Cavalry Corps. Napoleon retained the III Cavalry Corps in Mainz, until the provisional regiments were solid enough for service in the field.

French Artillery

The French artillery was also in a sad condition. The Grande Armée in Germany had 48 artillery companies that had not taken part in the Russian campaign. Napoleon designated 20 of them to be assigned to the field army, and 28 to man the various garrisons in Germany. Eugène was organizing another 52 companies in Magdeburg.

To reinforce the morale of his raw infantry, Napoleon chose to organize the artillery of the army so that there would be two batteries (sixteen guns) for each infantry division and two horse batteries (twelve guns) for each cavalry division. Each army corps was to have two horse batteries (six guns each) and two reserve batteries (eight guns each).[22] Only about 20 organized artillery company cadres had returned from Russia, plus a small number of officers and about 1,000 gunners whose units had collapsed during the retreat. This force was sent to Magdeburg, where they joined several incomplete artillery companies. They were merged with other fragments that had been posted about Germany. As they were joined together to form functional artillery companies, the 52 National Guard artillery companies assigned to the infantry cohorts, totaling 5,000 men, were also dispatched from France to form companies for service under Eugène.

Certainly those men remaining in the various depots were quickly sent forward, but in addition naval gunners and a draft of ten men per company from the artillery companies serving in Spain brought more men. These men, plus extraordinary drafts from the schools at Metz and Saint-Cyr were used to reform the Old and Young Guard artillery. The Guard was to be raised to 26 batteries, six Old Guard Foot, 14 Young Guard Foot, and 6 Old Guard Horse Batteries.

Military Train

The military train was in even worse condition. Most of it had gone into Russia and simply vanished. To address this, Napoleon ordered a complete restructuring of the train. It was to be organized into four regiments, each with nine companies. This effort, however, required the allocation of 4,480 men and 8,000 horses. The problems that haunted the infantry and cavalry also haunted the train.[23]

The Guard Cavalry

When the Guard cavalry was reconstituted, only five of the six regiments were reorganized. The 3rd Lancer Regiment was not re-raised. The Guard cavalry regiments were reformed from the debris in Hanover and Brunswick and every man that could be drawn from the Guard depots. New drafts of veterans were drawn from the gendarmerie and from the armies of Spain. Each line regiment surrendered 25 veterans for the Imperial Guard. Napoleon further directed that Eugène surrender all mounted Guard cavalry that remained with him, so that it might join the reorganizing regiments, bringing the total to about 5,000 men. When five dismounted squadrons of the Guard arrived in Fulda, they found material to fill their every need except horses. Those were being gathered in France.

One interesting reinforcement for the Guard cavalry came when Eugène directed the incorporation of 200 of the Lithuanian Gendarmerie to be incorporated into the Polish or 1st Guard Lancers. Napoleon, who might otherwise have discouraged such acts, approved this in a letter dated 26 January.[24]

THE GUARD INFANTRY

Rebuilding his Guard presented Napoleon with another problem. The Guard had traditionally consisted of experienced, elite soldiers. His first step was to reorganize those guardsmen who had escaped Russia. The second step was to recall 25 veteran soldiers from every battalion from Spain, as well as men from every veteran formation in the French army that were suitable for the Guard. A total of 3,000 veterans were collected by this method. The Young Guard was reformed using the draft and an additional ten regiments were raised from the best men found in the recruit depots.[25] The goal was to raise the guard to 36,000 men and by 1 March, there were actually 18,600 guard infantry. The goal of 36,000 men was never realized and with the decree of 3 April relative to the drafting of an additional 80,000 men, Napoleon earmarked 24,000 for the Young Guard.[26]

In general, Napoleon found himself with plenty of manpower with which to rebuild his guard, but he found himself desperately short of cadres and officers. On 21 January he wrote to Eugène stating that, "The Guard is being organized into a large force. I already have here a division of 10,000 men, and I have need of officers and of cadres to receive the men who are coming from all sides."[27]

THE FIELD ARMIES ARE REBUILT

Napoleon began the task of reorganizing the field armies with the establishment of the Corps d'Observation de l'Elbe. It was to have three divisions and a total of 48 battalions. On 15 February, it began organizing near Magdeburg. By 15 March it was complete and consisted of units that had been National Guard cohorts.

The I Corps d'Observation du Rhin was formed under Maréchal Ney around Mainz in March. It was to have four divisions totaling sixty battalions. The II Corps d'Observation du Rhin formed under General Marmont. It was to have fifty battalions. It began by forming three divisions around Mainz between late March and early April. A fourth division was not completed until late May.[28]

The Corps d'Observation d'Italie was formed with four divisions and a total of fifty-four battalions. The new I Corps was to be raised with four divisions and a total of sixty-four battalions. The new II Corps was to have four divisions and a total of forty-eight battalions. Durutte's division and the two divisions of Saxons became the new VII Corps and the Imperial Guard was reconstituted around the survivors of the Russian campaign and new drafts of veterans drawn from Spain.

The existing army under Eugène in Germany consisted of the remains of the first four corps of the Grande Armée that had invaded Russia. The reorganized I Corps was now to consist of sixteen regiments and remained under the Maréchal Davout. The old II and III Corps were combined and formed into a new II Corps under Maréchal Victor. This corps had twelve regiments. All of these regiments were to be reorganized with four battalions each.

On 17 February the I Corps consisted of 68 officers and 1,536 men.[29] By the end of April the 1st Division, I Corps alone had 11,508 men and the 2nd Division had 9,080 men.

To achieve this, detachments of 700 draftees from the class of 1813 were sent to the depots of the 28 regiments of these two corps. As the debris of the parent formations arrived in Erfurt, battalion cadres were organized from the excess officers and non-commissioned officers. These cadres were then dispatched to the depots and the 700 conscripts were formed about them. This conscript battalion was then designated as the 2nd Battalion of each regiment.

These 2nd Battalions were then converged in pairs as provisional regiments and dispatched to Magdeburg, where Davout and Victor could draw them into their reforming divisions. This process had begun by March and was placed under the control of Eugène, who had already received reinforcements in the form of Lauriston's corps of 20,000 men.

In order to re-raise the 1st, 3rd, and 4th Battalions of the various regiments for Davout and Victor's corps, Napoleon chose to use the conscripts from the last four draft classes, the debris which remained in Erfurt, and the cadres coming from Spain.

The first battalions re-raised were to be the 4th Battalions and they were to be on the Rhine by mid-March. The 1st Battalions were to come five or six weeks later. They too were organized into provisional regiments and marched from the Rhine to the lower Elbe, where they would join Davout and Victor. Once the provisional regiments arrived, they were dissolved and the 1st and 4th Battalions united with the 2nd Battalions already there. The newly re-raised 3rd Battalions were not to arrive at the Rhine until May. They were to be formed from the last cadres coming from Spain and conscripts of the draft class of 1814.

General Doucet had the responsibility of handling the debris arriving from Russia at Erfurt. After the first 28 regiments were reorganized, their cadres were sent to France for fleshing out. Doucet had the debris of five remaining regiments and their depots with which to work. Doucet was ordered to hold these men in Erfurt and organize them into cadres for ten battalions that would receive 4,000 conscripts of the class of 1813 and be filled out with further drafts from the classes of 1809, 1810, 1811, and 1812. However, Doucet's job was not to be easy. There were insufficient men to form cadres. Of the eight regiments of the I Corps that were forming their second battalions, no battalion had more than eight officers and five non-commissioned officers out of a requirement of 18 officers and 84 non-commissioned officers. Some, notably the 33rd Légère, had not a single officer or non-commissioned officer of its cadre.[30]

The lack of sufficient cadres was a universal problem. Some of this problem was alleviated by the drafting of 200 sous-lieutenants from the military school at Saint-Cyr, though these men were sent to the regiments formed from the National Guard, and a special draft of 100 corporals who were especially promoted to the rank of sous-lieutenant. These corporals all had a minimum of ten years service and were probably more than sufficiently capable of their new responsibilities.

The old IV Corps was to be dissolved. It had only six French regiments (9th, 35th, 53rd, 106th, 84th, and 92nd) and a large number of Italian formations, all of which had their depots in Italy.[31] The survivors of the six French regiments were not returned to Italy with the Italian survivors, but were sent to Augsburg where their regimental cadres were reformed. They were to be reconstituted by detachments of 700 conscripts of the class of 1813 sent from their depots in Italy.[32] By this means, six battalions were be formed. These battalions were then paired in provisional regiments and held for service in the Corps d'Observation d'Italie.

43rd Provisional Regiment	2/9th & 2/35th Line Regiments
44th Provisional Regiment	2/53rd & 2/106th Line Regiments
45th Provisional Regiment	2/84th & 2/92nd Line Regiments

It was also prescribed that the depots of the regiments of the first four corps be drawn to Stettin, Cüstrin, Glogau, and Spandau, where they were to be used to form eleven provisional battalions that were to form the garrisons of those cities.

Some corps had not entered Russia as far as the others, but were also disbanded, as the principal portions of those corps were not French, and Napoleon had little to say about their troops or the reorganization of those armies. Only the depots of the French regiments of Loison's

NAPOLEON REVIEWING THE GUARD ARTILLERY

and Marchand's Divisions, which had reinforced the IX Corps near Vilna, were available for his use. These regiments were blockaded in Danzig, but Napoleon drew their depots together and organized them into the "Hamburg Brigade."

The Poles

As a group, Napoleon had particular interest in the Poles. They were amongst his staunchest allies and superb soldiers. On 22 January 1813 he wrote Eugène and directed that the 4th, 7th, and 9th Line Polish Regiments, which were in French pay, were to be brought to strength as quickly as possible. The same effort was to apply to the four Vistula Legion Regiments and the three Lithuanian infantry and two cavalry regiments. All necessary expenditures to bring these twelve regiments to full strength were to be made against Napoleon's treasury rather than the Polish.[33]

It was Napoleon's intention to organize them into a single division, "under a Maréchal or Général de division of the first rank." In late January, however, each regiment had a force of little more than 150 men, or the normal strength of a single company. Only the 4th Vistula Regiment was in a condition to take to the field. However, these regiments were slated to receive 3,000 conscripts and draw their officers from those to be found in Kalisch.[34]

On 18 April 1813 Napoleon ordered the organization of a Polish corps in Wetzlar under the orders of General Dombrowski. It was to be formed with two infantry regiments, two cavalry regiments, and a horse battery. The infantry regiments were numbered the 2nd and the 14th. They were organized with two battalions each. Though each company was to have a captain and 3 lieutenants or sous-lieutenants, somewhat abnormal, the rest of the company was organized exactly like a French company.

The two cavalry regiments were organized like a French light cavalry regiment. The horse battery was organized like a French horse battery. They were also to be paid from the French treasury, which parallels the funding of the 4th, 7th, and 9th Polish Infantry Regiments.[35]

Other Allies in French Pay

The Portuguese Legion had been reduced to little more than a single battalion of 400 men. It was assigned to the III Corps and sent to Erfurt to recover. The Swiss were more important. All of the Swiss who were in bataillons de march or in various garrisons were to be sent to the II Corps and formed into one or two battalions, depending on their strength. All of the excess cadres were to be sent to Erfurt where the depots of the four Swiss regiments could send them replacements.

In early February he directed most of these foreign units to Erfurt. Napoleon intended to organize a corps in Erfurt formed with various foreign units. They were to include the 123rd, 124th, 127th, 128th, and 129th Line Regiments, the four Swiss Regiments, the 35th and 36th Légère Regiments, 31st, 32nd, and 33rd Line, the Illyrian Regiment, and the various Croatian provisional Regiments.

Bavaria

The Bavarian army had fought extensively in the Russian campaign. Most of its infantry had been in the VI Corps under General St.Cyr. It had fought on the northern flank of the French army around Polotsk, but suffered the heaviest losses from the weather. The Bavarian cavalry had fought with the main army at Borodino and other battles. It had entirely vanished. The 168 companies that had entered Russia had had 121 men each. Now they averaged 40 to 50 men each. The strongest company in the 2nd Brigade, VI Corps stood at 58 men. Only 20 guns out of the 58 that began the campaign remained and of the approximately 3,000 cavalry had been reduced to a single combined regiment of 326 men.[36]

The Bavarian infantry was rebuilt by reforming the 1st Battalions of each regiment and by merging the 2nd Battalions with the depots. Men who had completed their military obligations or who were still fit for service were assigned to the second battalions. The force created by the joining of the 2nd Battalion and the depot was designated as the reconstituted regiment and serviced as such in the field, however, it had only a three company strength, in contrast to the former six company strength. The light battalions were reorganized in a similar fashion, but each had only two companies.

The cavalry was reformed when a single division (two squadrons) was organized in March 1813. It was formed by mounting men who had been previously released from the military and from horses that had been earlier rejected for service. This division quickly expanded into a regiment of six squadrons and was sent to the northern border of Bavaria. On 26 March the National Chevauxleger Regiment was raised. The rest of the Bavarian cavalry was not re-raised until August 1813.[37]

Early in the 1813 spring campaign the VI Corps was reorganized into a single infantry division with two brigades, a cavalry regiment and an artillery detachment with four batteries.

The infantry regiments in the field were reorganized into single battalions and two were combined to form combined line regiments. On 10 and 13 January the fourth and fifth replacement columns arrived to the corps with 33 officers and 2,315 men. However, these reinforcements were quickly offset by an almost continuous stream of sick and disabled being sent back to the homeland.

WESTPHALIA

The Westphalian army had not suffered too severely during the Russian campaign. A number of regiments had not participated in it or had not advanced very far into Russia. The 1st, 4th, and 5th Regiments remained mostly intact and at full strength as did the newly formed 9th Regiment. The 2nd, 3rd, 7th and 8th Regiments had to be completely rebuilt by filing out the depot battalions with conscripts. The 6th Regiment was never reformed. The 1st, 2nd, and 4th Light Battalions were formed from new conscripts. The 3rd Light Battalion was reformed with conscripts and a cadre drawn from the light battalion then serving in Spain.

The Guard Grenadiers and Guard Jägers were re-raised by drawing the voltigeur and grenadier companies from the Königin Regiment. The remaining eight fusilier companies were used to form the Guard Fusilier Regiment.[38]

The two hussar and two cuirassiers regiments were completely rebuilt and the depots filled out with new drafts. One single new cavalry formation, the Jérôme Hussar Regiment, was raised for the Westphalian army, but it consisted principally of German speaking Frenchmen from the Alsace/Lorraine area. This formation saw no action in the 1813 campaign and returned to France when Westphalia was overrun and the last of the native Westphalian troops defected.

WÜRTTEMBERG

All of the Württemberg army had, with a few exceptions, joined the French invasion. It was part of Ney's III Corps, though some of the cavalry was assigned to the II Reserve Cavalry Corps. Of all the contingents it was, apparently, the first to vanish. By the time it was engaged at Borodino the Württemberg brigades had been reduced to the strength of battalions. It ceased to exist and very few survivors returned to Württemberg. In reaction the Württemberg military re-raised all four cavalry regiments that had been sent into Russia. They were raised between 29 January and 3 February. On 27 December the Württemberg contingent was ordered back to Württemberg by their king. Only 182 men remained capable of bearing arms. This tiny force was organized into the "Provisional Battalion" on 22 February. In addition, the 100 artillerists in Danzig were released and sent back to Württemberg. By 1 April, 173 officers and 760 men of the original 1812 contingent had returned to Württemberg. The first step, before the 1813 campaign began, was to organize three infantry regiments, each with two battalions, a cavalry regiment with four squadrons, a horse battery and a foot battery, the Garde zu Pferd Regiment and the Guard Horse Battery. A total of 2,430 men, 339 cavalry, and 103 artillerists were in the depots. They were quickly fleshed out and by late December 1812 the Württemberg army had 7,204 infantry, 1,449 cavalry, 621 artillerists, and 12 guns ready for the field.[39] The 7th Infantry Regiment was rebuilt from the survivors of the original regiment, the 2nd Battalion of the 8th Infantry Regiment and new recruits. Using similar methods, all eight regiments were eventually rebuilt. The new 9th and 10th Infantry Regiments were organized from the survivors of the Jäger and Light Infantry Battalions. Various sources of troops were used, including the Garrison Regiment and new drafts.[40] By 6 April 1813, The 1st, 2nd, 4th, 6th, and 7th Infantry Regiments were reorganized with two 717 man battalions. The 9th and 10th Line Regiments consisted solely of one 715 man battalion each. The 1st, 2nd, 3rd, and 4th Cavalry regiments had four squadrons and a total of 541 men each. There were also two horse batteries (6 guns and 274 men each) and a foot battery (10 guns and 202 men). The total force had 11,396 men and 2,649 horses.[41]

BADEN

The army of Baden had consisted of four infantry regiments, a light infantry battalion and two cavalry regiments. The light dragoon regiment had remained in Baden during the campaign and the 4th Infantry Regiment was serving in Spain. The other infantry regiments shared the fate of every other Confederation of the Rhine contingent and vanished. The hussar regiment was shattered and nearly obliterated in the heroic cavalry charges conducted to defend the Berezina crossings. Only the Ersatz-Batallion of 1,200 men remained, and it was in Glogau. When 1813 arrived, and the survivors returned, the Baden army was rebuilt completely. Only 336 men returned from Russia, out of the total contingent of 7,100 men. By the end of March, two infantry regiments, one depot battalion, one half 6pdr battery, and the Light Dragoon Regiment with five squadrons were serving in the 9th Division. The Hussars were not reorganized.[42]

CLEVES-BERG

The army of Cleves-Berg had consisted of eight infantry battalions formed into four regiments and two cavalry regiments. One of the cavalry regiments and all of the infantry had participated in the Russian campaign. The cavalry was assigned to the Imperial Guard and fared as did the French Guard cavalry. The infantry had not been in the front line prior to the Berezina crossings where it fought bravely to keep the Russians away from the bridges. The infantry was noted for its high desertion rates and once the morale disaster of the retreat struck home, the Berg infantry contingent vanished. In January 1813, the infantry consisted solely of the 2nd Battalion, 3rd Infantry Regiment. A total of 5,000 draftees were swept up and used to organize a new army consisting an infantry regiment, a cavalry regiment and a horse battery.[43]

HESSE-DARMSTADT

The Hessian army had sent two of its three infantry regiments and its only light dragoon regiment into Russia. The Hessian infantry served as rear-area garrisons during the campaign, and did not suffer until the retreat, where it vanished. The light dragoons were brigaded with the Baden Hussars and, for all practical purposes, ceased to exist after the Berezina bridge crossings. The infantry was reorganized and put back into combat status. Initially a single battalion was organized for the Leib-Regiment and as recruits became available, the other regiments followed suit. The cavalry regiment returned from Russia with 5 officers, 83 men, and 36 horses. In February it was directed to be reformed with four squadrons and by 28 February it was operational. On 23 February the regiment contained 338 men.

THE RUSSIAN ARMY

The Russian Army had suffered as badly as the French, losing 150,000 soldiers dead and nearly 300,000 crippled by frostbite and other causes. None of these men would fight again.

In an effort to make good these losses, the Russian depot systems were processing as many men as possible, but the winter made training difficult. A further impediment was the stripping out of the depot during the height of the 1812 campaign. The elite companies had been withdrawn from the depot battalions, as well as any men that were serviceable in the field. This reduced the training cadres to the bare minimum.

The system of reserve battalions had also begun during the war. This amounted to a fourth battalion being added to the standard three battalion organization. These reserve battalions were found in large numbers in early 1813, but they were eventually absorbed into the 1st and 3rd Battalions.[44]

Further drafts of roughly trained men were available from the various militias or opolochenie, which had been raised during the invasion. The combat value of the opolochenie was low, but once the retreat started there was truly very little combat against the French that required fully trained soldiers. Both sides spent more time fighting the weather to stay alive than fighting one another.

The Opolochenie were raised by provinces and cities, and dispatched in battalions or cavalry regiments. Initially they lacked even muskets, but by January 1813, they had all been equipped by English subsidies and shipments of equipment. During the 1812 campaign, they had fought as independent formations. Occasionally, they were coupled with veteran line formations in a manner quite similar to French Amalgamations of line and national guard units during the French Revolution. By early 1813, very few of the Opolochenie units remained in the field as independent organizations. Ever since the battle of Malo-Jaroslavets, they had been used as replacements to fill out the depleted ranks of the line formations.[45]

In contrast to the French, the Russians did not need to completely reorganize and reestablish their formations. They had succeeded in sending a steady stream of replacements to their units during the campaign and kept them from falling apart. There was, as a result, no frantic raising of new formations or increased drafting of new recruits. As 1813 came, the Russian army could still perform in the field, though few regiments had a strength equal to more than a single prewar battalion.

THE AUSTRIAN ARMY

Of the Austrian army, only one small corps of about 30,000 men had fought in Russia. Austria had one of the largest armies in Europe and it was, for all intents and purposes, untouched by the recent campaign. The main Austrian army had not mobilized for the campaign and remained in a stand down condition. This was the legacy of both the defeats it had suffered in 1809 and the terrible condition of the Austrian treasury. In order to prepare for an active campaign, both time and money would be necessary in copious amounts in order to bring the Austrian army into a condition fit for combat.

THE PRUSSIAN ARMY

The Prussian army was an untried weapon. The defeats at Jena-Auerstädt in 1806 had destroyed the army of Friedrich the Great and forced the Prussians to totally reorganize and rethink their military situation. The first consideration was the Treaty of Tilsit, which limited the size of the Prussian army and posted French garrisons throughout Prussia.

In an effort to evade the limits on the Prussian military, the "krümper" system of rotating recruits into the army and putting trained soldiers on leave was developed. Each squadron and company, at fixed intervals, discharged trained soldiers and took in new recruits for training. This method of constantly passing untrained men into the system allowed the Prussians to evade the restrictions laid on them by the French after Jena-Auerstädt.[46] The krümper system had allowed 39 of the 46 infantry battalions in the Prussian army to organize clandestine reserve battalions. Batch after batch of recruits was trained until it came time to call them back to arms. When this recall occurred, the 39 reserve battalions appeared almost magically.

In January 1813, this system began producing its fruit. It is estimated that 70,000 soldiers had been raised, trained, and silently put on leave. These men were ready for a quick return to the army. It was these men who responded to the succession of calls from the king. When called, the individual soldiers evaded French observation by traveling by night, long detours, and other ruses in an effort to move to their rendezvous.

At the end of 1812, the Prussian army had eleven infantry regiments, five grenadier battalions, three jäger battalions, five battalions of guard infantry, eighteen line and two guard cavalry regiments, 45 artillery companies, six pioneer companies and a few garrison battalions.[47] Once these units were filled to strength, sometime after the June armistice, a twelfth infantry regiment was raised and a fifth squadron was added to every cavalry regiment. By the end of 1813, a total of 52 new reserve battalions were raised, as were 20 new artillery companies, and the number of garrison battalions was raised to 24. Because the krümper system provided cadres as well as trained soldiers, the Prussians were able to quickly structure new battalions and form recruits around those trained cadres. This process required slightly over 20,000 new recruits.

The expansion of the forces under Bülow provide an excellent example of the process of expansion. At the beginning of 1813, Bülow's force in Prussia consisted of five infantry battalions, depots of four infantry regiments, four cavalry depots, four garrison companies, four brigade garrison companies, seven foot artillery companies, an artisan company, and a pioneer company. This force had 8,138 men and 500 horses.[48]

When the Krümper began, Bülow's force quickly received eight "marsch-kompagnien" of infantry with 1,062 men and two "marsch-eskadrons" of cavalry with 263 men, and a Rekonvalenszenten-bataillon with about 300 men.

This force moved to Graudenz, where it began a further growth process in mid-January. Eight reserve battalions were organized between 11 and 13 January. Three were formed from the depots of the 2nd, 3rd, and 4th East Prussian Infantry Regiments. The depot of the 1st East Prussian Infantry Regiment was in Memel, where it was receiving prisoners from various German states captured by the Russians during the 1812 campaign. This force became Reserve Battalion #1 and served as the depot battalion for a newly forming regiment. The first four reserve battalions were used to form the 3rd Battalions of the 1st, 2nd, 3rd, and 4th East Prussian Infantry Regiments. The 5th, 6th, 7th, and 8th Reserve Battalions became the 1st, 2nd, 3rd, and 4th East Prussian Reserve Battalions.

The depots of the 2nd, 3rd, and 4th East Prussian Infantry Regiments drew only men from the Krümper and were built up to a strength of 80l veteran soldiers. The 1st, 5th, 6th, 7th, and 8th Reserve Battalions were formed half with Krümper and half with new recruits.[49]

In Pomerania a similar process went on as well. The 1st and 2nd (Colberg) Pomeranian Infantry Regiments had 7,222 men in early January 1813. Eight reserve battalions were organized with a total of 7,008 men by 12 January.[50]

In an effort to assure this process of sufficient horseflesh, Scharnhorst had provided a peacetime system for the continual identification of all appropriate horses. Once the need arose, the appropriate communications were made and the horses flowed into the depots. The royal treasury was unable to pay for this, so the provinces provided much of the funding to cover this expense. In addition, during this period three new cavalry regiments were raised and sent into the field. They were the Pomeranian, Silesian, and East Prussian National Cavalry Regiments.[51]

Scharnhorst had gathered up 100,000 muskets for the infantry and placed them with 400 mounted cannons into magazines to cover the equipment needs of this force. Other materials were prepared and gathered together by a massive reallocation of civilian assets to military production. However, this did not prove adequate in the long run, and many uniforms and much equipment was supplied by England.

The new officers for this expanded army were raised by recalling officers from leave and promoting senior non-commissioned officers from the existing cadres to the rank commissioned officer. Also, many officers were drawn from the masses of freiwilligerjägers, who were streaming to the army as a result of the orders of 3 and 9 February. These men were generally the best educated men in the country and their talent was not wasted. The Decree of 3 February, laid out that they would be young men aged 17 to 24 and that they would equip themselves or would be equipped by their neighborhood. This decree also set the strength of a jäger detachment at four officers, fifteen oberjäger, three buglers and 182 jägers.[52] The Decree of 9 February laid out the limits of exemptions and the penalties for not belonging to either the regular army, landwehr, or to the "freiwilliger jägers." The amount of "free will" appears to have been somewhat limited.[53]

Irrespective of the willingness of these men, the process raised a large number of men in a very short time. In the period before the June Armistice, the following were raised:

43 Foot Detachments	5,300
23 Mounted Detachments	2,050
3 National Cavalry Regiments	450
Attached to the artillery	220
Attached to the pioneers	156
Jägers moved to regular army	300
	8,476 men[54]

In addition, the Prussians began the recruitment of foreign volunteers. Many officers came from this source as well. Major Lützow began the formation of his famous partisan corps. The Elbe Regiment was raised from the provinces torn from Prussia in 1807, von Hellwig began raising his "streifkorps" of three squadrons and a jäger detachment.

Scharnhorst's actions of 17 March began to mobilize the other military formation, the landwehr. It was to consist of 32 battalions of 825 men each, and 100 squadrons of at least 100 men each. This was to be a reserve of 120,000 men, but they lacked muskets. These were to be found abroad, mostly in England. Until muskets were available, the King of Prussia ordered the manufacture of pikes, so that they had some armament.

On 1 March the Silesian Corps, commanded by Blücher, contained the Brandenburg Brigade (eight battalions, eight squadrons, three batteries), the Lower Silesian Brigade (six battalions, six squadrons, three batteries), the Upper Silesian Brigade (seven battalions, six squadrons, three batteries), a cavalry reserve (two squadrons and two Batteries), and an artillery park (1½ batteries, three park columns, and two pioneer companies).

Yorck's Corps consisted of Hünerbein's Brigade (ten battalions, four squadrons, three batteries), Horn's Brigade (nine battalions, four squadrons, three batteries), a cavalry reserve (eight squadrons, one horse battery), and a park (1½ batteries, four park columns, one laborer column, three pioneer companies). General von Bülow's corps consisted of ten battalions, eight squadrons, three batteries, and a pioneer company. General Borstell's forces consisted of seven battalions, ten squadrons, three horse and four foot batteries, two park columns, a train column, and a pioneer company.[55]

By the first days of April, the Prussians had 46,000 men and 200 cannon in their main army. The second line troops consisted of 44,000 men partially organized and equipped. The third line troops, including the various garrisons consisted of 28,000 men. The total force, without the few thousand men in the various partisan corps, came to about 128,000 men. This force was to be joined by the 20,000 militia or "Landwehr" raised in East Prussia, for which the Russians had provided 15,000 muskets.

The British began providing material to equip this force. On 24 April a major shipment of powder arrived. On 14 May another ship arrived with 18 cannons, 5 howitzers, 5,000 muskets, and ammunition. Eight days later another ship arrived with 190 barrels of powder, coats, hats, shoes, and other uniform equipment. A third ship, similarly loaded, arrived two days after that.

However, it was in June that the principal shipments of material arrived. A total of 64 cannons, 16 howitzers, 6,000 sabers, 15,000 bayonets, 2,000 carbines, 4,000 pistols, 4,200,000 cartridges, and 1,955 90 pound casks of powder were delivered on 16 June alone. On 24 June 15,000 muskets, 3,000,000 cartridges, 2,000 sabers, 1,045 90 pound casks of powder, 2,375 bayonets, 2,368 bandoleers, as well as thousands of coats, shakos, shoes, jackets, and hats arrived.[56]

With its armed might restored by the tireless efforts of Scharnhorst, the Prussians, once they broke away from the French alliance, were ready to renew the struggle. The "befreiungskrieg," or war of liberation, had begun.

[1] Rousset, Grande Armée, pg 2.

[2] Rousset, Grande Armée, pg 11.

[3] Belhomme, Infanterie en France, Vol II, pg 596, & Bonaparte, Correspondance, #19437.

[4] Rousset, Grande Armée, pg 18.

[5] Charras, La Guerre de 1813, pg 289.

[6] Rousset, Grande Armée, pg 31.

[7] Belhomme, Infanterie en France, Vol II, pg 602, & Charras, la Guerre de 1813, pg 269.

[8] Rousset, Grande Armée de 1813, pg 21.

[9] de Marmont, Memoires, pg 12.

[10] Napoleon, Correspondance, #19485.

[11] Rousset, Grande Armée de 1813, pg 20.

[12] Rousset, Grande Armée de 1813, pg 25.

[13] Napoleon, Correspondance, #19482.

[14] Napoleon, Correspondance, #19559.

[15] Bonaparte, Correspondance, #19504.

[16] Charras, La Guerre de 1813, pg 263.

[17] de Mazade, Davout, #1287 & #1314.

[18] Charras, La Guerre de 1813, pg 282.

[19] It is possible that this was one of the final straws that broke Napoleon's political hold on France as it disenchanged many politically important men whose support was necessary for Napoleon's continued rule of France.

[20] Charras, La Guerre de 1813, pg 315. & Boucquoy, Gardes d'Honneur, pgs 354–362.

[21] Bonaparte, Correspondance, #19768.

[22] Bonaparte, Correspondance, #19520, & Holleben, Fruhjahrsfeldzuges, pg 181.

[23] Bonaparte, Correspondance, #19532.

[24] du Cassé, Prince Eugène, Vol 8, pg 261.

[25] Charras, La Guerre de 1813, pgs 276–277.

[26] Rousset, Grande Armée, pgs 61–62.

[27] du Cassé, Prince Eugène, pg 233.

[28] Charras, la Guerre de 1813, pg 272.

[29] Holleben, Frühjahrsfeldzuges, pgs 183–184.

[30] Rousset, Grande Armée, pg 32.

[31] Bonaparte, Correspondance, #19670.

[32] Charras, la Guerre de 1813, pg 281.

[33] du Cassé, Prince Eugène, Vol 8, pg 234.

[34] du Cassé, Prince Eugène, Vol 8, pgs 301–302.

[35] Chuquet, Ordres, pg 271–272, #5971.

[36] Nafziger, Bavarian and Westphalian Armies, pgs 10–11, & 19.

[37] Königlich Bayerischen Kriegsarchiv, Darstellungen, pgs 46.

[38] Nafziger, Bavarian and Westphalian Armies, 1799–1815, pg 52

[39] Holleben, Frühjahrsfeldzuges, pgs 226–227.

[40] Nafziger, Württemburg Army, pgs 14, 26, & 34.

[41] Holleben, Frühjahrsfeldzuges, pgs 227–228.

[42] Holleben, Frühjahrsfeldzuges, pg 238. & Sauzey, Le Contingent Badois, pg 72. & Vollmer, Bewaffnung, pg 124.

[43] Thomas, Un régiment Rhénan, pgs 64–67.

GNEISENAU

[44] Nafziger, Russian Army, pg 9.

[45] Nafziger, Russian Army, pgs 54–55.

[46] Petre, Napoleon's Last Campaign in Germany, pg 22.

[47] Charras, La Guerre de 1813, pg 210.

[48] Holleben, Frühjahrsfeldzuges, pgs 40–41.

[49] Holleben, Frühjahrsfeldzuges, pgs 59–60.

[50] Holleben, Frühjahrsfeldzuges, pg 112.

[51] Charras, La Guerre de 1813, pg 211.

[52] Holleben, Frühjahrsfeldzuges, pg 103.

[53] Petre, Napoleon's Last Campaign, pg 23.

[54] Holleben, Frühjahrsfeldzuges, pg 104.

[55] Holleben, Frühjahrsfeldzuges, pg 114.

[56] Preussischen Grossen Generalstab, Das Preussische Heer der Befreiungskriege, pgs 177–179.

Befreiungskrieg!
The War of Liberation Begins
March 1813

On 26 February, in preparation for the withdrawal from Berlin, Poincot's Division (four battalions) occupied the villages of Glienicke, Nowawes, and Neudorf, near Potsdam. They posted themselves to seal off the Baumgarten bridge. A further 3,000 men were sent from Magdeburg into Brandenburg, along the Plauensche Canal to seal it off. On 21 February the bridge by Crossen was burnt, and on 23 February the bridge at Frankfurt-am-Oder was also burnt. On 26 February the bridge at Schmökwitz was burnt.

Finally on 4 March, the French army began its withdrawal. Eugène's headquarters moved to Saarmünd. The detachments in Brandenburg moved to Glozow. The 155th Infantry Regiment moved from Möckern to Zerbst and Dessau. The battalion at the Baumgarten bridge burned the bridge and withdrew. Poincot's division, forming the rearguard, remained in its positions around Potsdam.

On 5 March, Eugène had the advanced posts reconnoiter the areas between Jütergolz and then ordered Poincot's division to abandon Potsdam. The French advanced lines were reestablished between Saarmünd and Belitz. On 6 March the advancing Russian forces engaged in a light skirmish with the Poincot's division by the village of Kähnsdorf, between Saarmünd and Beelitz.

Based on orders issued by Napoleon on 2 March, by 10 March the French army had assumed positions on the left bank of the Elbe.[1] General Reynier's corps, consisting of his Saxons, a small force of Poles, Durutte's French 32nd Division, and Rechberg's Bavarian Division (73 officers, 1,588 men, 200 cavalry and 6 guns), covered Meissen and Dresden.[2] Generallieutenant Thielmann occupied Torgau with a corps of 5,000 to 6,000 Saxon recruits. Maréchal Victor was in Wittenberg, Rotzlau, Dessau, and Alten with the newly forming II Corps (1st Division, I Corps and 4th Division, II Corps with 10,000 men) and the XI Corps of Général de division Grenier (35th and 36th Divisions with 17,500 men). Eugène's Guard Division, under Roguet, was in Leipzig with 3,084 infantry and artillery, 944 cavalry, and 9 guns.[3]

The Corps d'Observation de l'Elbe, under Lauriston, was in Magdeburg with 23,087 men and 92 guns. The left wing was formed in the 32nd Military Division with the Corps of General de division Count Vandamme. Under him was J. Morand's Division (71 officers, 2,471 men, 224 horses, and 12 guns on 9 March) in Swedish Pomerania. He occupied the cities of Hamburg, Lubeck and Bremen. A further two reserve cavalry corps (I Cavalry Corps - 1,373 men, and II Cavalry Corps - 1,808 men) and the Imperial Guard were on the Rhine organizing themselves. Further new troops were coming into Germany from Italy, as General Bertrand's division crossed the Tyrolian Alps.

Though his force was assembling, it was still weak and not able to assume the offensive. Napoleon estimated that he would be able to assume an offensive posture in mid-May, which is a very strong statement of what he felt his strength and offensive capabilities were vis-a-vis the Russians. His intentions were plainly to hold the fortified positions of Magdeburg, Torgau, and Wittenberg, using them to prevent any major Russian advance, until he was able to strike back. He gave very specific instructions to Lauriston on how he wanted those cities garrisoned and defended.[4]

THE RUSSIAN SITUATION

When the Russians and Prussians signed the Convention of Kalisch on 28 February, the Russian army had been considerably diminished. The obligations of blockading Danzig and the other Polish fortresses as well as the detachment of a force to observe Schwarzenberg, Reynier, and Poniatowski to the south, reduced their army to 56,000 men. This force consisted of 10,000 cossacks and cavalry plus 46,000 regular infantry divided into two unequal forces, under Wittgenstein and Kutusov, separated one from the other by 50 leagues.

Wittgenstein's corps with 8,000 Russians was located in Driesen, 25 leagues from the Oder and 50 from Berlin. He quickly found himself obliged to detach a further 4,000 men under General Repnin to support the cossacks. Though initially a seeming problem, this force would eventually achieve a major success when it convinced Eugène to abandon Berlin.

Kutusov had his headquarters in Kalisch and his army was encamped around the Kalisch, Rawitsch and Gostyn. This force contained the corps of Tormassov, Miloradovich, and Winzingerode. As he moved to the Silesian border, the Czar left Docturov, with 11,000 men behind him blockading Modlin and as a garrison in Warsaw. His force had been reinforced by 3,000 men drawn from Sacken. General Radt, reinforced with 3,000 opolochenie, was detached to blockade Zamosc. Sacken departed Warsaw with 9,000 men on 9 March, to observe Schwarzenberg and Poniatowski in the neutralized zone.

The Czar had the three columns of Winzingerode, Tormassov, and Miloradovitch deployed to enter Silesia. There were approximately 40,000 men and 4,000 cossacks in these columns. In addition Wittgenstein's forces, totaling 12,000 men, and the cossacks of Czernichev, Tettenborn and Benkendorf totaling a further 5,000 men, were moving on the Czar's right. This was the Russian force, 57,000 men, less cossacks, that faced Eugène.

To counter the Russians, Eugène had the divisions of Grenier, Charpentier, Lagrange, and the other forces moved to Posen, or 33,000 men, under his immediate control In addition, J.Morand (who was watching Swedish Pomerania with 3,000 men), Rechberg, and Reynier could join him quickly. This was more than sufficient to face the Russians and should have allowed him to easily hold the Oder line.

Wittgenstein received orders on 2 March to detach 3,000 to 4,000 cavalry under General Repnin to advance on Berlin. The Prussians, who were to support him, were still awaiting instructions from their king. Generalmajor Repnin's forces consisted of three cossack regiments, two hussar regiments, three chasseur regiments, Horse Battery #23, and Light Battery #28.

The King of Prussia and the garrison of Potsdam, which contained 8,000 to 9,000 men, were now cantoned in Silesia with Blücher's strong army corps containing 27,000 men. Generalmajors Bülow and Borstell had formed two other new divisions in Neu Stettin (8,000 men) and Colberg (6,000 men) respectively. Yorck had raised his own corps to 20,000 men. The total army available to the Prussians was about 61,000 men. This combined with the 56,000 Russians gave a total allied army of 117,000 men.[5]

The allied army was distributed along a line of operations from Frankfurt and Posen to Warsaw, when it was proposed by the Prussian Colonel Knesebeck that this force advance resolutely against Eugène's army, located around Berlin, in an effort to throw him back to the Elbe. He proposed that they should demonstrate incessantly and advance detached units towards the Elbe and Hamburg. Hamburg, which was lightly garrisoned, was to be targeted by a corps of 20,000 men, including 4,000 to 5,000 cavalry. Its capture would provide a solid base for the fermenting insurrection against the French between the Elbe, Weser, Ems, and Rhine.

A second plan, proposed Blücher's Chief of Staff Scharnhorst, would have the allies operate against the French right in the direction of Dresden. Eugène would be obliged to concentrate his army there and the combined Prusso-Russian army could defeat him easily. This would break Saxony and Bavaria from their alliances with Napoleon. At the same time the greatest part of the allied light cavalry and cossacks would be sent between Magdeburg and Hamburg, where they would ferment revolts against Jérôme and Napoleon.

The execution of either plan required a quick concentration of the allied army and a quicker advance against Eugène. Unfortunately for the allies, there were three problems. The Prussian generals hesitated, because of the failure of their King to declare war against France, Eugène preempted the initiative by voluntarily evacuating Berlin and Kutusov could be counted on for an endless stream of objections to any advance.

Especially after Kalisch, Kutusov felt he was too far removed from his base of operations. He wanted to wait for the arrival of reinforcements. He had little faith in the strength and enthusiasm of the Prussians. Above all he saw the French held fortresses on his lines of communication in the Grand Duchy of Warsaw, Poniatowski's corps on the Galician frontier supported by an Austrian army whose neutrality he didn't trust, and the knowledge that the Austrian cabinet was sitting on the political fence. A major allied disaster could shove the Austrians into the French camp very quickly.

Kutusov feared that if he advanced too far forward, he could find a hostile Austrian force advancing into his rear, cutting his lines of communication, and a disaster of unprecedented scale befalling the Russians.

The Czar was also restrained by the lack of a Prussian declaration of war and an unwillingness to pressure Kutusov into action. As a result, no decisive decision was made and opportunity slipped past the allies. The only decision was that the allied forces would provisionally operate in two columns of nearly equal strength.

The right column, under Wittgenstein, was ordered to move immediately on the Oder and, if possible, on Berlin. Yorck, Bülow, and Borstell were to advance behind him and be ready to take part in operations, once the Prussian declaration of war was issued. Voronzov was detached from the Army of the West and assigned to Wittgenstein.

The left column was under Blücher, who had Winzingerode's corps as its advanced guard. Winzingerode was to begin movement on 8 March and advance by Köben and Bunzlau towards Dresden. Blücher was to begin his movement on 16 March.

Miloradovich was sent to Glogau to blockade that fortress. He was to remain there, until relieved by the Prussian corps of General Schuler von Wenden, then forming in Silesia with various reserve battalions. Once relieved, Miloradovich was to move to Sagan, where he would receive new orders. Tormassov was to move behind Blücher and serve as a reserve for him, as well as for Wittgenstein should the two forces approach one another sufficiently.

PRUSSIAN MANEUVERS

Earlier, on 23 January, Yorck had moved his corps from Tilsit and Königsberg to the area between Elbing and Marienburg, in order to take advantage of magazines and materials abandoned by Murat and Macdonald. From here he could support the Russian siege force at Danzig or Wittgenstein, depending on which action seemed appropriate. His corps consisted of 20,000 men, but there were a further 13,000 men in his depots between the Vistula and the Niemen Rivers.

On 17 February, Yorck moved his corps to Konitz and on 22 February he participated in a conference with Wittgenstein and Bülow. Bülow had a corps of a few thousand men, who had followed the French withdrawal, evading both French and Russian forces until it arrived in Neu Stettin in Pomerania on 17 January. Here he had begun filling out his corps from the resources made available to him by the provincial government.

While in Neu Stettin Bülow had evaded the technically legal orders he received from Eugène to support the French. He mounted his cavalry units, raised a force of artillery, and reequipped his force which now totaled around 8,000 men. Though the Prussians were unable to take active part in the hostilities against the French, they agreed to act in concert with the Russians.

Wittgenstein departed for Berlin and arrived there on 27 February. The Czar ordered him to remain there and he did not advance again until 2 March.

Yorck's corps moved towards Soldin by way of Schloschau and Markisch-Friedland on 27 February, and Bülow moved to Stargard. On 2 March Bülow arrived there where he found himself joined by Generalmajor Borstell with 6,000 men. Borstell's force had been organized in Pomerania, near the city of Colberg. It consisted of reservists, volunteers and recruits. In late February, he departed Colberg with all the forces available to him, writing the King of Prussia that he was moving on Königsberg where he would wait for orders. He also took the liberty of sending an aide de camp to London, to demand that the English government send subsidies, arms and munitions to support him.

Yorck continued his movement westward, while Bülow remained around Stargard. Bülow advised Wittgenstein that he had still received neither advice or orders and therefore could not cross the Oder without the orders of his king. Despite this expressed sentiment, the actions of Yorck, Bülow, or Borstell showed little concern if their sovereign approved or disapproved of their movement towards the Oder.

On 6 March the King of Prussia advised Yorck of the Treaty of Kalisch and directed him to take Bülow and Borstell under his orders. He also directed that he operate in concert with Wittgenstein, but that he avoid all hostilities with the French until the formal declaration of war. To this Scharnhorst added that the Prussian forces were to advance on the Oder as quickly as possible and cross it if unopposed.

Yorck received these dispatches as he arrived in Arnswalde. He advised Wittgenstein, then enroute to Berlin, that his Prussian force would advance by way of Königsberg and Schwedt to join him. Yorck ordered Bülow to move on Stettin to observe it and the French bridgehead at Damm. If possible he was to occupy both sites.

THE BLOW WESTWARD

On 13 March Borstell led a small force westward in an effort to strike at the French in Mecklenburg. His command consisted of the Pomeranian Grenadier Battalion, the 1/,2/,Fus/ 1st Pomeranian Infantry Regiment, the Königin Dragoon Regiment, 75 men each from the Brandenburg, and Pomeranian Hussar Regiments under Major Graf von Lottum, 6pdr Foot Battery #10, Horse Battery #5, a pioneer detachment, and half a park column. However, before this force advanced very far, Borstell received orders calling him back.

The commando raid into Napoleon's rear was to be executed by the Russian Colonel von Tettenborn. Borstell's force was divided and one battalion, two squadrons, and four guns were detached with Tettenborn. The rest was to pass over the Elbe at Havelberg under the command of General von Dörnburg.[6]

On 11 March Wittgenstein arrived in Berlin at the head of 6,000 Russians. He had been obliged to detach 2,000 before Cüstrin, which was still garrisoned by the French, and his cossacks and Repnin's detachment were seven days ahead of him.[7] Blücher's Corps (21 battalions, 40 squadrons, 12½ batteries, two pioneer companies, and three park columns totaling 645 officers, 26,510 men, and 100 guns), was moving west from Breslau towards Saxony. Miloradovich's corps (15,687 men and 98 guns), and the rest of the main army (17,100 men and 176 guns), remained in Kalisch.[8]

BERLIN IS LIBERATED

Wittgenstein's main body continued its advance over the bridge at Schiff on 6 and 7 March. On 11 March they entered Berlin. His headquarters was to remain there until 28 March. Berlin erupted in a delirious celebration of their liberation from the French, and he was received like a conquering hero. Repnin had rested his forces since he had arrived, but Czernichev's and Benkendorf's cossacks had continued after Eugène as he withdrew to the Elbe.

BASHKIRS FRATERNIZING WITH BERLINERS

Eugène had known that it was important to remain in control of Prussia, to hold Berlin and to retard the Russian advance. He had not lacked the means, as he had 30,000 men under his immediate control and could call on 3,000 more under J. Morand in Swedish Pomerania. That would have been more than sufficient to contain Wittgenstein's paltry force of 12,000 regular troops and 6,000 cossacks, before Prussia declared war on France. Indeed, if necessary he could call 60,000 men to Berlin in a few days if he chose to do so.

Eugène had consulted Maréchal St.-Cyr, who had advocated holding the line of the Oder. St.-Cyr had advocated remaining before Berlin, but morale issues, not bayonets, caused Eugène to withdraw. He withdrew and by 8 March was in Wittenberg, abandoning the entire country between the Oder and the Elbe to the Russians without a single shot fired in its defense. This vacuum was filled only by a few thousand cossacks supported by Repnin's 4,000 men.

Stettin, Cüstrin, Glogau and Spandau were abandoned with strong, well provisioned garrisons. Stettin's garrison had been reduced from 8,000 to 6,000 by Eugène. Cüstrin's garrison had 3,500 men; Spandau's had 1,800 poorly equipped Polish conscripts and 1,700 veteran troops; Glogau's garrison had 4,000 men. All of these garrisons were formed with provisional battalions, organized in February with the survivors of the Russian campaign, and a few companies drawn from ship garrisons stationed in Texel and the Escaut.

Eugène's withdrawal necessitated a parallel movement by Reynier and Rechberg's Bavarian division, which maintained communication between the two armies. Reynier moved from

Maßstab 1:1100000.

10 5 0   10   20   30   40 km

THEATRE OF WAR IN THE NORTH

Bautzen towards Dresden, while Rechberg moved from Guben to Meissen. Eugène then directed J.Morand to evacuate Swedish Pomerania with his 3,000 men and that he occupy Hamburg.[9]

Berthier, Napoleon's able chief of staff, was still ill and had been recalled to Paris. His functions in the general staff were being carried out by General Monthion. Maréchal St.-Cyr had come down with typhus and had turned command of his army corps over to General Grenier.

This corps consisted of the divisions of Grenier, Charpentier and Lagrange. Seven of Lagrange's battalions had been detached to Stettin as a garrison. Because it was reduced in strength, it was merged with Gérard's division to form a single division. Girard's Polish division was disbanded. Two thousand men from it were used to form the garrison of Wittenberg under General Lapoype. The remainder were used as cadres around which the recruits from Posen were to be organized. This force of cadres and recruits was sent to Westphalia to be organized into a functional force. With the various garrisons established, Eugène withdrew his 34,000 man force, organized in four infantry divisions, the Imperial Guard under Roguet, and a small cavalry division behind the Elbe.[10]

A total of 15,000 to 16,000 Russians were posted before the various French occupied fortresses. Voronzov's flying corps was sent to Cüstrin because it was useless in Posen and Barclay had no use for it at the siege of Thorn.

THE POLISH RESERVE ARMY IS FORMED

For the sake of smooth administration, the Russians needed a third formalized military body with the appropriate command and control structure. This force was necessary to take care of the military activity in the Grand Duchy of Warsaw, while the main armies advanced to engage the French. It was established by the Imperial Order of 5/17 February 1813, under Prince Labanov Rostowski and consisted of 73 battalions, 92 squadrons, and a large artillery force.

The actual formation of this force, soon to become known as the Polish Reserve Army, was slow because of the advanced season, the long distances to be covered and the lack of qualified officers. After the occupation of Berlin, this process was expedited by the return of several front line forces.

BÜLOW CROSSES THE ODER

Bülow had on 7 March sent a battalion, 200 horse and a half battery over the Oder. These troops crossed near Schwedt. On 10 March they were followed by Bülow's advanced guard of three battalions and a further 200 horse under Major Prinz von Hohenzollern. They were followed on 11 March by Horse Battery #11. Bülow held his pioneers in Schwedt on the eastern bank of the Oder and the three cossack regiments under General Illowaisky III were poised to cross the Oder.[11]

Bülow brought the rest of his forces into Königsberg on 10 March, and established his headquarters there. In Graudenz he left a newly mobilized reserve battalion and a 12pdr battery. On 12 March, Bülow's advanced guard reached Garz, as two further battalions and 6pdr Battery #16 crossed the Oder. On 14 March Bülow sent his remaining Feld-Bataillons over the Oder with 6pdr Battery #5, where they established a line from Schwedt, Garz, Benkun, and Löcknitz.

On 16 March, Bülow led his force, consisting of 1/,3/4th East Prussian Regiment, 1/,3/,Fus/ 3rd East Prussian Regiment, 1/,3/2nd East Prussian Regiment, East Prussian Grenadier Battalion, three Russian cossack regiments, 200 Prussian cavalry, 6pdr Foot Batteries #5 and 16, Horse Battery #6, and Pioneer Company #1, into line on the left bank of the Oder between the fortress of Stettin and Schwendt and on to Löcknitz. Two further battalions, (3/1st Pomeranian & 3/Colberg Infantry Regiments), were left on the right bank of the Oder, south of Damm stretching to the suburbs of Stettin. Bülow established his headquarters in Graz.

On 17 March two Pomeranian reserve battalions moved across the Oder north of Stettin and into positions where they could support the Prussians in Löcknitz.

On 20 March the blockade of the fortress of Stettin was completed, as three further Pomeranian reserve battalions, the two Pomeranian Regiment's Garrison Battalions, a Marsch-Bataillon,[12] and a Marsch Eskadron from both the Brandenburg Dragoon Regiment and the Pomeranian Hussar Regiment moved into position. The 6th, 7th, and 8th Pomeranian Reserve Battalions were left in Kolberg.[13]

Bülow's corps began to move forward. It consisted of the Combined Leib Hussar Regiment, the Combined Lithuanian Dragoon Regiment,[14] four East Prussian Reserve Battalions, 2/3rd East Prussian Regiment, 2/4th East Prussian Regiment, 12pdr Battery #1, 1/2 10pdr Howitzer Battery, a park column, a horse depot, and a flying field hospital. The 3rd East Prussian Reserve Battalion was left in Graudenz with a Field Pioneer Company to defend the fortress.[15]

On 26 March a Swedish legation arrived in Bülow's headquarters to announce that a Swedish Division (7,000 to 8,000 men) had landed in Stralsund and Rügen. This force was 50 miles to the west of the Oder and Bülow's forces around Stettin. It secured him from any but the most serious assault.[16]

STATUS OF THE REBUILT FRENCH ARMY

By the end of February, the Corps d'Observation de l'Elbe, commanded by General Lauriston, was organized around Magdeburg. On 5 March his 3rd Division was in Dessau, and the 1st and 2nd Divisions were in Magdeburg on the 9th, except for the 152nd Regiment which was posted to the lower Elbe to contain the local population. Lauriston's 4th Division was moving from Mainz via Kassel and was in Halberstadt on 16 March.

Lauriston's corps consisted of twelve of the four battalion regiments organized from the 88 cohorts of national guard and two elite battalions of the 3e Régiment Etranger.[17] It should have had a total of 42,000 men, but detachments, desertions and other losses in transit to the front had reduced it to 36,000 men. It was well provisioned with artillery, having an artillery train of 96 guns. Each division also had an engineering company.

Davout was in Leipzig with the 16 battalions of the 1st Division of his newly forming corps. This force was being formed around new conscripts and debris from his command during the Russian campaign; he had 12,000 men. Victor was marching into the lower Saal basin with the twelve battalions that were to form the 1st Division of his corps. Victor's command consisted of only 7,500 men. A further 1,500 had been lost during the march to Erfurt.

The cavalry corps forming in Magdeburg contained the 1,600 men organized in Hanover and another 1,800 from Brunswick. Latour-Maubourg commanded the first group and Sébastiani the second. The various reinforcements received raised Eugène's available forces to about 90,000 men, including about 5,000 cavalry. This figure did not include Rechberg's Bavarians or Reynier's corps in Dresden.

Eugène directed Lauriston to leave two of his divisions in Magdeburg and to move the other two a few leagues south of the city to form a line on the left bank of the Elbe. He also attached Sébastiani's cavalry corps to Lauriston. Grenier, from whom Eugène would take Gérard's division and to whom he would give Latour-Maubourg's cavalry, was to remain in Wittenberg, with his left supported by Lauriston and his right by Torgau. Rechberg's Bavarians were to remain in Meissen and guard the bridgehead on the Elbe. Gérard was sent to Dresden to reinforce Reynier.

The Guard was sent to Leipzig, where, on 9 March, Eugène established his headquarters. Once the dispositions were complete, Eugène held a conference with Davout in Dresden. Davout was given command of the Elbe line from the Bohemian mountains to Torgau. Davout sent 16 battalions of his 1st Division to support this line. Ten other battalions were sent to Bernberg and

THE BRIDGE AT DRESDEN IS BROKEN

Magdeburg, with orders to join the twelve battalions of Victor's 1st Division which were to arrive shortly.

EUGÈNE'S DEFENSIVE POSITIONS

Eugène had neglected the lower Elbe in his effort to guard the upper and middle Elbe. To do this he had merely placed his forces behind the river and spread them out in a weak cordon. Napoleon had written him earlier, reproaching him for abandoning the Oder without a shot. He had directed that he retain his forces before Berlin as long as possible, using force, terror, and devastation to keep the Prussians in line. In the same letter he directed that Eugène draw his forces together two or three leagues before Magdeburg, in an entrenched camp as appropriate, and extend his left below the river between Magdeburg and Hamburg. He was to give secondary importance to Dresden and the upper Elbe. Wesel was to be his base of operations and he was to occupy himself, above all, with the defense of Westphalia, and the 32nd Military Division (Departments of the Upper Ems, Mouth of the Weser, and Mouth of the Elbe).

Napoleon felt that if Eugène supported himself in Magdeburg, he could not be turned by any Russian advance and that it would take an army of over 100,000 men to force him to abandon Magdeburg. Furthermore, any army that attempted to turn Magdeburg by its right would find itself struck in the flank by the I Corps d'Observation du Rhin, which was forming in Frankfurt and Aschaffenburg.

In a letter dated 5 March, Napoleon directed that if Eugène was pushed out of Magdeburg, he was to withdraw into the Harz mountains, covering Kassel and Hanover, using Wesel as his base of operations.[18] Unfortunately for Napoleon, these dispatches arrived at Eugène's headquarters at about the same time Eugène's dispatches arrived in Paris, announcing his evacuation and abandonment of Berlin. Napoleon's response was not flattering to Eugène's military prowess.

EUGENE ATTACKED BY COSSACKS OUTSIDE MAGDEBURG

In his response, Napoleon told Eugène to defend the lower Elbe obstinately in an effort to contain the explosion of German nationalism Napoleon feared would erupt if it were also evacuated. A failure to contain the population there would quickly lead to a revolt in Westphalia, the kingdom of Napoleon's brother Jérôme. From there the revolt could spread to Holland, which would be a disaster for Napoleon's plans.[19]

Napoleon restated his desire that Eugène mass the bulk of his army around Magdeburg and pointed out the weaknesses of Eugène's dispositions on the Elbe. Eugène was given clear direction as to how he was to conduct the campaign and delay the declaration of war by Prussia.

Before these directions could reach Eugène, Davout had already marched his force to Dresden, passing through Meissen where he burnt the bridge and all the mills, boats, and barges he found on the Elbe. Typhus had reduced Rechberg's force to 1,400 infantry and 200 cavalry, not including a small number of unemployed cadres. Davout directed these 200 horsemen on Dresden and directed Rechberg to guard the left bank of the Elbe with his infantry between Starehla and Dresden, centered on Meissen.[20]

When Davout arrived in Dresden on 13 March, he found Reynier busy with its defenses, but the King of Saxony was absent. Friedrich-August had fled on 25 February at the first sound of Winzingerode's cossacks in Lusace. He sent his archives and his treasures to the Königstein fortress. He and his family then moved on to Plauen, where he reestablished his court. When he went, he took with him his two regiments of cuirassiers and all his light cavalry. In other words, he stripped Reynier of all his cavalry support. This cavalry force consisted of eight cuirassier squadrons and six squadrons of hussars and uhlans.[21]

Friedrich-August had refused the Austrian offer of sanctuary in Bohemia. The threat of cossacks caused him to issue proclamations that spoke of the strength of his alliance with France, but his actions in withdrawing his cavalry, indicated a level of insecurity and insincerity. Though he had left his infantry with Reynier, he sought a pretext to withdraw them as well.

He was pressed by his ministers to embrace the cause of German nationalism, place his army under the Saxon general Thielmann, and to take no part in the upcoming campaign. His subjects were also in a ferment. Between the threat of cossacks and the nationalistic rhetoric from the rest of Germany they too were swept up with a desire to break away from their French allies. Though the people were openly hostile, the Burgergarde[22] was more prudent. The line forces remained aloof from this out of discipline and probably respect and affection for Reynier who had seen them through the Russian campaign.

Reynier's corps had been reduced by typhus to 1,700 or 1,800 Saxons under arms, Durutte's 32nd French Division (3,000 men), 3,000 disorganized Poles, and Gérard's French 35th Division. The six battalions arriving with Davout, were a major reinforcement. Including Rechberg's small force, Davout had about 20,000 men.

Davout chose to undertake a vigorous defense of the city and continued the defenses begun by Reynier. This effort was facilitated by the old wall that was still around Dresden. In addition, he had a mine placed in the bridge over the Elbe, so that it could be destroyed should it become necessary. Wooden palisades were raised and a Saxon garrison established in the city.[23]

He called on Thielmann, commandant of Torgau, to assist him, but the Saxon general, who was later to desert to the Prussians, refused to cooperate in any manner. Before Davout had completed his dispositions, orders came from Eugène to bring all his forces to Magdeburg. On 19 March Davout fired the mine, destroying two spans of the bridge over the Elbe and evacuated Dresden. Though Eugène had ordered the bridge destroyed, Davout was blamed for it by the public. The damage was minimal and easily repaired, but it caused a tremendous furor to arise against Davout. He was called a vandal, a barbarian, and decried as a desecrator of the civilized world.[24]

Davout sent his Polish troops to Westphalia, where they were to be organized under the command of General Dombrowski. The protection of the upper Elbe was left to Durutte. Reynier, unhappy being under Davout, declared himself ill after a few days and withdrew to France without authorization.[25]

After the six battalions of the I Corps departed, Dresden was guarded only by Durutte's division and the Saxon garrison. On 20 March the Russian partisan corps under Colonel Davidov arrived before the Neustädt suburb of Dresden. Davidov's forces consisted of 1,500 cavalry and a small artillery detachment.[26]

On 21 March the Saxon forces under Generallieutenant von Lecoq were reorganized into a single brigade of 1,436 commanded by Generalmajor von Steindel. Once organized, this Saxon brigade marched out of Dresden towards Torgau. They arrived on 27 March with a total of 74 officers, 1,762 men, and 309 horses. The command of this force was then passed over to Generallieutenant von Thielmann.

After the departure of the Saxon forces from Dresden, General Durutte remained there with his small division. Immediately after the Saxons left, the Prussian declaration of war was announced. Durutte suddenly found himself facing allied reconnaissance forces formed not with just cossacks, but regular cavalry armed with artillery. Durutte's position was being probed by the advanced guard of Winzingerode's corps and the Prussian forces of General Blücher.

The Russians offered Durutte an armistice on 21 March, at 5:00 P.M. Durutte quickly accepted it, using the time to evacuate his wounded and ill from Dresden. The armistice was negotiated with the Russians in Neustädt, on the noon of 22 March, and covered a distance of two leagues above and below Dresden. It could not be broken without 12 hours prior notice. The Russians broke it on the evening of the 24th.[27]

Durutte quickly sent Rechberg orders to join him behind Dresden, with his division of Bavarians. Two Bavarian regiments were pulled into Dresden and the rest drawn closer to the city. Only the 1st Combined Regiment[28] remained in Meissen by 20 March.[29] When Durutte

THE BATTLE OF MOCKERN

learned the enemy had passed heavy forces of cavalry over the Elbe above and below Dresden, he evacuated Dresden on 26 March. Durutte's forces joined the Bavarians at Wilsdurf. From there he moved his tiny force of 3,000 French and 1,000 Bavarians to Rochlitz, where he joined Eugène's forces.

On 29 March, Oberstleutnant von Hertling and 300 men of the 3rd Bavarian Combined Light Infantry Battalion (322 men from the 1st, 3rd, and 6th Light Battalions), a detachment from the 4th and 13th Line Regiments, a detachment of chevauxleger, and two guns were at Golditz, north of Rochlitz.[30] During the night of 29 March the city was attacked by a force of Russian cavalry, about 250 to 280 strong. This force charged across the bridge in an effort to take the city by a coup de main. The accurate fire of the detachments of the 1st and 6th Light Battalions broke the charge, causing them several casualties. Though the Bavarian losses were light and the attack not too severe, the Bavarians were quickly supported by the VII Corps and the Russians broke off the attack.[31]

Eugène had left Leipzig on 20 March, and sent the troops he had there to Magdeburg. This force consisted of Roguet's Guard division; the XI Corps under Grenier; the 16th, 18th, and 19th Divisions of the V Corps, less the 152nd Line Regiment, under Lauriston and the I Cavalry Corps under Latour-Maubourg. He re-directed the newly forming Guard Cavalry Division from Fulda to Magdeburg.

In an offensive move, Eugène had moved his headquarters on the right bank of the Elbe along with most of his forces in an effort to establish the offensive position Napoleon had directed him to form.

Puthod's 17th Division, V Corps, was in Lüderitz. The 1st Division, I Corps under Philippon, consisted of the six battalions and eight guns that Davout had drawn out of Dresden. Philippon

PRUSSIAN CAVALRY IN ACTION AT MOCKERN

had moved his division to Stendal and had not yet rejoined the rest of I Corps. The 2nd Cavalry Corps, under Sébastiani was en route to Stendal.

The eight battalions of the 4th Division (Dubreton), II Corps, were in Bernberg on the lower Saal River. On 31 March they were joined by the pathetically weak 9th and 19th Chasseur à Cheval Regiments. On 15 April the 9th Chasseurs had three squadrons with a total of 70 men and the 19th Chasseurs had two squadrons with a total of 130 men.[32]

THE ALLIED PLANS

Kutusov's plans for the immediate campaign were to have Wittgenstein mask Magdeburg with a few thousand men, while the main Russian army marched to join Blücher on the right bank of the Elbe. After the juncture, the combined force would advance on Leipzig.

Wittgenstein protested, stating that it would expose Berlin to a French thrust and advocated an advance on Magdeburg. At the same time he proposed putting a bridge over the Elbe at Rosslau and, in concert with Blücher, cross the Elbe. Thus, by a rapid thrust into the lower Saal basin, he would oblige Eugène to move to face this threat. At the same time Wittgenstein proposed sending Czernichev across the Elbe below Magdeburg at Havelberg, and west into Hanover and Westphalia.

EUGÈNE RESPONDS

Eugène had initially responded to Napoleon's order to occupy the eastern bank of the Elbe by dispatching a small force across the Elbe. Maison's division lead the advance covered by a screen of cavalry. The 151st Line Regiment acted as the advanced guard and encountered a light force of allied cavalry, which it successfully pushed back inflicting on it 60 dead, wounded, or prisoners.

Möckern was then occupied by Maison's division, with a cavalry screen spread down the main roads to the village. The two battalions of the 151st were posted on the same roads with four guns. The two other battalions of the 151st were posted in the village and the 153rd Line Regiment was posted to the rear with the divisional artillery.[33]

In response to the allied movements, Eugène had kept his main army on the left bank of the Elbe. He withdrew Maison's division of the V Corps, which he had earlier advanced to Möckern. On 31 March he learned that Wittgenstein had left Berlin and appeared to be moving towards Rosslau, planning a passage over the Elbe. In response to this maneuver by the Russians, Eugène returned to Napoleon's original instructions and took the main body of his forces across the Elbe. Eugène's force consisted of 50,000 men, including 4,000 cavalry and 180 guns.

Victor was left to guard the lower Saal and twelve battalions were left to watch the lower Elbe, between Magdeburg and Tangermunde.[34] In case the Russians pushed over the Elbe these twelve battalions were to be supported by Davout with 11,000 men.

The combined allied army of Wittgenstein and Blücher moved towards Möckern on 23 March, with 10,000 infantry and 1,500 cavalry. By the 29th the greatest part of the allied army was between Möckern and Zerbst. The advanced guard under General Kleist observed Wittenberg. Yorck's Corps lay in and around Zerbst in canton. Generallieutenant Bülow marched his force to Ziesar and the Russian division under General Berg moved on Liezo, three hours from Zerbst. General Borstell had remained in Gloina.

STATE OF THE FRENCH ARMY

On 31 March Eugène responded to Napoleon's latest request for the status of the reorganization of the French army. He reported that General Bourcier still had about 6,000 dismounted cavalry for whom he was seeking remounts. The mounted cavalry was organized into two corps with 3,340 men and 3,485 horses. A column of 9,907 men and 6,655 horses were dispatched from the remount depots in France, bringing the total to 13,247 men and 10,120 horses. Of the 13,247 men, however, 80 were eligible for discharges, 814 were in various hospitals, a further 710 were sick and convalescing, leaving a total of 11,643 effective troopers, but as there were only 10,120 horses, 1,523 were not of immediate use in the campaign.[35] Unfortunately for the French the Russian cavalry still significantly outnumbered the French cavalry. The Russians were entirely veteran troops, but though much of the French cavalry was veterans, there was significant number of new recruits in the force.

THE BATTLE OF MÖCKERN

Dessau was occupied by 1/, Fus/Leib Infantry Regiment, a half horse battery, and a squadron of hussars. The bridgehead by Rosslau was defended by the 2/Leib Infantry Regiment and another hussar squadron. A cossack regiment was on the other side of the Elbe as a picket, and to provide communication with Winzingerode's corps. On 4 April General Hünerbein, with three battalions, six squadrons, a foot battery, and a half horse battery, moved from Zerbst, over the Schörrau, and into Leitzkau.[36]

In the morning of 5 April, the allies learned of the French army's advance across the Elbe. General Wittgenstein concentrated his forces, expecting to do battle on 6 April. He planned to engage Eugène's front with Bülow and Borstell, while the divisions of Yorck and Berg, moving from Zerbst on Gommern would strike him in the flank and cut him off from his lines to Magdeburg.

The XI Corps, commanded by General Grenier, occupied a plateau that was slightly elevated above the surrounding terrain. His left was formed by the 35th Division, which he commanded personally, and stood before Nedlitz. His right, the 31st Division, was before Carith. The 36th

Division, under Charpentier, occupied Wahlitz, which was about five kilometers to the rear of the 35th Division. Lauriston had two of his divisions, the 16th under Maison and the 19th under Rochambeau, in Gerwisch and Woltersdorf respectively. Lauriston supported his right with Grenier's 35th Division. His third division, Lagrange's 18th Division, was in the second line near Wahlitz, where it occupied the roads to Berlin and Wittenberg. The Imperial Guard formed the third line with its head in Clussdamm, and its main forces in Pechau.[37]

The I Cavalry Corps of Latour-Maubourg was deployed with the 1st Light Cavalry Division in Zehdenik, with 100 horse deployed in Möckern and another 100 horse in Trippehne. The 3rd Light Cavalry division was in Wehlitz, and had 100 horse in Danigkow. The 1st and 2nd Cuirassier Divisions, with their supporting horse artillery, were in Wahlitz and Gommern.[38]

The front of the army was covered with a series of posts, each occupied by 2 to 4 companies, in Danigkow (two companies), Vehlitz (four companies), Zehdenik (four companies) and Ziepel. Charpentier's 36th Division provided a garrison for Gommern, Rochambeau's 19th Division provided a garrison for Buden and Maison's 16th Division provided a garrison for Corbelitz.[39]

Grenier was covered along his front by the Ehle River, which was neither deep nor wide, but its banks were swampy and difficult to pass. This stream ran from Zehdenik to the south, past Vehlitz and behind Danigkow. At Danigkow it turned east to Grommen, which was on its right bank. It continued east to Clussdamm and on into the Elbe a few leagues below Magdeburg.

The allied attack came in three columns. The first column was formed with General Hünerbein's detachment (two battalions, six squadrons and a horse battery), and the men from General Yorck's 1st Division, which had advanced from Zerbst and arrived around 11 A.M. on 6 April. Hünerbein's advanced guard consisted of two hussar squadrons and four tirailleur züge from the 1/1st East Prussian Infantry Regiment under the command of Premierlieutenant von Rosenberg-Gruszynski. The remainder of the 1/1st East Prussian Infantry Regiment followed to support the advanced guard.[40]

Yorck's force consisted of the 5th and 6th Combined Infantry Regiments, the Fus/1st East Prussian Infantry Regiment, the 1st Dragoon Regiment, two foot batteries, and Lt. Hensel's horse battery. This force posted itself before Leitzkau. Hünerbein posted his forces between Leitzkau and Danigkow. His advanced guard struck the French quickly. The two squadrons of hussars drove forward, followed quickly by the Prussian tirailleurs. They slowly pushed the French back to Danigkow.[41]

Under Yorck, the Fus/1st East Prussian advanced behind a screen of 20 hussars from the 2nd Leib Hussar Regiment. They passed over the Leitzkau at Gommern, as the left flank guard of Yorck's forces and to threaten the French right. They marched through Klein-Lübs and Dörnberg. At 1:00 P.M. Hünerbein was in Leitzkau, with his advance guard on the road to Gommern. His orders were not to become engaged with any strong enemy force, but only to pin it in place. His right flank was tied to Berg by the Illowaisky #5 Cossack Regiment.

Danigkow was the key to the French position and it was, stubbornly defended by two companies of the 154th Infantry Regiment. Two squadrons of French cavalry posted before the Danigkow struck two squadrons of the Prussian 2nd Leib-Hussar Regiment, but were driven back. The Prussian hussars advanced on the village until French skirmishers took them under fire, inflicting a number of casualties on the Prussian hussars and forcing them back.[42]

The French garrison of Danigkow was reinforced by the arrival of a grenadier company from the 154th, sent by Eugène to face the allied force of four battalions of infantry, six regiments of cavalry and an eight gun battery. Hünerbein sent the skirmishers of his first battalion forward supported by skirmishers of the second battalion and the fire of half of Lieutenant Hensel's horse battery. There were now three French companies forming the garrison of the village and a few squadrons. The Prussian skirmishers were driven back.

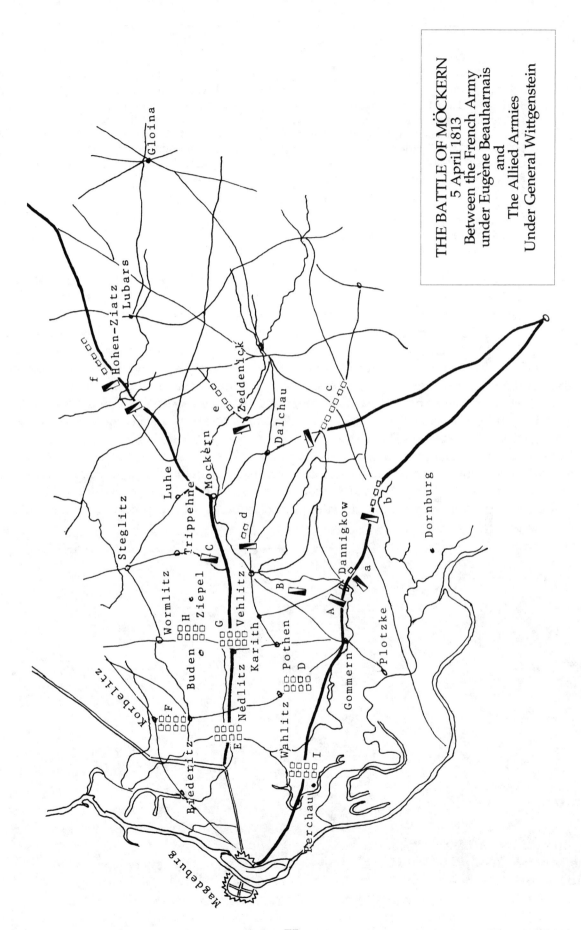

THE BATTLE OF MÖCKERN
5 April 1813
Between the French Army
under Eugène Beauharnais
and
The Allied Armies
Under General Wittgenstein

Gloina

Lubars
Hohen-Ziatz
f

Zeddenick
e

Dalchau
c

Mockèrn

Steglitz

Luhe

Trippehne

Dannigkow
b

a

Dornburg

C
d

Wormlitz

Ziepel
H

B

Vehlitz
G

A

Plotzke

Buden

Karith

Pothen

Gommern

Korbelitz

F

Nedlitz

Wahlitz

D

Biederitz

E

I

Perchau

Magdeburg

75

THE BATTLE OF MOCKERN
5 APRIL 1813

FRENCH:
A 3rd Light Cavalry Division, Chastel
B 1st and 3rd Cuirassier Divisions,
   Bordesoulle and Doumerc
C 1st Light Cavalry Division, Bruyére
D Lagrange's Division
E Rochambeau's Division
F Maison's Division
G Fressinet's Division
H Charpentier's Division
I Imperial Guard Division, Roguet

ALLIES:
a Yorck's Advanced Guard
b Yorck's Main Body
c Berg's Main Body
d Berg's Advanced Guard
e Borstell's Main Body
f Bülow's Main Body

The French garrison had occupied the houses and loopholed them to improve their defense. As the French supply of ammunition fell dangerously low, the Prussians launched a bayonet assault. It was lead by Major Lobenthal, commander of the 1st East Prussian Infantry Regiment, and consisted of the two musketeer battalions of the regiment, supported by the skirmish line, four squadrons of the 2nd (1st West Prussian) Dragoon Regiment, and Horse Battery #2. The attack dislodged the French from the village. The Prussian assault passed through the village, pursuing the French as they withdrew on Gommern. However as the Prussians came out the far side, they were greeted by the French cavalry of the 1st and 3rd Cuirassier Divisions and their supporting artillery. Major Lobenthal quickly pulled his forces back into Danigkow. The French pursued him and recaptured Danigkow.[43]

During the attack, Hensel's horse battery had inflicted heavy casualties on the three French companies in the village, while the Prussian cavalry, on the left of the village, engaged in a heavy skirmish with a force of French cavalry. Major Crammond had advanced with Fus/1st East Prussian Infantry Regiment and 20 hussars from Dörnberg. He was preceded by a skirmish

HELLWIG'S HUSSARS ATTACK THE BAVARIANS

screen, but his attack was not as successful as the earlier assault on Danigkow. His small column recoiled from Danigkow, while the rest of Yorck's 1st Division (six battalions, four squadrons, a horse battery, and two foot batteries) advanced on to the battlefield. Yorck left two fresh battalions behind the village as a reserve and sent his artillery forward. The Prussian artillery engaged in a cannonade with the French, but nightfall ended the battle.[44]

The second column was the Russian division of Generallieutenant Berg. General Roth's forces formed its advanced guard. The division marched from Liezo, over the Dalchow towards Vehlitz, and had General Borstell's forces behind it as a support column. Borstell's forces (four infantry battalions, four squadrons of dragoons, one foot battery, and a half horse battery) had apparently found a back road that lead to Zehdenik and arrived there at 4:00 P.M. in time to hear the battle at Danigkow.[45]

This position was important as the left flank of the French line stood here. The Maison's 16th Division was posted on the road to Burg. Lagrange's 18th Division was posted in Wahlitz, as the XI Corps Reserve. The French line ran from Danigkow, Vehlitz, Zehdenik, and Ziepel and was covered principally with infantry. General Rochambeau's 19th Division stood in Woltersdorf.

When Borstell heard the artillery fire, he took his dragoons and horse battery and set out as quickly as he could, marching to the sound of the guns. His infantry was expected to follow as best it could. When he arrived in Vehlitz, he encountered the French infantry garrison and two guns. The half of Horse Battery #5 Borstell commanded, unlimbered and took both under fire. When the infantry arrived, Foot Battery #10 also unlimbered and began fire.

The garrison of the village of Vehlitz consisted of four companies of infantry. However, when the attack began on Danigkow, Eugène ordered Grenier to move the 35th Division on the right of the road which leads from Carith to Vehlitz. The 1/112nd Line Regiment was detached by General Grundler with two 6pdrs to defend the village.[46] General Zucchi also detached a battalion to the village. The allies attacked at 3:00 P.M.

Borstell's infantry struck the village from opposite sides. The Fus/4th East Prussian Infantry Regiment, with the Pomeranian Grenadier Battalion as support, struck the left or southern side of the village. The right (north) was struck by the 2/2nd Pomeranian Infantry Regiment, while the 1st Battalion of the same regiment advanced behind it as support. The attack by the 1/2nd Pomeranian Infantry moved to cut off the 1/112nd Line Regiment and the voltigeurs who were screening it, as it withdrew from Vehlitz and took up positions behind the bridge.

The middle column, commanded by General von Roth, was lead by the Russian 26th Jager Regiment, supported by the Olonetz and Volodoga Militia Battalions. In addition, a company of Russian jagers was combined with the Prussian sharpshooters. This force filled the gaps between the three columns. Two squadrons of the Königin Dragoons formed the link with Bülow's corps in Zehdenik.

The remainder of General Berg's forces served as a support for the assaulting columns. The French defense of the bridge was such that the attacking column chose to advance through the stream instead. The stream was two to three feet deep and about twelve feet wide. Despite the intense musketry and artillery fire, the Prussians crossed the stream. The skirmishers of the East Prussian Fusilier Battalion, commanded by Hauptmann Meyer, struck the French, drove them back, spiking two French guns.

At this time a regiment de marche of 600 to 1,000 French cavalry charged, striking at the skirmishers as they passed through the stream. Hauptmann Meyer, four of his officers, and the bulk of his men were killed or wounded. However, the defensive fire of the infantry was sufficient to drive the French cavalry back behind the village.

The northern attack was more successful and both Prussian battalions crossed the Ehle without problems. The 2/1st Pomeranian Infantry Regiment turned left against Vehlitz. Almost as quickly as it turned, it was struck in the flank and driven back by cavalry from the 3rd Light Cavalry Division. It formed square and fired on the attacking cavalry at a range of 40 to 50 paces.

The charging cavalry broke and passed to the right and left of the square. Part of the French cavalry swung to the north and reorganized itself behind Vehlitz. The other part swung to the south. When the southern cavalry force passed the Prussian infantry the Prussian infantry square quickly slipped across the stream and under the protection of the Königin Dragoons.[47]

As the French cavalry that moved to the south passed before the Russian Grodno Hussars and the 1st West Prussian Dragoon Regiment, it was struck and driven back. The Prussian pincer attack was successful, despite the set back to the north, and the village of Vehlitz passed into Prussian hands. The 1/1st Pommeranian Infantry Regiment, the Pomeranian Grenadier Battalion, and a battalion of the 26th Russian Jager Regiment, struck northward against a hill position defended by men of the French 35th Division. The skirmishers of the Pomeranian Grenadier Battalion captured a cannon.

The Prussians detached two squadrons of dragoons to face three French battalions, which were observed to be enroute to Vehlitz. They were quickly supported by a force of allied infantry and the French withdrew. The French were beaten, but not broken, when night fell. Zucchi disengaged himself, supported by the rest of the brigade which Grenier had sent down from the plateau. Grenier himself was grievously wounded by a musket ball in the face.[48] This allied column lost about 250 men hors de combat, but had captured one cannon, two caissons, 250 prisoners, and 60 horses.[49]

The third column, or the corps of General Bülow left Ziesar in the morning and moved down the main road. This force consisted of five battalions, eight squadrons, a horse and two foot batteries. The advanced guard, with which Bülow marched, arrived in Hohenziatz at 12:30 P.M. The advanced guard was under the command of General Oppen and consisted of four squadrons of the Combined Leib-Hussar and Combined Dragoon Regiment, Fus/3rd East Prussian Infantry Regiment, and Horse Battery #6. In Hohenziatz, they found the Illowaisky #4 Cossack Regiment, which joined them. By 3:30 P.M., when Bülow began to move again, the main body of his infantry had caught up with him in Hohenziatz.

Bülow's column advanced with the Illowaisky #4 Cossacks and the Leib-Hussars in the lead, behind a strong screen of cossacks. This force moved through Trippehne and Wörmlitz in an effort to seize the road from Burg to Magdeburg. About a league from Möckern he was observed by the Italian general Zucchi, who was advancing with two companies. Zucchi quickly withdrew his forces to Zehdenik, where he joined them with the four companies forming the garrison of the village.

Zucchi moved his small force behind Zehdemick and formed it into three small squares. Each square was apparently formed with two companies of infantry, which was an unusual occurrence. He then covered the squares with 1,200 French cavalry of the 1st Light Cavalry Division from Latour-Maubourg's corps, and a horse battery, which had just joined him.

The French cavalry withdrew behind the infantry so as to allow the French artillery a clear field of fire on the Leib-Hussars. The Combined Dragoon Regiment (formed from the Lithuanian and West Prussian Dragoon Regiments) and Captain Steinwehr's Horse Battery #6 (four guns and two howitzers) arrived, and General Oppen detached a single squadron of the Leib-Hussars to protect the battery while he led the remaining seven squadrons forward.[50]

The French were covered by a wide ditch and greeted his attack with musketry from the French infantry. The charging Prussian cavalry leapt over the ditch and struck the French, losing 150 men in the attack. General Zucchi began withdrawing with his cavalry and the six companies of the 2nd Italian Légère Infantry Regiment. He was pushed by numerous allied cavalry and artillery. When he was obliged to open a passage for his two guns, a Prussian officer called upon him to surrender, but the response was made with muskets. Zucchi continued his withdrawal.[51]

The terrain did not permit a Prussian infantry attack on the squares. As twilight fell, the horse battery closed on the French squares and began to shell them once again. This ceased when six fresh French squadrons appeared and forced the Prussian horse artillery to withdraw.

The Prussian infantry followed up the cavalry pursuit of Zucchi, but night fell, ending the engagement. During the night the allies pulled their forces onto the battlefield. Bülow concentrated his forces around Boden, Yorck by Danigkow, and Generals Berg and Borstell by Vehlitz.

An erroneous message stating that Wittgenstein had crossed the Elbe at Rosslau, caused Eugène to fear for his communications with Magdeburg, and once again he issued the order to withdraw behind the Elbe. The French fell back towards Magdeburg, with their advanced posts behind the Clussdamm stream and Königsborn. At 7:00 P.M., the 35th Division retired in echelon. The first brigade took up positions at Carith and the second resumed its former positions to the right of Nedlitz. The 1st Brigade, 36th Division moved before and to the left of Nedlitz. Because of Eugène's fear of the allies, he destroyed two pontoon bridges, one near Magdeburg and the other near Grossschönebeck.

In the battle of Danigkow, or Möckern, the French had lost a total of 21 officers and 738 men hors de combat, about 100 prisoners (nearly all from the 1st Light Cavalry Division), one gun and two caissons. Generals Grenier and Grundler were wounded.[52] The three separate engagements had cost the Russians and Prussians 28 officers and 953 men hors de combat.[53] Eugene's heart was not in the campaign or battle and his lack of confidence lead to an unwillingness to engage in a major battle. This resulted in the Russians being able to bluff him out of his position after his advanced posts were engaged.

The results of the battle of Möckern were not what Eugène had hoped. He had only drawn part of Wittgenstein's forces into battle, and his failure allowed the allies to claim a great victory. Though it was not an allied victory, it enabled them to harvest amongst the German populace the morale effect of a victory.

This battle had several results. First, it showed that the Prussians were a viable military force and gave faith in such to the Russians. Secondly, it was another set-back for French arms and finally, the allies had crossed the Elbe and not been driven back. On 6 April the allied advanced guard under General Yorck was in Kluskrug and the village of Wahlitz. Bülow's advanced guard was in Königsborn and Mertz. Bülow's division had been merged with General Borstell's division and was in Nedlitz. Yorck continued the allied advance and moved his column across the bridge at Roslau towards Cöthen. Berg's Russian division provided supported him and held the bridgehead.

The French continued their withdrawal, and on 7 April there were no French columns on the left bank of the Stromes or the lower Saal valley. On 13 April a newly formed infantry battalion from the Saxon Ducal Houses was surrounded by a small Prussian detachment of hussars under the command of Major Pinto. The battalion, under the command of Major Lynker surrendered, "without hesitation." The battalion was taken to Altenburg, where Blücher had his headquarters. Major Lynker transferred his allegiance to the Prussian army and the entire battalion, except Lieutenant von Wangenhiem, did the same.[54] This battalion became known as the Thuringian Battalion.

In the days after the battle, Eugène withdrew his army to the lower Saal, where he set up positions between the river and the Harz mountains.[55] They stood in great strength in the cities of Alseleben, Bernberg, Nienburg, and Calbe. On 16 April Eugène advanced again, this time from Bernberg. He now faced the combined forces of Wittgenstein and Blücher, on the left bank of the Elbe.

Rechberg's Bavarian division, recalled by its king, had departed Stolberg and was to become the cadre for the soon to be reformed Bavarian army. On 17 April it was attacked in Langensalza, between Gotha and Mülhausen. The attacking force was commanded by the Prussian Major von

Hellwig and contained about 1,400 infantry, 400 cavalry, and 6 guns. Though the division consisted of only 1,052 men, 185 cavalry, and 6 guns it repulsed several attacks. Losses on both sides were light, each losing a about a dozen men killed, wounded, and prisoners.[56]

ASSAULT ON WITTENBERG

General Wittgenstein's position on the left bank of the Elbe was handicapped by his lack of a strong fortress, from which to base his operations. The ideal position to hold was Wittenberg, but the French had left a garrison under Commandant Lapoype in the city. Lapoype had fortified the suburbs and denied use of the city to the allies.[57]

On 17 April the Prussian siege commander, General Kleist, ordered an attack on the suburb. The attack force was under the command of General Diebitsch II. His forces consisted of the Russian 23rd and 24th Jager Regiments, Position Artillery Battery #21, Capitän Zinken's (Prussian) Horse Battery #1 with two howitzers and three cannon, a squadron of hussars, and a squadron of cossacks at Traguhne. This force was to attack the suburbs that lay before Traguhne.

The Prussian forces stood in Teichel and consisted of the 2/, Fus/Colberg Infantry Regiment, six guns of the Russian Position Battery #4, and a squadron of hussars. The goal of this force was the suburbs between Weinberge and the city, as well as right of the road to Berlin.

Under the command of Oberstlieutenant Steinmetz were the 2nd East Prussian Infantry Regiment, Fus/Colberg (2nd Pomeranian)[58] Infantry Regiment, three guns of Capitän Zinken's Horse Battery #1, Capitän Ziegler's Foot Battery #3, and a squadron of cossacks. [59]

Oberstlieutenant Steinmetz assembled his forces at midnight in Major Funk's camp. As soon as the organization was complete, he moved through Rheinsdorf towards the new mill against the Red Mark. The front of the assault was completely covered with woods.

Steinmetz's artillery was posted behind Rheinsdorf. When the attack began, he withdrew the three guns of Capitän Zincken's battery from Rheinsdorf and sent them behind Piestritz where they covered the assault. Capitän Ziegler's Foot Battery #3 remained by Rheinsdorf.

Major von Funk's attack began at 3:00 P.M., between the road to Belziger and the Elbe. He detached a fusilier company towards Pelstritz, where it was to occupy a position behind the village and on the far bank of the Elbe. It deployed in Scharfrichterei and Ziegelei. The company had to move quickly because it came under the artillery fire of the fortress.

The 1/2nd East Prussian Infantry Battalion was moved from Piestritz, as a support for this attack and remain with it in case of a counter attack. Funk's three other fusilier companies made an attack on the suburb between Belziger and the road to Coxwig. This attack was timed to go with the previous attack and was to be supported by the 2/2nd East Prussian Infantry Regiment and 1/Colberg Infantry Regiment.

A battle raged and the French were forced back out of the suburb. The Prussians pushed to destroy the source of the garrison's drinking water, defended by two French battalions (800 to 1,000 men). However, the Prussian skirmishers were driven back behind a deep, dry ditch. The supporting battalions then detached their sharpshooters to support the fusiliers, but remained in column in the shelter of the houses where they were not exposed to the artillery fire of the fortress.

A hussar squadron, operating with the 1/Colberg Infantry Regiment, moved from the woods and moved to the left of the attack. It joined the combined 1/, and 2/Colberg Infantry Regiment. The 2nd Battalion was posted in Weinberge. The four hussar squadrons, which had stood in Coswig, moved to Piestritz and supported the 1/2nd East Prussian Infantry. These four squadrons remained in the interval between the infantry and the Eichwalde.

The Fus/Colberg Infantry Regiment was between the road to Berlin and Weinberge. It advanced and drove the French back out of the suburb and across the glacis of the citadel.

As it reached the foot of the glacis its commander, Major Rekow, heard the fire of the 1/2nd East Prussian Infantry and detached a company under Capitän Hugo to strike the two French battalions in the rear. The French fell back behind a large ditch and a palisade, where they took the Prussians under heavy musketry fire. The French were also able to bring the artillery of the citadel to bear and showered the Prussians with heavy cannister fire, inflicting heavy losses, and causing General Kleist to withdraw his troops out of range.

The suburbs between Elsterhore and the Traguhnerbusch had been only lightly held by the French. The two Russian jager regiments struck there and drove the French out with little trouble. The entire assault on the suburbs ceased at 10:00 P.M., when it became too dark to advance further. Both sides had lost heavily. The French had lost as prisoners a lieutenant colonel, a captain, and 126 soldiers.

The next morning Wittgenstein organized four batteries. The two largest were the Russian position batteries and had eleven or twelve guns each. Two smaller batteries were organized with two howitzers each. Prior to commencing a bombardment, Wittgenstein sent Rittmeister von Strautz to ask the fortress to surrender. The French commander, Lapoype, refused and at 9:00 A.M., the allies' 27 guns began to fire shell and incendiary shot. The French responded with their own artillery.

The bombardment resolved nothing and by nightfall the blockading allied forces had withdrawn to their positions of two days prior. Only a small vedette remained in the suburbs.

ASSAULT ON ALSLEBEN

On the same day that the allies attacked the suburbs of Wittenberg, Major Rudolphi struck the French garrison of the city of Alseleben. On the 18th the cossacks of General Radinov skirmished with the French near Güsten and Major Seliwanov's cossacks hit Alseleben again.

On the 19th the battle around the bridge at Alsleben grew such that the French force in Alseleben consisted of 5,000 to 6,000 men and ten guns. General Yorck and the three cossack regiments of Radinov moved to support the allied forces at Alsleben. Later in the day Wittgenstein learned that Napoleon was advancing to join his army with that of Eugène. He directed Yorck to withdraw to a position by Cöhen near Zörbig and leave the lower Saal to be watched only by light troops.

General Kleist withdrew most of the forces around Wittenberg, leaving only two infantry battalions, a hussar squadron, a cossack regiment, and the horse battery. The two jager regiments and a heavy battery moved to defend the bridgehead at Roslau. The rest of the forces moved on Dessau.

On 22 April Eugène dispatched a column of 6,000 infantry, 1,000 cavalry, and 12 cannon against Cöhen, where General Helfreich was posted. A second, weaker column was sent against Alsleben. The goal was to provoke Wittgenstein into moving. If Wittgenstein advanced against Eugène he would expose his flank to attack by Maréchal Ney's forces. If he advanced on Düben, Eugène would advance and do the same.

Instead Wittgenstein chose to march by night and moved quickly to Hinsdorf and Qualmdorf. Here he prepared for battle, but Eugène withdrew back across the Saal.

THE FRENCH ARMY REORGANIZES AGAIN

The French army was to be reorganized again. On 28 March the Minister of War wrote to Eugène that Napoleon had decided to reorganize the army as follows: The I Corps was to consist of the 1st, 2nd, and 3rd Divisions. The 1st Division was to be composed of the 16 second battalions of the regiments then forming the I Corps. The 2nd Division was to be formed of the 16 fourth battalions and the 3rd Division was to be formed from the 16 first battalions. When the regiments had drawn together they were to reorganize themselves such that the battalions would be reorganized by regiment and two divisions would be formed with five regiments and the third division would be formed with six regiments.

The II Corps was to be organized with the 4th, 5th, and 6th Divisions. The 4th Division was to be formed with the 12 second battalions of the II Corps, the 5th Division with the 12 fourth battalions and the 6th Division with the 12 first battalions. When the corps was drawn together the battalions were to be organized into their respective regiments with each division having four regiments.

The III Corps was to be formed with the 8th, 9th, 10th, and 11th Divisions. The 9th Division was formed from the 2nd Division of the I Corps d'Observation du Rhin. The 10th and 11th were to be formed from the 3rd and 4th Division of the same corps.

The IV Corps was to be formed from the Corps d'Observation d'Italie with its four divisions being numbered 12th, 13th, 14th, and 15th. The V Corps was to be organized with the 16th, 17th, 18th, and 19th Divisions which were organized from the four divisions of the Corps d'Observation de l'Elbe. The VI Corps was formed from the II Corps d'Observation du Rhin and formed with the 20th, 21st, 22nd and 23rd Divisions. The VII Corps was to be formed from the two Saxon divisions which were renumbered the 24th and 25th Divisions as well as Durutte's 32nd Division, which retained its designation as the 32nd Division.

The VIII Corps was to be smaller and contained only two divisions, the 26th and 27th. The IX Corps (Bavarians) also had only two divisions, the 28th and 29th. The X Corps was to be formed from the three divisions in Danzig which conserved their designations as the 7th, 30th, and 33rd Divisions. The remains of the old 34th Division were to be incorporated into the 30th Division.

The XI Corps was to remain as it was then organized with the 31st, 35th, and 36th Divisions, Gérard's division of five battalions (3/3rd Line, 3/105th Line, 3/127th Line, and two Neapolitan battalions).

The Westphalians were to form the 37th Division, the Württembergers to form the 38th Division, and the contingents from Baden, Hesse-Darmstadt, and the Prince Primate (Frankfurt) were to form the 39th Division. The four Vistula Regiments, the 4th, 7th, and 9th Polish Regiments, and the various Lithuanian Regiments were to be organized into the 40th Division.

The 41st Division was to form in Erfurt with the 2/,3/123rd, 2/,4/,124th, 2/,3/,127th, and 2/,3/129th Line Regiments.[60]

SIEGE OF GLOGAU

With the French withdrawal to the Oder a second line of fortresses was abandoned behind the allied lines. The fortress at Glogau had a garrison of 6,000 men. The French (two companies of the 92nd Regiment, one company of the 127th Regiment, and three other battalions totaling about 1,600 men and a foot battery of 120 men), Saxons, Frankfurt, Baden (one battalion with about 1,200 men), Croatian and Spanish troops were under the command of Général de division Laplane. Among the garrison was the depot battalion of the reorganized 8th Légère Regiment. This regiment's single battalion totaled six officers and 230 men, organized into two companies. They formed part of the detachment of three French battalions that garrisoned the city.[61] The garrison also contained about 60 men of the 5/9th Sapper Battalion. The city garrison had a force of artillery that totaled 73 12pdr guns, twelve 6pdrs, six 3pdrs, six howitzers, and five mortars.

On 28 February the city was surrounded by a screen of cossacks. The fortress was blockaded by General St. Priest, with the advanced guard of Count Miloradovich's Corps on 15 March and he remained until to 30 March. His force consisted of 8,000 infantry, 2,000 cavalry, and 20 guns. He summoned the fortress to surrender, but the answer was negative. Two sorties by the garrison on 19 and 25 March proved damaging to his siege works. On 31 March Prussian Generalmajor Schüler had assumed command of the siege with a combined force of Prussians and Russians. The Prussians consisted mostly of Silesian reserve battalions.

After a new demand to surrender, which was also refused, St. Priest began to bombard the fortress with a battery of 16 heavy guns. This battery was destroyed by a sortie on 1 April. Another sortie on 12 April destroyed the Prussian trenches around Lindenrhone. On 16 April the Prussians attempted through a ruse to deceive the garrison into surrendering. They passed the word into the garrison that the garrisons of Thorn and Cüstrin had capitulated. This too failed.[62]

Because of food shortages the French garrison pushed 258 civilians out of the city. On 7 May, a sortie of 800 men and two guns exited through the Breslau gate and destroyed a number of allied works. The battle was hard fought and the garrison lost 11 killed and 54 wounded. The Prussians reportedly lost 90 dead, 180 wounded, and 50 prisoners.

On 17 May a formal siege battery arrived from Breslau. On 21 May the allies established a battery with five embrasures below Zerbau and attempted to once again destroy the fortress's bridge with artillery fire. About noon, 200 French, organized in four ranks, sortied from the city. Once across the bridge it broke into two groups. One group of 100 men, under Capitaine Roccassera, surprised and captured a Prussian post. The second, under Commandant Marthe, moved at the pas de charge to the left where it struck a force of 100 Prussians, killing 20 and putting the rest to flight. The battery was overrun, the guns spiked and the battery destroyed.[62]

In the morning of 27 May, the governor was surprised to find that his assailants had disappeared. He sent out a battalion on reconnaissance, but found nothing. On the morning of 29 May a squadron of French cavalry found itself under the walls of Glogau announcing the victories of Lützen and Bautzen to the garrison. The first siege was over.[64]

SIEGE OF CÜSTRIN

Wittgenstein had detached a corps under the command of Generalmajor Helfreich on 6 March, to surround and observe the fortress of Cüstrin. This force consisted of the Tenginsk and Estonian Infantry Regiments, Position Batteries #14 and #21, the Grekov #9 Cossack Regiment and the Tver Opolochenie Cossack Regiment. The garrison facing them consisted of 3,000 to 4,000 French, Poles, Hessians, Dutch, and Illyrians commanded by Général de brigade Fournier.

This force arrived at Cüstrin during the night of 8/9 March and took up positions on the right bank. After Generalmajor Helfreich's command was detached, the command of Generallieutenant Voronzov was dissolved on 17 March. The forces under his command were sent to Berlin where they were reabsorbed into the main army.

This obliged the Russians to provide further forces to fill the gaps around Cüstrin. To do this Wittgenstein brought a 6,000 man corps into position. He placed the six converged grenadier battalions and half of Light Battery #26 in Frankfurt-am-Oder. Around Lebus and near Ortschaften was Colonel Krassovsky and the 13th and 14th Jager Regiments. Two squadrons of dragoons were posted between Güsow and Seelow. Around Cüstrin were the two cossack Regiments of Panteleev #2 and Bihalev #2 and the other half of Light Battery #26.

The detachment of Generalmajor Orurk was posted between Züllichau and Crossen. It consisted of the Volhynie Uhlan Regiment, Pavlograd Hussar Regiment, the Diatschkin Cossack Regiment, the Melnikov #5 Cossack Regiment and Horse Batteries #11 and #18 with 14 guns.

In addition to Cüstrin, a small blockading force was sent to Spandau, that consisted of an infantry regiment and a heavy 12pdr battery. This force arrived around Spandau on 15 March.

On 20 March a reinforcement column of Russians was sent to the siege of Cüstrin. It was commanded by Generalmajor Sagraevsky and consisted of 120 cavaliers from the Niejine Chasseur à Cheval Regiment, 200 Polish Uhlans, 80 cossacks, and Heavy Battery #28.

On 14 April Kapzevich, commanding a slightly smaller corps, assumed the siege duties. Later still the siege duties were assumed by a corps of landwehr commanded by Generalmajor von

Hinrichs. After a long and bitter siege that lasted through the winter, the city capitulated on 7 March 1814 and on 30 March the fortress was surrendered.[65]

THE SIEGE OF SPANDAU

The fortress at Spandau was manned by 3,140 French, German and Dutch under the command of General Baron Bruny. On 4 March 1813, it was cut off as Eugène withdrew to the Elbe. The siege began on 14 March, when the fortress was surrounded by a small Russian force.

On 1 April Prussian Generalmajor Thümen relieved the Russian force blockading Spandau, with his 1,800 man brigade. This brigade consisted of the 4th East Prussian Infantry Regiment (3 battalions), 2 jäger companies, a freiwilliger jäger detachment from the East Prussian Infantry Regiment, and the 6pdr Foot Battery of Captain Ludwig.

On 9 April a battery of three 12pdr cannon and one 10pdr howitzer was established and began bombarding the fortress. On 14 April, a convention was signed by which the French would withdraw into the citadel and the city would be declared neutral.[66]

On 17 April the French garrison abandoned the city and moved into the citadel. This move was followed by a bombardment by three Prussian mortar batteries. On 18 April, a new mortar battery with four 10pdr mortars was established. It began shelling the citadel and before noon a shell had destroyed a powder magazine and a redoubt. By 11:00 A.M., the Königin Bastion had also been destroyed.

On 20 April, after a prolonged bombardment, the citadel was assaulted by three columns. The Prussians lost ten dead, four officers, six non-commissioned officers, and 31 men wounded, and three missing in the attack. The attack failed, but it obliged the garrison to negotiate. On 27 April, after negotiations were complete, the garrison marched out of Spandau and was escorted over the Elbe to the French lines.[67] This was to be the only allied success in the French policy of leaving garrisons behind their lines in the Spring campaign.

THE SIEGE OF STETTIN

Stettin had a garrison of 8,000 men commanded by Général de division Grandeau. He was initially blockaded by a force of cossacks, but on 18 March Generallieutenant Graf von Tauenzien, the Prussian military governor of the region, began a formal siege. He surrounded the city with 14 battalions of infantry, four squadrons line cavalry, and the Illowaisky #3 Cossack Regiment.

On 15 April the besiegers struck the customs house, customs bridge, and a blockhouse, but the assault was not successful. The artillery barrage began too late and was not accurate enough to bring the assault to a successful conclusion.

After the summer armistice command of the siege was assumed by Generalmajor von Plötz. On 21 November 1813, because of a lack of provisions, a capitulation was reached whereby 1,400 prisoners of war were sent out of the garrison. On 13 December 1813 the fortress finally capitulated.[68]

NAPOLEON'S USE OF THE FORTRESSES

It is difficult to assess the wisdom of Napoleon's campaign of garrisoning so many fortresses and then leaving them to their fate behind the allied lines. He is frequently criticized for leaving so many men and so much material behind, but it also tied down a considerable number of allied troops and obliged them to devote time and effort to the reduction of these fortresses.

To justify Napoleon's decision of leaving garrisons is relatively simple. If the French garrison outnumbers the besieging allied force an aggressive garrison can not only defeat it, but begin an active campaign in the surrounding territory, disrupting allied supply lines and communications. That would be a victory for the French.

On the other hand, if the allied besieging force outnumbers the French garrison, the French are obliging the allies to commit a larger military force than it has committed itself to the siege. That is also a victory for the French, as they have diverted more military power from the front than they have subtracted from their main armies by being "locked up" in the fortress.

The only serious argument against the policy is the loss of cadres and veteran troops at a time when the French army was being rebuilt and was overflowing with raw conscripts. However, not only did the conscripts fight well, but there is no evidence that the French suffered a shortage of cadres around which to form the new conscripts.

The policy of manning those garrisons can only be determined to be a success, as it did tie down large numbers of allied forces and denied free use of the various lines of communication to them. And if Napoleon is to be criticized for manning such garrisons, then Vauban and every other general of the previous century must be criticized for making the same decision.

1 Bonaparte, Correspondance, #19641.

2 Holleben, Fruhjahrsfeldzuges, pg 205. & Königlich Bayerischen Kriegsarchiv, Darstellungen, pg 73.

3 Holleben, Fruhjahrsfeldzuges, pgs 207–208.

4 Bonaparte, Correspondance, #19673 and #19675.

5 Charras, La Guerre de 1813, pg 391.

6 Holleben, Fruhjahrsfeldzuges, pg 151.

7 Charras, La Guerre de 1813, pg 403.

8 Holleben, Fruhjahrsfeldzuges, pgs 243–244.

9 Cazalas, Stralsund à Lunebourg, pg 13.

10 Charras, La Guerre de 1813, pg 408.

11 Holleben, Fruhjahrsfeldzuges, pg 257.

12 Marsch Bataillon is the German term for the French bataillon de marche and its function is identical.

13 Holleben, Fruhjahrsfeldzuges, pg 258.

14 Both the Prussians and Russians had dragoon regiments named "Lithuanian." The reader should be cautious of this and understand that these two regiments never served with forces of the other nation.

15 Holleben, Fruhjahrsfeldzuges, pg 256.

16 Holleben, Fruhjahrsfeldzuges, pg 262.

17 The 3e Régiment Etranger was also known as the Irish Legion. It had served in Spain and one battalion had fought the British during the 1809 invasion of the Scheldt. It was to see its first real combat during the 1813 campaign and was destroyed during the first few days of the fall campaign.

18 Bonaparte, Correspondance, #19664, & du Cassé, Prince Eugène, Vol 8, pg 406.

19 Bonaparte, Correspondance, #19696.

20 Charras, La Guerre de 1813, pg 417.

21 Sauzey, Les Saxons dans nos rangs, pg 205.

22 The Burgergarde was the city's police force and were a paramilitary force.

23 de Vaudoncourt, Prince Eugene, pg 146.

24 Charras, La Guerre de 1813, pg 425.

25 Holleben, Fruhjahrsfeldzuges, pg 245.

26 Holleben, Fruhjahrsfeldzuges, pgs 246–247.

27 The Combined Regiment was formed from one battalion of the 1st and another from the 9th Regiment.

28 Königlich Bayerischen Kriegsarchiv, Darstellungen, pg 77.

29 Königlich Bayerischen Kriegsarchiv, Darstellungen, pgs 81–82.

30 Holleben, Fruhjahrsfeldzuges, pg 249.

31 Holleben, Fruhjahrsfeldzuges, pg 251.

32 Schmitt, 151e Regiment d'Infanterie, pg 29.

33 Petre, Napoleon's Last Campaign in Germany, pg 45.

34 du Cassé, Prince Eugène, Vol 9, pgs 11–12.

35 Sporschil, Grosse Chronik, Vol I, pg 104.

36 de Vaudoncourt, Prince Eugene, pg 162.

37 Holleben, Fruhjahrsfeldzuges, pg 443, & Charras, La Guerre de 1813, pg 468.

38 de Vaudoncourt, Prince Eugene, pg 163.

39 von der Oelsnitz, Ersten Infanterie, pg 659.

40 Holleben, Fruhjahrsfeldzuges, pg 287, & Plotho, Krieg in Deutschland, Vol I, pg 68, & von der Oelsnitz, Ersten Infanterie, pg 659, & Sporschil, Grosse Chronik, Vol I, pg 15.

41 Holleben, Fruhjahrsfeldzuges, pg 388 & 444

42 von der Oelsnitz, Ersten Infanterie, pg 660.

43 Holleben, Fruhjahrsfeldzuges, pg 289.

44 Plotho, Krieg in Deutschland, Vol I, pg 68.

45 Holleben, Fruhjahrsfeldzuges, pg 444.

46 Holleben, Fruhjahrsfeldzuges, pg 291.

47 Holleben, Fruhjahrsfeldzuges, pg 29, & Charras, La Guerre de 1813, pg 474.

48 Plotho, Krieg in Deutschland, Vol I, pg 68.

49 Holleben, Fruhjahrsfeldzuges, pg 293.

50 Holleben, Fruhjahrsfeldzuges, pg 445.

51 du Cassé, Prince Eugène, Vol 9, pg 49.

52 Holleben, Fruhjahrsfeldzuges, pg 294.

53 Sauzey, Le Régiment des Duchés de Saxe, pg 16y, & de Vaudoncourt, Prince Eugene, pg 167.

54 Petre, Napoleon's Last Campaign in Germany, pg 46.

55 de Vaudoncourt, Prince Eugene, pg 172, & Königlich Bayerischen Kriegsarchiv, Darstellungen, pg 89.

56 Charras, La Guerre de 1813, pg 482.

57 Sporschil, Grosse Chronik, Vol I, pgs 109–111.

58 The Prussian 2nd Pomeranian Regiment was also knows officially as the "Colberg" Regiment, after the defense of that city in 1806.

58 du Cassé, Prince Eugène, pgs 195—198.

59 Pitot, 83e Regiment, pg 125.

60 Spectateur, Siège de Glogau, Vol LX, pg 206.

61 Pitot, 83e Regiment, pg 126.

62 Spectateur, Siège de Glogau, Vol LX, pg 208.

63 Sporschil, Grosse Chronik, Vol I, pg 79.

64 Holleben, Fruhjahrsfeldzuges, pg 354.

65 Sporschil, Grosse Chronik, Vol I, pgs 79–80.

66 Sporschil, Grosse Chronik, Vol I, pgs 80–81.

FRIEDRICH WILHELM ENTERS BRESLAU 25 JANUARY 1813

The Cossacks Strike West

Wittgenstein learned of Eugène's withdrawal to the Elbe and was excited by Eugène's timidity. The emissaries from the Hanseatic cities, Hanover, Oldenburg, and Westphalia told him of pending revolts against the French and he felt he had a chance to engage a morally weakened enemy. Wittgenstein sent Colonel Tettenborn's cossacks after the French in the direction of Magdeburg. The forces of Czernichev and Benkendorf moved towards Wittenberg in an effort to seize Hamburg.

Tettenborn arrived in Ludwigslust, residence of the Duke of Mecklenburg-Schwerin and found the duke a ready convert to the allied cause. The duke joined the allied cause, separated himself from the Confederation of the Rhine, and began to rebuild his single infantry regiment, which had been lost in Russia. He set his contribution to the allied cause at 2,000 infantry and 1,000 cavalry.[1]

From there Tettenborn moved towards Hamburg. Earlier, on 24 February, the city had erupted after a customs official had brutalized a citizen. Though unarmed, the crowds attacked soldiers, customs officials, and any other Frenchman they found. Though peace was restored with a liberal use of musketry and the appearance of some Danish cavalry in Altona, the situation remained tense.

The garrison of Hamburg initially consisted solely of three infantry companies, but it was enlarged after this incident with the addition of some gendarmes, a number of armed customs, and two battalions of the 152nd Infantry Regiment, which were dispersed along the Elbe below Hamburg. The force totaled about 800 men.

As Tettenborn advanced to the Elbe he didn't encounter a single Frenchman and felt safe in his advance. However, he didn't know that General J. Morand was advancing towards Hamburg with his division from Swedish Pommerania. Morand had departed Stralsund on 9 March. He decided to move on Hamburg despite the ferment and Carra St-Cyr's movement towards Bremen.

When General J. Morand was within five or six leagues of the city, the Danish general Ewald indicated that under orders from his king, he would oppose with his forces any effort by the French to occupy Hamburg. The King of Denmark was trying to reopen the failed negotiations with the allies.

Ewald held 5,000 to 6,000 men on the frontier of Holstein and General J. Morand only had 2,500 to 3,000 men. Morand chose not to provoke the Danes and moved into Bergedorf on 16 March. This move put him directly into the path of Tettenborn. Morand had barely established his bivouacks when the cossacks descended on him. Morand was out classed and crossed the Elbe quickly, abandoning six guns to the cossacks.

THE CAPTURE OF HAMBURG

Once General J. Morand had been pushed aside, Tettenborn resumed his march to Hamburg and entered it on 18 March. Hamburg responded by reestablishing its old government and proclaimed its independence. This action raised the flag of revolt in Lübeck, Lüneburg, Harburg, Buxtehude, Stade, and nearly the entire lowlands between the Elbe and the Weser. The French officials who chanced to be there were quickly hustled on their ways and all emblems and signs of the French domination were burnt.

However, on 20 March the alarm sounded on the banks of the Ems. The British, who had maintained a force on the island of Helgoland, landed a small detachment in Cuxhaven and their ships moved up the Elbe to Hamburg. Another detachment was disembarked on the right bank of the Weser near Bremerlehe. Here the coastal artillerists and the 7th National Guard Cohort had joined the revolt. The sight of the red British uniforms also brought the gunners of Fort Blexen over to the allied side.

The French reacted quickly. General Carra St.-Cyr and General J. Morand acted to suppress the revolt. St.-Cyr quickly rallied the two battalions of the 152nd Infantry Regiment, joined Morand to his forces and advanced to control the revolt. Two mobile columns, each of 1,200 men were dispatched, one on Bremerlehe and the other on Blexen on 23 March.

On the 24th, the French column in Bremerlehe encountered 1,500 to 1,800 ill armed peasants and bourgeois under the command of an English lieutenant. After an hour of combat, the small column was crushed and all the prisoners were executed without pity. The village was pillaged and, in a terrific rush out of the village, the coastal battery was overrun and its "traitorous occupants and their British accomplices," one officer and 19 soldiers, were killed.[2] In addition to the 20 British soldiers killed in combat a further 15 were taken prisoner.[3]

The second column struck Blexen at noon. The peasants ran to arms, but were quickly dispersed. The rebel gunners in Fort Blexen attempted to resist and fired a few rounds before a company of customs troops overran the fortress. The commander of the fort, a sergeant, was taken prisoner and executed. Blexen was pillaged and obliged to pay a 15,000 franc war contribution. In addition, the 20 prisoners taken during the actions were marched into the cemetery and shot.

This column then marched into Bremen where two of the leading citizens were shot. Under the direct orders of Eugène and Napoleon, Carra St.-Cyr acted with swift violence to suppress any further thoughts of revolt.

Tettenborn, whose cossacks had provoked this massacre, had moved his men to the left bank of the Elbe to continue the revolt. His men passed near Bremen and danced about the flanks of St.-Cyr's forces. Tettenborn had sent one of his officers to London to request that they provide money, arms, and munitions to support the creation of a corps of volunteers. This force was to consist of 6,000 men of all arms and be known as the Hanseatic Legion. He also helped to raise the Hamburg Civil Guard of 7,000 to 8,000 men.

When Wittgenstein, still in Berlin, learned of Tettenborn's entrance into Hamburg, he was delighted. He organized a second force, which he detached from Yorck's corps. It consisted of three officers and 200 men and they were to form the cadre of the Lubeck Battalion. A further force of 400 Mecklenburg Guardsmen moved into the city on 28 March.[4]

Wittgenstein ordered Benkendorf to break off from his position around Wittenberg and join Dörnberg, bringing the force to 1,200 infantry and 2,000 cavalry. Benkendorf was to move on Hanover and push as far as possible into the Kingdom of Westphalia.[5] He was to be further supported by Czernichev with his 2,000 men. Westphalia appeared to be devoid of troops and Wittgenstein wished to recreate the success of Hamburg in Westphalia. Dörnberg's union with Benkendorf occurred and the combined force crossed the Elbe during the night of 25/26 March. That night, as they crossed near Quitzöbel, they seized the small town of Werben.

Dornberg's force now consisted of a Prussian force consisting of the Fus/1st Pommeranian Regiment (520 men), ½ Horse Battery #5 (four guns and 74 gunners), and the Russian 2nd Jager Regiment (300). Dornberg's Russians were divided into two groups. The force under Benkendorf consisted of a battalion of the 2nd Jager Regiment (300 men), Finland Dragoons (two squadrons), Grodno Hussars, Melnikov IV Cossack Regiment, Andreiev II Cossack Regiment, a Bashkir Regiment, and two guns totaling 1,400 cavalry, and 300 infantry. The second force, under Czernichev consisted of the Riga Dragoons (two squadrons), Finland Dragoons (two squadrons),

Isoum Hussars (4 squadrons), Illowaisky XI Cossacks, Chourov Cossacks, Vlastov II Cossacks, Sissoiev or the Grekov XVIII Cossacks, and four guns, totaling 1,800 men.[6]

EUGÈNE'S RESPONSE TO HAMBURG

When Eugène arrived in Magdeburg, he became involved in the preparations of his offensive encampment. He moved the three divisions of Lauriston's Corps (Maison—16th Division, Lagrange—18th Division and Rochambeau—19th Division) across the Elbe. Puthod's 17th Division, detached from Lauriston's Corps, remained on the left bank of the Elbe.

Eugène had ordered General J. Morand to expedite his movement from the Weser and to move without delay into Lüneburg. The rest of his dispositions were in accordance with the directions he'd received from Napoleon.

Davout was given command of the Elbe from Magdeburg to Hamburg, including the 32nd Military Division, and the forces under Vandamme. This was principally because

TETTENBORN

Napoleon felt he knew the territory and his command of Hamburg would be "quite useful." Davout arrived in Stendal on 28 March. Sébastiani's cavalry corps and ten battalions of Davout's 1st Division were posted Lower on the Elbe near Stendal, to cover the flank.

On the same day Eugène abandoned Napoleon's instructions and abandoned the offensive position he had assumed. He learned of the Russo-Prussian alliance. He was unsettled by the insurrections in the north and the cossacks to his front. Eugène feared that the allies were converging below Werben and that they would move on Hanover. He moved the divisions of Maison, Lagrange, and Rochambeau to the Ohre, a river on the left of the Elbe a little below Magdeburg. He directed Grenier, Latour-Maubourg, and the troops coming from Dresden to move there as well. Victor, with his 4th Division, was to remain on the lower Salle. He had already forgotten Napoleon's lesson that the best way to protect Hanover was to threaten Berlin.

As the French reconnaissance forces moved from Stendal towards Werben, they encountered Dörnberg's forces. A force 2,000 infantry and 500 horse under French General Montbrun pursued Dörnberg as far as Neukirch, inflicting about 100 casualties on him. Realizing that he was greatly outnumbered by the total of the French forces in the area, Dörnberg quickly recrossed the Elbe.

Dörnberg, supported by Czernichev, who had left the area before Magdeburg to the French, recrossed the Elbe on 31 March, ten leagues south of Werben. He quickly occupied Dannenberg and Lückow. Czernichev occupied Wustrow.

He planned to advance on Hanover once again, but learned that General J. Morand was approaching Lüneburg. Lüneburg had been in revolt for about 12 days and had raised a small, poorly armed civil guard of a few companies. Dörnberg and Czernichev resolved to move to their defense. Unfortunately, when they arrived outside Lüneburg they found the French flag flying over the city.

General J. Morand's force had been reorganized in Bremen and consisted of the Saxon Prinz Maximilian Infantry Regiment with two battalions (1,492 men), the 4/152nd Infantry Regiment

TETTENBORN'S COSSACKS ENTER HAMBURG

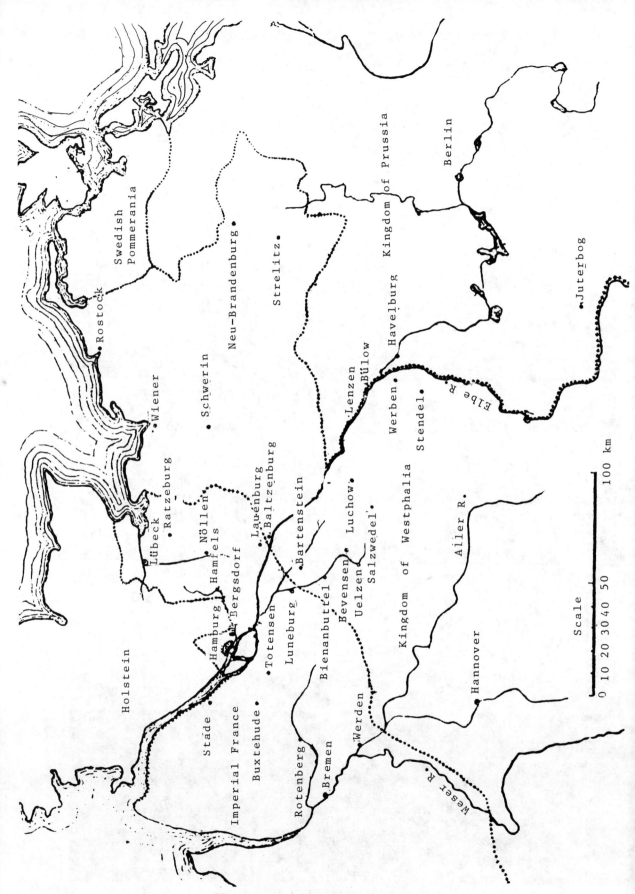

THEATRE OF WAR ON THE ELBE

CZERNICHEV

(468 men), two companies of customs guards (147 foot and 25 horse), 3/8th and 17/8th Foot Artillery Companies (two 6pdr guns and 193 men), the Saxon battery of Hauptman Essenius (four 8pdrs, two howitzers, and 170 men), and 45 gendarmes and cavaliers.[7]

On 1 April Morand had reached Lüneburg. His column arrived at about noon. As his advanced guard reached the barricaded gates of the city it was greeted with a hail of musketry. A small force of cossacks, volunteer sharpshooters and a few Bürger militia companies faced them in the terrain before the city.[8] The Saxon skirmishers riposted that attack and, reinforced by two Saxon companies and three cannons (two French and one Saxon), pushed forward. Under the protection of this force Morand's column formed by pelotons at half distance and began their advance. On the third cannon shot and the threat of the advancing French the cossacks dispersed and the musketry diminished significantly.

The two Saxon companies under Major von Ehrenstein, moved forward, cleared the barricade and seized the Neue Gate. From there they pushed through the city, chasing the cossacks out the Bardowick gate. At the same time the Saxon skirmishers, under Unterleutnant von Metzsch, attacked the old rampart situated between the Neue and Rouge Gates. They passed over the wall and penetrated into the city. The 4/152nd Line Regiment moved to the north of the road while the remainder of the Saxon Prinz Maximilian Infantry Regiment, with Morand at its head, moved at the pas de charge down the main road in "colonne serrée." When Morand's column reached Neue Gate the enemy fire from the ramparts had completely ceased.

General J. Morand's column entered the city, drums rolling. The Saxons formed square in the city square with its artillery and equipment in the middle. The French installed themselves at the Sander-Platz. The rearguard, which had remained on the heights to the west of the city, joined the main force after about an hour and a half, leaving their guns at the Neue Gate.[9]

As the French entered into the city they were greeted by occasional sniper fire, but it was quickly and brutally stopped by the French. When Morand passed through the city's gate he found numerous dead civilians, who had opposed the French and Saxons. Because of the popular support of the cossacks, Morand felt he had to take severe actions to impress on the populace that the French were in charge. He established a military commission, shot two burgers who were caught with guns in their hands,[10] and incarcerated 30 of the most prominent citizens of the city.

Not knowing what to expect, Morand established his defensive positions with an attack by regular forces in mind. He felt it was wasteful to establish advanced posts because of the enemy cavalry superiority and chose instead to barricade the city's gates.

He established garrisons at each gate that consisted of an officer and 50 men. In addition, a cannon was placed at the Lüne, Bardowick, and Rouge Gates. Those men who were not assigned to the gate garrisons were dispersed throughout the city.

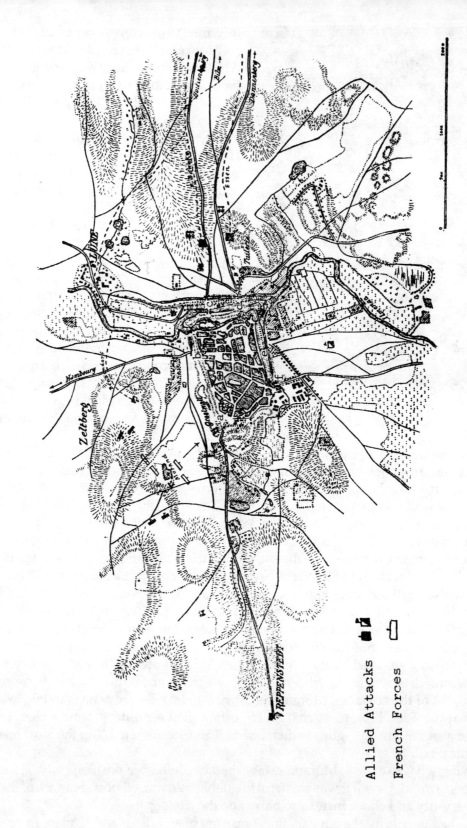

Battle of Lüneburg
2 April 1813

a – Neue Gate   d – Oldenbruck Gate
b – Bardowick Gate   e – Rouge (Red) Gate
c – Lüne Gate   f – Sulz Gate

Allied Attacks

French Forces

ACTION AT LÜNEBERG

94

At 6:00 A.M. on 2 April, the French sounded the alarm at the sight of cossacks approaching in the distance. Their posts remained manned until the order to stand down was issued. The only revision was the establishment of an officer and a 100 man reserve in the citadel.

The first shots of Dörnberg's and Czernichev's attack occurred at about 10:00 A.M., but they amounted to little more than stray shots from cossacks attempting to harass the garrison. They illicited no response from the French and Saxon infantry. At 11:00 A.M., Major von Ehrenstein was touring his posts when word came that strong columns of cavalry were visible to the south of the city before the Sulz and Rouge gates.

The attacking allied force consisted of a battalion of the Russian 2nd Jager Regiment, 300 men under Major von Essen, four squadrons of the Isoum Hussars, two dragoon squadrons, a weak Bashkir Regiment, three weak cossack regiments, two horse guns, the Fus/1st Pommeranian Infantry Regiment (500 men) under Major Borcke, and half of Prussian Horse Battery #5 (three guns).[11]

The city was surrounded by an old wall pierced with five gates. The Russian commander sent a false attack under Pahlen against the southern and western gates (Rouge and Sulz), while the main attacks were against the Lüne and Oldenbrück Gates.

The column which struck Lüne Gate consisted of von Borcke's Fusilier Battalion,[12] three cannons and Benkendorf's cavalry. A battalion of the Russian 2nd Jager Regiment, three guns and Czernichev's cossacks struck the Oldenbrück Gate.[13]

Around noon Morand ordered Captain Pariset with two guns and a small force of cavalry supported by the skirmishers of the Saxon regiment to the heights situated to the south east of the tile works in an effort to take the Russian cavalry in the flank. However, as they attempted to set up their battery they were taken in their flank by a Prussian battery of four guns to their east and attacked by a squadron of the Russian Isoum Hussars. Both guns and a major portion of the men were captured by the Russians, while the rest were driven back to the the Oldenbrück Gate.[14] Shortly later the commanders of the Rouge, Bardowick, and Neue Gates announced that they were under heavy assault. A reinforcement of 50 men was sent to Rouge, while two detachments of 100 men were dispatched, one to the Neue Gate and the other to the Bardowick Gate.

The French had posted the Saxon skirmishers on the walls and in the houses. The 2nd Saxon Battalion stood on the northwest, watching the Neue Gate. This force was covered by two Saxon howitzers. The 4/152nd Infantry Regiment and a single 4pdr gun stood at the Oldenbrück Gate.

Major von Ehrenstein, responding to the attack, directed the reserve in the citadel (under Lieutenant von Döring) to the Rouge Gate with a single Saxon gun to repulse the Russian attack at that gate.

Just as these forces arrived at the gates, Dörnberg ordered his two columns to attack the city. The right column, three Prussian companies under the command of Major von Borcke, advanced on the Lüne Gate. The left column, a battalion of the Russian 2nd Jagers under Major Essen, moved against the Oldenbrück Gate. They were supported by six cannons placed 500 to 600 paces to the east of the gates.[15]

The allies were able to advance quite close to the city without coming under significant fire, because of the covering terrain. Once close enough, they engaged the French garrison with musketry, supported by artillery fire, but their attack met with great difficulties. The French position was covered by an arm of the Ilmenau River and it was necessary to force the bridges that were swept by French fire.

Major Borcke, leaving only two pelotons before the Lüne Gate, moved the rest of his force (two companies) against the village of Lüne with the intention of forcing his way across the first arm of the river out of view of the enemy.

General J. Morand had posted himself at the Lüne Gate and saw the allied infantry. He quickly realized that the battle would require more than a few shots to chase off some overly aggressive

JOHANNA STEGAN WINNING THE NEWLY-CREATED IRON CROSS BY
DISTRIBUTING CARTRIDGES UNDER FIRE TO THE
POMERANIAN FUSILIERS AT LUNEBURG

cavalry. He called for the two Saxon reserve companies that remained in the city market, but it was too late to stop Borcke.

Borcke's forces crossed successfully and threw themselves at the gate's defenders. These were overwhelmed and nearly all taken prisoner. The breach was made and the allies began to move into the city.

Just as the gate was overrun, the two Saxon infantry companies that had been held in reserve in the city market arrived. The Prussians pushed on as the Saxons withdrew under Morand's orders. Once in the city the two allied columns began a terrific battle with the French, assisted by the citizens of the city firing on the French from their windows. The battle become one of hand to hand combat with a Prussian officer attempting to seize the flag of the 2/Maximilian Regiment from the hands of Unterleutnant von Milkau. Though the Saxons retained their standard this time, it would not remain in their hands for long.

As the Franco-Saxon force withdrew into the market place, Leutnant Kunze arrived with two howitzers, put them into battery, and poured cannister into the advancing Prussians. This permitted the 2/Prinz Maximilian Regiment to disengage and reach the Neue Gate.

Realizing that the day was lost, Morand escaped out of the western gate with 500 to 600 men and two guns. The French forces formed themselves into column and marched down the Harburg road. He hoped to reach a position on the heights to the west of the village.[16]

The French defenders at the Oldenbrück Gate had been more successful in holding off the allies, but did not receive the word to retreat. They continued to hold their position and fight the Russians until they found their position turned by the Prussians. Most were obliged to surrender and only a few succeeded in rejoining their comrades.

To the north, at the Bardowick Gate, the attacking allies consisted only of cavalry and were never a serious threat. When the Saxon garrison at the gate found themselves surrounded, they vainly counter-attacked and were eventually forced to lay down their arms. The southern, under Leutnant von Döring, held out as well, only to surrender when the wounded Major Ehrenstein was brought forward to tell von Döring that continued efforts were hopeless. Only the defenders of the Sulz Gate succeeded in escaping and joining the retreating Morand.

General J. Morand marched into Reppenstädt, a half league from Lüneburg. The Saxon 2/Prinz Maximilian and one company of the 1/Prinz Maximilian Regiment formed in column, by zügen to the right, with a 6pdr cannon on one flank and a howitzer on the other. There were only 480 Saxon infantry remaining. To the right of the Saxons marched a French battalion, the 54th National Guard Cohort (also known as the 4/152nd Line Regiment) formed in colonne d'attaque. The entire force was surrounded by skirmishers.

Once in Reppenstädt, Morand found himself attacked by a number of cossacks, the Isoum Hussar Regiment, and four cannons. The initial charge by the Isoum Hussars was driven back by a hail of cannister and musketry.[17] The Isoum Hussars suffered heavily from the cannister fire. The cossacks, choosing not to act in mass, were held at bay by the French and Saxon skirmishers. The Russians artillery showered the escaping column with cannister and quickly dismounted both Saxon guns. Dörnberg had divined Morand's plan and had marched to intercept him.

Seeing he was terribly disadvantaged by the superior allied cavalry, Morand chose to return to Lüneburg, where one of his battalions fought on; it had failed to escape with Morand when he left earlier. The Saxons charged forward with Morand at their head, holding their flag and crying, "Vive l'Empereur!" The allied battery that had closed to engage the Saxons was overrun and its gunners fled. The Saxons, now 250 strong because two companies had been detached to face the cossacks who suddenly chose to attack, found themselves in a desperate situation. The 4/152nd did not follow their movement and Morand sent two aides de camp to them to urge them on, but it was too late.

At that time General J. Morand was struck down by a shot. Colonel von Ehrenstein, despite already being wounded, assumed command. He sent Captain Erdtel forward to Dörnberg to negotiate their surrender.

The 54th National Guard Cohort (4/152nd) and the two Saxon companies stood defiantly on the heights, surrounded by a sea of enemies. Their muskets blazing at any, who were foolish enough to venture too near while they suffered under the allied artillery fire. Slowly, however, their ammunition began to run out and the circle of enemies closed in. In a last desperate gasp the battalion commander cried, "En avant! Vive l'Empereur!," the drums rolled the attack, and the battalion square moved forward in an effort to gain the shelter of the nearby village. However, cries of, "Don't shoot!" from the skirmishers were quickly heard as they ran out of ammunition and the morale of the entire force collapsed before it had advanced 60 paces. The battalion surrendered.

General J. Morand died surrounded by his men, and the few hundred men that remained with him surrendered. The battle had lasted from noon to 5:00 P.M. A total of three flags, 2,300 prisoners, and seven guns were taken by the allies.[18] From among the 400 Saxon prisoners many deserted to the allies and enrolled in the Russo-German Legion. They were transported to Königsberg. The French and Saxons reported losing one officer killed and eleven wounded. About 130 men were killed and 220 wounded. The allies lost five officers and 41 men dead and wounded.

On 3 April Dörnberg and Czernichev left Lüneburg and recrossed the Elbe. They had learned of the approach of Davout's forces. Only a few hours after their evacuation from Lüneburg the advanced guard of Davout's corps, 4,000 men of Lagrange's 18th Division, under General Montbrun, marched into Lüneburg. The following day Davout arrived at the head of 5,000 more. Vandamme's corps also began arriving in the area. Dufour's 5th Division and Carra St.-Cyr's divisions moved into Bremen and Dumonceau's 2nd Division occupied Minden.[19]

Davout was charged with complete civil authority over the 32nd Military Division in order to grind out the revolt. He had the muscle to do the job. Vandamme, at the head of 28 battalions, as well as 33 other battalions, were en route. A total of 61 battalions were dispatched to the 32nd Military Division to enforce French rule.

Of these 61 battalions 53 were formed with conscripts of the Class of 1813. They were to form the 2nd and 3rd Divisions of Davout's and Victor's Corps. Davout's 2nd Division was commanded by Dumonceau and Victor's 5th Division by Dufour. The two 3rd Divisions were not destined to be complete until the end of April. In addition, five battalions of infantry, not assigned to either corps, were organized into the Hamburg Brigade and posted in Bremen. Eugène had also provisionally left Puthod's 17th Division and Sébastiani's cavalry, with 2,000 men, at Davout's disposition. This force was to operate, if necessary, with the 16 battalions of Davout's 1st Division that were posted between Stendal and Werben.

On 2 April Eugène received a dispatch from Napoleon which repeated his preceding instructions and recommended that he select a battlefield 3 to 4 leagues in front of Magdeburg, that he cover it with redoubts, and that he establish a line of advanced posts from Dessau to the junction of the Plauen Canal and the Elbe.[20]

[1] Holleben, Fruhjahrsfeldzuges, pg 210.

[2] Charras, La Guerre de 1813, pg 435.

[3] de Vaudoncourt, Prince Eugene, pg 167.

[4] Holleben, Fruhjahrsfeldzuges, pgs 210–211.

[5] Charras, La Guerre de 1813, pg 440.

[6] Cazalas, Stralsund à Lunebourg, pg 30.

[7] Holleben, Fruhjahrsfeldzuges, pg 270, & Charras, La Guerre de 1813, pg 445, & Sporschil, Grosse Chronik, Vol I, pg 127, & Cazalas, Stralsund à Lunebourg, pg 37.

[8] Jacobi, B., Hannover's Theilnahme, pg 41.

[9] Cazalas, Stralsund á Lunebourg, pgs 38–39

[10] Jacobi, B., Hannover's Theilnahme, pg 41.

[11] Jacobi, B., Hannover's Theilnahme, pg 43.

[12] A company of Prussian fusiliers and a cossack pulk were left in Dahlenburg. They drew back to Dannenberg to watch the Neetze bridge.

[13] Holleben, Frühjahrsfeldzuges, pg 271, & Plotho, Krieg in Deutschland, Vol I, pg 57, & Jacobi, Hannover's Theilnahme, pg 46.

[14] Jacobi, B., Hannover's Theilnahme, pgs 47–48.

[15] Cazalas, Stralsund à Lunebourg, pg 45.

[16] Jacobi, B., Hannover's Theilnahme, pg 49.

[17] Jacobi, B., Hannover's Theilnahme, pg 50.

[18] Holleben, Fruhjahrsfeldzuges, pg 272.

[19] de Vaudoncourt, Prince Eugene, pg 159.

[20] Bonaparte, Correspondance, #19779.

BENCKENDORFF ROUSING SUPPORT IN LUBECK

The Political Situation
April — May

At 4:00 A.M. on 15 April, Napoleon left his palace in Saint-Cloud en route for Mainz. He had hoped to delay his departure until the first week of May, but the military situation in Germany demanded that he return to the front. France had never been so unsettled as it was now. Massive drafts were made on its young men to replace those lost in Russia. France stood at the end of 20 years of armed struggle with the rest of Europe.[1]

Napoleon was still having problems with Pope Pius VII and the catholic clergy were an almost constant source of agitation. Malet's abortive coup d'etat had shown the weakness of his regime. He needed to stay in Paris and reassure his subjects, but Eugène, his step-son and commander in Germany, was unable to handle the military situation.

In Spain, Wellington was leading an army of 90,000 British and Portuguese and 50,000 Spanish supported by ubiquitious guerrillas. Napoleon's army had only 100,000 men. Napoleon had recalled Soult and Napoleon gave serious thought to a complete withdrawal from the Iberian peninsula, establishing lines along the Pyrenees.

Murat, his lieutenant and now King of Naples, was behaving in a most suspect manner. He was thought to have contacts with the English and was dealing with Metternich. In fact, Murat had, in return for guarantees from Austria, declared himself ready to support Austria with all his forces. As a further indication of his infidelity Murat had refused Napoleon's summons for him to return to the Grande Armée.[2]

Murat also refused to send more troops to assist Napoleon, though his army already numbered 40,000 and he raised another 10,000. This cost Napoleon not only a potential ally, but obliged him to retain an unnecessarily large force in the Kingdom of Italy, lest Murat choose to attack it.[3]

The political situation on the far side of the Rhine was no better. Davout was stamping out the revolt in the 32nd Military Division. Napoleon felt it was both politically and militarily necessary to control this region. This region and Westphalia bordered directly on metropolitan France, Holland having been incorporated into metropolitan France in 1810.[4] If they fell, France was open to assault. Napoleon actively feared landings by the English, Swedish, and Russian armies in this area if he lost control of it.

Even though Davout was ready to resume his advance into the lower Elbe basin, he had the Dutch and Belgians in his rear. Any reverse could cause these people to rise up against the French. This could spell disaster both to Davout's army and Napoleon.

Napoleon's reaction to the revolts was harsh. His generals were given carte blanche to end all active resistance to French domination. In Bremen alone, by 25 April a total of 173 people had been arrested, 21 were executed, 76 were in prison awaiting trial, and a further 76 had been released. The mayor of Varel was convicted of instigating insurrection, banished, and had all his goods confiscated. Despite the French reaction, incidents still occurred and during the night of 20/21 April, the French postal station in Lilienthal was burnt to the ground. Vandamme's situation in Bremen was not strong. He had only a poorly trained infantry and totally lacked artillery and cavalry.

France's relationship with Denmark had also decayed. Though it had obligations to France as a result of the Treaty of Fontainbleau,[5] it was actively negotiating with England and Russia. It offered to provide its army to the allies for use against the French. Though the allies would not

DUKE KARL OF MECKLEMBURG STRELITZ SERVED AS
A GENERAL IN THE RUSSIAN AND PRUSSIAN ARMIES

accept the Danes as a full ally, the Russian ambassador did sign an convention of armed neutrality with the King of Denmark. This action prohibited nearly all military actions by Davout on the lower Elbe and against Hamburg.

In the Confederation of the Rhine the situation was also deteriorating. Reports from every state, Würzburg, the Grand Duchy of Frankfurt, Württemberg, Cleve-Berg, Westphalia, Hesse-Darmstadt, Saxony, and Bavaria spoke of popular agitation against France and Napoleon. The monarchs of these various states spoke of their support of Napoleon, but the support of some, most notably the King of Saxony, was very questionable.

As Napoleon entered the campaign, an incident brought to light the true sentiments of the Bavarians. In March, General Raglovich, commander of the Bavarian corps destined to join the Grande Armée, visibly hesitated to obey Ney's lawful orders for him to leave Bavaria. He claimed that he could not cross the Bavarian frontier without the authorization of his government in Münich.[6]

As Bertrand and the IV Corps moved into Bavaria, the question arose again. Raglovich actively refused to cooperate with the French, without orders from his King. The other Bavarian corps, commanded by General Beckers, also refused to move. His attitude was more hostile than that of Raglovich.

Napoleon's reaction was swift. He wrote the King of Bavaria, demanding that General Wrede, who he felt was more disposed towards France, be given command of the Bavarian army. He requested of the King of Bavaria that the instructions of the French generals be obeyed without restrictions and he demanded that Raglovich concentrate his forces in Ebersdorf.

The Saxon Ducal States remained calm. They were the point of convergence of the massive French columns, and because of that or true sympathy with France, their people expressed no opinions. Despite that, the battalion raised by these states containing 13 officers and 429 men, surrendered to a detachment of 20 Prussian Hussars on 13 April.[7] The battalion passed into service of the allies. The Duke of Weimar had strong ties with Prussia and his forces had fought with the Prussians in 1806. Napoleon had no doubts about his actual sentiments.[8]

Westphalia was a state that Napoleon had created from the remains of several smaller German states, which had strong ties with England. The French control of the people was weak, while the sentiments of German nationalism and the anti-French attitudes were strong. Napoleon feared that two or three allied squadrons could chase Jérôme out of his capitol. His fears were well founded.

In northern Germany, Mecklenburg had renounced its alliance with France and declared for the allies at the end of March. Militarily it was insignificant, but it had been a member of the Confederation and it was the first defection from that Confederation. It was important from the political point of view to occupy Mecklenburg as soon as possible. However, the reoccupation of Mecklenburg by Davout was made difficult by the active intervention of Sweden, even though at that moment Sweden's forces in Germany consisted of a few thousand men in Stralsund who were far from ready to enter the campaign.[9]

Napoleon's greatest concern was that Austria would openly declare for the allies. This would be grave from the domestic political point of view, as well as from the military point of view. This alliance was the most visible gage of the stability of Napoleon's political system. If it defected, the French morale would crumble and that of the allies would soar. France had lost the support of the huge Austrian army already. If the Austrian court declared for the allies, it would face him from the opposite side of the battlefield. Napoleon needed to secure Austria's neutrality, if he couldn't secure its active cooperation.

Napoleon's peril from the Austrians was more than illusion. By April, the Austrians had already decided to declare for the allies. They were only waiting for the right moment. In the meantime, they actively courted Napoleon's German allies in an effort to pry them away from the Confederation of the Rhine. Württemberg, and Bavaria were the most important targets.

Metternich had written their sovereigns, urging them to take arms against Napoleon, if he refused to enter into negotiations on the basis proposed by the Austrians. On 17 April, Metternich wrote to Lebzeltern, his envoy in the allied camp, expressing his greatest hope that the coalition should beat the French army.

On 29 April Metternich again wrote his envoy, directing him to give the allies formal assurances of Austrian cooperation. He asked that the allies be assured that the Austrian army in Bohemia was acting solely in their interests and was not intended to attack them.

Narbonne, Napoleon's ambassador in Vienna, reported that the Austrians were building magazines in Wels, Ems, and Liz, as well as on the Bavarian frontier. Word was sent on 1 April, that the Austrian army consisted of three corps: the Auxiliary Corps—39,712 men and 6,805 horses; the Galician Corps—33,231 men and 6,458 horses; a corps in Silesia and Moravia—27,740 men and 5,359 horses. The total Austrian army consisted of 100,683 men and 18,623 horses ready to enter "en campagne."[10]

Though Metternich attempted to conceal the final destination of the corps in Silesia and Moravia, Napoleon knew it to be Bohemia, where it could threaten the frontiers of Saxony and Bavaria. On 16 April Narbonne reported that the Austrians were selling 45,000,000 florins worth of bonds, which Narbonne correctly interpreted as preparations to finance war.

About 24 April, Napoleon learned that the Austrian corps of Schwarzenberg had resumed its withdrawal towards Galicia. He also learned that Poniatowski, commander of a corps of Poles trapped by the Austrian movement, had concluded a convention allowing the Poles to rejoin the Grande Armée across Moravia and Bohemia. Their movement was to begin on 3 May.

Part of this convention was that Poniatowski's force was to place its weapons in wagons that would follow the troops. Napoleon felt that this was an attempt to disarm them so that they could be quickly overcome. With regards to this, Berthier wrote to Poniatowski, "The Emperor prefers the death of the 15,000 French and Poles who are in Cracow, before he sees them lay down their arms. His majesty will make no case for the lives of men who are dishonored."[11] The military activity of the Austrians and their actions vis-a-vis the Poles, visibly signaled their hostility. Napoleon calculated that Austria could not enter the war until the month of July, by which time it would have completed the organization of its army. Time was short. Napoleon had to defeat Prussia and Russia before the Austrian army was ready to march against him.

In April, Saxony was the most important German state to Napoleon. It was nearly totally occupied by the allies, but it had not followed Prussia's example. Its defection would have a profound effect on the rest of Germany, both politically and militarily. In addition, the King of Saxony was also the sovereign of the Grand Duchy of Warsaw. The Poles had been Napoleon's strongest allies. The loss of that alliance would also be disastrous.

In Torgau, Saxony had 5,000 to 6,000 infantry, that would greatly add to either Napoleon's or the allies armies. They also had a brigade of cavalry totaling 1,600 men. For Napoleon this was a precious prize, in view of his desperate lack of cavalry. Torgau, with Wittenberg and Magdeburg, occupied by French or allied garrisons, would give Napoleon total command of the course of the Elbe.

As it was nearly totally occupied by the allies, Saxony found its strongest defender in Austria. On its side, Austria sought to gain Saxony's support for its proposed mediation. Initial contacts had begun in March, but they were finalized on 20 April with the signing of the Convention of Torgau.

Saxony signed the convention which gave its support to the Austrian mediated peace. In exchange Austria guaranteed the King of Saxony his hereditary territories and promised a territorial compensation for the loss of the Grand Duchy of Warsaw. These negotiations had been held in secret. The withdrawal of the King of Saxony and the concentration of the Saxon army in Torgau, appeared superficially to be a simple withdrawal from the advancing allied army. There were some indications that more was afoot than a simple withdrawal, however. Most notably was General Thielmann's refusal to cooperate with the French. He was commander of the Torgau garrison and he refused to open the city to French or ally. There was also the refusal of the King of Saxony to send either his infantry or his cavalry to join the Grande Armée, as requested by Napoleon.

On 24 April, Napoleon learned of the Convention of Torgau from the King of Württemberg. Napoleon then realized that Austria was actively campaigning in the political arena against him. He directed Narbonne, his ambassador to the Austrian court, to explore this situation as delicately as possible. As to Saxony, the Emperor no longer counted on diplomatic negotiations to keep the King of Saxony on the French side. Napoleon ceased all diplomatic correspondence with Saxony until after the battle of Lützen.

Napoleon needed something to knock the pieces of the puzzle back into place. Diplomacy was failing him. He needed to show that France was still a military power to be respected and feared. A military victory was what he needed: a smashing victory, an Austerlitz! With a single crushing military blow Napoleon would defeat his enemies and bring his wavering allies to heel.

At 4:00 A.M. 15 April, Napoleon left his palace in Saint-Cloud en route for Mainz.

[1] Charras, la Guerre de 1813, pg 490.

[2] Tournes, Campagne de Printemps, pg 30.

[3] There was a small Neapolitan contingent of infantry, some cavalry, and artillery operating with the Grande Armée that would remain there throughout the spring campaign.

[4] Margueron, Campagne de Russie, Vol I, pg 130–132, Imperial Decree of 18 August 1810.

[5] Margueron, Campagne de Russie, Vol IV, pg 400–402.

[6] Demmler, "Anteil der bayerischen Division", Darstellungen , Vol 16, pg 188.

[7] The details of this defection are discussed in Chapter 4.

[8] Sauzey, Regiment des Duches de Saxe, pg 166.

[9] Tournes, Campagne de Printemps, pg 42–43.

[10] Tournes, Campagne de Printemps, pg 49.

[11] Tournes, Campagne de Printemps, pg 52.

The French Offensive Begins

THE MAIN ALLIED ARMY

On 25 March Kutusov, in the name of the King of Prussia and the Czar of Russia, issued the Convention of Kalisch. It formally declared war on France and called on all Germans to join the allied cause.

The 11,000 man corps of General of Infantry Miloradovich formed the advanced guard of the main Russian army on 31 March. Generallieutenant Count St. Priest formed Miloradovich's advanced guard, Generallieutenant Count Markov commanded the first column, Generallieutenant Volkonski commanded the second column and Generallieutenant Baron Korff commanded the cavalry. Miloradovich's headquarters marched with the first column. On 31 March this force crossed the Elbe near Milzig and arrived in Dresden on 15 April. On 22 and 23 April it was in Freiberg and by 29 April it was in Penig, with the advanced troops under Generalmajor Emanuel in Zwickau, Lobenstein and Saalfeld.

On 7 April the main Russian headquarters moved from Kalisch, where it had been since 24 February. On 14 April it was in Steinau and on 18 April it was in Bunzlau where the ill Field Marshal Kutusov had gone. The army marched in two columns. The left flank column was commanded by General of Cavalry Tormassov and consisted of the Guard Infantry Corps under Generallieutenant Lavrov, the 3rd (Grenadier) Corps under Generallieutenant Konovnitzin, and the lst Cuirassier Division under Generalmajor Depreradovich.

The second column consisted of the 8th Infantry Corps with four artillery companies commanded by Generallieutenant Gorchakov II and the 2nd Cuirassier Division under Generalmajor Duca.

On 25 April the two monarchs entered Dresden at the head of the Russian Guard, two battalions of Prussian infantry, a Prussian light cavalry regiment, and an artillery park of 60 guns. They were greeted by ringing bells and showers of flowers.

On 28 April the Russian Reserve Army (the columns of Constantine and Gallizin), received orders to advance out of Dresden. The Grand Duke Constantine, because of illness, remained in Dresden. On 29 April the first column was in Geringswalde and Waldheim, while the second was in Mitweyda. On 1 May both columns had joined together and were lagered in Lobstädt. The Czar established his headquarters in Borna.

Barclay de Tolly had 14,000 men blockading Thorn. The siege of Thorn ended on 18 April, freeing his army, and the siege of Spandau ended on 21 April, freeing yet another brigade.

In late April the allies rebuilt the bridge at Dresden that Davout had destroyed. They also raised two new bridges in Dresden and others at Meissen and Mühlberg. Though his country was occupied, the King of Saxony remained neutral and ordered Thielmann to refuse entry of either side into Torgau.

THE FRENCH ARMY

Napoleon departed Paris during the evening of 15/16 April, and 48 hours later he was in Mainz. Eugène's withdrawal behind the Saal, the insurrections in Germany, the Saxon King's equivocation, the Austrian attitude, the weakness of the Confederation of the Rhine, and the arrival of the campaigning season provoked Napoleon to move quickly.

The resources remaining to Napoleon were immense. He had 357,000 men on 25 April, who were yet to be made into soldiers. The conscription of 1813 and the review of other draft classes had produced 127,000 men since March, who were not yet incorporated into the first line formations. In March the depots received 80,000 men of the six classes and a further 150,000 men of the Class of 1814. In addition to these men the various allies, the Confederation of the Rhine, the Kingdom of Italy, Naples, and the Swiss Confederation were to provide further men. Further forces were to arrive because Poniatowski was about to rejoin the Grande Armée and cadres were being drawn from Spain.

Eugène had massed the bulk of the Grande Armée on the lower Saal. He had Roguet's Guard Division, Grenier's Corps, three of Lauriston's four divisions, the remains of Durutte's division, the eight battalions of the 4th Division of Victor's II Corps, 10 battalions of the 1st Division of Davout's I Corps, Latour-Maubourg's cavalry and 186 cannon with him. The total force was 73,000 men, but the quality was mixed.

A second major force was Davout's, placed to put down the insurrection on the lower Elbe. This force consisted of Puthod's 17th Division of Lauriston's Corps, Sébastiani's II Cavalry Corps, St. - Cyr's small division, Dumonceau's 2nd Division, and Dufour's 5th Division) (Dumonceau and Dufour were, respectively, the second divisions of Davout's and Victor's newly forming corps).

A third army was forming and consisted of the 1er and 2e Corps d'Observation du Rhin, the Corps d'Observation d'Italie and the Imperial Guard. The 1er Corps d'Observation du Rhin was commanded by Maréchal Ney and contained four French divisions (Souham—8th, Brenier—9th Girard—10th, and Ricard—11th), a German division (Marchand's 39th), a mixed German and French cavalry brigade and 122 cannon (almost all French).[1]

The four divisions of Ney's III Corps were formed from mobilized national guardsmen and 28 battalions of conscripts formed around cadres taken from the regiments serving in Spain. Marchand's 29th Division consisted of the contingents of the Confederation of the Rhine: Baden, Hesse-Darmstadt and Frankfurt. It had only 11 battalions, all of which were formed with new recruits. Ney's III Corps contained 53,000 men, of whom 44,000 were French and 9,000 were German.[2]

Ney slowly moved his force through south western Germany, imposing the French will on the populations of Franconia and Thuringia. He also menaced France's wavering allies in Bavaria and Saxony.

The 2e Corps d'Observation du Rhin was, at this time, not in as ready a state as the 1er Corps. It was commanded by Maréchal Marmont and contained four French divisions (Compans—20th, Bonnet—21st, Friederichs—22nd and Teste—23rd), 88 cannons and a cavalry force formed with the 250 Chevauxlegers-lanciers of the Grand Duchy of Berg.[3]

Among his four divisions were 15 battalions of marine artillerists, who though veteran soldiers were ill drilled, as well as 32 battalions of conscripts, the 37th Légère Regiment formed from departmental reserve companies, and the Spanish infantry from the 1/Joseph Napoleon Regiment.[4]

When Marmont marched his corps into Germany from Mainz, he was obliged to leave Teste's 23rd Division behind, as it had not yet completed its organization. It was decided that a force of infantry was necessary to maintain the order in Westphalia and Cleve-Berg, where the citizens were aroused by thoughts of freedom from France. Teste's 23rd Division was to perform these duties. Marmont's advancing army contained about 27,000 men of all arms and had 78 cannon. He paralleled Ney's advance and on 17 April, he was in Eisenach.

The Corps d'Observation d'Italie was organized by General Bertrand. Work had begun on 13 March near Verona. The corps consisted of three French divisions[5] (C.Morand—12th, Pacthod—13th, and Lorencz—14th), the Italian infantry 15th Division (Peyri), a cavalry division and 80 cannons, soon to be 102 cannons. The French divisions were formed with two regiments formed from national guardsmen (137th and 156th), two old regiments (13th and 23rd), 16 battalions of conscripts of the class of 1813 and a few with conscripts of the class of 1812. In addition there were three Neapolitan and two Croatian battalions. The Italian division contained 13 battalions. It was formed was formed of soldiers with many years of service, yet with no combat experience. The cavalry division had 11 squadrons, none of which had any combat experience. The Corps d'observation d'Italie had a total of 42,000 men.

As Bertrand marched through Augsburg he found the six battalions, which had been organized with conscripts of the class of 1813[6] and the cadres of Eugène's old corps that had survived Russia. He disbanded these battalions, sent the cadres to Italy and incorporated the conscripts into his weakest regiments. He did the same to the "Würzburg batallion de marche" formed from ships' companies and initially destined to garrison Glogau. He raised his corps to total of 45,000 men.[7]

The Imperial Guard was a powerful force, but less numerous than hoped. It consisted of 16 battalions in Mainz, 2 Old Guard and 14 Young Guard. In addition there were 3,000 cavalry and 80 cannon in Mainz, as well as another 3,000 Guard cavalry that Eugéne had taken with him in January. The Guard contained 18,000 men.

On 25 April the 2nd Guard Division, commanded by General Barrois, was broken into two parts. The lst Brigade, commanded by General Decouz, had 2,219 men. It departed Frankfurt on the 24th and moved to Eisenach. The second part, two other brigades totaling 5,935 men, did not leave Frankfurt until the end of the month. Two further Guard divisions were forming. The 3rd Guard Division, under General Delaborde, was sending its initial elements to Mainz, but was still an insignificant formation. The 4th Division, under General Friant, was organizing in Paris.

The two divisions of "cavalerie de marche" destined to reinforce the corps of Latour-Maubourg and Sébastiani were organizing in Mainz. On 21 April the lst Division of the I Cavalry Corps, totaling 1,824 men, was under the command of General Milhaud. It had only four regiments. The lst Division of the II Cavalry Corps, totaling 1,910 men, was commanded by General Saint-Germain. This division had only three regiments.[8] The two divisions were unified under the command of General Lebrun, the Duc de Plaisance. On 21 April this corps was dispatched to Gotha.

After they had departed, General Margaron continued to organize regiments de marche with stream of reinforcements that arrived in Hanau and eventually, he completed each of the two divisions to a strength of four regiments. And as more men came in, he constituted two new divisions de marche. However, by 5 May these two new divisions had a strength of only 786 men, less than a single full strength cavalry regiment.

The 3rd Cavalry Corps, commanded by the Duc de Padoue, had only just begun organizing in Metz. On 25 April it contained only 1,026 men and 1,057 horses. It was to fill in where the first two cavalry divisions de marche had been stationed and was sent to Hanau. For this move, it was organized into four regiments (15 officers and 977 men) and departed Metz on 26 April. Those that remained in Metz were eventually raised to 4,000 men by 4 June.

Not only did the cavalry gradually grow with reinforcements, but so did all of the formations of the Grande Armée. On 5 May, Berthier reported to Napoleon that 8,449 reinforcements designated for the III, VI, and XII Corps, as well as the Guard, were spread between Eisenach and Frankfurt. Between 1 and 31 May, a further 6,780 men left Italy to join the IV and XII Corps. The members of the Confederation of the Rhine, notably Bavaria and Württemberg, were working hard to organize their obligated contingents. Bavaria had reorganized and strengthened the 29th Division commanded by General Raglovich in Bayreuth. It now had nine battalions of infantry, six squadrons of cavalry, and 16 cannon totaling 8,000 men.

A Württemberg 38th Division, commanded by Generallieutenant Franquemont, was forming at Mergentheim. It had ten battalions of infantry, eight squadrons of cavalry and 12 cannon

SAXONY AND CENTRAL GERMANY

Scale 1:1,000,000

| | | | | | |
|15|30|45|60|75|90 miles|

totaling 6,500 men. Württemberg raised and sent into the field 4,789 infantry, and 1,596 cavalry, on 15 May. Early in the campaign Bavaria had 12,183 men, but in March and April it raised a further 14,845 men. Baden also raised a small contingent of 2,718 men.

Jérôme Bonaparte, King of Westphalia, was also organizing a contingent for Napoleon. Eight battalions, eight squadrons and 16 cannon were raised and placed under the command of Generallieutenant Hammerstein. Outside of this force, Jérôme retained his guard (2,200 infantry, 1,100 cavalry, and 1,200 artillerists)[9] in Kassel. This force consisted of the Garde du Corps, the Garde Chevauxlegers, the Grenadiergarde, the Chasseurgarde, the Chasseur-Karabinier, the Guard foot battery and various depots.[10] However, because of the threat of Russian and Prussian partisans, Jérôme was obliged to keep the rest of his army on his borders, lest his country revolt.

On 25 April, the Westphalian 37th Division of General Hammerstein contained 5,950 raw recruits. They were totally incapable of combat and desertion was a major problem. The second division forming in Westphalia was Dombrowski's Polish division. It contained 3,024 men formed from cadres that had escaped the disaster from Russia. Though veteran troops, they were incapable of any service, until they had been rested and refitted. Napoleon needed these men, however, and they were provisionally attached to Teste's division (23rd Division, I Corps). They were organized in Giessen and sent to Cassel. Once in Cassel, they then began their task of ensuring order and tranquility in Westphalia.

In late April Napoleon abolished the various old corps designations and eventually reassigned them as follows:

Davout	I Corps (1st, 2nd, 3rd Divisions)
Victor	II Corps (4th, 5th, 6th Divisions)
Ney	III Corps (8th, 9th, 10th, 11th, 39th Divisions)
Bertrand	IV Corps (12th, 13th, 14th, 15th Divisions)
Lauriston	V Corps (16th, 17th, 18th, 19th Divisions)
Marmont	VI Corps (20th, 21st, 22nd, 23rd Divisions)
Reynier	VII Corps (24th, 25th, 32nd Divisions)
Poniatowski	VIII Corps (26th & 27th Divisions)
not named	IX Corps (28th, 29th Divisions)
Rapp	X Corps (7th, 30th 33rd Divisions)
St. Cyr	XI Corps (31st, 35th 36th Divisions)

The 1er Corps d'Observation du Rhin had become the III Corps, the 1er Corps d'Observation d'Italie had become the IV Corps, the Corps d'Observation de l'Elbe had become the V Corps and the 2e Corps d'Observation du Rhin had become the VI Corps. Reynier's feeble force of Saxons and Durutte's French 32nd Division had become the VII Corps. Poniatowski's force of Poles, still trapped in Galicia, became the VIII Corps. The Bavarian contingent was to become the IX Corps, the title X Corps was given to the garrison of Danzig under General Rapp, and Grenier's corps became the XI Corps.[11] Initially Napoleon decided to keep the IX Corps vacant. The IV Corps was formed with only two of its intended divisions (Morand's 12th and Peyri's Italian 15th), the Italian cavalry and the Württemberg 38th Division under Franquemont. A XII Corps was then organized with Bertrand's other two divisions (Pacthod—13th and Lorencz—14th) and the 29th (Bavarian) Division of Raglovich. Oudinot was given command of the XII Corps. The entire Grande Armée commanded by Napoleon in Germany consisted of 269,000 men: 230,000 infantry, 15,000 cavalry and 24,000 artillery, engineers and train.

In addition, there were several divisions outside of these corps that were to play a part in the 1813 campaign. The Westphalian forces formed the 37th Division, those of Württemberg formed the 38th Division, the combined forces of Hesse-Darmstadt, Baden and Frankfurt formed the 39th Division. The four Vistula regiments, the 4th, 7th, and 9th Polish Line

Regiments and a few Lithuanian regiments were used to form the 40th Division and ten further battalions were being organized into the 41st Division in Erfurt.

On 4 May, the Westphalian 37th Division was assigned to the VI Corps. The 38th Division was assigned to the IV Corps and the 39th Division was assigned to the III Corps. The 6th Division of the II Corps remained in Wesel until the beginning of June. At the end of April the lst Division I Corps was under Victor in the II Corps and the 5th Division, II Corps was under Davout and serving with the 3rd Division, I Corps in Wesel.

The Imperial Guard Infantry served under Maréchal Mortier and the Imperial Guard Cavalry under Maréchal Bessières. The I Cavalry Corps was under General Latour-Maubourg and the II Cavalry Corps was under General Sébastiani.[12]

Though it sounded impressive, many of the soldiers were recent conscripts. They lacked every type of equipment and support. Many of the battalions had not formed their elite companies. Napoleon directed that they be organized quickly, but as they were often conscripts, they were "elite" only in name.

Only the garrison of Danzig, the Imperial Guard, some of the battalions under Bertrand and Marmont, and a few thousand cavalry and artillerists were veteran troops. The rest were conscripts.

Many of the corporals had only four or five months of service and many of the non-commissioned officers had never been to war. Many of the units were thrown together quickly and their men had not had the necessary time to form the interpersonal bonds within their companies, battalions, and regiments that gave them the morale strength necessary to wage war successfully. These men also lacked many of the skills necessary to survive on campaign, to forage for food, and to march endlessly.

Despite it all, the army's morale was high. The veterans of the Russian campaign had regained their faith in Napoleon. But the recruits and the contingents from the Confederation and the Kingdom of Italy found mixed satisfaction in their situation. There were problems and many units suffered from desertion. The 7th Italian Line Regiment lost 250 deserters in a single night. The Hessian and Baden regiments suffered notably from desertion. As the Croatian regiments passed by Bohemia, the Croatians slipped away in great numbers. However, much of this was overcome by the personality of Napoleon, who still excited loyalty and fanaticism in the troops he commanded.

NAPOLEON TAKES COMMAND

In mid-April Napoleon began sending orders directly to his marshals in the field. He directed Davout to send Vandamme's division towards the Elbe and against Hamburg. He ordered Eugène to move up the Saal by the right bank and to occupy the bridgeheads at Halle and Mersburg.

Bertrand was ordered from Bamberg to Coburg and on to Saalfeld. He was given temporary command of the Bavarian division and told to send it to the heights above Ebersdorf. Bertrand was also made subordinate to Ney. This force became known as the Armée du Mein.

Ney was in Weimar on 18 April. From there he was ordered to Jena and the other passages over the Saal from Kamburg to Auerstädt. Marmont was to move by Langensalza and Weissensee to the heights of Weimar, Colleda, and Erfurt. The Imperial Guard, commanded by Maréchal Bessières, was sent to Erfurt. Pacthod and Lorencz were ordered to quickly join the Bavarian division and form the XII Corps under Maréchal Oudinot, then to advance on the left of General Bertrand.

All movements centered on Erfurt. The city was surrounded by a strong wall and had two citadels. It sat on the main road from Dresden and Leipzig to Mainz, and gave Napoleon's army a solid base of operations, a strong position for vital depots, and a central position from which to operate.

The city of Würzburg was of similar value and it too was organized as a center of communications. It was positioned on the road from Dresden to Mainz by Hof. A strong French garrison was posted in both Erfurt and Würzburg. However, the garrison of Würzburg was formed with the 2/127th, 2/128th, and 2/129th Infantry Regiments. These 1,886 men were recruited from the 32nd Military Division (Hamburg) where there was currently open revolt against the French. They had been moved to Würzburg from Erfurt because their morale was low and their master's faith in them was even lower. Erfurt's new garrison was formed with two battalions from the 123rd and 124th Infantry Regiments, Dutch conscripts, and a battalion of the 134th Infantry Regiment.[13] The garrison was still not composed of such troops as to inspire a commander's faith and trust.

Augereau was appointed military governor of the Grand-Duchies of Frankfurt and Würzburg[14] and charged with organizing two reserve corps d'armée on the Mein with the conscripts from the last class called, as well as the class of 1814.

In Erfurt, General Doucet was organizing a force with 100,000 conscripts of the class of 1813 and the debris of the regiments from the I, II, and III Corps that had been destroyed in Russia, which had not been used to organize Davout's and Victor's new I and II Corps. It was in no condition to join the campaign and Napoleon chose to leave it in Erfurt.[15]

FRENCH OPERATIONS BEGIN

Eugène recrossed to the right bank of the Saal and destroyed the bridgehead at Wettin abandoned by the allies. On 28 April he sent Lauriston against Halle. It was strongly defended, but a successful assault gave the French a bridgehead and forced the allies to destroy their own bridges.

Eugène established his headquarters in Eisleben, occupied Querfurt with a division, and ordered Macdonald to move on the following day on Mersburg and take it.

Ney's five divisions were in Naumburg, Camburg and Dörnburg along the Saal. Marmont had a division in Weimar, one in Naumburg and a third on Freiburg. The Imperial Guard was in Auerstädt. Bertrand was in Jena and occupied all the passages over the Saal between Jena and Saalfeld. Oudinot was to arrive the next day.

The Russian and Prussian partisans had completely disappeared from the left bank of the Saal. The French reconnaissances encountered only light cavalry opposition.

THE ALLIED ARMIES

On 17 April Wittgenstein's army (31,510 men) was located on the lower Saal, on both sides of the Elbe north and west of Wittenberg. His army contained the two Prussian corps of General von Bülow (7,270 men) and General von Yorck (8,540 men), the Russo-Prussian corps of General Kleist (6,200 men) and the Russian corps of General Berg (9,500 men.)

General Blücher's army (39,600 men) was located between Leipzig, Zwickau, and Mittveida. It consisted of the 1st Prussian Corps (25,110 men) and Winzingerode's Russian corps (14,550). The Russian main army (31,060 men) was marching towards Dresden. It contained Miloradovich's corps (12,960 men) and the "principal army" under Tormassov (18,100 men). The total allied armies consisted of 102,230 men. The allies faced a total French army of 151,000 men, but for their operations in Saxony, the allies had 30,710 cavalry, while the French had only 8,540 very mediocre cavalry.[16]

All of the allied forces operating north of Magdeburg, on the lower Elbe, were placed under the command of General Wallmoden. This force was to eventually be reinforced by the Russo-German Legion, which was supported financially by the British. The British even provided drafts from the King's German Legion to train and form the cadres of the new units. A force of 400 infantry under Lieutenant Colonel Martin, a cavalry force of 60 men and 40 horses under

FREIWILLIGER OF 1813 IN BRESLAU

Rittmeister Krauschenberg and Lieutenant von Estorff, and an artillery detachment of 43 men and six guns under Captain Wiering was assembled and sent to Hamburg.[17]

Wittgenstein's Order of the Day of 13 April placed Czernichev, Dörnberg, Tettenborn and Benkendorf under Wallmoden's command. This force was broken into three formations. General Tettenborn was in Hamburg with 1,400 cavalry. General Dörnberg was in Celle with 2,460 men, and General Czernichev was in Uelzen with 3,000 men. This force was soon to be reinforced by a corps of 5,270 men being formed in Hamburg and Mecklenburg. The effective strength of General Wallmoden's force would rise to 11,630 men.

In addition, the allies had many men tied up in their rear areas. General Barclay de Tolly commanded the Army of the West (13,210 men) which surrounded the fortress of Thorn. Thorn surrendered on 16 April, but Barclay was unable to return to the main army until the middle of May.

To the south, General Osten-Sacken faced Poniatowski and Frimont with 9,110 men. At the same time 5,000 men under General Pahlen were occupying the Grand Duchy of Warsaw. In addition there were 60,200 men watching various other fortresses still occupied by the French.

Of the forces available for operations in Saxony, the 43,760 Prussians were formed almost entirely of veterans and reservists called up since January. All of the "volunteers" were organized into "freiwilligerjäger" detachments of up to 200 men and attached to each regiment

WITTGENSTEIN

of the army. There were no more than 7,800 of these volunteers. The 58,470 Russians were entirely veterans.

These soldiers were both the military and morale superiors of the French. Though the Russians were no longer motivated by the desire to throw the "satanic invaders" from the motherland, many of them were hardened veterans, well disciplined, brave, tenacious, and totally devoted to their commanders.

The Prussian army was formed with trained soldiers, who were motivated by the ideas of German nationalism and the desire to throw off the oppressive "French yoke." In their spirit to liberate their homeland, they were the German equivalent of the French volunteers of 1792. The Germans still refer to this war as the "Volkerbefreiungskrieg," or People's War of Liberation.

Kutusov remained ill in Kalisch and died there on 28 April. He was officially replaced by General Wittgenstein as commander of the Russian armies. When he assumed command, he found that the allied armies were not structured to facilitate his job. His powers were far from absolute, and though he bore the title "Commander in Chief of the Army of the Combined Allied Powers" he in fact had only direct command of his own army, and those of Blücher and Winzingerode.

He was saddled with a chief of staff, d'Auvray, who had completely passed over the responsiblities of his position to General Diebitsch. Diebitsch did not have the experience or the capabilities to perform his new task.

Wittgenstein's problems were further exacerbated by the presence of both the Czar and the King of Prussia with his army. Friedrich-Wilhelm, the King of Prussia, was unable to make a decision. He constantly feared disaster and acted conservatively at every turn. On the day of the battle of Lützen, when Blücher went into battle, he was heard to say "Now, in the name of God, what shall come, let it not be another Auerstädt."

In contrast, the Czar, who had no military experience or education of note, was resolved to push the war energetically. He oversaw Wittgenstein's every action and often superseded his commander's decisions.

A substantial staff supported the allied commanders, but the Allied staff was not a smooth running, efficient organization. It was fraught with incompetence and petty rivalries. Factions fought each other almost as hard as they fought the French. This problem permeated every aspect of the staff's work. Its work was as much military as it was toadying to the vanities of superiors and competing for favor with the King of Prussia and the Czar.

The first plan generated in this environment and presented to the Czar was the work of generals Volkonski, Toll, and Knesebeck. Volkonski was chief of staff to the Czar, but exercised little influence over the Czar. In the beginning of the 1813 campaign it was General Toll who had the Czar's ear. By the end of the 1813 campaign, however, it was General Knesebeck who exercised the greatest influence.

Toll was an ardent admirer of Scharnhorst, while Knesebeck was Scharnhorst's declared enemy. Knesebeck was from the old Prussian school, and resisted all of the changes to the Prussian army that had been instituted after Jena and Auerstädt. Knesebeck bitterly fought Scharnhorst and his ideas at every turn.

The infighting and other organizational weaknesses of the allied command were tremendous. In contrast Blücher's staff was something remarkable. It was headed by Scharnhorst who was noted for his superior intelligence. He was the architect of the reorganization of the Prussian army after 1806, and was to have an influence beyond what might have been expected from one who was so junior.

Under Scharnhorst was yet another general of historical note: Gneisenau. It was from these two men, Scharnhorst and Gneisenau, that the Prussian army staff corps was to spring. That staff corps led directly to the German victories of 1870, 1914, and 1939.

THE ALLIED STRATEGIC SITUATION

The allies had no strategic plan when Wittgenstein assumed command. The corps of Tormassov and Miloradovich approached the Elbe, but no decision had been made if they should cross it or if they should deploy around Dresden.

Wittgenstein was stricken with indecision. He wanted to join all of the forces that had crossed the Elbe, but he did not have control of any of them other than those of Blücher. He was further handicapped by the location of the bridgeheads that he did hold over the Elbe.

Between Magdeburg and Wittenberg, both held by the French, he had only one bridge at Dessau. Torgau was still occupied by Thielmann's Saxons and despite all entreaties, it remained closed to them. Historical hind-sight indicates that Thielmann was a German patriot before he was a Saxon. He was eventually to lead one of the Prussian corps during the 1814 and 1815 campaigns. No doubt an enticement could have been found to open Torgau to the allies, but, unfortunately for the allies, it was not found. The allies did have five other bridges, one at Mühlberg, one at Meissen and three in Dresden.

Leipzig was a tempting goal, but if Wittgenstein were to move in that direction, nothing stood between Eugène and Berlin. If he detached Blücher north to block the road to Berlin, he would diminish the main army and might be seriously outnumbered by the French. Wittgenstein's information on the French armies was poor. He fooled himself into believing that Eugène had only 26,000 men and that it would abandon the lower Saal if pressed. In fact Eugène had 50,000 men.

In contrast Blücher's staff refused to believe that Eugène was likely to withdraw. They had information that Bertrand's corps of 45,000 men (in reality 40,367 men) was en route to Nürnberg and that Ney was moving towards Gotha and Erfurt with a force of unknown strength. Blücher's staff was predicting a French attack on the Russian army.[18]

This caused the Czar to hesitate about moving Tormassov and Miloradovich over the Elbe. On 17 April Scharnhorst proposed to the Czar and Wittgenstein a plan of action. He suggested that Tormassov and Miloradovich should be joined to the main army, bringing its strength to 129,000 men. He judged by the movement of Bertrand, Ney and Eugène that Napoleon was concentrating his forces between the Saal and the Elbe on a line from Leipzig to Zwickau.

This would bring a battle between Mulde and the Elbe or between Mulde and the Saal. A battle between the Mulde and the Elbe had grave consequences, as it was located such that all of the French forces were perfectly posted to strike there. In contrast, the position between the Mulde

115

and the Saal was positioned such that the conditions were best for the allies. It would oblige the French to concentrate on the plains of Leipzig where the allied cavalry superiority could best be brought to bear.

Scharnhorst stated that if Tormassov and Miloradovich were not to cross the Elbe, but that Wittgenstein and Blücher were to withdraw across the Elbe and join them on its eastern bank, the French would find the road to Berlin and Hamburg open to them. Scharnhorst proposed that the allies then undertake an audacious plan. He recommended that as the French main army moved from Erfurt on the Saal, that Blücher rapidly join Wittgenstein and that their combined forces march towards Eisenach, Cassel and even Frankfurt.

Miloradovich and Tormassov were to defend the Elbe from Dresden to Mühlberg. If the movement of Blücher and Wittgenstein was faced by too great a force, they could withdraw on northern Germany, where their rear would be covered by the Danish and the Swedish armies.

Scharnhorst's proposal of movements towards Magdeburg had several problems. The first was Eugène's army, which would not remain immobile on the lower Saal. Could the allies survive a battle with their 60,000 men facing the potential 129,000 men army that Napoleon could bring against them?[19]

The indecision of the allied general staff was such that Scharnhorst's audacious plan was immediately dropped and his plan gained no favor. Plan after plan was presented, discussed and discarded on the sea of petty infighting. When it was finished only Scharnhorst stood out. It was he who had projected Napoleon's target and the location of the battle of Lützen. Unfortunately for Scharnhorst, Lützen was to be his last battle.

Napoleon's Plans

Napoleon envisioned a maneuver from the lower Elbe, whereby he could in a short campaign regain the Vistula and drive the Russians out of western Europe. He had been developing this idea since February. Its execution had been hampered by the situation in northern Germany, and the fear of an English or Swedish landing at Hamburg, which obliged Napoleon to have the Armée de l'Elbe watch all of Westphalia and the 32nd Military Division. To this end Napoleon had ordered Eugène to cover Magdeburg as long as possible. He had accepted the possibility that the allies might invade Saxony, as well they did. Ney's Armée du Mein was to maneuver on Eugène's right and to stop any enemy thrust from Dresden.

All of Napoleon's plans were evolved in these terms: if, at the moment of the resumption of operations, the French were still masters of the Elbe, they would cross at Magdeburg and march to the north towards Küstrin, Stettin, and Danzig. If the allies were to cross the Elbe at Dresden it would be necessary that they first be pushed back across the Elbe, but only after Napoleon's contemplated march on Danzig.

In a letter dated 11 March, Napoleon explained to Eugène his thoughts. He counted on converging at the beginning of May, the Armée du Mein, under Ney, at Würzburg, Erfurt, and Leipzig. The Armée de l'Elbe, under Eugène, would be at Magdeburg, holding Havelberg and Wittenberg. Napoleon presumed that at the same time the allied army would be still to the east of the Elbe, stretched between Danzig and Glogau.[20]

If these conditions existed, the goal of the French army would be to march immediately to the succor of the garrison of Danzig. The entire Armée de l'Elbe, followed by the Armée du Mein would march by Havelberg on Stettin. After having made feints to cause the allies to believe that he was moving on Dresden and into Silesia, he intended to move through Havelberg and on to Stettin with a force of 300,000 men using the Thuringian mountains as a screen. Once there he would continue his march on Danzig, where he estimated this force would arrive in 15 days, 20 days after crossing the Elbe. Once there he would break the siege of Danzig, take Marienburg, the island of Nogat and all the bridges on the lower Vistula. This would free 50,000 veteran soldiers that were trapped in various garrisons and provide a tremendous reinforcement for his army, as well as making good the losses of the long march.[21]

If this march were to succeed, it is unquestionable that the allies would be obliged to withdraw and Napoleon would have recovered all of the territory that had been lost since December 1812. However, this maneuver runs contrary to his historical preference for marching on and destroying the enemy's army. It is possible that he feared marching towards Saxony, where the enemy's cavalry superiority could be fully employed on the plains of Leipzig. It is also possible that Napoleon feared risking everything in a massive battle with his army of relatively raw recruits. Whatever the truth may be, no documents were left behind to explain his preference for geographical goals.

It is essential to note that Napoleon's maneuver was based on the premise that the allied armies were in force near the Elbe, but that they had not yet crossed it. The maneuver was not desirable if the allies had massed their army near Leipzig. By May, Napoleon could no longer count on the allied armies being east of the Elbe, but he persisted in his plan.

On 13 March he had issued the orders necessary to concentrate the III Corps in Würzburg in the first half of April.[22] At the same time the XI Corps was to concentrate in Aschaffenburg and Hanau, and the Guard in Frankfurt. Napoleon told Ney that it was his plan to vigorously retake the offensive and retake Dresden, break the blockade of Danzig and the fortresses on the Oder, as well as driving the allies behind the Vistula. Unfortunately for Napoleon, the two corps d'Observation du Rhin and the Corps d'Observation d'Italie were in no state to undertake this ambitious plan.

Initially the declaration of war by Prussia changed nothing. But the arrival of Blücher in Dresden in early April, the increasing hostility of Austria, and the attitude of Saxony did change the situation. Napoleon now felt it was necessary to give an example of the consequences of defection from the Confederation of the Rhine. Napoleon determined to resume the offensive in the direction of Dresden, and Saxony was to provide the example "pour encourager les autres."[23]

Napoleon believed that Blücher had not crossed the Elbe. He ignored the fact that Eugène had withdrawn behind the Elbe himself. He believed that the Russians had held the bulk of their forces around the various French garrisoned fortresses in their rear. He still held his plan to strike through to Danzig.

Eugène's goals were not changed. The Armée de l'Elbe was to maintain its positions to the east of Magdeburg. The Armée du Mein was placed under Ney until the arrival of the Emperor, and the VI Corps and the Guard were formed into an army group under the command of Bessières.

Between 15 and 18 April, the II Corps was to arrive in Meiningen, the VI Corps and Guard were to be behind it, and the IV Corps was to be in Coburg. If Ney could move to Erfurt without risk he was to move the III Corps there to support Eugène and cover Westphalia. The VI Corps and the Guard were to move to Gotha.

Bessières was to pass to Marmont the command of his two corps, move to Erfurt and join Ney. He was to form under his command the Guard cavalry, the III Corps cavalry and that of the Bavarians to form a corps of 7,000 to 8,000 cavalry. Bertrand was to continue on towards Jena and support Ney's side facing Erfurt or Meiningen, if the allies marched from Dresden to Bayreuth.[24]

Napoleon was overly optimistic about the amount of cavalry that Bessières could gather together in Erfurt. The total was in fact only about 5,500 cavalry.

The French information on the allied intentions were very poor. There was insufficient information upon which to base a sound maneuver. It was possible that the Prussians might advance from Dresden towards Bayreuth, in hopes of attacking the IV Corps as it moved through Bamberg. This would have been the most timidly aggressive possible movement by the Prussians. It would have also been a very advantageous situation for the Armée du Mein.

Napoleon held himself ready to profit from this maneuver. He stated that it was his intention to refuse his right and let the enemy penetrate into Bayreuth. He would make the inverse of the movement he had made during the Jena campaign. However, the Prussians did not comply with Napoleon's desires and this maneuver was never executed.

The Maneuvers Begin

After the battle at Möckern, Eugène had abandoned his positions on the east bank of the Elbe and moved into the lower Saal basin. He reported that Wittgenstein had crossed the Elbe at Dessau with 40,000 men and seemed intent on massing his army with Blücher's 24,000 men behind the Mulde.

Napoleon judged that the concentration of the Armée du Mein before Coburg and Erfurt, risked being struck by an allied offensive from either Leipzig or Altenburg. He responded by directing Ney's III Corps on Meiningen, and the VI Corps and the Guard to Eisenach. The IV Corps' movement on Coburg and Bamberg became too dangerous as a result of Blücher's presence in Altenburg and was withdrawn on Schweinfurt. This allowed the four corps, totaling 100,651 men, to converge quickly for a battle in the environs of Meiningen.

When Napoleon arrived in Mainz on 17 April, he immediately began assessing the situation. He poured over the intelligence reports of his generals. On the same day, he issued orders for a concentrations of the armies of the Mein and the Elbe on a line running form Erfurt to Coburg.

The Armée de l'Elbe had signaled Napoleon that Wittgenstein was moving on the Saal, towards Halle and Mersburg and that Wittgenstein's advanced guards were in Eisleben and Leimbach. This was soon found to be in error, and Eugène signaled that Wittgenstein had remained immobile near Dessau and Cöthen, and that only patrols had been seen in Halle, Eisleben and Leimbach. Napoleon's information on Blücher was less precise. According to the various German and Austrian newspapers, Blücher's corps was moving towards Freyberg and Chemnitz. They also stated that Winzingerode's corps was in Leipzig on 1 April.

The French minister in Münich, signaled that on 10 and 11 April, Prussian cavalry patrols were seen in Plauen, Hof, and Schleiz. Bertrand confirmed this on 16 April, as he passed through Bamberg. The most significant news came from the French minister in Weimar, who signaled that Blücher's army was in Leipzig, Borna, and Penig, that his cavalry was in Altenburg and that four squadrons of Prussian cavalry occupied Jena. The Russian army was, based on Austrian newspaper articles, believed to still be around Glogau and before Frimont and Poniatowski. Napoleon did not believe that there was a Russian army en route to Dresden.[25] The news from northern Germany was encouraging. Napoleon learned from an agent in Stralsund that as of 29 March, there were no Swedish forces there and that the force that debarked in April consisted of only 7,000 to 8,000 men. Eugène reported that the insurgents in Hamburg and on the lower Elbe had raised only 3,000 to 4,000 cavalry and 2,000 infantry.

Napoleon estimated that Wittgenstein had 25,000 to 31,000 men, that Blücher and Winzingerode had a combined strength of about 40,000 men. Napoleon's analysis of the intelligence information indicated to him that the allies intended to undertake nothing serious for the time being.

On 19 April the Armée de l'Elbe was in position between the Harz mountains and the Elbe. The Armée du Mein and the III Corps had converged at Erfurt. The Guard and VI Corps were in Gotha and the IV Corps was in Coburg. After all of the corps had reached their designated positions the Emperor issued new orders, to continue the movement on the Saal. He ordered the III Corps, the Imperial Guard and the VI Corps to move on Naumburg and Dörnburg. The 39th Division was to act so as to provide liaison between Ney and Bertrand's corps. Once there, Ney was to move on Saalfeld and then to Jena. On the same day as he issued these orders Napoleon learned of enemy forces between the Armies of the Mein and the Elbe. This news profoundly troubled him.

On 11 April Major von Laroche, under Blücher's command, had departed from Naumburg enroute to Erfurt and Magdeburg with one of the two squadrons of the 2nd Silesian Hussar Regiment he commanded. On 12 April, the commander of this squadron, Major Hellwig, learned that in Langensalza there were about 2,000 men. This force was the debris of the Bavarian division of General Rechberg, which totaled 1,700 infantry, 400 cavalry and six guns. Hellwig's squadron attacked them, capturing two howitzers, three cannons, and three munition wagons. The Bavarian casualties totaled 30 to 40 dead and 12 prisoners. Hellwig lost one officer and five men.[26] On 17 April, von Hellwig was in the area around Wanfried, where he fell on a Westphalian cavalry squadron and a company of voltigeurs. He captured 32 men and withdrew on the Saal.[27]

This cavalry raid, with no support, threw the entire Westphalian army and the court of Jérôme into a panic. His cavalry forces consisted solely of the two squadrons of Guard Chevauxlegers under Major von Löwenstern, then in Nordhausen. Even this tiny force was not safe. It was struck by Lanskoi who captured 3 officers and 102 men. General Hammerstein judged that Lanskoi had moved to Heiligenstädt and withdrew to the west. He felt that the presence of these forces signaled the presence of a corps of Russian cavalry, supported by a regiment of jagers and six guns marching from Nordhausen to Heiligenstädt, while another enemy corps occupied Mülhausen. Jérôme instantly cried for assistance from Napoleon, Ney, and General Teste.

Napoleon felt these numbers were grossly exaggerated and estimated that there were only 3 to 4 squadrons, 2 to 3 battalions and six guns maximum in the indicated areas. However, the Westphalian position in his rear was important. Napoleon directed Bessières to send a small force of Guard cavalry, supported by Bonnet's Division towards Langensalza. He then ordered General Teste to move his division to Cassel.

The orders issued by Napoleon on 19 April were received by the various corps between 20 and 22 April. These directives guided their actions between 24 and 25 April. On 22 April new information caused Napoleon to issue new instructions. The strategic initiative still rested with the allied cavalry forces and streifkorps.

ALLIED REACTIONS

On 18 April Wittgenstein and Blücher learned that Ney had arrived in Erfurt, with an estimated 70,000 men. They knew Marchand was moving from Coburg to Erfurt and that Bertrand, with 25,000 French and 10,000 Bavarians, was moving on Coburg or Hof. They also knew that the Armée de l'Elbe was still immobile on the lower Saal near Eisleben and Quedlimburg.

The movement of the Armée du Mein towards the Saal, struck Wittgenstein as the prelude to a general offensive designed to cut off Blücher. On the evening of 19 April, he ordered the concentration of his army. Movement began on 20 April and on 21 April, Kleist was between Dessau and Rosslau, Yorck was at Düben, Berg was in Eilenburg and Bülow continued to observe Magdeburg from the right bank of the Elbe. Only a few light detachments were left along the Saal River.

EUGÈNE'S ACTIONS

The Armée de l'Elbe was immobile in the positions prescribed by Napoleon, stretching from Magdeburg towards the Harz mountains. It was well placed to coordinate a concentration with the Armée du Mein. Napoleon had positioned it to hold Wittgenstein on the lower Saal. It was able to strike the flank of any enemy, who departed the region around Leipzig and was positioned to strike towards Weimar or Erfurt as necessary. Eugène sat impatiently and towards mid-April, he began to request a mission from Napoleon. This mission came on 22 April.

On 17 April Ney's forces were advancing towards Weimar, and had no idea that there were any enemy forces near his army. Souham's division concentrated on 19 April in Weimar, and acted to cover the concentration of the rest of Ney's forces. Souham's lst Brigade and the corps brigade of cavalry (Baden Dragoons and 10th Hussars) moved on Erfurt and quickly encountered two squadrons of Major Blücher's Prussian cavalry. The Prussians were caught totally by surprise.[28] The Baden Dragoons struck their front, while the 10th Hussars struck them in the flank. The French and Baden cavalry chased them through the streets of Weimar, sabering them as they went. The Prussians lost 70 killed or wounded and 25 prisoners. The French losses were two killed and two wounded. This contact with what was estimated at three squadrons of cavalry was interpreted as an indication of the region being heavily occupied by the allies. A Prussian officer taken prisoner in this engagement, announced that Winzingerode commanded a corps of all arms in Leipzig.[29]

Souham began to fear that he was closing on an infinitely superior enemy. This fear was further corroborated by an officer sent on reconnaissance towards Jena, who reported that the village was filled with infantry, that he had seen ten guns, and that the inhabitants reported seeing columns of at least 40,000 Prussians near Gera and Altenburg. He reported that two corps were marching on Jena.

This information was completely false, but Ney did not know that and became very agitated at the prospect of an unanticipated encounter with a major allied formation. Ney expected to give battle on 21 April around Erfurt and disposed his two divisions of III Corps and one of VI Corps with that in mind.

The French knew little about Blücher's army. Eugène, fooled by the skirmish with Major Blücher's cavalry, announced that General Blücher had already passed the Saal. However, a subsequent reconnaissance towards Jena proved that to be false except for a few units of allied light cavalry. Two other reconnaissances advanced as far as Cölleda without encountering any enemy. A third reconnaissance towards Saalfeld encountered 120 hussars. All of these reconnaissances brought back reports from the local inhabitants of large concentrations of the allied forces in and around Leipzig.

Ney's concern relaxed and he dispatched agents to Leipzig, Altenburg and Dresden. He issued orders on the 20th to the III Corps to assemble at Erfurt and Weimar, the 39th Division was to move from Coburg to Ilmenau and allow liaison with the advanced guard of the IV Corps then moving towards Saalfeld.

The movement of the second line of troops, under Bessières, was uneventful. Ney's actions prevented the VI Corps from passing Gotha before the 26th, by which time the III Corps had completely cleared it and was deployed to the east of the village. The Guard continued to move from Hanau towards Eisenach with the exception of a detachment of 500 cavalry and six guns, under Lefebvre-Desnouëttes, which had been posted in Gotha since 18 April.

On the 19th, Marmont ordered Compans to advance along the Eisenach-Langensalza road the following day and to continue towards Leipzig. Ney directed Marmont and Bessières to move a division of the VI Corps to Cassel, and the two others to Langensalza and Mülhausen, if the enemy continued to move towards the west. This was not in conformance with the instructions received from Napoleon.

Eugène estimated that between 20 and 22 April, Wittgenstein had about 52,000 men and that his forces were immobile around Dessau and Cöthen. He was unaware of Wittgenstein's retreat that began on 20 April, other than noting the parties of allied light cavalry were no longer to be seen on the lower Saal. He knew of the attack on Wittenberg on 15 April, and that the citadel still held out against the allies.

On 22 April, the French corps reached the designated positions and it was necessary to send them orders to continue the movement. The Armée de l'Elbe moved on Halle and then on to

Mersburg, occupying both cities. Its force was positioned to march to the east of the Saal. Its right wing moved on Querfurt to facilitate Ney's communications with Naumburg.

Eugène held his army alert and ready to march offensively towards Jena and Naumburg. The bridge at Wettin had been destroyed and the presence of the II Corps on the lower Saal assured the left flank and rear of the Armée de l'Elbe. The III Corps was to occupy Naumburg and Jena. The VI Corps was provisionally to remain in the emplacements of 22 April, but the Guard continued on to Erfurt. The IV Corps moved to Saalfeld. Bertrand was ordered by Ney to move on Coburg by way of Ilmenau.

Eugène's orders of the 22nd, arrived on 25 April. Ney and Bertrand received theirs on 24 April. However, the two French armies were unable to execute these orders until the 25th and 26th. On 21 April, Eugène responded to a request from Ney, and pushed the XI Corps on Wipper and Lembach. This was done to facilitate communications between the two corps. Eugène's army remained in these positions until 26 April.

THE ALLIES

On the 22 April Wittgenstein conformed to his orders of 20 April. He remained in his positions, but sent out strong reconnaissance patrols that were pushed back from Cöhen and Alseleben towards Cönnern by the Armée de l'Elbe.

He decided to concentrate his forces and ordered Kleist and Berg to join Yorck. Bülow moved into Dessau as Kleist evacuated it. Voronzov was left alone on the right bank of the Elbe to observe Magdeburg. This allied redeployment began on 24 April and was complete the next day.

On 25 April, Bülow's corps was in Dessau and his advanced guards were in Cöhen and Aken. Yorck was in Zörbig, Berg was in Landsberg, and Kleist was in Halle, which he occupied with two battalions and Knorring's cavalry brigade. On the right bank of the Saal, the various cavalry vedettes observed the entire bank of the river from Wettin to the Saal's confluence with the Elbe. The cossack regiments remained on the left bank, to the north west of Wettin, where they watched the movements of the French V and XI Corps.[30]

Because of their cavalry superiority, the allies had complete knowledge of the movements of the Armée de l'Elbe and the III Corps. Gneisenau wrote Hardenberg on 25 April that the French had crossed the Saal.

EUGÈNE ACTS WITHOUT ORDERS

Unfortunately, Napoleon had continued to leave Eugène without specific orders. Eugène became more and more impatient to receive precise orders that would indicate what Napoleon expected of him. He wrote Napoleon, proposing a diversion by his army on Wittenberg and occupying Mersburg and Weissenfels.

Acting without orders but executing his desired action, Eugène detached Sébastiani with the II Cavalry Corps and Puthod's 17th Division, V Corps, into the region north of Brunswick. Eugène declared that this action was to cover Westphalia and Davout's organization of his divisions. On 25 April, Sébastiani was in Uelzen with 10,748 men, facing Dörnberg's and Czernichev's 4,450 cavalry. He was 150 kilometers from the Armée de l'Elbe, which put him too far away to participate in any actions south of Magdeburg.[31]

Later a report arrived from General Haxo, Governor of Magdeburg, which announced the passage of 10,000 allies over the Elbe at Sandau and Havelberg. Though Eugène judged this to be an exaggeration, he detached a force of 8 battalions and 80 cavalry to Stendal.

NEY'S NEW ORDERS

Ney received Napoleon's orders of the 22nd, on the evening of 24 April. He responded by directing the III Corps towards the Saal. On the 25th, Souham's 8th and Ricard's 11th Divisions were echeloned on the route to Erfurt and Naumburg. Kamburg was occupied by a detachment from Souham's 3rd Division. Brenier's 9th Division was in Jena and Dörnberg with the Girard's 10th Division and Marchand 39th Division behind him. The aggressive reconnaissance patrols that pushed towards Naumburg and Röda encountered only light allied cavalry patrols.

General Bertrand pushed an advanced guard past Coburg on 21 April, that consisted of two battalions of the 13th Line Regiment, one of the 8th Légère Regiment, twelve cavaliers, and a single gun under the command of Colonel Larcilly. Larcilly pushed his force into Saalfield, where he found no trace of the allies. He did, however, receive news of significant allied forces in Schleiz and Kahla. Ney passed this news to Napoleon. In response, Napoleon ordered the withdrawal of Larcilly's force and the advancing of Morand's 12th Division on the road between Coburg and Saalfeld to support the advanced guard. He felt that it was necessary to know exactly what enemy forces lay in Schleiz, Zwickau, and Plauen.

Napoleon's instructions advocated caution, which coupled with the lack of significant enemy forces on the right of the Saal, caused Bertrand to send Larcilly to Gräfenthal and Morand to Neustädt and Sonneberg. The fears raised in Bertrand by the orders of 21 April, were heightened by the orders of 24 April, which directed him to move to Saalfeld. He feared major enemy forces lay in the vicinity of Schleiz, Zwickau, and Plauen.

Bertrand chose to keep his advanced guard under Larcilly in Saalfield and refused to put his corps in motion on the pretext that it was possible that Ney might send him an order to move on Erfurt by Ilmenau. On 24 April, he received an order from Berthier and the IV Corps moved into Saalfeld and Peyri's 15th Division was moved to the west of Gräfenthal, into the mountains of Thuringia.

On the 25th Raglovich received directions from the King of Bavaria to conform to Napoleon's orders and commenced to concentrate his forces in Cronach and Lichtenfeld. The XII Corps, whose head was in Bamberg, continued on Coburg with Fresia's cavalry brigade in the lead. They arrived in Coburg on 27 April. The 38th (Württemberg) Division arrived in Hildburghausen on 26 April.

On 25 April Napoleon had at his disposal a numerically superior force poised and ready for a battle between the Elbe and the Saal. He had the II and XII Corps disposed defensively, but could draw into battle 150,000 men of the Armées de l'Elbe and du Mein. The allies forces had 102,180 men west of the Elbe. If Blücher were to remain stationary before Victor, they would have only 95,000 men.

THE ALLIED PLAN

As the Armée du Mein now stood on the Saal, the allies renounced their earlier plans to attack west of the Elbe. Their first operation was to concentrate their army east of the Saal, abandoning the advantages of the offensive to the French. Their freedom of action was further constrained by the bridges at their disposal over the Elbe. In case of a major defeat, they would only be able to move south to the line of Leipzig-Würzen, given that their center was not pierced. The French III Corps and the Armée de l'Elbe were only 60 and 70 kilometers respectively from Leipzig. The only saving grace was that if either of these formations crossed the Saal, their movement would be immediately reported by the numerous allied light forces disposed to watch the Saal.

Despite this, the danger to the allied army on the 25th was significant. This danger was further exacerbated by the problems of the allied staff. Wittgenstein had been made commander in chief on 25 April, but didn't receive notification of this until 27 April. As if the problems contained within his newly inherited staff weren't enough, his powers were limited by the presence of two sovereigns. The only blessing, which was also a curse, he accrued when he assumed command, was that his headquarters and that of the Czar were separated by a significant distance. This significantly delayed all consultations on strategy. It gave him tactical freedom, but tied his hands strategically.

On 23 April, Toll expressed the gravity of the developing situation to the Czar. Ney in Erfurt and Bertrand in Bamberg indicated to him, a pending general offensive by the French. It was urgent, he felt, that the allies decide if they intended to defend the right bank of the Elbe or if they wished to give battle on the left bank.[31]

Holding the line of the Elbe was impossible, as long as Napoleon held or denied them Wittenberg, Magdeburg, and Torgau. He was in the position to rapidly descend on the allied flank at a time and location of his choosing. Such a blow would oblige the allies to rapidly withdraw into Silesia or perhaps as far as Poland.

On the other hand, if the allies were to give battle, where was the best place to give a battle between the Mulde and the Saal. On this, Toll differed slightly from Scharnhorst. He felt that Napoleon would repeat his 1806 maneuver and slide along the frontier of Bohemia, along the flank of his "allies" the Austrians. Toll advocated advancing the allied right, to isolate the bulk of the French south of the line from Altenburg and Jena. If, to the contrary, the French moved from the Saal east in the direction of Naumburg and Leipzig, Toll proposed to attack their left flank. Either maneuver, he advocated, could be executed, if the army was united near Altenburg. These ideas were not new to the Czar, but the danger of the French advance did not strike him as sufficient to issue the orders. Toll was, however, sent to Wittgenstein's headquarters and later to Blücher's to acquaint them with the Czar's wishes.

While in the front lines, Toll's observations of the French maneuvers further convinced in him, that his proposed plans for the allies were correct. On 27 April, Toll was in Dresden and shortly thereafter he was in the Czar's headquarters. He found absolute calm. The King of Prussia was totally disinterested in the conduct of operations and the Czar had judged the situation quiet enough, to have gone to Toeplitz to take the waters with his sister, the Grand Duchess Catherine. Miloradovich's and Tormassov's corps had not been issued any orders.

In contrast, Wittgenstein's headquarters between 24 and 26 April, were in a near panic of activity. Still ignorant of his appointment as commander in chief, he did not know if he could give Blücher orders. He didn't know what if any support could be expected from Miloradovich and Tormassov. Being trapped by the French and his inability to control the other allied corps, he chose to withdraw towards the region of Leipzig and Würzen, where the troops were under his direct control. His movement began on 27 April. Yorck moved to Landsberg, Berg to Schkeuditz, Kleist remained in Halle, and Winzingerode moved to Naumberg as the advanced guard. Bülow was left on the lower Saal to watch Eugène's movements, the bridge at Rosslau, and pursue the siege of Wittenberg. He knew a battle was coming and if defeated he planned to withdraw into Prussia and defend Berlin.[33]

On 26 April, the Armée de l'Elbe began to move and Wittgenstein modified his first orders. He ordered a concentration towards Leipzig as quickly as possible. Yorck was sent to Schkeuditz. Kleist and Bülow were to send their cavalry over to the left bank of the Saal, to slow down Eugene. If Kleist was obliged to abandon Halle because of Eugène's movement, he was to move on Landsberg.

When the allied move began, Radianov moved his cossacks from the Saal to Halle, slowing the progress of the French V Corps. Winzingerode put Lanskoi's cavalry and a horse battery in Naumburg, to slow the French in that region. He quickly came into contact with Souham's division and later that day bivouacked near Plötha. The other allied forces remained immobile.

The peak of the allied command failure was reached, as Napoleon joined the Armée du Mein on 25 April in Erfurt. French spies gave Napoleon a complete perspective of Wittgenstein's forces and their movements. Knowledge of the allied forces near Leipzig were blurred by contradictory reports, but it was certain that Winzingerode was there. Napoleon became more and more assured that Blücher was in the vicinity of Altenburg with 25,000 men. Napoleon's knowledge of Tormassov and Miloradovich was very sketchy. He believed that Miloradovich was at Bautzen, 50 kilometers from Dresden with 20,000 men. Kutusov, he thought, was in

Lübben, 80 kilometers north east of Torgau. His sources also indicated that Barclay de Tolly was still at Thorn with 20,000 men. With this information in mind, Napoleon decided that the bulk of the enemy was south of the line from Leipzig to Torgau.

Napoleon's plans remained unchanged. He planed to march on Leipzig with his left in advance. He wished to draw the allies south towards Bayreuth. He saw that the advantages lay in crossing the Saal as quickly as possible. The concentration of his armies was to occur near Halle, Mersburg and Naumburg. The III, IV, and XII Corps would march down the valley, forming a refused left always at his disposal. He intended to perform the opposite of the 1806 Jena maneuver, reach Dresden behind the allies, and cut them off from Prussia.[34]

The III Corps concentrated around Auerstädt, Naumburg and Dörnburg. Marchand's 39th Division departed that region only when relieved by the IV Corps. Marmont detached Bonnet's 21st Division from the VI Corps and sent it between Erfurt and Weimar. Friederichs' 22nd Division was sent between Gotha and Erfurt. Compans (20th Division) moved his advanced guard into Kölleda, seeking contact with the Armée de l'Elbe.

The III Corps was supported by the Guard cavalry just east of Weimar. The Guard infantry passed through Weimar and would conform to the movements of Friederich's and Bonnet's divisions, moving on Jena or Naumburg if necessary.

On 26 April, the Armée de l'Elbe advanced only 12 to 15 kilometers. Two divisions of the V Corps were between Alseleben and Wettin. The Guard was behind their right wing, Latour-Maubourg's cavalry (less the lst Light Cavalry Division which was with the XI Corps and the 3rd Light Cavalry Division which was with the V Corps) was in Gerbstädt.

During its advance, the V Corps had encountered the 1,500 cossacks of Radianov, who promptly retreated to the south. After destroying all boats and other means of passage over the Elbe up to Alsleben, the V Corps arrived in Wettin. The bridge was intact, but protected by an earthwork on the far bank. Lauriston estimated that it was defended by 3,000 infantry, 1,300 cavalry and a force of artillery. In fact the garrison was 700 to 800 infantry, 4 guns and a few hundred cavalry, mostly cossacks. Lauriston sent a message to Eugéne asking if he should attack.

Ney conformed to Napoleon's orders and set the III Corps in motion. Souham's 8th Division quickly encountered the 400 cossacks and 200 Prussian hussars near Naumburg. This signaled that an allied cavalry brigade, Lanskoi's 1,200 men, was in the vicinity. Ney dispatched Ricard's 11th Division to Naumburg and Girard's division to Auerstädt. During the day Marchand's 39th Division had arrived in Weimar. The Guard had not moved on the 26th.

Marmont too followed Napoleon's directions. The IV Corps, under Bertrand, was in Rudolstädt and the rest of the corps was stretched back to Gräfenthal. The 38th Division (Württembergers) was still in Hildburghausen. The passage through the steep Thuringian mountains obliged the French to constantly double up their artillery teams and greatly slowed the advance.

On the 27th, Souham's 8th Division continued contact with Lanskoi's brigade. A few cannon shots were exchanged and Lanskoi withdrew into the night towards Plöha. One of Ney's staff officers estimated Lanskoi's force at 1,500 cavalry, two infantry battalions and three guns. There was no infantry, but assuming that there was, Ney felt obliged to move all his divisions to Naumburg as quickly as possible.[35]

Bertrand's travels were exhausting and he requested a day of repose, as soon as possible for his corps. The XII Corps was south of the Thuringian Forest, 60 kilometers behind the IV Corps. The 29th (Bavarian) Division, his advanced guard, was in Lichtenfeld, while Pacthod (13th Division) and Lorencz (14th Division) were in Bamberg.

Oudinot began his movement on the 28th, and anticipated arriving in Saalfeld on 1 May. His forces carried insufficient supplies, and the IV Corps had depleted the region along the road between Coburg and Saalfeld, making progress difficult.

During the evening of 27 April, an important decision was made by the chief of staff of the allied army. In Dresden, on the insistence of General Toll, Prince Volkonski, without consulting the Czar, ordered General Tormassov to depart Dresden and move so as to be in the vicinity of Frohburg and Kohren (30 kilometers east of Altenburg) on 30 April.

THE ALLIED PLANS

Wittgenstein issued a general order to govern the movements of the allied armies should the French cross over the Saal. These instructions directed that Kleist should defend Halle, but if attacked by superior forces, he should withdraw on Schkeuditz, where he could be supported by Yorck. If required, the two generals should retire as far as Leipzig. Yorck was to watch the defile at Mersburg. The surveillance of the most probably line of attack, Naumberg, was given to Berg and Winzingerode. Berg was posted west of Leipzig and Winzingerode was posted such that his advanced guard was in Weissenfels, his cavalry was in Lützen and his infantry was in Zwenkau.

Blücher was to watch the Saal, towards Jena, and concentrate his forces in Altenburg and Borna. His cavalry was to move to Gera. Miloradovich was to watch the allied left flank as far as Zwickau. Tormassov was to move on Rochlitz.

Wittgenstein believed that the French concentrations were aimed at a thrust towards Naumberg, with a movement along the axis towards Leipzig and Torgau, with the goal of turning the allied right wing. He envisioned a movement across the Saal, by Halle, moving on Altenburg, or by Gera or Plauen and moving on Zwickau.

If the attack came by Halle, Wittgenstein saw two French alternatives. If they came in mass, Wittgenstein planned to unify the allied armies between Leipzig and Wurzen, including Miloradovich and Tormassov, so as to be able to execute a general counterattack.[36]

If the French assault was weak, Blücher, Tormassov and Miloradovich were to content themselves with covering the west of the allied counter-attack to be executed towards Halle by the rest of the allied army. He also proposed the possibility of Kleist and Yorck slowing the French advance to allow an allied concentration west of Wurzen.

If the French were to pass through Mersburg and Naumburg, Wittgenstein directed that the allied armies should still concentrate between Leipzig and Wurzen. Winzingerode was to act as a rearguard, covering the allied retreat. Once concentrated the allies would pass over to the offensive led by Winzingerode and supported by Blücher coming from Pegau. Yorck, Berg, Tormassov, and Miloradovich were to watch for French attacks from the directions of Jena and Halle.

The plans based on the premises of a French attack south of the line from Jena to Altenburg, were quite simple. They envisioned Blücher, Tormassov, and Winzingerode concentrating behind the Mulde River, between Rochlitz and Colditz, while Yorck and Berg were to operate on the left flank and Miloradovich was to maneuver on their right flank.

If the French passed from Gera and Plauen towards Zwickau, they were to be stopped by Miloradovich, Tormassov, and Blücher, at Flötha, and struck in the flanks by the other corps that were to concentrate between Altenburg and Borna.

Bülow was charged with a separate mission from the rest of the army. He was to operate on the left and front of Eugène, while continuing to cover Magdeburg and Wittenberg. His line of communications was to run by Rosslau to Berlin and the lower Oder.

Scharnhorst severely criticized these orders. They left several things hanging. The execution of these measures at the critical moments were left up to the corps commanders. They were to determine if the attacking enemy forces were significant or insignificant. And, most importantly, they left the initiative to the French.

THE RUSSIANS BEGIN TO MOVE

The allied reconnaissances made on the morning of 28 April, indicated that the passages on the lower Saal were completely occupied. During the evening Bülow learned of the French attack on Halle. He concentrated his forces at Cöthen, in the hope of falling back on Kleist or escaping towards Berberg. North of Leipzig, Kleist's corps encountered Maison's 16th Division of the V Corps at Halle. Yorck remained in Skeuditz, with a detachment of two battalions, four guns, and 240 cavalry in Mersburg. Berg was still in his cantonments.[37]

In the center, Winzingerode concentrated his infantry around Rötha and Borna. He pushed Pantschoulidzev's cavalry brigade into Lützen and Lanskoi's towards Plötha. Knorring's brigade crossed to the right bank of the Saal and established itself east of Mersburg. Winzingerode had concentrated his 4,500 to 5,000 cavalry in a small area.[38]

Blücher, moved the Prussian Guard cavalry brigade (1,350 men and a horse battery) towards Naumburg and Miloradovich occupied Zwickau with Emmanuel's brigade (600 to 700 cavalry). Tormassov's corps arrived in Nössen.

THE FRENCH ADVANCE

Napoleon's knowledge of the allied positions and maneuvers were much as they had been before. He knew Wittgenstein's and Blücher's positions well. Winzingerode's movements were less clear, and the positions of Tormassov and Miloradovich were quite vague. Napoleon judged the situation quite favorable and expected to find only Wittgenstein and Blücher on the west bank of the Elbe.

He felt the allies had committed a serious fault, giving him the chance to concentrate his army and smash two allied corps. Leipzig remained the objective of both the Armée du Mein, which was to advance by Naumburg and Lützen, and the Armée de l'Elbe, which would advance by Halle and Mersburg. The orders were in place. The movements began on 28 April.

1   Bonaparte, Correspondance, #19714.

2   Fabry, Opérations des IIIe et Ve Corps pgs 105–107.

3   Charras, La Guerre de 1813, pg 493.

4   Boppe, Les Espagnols, pg 160.

5   Though nominally "French," these divisions were recruited in what is modern Italy and the soldiers were ethnic Italians.

6   These six battalions were as follows: 43rd Provisional Regiment—2/9th and 2/35th Line; 44th Provisional Regiment—2/59th and 2/106th Line; 45th Provisional Regiment—2/84th and 2/92nd Line.

7   Charras, La Guerre de 1813, pg 496.

8   Though this number seems large, it probably includes train, troops, and various engineering troops.

9   Spectateur Militaire #137

10 von Kaisenberg, König Jérôme, pg 261.

11 Charras, La Guerre de 1813, pg 504, & Holleben, Fruhjahrsfeldzuges 1813, pgs 181–182.

12 Holleben, Fruhjahrsfeldzuges 1813, pgs 182–183.

13 The 134th Regiment had formerly been the Garde de Paris, a police force, that was taken into the army and organized into an infantry regiment.

14 Bonaparte, Correspondance, #19824.

15 Charras, La Guerre de 1813, pg 512.

16 Tournes, Campagne de Printemps, pgs 141–142.

17 Schwertseger, Königlich Deutsch Legion, pgs 502–504.

18 Tournes, Campagne de Printemps, pg 149.

19 Tournes, Campagne de Printemps, pg 152.

20 Bonaparte, Correspondance, #19697.

21 Tournes, Campagne de Printemps, pgs 158–159.

22 Bonaparte, Correspondance, #19714.

23 The phrase comes from Voltaire's description of the execution of British Admiral Byng— "pour encourager les autres"—to encourage the others. In much the same draconian sense, Napoleon would have turned his own artillery on his own allies to enforce discipline in the ranks.

24 Bonaparte, Correspondance, #19839.

25 Tournes, Campagne de Printemps, pg 169.

26 Holleben, Fruhjahrsfeldzuges 1813, pgs 333–334.

27 Tournes, Campagne de Printemps, pg 172.

28 de Vaudoncourt, Prince Eugene, pgs 170–171.

29 Tournes, Campagne de Printemps, pg 177.

30 Plotho, Krieg in Deutschland, Vol I, pgs 86–87.

31 Tournes, Campagne de Printemps, pg 190.

32 Tournes, Campagne de Printemps, pg 198.

33 Plotho, Krieg in Deutschland, Vol I, pg 88.

34 Chandler, The Campaigns of Napoleon, pg 878.

35 Tournes, Campagne de Printemps, pg 212.

36 Tournes, Campagne de Printemps, pg 219.

37 Sporschil, Grosse Chronik, Vol I, pgs 115–116.

38 Tournes, Campagne de Printemps, pg 222.

COSSACKS FORAGING

Davout's Operations in the North

FRENCH ACTIONS IN THE 32ND MILITARY DIVISION

On 2 April, Davout organized what was to be known as the "Hamburg Division." It consisted of a single brigade with five battalions, which included 900 customs guards and gendarmes organized into two battalions.[1] By 15 April this force had been expanded to seven battalions and contained 3,961 men. This division was to form the principal garrison of the 32nd Military Division.[2]

Those arrangements being made, Davout began to act offensively against the insurgents. He directed Montbrun's advanced guard to Luckow. From there Montbrun was to move to the Elbe by Dannenburg, and up the river until he reached Lüneburg. Davout was seeking to confirm the Russians were withdrawing, as reported by the assistant prefect of Salzwedel.[3]

Vandamme found English men-of-war in the mouth of the Weser, obliging him to spread his forces along the coast in an effort to prevent any landings. Dufour's 5th Division was posted in Varel and Elsfleth on the left bank of the Weser and on the right bank of the Weser from Osterholz, Lehe, and to Dorum.[4]

On 6 April, the 2nd Cavalry Corps and Pacthod's 17th Division were posted around Lüneburg and along the Elbe. This force was spread from Dannenberg, and Uelzen to Göhrde and from there through Wustrow and Lüchow. On 8 April Davout wrote Vandamme, then in Lüchow, that Eugène had ordered Vandamme to move closer to Davout. Vandamme was to concentrate his forces near Salzwedel because of information that the allies had built a bridge at Dessau. Eugène intended to defend his positions foot by foot and, if seriously pressed, he planned to withdraw into Brunswick where he would concentrate his forces. Davout was to position himself on the Weser and establish a bridgehead.

Vandamme responded to this by writing that Bremen and Minden were secure and that all the bridges over the Weser were destroyed, as well as the bridge by Verden over the Aller River. The bridge at Nienburg was defended by fieldworks.

Davout departed Lüneburg on 9 April and moved to Brunswick. He had directed Sébastiani to move his forces to Salzwedel and Wustrow, with Puthod's forces. However, Sébastiani detached 500 horse to Montbrun's command.[5] On 10 April, three battalions of the 148th Regiment, detached from Puthod's 17th Division, were sent to Uelzen on the Celle and the rest of the 17th Division was posted in Salzwedel. General Montbrun's cavalry moved from Lüneburg to Salzwedel. The 148th occupied the Celle on 11 April, with a total of four battalions (2,000 men), 500 cavalry and four guns. The rest of the 17th Division departed on 12 April and moved to Brome between Salzwedel and Gishorn where it rejoined Davout's forces.[6]

As the French maneuvered to support Eugène, the pressure on the various streifkorps faded. When Davout ceased to be a threat to Dörnberg's forces, he recrossed the Elbe and occupied Lüneburg. On 11 April Dörnberg arrived in Uelzen, announcing that he was followed by a Swedish corps, though Davout felt this was purely bluff.[7] Benkendorf departed Hamburg with part of the Hanseatic Legion and moved to Ottersberg, just outside of Bremen. Scattered parties of cossacks spread across the countryside and occupied Verden, where, on 17 April, they skirmished with a French advanced post.

Davout found it necessary to return to Bremen. General Sébastiani was charged with covering the left wing of Eugène's forces, with his force of 1,500 cavalry and Lagrange's 18th Division.

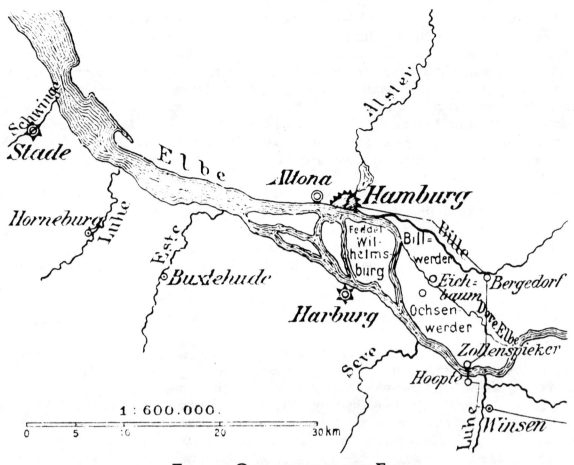

ZONE OF OPERATIONS ON THE ELBE

He positioned himself in Brunswick and detached a strong force, under General Maurin, to Celle.[8]

On 17 April General Maurin departed Celle, and Dörnberg hastily slipped 700 to 1,200 cossacks into the city. Maruin was returned to Celle by Sébastiani on 18 April, with four battalions, 300 cavalry, and some artillery. He drove the cossacks out of the city with some slight losses and recaptured it. At the same time Sébastiani, leading six battalions and the rest of his cavalry, moved from Brunswick on Uelzen by way of Gishorn. Before Gross-Oesingen, he encountered 600 cossacks, who withdrew into Sprakensehl, where they were joined by another 900 cavalry. General Sébastiani charged them with his light cavalry and drove them from the village. The French killed four cossacks, wounding another 50 and capturing two officers. These prisoners informed the French that only the forces of Czernichev, Tettenborn, and Dörnberg were on the left bank of the Elbe.[9]

Davout then ordered General Dumonceau to leave for Niemburg on 22 April, with five battalions and a battery of eight guns. Once there, he was to move directly on Bremen by the shortest route. The two battalions in Minden and another battery were also dispatched on the 22nd for Bremen.

Dufour and Carra St-Cyr's divisions were drawn together in Bremen and Dumonceau's division in Minden. On 22 April Davout began to move. Carra St-Cyr's division attacked the allies posted between Ottersberg and Rothemburg.[10] Vandamme's advanced guard encountered 1,500 allied cavalry, part of the Hanseatic legion, and three guns. The advanced guard, under the Prince von Reuss, attacked the allies posted before Rothemburg, which he defeated and

129

drove back to Harburg. The allied losses were estimated at 50 to 60, while the French lost two or three wounded.[11] At the same time Sébastiani occupied Lüneburg.

It was at this time that Davout learned from the Hamburg newspapers that Bernadotte had arrived in Stralsund and made a trip to Rostock to visit the Prince of Mecklenburg. Davout understood that there were both Swedish and English forces on the left bank, but this information was "vague" and he did not believe them. He also learned that the former Hanoverian minister Decker had arrived in Stade, from England. Here Decker had established a commission, that overthrew all vestiges of French authority in the area. Davout's response to this was to commit to Jérôme, that he would execute everyone who carried out the orders of this commission.[12]

On 27 April Vandamme's advanced guard arrived before Harburg. A company of voltigeurs from the 152nd Line Regiment stood before the fortress. A detachment, lead by sous-lieutenant Roulle, found an unguarded sally port and entered the city. They opened a gate to the French, who quickly pushed into the city, capturing it and a British 12 gun cutter. On the same day, other forces of Prince von Reuss captured a British brig in Zollenspicker.[13] The guns from the cutter in Harburg were used to arm the fortress at Harburg.

The British had, in April, begun to send a very steady stream of material into the Hamburg area to support the newly forming Hanoverian forces. This British cutter and brig were but part of supply line.[14]

Tettenborn responded to Vandamme's presence by sending a detachment under Benkendorf forward to observe Vandamme. This force consisted of most of the cossacks, the Isoum Hussars, most of the newly raised Hanoverian cavalry and two horse guns.[15]

On 30 April Davout arrived in Lüneburg. Sébastiani was already there with his forces. The allies had withdrawn their forces to Winsen. Davout ordered Dumonceau to move out at the break of dawn on Winsen, with 2 to 3 battalions and two guns, to chase the allies from Winsen and to force them to recross the Elbe. The rest of Dumonceau's 2nd Division was to move on Lüneburg and establish observation posts on the Elbe. Vandamme was concentrating his forces in Harburg.[16]

Carra St.-Cyr wrote Davout, announcing the pending arrival of the Danes. Four companies, each with 470 marines, were to arrive beginning on 5 May. Davout responded by directing that an officer be assigned to coordinate the Danish activities and to determine the status of the allied forces in Hamburg.

The Allies In Hamburg

In mid April General-Lieutenant Graf Wallmoden, a general in English and Russian service, arrived in Hamburg to assume command of the fledgling corps. By the end of the month he commanded a force consisting of Tettenborn's 1,500 cossacks and two guns, a newly raised Haneastic Legion consisting of three infantry battalions and eight squadrons totaling about 3,000 men, a battalion of Mecklenburg infantry totaling about 700 men, the three battalions of Lauenburg, Lüneburg, Bremen-Verden as well as the Feldjägerkrops of Hanoverian levies totaling about 1,600 men, and six battalions of Hamburg Bürgergarde or city guard.[17] On 23 April the Bürgergarde consisted of:

Jägercorps under Graf Kielmansegge	170 men
Lauenburg Legion under Major von Burger	888 men

Lüneburg Legion under Oberstleutnant	
von Estorff	
Cavalry/Hussars	388 men
Infantry	291 men
Bremen Legion under Major von der Busche	
Cavalry under Capitain von der Decken	324 men
Infantry under Capitain von Zesterfleth	519 men
Lauenburg Militia under Major Gragetopf	800 men
New Recruits	400 men
Total	3,780 men[18]

The city of Hamburg had heavy artillery defending its walls, but it lacked munitions and trained personnel.

On the western point of Wilhelmsburg and by Zollenspicker there were two heavy batteries, each armed with four guns. The city walls were repaired and the moat flooded in anticipation of an eventual French assault. Wallmoden posted Czernichev and Dörnberg between Boitzenburg and Dömitz to deny the French easy passage over the Elbe.

DAVOUT'S OPERATIONS AGAINST HAMBURG

Davout began an aggressive campaign against the rebellious German cities. His goal was to crush German nationalism back into meek subservience to the French will. In the beginning of May, Davout moved his forces north, occupying Uelzen, Bremen, Rothemburg, and Lüneburg. Davout continued to act aggressively to put down all signs of the rebellion. All rebels were to be executed and the first village to sound the alarm, was to be decimated by the French.

By early May, Tettenborn could muster a force that consisted of about 1,500 cossacks and Russian cavalry, with two guns, the newly raised Hanseatic Legion with three infantry battalions and eight squadrons, totaling about 3,000 men, the Mecklenburg Garde-Bataillon of 700 men, about 1,600 Hanoverian militia levies. The six battalions of Hamburg Bürgerwacht were not capable of taking to the field. His total force came to about 5,000 to 6,000 men, but he had only about 3,000 muskets with which to arm the newly raised German forces.[19] Tettenborn had a force of heavy artillery in the city that consisted of two batteries of 24pdrs and three smaller batteries.

Tettenborn organized his forces and prepared his defense of Hamburg. He placed the Kielmansegge Jägers under Oberstleutnant von Beaulieu, the 1st Hanseatic Battalion under Major von Stelling, two companies of the Mecklenburg Garde-Bataillon, two Russian guns, and 50 cossacks on the Wilhelmsburg Island. On 5 May the Bremen and Verden Battalion, 136 men under Capitain von Zesterfleth, were sent to reinforce Keilsmansegge, who commanded all the forces on Wilhelmsburg.

On Oschsenwerde stood the 2nd Hanseatic Legion Battalion and by Zollenspiecker stood the 3rd or Lübeck Battalion under Capitain von Lucadou. To support these troops Major von Berger's battalion stood in Bergedorf, 300 cossacks, a weak squadron of Hanseatic cavalry, and the militia stood on the left wing.

In Hamburg proper, there remained only two companies of the Mecklenburg Garde-Bataillon, the remainder of the Bremen-Verden Battalion, and the Bürgerwacht.[20]

Davout then began preparing for his operations against Hamburg proper. However, in order to take the city, it was necessary for him to occupy a number of islands in the river, as well as control traffic on the river. His first step was the establishment of a number of batteries that commanded the critical stretch of river. Then came the preparations for assaulting the islands.

During the night of 8/9 May, Vandamme seized several small islands near Harburg and pushed a reconnaissance force onto the Island of Wilhelmsburg. In the dark, a sharp bayonet attack by the French drove towards the allied lines. The garrison of Wilhelmsburg, the

Kielsmansegge Jägers and 136 men of the Bremen-Verden Infantry Battalion,[21] could not repulse the French assaults and had to withdraw. Tettenborn withdrew his forces from the islands and posted them in Feddel.[22] The allies lost 200 to 300 killed and wounded, 150 prisoners, and eight guns. The French lost about 60 dead and wounded. That same night the Lauenburg Battalion under Major von Berger, which occupied Ochsenwerder, repulsed the French attack on that island as well.

At 9:00 A.M., Kielsmansegge sent the Hanseatic Battalion, the Bremen-Verden Battalion and the two companies of the Mecklenburg Garde-Battalion forward in a counter attack. The initial attack by the Hanseatic Battalion and the Bremen-Verden Battalion stalled as the French counter-attacked. The Mecklenburgers gallantly made a bayonet attack against a large French column to cover the withdrawal of the Hanseatic Battalion and the Bremen-Verden Battalion. The Kielsmannsegge Jägers took the column in the flank with their skirmishing fire and the combined efforts of both units brought the assault to a halt.[23]

Vandamme withdrew losing, according to allied accounts, 300 men, spiking the captured guns. The counter attack cost the allies about 163 officers and men dead, wounded, and captured.[24] It is worth noting that amongst the prisoners taken by the French, many were found to have been part of the King's German Legion. They reported that there were only 450 of them, but that they had the equipment to outfit 18,000 men with them.[25]

The French attack on Oschenwerder consisted of about 1,500 men who struck the 2nd Hanseatic Battalion and drove it back to Fünfhäuser after a two hour fight. Major von Berger with the Lauenburg Battalion (about 800 men strong) stood in Bergedorf as a reserve. He led his battalion against the French in Fünfhäuser and drove them back losing 13 dead and 32 wounded.[26]

On 11 May Vandamme made a renewed attack against Wilhelmsburg, and the brigade of General Gengoult (Dufour's 5th Division) occupied the island. The following day the allies landed 1,200 to 1,500 men on the island, directly across the river from Hamburg. This force consisted of two companies of Mecklenburger Guard, two companies of the Danish Schleswig-Holstein jägers,[27] a Hanseatic infantry battalion, 150 men from the Hamburg Bürgergarde, the Kielsmansegge Jäger, and a detachment from the Bremen-Verden Battalion.[28]

The allied advance drove back the light forces of Gengoult's brigade. Vandamme responded by calling forward forces from Dufour's division. The French counter attack was met with cannon fire from the fortress of Hamburg, but the French repulsed the attack.

In light of the potential for repeated landings, Vandamme posted Reuss's brigade on the island. The second landing occurred and the two brigades of Reuss and Gengoult counterattacked, driving the allies off the island and capturing 6 guns and 800 prisoners. Davout was very pleased with the actions of the young and inexperienced troops involved.

On 14 May, in the course of preparing the forts at Kuxhaven against a coup de main, an English merchant ship was seized. The ship's estimated 2 million francs of cargo was treated as contraband and sent to Bremen, while the papers were examined to determine who had negotiated for the merchandise. Appropriate action was to be taken against those who violated the terms of the Continental System.

On 13 May Tettenborn advanced from Ochensenwerder. He attacked the brigade of the Prince de Reuss, at Zollenspeiler, with the Lauenburg Battalion under Major von Berger, two companies of the King's German Legion (KGL), and a Hanseatic battalion. Two 24pdr howitzers, served by the KGL and Hanseatic artillerists supported the attack. A parallel allied attack landed from Wilhelmsburg, but both were repulsed.[29] Davout now began his operations to oblige Hamburg to surrender. On 17 May, he was authorized, if necessary, to fire heated shot and howitzers into Hamburg in an effort to bring the city to submission. On 19 May Vandamme occupied the remaining islands in the Elbe and began to bombard Hamburg.

At the same time, the forces of Dörnberg and Czernichev, with about 4,000 cavalry, 3,000 infantry, and 12 guns, recrossed the Elbe at Domitz, evacuating the western bank of the Elbe.[30]

By 20 May Davout was making serious preparations for the assault on Hamburg. He had 32 siege guns due to arrive in Bremen shortly. He directed Vandamme to fire a few howitzer shells and 24pdr balls into Hamburg periodically, so as to acclimate the garrison of Hamburg to the sound of French fire. This was an effort to cause the garrison to be less alert when the actual assault did begin.

However, the plans for the assault were delayed because of the uncertainty of Danish actions and the pending negotiations. When the interim treaty with the Danes was signed some days later, the preparations went on. Davout wrote Vandamme on 25 May to announce that the King of Denmark had ordered his troops, 8,000 to 10,000 men, then posted in Holstein, to cooperate with the French.[31] The command of General Schulemburg was at the disposition of Davout and sealed the fate of the Hamburg revolt.

The allied forces maneuvered in an attempt to dissuade Davout from his purpose and a column of 400 to 500 cavalry, 3,000 to 4,000 infantry, and twelve guns were maneuvering near Dahlemburg. Davout dispatched Dumonceau's 2nd Division to push them back. Dumonceau was then directed to place seven guns and a battalion of the 152nd Line Regiment in Haarburg.

On 23 May Davout reported to Berthier, that there were Swedish troops in the Hamburg garrison and that further Swedish forces were pushing to reach the beleaguered city. All indications were that Tettenborn had every intention of defending the city as long as possible.[32] By 26 May Davout had heard that the Swedes had seven or nine battalions actually in Hamburg. By 28 May he understood that Dörnberg had moved his forces back into Hamburg.

Colonel von Haffner, the Danish liaison officer, advised Davout that General Wallmoden's corps consisted of the forces of Czernichev, Dörnberg and Tettenborn, as well as a corps commanded by Voronzov. Haffner reported that the entire force was commanded by Bernadotte, King of Sweden, and that it contained 60,000 men. However, Davout, knowing the tendency of people to exaggerate, discounted the figure and evaluated the allied force at about 20,000 Swedes and 8,000 to 9,000 under Dörnberg, not including the Hamburg "sugar merchants." He had no idea what Voronzov commanded. He also received reports that the Swedish had 20,000 to 25,000 men in Stralsund and the British had 40 transports in Heligoland with 4,000 to 6,000 men of the King's German Legion.[33]

On 29 May Vandamme once again attacked the island of Ochsenwerder. The Lauenberg Battalion was posted on Ochsenwerder. It had two companies as advanced posts in Elbdeiche and Wilhelmsburg. In addition, 130 men of the King's German Legion, under Lieutenant Dehnel, stood by the Ochsenwerder Church as a supporting reinforcement. At 4:00 A.M. the night exploded with the sounds of French cannon and the assault began. The Lauenberg Battalion advanced posts were struck and the battalion was joined by the KGL detachment in resisting the French. An assault force of 180 to 200 French came across the water and appeared out of the fog to strike the allies. The French landed and a fire fight began. An allied advanced guard, 40 skirmishers under Fähnrich Schulz, was sent forward. It was reinforced by men drawn from the KGL detachment, but the inadequacy of artillery support on the allied side began to tell. Despite at least one allied counter attack, the French attack was completely successful. The island, 200 prisoners, and a cannon were captured. Vandamme was now a half mile from Bergedorf.

The Danish corps was united in Altona and Vandsbeck. The Danes were ready for action against Hamburg. On 30 May they dispatched some of their cavalry to Billwerder to provide for communications with the French. In addition, several French positions were taken over by the Danes. Five of General Dumonceau's battalions were transported to Haarburg in Danish vessels after they were relieved.[34]

COSSACKS ON WATCH

HAMBURG FALLS

During the night of 30/31 May Tettenborn evacuate Hamburg and took with him 3,000 men of the Hanseatic Legion, 1,000 Prussians, 1,200 Mecklenburgers and his Russian corps. It was the arrival of the Danish corps, which made Tettenborn's position in Hamburg untenable. He moved to Boitzenburg. On 31 May the Danes entered Hamburg from the east, while the French entered from the west.[35]

Once the allies had departed and established themselves at Boitzenburg, General Dumonceau moved three battalions to the left bank of the Elbe, where he could observe Boitzenburg and Lauenburg. He sent three other battalions and his artillery to Zollenspicker, while four other battalions moved into Hamburg and one remained in Haarburg.

Once Hamburg was occupied, the war material there was inventoried. Over 150 guns, the smallest of which were 6pdrs, were captured. A total of 800,000 infantry cartridges, of which 600,000 were English, were found in the city's magazines. It was estimated that 10,000 English muskets had been distributed to the Hamburg Civil Guard. Davout wasted no time in disarming this militia. Those individuals who had taken part in the Hanseatic Legion, had departed with the Russians or had dispersed in the countryside. Some even fled to Denmark. All of the officers of the Hanseatic Legion captured by the French were found to be foreigners, mostly Prussians.

Once Hamburg was taken Davout's problems continued. On 1 June, General Dumonceau occupied Bardowick and arrested the five principal inhabitants of the city. They were imprisoned at Fort Hope pending the outcome of the investigation of the assassination of a French sentinel.

If the inhabitants of the city did not turn over the assassins in three days, Davout ordered that the five prisoners should be shot.

Davout settled in for the long occupation of the city and 32nd Military Division. He deployed his troops around Hamburg so as to protect it from a renewed allied assault. All of the enemy works were occupied by the French. He continued a mopping up operation in the province, and on 2 June he moved a Danish division to Lübeck to occupy the city.

THE COSSACKS' IMPACT ANALYZED

Principally, the impact of the cossack raids on the west has two major and some minor aspects. The most significant impact was the dispatching of Napoleon's most capable general, Maréchal Davout, away from the main battle to the far north. This was done because Napoleon felt that the 32nd Military Division was extremely important to his overall goals. It was an industrial and commercial center, so its loss would be felt by his military machine. However, it had been incorporated into metropolitan France since 1810 and its loss, the loss of French national territory, would be a moral blow that he did not want to suffer.

The second major impact was the dispatching of 61 French battalions to the 32nd Military Division to enforce French rule. This force totaled 16,174 men, including some sorely needed cavalry. The 37th (Westphalian) Division, eight battalions, eight squadrons, and 16 cannon, and the Westphalian guard and Kassel garrison (2,200 infantry, 1,100 cavalry and 1,200 artillerists) were held in Westphalia to keep it under control. The 27th (Polish) Division, with 3,024 men, was also held in Westphalia. In addition, on 17 April the allies had 30,710 cavalry in the main theater of operations, while the French had only 8,540 very mediocre cavalry.[36] The detachment of 4,493 French cavalry to the 32nd Military Division or held in Westphalia because of the cossack threat constituted 35% of the total French cavalry Force.

The total forces held out of the French army during the 1813 Spring campaign were as follows:

Strength of French Forces Committed to the 32nd Military Division[37]

	Infantry	Cavalry	Engineers, Artillery & Train	Guns
2nd Division	8,680		113	8
5th Division	5,959		120	8
Hamburg Division	3,397	367	?	8
II Cavalry Corps		1,852	125	6
17th Division	7,142		?	8
18th Division	6,931		480	16
27th Division	3,024	?	?	?
37th Division	3,209	1,174	156	16
Westphalian Guard	2,200	1,100	1,200	?
Total	40,542	4,493	2,194	70

Total Allied Forces Committed

Tettenborn	1,400
Dörnberg	894
Benkendorf	1,700
Czernichev	1,800
Total	5,794

As can be seen, for the investment of approximately 6,000 men, about 3,000 Cossacks, some line cavalry, three infantry battalions, and a horse battery, the Russian raids drew at least 30,000 French, Westphalian, and Polish soldiers out of the main theater of the Spring campaign.

One can only speculate what the impact would have been if Napoleon had had this force with him at Lützen and Bautzen. It is not beyond the realm of possibilities that this force, under the command of the able Maréchal Davout, could have converted Napoleon's tactical victories at Lützen and Bautzen into strategic victories and forced a termination of hostilities. That would have resulted in a major change to the course of history.

On a less significant side, J. Morand's 2,500 to 3,000 men were lost to the French. Included in that number was the first major defection in the 1813 campaign, the Saxons who became the 6th Battalion of the Russo-German Legion. Another such impact on the relative strengths of the two belligerent camps was the addition of the Hanseatic Legion and the Mecklenburg forces to the allied armies. This force, though not huge, would contain about 10,000 men in July 1813. Between the loss of Morand's force and these allied reinforcements, Napoleon suffered a shift of 12,500 men to the allied cause. This force was the size of a normal division.

One can then legitimately argue that the 6,000 partisans under the four cossack leaders used in these operations had the effect of shifting the effective manpower resources available in the main theater away from the French and to the allied cause by a total of 53,042 men.[38]

The total loss to the Cossacks, their supporting infantry and artillery was only a few hundred casualties. The exchange was one that any commander would find most gratifying.

As a result of this, the Cossack raids in the west can be counted as a highly successful operation that contributed significantly to the eventual Allied victory in the 1813 campaign.

THE FRENCH CONSCRIPTS GO INTO ACTION

1   The other units present were the 3/3rd, 3/29th and 3/l05th Line Regiments.

2   Holleben, Fruhjahrsfeldzuges, pgs 184–185.

3   de Mazade, Correspondance du Davout, #1254.

4   Holleben, Fruhjahrsfeldzuges, pgs 305–306.

5   de Mazade, Correspondance du Davout, #1265.

6   Holleben, Fruhjahrsfeldzuges, pg 306, & de Mazade, Correspondance du Davout, #1266.

7   de Mazade, Correspondance du Davout, #1267.

8   Viger, Davout, Marechal d'Empire, pg 119.

9   de Mazade, Correspondance du Davout, #1274.

10 Viger, Davout, Marechal d'Empire, pg 119.

11 de Mazade, Correspondance du Davout, #1278.

12 de Mazade, Correspondance du Davout, #1281.

13 de Vaudoncourt, Prince Eugene, pgs 172–173.

14 Shipments for April were as follows:

Material	Sailed on	Destination
Arms, accoutrements, and munitions for 10,000.	10 April	Cuxhafen
Ditto for 5,000.	16 April	Cuxhafen
Arms & munitions	27 April	Cuxhafen
5,000 stands of arms, accoutrements, munition & 1,045 barrels of powder.	27 April	Cuxhafen
Arms, accoutrements, & munitions for 15,000 infantry & 8,000 light cavalry, 65 cannon & 1,955 barrels of powder.	Ready & under orders to sail	Cuxhafen

15 Jacobi, Hannover's Theilnahme, pg 73.

16 de Mazade, Correspondance du Davout, #1284.

17 von Sichart, Hannoverschen Armee, pg 107.

18 Jacobi, Hannover's Theilnahme, pg 99.

19 Jacobi, Hannover's Theilnahme, pg 114.

20 Jacobi, Hannover's Theilnahme, pgs 116—7.

21 von Sichart, Hannoverschen Armee, pg 108.

22 Schwertseger, Königlich Deutsch Legion, pg 506.

23 Jacobi, Hannover's Theilnahme, pg 121.

24 von Sichart, Hannoverschen Armee, pg 108.

25 de Mazade, Correspondance du Davout, #1310.

26 von Sichart, Hannoverschen Armee, pg 108.

27 During this period the diplomatic situation of the Danes was nost unsettled. During a very short period the Danes actively fought on both sides. However, the diplomatic intrigues of Bernadotte finally were to push them into the French camp.

28 von Sichart, Hannoverschen Armee, pg 109, & Jacobi, Hannover's Theilnahme, pg 125.

29 Viger, Davout, Marechal d'Empire, pg 122, & von Sichart, Hannoverschen Armee, pg 109.

30 de Mazade, Correspondance du Davout, #1324.

31 de Mazade, Correspondance du Davout, #1337 & #1342.

32 de Mazade, Correspondance du Davout, #1334.

33 de Mazade, Correspondance du Davout, #1342.

34 de Mazade, Correspondance du Davout, #1345.

35 Viger, Davout, Marechal d'Empire, pg 122.

36 Tournes, Campagne de Printemps, pgs 141–142.

37 Tournes, Campagne de Printemps, pgs 141–142, & French Army Archives, Carton C2 541 and C2 706.

38 This figure is developed from the 30,000 men under Davout, the 2,500 Morand lost at Lüneburg and the 10,000 men raised by the allies in the form of the Hanseatic Legion and the defecting Mecklenburg forces.

IX
Prelude to a Battle

KLEIST HOLDS HALLE

The city of Halle is situated on the right bank of the Saal and was surrounded by a stout wall. A single bridge gave access to the left bank. Since 26 April, Kleist had occupied the city with 1/, 2/2nd East Prussian Infantry Regiment, a squadron of hussars, Horse Battery #3, the Russian 23rd and 24th Jager Regiments, Antropov's Russian 12pdr battery, and a cossack regiment (7,200 men, 600 cossacks, and 22 cannon).[1] Kleist had built several earth works, which dominated the passages over the Saal. The 23rd and 24th Russian Jager Regiments were detached to the south, to defend the ford at Wörmlitz. To the north, a few weak detachments of infantry watched Gibichenstein and Trotha, where the Saal was very fordable.[2]

Kleist's job was to prevent the French from crossing at Halle, but he judged his mission almost pointless. He estimated that the French would ignore Halle and pass across the Saal, either above or below the city. He anticipated having to withdraw on Leipzig, shortly after the French appeared.

Eugène was well informed of the Halle garrison and knew that they were fortified. He also knew that it was necessary to seize the passage quickly, but the orders he issued only resulted in the V Corps engaging in a fruitless battle. He ordered Maison's 16th Division to attack the bridge at Halle, and if stubbornly defended, he was to renew the attack supported by Lagrange's 18th Division.

Maison's strict interpretation of his orders led him to execute a simple reconnaissance, not a general attack on Halle. His division departed for Niedleben at 2:00 pm. The 151st Infantry Regiment advanced with six guns under the command of General Avril. The 153rd advanced with six guns under the command of General Penne.[3] Maison contented himself with advancing four companies detached from two battalions of 151st and 153rd Regiments supported by a screen of cavalry in skirmish order. The infantry deployed as skirmishers and closed on the bridge over the Saal at Halle. Once at the bridge, they engaged in a lively fusillade with the Prussian infantry.

Twelve guns supported the French advance. The 3rd Light Cavalry Division moved in support, as the 1st Brigade moved to attack the left of Nidleberg and the second moved to flank the right of the village. The 2nd Brigade covered the road to Mersburg. The 134th Line Regiment moved to a position, where it could observe the Saal and the Prussian movements.

A total of twenty-four guns supported the French, while twenty-one supported the Prussians.[4] The Prussians began to fire their artillery on the French left wing—the 151st Line Regiment.

Maison detached a battalion of the 153rd to the Giermeritz farm, on an island formed by two branches of the Saal. The battalion's voltigeurs took up a position, where their fire began picking off the gunners serving the Prussian batteries in the earthworks on the far side of the river. The two 6pdr cannon and howitzer posted in the earthwork, were soon withdrawn because of the intensity of the fire.

The French right column threw a company of voltigeurs up to the bridge. It advanced under the arches of the bridge, where it was subjected to heavy cannister fire by the Prussians on the far bank. The skirmishers dispersed and took up positions where they could shower musket fire on the Prussian batteries.[5]

KLEIST

When by 5:00 P.M., the French had shown no intention of seizing Halle, Kleist decided to hold the city. His casualties were serious, having lost 200 to 300 men killed and wounded as well as 5 guns dismounted. The French losses were reportedly quite light, 8 killed and 58 wounded.

Lauriston witnessed the engagement and evaluated Kleist's forces at 6,000 infantry supported by 21 guns. When Napoleon learned of the Prussian resistance in Halle, he recommended that Morand move to Mersburg and force the Prussians to evacuate their positions in Halle.

NEY'S MOVEMENTS

Ney arrived in Naumburg during the evening of 28 April. He had no idea of Eugène's position, and as the enemy cavalry continued to be visible along the left of the Saal north of Freiburg and towards Nebra, Ney estimated that the Armée de l'Elbe was most certainly not in Mersburg. Ney judged it prudent to modify the orders of the Emperor to account for this and directed the III Corps to occupy Weissenfels. Souham's 8th Division remained to the east of Naumburg and moved Larboissière's cavalry brigade, supported by a few battalions, towards Weissenfels.

Labroissière encountered and drove back a large party of Prussian cavalry. The Prussians fell back on Zeitz. On the left of the Saal, Ricard's 11th Division was in Freiburg, Girard's 10th Division moved to Kösen, Brenier's 9th Division sent a brigade to Kamburg and a second brigade to Eckartsberga. Both Brenier's and Girard's divisions were posted to where they could move to support Souham.

Behind the III Corps, the Imperial Guard moved towards Eckartsberga. The VI Corps was deployed such that Bonnet's 21st Division was east of Weimar, Friederichs' 22nd Division was east of Erfurt and Compans' 20th Division was near Kölleda. The IV Corps was spread over a distance of 34 to 35 kilometers. Morand's 12th Division was between Jena and Kahla. Peyri's 15th Division was between Uhlstädt and Saalfeld. The Württemberg 38th Division was in Königsee where it was receiving an indispensable rest from its marches.

The XII Corps was posted such that the 29th (Bavarian) Division was between Neustädt and Kronach. Pacthod's 13th Division was in Coburg and Lorencz's 14th Division was in Lichtenfeld. The various elements of Hammerstein's 32nd (Westphalian) division were not expected to be unified in Sonderhausen before 30 April.

ALLIED FUMBLING CONTINUES

During the day of 29 April Wittgenstein studied the effects of his orders of 27 April. He also learned that day that his plans had been overturned by a communication from the Czar, who had by now adopted Toll's plans. The allied armies would concentrate near Altenburg.

On 29 April Toll returned the allied headquarters from his trip to Altenburg. Once there, he was surprised to read Wittgenstein's instructions of the 27th. No one in the general headquarters understood why Wittgenstein had modified the dispositions previously ordered by the Czar.

Toll wrote to d'Auvray, Wittgenstein's chief of staff, advising him that the French offensive was coming towards Leipzig and Altenburg, putting the left of allied armies in grave danger. He reiterated that the concentration at Altenburg would permit the allies to strike the French head on.[6]

During the evening, the allies learned of the engagement near Weissenfels. Toll told Volkonski, chief of staff to the Czar, this indicated that the French line of advance was from Mersburg and Naumburg on Leipzig. The allied reconnaissances indicated that the area of Hof was free of French troops. With this idea, Toll continued to press for the allied armies to move on Altenburg.

When the Czar learned of Wittgenstein's orders of the 27th, he persisted in advocating Toll's plans. During the evening of the 29th this was communicated to Wittgenstein. Volkonski and Wittgenstein then decided to unite the allied armies between Leipzig and Borna, with the goal of attacking the flank of the French moving from Naumburg on Leipzig.

KLEIST WITHDRAWS

Kleist still held Halle on 29 April, when he learned of the French capture of Mersburg. He feared being cut off from Schkeuditz and prepared to move. At the same time Wittgenstein, in the center, dispatched a large reconnaissance force north, towards the French in Naumburg in an effort to determine the strength of the French moving, on Leipzig. This force was commanded by Winzingerode.

At the head of all of his cavalry, Winzingerode moved from Rötha towards Lützen. When he arrived there, the French had already struck Weissenfels and had thrown Lanskoi's brigade across the Rippach ravine. Winzingerode's 6,700 cavalry remained inactive that evening, bivouacked near Starsiedel. His infantry was in Zwenkau and Meyhen.

FRENCH INTENTIONS

If the allied intelligence was bad, the French intelligence at this point was very good. Napoleon learned that Yorck was in Schkeuditz and Wittgenstein was in Leipzig. He knew that there was a combined force of 6,000 Russians and Prussians in Halle and that Wittgenstein's main army was probably posted between Halle and Leipzig. Blücher's position was verified and reverified to still be Altenburg. However, vague reports of a Prussian force moving on Gera were received, with indications that Blücher's forces were to move in that direction in an effort to join Wittgenstein.

Napoleon learned of Tormassov's and Miloradovich's forces being west of the Elbe, from an ambassadorial secretary detached to Prague. The Saxon General Gersdorf advised the French that on 22 April, Miloradovich was between Dresden and Zwickau with 18,000 men and that the head of Kutusov's corps had arrived in Dresden, the same day. With this intelligence, Napoleon found himself in possession of a relatively exact description of the allied positions.

Under these conditions, Napoleon deemed a general offensive of the Armées de l'Elbe and Mein in the direction of Leipzig to be the most fruitful. Napoleon planned to move with his combined forces east of the Saal on 30 April. The Armée de l'Elbe was directed to move as much of its force as possible on Leipzig, parallel to the Armée du Mein, which was also to advance on Leipzig. This two-pronged thrust contained about 200,000 men.

MERSBURG IS SEIZED

Mersburg, situated on the left bank of the Saal, was surrounded by a wall averaging slightly under ten feet in height, and in a few places, by an earthen parapet. Only one bridge permitted access to the city from the Neumark suburb on the right bank.

Since 28 April, the city had been occupied by a Prussian detachment from Blücher's corps, commanded by Major Löbenthal. Löbenthal's force consisted of two battalions, a detachment of freiwilliger jägers, a half squadron (100 men) of regular cavalry, and about 200 cossacks. This force of 300 cavalry and 1,300 infantry was supported by four guns.[7]

Löbenthal placed his men around Mersburg, holding the 100 line cavalry and two guns on the right bank in the Neumark suburb. About noon, Bruyère's cavalry division, I Cavalry Corps, chased back the few cossack patrols and reached the edge of Mersburg. Maréchal Macdonald directed the Gérard's 35th Division to seize the village.

Under the protection of three batteries, the 35th Division deployed a strong line of skirmishers, indicating an attack on the wall from the north, west and south. The attack began quickly; the doors were broken in and the walls scaled. The French quickly arrived at the unbroken bridge and prepared to pursue Löbenthal's beaten detachment to the far bank. However, Macdonald stopped the French advance and contented himself with occupying the city.

At the same time Eugène, in reaction to Kleist's positions, definitively renounced his efforts to force a passage over the Saal in that region. At 2:00 P.M., he set the V Corps in motion towards Mersburg, leaving only Chastel's 3rd Light Cavalry Division and Maison's 16th Infantry Division before Halle to watch Kleist.

When Eugène learned of the passage available at Mersburg, he wrote Napoleon announcing the movement of the Armée de l'Elbe through Mersburg towards Leipzig would begin on 30 April. Maison and Chastel were to be left at Halle.

GERARD'S INFANTRY TAKE THE BRIDGE AT MERSBURG
KNÖTEL

General Souham's 8th Division formed the advanced guard for the III Corps. His lead elements were commanded by General Laboissière and consisted of Kellerman's cavalry brigade (10th Hussars and the Baden Light Dragoons), two battalions of the 6th Provisional Légère Infantry Regiment, and four horse guns. On 30 April, about 2:00 A.M., the advanced guard passed through Weissenfels without incident and continued to move on Lützen. The III Corps' column was formed such that Souham's 8th Division led, followed by the divisions of Girard (10th), Brenier (9th), Ricard (11th), and Marchand (39th). Each brigade was allocated a 200 meter interval and marched in columns by division, at a full interval.[8] This would allow them to quickly form square if attacked by cavalry. Each division was preceded by its artillery and followed by its baggage.[9]

Tarayre's brigade, of Ricard's 11th Division, had attempted to establish a bridgehead towards Kirchdorf, but failed and rejoined the division as it passed through Weissenfels. Napoleon had directed them to advance with their left on the Saal. The cavalry of the advanced guard was ordered to cover the right. This force was supported by 3,245 Imperial Guard cavalry, advancing in echelon to the right rear of the corps.

The advance went well and the allied cavalry encountered west of Poserna quickly fell back. The French lead elements suddenly encountered Lanskoi's Russian cavalry division (two cavalry regiments, 3 to 4 cossack regiments—1,200 to 1,500 men), supported by a jager battalion, deployed in skirmish formation, and a horse battery of twelve guns.[10] Lanskoi was defending the defile across the Rippach stream, near Gross-Göhrey.

A heavy exchange was in progress and Souham was making slow progress across the ravine. At 12:45 P.M., Napoleon ordered Bessières to cross the ravine and push back Lanskoi's cavalry. Bessières moved forward attended by his orderly, Sergeant Jordan of the Polish Lancers. His orderly was struck by a cannon shot that blew off his head.

As he stood inspecting the situation, another Russian artillery round struck Maréchal Bessières, throwing his mutilated body beneath his horse's hooves.[11] He fell 50 feet in front of the Baden Dragoon Regiment.

Larboissière soon found himself attacked by so much enemy cavalry that he decided to stop his forward movement until the rest Souham's 8th Division could move up in support. Maréchal Ney arrived with this division and pushed Chemineau's brigade forward rapidly to support Larboissière. Girard's 10th Division obliqued to the east towards Starsiedel, while Ricard's, Marchand's (11th), and Brenier's (9th) divisions advanced behind Souham.

Souham's 8th Division formed squares and the attacks by the Russian cavalry were easily repulsed. Chemineau's brigade was also formed in squares. It moved rapidly onto the clear plateau to the east of Weissenfels, despite the repeated charges of the Russian cavalry. Slowly Chasseraux's infantry brigade edged onto the plateau and took up position next to Chemineau's brigade.

Each square was placed 500 yards from the others. The sixteen regimental guns were posted such that four guns were between each square. The 10th Hussars and the Baden Dragoon Regiment were placed in line under the command of General Count de Valmy. Girard and Marchand advanced their divisions at the "pas de charge" in squares formed by echelons, driving the Russians back on Lützen.[12]

Lanskoi's cavalry withdrew towards Winzingerode's cavalry (4,700 men), posted near Starsiedel and all of the allied artillery (30 guns) moved to Starsiedel in an effort, by its combined fire, to stop the advance of Girard's 10th Division. Souham's 8th Division ceased moving towards Lützen and moved against Kaja to threaten the northern flank of Winzingerode's forces. The Imperial Guard cavalry moved to position itself on his south. This proved too much for Winzingerode, who prudently chose to withdraw back across the Flössgraben canal to Meyhen, where he joined his infantry.

FRENCH CONSCRIPTS AT WEISSENFELS

Souham's conscripts had tasted their first battle and had performed soundly, showing no sign of weakness. Ney was pleased with their actions. Lanskoi's forces later moved to Thesau and Knorring's moved to Pegau.[13] Winzingerode deployed elements of his cavalry in a string of posts along the Saal to maintain contact with the French.[14]

WITTGENSTEIN REACTS

During the night of 29/30 April, as soon as Wittgenstein had consulted with Volkonski, he gave the orders for a general concentration on Borna. Toll took the initiative, on the morning of the 30th, to invite Miloradovich to move on Altenburg to replace Blücher. The events of the previous two days left no doubt in the allied headquarters as to the line of advance of the French army. However, it does not seem that Wittgenstein had any notion of the danger to his right wing. The mass of his forces, except Kleist, Yorck, and Berg (24,000 men), were about to execute a flank march, 25 kilometers from the French XI Corps, I Reserve Cavalry Corps, and III Corps. Without a doubt Winzingerode (14,500 men), could slow the enemy offensive, but even if the entire allied right (38,000 men) was available, it faced 73,000 men. Despite the opportunity that Wittgenstein's move offered the French, the French armies unwittingly stopped on the 30th and permitted the allied concentration.

During the 30th, the III and XI Corps remained in their bivouacs of the previous night, without renewing their movement towards Leipzig. When Kleist learned that Macdonald was in

143

Mersburg, he immediately evacuated Halle, fearing to be cut off from Schkeuditz. He withdrew during the night without incident to the west of Leipzig, where he established his bivouacs in accordance with Wittgenstein's instructions of 28 April.

On the Allied left, Blücher assembled his forces near Borna. Tormassov stood between Kohren and Frohburg. Miloradovich remained stationary in Penig, ignoring Toll's directive, on the basis that he required a regular order coming from the Czar's headquarters. Miloradovich was content to place his cavalry so as to watch the various routes. He had detached Generalmajor Emmanuel to Zwickau with two dragoon regiments, two cossack regiments, and four artillery pieces. Generalmajor Lissanevitch moved to Gera with an uhlan regiment, a cossack regiment and two guns. Generalmajor Jusefovich was sent to Zeitz with two dragoon regiments, a cossack regiment, two guns, and a regiment of infantry.[15]

THE FRENCH REORGANIZE

On 30 April the French army concentrated so as to march to the east in a "masse." New instructions were issued which directed that the Armée de l'Elbe concentrate around Mersburg in such a manner as to be able to move on 1 May towards Leipzig.

The VI Corps moved two divisions into Naumburg. The IV Corps took the shortest route towards Stössen, where Napoleon directed that it concentrate on 1 May, its three divisions. From here both corps observed Pegau and Zeitz, the two bridges over the Elster, and were positioned to move against Blücher if he moved from Altenburg on Weissenfels or Naumburg. Ney concentrated the III Corps around Weissenfels, recalling Marchand's 39th Division to join him. The 30th passed quietly around Weissenfels, as the four French divisions organized themselves. Marchand was still in Stössen.

A small reconnaissance towards Tuchern encountered a few cossacks and learned from the local peasants that approximately three enemy cavalry regiments had been in Zeitz, but had retired to Altenburg. In contrast, the advanced guards of Kirchdorf and those of Souham's division encountered 2,000 to 3,000 enemy cavalry. This mass of cavalry near Lützen occupied Ney's attention. He decided not to push his advanced guard into Lützen. He judged that Napoleon had not ordered him to engage Winzingerode with the III Corps and with the presence of enemy cavalry north of Weissenfels, it was impossible to establish contact by the right bank of the Saal with the XI Corps. Prudence dictated caution rather than a headlong rush.

The Armée du Mein advanced without incident. The XI Corps and the I Cavalry Corps occupied Mersburg and crossed the Saal, advancing seven or eight kilometers along the route to Leipzig. Roguet's Imperial Guard division moved into Mersburg, where Eugène established his headquarters. Durutte's 32nd Division was in Schafstädt. The V Corps moved east. Maison's 16th Division entered Halle at 4:30 A.M., after seeing Kleist withdraw the previous night. It advanced the next day when relieved by the 135th Infantry Regiment. This regiment had abandoned its positions on the passages over the Saal in Rotenburg and Wettin, executed a night march, and arrived in Halle in the morning of 1 May. At the same time the leading divisions (Rochambeau's 19th and Lagrange's 18th) of the V Corps arrived near Mersburg. All indications were that the allies were withdrawing on Leipzig. Eugène directed Victor to concentrate his forces to the east of Bernberg and to push a strong reconnaissance on Dessau, to determine if Wittgenstein had left a guard at the bridges.[16]

Situation of the French Army on 1 May

Armée de l'Elbe

V Corps (Lauriston) Ginstherdorf	22,000
XI Corps (Macdonald) Quesitz & Markranstädt	22,000
I Cavalry Corps Between Schladebachand (Latour-Maubourg) Vetzh	4,000
32nd Division (Durutte) Mersberg	4,500

Armée du Mein

Imperial Guard

Cavalry Lützen	4,000
Old Guard (Curial) Weissenfels	3,500
Young Guard (Dumoustier)	11,000

III Corps (Ney)	45,000
8th Division (Souham) Around Gross Görschen	
9th Division (Brenier) Near Lützen	
10th Division (Girard) Starsiedel	
11th Division (Ricard) Near Lützen	
39th Division (Marchand) In Lützen	

IV Corps (Bertrand)	30,000
12th Division (Morand) In Stössen	
15th Division (Italians) In Gross-Gessewitz	
38th Division (Württemberg) In Jena	

VI Corps (Marmont)	25,000
20th Division (Compans) Near Lösan	
21st Division (Bonnet) East of Rippach	
22nd Division (Friederichs) In Naumburg[17]	

ALLIED MOVEMENTS

During the day of 1 May, Wittgenstein received a flood of accurate information on the strength and location of the French armies. Winzingerode provided him with a complete description of Lanskoi's action and the size of the French forces Lanskoi had engaged. He also pointed out that the French line of advance was towards Lützen. However, for some reason he failed to advise Wittgenstein of Souham's division bivouacking at Gross-Görschen.

Winzingerode's movement backwards was a great surprise for Wittgenstein. He had counted on the advanced guard maintaining itself in Meyen and holding the line of the Flössgraben canal. This would have permitted Yorck and Berg to safely cross the Elster at Zwenkau. Now the plans were totally disrupted. Wittgenstein now possessed only the two permanent bridges at Storckwitz and Pegau.

News of the arrival of the IV Corps at Stössen, also disquieted Wittgenstein. He felt it was necessary to guard himself against the French troops, which could intervene from the direction of Altenburg. Miloradovich was advised by Volkonski of the Czar's resolution to attack the French near Lützen and that he was to move on Predel and to hold himself ready to intervene in the battle if necessary. However, Wittgenstein decided that this was not the best position for Miloradovich and decided it would be more adventageous if he was posted in Zeitz, where he would be better able to face the French IV Corps if it should choose to intervene in the battle.

Wittgenstein realized because of the late hour that if he wished to attack the French in the morning, he would have to move his forces across the Elster immediately. He directed that Blücher's corps cross first, followed by Yorck and Berg. Blücher was directed to move from Rötha and march on Pegau, where he was to prepare to attack the French in the morning.

In his battle instructions, Wittgenstein directed that Blücher, Yorck, Berg, and Winzingerode should join their forces between the Flössgraben and a line from Werben to Dömsen. Tormassov was to have the head of his corps in Pegau and Storckwitz. At 5 A.M., Blücher's corps, formed in two columns, was to cross the Elster and move on the Flössgraben. His right column would cross at Storckwitz and Werben. His left column would cross at Pegau and Stönzsch. Berg would follow Blücher's right hand column, while Yorck would follow Blücher's left column. Winzingerode was to cover the crossing by being positioned west of Werben. He was to be reinforced here by Blücher's cavalry reserve. This cavalry force totaled about 9,700 cavalry. Winzingerode was to detach three infantry battalions, eight guns, and three cossack regiments to guard the bridge at Zwenkau and maintain liaison with Kleist then in Leipzig.

Blücher was to form the first line of battle and support his left flank on the Grünabach stream and his right flank was to extend to the Rippach Stream. The cavalry and artillery were to be formed in a refused echelon that was supported by the Flössgraben.[18] Yorck, Berg, and Winzingerode were to form the second line and Tormassov was to be the general reserve. Kleist was to remain to the west of Leipzig with orders to assume the offensive when he heard the sound of the battle. If he was faced by a superior enemy force, he was to withdraw on Wurzen. Wittgenstein also added to his instructions that if the allied army was beaten, it was to withdraw on Altenburg and Frohburg.

THE FRENCH MOVEMENTS

The French cavalry was busily probing the allied lines in an effort to locate the principal allied armies, but it had located only Winzingerode's Corps. Winzingerode's withdrawal, therefore, drew Napoleon like a magnet. The reports of various agents indicated that the forces in Leipzig were insignificant. Those agents also reported that Wittgenstein was in Zwenkau, and that Yorck and Winzingerode were in Borna, where they were joined by Blücher. To the south they reported a Russian corps had passed through Chemnitz and that the Czar and King of Prussia had established their headquarters in Rochlitz. Napoleon also learned that Wittgenstein had replaced Kutusov as commander in chief of the allied armies.

Not knowing the allied intentions, Napoleon positioned his forces, so as to riposte any aggressive movement by the allies. The XI Corps advanced, with the V Corps in echelon to the right behind it, until it occupied the crossroads of the roads to Lützen, Leipzig, Mersburg and Zwenkau. The Imperial Guard was in Lützen and III Corps was nearby in Kaja. The VI Corps was to move around Poserna and scout the road to Pegau. On the right, the VI Corps was to leave Stössen at 4:00 A.M. and send its two divisions towards Starsiedel. The XII Corps, the Württemberg division and all of the fragments of the VI Corps, notably Frésia's cavalry division, were to move on Naumburg. Peyri's Italian 15th Division was to move to Gleitsberg and from Naumburg, the 38th Division (Württembergers) was to move on Stössen, so that the VI Corps could move on Pegau on the 3 May.

On the morning of 2 May, Napoleon had organized his army such that the Armée du Mein had 87,000 men between Lützen and Poserna, a distance of six to seven kilometers, facing the bridges at Zwenkau and Pegau. At 8:00 A.M., the VI Corps (20,876 men) would appear at Aupitz. To the left, the Armée de l'Elbe (49,000 men) was ready to move on Zwenkau or Leipzig, as appropriate. The allies, who thought they would be facing about 80,000 men, would in fact find themselves confronted with 157,000 men.

1   Holleben, Frühjahrsfeldzuges 1813, pg 386.

2   Tournes, Campagne de Printemps, pg 230.

3   Schmitt, 151e Regiment d'Infanterie, pg 36.

4   Tournes, Campagne de Printemps, pg 320.

5   Schmitt, 151e Regiment d'Infanterie, pg 38.

6   Tournes, Campagne de Printemps, pg 236.

7   Tournes, Campagne de Printemps, pg 243.

8   A battalion column by division at full interval means that the battalion is broken up into three divisions, each division being two companies. The first division, two companies facing in the same direction and formed in a single line, was followed by the second division at an interval equal to the length of the two companies side by side, i.e. approximately 150 feet. The third division followed the second at the same distance. This interval permitted a division to wheel to the left or right and not collide with the other divisions.

9   Tournes, Campagne de Printemps, pg 280.

10 Weil, Campagne de 1813, La Cavalerie, pg 32.

11 Lachouque, The Anatomy of Glory, pg 291.

12 Plotho, Krieg in Deutschland, pg 99, & Sauzey, Contingent Badois, pg 76, & Thiry, Lutzen et Bautzen, pg 173.

13 Sporschil, Grosse Chronik, Vol I, pg 141.

14 Weil, Campagne de 1813, La Cavalerie, pg 32.

15 Weil, Campagne de 1813, La Cavalerie, pg 33.

16 Tournes, Campagne de Printemps, pg 283.

17 Camon, Guerre Napoléonienne, Vol IV, pg 374.

18 In this situation "refused" means that the line of battle is angled back, away from the enemy. Echelon means that the units are organized in echelon so the formation appears as follows:

French Lines   ————————————————
Allied Lines   ————————

                          ————————

                                        ————————

THE ALLIES RETREAT FROM LÜTZEN
KNÖTEL

The Battle of Lützen
2 May 1813

The French Plans

At 5:00 A.M., an order arrived in the headquarters of Ney's III Corps for the five divisions to "rally" and to send out two strong reconnaissance forces, one towards Zwenkau and the other towards Pegau. However, Ney chose to pay little heed to these directions and during the morning his divisions remained in their positions. Marchand's 39th Division remained on the right bank of the Flössgraben, east of Lützen, and the divisions of Ricard (11th) and Brenier (9th) remained on its left bank. Girard's (10th) Division was in Starsiedel while Souham's 8th Division and Kellerman's advanced guard remained in Gross-Görschen.

General practice implied that the order for two "strong reconnaissance" forces required a force of combined arms be sent down both roads. Ney's advanced guard consisted of only two battalions and seven squadrons, yet he directed it to perform these reconnaissances. Kellerman, the commander of the advanced guard, interpreted this to be a very low level reconnaissance and dispatched only a few weak cavalry detachments down each road. These detachments were too weak to pierce the screen of cossacks before the allied positions and learned nothing.[1]

Ney had established very few advanced posts. Girard's and Souham's divisions had posted only a few sentinels around their positions in Starsiedel and Gross-Görschen. Kellerman pushed a cavalry post to Hohenlohe on the Flössgraben. Though cossacks were observed on the heights of the plateau between the Elster, Flössgraben, and Rippach, the French thought nothing of it. They had been continually surrounded by cossacks and Russian cavalry since they entered Saxony. The allies' sense of security was furthered by the convergence of 75,000 men behind the ridge at Monarchenhügel, 2,500 meters behind Souham's division.

At 10:15 A.M., Marmont received the order to advance on Pegau and chose to execute this, by passing his corps along the right bank north and east of the Rippach, so as to remain in liaison with the III Corps. At 11:00 A.M., Bonnet's (21st) and Friederich's (22nd) divisions crossed the ravine, followed by the rest of the corps, and moved so as to pass between Starsiedel and Kölzen. They marched in the anti-cavalry formation directed by Napoleon and used by III Corps when Souham's division encountered Lanskoi at Weissenfels.

Eugène's Advance

Between 6:00 A.M. and 11:00 A.M., Eugène's forces clashed with the allies twice, once at Halle and the second time west of Leipzig.

When Eugène left Halle, he left the 1st Brigade, 19th Division, V Corps (four battalions of the 135th Line Regiment) supported by a half battery of four guns and a company of engineers there as a garrison. The city gates were barricaded and houses had loopholes cut in them.

Bülow, who was in Oppin, received an order from Wittgenstein to take Halle and to then act on the French rear and left flank. At 3:00 A.M., Bülow led his detachment of 4,500 men and 24 guns towards Halle, arriving there at about 6:00 A.M. Six squadrons of cavalry and a horse battery blockaded the south of the city, while General Lacroix, the French garrison commander,

148

sounded the alarm and prepared to defend the city. Two French battalions manned the walls, while the other two formed a ready reserve.

The initial Prussian attempts to scale the walls were easily repulsed and General Lacroix chose to attack the Prussians with his two reserve battalions and four guns. However, as he sortied from Halle, he immediately encountered Bülow's main column. A sudden attack by two squadrons of Prussian cavalry into the French infantry's flank drove them back in complete disorder. As they fled, the French abandoned three guns to the allies.

Despite this disaster, the French engineers and one infantry battalion established themselves strongly and repulsed the efforts of the Prussians to seize the passage. They covered the withdrawal of the two shattered battalions and one formed battalion by Mersburg. At 11:00 A.M.,

NAPOLEON MAKING HIS PLANS OF BATTLE

the French force holding the bridge withdrew in good order on Mersburg, holding the Prussian cavalry at bay. The affair cost the French 13 officers and 650 men hors de combat.

Around 9:00 A.M., Lauriston learned of the attack on Halle. He detached Général de brigade Harlet and his brigade, sending them towards Halle to rescue the garrison. About the same time, he was ordered by Eugène to move immediately on Leipzig. The 16th Division (Maison) led, followed by the 18th (Lagrange) and the 19th (Rochambeau). Maison quickly encountered 400 to 500 allied cavalry near Leutszch. He responded by forming himself to attack and soon found himself facing Kleist's corps.

Kleist had a force of about 6,000 men and 34 guns. He knew he was facing a major French force and judged it impossible to hold his position west of Leipzig. Without waiting for the attack, he recoiled before the leading elements of Maison's division, the 151st and 153rd Line Regiments. The French skirmishers pursued him so closely, that he was unable to burn the bridges over the

Elster as he withdrew into Leipzig. At 12:30, as Lauriston was preparing to push Lagrange's division into Leipzig, he received orders from Eugène ordering him to stop his movement. By that time Souham was engaged at Gross-Görschen and the sounds of the battle could be heard in Leipzig.

THE BATTLEFIELD

The battlefield where the two armies collided at Lützen was undulating and generally rises towards Lützen. The greatest elevation was a mound a quarter league south of Gross-Görschen, now known as the "Monarchenhügel" or "Monarch's Hill," because the two monarchs were on that height when the battle occurred. This height dominated all the plain and from there the entire battlefield could be observed.

Between Starsiedel and Rahna, there was a muddy ravine that ran east towards the Elster and westward towards the Rippach. In good weather it could be traversed easily, with the exception of where the road left Starsiedel. To the north, parallel to this ravine, ran a low ridge.

The Flössgraben canal, which crossed the battlefield from north to south, was used to transport logs. It was usually fordable, but its bank represented a substantial obstacle to the movement of cavalry and artillery, forcing them to use the few bridges. Its banks were planted with cherry trees that blocked the view but offered no shelter.

Between the villages of Rahna, Görschen and Kaja were fields cut with ditches, hedges and low bushes. The main road from Görschen to Lützen had ditches on both sides that contained standing water. The rest of the battlefield was crisscrossed with sunken roads that constrained the movements of cavalry and artillery. The houses were built of wood and brick. Their courts were formed by earthen walls and hedges.

ALLIED MOVEMENTS

During the night of 1/2 May, the allied armies moved in two columns. At 5:00 A.M., Generals Yorck and Berg moved their forces on the main road from Zwenkau via Audigast to Pegau. Yorck's column was led by an advanced guard, under Oberstlieutenant von Steinmetz, which consisted of the 2nd Leib Hussar Regiment, three battalions of the Colberg Infantry Regiment, and a half foot battery.[2] Berg's corps followed Yorck, but turned off to cross the Elster at Storckwitz, where it assumed a position to form the right wing of the second line of battle. Blücher's corps moved to the right, as did the left wing of the second line, through Storckwitz, through Pegau, crossed the Elster and then crossed the Flössgraben by Carsdorf to Dölben.

At the same time, General Blücher moved his forces from Rötha to Storckwitz below Pegau in order to cross the Elster. He was destined to form the first line and Yorck was to become the second line. Blücher advanced in two columns. The first column on the right flank was commanded by Oberst von Klüx. It consisted of the Lower Silesian Brigade. The second column consisted of the Upper Silesian Brigade of Generalmajor Ziethen, the Brandenburg Brigade of Generalmajor Röder, and the reserve cavalry of Oberst von Dolffs.[3]

The reserve cavalry was ordered to move to the left, to control the road from Weissenfels. General Miloradovich moved from Altenburg to Zeitz, in order to occupy the road from Naumburg to Leipzig. General Kleist, who had moved from Mersburg to Leipzig, was ordered to remain in Leipzig and, if necessary, direct his retreat on Wurzen.

When the two columns arrived in Audigast, the earlier order of march was changed and the general rate of advance stopped. Only Ziethen's Prussian brigade and Berg's Russian division passed Storckwitz. The rest of the army remained on the road to Pegau and paraded through that village in review for the two sovereigns. After they crossed the canal, they were arranged in order of battle between Werben and Domsen, where they found themselves masked by a row of trees. The battalions were formed in masses on the center, the divisional artillery was in front of the infantry, and the reserve artillery brigades were held in reserve.

Tormassov's reserve broke its camp by Lobstädt and moved in one large column to Groitsch. There it broke into three columns. The first column, under Konovnitzin, contained the Grenadier Corps, the Russian Guard Infantry Corps, and the reserve artillery of Generallieutenant Yermolov. It moved through Pegau and crossed the Flössgraben by Stönzsch. The second column, under Gallizin V, contained the two cuirassier divisions and the Guard Light Cavalry Division. It crossed the Elster by Pegau. The third column, under Gortschakov II, was formed by the 8th Infantry Corps. It crossed at the bridges by Werben, Storckwitz, Pegau, Stönzsch and Carsdorf. At 7:00 A.M., the reserve had arrived in Groitsch, where it stopped until the other troops passing through Pegau had cleared the area.[4]

At 7:00 A.M., the Russian army stood by Pegau and Storckwitz. Its infantry and light artillery filled the defiles by Stönzsch, Carsdorf, Werben, and Storckwitz. It was ready to serve as the general reserve. Blücher had received orders to position himself such that the left of his line ran extended to the course of the Grünabach stream, which ran from Grossgrimma to Delitzsch.[5] The second line and reserve were placed behind him, close enough to support him, but far enough back to be sheltered from the French artillery fire.

Blücher's left flank was secured with cavalry and horse artillery, positioned so that it could control both the banks of the stream and the heights before them. The right flank was to move between the two streams known as Rippach and Flössgraben and hold its position there. If the French attempted to attack it, the infantry was to fall back behind the artillery, supported by the cavalry, and allow the artillery to defend the flank.

General Winzingerode's corps organized itself at 6:00 A.M., at Werben and was covered by the cossacks of the advanced guard. The cossacks manned various forward posts spread between the Flössgraben stream, Kreischau, and Weissenfels.

General Winzingerode's corps moved towards the battlefield. Two battalions of the Krementsoug Infantry Regiment, a battalion of the Riajsk Infantry Regiment, a light battery and the Grekov #3 Cossack Regiment were left in Zwenkau to cover the bridge over the Elster and act as an advanced post. Two cossack regiments were posted in the defile at Zwenkau in order to slow any French movement against Zwenkau.[6] Tormassov had detached three infantry battalions, two engineering companies, a battery of 12 guns, and 100 cossacks to watch the bridges at Werben, Storckwitz, and Pegau, as well as to garrison Stönzsch. This force totaled about 1,600 men.

The Czar and King of Prussia left their headquarters in Borna at 2:00 A.M. and rode from Lobstädt to Pegau, where they arrived at 5:00 A.M. From there they watched Blücher's corps pass through the village.[7] Slowly the entire allied army wound itself out onto the battlefield, assuming its positions for the battle.

ALLIED POSITIONS

The first line was commanded by General of Cavalry von Blücher. It was positioned with Upper Silesian Brigade of Generalmajor von Ziethen on the right flank. The brigade was deployed, right to left, as follows: The extreme flank was held by the cavalry under Major Laroche von Starkenfels with the 1/,2/Silesian Uhlan Regiment, 2/,4/1st and 3/,4/2nd Silesian Hussar Regiments, and Horse Battery #9. The infantry, under Oberst von Pirch I was arranged, right to left: Silesian Grenadier Battalion, Russian Position Battery #1, 1/,3/ 1st Silesian Infantry Regiment, 6pdr Foot Battery #11, 1/,3/2nd Silesian Infantry Regiment, Fus/1st Silesian Infantry Regiment, Silesian Schützen Battalion, 6pdr Foot Battery #13, Russian Position Battery #33, and a half of Prussian 12pdr Foot Battery #3.

The left was held by the Lower Silesian Brigade commanded by Oberst and Flügeladjutant von Klüx. The brigade was deployed, right to left as follows: the infantry under Major von Jagow consisting of West Prussian Grenadier Battalion, 2/,3/1st West Prussian Infantry Regiment,

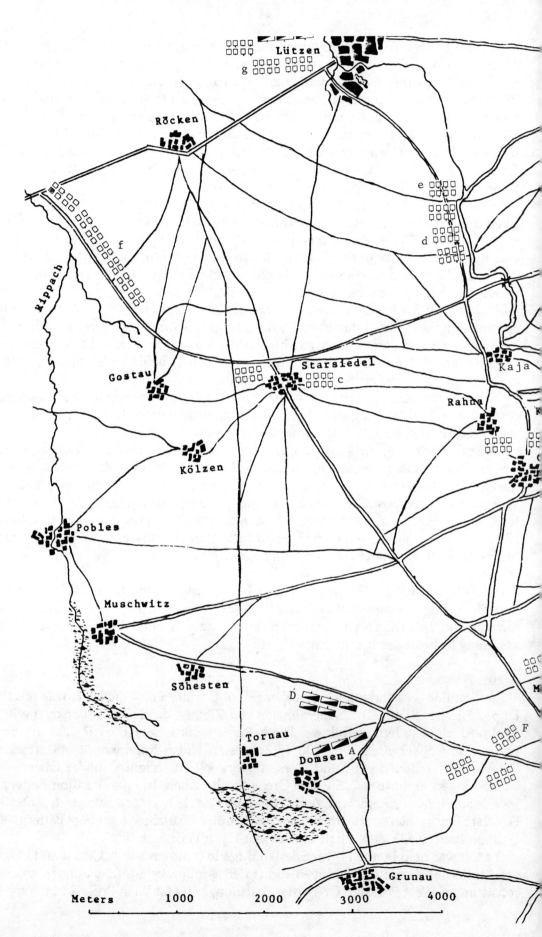

Lützen

g

Röcken

Rippach

e

d

f

Gostau

Starsiedel

Kaja

c

Rahna

Kölzen

Pobles

Muschwitz

Söhesten

D

Tornau

F

Domsen

A

Grunau

Meters   1000   2000   3000   4000

152

Meuchen

Meyhen

Gross Schkorlopp

Klein Schkorlopp

Eisdorf

Kitzen

rschen

rschen

Hohenlohe

Thesau

Sitteln

Löben

Scheiden

Peissen

B

hugel

Segel

C

Werben

Flossgraben

Pegau

The Battle of Lützen
2 May 1813
11:00 a.m.
Between
the Grande Armée under
Napoleon Bonaparte
and the
Combined Allied Armies
under their Majesties
King of Prussia
and the
Czar of Russia

153

a	Laboissiere's Cavalry Brigade, III Corps	A	Knorring's Cavalry Brigade
b	Souham: 8th Division, III Corps	B	Blücher's Corps
c	Girard: 10th Division, III Corps	C	Berg's Corps
d	Brenier: 9th Division, III Corps	D	Dolff's Reserve Cavalry
e	Ricard: 11th Division, III Corps	E	Winzingerode's Corps
f	Marmont: VI Corps	F	Yorck's Corps
g	Imperial Guard	G	Russian Guard & Grenadier Divisions
h	Marchand: 39th Division, III Corps		

6pdr Battery #7, 2/,3/2nd West Prussian Infantry Regiment, 6pdr Foot Battery #8, Russian Position Battery #14, and Fus/1st West Prussian Infantry Regiment.

Immediately to the left of this was Oberst von Mutius' force, which consisted of Horse Battery #7, 1/,2/,3/,4/Neumark Dragoon Regiment, and 2/,4/1st West Prussian Dragoon Regiment.

The first line's reserve, the Brandenburg Brigade, was under Generalmajor and General Adjutant von Röder. Oberstlieutenant von Katzler commanded the 1/,2/,3/,4/West Prussian Uhlan Regiment, 1/,2/Brandenburg Hussar Regiment, and Horse Battery #8. Oberstlieutenant von Tippelskirch commanded three battalions of the Garde zu Fuss, the Normal Infantry Battalion, the Garde Jäger Battalion, the von Wedel Guard Freiwilliger Jägers, the Leib Grenadier Battalion, 3/Leib Infantry Regiment, the East Prussian Grenadier Battalion, Guard Foot Battery #4, and 6pdr Foot Battery #9 von Grevenitz.

The second line, under Generallieutenant von Yorck, was formed with the right wing commanded by Generallieutenant von Berg. Under him was Generalmajor Alexeiev commanding the Mitau Dragoon Regiment (three squadrons); Position Battery #5, the 5th Infantry Division of Generalmajor Lukov,[8] a brigade of the 14th Infantry Division under Generalmajor Helfreich.[9]

The left wing of the second line was commanded by Generalmajor von Hünerbein. It had the 1/,2/,3/,4/Lithuanian Dragoon Regiment on the right flank. The right flank was formed, right to left, under Major von Lobenthal consisted of half of 6pdr Foot Battery #3, 1st Combined Infantry Regiment (2/1st East Prussian, 1/2nd East Prussian, and Fus/1st East Prussian Infantry Regiments)[10] and 6pdr Foot Battery #1. Under Oberst Horn was Major von Schmalensee with the 5th Combined Infantry Regiment (Fus/Leib [this should be read, "Fusilier Battalion/Leib Regiment], 1/2nd West Prussian, and Fus/2nd West Prussian Infantry Regiments).[11] The infantry was formed in columns on the middle.[12] Major von Lessel commanded the reserve, consisting of the 6th Combined Infantry Regiment (2/1st Silesian, 2/2nd Silesian, and Fus/2nd Silesian), 6pdr Foot Battery #2, 1/2 12pdr Foot Battery #3, 1/,2/1st West Prussian Dragoon Regiment, and 1/,2/Brandenburg Dragoon Regiment.

The reserve of the right wing of the second line was commanded by Generalmajor Kasatschkovsky. He commanded the Ataman Cossack Regiment, a Don Cossack Horse Battery #1, 1st Grenadier Division Reserve with 5 battalions, and four converged grenadier battalions from the 5th and 14th Infantry Divisions.

The reserve of the left wing of the second line was commanded by Oberstlieutenant von Steinmetz. It consisted of the 1/,2/,3/,4/2nd Leib Hussar Regiment, 6pdr Horse Battery #2, 1/,2/,Fus/Colberg Infantry Regiment and 3pdr Foot Battery #1.

The first reserve was commanded by Generallieutenant and General Adjutant Baron von Winzingerode. His forces included the Prussian Reserve Cavalry Brigade commanded by Oberst von Dolffs. Under him Oberst von Jürgass commanded Horse Battery #10, 1/,2/,3/,4/

East Prussian Cuirassiers, 1/,2/,3/,4/Brandenburg Cuirassiers and 1/,2/,3/,4/Silesian Cuirassier Regiments, and 6pdr Horse Battery #3 from Yorck's corps. The other half of the reserve, under Oberstlieutenant von Werder, contained five squadrons of the Gardes du Corps, Guard Horse Battery #4, and six squadrons of the Guard Light Cavalry Regiment.[13]

The reserve for the second line consisted of three horse batteries (#2,7, and 8) under Generalmajor Nikitin, five cossack regiments under Generalmajor Illowaisky XII, Prinz Eugene von Wurttemberg's Corps and the Cavalry Reserve of Generalmajor Count Troubetzkoi. This Cavalry Reserve was formed in two groups. The first, under Generalmajor Lanskoi, consisted of the Alexandria and White Russian Hussar Regiments, two squadrons of the Soum Hussar Regiment, the Lithuanian Chasseur Regiment, and Horse Batteries #1 and 3. The second force was commanded by Generalmajor von Knorring and consisted of the Converged Dragoon Regiment, two squadrons of the Lithuanian Uhlan Regiment, and the Tartar Uhlan Regiment.

Prinz Eugene of Wurttemberg's corps was organized with two divisions. The first, the 3rd Infantry Division was commanded by Generalmajor Schachafskoi and contained the 1st Ukrainian Cossack Regiment, Light Batteries #6 and #7, three infantry and two jager regiments. The 4th Division was commanded by Generalmajor Pischnitzki and contained three infantry and two jager regiments, Light Battery #33, and 3rd Ukrainian Cossack Regiment.

The Reserve, commanded by General of Cavalry Tormassov, was broken into two lines. The first line was commanded by Generallieutenant Konovnitzin during the illness of the Grandduke Constantine. It contained a brigade from the Guard Light Cavalry Division commanded by Generalmajor Schaevitch. This brigade consisted of the Guard Hussar and Guard Uhlan Regiments, and Horse Battery #4 . Next was the 1st Grenadier Division, which consisted of two grenadier regiments under Colonel Kniaschnin II, two grenadier regiments under Colonel Acht, Position Battery #30 and Light Battery #14. Then came the 2nd Grenadier division with six grenadier regiments commanded by Colonels Pissarev, Golowin and Hesse, and Position Battery #32. Operating independently was the second brigade from the Guard Light Cavalry division under General Major Tichischerin consisting of the Guard Dragoon Regiment, Guard Cossack Regiment, and Guard Black Sea Cossack Sotnia.

The second line of the reserve was commanded by Generallieutenant Gallizin V. On the right was General Deperadovich's 1st Cuirassier Division (Chevalier Guard, Horse Guard, four cuirassier regiments), and Guard Horse Battery #1 under Gallizin's personal command.

Next was the 1st Guard Infantry Division under Generalmajor Rosen. It contained the four guard battalions under Generalmajor Potemkin, four battalions under Generalmajor Krapovitzky, Guard Light Battery #1, and Guard Position Battery #1 . The infantry was formed in columns of attack.[14]

To the left of the 1st Guard Division was the 2nd Guard Infantry Division of Generalmajor Udom II. It contained Colonel Krischanovsky's brigade, formed with the two battalions of the Lithuanian and two battalions of the Finland Guard Infantry Regiments; the brigade of Generalmajor Scheltuchin II, formed with the Leib Grenadier Regiment and the Pavlov Grenadier Regiment, and Guard Light Battery #2 and the Guard Position Battery #2. The infantry was also formed in columns of attack.

On the far left was the 2nd Cuirassier Division of Generalmajor Duca. It contained six cuirassier regiments under Generalmajors Leontiev, Gudovich, and Colonel Massalov, as well as Guard Horse Battery #2. The artillery reserve consisted of two heavy and four light Russian batteries under Generalmajor Euler.

In addition, the advanced guard and "streifkorps" consisted of 16 cossack regiments, one bashkir regiment, and a Kalmuck regiment plus the streifcorps commanded by Mandatov and Davidov.[15]

PRUSSIAN CHARGE AT GORSCHEN

THE FRENCH DISPOSITIONS

On the morning of the battle, the first offensive action occurred when a squadron of the Gardes du Corps was detached to reconnoiter the French lines. Captain Zollikofer, the commander, found his force repulsed by the French patrols situated in the villages along the Grünabach. He captured a French soldier near Gross-Görschen and learned that it was Souham's 8th Division, part of Ney's III Corps, that occupied the village. Everywhere else that Zollikofer saw was free of French soldiers.

The French army had begun the day with the four divisions of Ney's III Corps posted between Starsiedel and Görschen. Their task was to cover the French right flank. The 39th Division (Marchand), formed of troops from Baden and Hesse-Darmstadt, was moving on Leipzig, but had been stopped where the road from Dürrenberg joined the main road. The Imperial Guard was in Lützen. The VI Corps was near Poserna, the IV Corps had departed Stössen to move to Poserna, the XII Corps was near Naumburg, the V Corps was moving from Mersburg towards Leipzig, and the XI Corps was near Markranstädt, moving on Schünau. The French army had formed itself into large strategic squares formed by the various corps that were aimed at the battlefield.

THE OPENING SHOT

Wittgenstein saw before him only weak elements of a French advanced guard and ordered his forces to take the villages of Klein-Görschen, Gross-Görschen, Rahna, and Kaja from them. Müffling, a staff officer from Blücher's Corps, advised him that there were about 2,000 French infantry in Gross-Görschen and that Starsiedel did not appear to be occupied. He did, however, state that he had seen dust on the road from Weissenfels to Lützen. In fact there were 12,227 Frenchmen in Gross-Görschen and a further 9,887 in Starsiedel.

Wittgenstein's forces were to march forward in their battle order supported on the right by the Flössgraben. The immediate tactical goal was to take the French right wing in the flank. General Winzingerode was charged with executing this maneuver which, it was hoped, would cut off the French retreat. The Prussian cavalry was pushed forward on the allied left, with a goal of taking the French in the flank and it moved between Görschen and Rahna. The first goal was the capture of the villages of Rahna, Kaja, Gross-Görschen, and Klein-Görschen. As the cavalry advanced it was supported by Prussian Horse Batteries #4 and #10 and a large number of Russian guns.[16]

The entire allied army began its movement, with Ziethen's brigade holding the extreme right, Klüx's brigade the left, and Röder's brigade remained in reserve. The second line consisted of the four battalions of Generalmajor von Hünerbein forming the right wing and the five battalions of Oberst von Horn forming the left (his sixth battalion remained in Skeuditz). The battalions of the second line were formed in a single line. Steinmetz's brigade was placed in reserve.

As Klüx's brigade began the assault, it was 1,000 yards from the village of Görschen and formed in the classic brigade assault formation described in the 1812 Prussian Infantry Regulation:[17]

Front of Formation

Prussian Battery #9		Russian Heavy Battery #14
3/1st West Prussian IR		Fus/1st West Prussian IR
3/2nd West Prussian IR	2/2nd West Prussian IR	1/1st West Prussian IR
	2 Silesian Schützen Cos.	West Prussian Grenadier Battalion
Jägers & 1/Silesian Uhlans	2/,4/1st West Prussian Dragoons	2/Silesian Uhlans

Berg's Russian division was deployed to the left of these forces. All of the supporting cavalry was posted to the rear as reserves. The Prussian reserve cavalry, commanded by Oberst von Dolffs, was on the left and formed a single line with intervals the width of squadrons. The Silesian Cuirassier Regiment was on the right. Next to them stood the Garde du Corps, then the East Prussian and the Brandenburg Cuirassier Regiments. The freiwilliger jäger squadrons of the cuirassier regiments were in reserve. General Winzingerode deployed his cavalry near Domsen. He deployed Eugene of Wurttemberg's infantry behind the cavalry in column.

The French dispositions were such that Souham's 8th Division was deployed with one brigade in Gross-Görschen and the other in Rahna. The III Corps cavalry brigade (10th Hussar Regiment and the Baden Dragoon Regiment) stood before Gross-Görschen. Brenier's 9th Division was in Kaja, Girard's 10th Division was in Starsiedel, and Ricard's 11th Division was in reserve behind Kaja.

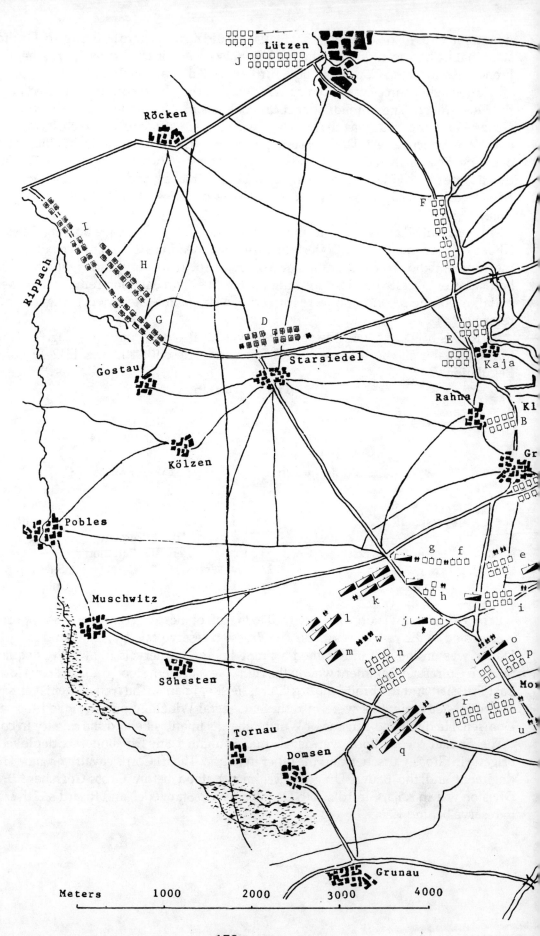

Lützen

J

Röcken

Rippach

I

H

G

Gostau

D

Starsiedel

F

E

Kaja

Rahna

Kl

B

Gr

Kölzen

Pobles

g   f

e

h

Muschwitz

k

i

l

j

Söhesten

w   o

m   n   p

Mo

r   s

Tornau

Domsen

u

q

Grunau

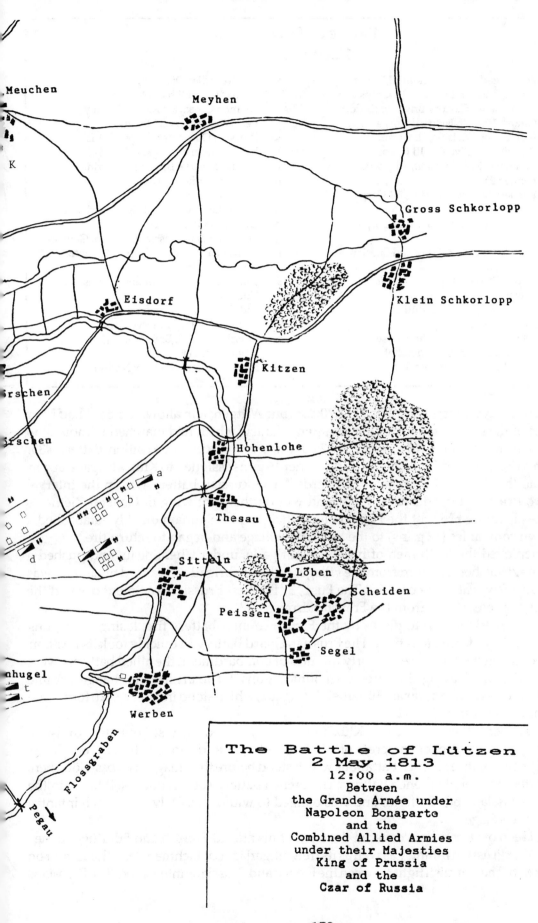

Meuchen

K

Meyhen

Gross Schkorlopp

Klein Schkorlopp

Eisdorf

Kitzen

rschen

rschen

Hohenlohe

a

b

Thesau

d

v

Sitteln

Löben

Scheiden

Peissen

Segel

nhugel

t

Werben

Flossgraben

Pegau

**The Battle of Lützen
2 May 1813**
12:00 a.m.
Between
the Grande Armée under
Napoleon Bonaparte
and the
Combined Allied Armies
under their Majesties
King of Prussia
and the
Czar of Russia

The allied maneuvers were complete at 11:30 A.M., but Wittgenstein allowed them a half hour rest, because of the state of fatigue of the Prussian infantry, which had marched without stop for the last ten hours. The battle began at 12:00 A.M. when a Russian Position Battery #33, Mandelsloh's Prussian 6pdr Battery #11, and another 16 guns assigned to Klüx's brigade began to cannonade the French at a range of 800 yards.[18] The Russian battery was in the interval between two Prussian brigades and the second was on the right wing of General Ziethen's brigade. The allied fire brought the French out of their torpor. Souham quickly established a battery of two companies (12 guns) to the left of the village and began to return fire.[19]

Souham deployed the 6,215 men of his second brigade, under Chemineau, and pushed a strong line of skirmishers forward from the village. As Klüx's brigade advanced his assault was proceeded by a few scattered cossacks. The Fus/, 3/1st West Prussian Regiment covered the two batteries to protect them from the French skirmishers.[20]

Prussian Battery #3 was cut to pieces by the French counter-battery fire, losing three guns dismounted, and was forced to retreat. The Prussian Guard Battery #4 quickly took its position and resumed fire on the French. After forty minutes of bombardment, the allied batteries were obliged to withdraw, leaving the three dismounted guns.[21] The artillery exchange became general and shot was falling as far as Hünerbein's brigade, which stood in reserve. No formation was safe from its attention.[22]

While the artillery duel progressed, Klüx's brigade advanced against Souham's division. Klüx's 5,200 men passed over the crest of Monarchenhügel and moved directly on Gross-Görschen. The two or three French battalions which stood before the village of Gross-Görschen, were supported by a single French battery. The French battery soon found itself taken in the flank by two Prussian 6pdr batteries and was obliged to withdraw. Only the French infantry remained in the village.

A strong screen of skirmishers covered the front of his attack. The 4th and 5th Züge of the 3/,Fus/1st West Prussian Infantry as well as its freiwilligerjäger detachment lead the assault on Gross-Görschen. The skirmish fight between the French and Prussians intensified. The Prussians reacted by deploying the 3rd and 6th Züge of both battalions as skirmishers and eventually both battalions of their first line were totally deployed as skirmishers.

As Klüx pushed into Gross-Görschen at the "sturmschritte [assault pace]," his entire force was deployed and utilized. He had no fresh forces left as he drove Chemineau out of Gross-Görschen. The French were driven out with the loss of about 100 prisoners.[23] Once in Gross-Görschen, all three battalions of the 1st West Prussian Regiment deployed into skirmish order to occupy the village.[24]

Chemineau withdrew his brigade back towards Kaja, where Souham's first brigade (6,019 men under Colonel Lamour) had been moved, as soon as Souham heard the first shots fired. The 2/2nd West Prussian Infantry Regiment pursued Chemineau with a column of three companies and advanced to strike a French column by Kaja. Dolffs' cavalry also caught up with the fleeing French, but the Prussians were taken in the flank by a battery of four French cannons firing cannister as they passed out of Gross-Görschen. This fire forced them to withdraw back into the village.[25]

The Prussian cavalry pulled back and stood in the allied line. It was to remain in these positions for several hours, standing under a heavy and continual French artillery fire. It suffered heavy casualties while it stood motionless.

Eugene von Wurttemberg moved his 2nd Corps to a hill between the Monarchenhügel and Tornau. From here, if necessary, he could move on Starsiedel to reinforce Winzingerode and threaten the French right flank. However, neither Winzingerode nor Wurttemberg chose to act and let the opportunity slip past. The only action the 2nd Corps took was to detach the Russian 6th and 7th Light Batteries of Lieutenant Colonels Dietrich and Talusin forward where they cannonaded the French garrison of Starsiedel. The 2nd Corps deployed in line of battle, but shortly after reformed itself into columns as if on parade. It was about then that Winzingerode's cavalry was moved forward. Unfortunately for the Russians, the French had taken advantage of the Russian slowness to ram divisions of the VI Corps and Morand's 12th Division of the IV Corps into Starsiedel.[26]

To the right of this, the 2/5th Combined Infantry Regiment had pushed the French back to Kaja. Its skirmishers pushed into the village and the village changed hands twice. The second time the 2/Prussian Garde zu Fuss Regiment and two Russian battalions supported the attack.

Girard's 10th Division was posted north of Starsiedel. The artillery fire had roused him to action and his forces rushed into Starsiedel. A battery was posted to the east of the village, on a crest which descends towards Kaja. From there the French battery had a clear view of the 2,650 men of the Prussian reserve cavalry. This force contained 17 squadrons and 16 guns under the command of Oberst Dolffs. Dolffs had been ordered to maneuver his forces in an enveloping maneuver with Klüx. He was to cut off the retreat of the weak French rearguard that was chased out of Gross-Görschen.

Dolffs' Prussian cavalry closed on Starsiedel at a trot and deployed into line 2,000 paces from the village as Blücher closed on Gross-Görschen.[27] Dolffs' cavalry was cannonaded by Girard's divisional artillery, which had just moved up to the heights overlooking the Prussian advance. The Prussian cuirassiers vainly attempted to throw back the three battalions which advanced out of Starsiedel.

Dolffs then learned that the French VI Corps was moving on Pegau by the northern bank of the Rippach. He felt it was impossible for his cavalry force alone to take Starsiedel and that it would be equally dangerous to neglect Starsiedel and move on Kaja. Instead he chose to stop, deploy his artillery and return the French fire with his 16 guns. He then sent an officer to Wittgenstein requesting Eugene von Wurttemberg's corps (6,400 infantry by Domsen) be sent to support him as he attacked Starsiedel. This request, however, was rejected by Wittgenstein, who did not realize the importance of the village and whose attention was locked on the attack on Gross-Görschen. Dolffs was left to continue his counterbattery and the initiative passed to the French.

MARMONT ADVANCES ONTO THE BATTLEFIELD

Maréchal Marmont was marching on Starsiedel at the time of the artillery duel with Dolffs. He was acting in accordance with Napoleon's instructions and moving on Pegau. He advanced his forces in nine columns on several lines, ready to form square instantly and advancing in echelon.[28] As a result Compan's 20th Division crossed Starsiedel at the "pas accéléré"[29] with Bonnet's 21st Division en echelon to the left and Friederich's 22nd Division in the rear.[30]

Prinz Wilhelm von Preussen placed himself at the head of the Brandenburg Cuirassier Regiment, on the extreme left of the Prussian line, attacked the leading French elements of Marmont's corps. This Prussian regiment was detached from Dolffs' force, which had been pulled behind the crests to the west of Monarchenhügel to avoid the artillery fire.

Maréchal Marmont was surprised by the presence of a large force of allied cavalry. He was obliged to dismount and take shelter in a square formed by the 37th Légère Regiment as it came under cavalry attack.[31] However, the 37th Légère Regiment broke and fled in terror. Marmont and his escort then moved towards the rear, where they were taken for the enemy and fired on by French troops. He then found himself obliged to throw himself into a ditch beside the road in order to escape capture.[32]

The 1st Marine Artillery Regiment, outfitted as an infantry regiment, formed the right of Compan's 20th Division. It formed in squares to the east of Starsiedel, when it was charged by the Brandenburg Cuirassier Regiment. Though the Brandenburgers had caused the 37th Légère Regiment to break, the 1st Marines repelled them easily.[33]

Marmont withdrew Compan's 20th Division to the edge of Starsiedel and to its north. He formed his forces into several squares, so that any new attack would not throw them into the same disorder that had struck the 37th Légère Regiment. These squares were placed so close that they could not fire unless the enemy cavalry actually passed between them.[34]

Marmont then deployed all 46 pieces of his artillery along side of the 16 belonging to Girard's division, on the crest running between Starsiedel and Kaja. About 1:30 P.M., the combined 62 guns roared, spitting shot and shell at Dolffs' sadly outnumbered force of two horse batteries. On this edge of the battle, the conflict once again settled down to an artillery duel into which the allies fed more guns. Girard, relieved by the arrival of Marmont, felt he should return to the assistance of his fellow division officer, Souham, and marched towards Kaja.[35]

As Compans' 20th Division of the VI Corps moved into line near Starsiedel, it was struck by and stopped the Prussian assault through Starsiedel. When the Prussians recoiled, Compans advanced through to strike Winzingerode's forces. General Berg's corps, supported by a Russian cuirassier division, the Guard Light Cavalry Division, and its horse artillery moved to the attack. This cavalry was commanded by General von Gallizin V, who formed it to meet any possible French counter attack.[36]

As an attack led by two battalions of Klüx's brigade (1/, Fus/1st West Prussian), attempted to push beyond Gross-Görschen, they found themselves facing a large French force.[37] Ziethen and Horn were sent to his assistance and ordered to turn the village's flank, moving towards Klein-Görschen. His attack was supported by 68 artillery pieces. The 2/1st East Prussian Infantry Regiment found itself confronted by two counter-attacking French battalions in column. It deployed into line and engaged them with salvo fire. Prussian skirmishers from the 12th Company, Fus/1st East Prussian engaged the French in the flank at a range of 50 paces. The combined effects of this fire stopped the French attack and drove them back.[38]

The Neumark Dragoon Regiment executed a successful attack against the French infantry, driving another column back. About 2:00 P.M., Souham's division was pushed back to the edge of Kaja. It was at this time that Ney arrived on the battlefield.

VIVE L'EMPEREUR! NAPOLEON'S ARRIVAL

Ney's absence had caused the French movements to be uncoordinated and without general direction. Ney's arrival resolved that. When he passed by Lützen, he had ordered the 39th Division (Marchand) to march to the sound of the guns. Shortly afterwards, about 1:00 P.M., he encountered Brenier's 9th Division and Ricard's 11th Division. He immediately sent these divisions in haste marching towards Kaja.[39] When he arrived in Kaja, Ney found Souham's 13,103 men deployed, but greatly fatigued from the earlier battles. Girard's 10th Division was also there with 8,693 men, intact and ready for battle. As he surveyed the situation Ney watched Brenier with 9,398 men move into sight south of Lützen, followed by Ricard (8,501 men). To the east of Flössgraben, Marchand's division (7,200 men) moved towards Meuchen, surrounded by Cossacks.

Ney immediately sent Souham's and Girard's divisions forwards on Klein-Görschen and Rahna respectively with Brenier's division in support. Both villages were recovered, but Gross-Görschen remained in allied hands.

THE PRUSSIAN GUARD ATTACKS THE FRENCH

In response to Ney's attack, Blücher was obliged to commit Röder's brigade (7,550 men). Röder spread his brigade over a wide area stretching from the right of Klein-Görschen and Rahna on the left. Two of Röder's battalions were sent to Eisdorf, where they established themselves to hold off Marchand's division that was just appearing to the southeast of Meuchen. All of Blücher's artillery, 104 guns, was dispersed in the brigade's line, but their effect was dissipated by the terrain, which had obliged it to be deployed and act as independent batteries. In contrast, Ney's position allowed him to deploy 65 to 70 guns on the crest between Starsiedel and Kaja, reinforced by Marmont's 46 guns. He found himself with a tremendous artillery concentration that could effectively intervene in the battle that was about to begin in earnest.[40] Despite Ney's advantages, Röder's brigade was able to advance against the fatigued forces of Souham's and Girard's divisions and push them back. The Prussians paid for their success with heavy casualties.

163

Blücher was able to recapture Rahna and Klein-Görschen and threaten Kaja again. Horn's brigade was originally directed against Rahna. Redirected, it now struck towards Kaja with the Fusilier Battalion and the schützen of the 1/2nd West Prussian Infantry Regiment. The fusiliers advanced behind a screen of skirmishers. These skirmishers engaged a French battalion at the edge of Kaja at a range of 30 paces, forcing them back. Ney's batteries, being so close to Kaja, were obliged by the advancing Prussians to withdraw to the north at the exact moment that their assistance was desperately needed by the French infantry.

Wittgenstein was in a position to seize Kaja or attack Starsiedel, and open a second gate to the plain of Lützen, or to shift his forces to support Blücher, if he acted quickly. Fortunately for the French, Marmont saw the hole forming in the French lines and shifted Compans' division to the north-east and blocked the hole created between the VI and III Corps. He supported Compans and Bonnet with Friederich's division which was closing to their rear.

In fact, the threat to the French had been minimal. Wittgenstein did not see the hole and sent no order to his forces. At the same time, the Czar had sent a message to Tormassov, then four kilometers from Monarchenhügel, that there was no reason to push his forces to the battle. His only action was to dispatch from Berg's Corps the Mohilev, Kaluga and Perm Infantry Regiments to the right where they formed a reserve behind Blücher's Corps on the left facing Starsiedel. They marched behind the Prussian reserve cavalry and advanced to attack with their supporting artillery.[41]

NAPOLEON ARRIVES

Napoleon had departed Schöna at about 12:30, after sending instructions to Prince Eugène for the Armée de l'Elbe. At the head of the Guard cavalry, he moved quickly through Lützen and he was in Kaja at about 2:30. Napoleon quickly developed his plans. Ney's corps was to hold the allies in place. Eugène's Armée de l'Elbe was to move to the battlefield and hold Ney's left, while Maréchal Marmont's corps was to assume a position on Ney's right wing. Bonnet's division was to be detached for a flanking maneuver that would pass through Poserna and strike them in the flank and rear. He was to cut the road to Weissenfels if possible. The French forces initially on the battlefield consisted solely of elements of Ney's corps. The rest of the French army was positioned such that it was some miles away and concealed from allied view.

While doing this, he watched Ney's batteries withdrawing and the young soldiers throwing their arms away as they fled to the rear. Napoleon ordered that the fugitives were not to be allowed to pass behind the formed French cavalry, but that they be obliged to pass behind the French left wing. Those that could be reorganized were pulled together quickly. These were the veteran soldiers, who had held out the longest in the villages.[42]

The Imperial Guard infantry arrived shortly afterwards. The Guard Grenadiers led, followed by the Chasseurs, and the Italian Guard. Behind them came the brigades of Tindal,[43] Lanusse,[44] Berthezène,[45] a battalion of the Fusilier-Grenadiers and a battalion Fusilier-Chasseurs.[46] Napoleon placed the Imperial Guard in echelons by battalion in square between Lützen and Kaja. The two Guard cavalry regiments that he had were sent to the right to reinforce that wing, and, by repeated charges, they were to give the allies an exaggerated opinion of their numbers.[47]

Napoleon then passed amongst his troops, allowing them to see he had arrived and electrifying them with his presence. Cries of "Vive l'Empereur!" rang out in the ranks. Even the wounded cried "Vive l'Empereur!" as they lay awaiting the hour of their death. The morale of the French army grew by the second as the word of Napoleon's presence swept across the battlefield.[48]

As Napoleon studied the battle, he felt that the withdrawal of Souham and Girard were only the inevitable fluctuations of any battle, but that it was important to prevent the allies from exploiting their withdrawal by capturing Kaja and deploying the numerous cavalry on the plain of Lützen. Souham and Grenier's divisions were fatigued, but Brenier's was still capable of an

THE PRUSSIAN GUARD ATTACK

effort. Ricard's 8,500 men were still intact and the Imperial Guard was about to arrive with 14,128 men. That gave Napoleon a total of 30,000 men to deploy in his next move.

Napoleon's concept of the battle resolved around two things. First was the necessity to continue the battle around Kaja with the III and VI Corps, and the Guard, with the greatest economy so as to keep the allies away from Lützen. The second was to hold the enemy in position until such time as the IV Corps, which was positioned and marching in a maneuver that would envelop the allies, had time to arrive on the battlefield and intervene decisively.

Napoleon had sent verbal orders to the Armée de l'Elbe between noon and 1:00 P.M., directing that it was essential for the XI Corps and the I Cavalry Corps (25,513 men) to move towards the battlefield by Räpitz. The V Corps was to leave a division facing Leipzig and follow the other two corps en echelon.

This maneuver had the XI Corps and the I Cavalry Corps moving to the battlefield by the shortest route and strike at the bridge at Pegau. The V Corps would protect its flank against a counter strike by any enemy force that might be in the area.

The IV Corps, despite the sound of the guns, continued to act according to Napoleon's orders of 9:00 A.M. Morand's 12th Division was moving to Taucha and Peyri's 15th Division was moving on Aupitz. Indications are that no other action was taken by Bertrand until he received an order at 2:30 to move on the battlefield.

The orders addressed to the VI Corps were simpler. This corps contained 21,000 troops and was ordered to advance through Rippach to Starsiedel and reinforce the French middle.

Around 3:00 P.M., Ricard's 11th Division advanced on Kaja. It was formed by successive brigades, with Tarayre's brigade in the lead and Dumoulin's brigade held back as a reserve. As this force advanced, the remains of the three divisions of III Corps (Souham, Girard and Brenier) rallied and joined the advance. Kaja, Rahna and Klein-Görschen were recaptured. Elements of

Tarayre's brigade, 3/,4/9th Légère Regiment and 17th Provisional Regiment, actually penetrated into the first houses of Gross-Görschen.

In reaction, Yorck's corps deployed on a frontage of about 2,000 meters. Hünerbein's forces deployed to the right. Major von Lobenthal's 3 battalions and 2 detachments of freiwilligerjägers moved against Klein-Görschen.

Steinmetz commanded the forces moving towards Rahna. His force consisted the 1st West Prussian Uhlan Regiment, 2nd Leib Hussar Regiment, 1/,2/Silesian Cuirassier Regiment, 2/Silesian Uhlan Regiment and two squadrons of the West Prussian Dragoons and Horn's five battalions.[49]

A smaller force remained in reserve. Röder's Guard Brigade also advanced between both villages and supported both attacks.

The Guard Fusilier Battalion, commanded by Major von Block, had just advanced into the fields between Gross-Görschen and Rahna, when Blücher personally ordered it to take the village of Kaja. The Guard Fusiliers were supported by the Leib Grenadier Battalion and, it would appear, the 2/1st West Prussian Infantry which had reformed under the orders of Major von Stach.[50] At the same time Klein-Görschen was struck by a second column under Major von Alvensleben commanding the 1/,2/Garde zu Fuss Regiment and two companies of the Guard Jägers.

The attacking Prussians succeeded in driving the French out of both Rahna and Klein-Görschen, pushing the French back and established themselves behind both villages. The French were forced to withdraw behind the village of Kaja.

The Russians acted in concert with this attack. The Czar ordered Generalmajor Nikitin to move 40 horse guns into the position between Winzingerode's Corps and that of Berg. They began a tremendous fire when the Russian cavalry joined the Prussian left. The fire of this battery was such that Generalmajor Pantschoulidzev I was able to led the Nijegorod Dragoon Regiment and the Tchernigov Chasseur Regiment in a very successful attack against the disordered French.[51]

Block advanced his column on Kaja with the 2/1st West Prussian Infantry operating in line on his flank. The French left wing was placed before the village, facing Rahna. Major Block was obliged to turn the French flank in order to seize the village. He completed this maneuver, but suddenly encountered a French battalion formed in line. It is reported that the French battalion did not recognize Block's command as Prussian until they were quite close and quickly fled, offering no resistance. The Prussians pursued them "à la bayonette" as far as the bridge and seized the village. Simultaneously with Block's advance into Kaja, the Russian and Prussian artillery moved up and established itself between Rahna and Gross-Görschen.

The French had placed large numbers of skirmishers in the village of Kaja, who quietly waited for the Prussians to close. Once the fleeing French battalion was clear, they began to pepper the Prussians with fire.

Ney, responding to the Prussian attack, sent two columns against the two flanks of the village, with the intention of cutting off the Prussian retreat. Seeing that he had no support, Block quickly withdrew his battalion and rejoined the main Prussian lines.

The battle seemed to be totally confined between the four villages. Fresh troops continued to arrive and were sent into the battle. The French 11th Division (Général Ricard) moved into the French battle line, facing Berg's Russians, and advanced. The terrain was very cut up, and the interval in which he formed his forces was so small, that he was obliged to concentrate his forces far more than was desirable. When a battalion was badly handled, rather than withdraw it, it was dispersed into skirmishers to allow a fresh battalion to move into its place. His attack became quite static with heavy losses on both sides, as it settled down into a bloody firefight.

A French battery posted on the hill between Rahna and Kaja was posted so that it could cover much of the battlefield. Its fire cause heavy allied casualties. A Russian battery was detached to take this battery under fire. It was placed next to the Gross-Görschen mill and covered by the Prussian Lithuanian Dragoon Regiment.

Ney moved into the front of the battle to better control the action. On both sides, the presence of these senior officers had a positive effect, but proved to have risks. Blücher had his horse killed under him and was wounded by a shot in the back. Yorck assumed command when he fell. Scharnhorst was mortally wounded. Ney, while leading an attack of his cavalry was wounded and his chief of staff, General Gouré was killed. All of the senior officers in Souham's 8th Division, save Souham himself were killed or wounded. The staff of Girard's 10th Division lost two generals badly wounded, and 75 percent of its regimental commanders were killed or wounded.

On the allied left wing, Horn's brigade advanced on Rahna. The two battalions of the Prussian 5th Combined Regiment[52] moved directly on the village, while the three battalions of the Prussian 6th Combined Regiment[53] turned its left. Oberstlieutenant von Steinmetz followed as a reserve. Horn put his three battalions[54] in the large intervals between the infantry and the cavalry of the left wing. The 2nd Combined Dragoon Regiment,[55] which had been sent to the right wing since the beginning of the battle, covered a battery posted in the area.[56]

The two battalions of the 5th Combined Infantry Regiment[57] charged and seized Rahna. Though under continual musketry, the regiment advanced through the village and up the hill behind it, throwing back two French battalions.

Oberst von Horn felt his forces were too weak to hold this position so close to the French lines and called for cavalry support from the second line. Steinmetz's cavalry (the West Prussian Uhlan Regiment, the 2nd Leib Hussar Regiment, the 1/,2/Silesian Cuirassier Regiment, two

squadrons of the 1st West Prussian Dragoon Regiment and the 2/Silesian Uhlan Regiment) advanced successively, attacking Souham's infantry.

In response Ney advanced his cavalry, placed himself at the head of the Baden Dragoons and counterattacked. The Baden Dragoons formed line to the right by squadron. The Silesian Uhlans only momentarily stopped this attack, when they pushed back the French 10th Hussar Regiment, which was attacking a force of Prussian skirmishers.[58] Then they were overwhelmed by the force of the Baden Dragoons' attack and fell back.

The Baden Dragoons struck the Prussian Guard Fusilier Battalion, formed in square. The Prussian square was broken and the Prussians fled behind a small woods to reorganize. The Baden Dragoons continued their charge and closed with a number of allied batteries, where they sabered several gunners. Finding themselves overextended, the Baden Dragoons withdrew. Ney, following this attack, had his horse killed underneath him.[59]

St. Priest

About the same time Ney's cavalry attacked (3:00 P.M.), Compan's 20th Division, formed in divisional square, advanced past Starsiedel. His heavy artillery drove back the Prussian cavalry. In response Winzingerode sent a 12pdr Russian battery and a 6pdr Prussian battery into position, where they covered the Prussian cavalry and took Compan's division under fire at a range of 800 paces. The French artillery was, in its turn, pushed out of its positions.[60]

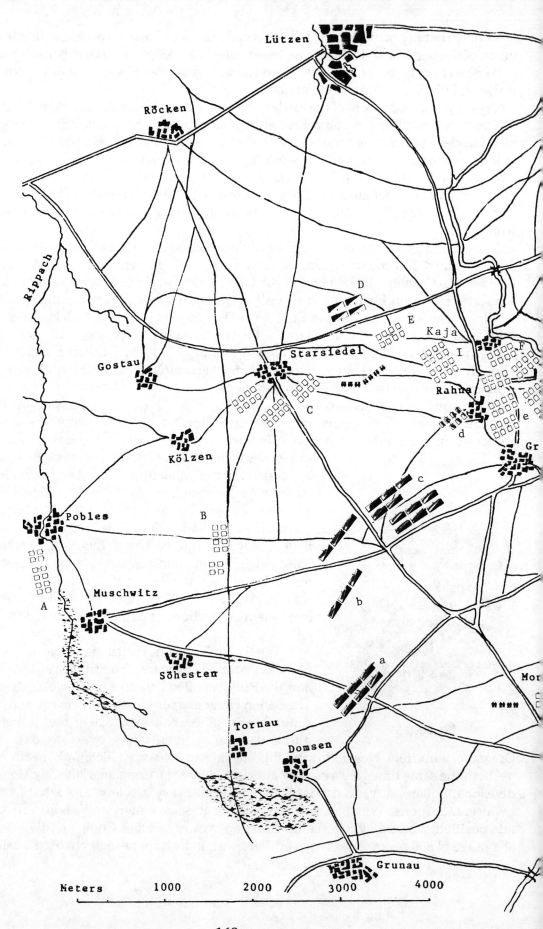

Lützen

Röcken

Rippach

Gostau

Kölzen

Starsiedel

Kaja

D

E

I

F

Rahna

e

d

Gr

c

C

B

Pobles

A

Muschwitz

b

Söhesten

a

Tornau

Domsen

Mor

Grunau

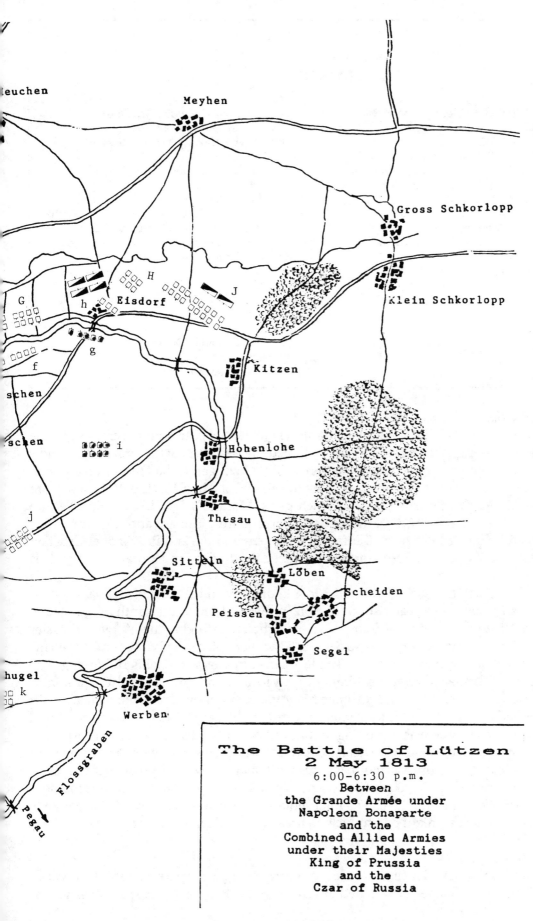

The Battle of Lützen
2 May 1813
6:00-6:30 p.m.
Between
the Grande Armée under
Napoleon Bonaparte
and the
Combined Allied Armies
under their Majesties
King of Prussia
and the
Czar of Russia

THE FRENCH IV CORPS

Around 3:00 P.M., the IV Corps was advancing slowly towards Pobles and the crossing of the Grünabach. It was facing Winzingerode, who occupied the east bank of the stream. Morand's 12th Division was stopped momentarily by batteries that Winzingerode had placed on the edge of a stream. This artillery force was reinforced by the arrival of a half 12pdr battery sent from Yorck's corps. Under the cover of sixteen French guns, Morand's 12th Division broke into columns, crossed the stream, and reformed itself into squares. The advanced guard of his division, formed by the 3rd Provisional Infantry Regiment and the 2nd Provisional Croatian Regiment,[61] led the advance. The French artillery rejoined the division and Morand resumed his advance.

At 5:30 P.M., Peyri's 15th Division was still 3 to 4 kilometers to the west of Grünabach, but Morand's 12th Division was already south of Kölzen. Before him, to the south of Starsiedel, Morand found Winzingerode's cavalry corps. On his right flank stood Gallizin's two cuirassier divisions, 10,000 cavalry not counting cossacks, and 73 artillery pieces. This force enveloped his 10,000 man division and began to attack it. The Russian cuirassiers struck his right wing. The 23rd Line Regiment, formed of veteran soldiers, quickly formed square and repulsed the attack. When the attacks faded away, Morand resumed his advance and moved onto the plateau south west of Starsiedel. He continued his movement towards Rahna and Kaja.

For Wittgenstein, the battle was beginning to turn unfavorably. His two Prussian corps had been heavily engaged all day and were nearly expended. Allied reserves were becoming very scarce. Berg had to be left before Marmont, where an offensive move was greatly feared. Only Eugene von Wurttemberg's 6,400 infantry and Tormassov's 10,800 infantry remained. Unfortunately for Wittgenstein, the Czar's intervention denied him easy use of Tormassov's forces. Wittgenstein needed night or a miracle to break the battle in his favor.[62]

THE RENEWED ALLIED ATTACK

Wittgenstein chose to strike. He sent an order to Wurttemberg to prepare his corps to advance to support Yorck and Blücher. The allied left, facing the French IV Corps, consisted of

Winzingerode's 6,700 cavalry, two divisions of cuirassiers, the Russian Guard cavalry and two horse batteries. The Armée de l'Elbe, north of the Flössgraben, was faced by nine squadrons, a cossack regiment and a horse battery hastily drawn from Blücher's, Yorck's and Berg's cavalry forces and placed under the command of General Alexeiev. Alexeiev was already operating in that area with a few squadrons and a horse battery. Wurttemberg's attack was to be a tactical envelopment formed by a frontal attack on Kaja coupled with a flank attack moving from Eisdorf, to the east of the Flössgraben, that would pass over the canal east of Kaja and strike Kaja in the rear. Schachafskoi's 3rd Division was to support Yorck and Blücher while Saint-Priest's division[63] was to move through Eisdorf. The plan was approved and put into execution.[64]

The allied left had been uncovered by the advance of the French VI Corps which was moving on Starsiedel. It would have been to the allied advantage to take the village before the VI Corps arrived. Before the VI Corps did do so, Berg's division, which had been ordered to take the village, had received an order to back track to its original positions. Only Winzingerode and his cavalry moved to Kölzen to extend the allied wing. Winzingerode moved his cavalry through Werben towards Tornau and then moved towards Starsiedel. The village was weakly held at this time, by the weak French infantry columns that had advanced out of Starsiedel and were thrown back by Dolffs' Prussian cavalry. Winzingerode positioned his cavalry to the left of Dolffs' cavalry about 2,000 paces from the Starsiedel and very near Rahna. Once here he began bombarding the French in Stariesdel with his horse artillery.[65]

Morand's 12th Division arrived in Kölzen and pushed Winzingerode's cavalry back from Rahna. Winzingerode's response to the French was solely to continue bombarding them with his horse guns. As Winzingerode's cavalry withdrew Prinz Wurttemberg personally led the 3rd Infantry Division (Schachafskoi's) to restore the situation between Rahna and Klein-Görschen.[66]

General St. Priest led the 4th Infantry Division towards Eisdorf to turn the French wing. A Prussian brigade from Hünerbein's force was "invited" to follow his advance. Schachafskoi led the 3rd Division forward to push back the French and lighten the pressure on Blücher. For this attack he deployed the Tchernigov, Mourmon and Revel Infantry Regiments to the right of Gross-Görschen. As he advanced the Prussians followed behind him. His thrust pushed the French out of Kaja for the last time.

St. Priest, a French emigre officer in Russian service, began his attack with his four battalions from the 4th Division, the 20th Jager Regiment and two batteries. He was to cross the canal at Eisdorf and take the village of Kaja from the rear. Two squadrons of the 1st Silesian Hussar Regiment, under the orders of Major Blücher, crossed the canal to cover the advance and chase out the French skirmishers covering the canal. They were followed by the Ataman Cossack Regiment, the Lithuanian Dragoon Regiment (Prussian unit) and a horse battery, and by the Russian dragoons attached to General Berg's division.[67]

As the Silesian Hussars crossed the canal they found themselves in a swampy pasture. Despite the difficulty of the terrain, they advanced against Marchand's 39th Division which showered them with musketry and cannister. However, when St.Priest saw the superiority of the French numbers and their movements threatening his flank he stopped short, moving the 20th Jagers into the village and placed the Volhynie and Krementsoug Infantry Regiments behind Eisdorf.

MARCHAND ACTS ON THE FRENCH LEFT

Marchand's division had remained inactive for most of the battle. About 5:30 P.M., it was stationary, south of Meuchen, with its artillery deployed. With the third loss of Kaja and the attack of Schachafskoi's division against the III Corps, Marchand, Ney's last fresh force, chose to attack.

Marchand positioned a battalion and two Hessian guns on a small hill to his left. Ten more guns were placed in battery at the foot of the hill. Marchand's division moved towards Klein-Görschen.[68] His attack was executed by successive brigades. Stockhorn's Baden brigade led the attack, moving on Klein-Görschen. Neufmayer's Hessian brigade supported Stockhorn's attack and deployed to his left. Neufmayer's Hessians marched in closed columns of companies.[69]

The Baden brigade moved against the Flössgraben and pushed back the allied skirmishers. The two Hessian regiments, on the left, moved against Klein-Görschen. As it deployed, the Hessian Leib-Garde Regiment's colonel was wounded by enemy fire, Despite this the regiment formed into square and continued advancing against Klein-Görschen. The Regiment du Corps moved in the second line to the left and the Fusiliers moved on the extreme left, formed in column and covering the whole advance. The force was covered by a screen of Hessian skirmishers and a redoubled artillery fire in support. The attack advanced at the "sturmschritte [assault pace]" to seize the bridge to Klein-Görschen. About 100 paces from the bridge, the regiment deployed into line to engage the allies holding the bridge. As it did so, it was threatened by allied cavalry on its flank and many of the young, inexperienced soldiers fled. Their regimental colonel had fallen wounded in the first seconds of the engagement, so Prinz Emil von Hessen personally rallied them.

The Fusilier Regiment and it supporting artillery had advanced successfully between Klein-Görschen and Kaja. The schützen and the flügel company of the 2nd Battalion were detached to push on to the Flössgraben. The 1st Battalion deployed its schützen in a skirmish line and advanced behind them in a "bataillonsmasse." The Leib-Garde Regiment, now reformed, advanced on their right. The regiment consisted solely of two companies because one had been detached with the schützen.

This attack drove into the village. The Hessians operated their regiments by divisions[70] operating behind lines of skirmishers and after more than an hour pushed the allies out of the village, capturing 150 Russian jagers, Prussian guardsmen, and freiwilliger jagers.[71]

The strength of the Hessian battalions was very low. The Meyer Company of the Fusilier Regiment was formed of veterans from the Russian campaign and numbered 3 officers, 5 musicians, 16 schützen and 48 fusiliers.[72]

The Regiment du Corps supported by their divisional artillery, pushed the Russians back towards Gross-Görschen. Marchand chose to deploy his artillery along the edge of the Flössgraben and bring the allied line between Kaja and Klein-Görschen under heavy fire. On his left, the first elements of the XI Corps were beginning to deploy.[73]

Maréchal Macdonald, commander of the XI Corps, had proposed to Eugène that he march on Kaja and assume a position behind the French army, but Eugène judged that it was essential to strike the allies in the flank and directed his march on Eisdorf.

The XI Corps marched with the I Cavalry Corps. The total force was 24,477 men, including 2,274 cavalry. The V Corps, with 18,380 men, remained en echelon before Leipzig. The XI Corps moved from Räpitz in divisional columns. Charpentier's 36th Division led, followed by the 31st Division (Fressinet), the I Cavalry Corps, and the 35th Division (Gérard). As they passed through Meyhen they easily pushed Alexeiev's cossacks out of the way and began to deploy to the east of Eisdorf when they contacted the leading elements of St. Priest's forces.

Eisdorf was attacked by Fressinet's 31st Division of the XI Corps, supported by the 36th and 35th Divisions of Charpentier and Gérard, who deployed before Kitzen in two lines. All of the corps artillery was positioned to cover the attack. Eugène retained the I Cavalry Corps and the 35th Division in reserve.

St. Priest and his Russians had reoccupied Eisdorf at the moment that Eugène occupied all the terrain before the village. Fressinet's division moved to attack the village just as the Russians began to advance out of it.

The renewed French assault, led by Fressinet (31st) and Charpentier's (36th) divisions of Macdonald's XI Corps, drove the Russian 20th Jagers out of Eisdorf. Wurttemberg sent all possible reinforcements to stop this attack. St. Priest sent the Volhynie Regiment into the right of Eisdorf, while Pischnitzki's brigade moved into its left. The French assault recoiled momentarily. Colonel Baikof's Light Battery #27 arrived to provide much needed support and was positioned on the Flössgraben to the right of Eisdorf. However, the French counterbattery fire soon killed so many of his gunners that he was forced to withdraw. Despite the French resistance, the allied attack still drove the French back and allowed the Russians to reoccupy the village. The French renewed their attack again and drove the 20th Jagers out again.[74] St. Priest reformed the Volhynie and Krementsoug Infantry Regiments and sent them once again into the fray with the support of a Prussian horse battery and the 20th Jager Regiment, which struck from the left.[75]

The French assault obliged the Russians to abandon the village, but they were quickly rallied by the arrival of General Konovnitzin, commanding three grenadier regiments of the 2nd Grenadier Division, and 50 cannons from the artillery reserve.[76]

The Russians renewed their assault on the village, recapturing it briefly, only to be driven out by Charpentier's 36th Division. Konovnitzin had been wounded and St. Priest chose to contain the French attack with musketry. With the French recapture of Eisdorf, night fell. Only the movement of the 31st Division, under Fressinet, to Kitzen continued. This maneuver forced Wurttemberg to withdraw back towards the Monarchenhügel. Eugène retained the 35th Division (Gérard) and the I Cavalry Corps as a reserve without attempting to envelop the allies from the east or force an exit from Eisdorf.[77]

THE IMPERIAL GUARD ADVANCES

As Winzingerode's attac drove the French back from Starsiedel, Napoleon saw that the allies had taken control of the ridge that dominated the entire battlefield, and that they were about to take his last position on the left. He also knew that the IV Corps was closing on Starsiedel and that Eugène was closing on the field. The allied pressure on his center was strong and if his line could be broken, the battle would be lost.

NAPOLEON SURVEYS THE BATTLEFIELD

Napoleon ordered Drouot to pull the 58 guns of the Imperial Guard artillery forward and join them with those of the III Corps (70 guns) and those of the VI Corps, forming a battery of 198 guns on the crest between Starsiedel and Kaja so that their fire would converge on the quadrangle between the four villages.

Napoleon then ordered Maréchal Mortier to lead forward the 16 battalions of Young Guard (9,804 men) posted near Kaja. The Young Guard was organized into four columns.[78] These battalions were organized into attack columns (colonne d'attaque), supported by six battalions of the Old Guard formed in four squares, and by the two divisions of Imperial Guard cavalry (3,335 men) formed in line.[79]

When the Young Guard began its assault, the order to advance was given by Maréchal Mortier. His order was greeted by the roar of a thousand voices shouting "Vive l'Empereur!" They then marched on Rahna and Gross Görschen as irresistible as the ocean, sweeping everything before them. One column broke away from the left and advanced on Klein Görschen.

The Young Guard assault coincided with the arrival of Konovnitzin's grenadiers at St. Priest's position. Bonnet's 21st Division, VI Corps, moved into the line near Starsiedel and thrust forward when Marmont saw that Kaja was about to be lost by Ney. He was ordered to conform with the movement of the Young Guard. Marmont was also ordered to advance his entire corps towards Rahna and to maintain liaison with the IV Corps. Morand's 12th Division of the IV Corps moved to their right, crossing the stream at Pobles to take up a position on the right wing.

At 6:30 P.M., Ney drove the III Corps forward in one further assault. Dumoustier's 1st Young Guard Division and Bonnet's 21st Division advanced with him. On the right, the VI Corps moved out of Starsiedel, with Compan's 20th Division leading. Friederich's 22nd Division was in echelon to the left rear and was in contact to its left with Bonnet's 21st Division. The allies concentrated 150 artillery pieces on the attack, but did not break it.[80] Blücher's and Yorck's corps were pushed back.

The Russians responded by dispatching Prinz Gallizin, with the Guard Light Cavalry Division and the 2nd Cuirassier Division, which moved from the left towards Grünabach. Prince Eugene of Württemberg's 2nd Corps again moved to support Blücher. His force consisted of the 3rd Division[81] and the 4th Infantry Division.[82] He was supported by the fire of the 3rd and 4th Artillery Brigades, which deployed at a gallop.[83]

Despite the Russian support, Oberst von Horn was not strong enough to maintain his positions on the hill before Rahna and was reduced to defending only the village. The French Young Guard recaptured Rahna. The French artillery, on the heights between Kaja and Starsiedel, began to rake the allied forces with heavy fire. This was the focal point of the main French attack.

The allies had already engaged their last reserve, except for the Russian Guard Corps. Czar Alexander ordered his Guard to advance. In the interval between Gross-Görschen and Eisdorf, there was already a reinforced infantry brigade and several grenadier regiments. This was now reinforced by the arrival of 38 squadrons of cuirassiers and 13 squadrons of light cavalry moving to the left wing. The cavalry took up positions about 800 paces behind General Pischnitzki's brigade of the 4th Division. The allied artillery increased its fire and the 14 battalions of Russian Guard advanced on the right, up to the heights of Gross-Görschen. It was 7:00 P.M., the Russian Guard Hussar Regiment, which had been engaged elsewhere, joined the infantry attack at this point.

At the same time, the French VI Corps attacked Rahna with a massive infantry attack under heavy artillery cover. Marchand's division crossed the canal at the bridge of Klein-Görschen and seized much of it, as the allied center was engaged by the Young Guard. The allied garrison of Klein-Görschen abandoned their posts and withdrew to Gross-Görschen. Once beyond the village, they rallied behind the Russian Guard.

At this time, the French line extended from Kitzen to Eisdorf, Klein-Görschen, Rahna, Starsiedel and Kölzen to Pobles. Fressinet's 31st Division had crossed the canal and was on the left bank between Eisdorf and Kitzen.

As night fell, the battlefield was lit by the fires of five burning villages. The Russians and Prussians rallied behind Gross-Görschen. The Silesian Cuirassier Regiment, the 2nd Combined Dragoon Regiment, the Lithuanian and Neumark Dragoons, and the Combined Silesian Hussar Regiment found themselves on the right wing, while the rest of the Prussian cavalry was on the left.

Though twilight was quite advanced, a sudden French attack struck between Starsiedel and Rahna, at the advanced posts of Steinmetz's brigade. Steinmetz was on a small hill, which favored the French as it hid the attack from its defenders. The Prussian infantry had bivouacked for the night, the 2nd Leib Hussar Regiment had dismounted and begun to settle down. With the first cannon shots the Prussians ran to their arms and pushed back the French with musketry.

Shortly after, Dolffs' nine Prussian squadrons advanced to disquiet the French. Towards the end of the day, the Prussians had drawn some of their cavalry together in an effort to move it against the French right flank. Dolffs pulled together a force consisting of three squadrons of the Garde du Corps, the Garde-Volontair-Kosacken squadron, and a squadron of the East Prussian Cuirassier Regiment. They were followed by the four squadrons of the Brandenburg Cuirassier Regiment formed by squadrons behind the right wing. They moved in two lines to attack the French, but became disoriented in the dark and lost their direction. They were further disordered by the narrow road they used.

Their situation was made worse by the capture of a drunken Prussian cuirassier from the Brandenburg cuirassiers who betrayed the pending attack to the French. This allowed the French to prepare a reception for the Prussians. They advanced several battalions forward from their line. The infantry formed square and remained in that formation through the night, awaiting the allied cavalry.

The allied cavalry advanced to the attack around midnight. They encountered the French 2/,3/32nd Légère Regiment (Compan's 20th Division) but were so disorganized that they were quickly driven back by cannister and musketry.[84]

The allies settled in to their bivouacs behind the canal, with the exception of Steinmetz's brigade, Winzingerode's cavalry, and the 16 Prussian squadrons that remained on the battlefield. The Russians admit to having lost about 2,000 to 3,000 men and the Prussians admit losing 8,000 to 8,500, including the Prince Hessen-Homburg. No doubt these figures are considerably lower than their actual losses. General Scharnhorst had been grievously wounded and would shortly die of his wounds. Few prisoners were taken. The allies had captured five guns and left two dismounted on the battlefield.

The French admit losing between 20,000 and 22,000 men hors de combat. Ney evaluated the French losses at 19,655 men, 2,757 dead and 16,898 wounded. The Young Guard lost 1,069 men and the Old Guard lost 55. The Guard Cavalry lost only 54.[85] Général de brigade Gouré, chief of staff to III Corps, was dead and Generals Girard, Brenier, Guillot, Chemineau, and five others were wounded.[86] A total of 55 superior officers were killed or wounded in the III Corps alone. During the battle the French had expended a tremendous volume of artillery. The munition consumption during the battle by corps was:

III Corps	12,150 rounds
IV Corps	110
VI Corps	3,630
XI Corps	2,600
I Cavalry Corps	70
Marchand's Division	5,000
Imperial Guard	5,813
Total	29,373

The Guard artillery had only been on the field from 6:30 to 8:30. During that time each gun fired an average of 50 rounds per hour or nearly one round per minute. Over 1,000,000 infantry cartridges were fired.

THE ALLIES WITHDRAW

The allied situation on the battlefield was impossible. They had not been broken, but their fresh troops consisted of only the Russian Guard and the 1st Grenadier Division, less than 6,400 men. If Miloradovich was able to bring his forces in during the night, that would only provide another 6,000 infantry. In view of the French positions on their flanks and their numerical superiority over the allies, Wittgenstein wisely chose to withdraw. Yorck, with part of Winzingerode's corps and Berg's division moved down the road from Fröburg towards Prödel and Ostrau. Blücher's army moved on Borna and the rest of the allies moved on Altenburg. Miloradovich, who had spent the day with his corps in Zeitz, received the order at 2:00 A.M., to join the army by the road to Prödel and act as a rear guard in conjunction with Wurttemberg's infantry division.

To the east, faced by Eugène's main force, Kleist abandoned Leipzig to the French and withdrew to Wurzen. When word of this reached the allies, so too did the news that the Russian artillery had expended its entire supply of shot and that it would not be replenished until the next day. There had been no choice but to retreat.

When day broke, only the allied cavalry remained on the battlefield. The villages were deserted save for a few groups of infantry near Kaja and a line of cavalry between Eisdorf and Klein-Görschen. At 8:00 A.M., a French column moved on Pegau, along the right bank of the Flössgraben canal. It was some of Eugène's forces. With that the allied cavalry moved out and passed over the Elster at Prödel.

Around noon Napoleon resumed his advance. MacDonald's XI Corps became the advanced guard and followed the Russian army through Borna, Colditz, Waldheim, Nossen and Wilsdurf. The V Corps moved on Zwenkau and then counter marched on Mölbis, Wurzen, Oschatz and Meissen. The IV Corps crossed the Elster at Prödel and took the route to Fröburg, Rochlitz and Mitweyda towards Dresden. The XII Corps moved through Zeitz, Altenburg and Penig. The III Corps moved towards Leipzig and after a few days rest moved through Eilenburg to Torgau to break the allied blockade of the fortress.

THE RESULTS OF LÜTZEN

The strategic maneuver which created the battle at Lützen, was begun on 17 April and is an incomparable example of Napoleon's ability to control the tactical situation with strategic maneuvers. He had positioned his forces so as to be able to strike at and crush the allied armies. The encirclements failed, not because of his planning, but because of events beyond his control. The battle began at noon and his forces were unable to arrive on the battlefield, deploy, and begin their attacks before the fall of night.

The French battle plan was one of improvisation based on those carefully laid grand tactical plans. The formation of Napoleon's advancing armies put him in the situation where he was able to evaluate the situation and react accordingly. He had, as a pinning force, Ney (III Corps) with 45,000 and Marmont (VI Corps) with another 20,000 men to hold the allies in position while he maneuvered his turning forces against the allied flanks and rear.[87]

The allies had two lines of retreat. The first was through Dresden and the second was through Berlin. Napoleon's turning forces were designed to cut those lines, but the French were too weak in cavalry to do it effectively.

The "masse de rupture" Napoleon used in the battle consisted of the 5,000 Old Guard, the 11,000 Young Guard, and the 4,000 Guard cavalry. In addition, there was the Guard artillery, but yet another 100 reserve guns had not yet joined him and this significant force was sorely missed. This massive, veteran force was the reserve that the allies did not have when the critical moment came.

Napoleon cannot be criticized for his conduct of the battle, nor for his plan. In contrast, Ney's actions can be severely and justly criticized. He had neglected to execute the ordered reconnaissances. His five divisions were not united, when the allies attacked. His divisional generals are not free of blame either. They failed to post adequate pickets, to perform adequate reconnaissance, and allowed themselves to be surprised by the enemy.

In addition, Bertrand had not marched when he heard the sound of the guns, but chose to remain immobile for three hours at Taucha. If he had arrived three hours earlier the battle would have been quite different. And Marmont, once he had arrived, did not show himself to be very aggressive. Perhaps Napoleon's personal intervention could have been far more decisive for if he had prevented the many faults of his subordinates, it is highly probable that Lützen would have been a solid French victory. However, this criticism is one of hindsight.

Despite the failings of Napoleon's generals, the new levies had fought superbly. Ney's corps had suffered the brunt of the attack for hours before the arrival of the rest of the Grande Armée. Eugéne wrote, "Each soldier was a hero; everyone did their duty; not a single man fled his ranks and it was only with difficulty that the wounded could find someone to accompany them out of danger. Ney stated that Napoleon had witnessed the enthusiasm of the troops and noted with pleasure their noble élan. Napoleon reputedly stated, "Valor can supplant experience, here is the unrealizable wish." On the other side of the battlefield, however, the Prussian and Russian officers were humiliated and felt they were dishonored because they were "overwhelmed by infants." Even the often maligned Marine Infantry were found to "march with the firm pace in the path of their predecessors."[88]

On the allied side, the errors were more grievous, as always are the errors of the loser. Despite their overwhelming cavalry superiority, they allowed the slow moving French infantry columns to maneuver against their flanks and rear. In contrast to 1805, when Napoleon used masses of cavalry to screen his maneuver against Ulm, in 1813 he had no screen whatsoever to hide his advancing columns, yet the allies either totally missed his advance or allowed themselves to be positioned where they could be surrounded.

As the latter is not at all likely, this indicates either a total break down in their ability to use their reconnaissance capabilities or an incredible job of mismanagement of that asset.

Once on the battle field the allies showed little indication of having a well developed tactical plan. Their planning beyond the strategic setting of the battle appears to have been non-existent. Indeed, their actions were little more than frontal assaults with no effort to use their initial superiority of numbers or cavalry superiority in any sort of enveloping action against Ney's corps. Much of this can be attributed to a failure to have adequately reconnoitered the battlefield and determined exactly what they were facing.

In addition to the failure of the allies to reconnoiter the battlefield, their failure to develop a tactical battle plan is almost inexcusable. Their initial maneuvers were solely a march against Kaja, Gross-, and Klein-Görschen. Though they eventually extended the wings of their army to face the approach of the various French corps as they marched onto the battlefield, the level of subtlety of their tactics is best compared to that of a sledge hammer. A sledge hammer that Ney deftly parried time after time, until Napoleon was able to bring overwhelming forces to bear and break the allied position.

The allied actions indicate that they had once again left the battle to divisional level command and lower rather than being guided by an army level tactician. Much of this is probably due to the presence of both the Czar and the King of Prussia. Both men, most notably the Czar, exerted a military influence far beyond their military expertise. It is probable that the inadequate military understanding of the Czar and the King, coupled with the advice of jealous courtiers, so muddled the tactical situation, that if there was an army tactical command structure, it was unable to operate in any mode of army level attack other than the frontal assault. There is enough evidence of this on the strategic level, i.e. Wittgenstein's resignation as allied military commander, to justifiably assume that it existed on the tactical level.

[1] Tournes, Campagne de Printemps, pg 313

[2] Plotho, Krieg in Deutschland, Vol I, pg 108.

[3] Plotho, Krieg in Deutschland, Vol I, pg 108.

[4] Plotho, Krieg in Deutschland, Vol I, pg 109.

[5] Plotho, Krieg in Deutschland, Vol I, pg 106

[6] Plotho, Krieg in Deutschland, Vol I, pg 105 & 108.

[7] Sporschil, Grosse Chronik, Vol I, pg 151.

[8] Lukov commanded the Perm, Sieversk, Kalouga, and Mohilev Infantry Regiments, plus the Grand Duchess Catherine Infantry Battalion.

[9] Helfreich commanded the Tenguinsk and Estonia Infantry Regiments and Russian Light Battery #27.

[10] This is how Plotho presents this formation. Holleben indicates that this formation was no longer the 1st Combined Regiment, but the 1/.2/,Fus/1st East Prussian Infantry Regiment.

[11] Detached to Hünerbein.

[12] A Prussian column formed on the middle means that the column formed with the 4th and 5th zügen in the front as the first line, followed by the 3rd and 6th zügen in the second line, the 2nd and 7th zügen formed the third line, and the 1st and 8th zügen formed the rear or fourth line. By forming on the middle, three zügen moved on each wing of the line and the greatest distance moved was only three zügen lengths. If the column was formed on the right or left two wing zügen, the one zug would have to move 6 zügen lengths, causing the formation change to take twice as long as if it were formed on the center zügen. von der Oelsnitz, Ersten Infanterie, pg 678.

[13] Both the Garde du Corps and the Guard Light Cavalry Regiment had a normal establishment of four squadrons. However, because of "popular subscription" to the war squadrons known as "freiwilliger jägers" were raised. These were wealthy young men who wished to "liberate the fatherland." The Garde du Corps had one such freiwilliger jäger squadron and the Guard Light Cavalry Regiment had two.

[14] Zweguintov, L'Armée Russie, pg 438.

[15] Sporschil, Grosse Chronik, Vol I, pg 148–150.

[16] Preussen Generalstab, Vol I, pg 38

[17] von Conrady, Sechsten Infanterie, pg 168 & Prussian General Staff, Exerzir Regelment für die infanterie, Plan #2, figure 3.

[18] Camon, Guerre Napoléonienne, Vol IV, pg 380.

[19] Grossen General, Plane der Schlachten, pg 8.

[20] von Conrady, Sechsten Infanterie, pg 164.

[21] Grossen General, Plane der Schlachten, pg 9.

[22] von der Oelsnitz, Ersten Infanterie, pg 678.

[23] Rehtwisch, Grossgörschen 2 May 1813, ppg 81.

[24] von Conrady, Sechsten Infanterie, pg 164.

[25] Tournes, Campagne de Printemps, pg 330, & Lewinski & Brauchitsch, Grenadier, pg 76.

[26] Fabry, Prince de Wurttemberg, pg 47.

[27] Weil, Campagne de 1813, La Cavalerie, pg 37.

28 Camon, Guerre Napoléonienne, Vol IV, pg 381.

29 The pas accéléré is a marching pace of 250 paces per minute and is, in essence, a cadenced run.

30 de Marmont, Memoires, pg 18.

31 Ternaux–Compans, General Compans, pg 253.

32 de Marmont, Memoires, pg 22.

33 de Marmont, Memoires, pg 23, & Thiry, Lutzen et Bautzen, pg 178.

34 de Marmont, Memoires, pg 23–24.

35 Tournes, Campagne de Printemps, pg 332, & Sporschil, Grosse Chronik, Vol I, pg 156.

36 Wagner, Plans de Combat, Vol I, pg 9.

37 Lewinski & Brauchitsch, Grenadier, pg 76.

38 von der Oelsnitz, Ersten Infanterie , pg 680.

39 Rehtwisch, Grossgörschen 2 May 1813, pg 84.

40 Tournes, Campagne de Printemps 1813, pg 334.

41 Rehtwisch, Grossgörschen 2 May 1813, pg 86.

42 Tournes, Campagne de Printemps 1813, pg 335.

43 Tindal's brigade consisted of the 1/,2/1st, 1/,2/2nd, and 1/,2/6th Voltigeur Regiments.

44 Lanusse's brigade consiste of 1/,2/1st and 1/,2/2nd Tirailleur Regiments.

45 Berthezène's brigade consisted of the 1/,2/6th and 1/,2/7th Tirailleur Regiments.

46 Rehtwisch, Grossgörschen 2 May 1813, pg 94.

47 Camon, Guerre Napoléonienne, Vol IV, pg 384.

48 Chandler, The Campaigns of Napoleon, pg 884.

49 Sporschil, Die Grosse Chronik, Vol I, pg 159.

50 von Conrady, Sechsten Infanterie , pg 164.

51 Zweguintov, L'Armée Russie, pg 438.

52 The Prussian 5th Combined Infantry Regiment was formed from the 2/, Fus/2nd West Prussian Infantry Regiment and the 1/1st West Prussian Infantry Regiment. The latter appears to have been detached at this time.

53 The Prussian 6th Combined Infantry Regiment consisted of the 2/1st Silesian Infantry Regiment and 2/,Fus/2nd Silesian Infantry Regiment.

54 1/,2/,Fus/Colberg Infantry Regiment.

55 The 2nd Combined Dragoon Regiment was formed with the 1/,3/1st West Prussian Dragoon Regiment and 1/,3/Brandenburg Dragoon Regiment.

56 Grossen General, Plane der Schlachten, pg 12.

57 1/, Fus/2nd West Prussian Infantry Regiment.

58 Weil, Campagne de 1813, La Cavalerie , pg 38.

59 Sauzey, Contingent Badois, pg 78.

60 Grossen General, Plane der Schlachten, pg 13.

61 Pitot, 83e Regiment d'Infanterie, pg 128.

62 Chandler, The Campaigns of Napoleon, pg 886.

63 According to Plotho, St. Priest appears to have been commanding portions of both the 3rd and 4th Infantry Divisions. Eugene of Wurttemberg indicates in his memoirs that during the advance on Eisdorf St. Priest commanded the "Krementsoug and Volhynie Infantry Regiments, the 20th Jager Regiment, and two artillery batteries drawn from different corps." Based on Holleben, St. Priest was probably the commander of the 4th Division and Pischnitzky was a brigade commander. However, St. Priest seemed to receive many special assignments leaving Pischnitzky as acting divisional commander.

64 Fabry, Prince du Wurtemberg, pg 49.

65 Fabry, Prince de Wurtemberg, pg 47.

66 Fabry, Prince de Wurtemberg, pg 48.

67 Grossen General, Plane der Schlachten, pg 14, & Weil, Campagne de 1813, La Cavalerie , pg 38.

68 Prussian General Staff, Plans de Combates, pg 16.

69 Bigge, Infanterie Kaiser Wilhelm, pg 150.

70 In this period there were two types of division. There is the Division which is a force of many regiments and the division which is two companies or pelotons of infantry. In this instance, the "division" referred to is two companies of infantry.

71 Sauzey, Soldats de Hesse et Nassau, pg 124.

72 Bigge, Infanterie Kaiser Wilhelm, pg 150.

73 Tournes, Campagne de Printemps, pg 347.

[74] Zweguintov, L'Armée Russie, pg 439.

[75] Fabry, Prince de Wurttemberg, pg 50.

[76] Plotho, Krieg in Deutschland, Vol I, pg 116.

[77] Tournes, Campagne de Printemps, pg 352.

[78] Rehtwisch, Grossgörschen 2 May 1813, pg 115.

[79] Lachouque, The Anatomy of Glory, pg 293.

[80] Ternaux–Compans, General Compans, pg 251.

[81] This was a weak provisional infantry force, probably the remains of the Revel Infantry Regiment, the Mourmon and Tchernigov Infantry and the 20th and 21st Jagers.

[82] Tobolsk, Volhynie, and Krementsoug Infantry Regiments and the 4th and 34th Jagers.

[83] Fabry, Prince de Wurttemberg, pg 44.

[84] Tournes, Campagne de Printemps, pg 356, & Grossen Generalstab, Plane der Schlachten, pg 18, & Wagner, Plans de Combat, pg 16.

[85] Lachouque, The Anatomy of Glory, pg 294.

[86] Plotho, Krieg in Deutschland, Vol I, pg 119.

[87] Camon, Guerre Napoléonienne, Vol IV, pg 377.

[88] Rousset, Grande Armée de 1813, pgs 83–5.

The French Advance Continues XI

BÜLOW AT HALLE

During the battle at Lützen, Bülow had advanced his forces against Halle and attacked it with 6,000 to 7,000 men. This force consisted of three battalions of the 3rd East Prussian Infantry Regiment, the East Prussian Grenadier Battalion, a company of East Prussian Jägers, two companies of fusiliers from the Fus/3rd East Prussian Infantry Regiment, four squadrons the Königin Dragoon Regiment, two squadrons of the 2nd West Prussian Dragoon Regiment, and three squadrons of the 1st Leib-Hussar Regiment.[1]

Halle was only weakly held by three battalions of the 135th Line Regiment, a Bataillon de Marche[2] and and battery of six guns. The French had barricaded only the Galgen gate and defended it with three cannons and a howitzer. The Prussian assault came in two columns. On the Prussian right wing were the jäger and two fusilier companies supported by three hussar squadrons and a half foot battery. This force extended from the Saal to the heights on the right. On these heights were the three battalions of the 3rd East Prussian Infantry Regiment, which were formed on the middle in column. They were supported by four guns and two squadrons of the 2nd West Prussian Dragoon Regiment as they advanced against the Galgen Gate. The 3/3rd East Prussian Infantry Regiment led the attack, supported by the other two battalions. The grenadier battalion stood to the rear as a reserve with four squadrons of the Königin Dragoon Regiment and a half horse battery.

French skirmishers peppered the attacking columns with fire, driving the Prussian right hand column back into the suburbs. However, the column of the 3/3rd East Prussian Infantry Regiment, supported by the two squadrons of West Prussian dragoons, struck the gate, carrying it and capturing two cannons and a howitzer. They drove into the city and encountered the two other battalions of the 135th Infantry Regiment. Aided by a local citizen, who opened another gate, and the timely arrival of the grenadier battalion, the French position was compromised and they were pushed out of the city.[3]

Bülow had easily defeated this small force and drove it back to the shelter of Durutte's 32nd Division at Mersberg. Though a minor success, it was far outweighed by the French success at Lützen and Bülow was obliged to withdraw and cover the approaches to Berlin.[4]

THE ALLIED WITHDRAWAL AFTER THE BATTLE OF LÜTZEN

When the dust of the battle settled, the allied commanders found that their only hope lay in an immediate retreat across the Elbe. The allies withdrew towards the Elbe in two principal columns. The Corps of General Yorck, the Brandenburg and Lower Silesian Brigades and the heavy artillery formed one column. Their advanced guard consisted of two squadrons of the Brandenburg Hussars and the Colberg Infantry Regiment. It passed through Pegau and Prödel, crossing the bridge by Ostrau and moved east until they reached Greifenhain, where they ceased their day's march. The Russian troops, consisting of the Reserve Corps and the corps of Berg and Winzingerode, advanced parallel to the Prussians and stopped in Frohburg.

The second column, that of General Blücher, consisting of the Upper Silesian Brigade and part of the reserve cavalry, moved through Droschwitz, where it crossed the Elster. His forces moved towards Borna, where they bivouacked for the night. Colonel Dolffs with ten squadrons formed his rear guard and the brigade of Oberstlieutenant Katzler marched as the advanced guard of

1st LeibHussar Regiment in Action at Halle
Knötel

this column.[5] The Guard Light Cavalry Regiment, which had been in Leipzig during the fight at Lützen, had withdrawn before the advancing French cavalry and moved into Borna.[6]

Once in Borna, it positioned itself to watch the road to Leipzig. General Bülow's Corps, which had defended Berlin, moved towards Roslau. Kleist and his corps, moved through Wurzen to the Elbe at Mühlberg, where the allies had a pontoon bridge. Kleist's forces consisted of the Russian troops under Generalmajor Roth, and the Prussian troops under Oberstlieutenant Zielinsky. Roth's command contained the Illowaisky #4, Radinov #2 and Selvanov #2 Cossack Regiments, the 23rd, 24th, 25th, and 26th Jager Regiments under General Vlastov, the Grodno Hussar Regiment, Position Battery #21, and Horse Battery #23. Zielinsky commanded the 1/, 2/Leib Infantry Regiment, the 1/1st West Prussian Infantry Regiment, Fus/2nd East Prussian Infantry Regiment, two companies of East Prussian Jägers, a horse battery, and four squadrons of the Prussian 3rd Combined Hussar Regiment. The command totaled about 15,000 men.[7]

The rearguard of the army was formed by General Winzingerode's corps. Under him, General Eugene von Wurttemberg commanded the infantry and Generallieutenant Korff commanded the light forces. As the French followed the Russian rearguard the day after the battle, the Russians took position between Luckau and Frohburg, where they began the first of many holding actions.

Three other detachments were made under the commands of General Lissanevitch, Jusefovich, and Emmanuel. The latter moved from Zwickau to Tharandt.

At 7:00 A. M. , Czar Alexander left Grotzsch and moved to Frohburg. The King of Prussia and the Crown Prince moved to Altenburg with the headquarters of General Wittgenstein.

The march continued on 4 May, with the Prussian right column moving to Colditz and the Russian column on their left moving to Rochlitz. The Prussian corps broke camp at Gräfenhain at daybreak and moved towards Frauenthal. The advanced guard, under Oberst Jürgass, consisted of the reserve cavalry, the horse artillery, and two squadrons of the Brandenburg Hussar Regiment. They were followed by the Brandenburg Brigade. Yorck's Corps, consisting of the brigade of Oberst Horn, the cavalry, and horse artillery, formed the rearguard.

That evening, in camp at Colditz, a converged battalion was formed from the fusiliers of the Prussian 5th and 6th Combined Infantry Regiments, which was posted in the suburb of the city. The bridge was guarded by a battalion of schützen, formed of the volunteer jägers of the Colberg Infantry Regiment and two guns. The Upper Silesian brigade of General Ziethen took quarters in Colditz and both Blücher and Yorck established their headquarters in Colditz as well.[8]

The Russian forces of the left wing passed through Rochlitz and moved to the right bank of the Mulde, around the village of Etzdorf. Miloradovich's rearguard was in Rochlitz. A detachment of Korff's light cavalry remained in Geithain, on the road to Brone. Wittgenstein established his headquarters in Rochlitz, while the two monarchs established their headquarters in Dresden.

On 5 May, the Prussians moved to Dölben and the Russians to Nossen. By 9 May, the entire main army stood on the right bank of the Elbe, with Blücher's headquarters in Brochkwitz and Wittgenstein's in Radeberg.

THE MAIN FRENCH ARMY

On 2 May Napoleon ordered Lauriston to withdraw his single division from Leipzig and prepare to pursue the retreating allies, with Latour-Maubourg's cavalry corps in support. As Lauriston withdrew, Kleist sent some cossacks into the city to reoccupy it, before he, too, was ordered to withdraw.

By 3:00 A. M. , Napoleon was certain that the allies were retreating and issued the orders for the pursuit. Ney's corps, shattered by the battle, was to remain in Lützen, to reorganize and recover from its struggles. The remainder of the army moved through Zwenkau, Pegau, Predel, and Ostrau, as they crossed the Elster.[9]

Except for the minor skirmish between Eugène and Miloradovich's rearguard, between Luckau and Frohburg, the French met no opposition. However, their pursuit was almost entirely an infantry pursuit, and the infantry was already exhausted from its exertions. Little progress was made on 3 May.

Macdonald's XI Corps and the 1st Cavalry Corps reached Podelwitz, five miles from Pegau. Lauriston was on his left in Peres. Marmont was in Löbnitz, to Macdonald's rear. Bertrand found the bridge at Predel had been destroyed, skirmished with Miloradovich, and had only reached Ostrau by nightfall. Napoleon's headquarters and the Guard were in Pegau. Oudinot, who had not been able to reach the battlefield, was spread between Jena and Naumburg.

The main allied army was in two masses between Borna and Frohburg. Napoleon was uncertain of the true direction of their retreat, until more information could be gleaned. Once he had a strong feel for their line of retreat, he chose to advance on Dresden and cut off their tail of stragglers and any convoys he could catch.

Napoleon also chose to organize an auxiliary army under the command of Ney. It was focused on Ney's exhausted III Corps, to which he joined the VII Corps (consisting only of Durutte's division in Mersburg and destined to contain the Saxons in Torgau), Victor's forming II Corps, the 2nd Cavalry Corps under Sébastiani and Puthod's 17th Division of the V Corps. Puthod had been released from his positions on the lower Elbe because Vandamme's command was moving below Magdeburg and would fill Puthod's vacated positions.[10]

Spandau
BERLIN
KUSTRIN
Potsdam
Frankfurt
Cottbus
Hoyerswerda
Wessig
Kamenz
Königswartha
Weis
Grossenhayn
Bautzen
DRESDEN
Bischofswerda
Neustadt
Löbau
Elbe R.
AUSTRIA
PRAGUE

**EASTERN SAXON THEATRE OF OPERATIONS
BETWEEN 3 MAY AND 6 JUNE 1813**

POSEN

Bunzlau

Lowenberg

auben

Jauer

Lann

Streigau

Schweidnitz

BRESLAU

Strehlen

Nimptsch

Reichenbach

30   60   90   120 Miles

Ney was directed to take this newly forming army and relieve the two besieged cities of Torgau and Wittenberg, as soon as Sébastiani joined him. This force would consist of about 60,000 infantry, (including the Saxons in Torgau), 4,000 cavalry, and 129 guns. Napoleon's main army consisted of 120,000 infantry, 11, 500 cavalry and 386 guns. Napoleon felt that Ney's advance on Torgau would oblige the allies to abandon their anticipated defense of the Elbe River line at Dresden.

By 4 May, the French armies had advanced such that the French left, V Corps, was in Stockheim, facing Wurzen. It had moved to the left in response to word that a strong Prussian column was marching on Mühlberg. In fact, it was only Kleist's column. Napoleon wanted Lauriston to move to the left, so as to be able to support Ney's march on Torgau if necessary.

The center, consisting of the 1st Cavalry Corps and XI Corps (acting as an advanced guard under Eugène), the VI Corps, Imperial Guard and Imperial headquarters, was in Flössberg and Borna. The right, consisted of the IV Corps and XII Corps, which were in Frohburg and Naumberg respectively. None of these French columns encountered the allies during their advance.

During 5 May, Lauriston continued to move in support of Ney, while the right and center moved against Dresden. As Eugène passed out of the Colditz forest, at about 11:00 am, he encountered Steinmetz's brigade, which was posted so as to defend the passage of the Mulde River.[11]

The Skirmish at Mulde Or The Battle of Colditz

Upon learning that the French were advancing after them, Oberstlieutenant von Steinmetz was detached with his 1st Brigade, Yorck's Corps, and sent to Dölben, which was the passage over the Mulde River by Colditz. When he got there he found that Miloradovich's rearguard was crossing the Mulde at Rochlitz at a leisurely rate.

The 1st East Prussian Infantry Regiment and the fusilier battalion of the Leib-Infantry Regiment positioned themselves to act as the rearguard, and hold Colditz until the main allied column had cleared the village. When the main column had withdrawn over the Mulde at 7:00 A. M., the rearguard cavalry burned the bridge. The 1/Colberg Infantry Regiment stood to the right of the village, and the 2/Colberg stood to the left of the village with the Colberg's fusilier battalion and that of the Leib Regiment behind it. The Prussian Lithuanian Dragoon Regiment was also posted on the left flank.[12]

At 9:00 A. M., the French divisions of Charpentier (36th) and Gérard (35th), part of Macdonald's XI Corps and under the direct command of Eugène, appeared and began a heavy bombardment of Steinmetz's position with a battery of 20 guns.[13]

On the right, the Prussians had deployed four züge of skirmishers behind a strong stone wall. When the French appeared, they pushed first against the right, in an effort to flank the larger forces on the left, but this assault failed. The French then turned their attention and their artillery on the Prussian left.

The cannister fire was too much for Steinmetz, and he began to withdraw. The French drove forward towards Waldheim and struck Miloradovich's rearguard, striving to cut it off from the Russian main body. The Russians detached a force under Generallieutenant St. Priest, consisting of the 2nd Grenadier Division, the Guard Uhlan Regiment and two artillery companies to support Steinmetz.

St. Priest's forces joined the Prussians by Gersdorf, and began to engage the French. The advancing French responded by forming their two divisions into three columns, which struck the allied positions. A bloody, but inconclusive battle raged for three hours, which the allies broke off once the Russian rearguard had cleared the Mulde River.[14] Lacking cavalry, the French were unable to mount an effective pursuit, and the allies slipped away relatively easily. The rearguard action was effectively ended by noon.

The Prussians assumed a new position near Waldheim, behind Zschoppau. Eugène did not advance his main body beyond Hartha, though he pushed his advanced posts to Zschoppau. The French losses were estimated to be 100 dead and 600 to 700 wounded. The Russians lost, according to French sources, 500 to 600 dead and 1,500 wounded, in addition to several hundred prisoners.[15]

THE FRENCH ADVANCE CONTINUES

As Eugène advanced after the encounter with Steinmetz, he passed the word to Napoleon that he saw a hostile force, alleged to be Kleist, on his left as he moved to Mühlberg. Indications were that the allied main body was moving to Meissen and Dresden. That being so, Lauriston's march on Wurzen was no longer necessary, and his orders were changed to redirect his movement and move by forced marches to Dresden. By the evening of 5 May, the French army was positioned as follows:

Imperial Guard & HQ	in Colditz
IV Corps	in Mulda
XI Corps & I Cavalry Corps	in and east of Hartha
VI Corps	Behind the XI Corps
XII Corps	in and behind Altenburg

When Napoleon read Eugène's report of the action at the Mulda, he was very displeased. Because it was hilly terrain and the allied cavalry advantage was largely negated, he felt that Eugène should have been able to capture 2,000 to 3,000 of the enemy as they withdrew.[16]

Napoleon then wrote to Ney, indicating that he was anxious that Ney should occupy Torgau and relieve Wittenberg as swiftly as possible.[17] Napoleon had deduced that the allies were now marching in two columns, one Prussian and one Russian, based on rumors and other information. He knew that the Russians would be more inclined to trust their own lines of communication through Bautzen, Görlitz, and Breslau and on to Warsaw, while the Prussians were tied to the north and Berlin. He also knew that with Ney in Torgau, 90 miles from Berlin, the Prussians would be anxious for their capital. Napoleon was watching their maneuvers for an indication of a separation of the armies, resulting from these divergent lines of communication. He planned to hold the Russians with a small force, and descend with the bulk of his forces on the fledgling Prussian army.

The chances of such a split are interesting to examine. It was not the most practical military maneuver, but the vacillating King Friedrich of Prussia was anxious to defend his capital, and political considerations might overcome military ones. The inflexible nature of the Russian supply system, would also cause them to be very hesitant to abandon their own lines of communication, so there was a reasonable possibility of this split occurring.

MILORADOVICH'S RETREAT ON DRESDEN

On 6 May Miloradovich was moving through Nossen and Wurttemberg commanded the rearguard, composed of Millesimo's cavalry in Waldheim, and a force of infantry consisting of the 22nd Infantry Division under Turscheninov,[18] and Karpenskov's Jager Brigade,[19] which was in Etzdorf, where they met the 2nd Corps.[20]

The terrain appeared clear to Wurttemberg, and as Millesimo had already received orders from Miloradovich to withdraw to Waldheim if threatened by the French, Wurttemberg ordered his forces to withdraw into a woods behind the village. General Karpenkov was placed in the village with his jagers, with the exception of a single regiment, which was deployed as skirmishers in the woods. Karpenkov's orders were that if he was pressed by the French, he was to withdraw to the right and left of the woods, so as to unmask the skirmishers and allow them to engage the French. The forces of Prince Schachafskoi were placed in reserve, with the bulk of the 2nd Corps. Turtscheninov and two batteries were directly behind the woods, and Wurttemberg was ready to act in concert with Millesimo, and strike the French from ambush, as they advanced into the village.

The French advance came towards Wurttemberg's trap. Millesimo's cavalry held the French between Waldheim and Etzdorf until 5:00 P. M. Then Millesimo led his cavalry across the stream before Etzdorf and placed them in the positions designated by Wurttemberg. General Karpenkov prepared to receive the French as they crossed the stream.

At 7:00 P. M. , a strong French column from the 35th Division, XI Corps, struck at Etzdorf, and two other columns passed on either side of the village. They quickly engaged Karpenkov in a lively fire fight. When the French encountered the skirmish line in the woods, their assault began to slow.

Wurttemberg then brought forward his artillery and the forces of Prince Schachafskoi. As they advanced, the skirmishers in the woods were forced to withdraw. The Russian cavalry fell back with them, and the French remained in control of Etzdorf. Wurttemberg's trap did not succeed as he had planned.[21]

On 7 May the Russian main body passed through Wilsdurf and crossed the Elbe at Dresden. The same day the Prussians crossed at Meissen, and Kleist's forces moved through Mühlberg. Wurttemberg continued his rearguard actions with the French as he covered the retreating allied armies.

Wurttemberg occupied Nossen during the morning of 7 May with the Murmon Infantry Regiment under Lieutenant Colonel Wolff. Karpenkov placed his three jager regiments in Eula, and Millesimo's cavalry stood to the right of Eula. Wurttemberg prepared to again engage the French advanced guard and formed his forces into several echelons.

The corps of Wolkonski and Markov, along with the cavalry of Lissanevitch, took up positions between Deutschenbora and Hirschfeld. The 4th and 20th Jagers formed a fourth echelon in the wooded defile behind Deutschenbora. The Krementsoug and Volhynie Infantry Regiments formed the fifth echelon, behind the defile of Tanneberg. The rest of the 2nd Corps, under Prince Schachafskoi, stood behind the defile at Limbach.

The French lead elements appeared before Nossen at 7:00 A. M. , Lieutenant Colonel Wolff was attacked at 8:30 A. M. , and remained in position until 10:00 A. M. , when he was forced to withdraw to Nieder-Eu. The French crossed the river at Freyberg Julde, below Nossen, and at Kloster Zellan, and moved in force against General Millesimo's detachment. Millesimo responded with his horse artillery and slowed their advance as he withdrew towards Ilkendorf and Wedischbora.

The village of Eula was disputed in a bloody battle. The Russians deployed artillery before a small copse, between Deutschenbora and Hirschfeld, supported on the left of this village by Karpenkov's jagers and on the right by a few regiments from Markov's corps and Lissanevitch's cavalry.

EUGENE OF WUTTEMBURG

This force engaged the French columns advancing out of Ober-Eu, which formed in line to the right and left of the village. The French responded with their own artillery. The French artillery was too much for Miloradovich, who was commanding the rearguard when the battle developed. He withdrew Volkonski's and Markov's corps through the defile at Tanneberg, and left the artillery between the two villages to hold the French until the last minute.

The 4th and 20th Jagers now began to feel the French assault as they stood in the woods between Deutschenbora and Tanneberg. They were also pushed back, but the Russian cavalry advanced to cover their withdrawal, as they moved back to Plankenstein.

At 5:00 P. M. , the French finally occupied Tanneberg and pushed forward, after the withdrawing Russian rearguard. The rearguard action had slowed the French advance down to a few miles and allowed the allied armies to slip a little further away.[22]

The Withdrawal Continues

Miloradovich passed through Dresden on 8 May over the same stone bridge that Davout had broken earlier. The Russian main army was already on the right bank of the Elbe. The Russians had temporarily patched the bridge, but as they crossed, they destroyed their temporary wooden repairs, as well as their pontoon bridges. By 2:00 A. M. , on 9 May, the bridges were gone and the Elbe was sealed. Unfortunately for the allies, the destruction was incomplete, and the French were able to salvage many of the boats.

On 8 May the French were deployed such that the XI Corps and the 1st Cavalry Corps were in Dresden, the VI Corps was west of Dresden, the IV Corps was between Potzschappel and Tharandt, the XII Corps was in Oederan, and the V Corps was in Meissen. The French advance had been terribly slow, only 12½ miles per day. Much of this was due to the poor state of discipline and the high level of straggling in the French infantry.

On 8 May the Prussian forces were still on the right bank of the Elbe. The French advanced against their positions in Meissen and a terrific but inconclusive artillery duel began across the Elbe.

The Russian Grenadier Corps and the 5th or Guard Infantry Corps were posted in Hirsch and in the bridge head, but they withdrew from those positions and moved to Radeberg, there they formed the army's left wing. The Grenadier Corps acted as a rearguard for the entire army, and held the bridgehead until all of the other Russian units had passed.

Both cuirassier divisions and Berg's corps marched left, on the road to Königsbrück, but moved only as far as Seifersdorf; there, they went into bivouac. The cuirassiers posted themselves between Waschau and Lepersdorf.

Along the Elbe River bank, a line of advanced posts were established and manned with infantry sharpshooters. The Dresden suburb of Neustädt was garrisoned with a very strong detachment. The detachment of General Major Count Troubetzkoi joined the main army. Lanskoi detached a cossack regiment to General Miloradovich, and marched with another detachment to Moritzburg. In addition, Miloradovich assumed command of General Major Tschailikov's forces.

The Prussians Cross the Elbe

On 9 May the Prussians crossed the Elbe at Meissen around noon and left behind a line of posts along the Elbe River as their two columns moved on Grossenhain. Blücher's corps remained on the right and Yorck's was on the left. Both columns took up positions behind the Röde stream. An advanced post was established in Lenz, where four squadrons of the 2nd Leib Hussar Regiment were stationed. That evening, three reserve and two "marschbataillone [replacement battalions]," under the command of Major Graf Dohna, arrived in Pulsnitz.[23]

FRENCH CROSSING THE BROKEN BRIDGE

The Russian main army remained in its positions in Radeberg. Czar Alexander had his headquarters in Bischofswerda. The next morning, the army was to reunite at Königsbrück in what was anticipated as a major effort to prevent the French from crossing the Elbe.

NAPOLEON CROSSES THE ELBE

On 8 May Napoleon had begun his preparations to cross the Elbe. The Russians still held Neustädt, the eastern suburb of Dresden across the Elbe, and it was not possible to repair the broken bridge across the Elbe. Napoleon chose to move to Briesnitz, a short way below Dresden, where the river makes an ox-bow bend to the southwest. Both banks were low and level with one another. Napoleon could arrange his artillery to sweep the peninsula, formed by this bend in the river, and cross without any significant interference.

Napoleon placed 60 guns to sweep the peninsula and another 40 (three 12pdr Old Guard Batteries and 16 Old Guard Horse Guns)[24] on the Brühlsche Terrasse, close to the stone bridge. The French crossing began in earnest at 7:00 A. M. , on 9 May. The French guns on the Brühlsche Terrasse, drove the Russians in Neustädt from the river's edge, enabling 300 French voltigeurs to cross in boats and effect a lodgement in a large building at the end of the broken stone bridge.[25]

General Miloradovich responded by ordering the 4th Infantry Corps of General Markov, and a detachment of cavalry to the village of Pieschen, on the eastern bank of the Elbe, to face the threat of the French engineers preparing a pontoon bridge.[26] The Russians also deployed 36 cannons to support their defensive effort, and a major artillery duel quickly developed across the Elbe at this position.

The Russian counter-attack moved forward to drive the French out of their positions, bringing four batteries (48 guns of the 2nd & 30th Position, 3rd Light and 6th Horse Batteries) with them. The Russian Archangel Infantry Regiment, under the command of Lieutenant Colonel Schindschin, advanced in a valiant bayonet assault against the French. This effort failed when the 80 French guns showered them with shot and shell, forcing them to withdraw. The last Russian defenders of Neustädt were the sharpshooters of the Schusselburg Infantry Regiment.[27]

190

Under the cover of French artillery, with the voltigeurs holding the far end of the bridge, the French slipped more voltigeurs across the river, and sappers and engineers moved to repair the broken span. The task was completed on 11 May. Once the bridge was complete, the French army poured across the bridge, and by the evening 70,000 French soldiers had crossed to the eastern shore of the Elbe.

On 11 May Ney also passed the river with the III, V and VII Corps, totaling about 45,000 men. He moved across a temporary bridge at Belgern and the bridges at Torgau. With the move of Saxony to formally join Napoleon, the VII Corps was reinforced by the addition of 9,000 infantry, 250 cavalry and three batteries.

On 10 May, the allies were withdrawing to the east, their rearguard being in Glauschütz, Laustiz and Hokendorf, watching the roads to Meissen, Radeberg, and Dresden for signs of French pursuit. Kleist and his corps were moving into Grossenhain. The Russian army, under Wittgenstein, moved to Bischofswerda.

ALLIED PLANS

The allies were not unified in their plans and Napoleon's passage of the Elbe increased their problems. The Prussians were concerned to cover their capital and the province of Brandenburg. This encouraged them to withdraw to the north.

In contrast, the Russians were concerned about their lines of communication with Warsaw, which ran through Bautzen, Görlitz, and Breslau. However, despite these fundamental disagreements, both allies agreed that a stand should be made somewhere west of the Oder. If such a battle was not accepted by the allies, the Austrians and other German princes would perceive Lützen as having been decisive and that would improve Napoleon's political position.

Wittgenstein was in favor of taking a position between Herzberg and Luckau, so he could attack the French flank as they crossed the Elbe. However, on 8 May, he had ordered the Russians to defend the river itself. The Russian troops were posted above Meissen, and the Prussians were posted below it. Kleist held the passage at Mühlberg. The Russian main body was in Radeberg and the Prussian main body was in Grossenhain.

With Miloradovich's failure to prevent the French passage of the Elbe at Briesnitz, the situation changed. Wittgenstein advocated retiring northwards, in an effort to support the Prussian concerns vis-a-vis Berlin. However, the Czar overrode this because he would not hear of the Russian army abandoning its lines of communication.

On 10 May Wittgenstein believed that Napoleon was concentrating on his left, for a march on Berlin. He felt that the threats on Dresden were only a ruse to divert his attention. This caused him to withdraw and take up new positions where he could react to his best advantage. He moved his Russian forces to Bischofswerda and the Prussians to Königsbrück. He felt that if he was attacked, he could withdraw on Bautzen, but if Napoleon moved towards Berlin, from his positions in Wittenberg and Belgern, he could attack the French flank.

When it was learned that the French were moving towards Bautzen, Königsbrück, and Reichenberg with three corps, Wittgenstein once again abandoned his plans. On 12 May he issued orders for his army to assemble at Bautzen. He also ordered his chief engineer to fortify those positions. All of these movements caused Napoleon to believe that the Russians and Prussians were about to separate.

The allies moved on Bautzen with Miloradovich acting as the rearguard. He was supported by Eugene of Wurttemberg when Macdonald caught his rear elements near Weissig on 11 May. When the action was over, Miloradovich moved to Schmiedefeld. Kleist was attacked by Bertrand, the same day near Königsbrück, and forced back to Kamenz. Miloradovich again had to fight off the French at Schmiedefeld on 12 May, while the main allied body crossed the Spree River at Bautzen. It was late in the evening when the Russian rearguard succeeded in withdrawing across the river, fighting every step of the way. Based on the interrogation of a deserter, General Hulot passed to his command, that the allied rearguard consisted of the 23rd, 24th, 25th and 26th Jager Regiments, the Grodno Hussar Regiment, two cossack regiments, and the Prussian forces of General Kleist —5 Prussian infantry regiments and a cavalry regiment. This was supported by 23 Russian and Prussian cannons.[28] On 15 May, the entire western bank of the Spree was evacuated by the allies.

The allies received a reinforcement of 13,500 men under Barclay de Tolly shortly after. Barclay's forces were freed by the capitulation of the French garrison at Thorn.

FRENCH PREPARATIONS IN DRESDEN

Napoleon also received reinforcements. While he received a division of Young Guard, four battalions of Old Guard, and two cavalry divisions de marche.[29] The Saxons had also formally joined the Grande Armée, with their infantry going to the VII Corps, and four cavalry regiments joining the I Cavalry Corps.

On 15 May, the French army consisted of the following forces:

Under Ney	Battalions	Squadrons	Batteries	Men
III Corps	66	8	12	30,000
V Corps	44		12	27,000
(Including Puthod)				
VII Corps	16	1		9,500
II Corps	22		2	13,000
Light Cavalry Division		8–9		1,800
(I Corps)				
II Cavalry Corps		15–20		3,000
Main Army				
IV Corps	34	4	7	25,000
VI Corps	39	4	10	22,000
XI Corps	31	2	8	17,000
XII Corps	33		7	24,000
Old Guard	6–7			4,000
Young Guard	25–30			15,000
Guard Artillery			14	
Guard Cavalry		20	3	4,000
I Cavalry Corps		45–50	4	8,000

The total strength of the two French forces was 203,300, and they were facing about 110,000 Russians and Prussians, including Barclay's corps and Bülow's forces covering Berlin.

EUGÈNE IS SENT TO ITALY

Napoleon formally dissolved the Army of the Elbe, which Eugène had commanded. Eugène was sent to take command of the army which Napoleon was organizing in Northern Italy for the defense of the kingdom and to hold the Austrian army facing the Italian border in place should they decide to join the allied cause.

DRESDEN BECOMES CENTRAL

Napoleon now established his major forward depot in Dresden. He appointed General Durosnel as the governor and garrison commander of Dresden. His command included about 6,000 men, including the depots of the IV, VI, VII, XI, and XI Corps. The depots for the II, III, and V Corps were established in Torgau, while the depots of the cavalry corps were established in Dresden and Leipzig.

Napoleon established three lines of communication to France. The principal line ran through Mainz, Frankfurt, Fulda, Erfurt, and Weimar. At Weimar it split, one leg going through Jena and Altenberg to Dresden, and the other leg going to Naumburg and Leipzig. A second branch ran from Leipzig to Wittenberg, and a third ran from Augsburg through Nürnburg, Bamberg, Schleiz, Gera, and Altenberg.

As forces were brought up these lines, they marched in 15 mile stages for six or seven days and rested on the next. As a protection against cossacks and streifkorps that might be wandering in the French rear areas, these reinforcements marched in "regiments de marche."[30]

To further enhance his position, Napoleon directed the repair of the old walls around Dresden's eastern suburb of Neustädt. This was designed to serve him as a fortified bridgehead. At Briesnitz, two pontoon bridges were built with rafts and boats, and the stone bridge in Dresden was repaired. Two further pontoon bridges were built parallel to the stone bridge.

On 11 May, Napoleon had the Guard and Oudinot in Dresden, on the left bank of the Elbe. The IV, VI, and XI Corps were on the eastern bank of the Elbe, making maneuvering room. The XI Corps and a cavalry division acted as an advanced guard, and moved to Weissig, where Wurttemberg waited for them yet again.

WESSIG FALLS

Macdonald's forces struck the Russians under General St. Priest near Durre Bühlau. As Wurttemberg's corps arrived, Miloradovich deployed it and that of St. Priest on the heights before Weissig. St. Priest made his maneuvers while under heavy pressure and a lively French cannonade.

Seeing St. Priest's situation, Wurttemberg ordered Princes Troubetzkoi and Schachafskoi to hasten their marches, but to move towards Erkmannsdorf and Yllersdorf in lieu of moving on Weissig in an effort to support Miloradovich's right and to not embarrass his withdrawal. Only Pischnitzki's brigade continued to march along the main road to Weissig.[31]

About noon the Russians had ceded Weissig to the French, who had continued their advance through the village. The French advanced in columns, covered by artillery and a heavy screen of skirmishers. They also threw a column around the Russian right and forced them to continue their withdrawal.

Wurttemberg positioned Pischnitzki's brigade and a position battery (12pdr guns), on a ridge, where he could cover the withdrawal of the rest of the Russian forces. Wurttemberg then moved his forces to Ullersdorf where he deployed his corps in two lines between the village and the Priessnitz stream. Each battalion formed itself in attack columns. All of the 20th Jagers' skirmishers were placed under the command of Major Sukhoulim and deployed before the main lines with two artillery batteries.

The French intended to turn Wurttemberg's flank by moving through the woods, but they were met by the Russian skirmishers and artillery who engaged them. The French pressed forward, and Wurttemberg was obliged to support his skirmishers with his first line. This was enough to stop the French advance and they began to withdraw. This allowed Miloradovich to disengage his forces and effect his retreat.

MARSHAL MACDONALD

NIKITIN

Wurttemberg withdrew his forces as well, once Miloradovich was clear. He formed his infantry in three lines and withdrew them with a heavy screen of skirmishers facing the French. He moved through Gross Erkmannsdorf and on to Volmsdorf with the French in pursuit. He then formed his forces into column and moved through Arnsdorf to Fischbach, where he rejoined Miloradovich. This combined force then marched on Schmiedefeld.

On 12 May Miloradovich's rearguard moved onto the heights behind Schmiedefeld, known as the Capellenberg. He placed a strong force of artillery to cover St. Priest's forces, which formed the first line, and the 2nd Corps which formed the second line. The XI Corps struck the battery about 11:00 A. M. , with dense masses, while other columns moved towards Schmiedefeld on his right. The Tobolsk Infantry Regiment was detached to dislodge the French in Schmiedefeld and quickly succeeded, threatening the French flank.

The French then moved towards the Fischbach woods, and threatened the right of St. Priest, who was, after a long fight, pushed back through the defile at Bischofswerda. General Lissanevitch covered this movement with a charge by the Tchougouiev Uhlan Regiment. Unfortunately for the last Russian column to pass over the Fischbach, it was not enough to keep the French artillery from inflicting heavy casualties on it.

General Nikitin placed a strong battery on the heights behind Bischofswerda, which quickly slowed the French advance again. French progress was further slowed by the deliberate burning of Bischofswerda.

Macdonald continued to push forward against Miloradovich, but without much enthusiasm. Marmont moved northwards to Reichenberg, with Beaumont's Westphalian cavalry brigade and three battalions, which moved into Grossenhain. On 13 May, Marmont directed Beaumont to remain in Moritzburg and moved east to Radeberg.

NAPOLEON'S PLANS

About 10 May Napoleon directed that on 16 May Ney's army be posted with the III Corps in Luckau, with its advanced guard in Lübben. The V Corps was to be in Dobrilugk, the VII Corps was to be in Dahme, and the II Corps and the II Cavalry Corps were to be in Schönwald.

By posting them in this manner, Napoleon was reorganizing the "battalion carré,"[32] that had served him so well as he moved onto the battlefield of Lützen. In preparing these dispositions, Napoleon was waiting to see in which direction he should move. He knew that the Russians were retiring on Breslau, but he had no idea where the Prussians were headed. He thought that they might either be moving with the Russians, or that they might be moving on Berlin. Napoleon hoped that the allied maneuvers would allow Davout to reoccupy Hamburg, as well as allow Napoleon to lift the siege of Glogau, seize Breslau, and move several divisions into Pomerania.

Watching the movements of the allies on 12 and 13 May, Napoleon realized that they had remained united and were moving on Bautzen. He was inclined to believe that they did not intend to stand and fight despite reports that they were fortifying the position.

During 12 May, Macdonald encountered Miloradovich's rearguard by Fischbach, near Bischofswerda. After an assault contested by Generalmajor Nikitin's artillery, and a number of Russian cavalry units,[33] the Russians evacuated the village and burned supplies stored there. Only three houses remained standing after the exchanges of artillery and the uncontrolled fires.[34] On 13 May the XI Corps continued its movement, and moved onto the road to Bautzen.

The IV and VI Corps stayed in Königsbrück and Reichbach while the Guard and XII Corps were in Dresden. The V Corps left Torgau and moved towards Obrilugk, and the III Corps marched on Luckau. The II Corps, under Victor, and the II Cavalry Corps reached Wittenberg. [35]

On 15 May, Macdonald again encountered Miloradovich's rearguard. This time Miloradovich was in Gödau. Macdonald advanced two columns of infantry, which were quickly attacked by the Kharkov and Kargopol Dragoon Regiments under General Jusefovich.[36] A further force of Russian cavalry under Uvarov operated against the French right. Once again, Macdonald pushed him out with great effort. He pushed the Russians across the Spree where they took up new defensive positions. Miloradovich formed his forces in two lines with Prince Eugene von Wurttemberg's 2nd Corps in the first line, on the eastern bank of the Spree and Gortschakov's corps in the second line. A reserve was formed with Markov's corps and a portion of the Russian cavalry reserve. Both flanks were secured with cossack detachments, and the light cavalry under Generalmajor Emmanuel was placed on the far left by Boblitz.[37]

Macdonald then took up a position on the western bank. The VI Corps was moving up behind him, the IV Corps was in Kloster-Marienstern, and the XII Corps was also close. From his position, Macdonald could see the allied camps on the plains of Bautzen.

NEY'S ARMY

On 4 May Ney, was in Leipzig with the III Corps and Durutte's 32nd Division, the French portion of the VII Corps. When the VII Corps was completed, it was to be commanded by Reynier. On 5 May Ney moved towards Torgau via Eilenburg. He sent two divisions of III Corps to relieve Wittenberg.

On 7 May Reynier arrived before Torgau, with Durutte's division. Here he found himself facing Thielmann, the Saxon commander, who still refused entry to both the allies and the French. Reynier was rebuffed. When Napoleon heard that Thielmann was pleading that his king's orders prohibited him permitting entry to Torgau, he took matters quickly in hand to resolve the problem.[38]

The French minister to the Saxon court advised the Saxon king that Metternich, the Austrian minister, had said that Austria would have nothing to do with either the Saxons or their king. He also passed to the king of Saxony three demands, 1.) Thielmann was to be ordered to leave Torgau and unite his troops to Reynier's corps, 2.) the king was to send his cavalry to Dresden at once, and 3.) he was to write a letter to Napoleon, admitting that his engagements of the past years were valid and that he intended to fulfil them.

If the King of Saxony failed to comply within the time allocated, he was advised that, "he would cease to reign."[39] With that terrifying threat ringing in his ears on 12 May, the King of Saxony capitulated immediately. Thielmann was ordered to join his forces to Reynier's corps, which he promptly did. But Thielmann, after he turned the fortress over to Maréchal Ney, deserted to the Prussians with his staff.[40]

Napoleon had no doubt that the King of Saxony would capitulate and did not wait for a reply. He ordered Ney to concentrate the III Corps and Durutte's 32nd Division south of Torgau. They were to build a bridge at Belgern, a half day's march above the fortress. Lauriston was to leave Meissen with a small garrison and move his forces to the left, taking a position close enough to Torgau that he could support Ney if necessary.

On 11 May, Ney was ready to cross the Elbe with 60,000 men. Sébastiani was not to come along, as he did not reach Bernberg until 12 May.

FRIEDRICH AUGUST
KING OF SAXONY

1. Sporschil, Grosse Chronik, Vol I, pg 258.

2. A Bataillon de Marche and compagnies de marche were ad hoc battalion and company formations formed in the various regimental depots. They consisted of newly trained recruits and a professional cadre. These battalions and companies were the preferred method used to transport recruits to the front and to minimize their chances of deserting.

3. Sporschil, Grosse Chronik, Vol I, pg 259.

4. Petre, Napoleon's Last Campaign in Germany - 1813, pg 91.

5. Plotho, Kreig in Deutschland, Vol I, pgs 125 - 126.

6. Sporschil, Grosse Chronik, Vol I, pg 175.

7. Sporschil, Grosse Chronik, Vol I, pg 167

8. Plotho, Krieg in Deutschland, Vol I, pg 128.

9. Petre, Napoleon's Last Campaign in Germany - 1813, pg 91.

10. Petre, Napoleon's Last Campaign in Germany - 1813, pg 92.

11. Petre, Napoleon's Last Campaign in Germany - 1813, pg 31.

12. von der Oelsnitz, A.C., Geschichte des Königlich Preussischen Ersten Infanterie - Regiments, pg 684

13. Plotho, Krieg in Deutschland, Vol I, pg 130.

14. Sporschil, J, Die Grosse Chronik, Vol I, pg 179.

15. Foucart, P.J., Bautzen, La Poursuite jusqu'a l'armistice, pg 47.

16. Bonaparte,., Correspondance, H. #19971.

17. Bonaparte,, Correspondance, H. #19972.

18. The 22nd Division, under Turscheninov, consisted of the Viatka, Olonetz, and Staroskol Infantry Regiments and 45th Jager Regiment.

[19] Karpenskov's jager brigade consisted of the 1st, 33rd and 37th Jager Regiments.

[20] Fabry, Prince de Wurttemberg, pg 55.

[21] Fabry, Prince de Wurttemberg, pg 56.

[22] Fabry, Prince de Wurttemberg, pg 58.

[23] Plotho, Krieg in Deutschland, Vol I, pg 136.

[24] Foucart, Bautzen, pg 116.

[25] Plotho, Krieg in Deutschland, Vol I, pg 137.

[26] Sporschil, Grosse Chronik, Vol I, pg 190.

[27] Plotho, Krieg in Deutschland, Vol I, pgs 137–138.

[28] Foucart, Bautzen, pg 170.

[29] A Division de marche is a divisional formation organized from other "marche" formations. It is, principally, a large scale formation organized solely for the transportation of new recruits to the front and is not intended for combat.

[30] Petre, Napoleon's Last Campaign, pg 102.

[31] Fabry, Prince de Wurtemberg, pg 60.

[32] The bataillon carré is a marching formation where the force that is marching forms itself into four or more smaller formations that march in a diamond square formation. This formation allows the formation to engage the enemy with a sizable force, no matter from what direction the enemy should approach. While the enemy is then tied in place by the engaging force, the two nearer points of the diamond swing to strike at the enemy's flanks and the farthest force advances to serve the engaging force as a reserve.

[33] Sporschil, Grosse Chronik, Vol I, pg 196.

[34] Plotho, Krieg in Deutschland, Vol I, pg 141.

[35] de Marmont, Memoires, pgs 100–101.

[36] Sporschil, Grosse Chronik, Vol I, pg 196. & Plotho, Krieg in Deutschland, Vol I, pg 143.

[37] Plotho, Krieg in Deutschland, Vol I, pg 144.

[38] Petre, Napoleon's Last Campaign in Germany –1813, pg 96.

[39] Petre, F.L., Napoleon's Last Campaign in Germany–1813, pg 97, & de Marmont, Memoires, pg 98.

[40] de Marmont, Memoires, pg 100.

XII

Prelude to Bautzen
16 May to 19 May

NAPOLEON CLOSES FOR THE KILL

Macdonald's reports back to Napoleon clearly indicated that the allies intended to stand their ground at Bautzen. It was the battle that Napoleon so greatly desired. He swiftly began concentrating his forces, in an effort to gain the decisive victory that had eluded him at Lützen.

He directed the IV, VI, and XI Corps to assume a position facing Bautzen. The IV Corps was to be on the left and the XI Corps on the right. This gave Napoleon a total of 64,000 men facing the allies. The XII Corps, then at Bischofswerda, was to be the reserve for the first line. It was also to detach three mobile columns of 1,200 men and artillery, to clear the woods between the Dresden-Bautzen road and Bohemia, the Austrian frontier, which lay about ten miles south of Bautzen. [1]

With this force of approximately 90,000 men covering his front, and acting as an impenetrable screen to the allied cavalry, Napoleon could bring up the Imperial Guard from Dresden, and swing Ney's army from the north into the allied right flank.

Mortier was to clear Napoleon's left flank, with the 1st Cavalry Corps, Beaumont's detachment, and a division of Young Guard, in an effort to ensure clear communications with Ney. Beaumont was assigned the task of clearing the numerous roving bands of cossacks and allied cavalry out of the area between Grossenhain and Königsbrück.[2] The numbers and strengths of the allied cavalry forces in this area were so significant, that dispatch riders were often escorted by detachments of 25 or more horsemen.[3]

On 16 May, Mortier directed Beaumont to take 600 to 700 cavalry to attack allied cavalry known to be in Grossenhain. The allied cavalry fell back on Elsterwerda, and on 17 May, Beaumont found himself in communication with Lauriston's corps. [4]

Mortier also detached Dumoustier's 1st Young Guard Division, and the 6,000 cavalry of Latour-Maubourg to Bischofswerda. Latour-Maubourg's forces were as follows:

1st Light Cavalry Division	
7 regiments	34 officers and 509 men
Jacquet's Brigade	
8th Chevaulégers	28 officers and 243 men,
1st Italian Chasseurs	23 officers and 681 men
Saxon brigade Hussars	10 officers and 368 men
Chevauxlegers	8 officers and 356 men
3rd Light Cavalry Division	
11 regiments	55 officers and 1,492 men
1st Cuirassier Division	
French	71 officers and 1,054 men
Saxon	40 officers and 1,092 men
3rd Cuirassier Division	
Cuirassiers	13 officers and 216 men
Dragoons	42 officers and 620 men
Napoleon Dragoon Regiment[5]	27 officers and 799 men

NAPOLEON GIVING INSTRUCTIONS
DESVARREUX

Now that communications were open, Napoleon directed Lauriston to move from Dobrilugk to Hoyerswerda. Ney was ordered to move from Herzberg to Spremberg. However, Napoleon and Berthier appear to have forgotten that they had earlier ordered Ney to move to Luckau on 15 May. Though Napoleon had intended Victor to act against Bülow, with the II and VII Corps, these new orders did not make that clear, and Ney assumed that the orders directed that his entire force, except for Lauriston, was to move on Spremberg.

This was a fortunate error, in that Ney was bringing all available forces with him, and maximizing the forces that could be brought to bear on Bautzen. Bülow's forces were small enough to be contained by a few thousand men.[6]

Napoleon's orders to Ney did not send him to Bautzen via the shortest route. It would appear that Napoleon feared that Ney's appearance on the main road would chase the allies back into Silesia and prevent the decisive battle.

On 16 May, Napoleon ordered Ney to move to Hoyerswerda. Ney was not receive a copy of this order until 19 May. A second order directed Ney to move with Lauriston, and to send Victor, with Reynier and Sébastiani to move towards Berlin, capture both Berlin and Spandau if possible, and to contain Bülow. Ney reacted immediately by giving appropriate directions to Victor and ordering Reynier to stop at Luckau. This action was to keep Victor and 25,000 men out of the pending battle at Bautzen.

By the morning of 17 May, Napoleon seems to have reconsidered Ney's original movements and redirected him to use Victor, Sébastiani, and Reynier as seemed most appropriate. He did, however, clearly indicate to Ney that he anticipated a battle at Bautzen.[7]

Ney changed his orders to Victor and Reynier once again. He directed them to march on Bautzen via Kahlau and Hoyerswerda. Unfortunately, enough time was lost to prevent the arrival of these forces on the battlefield in time to take a decisive part in the coming battle. Napoleon appears not to have realized that his dalliance with secondary objectives had cost him critical time, and failed to realize that Victor's and Reynier's forces had been decisively delayed.

Napoleon's following instructions to Ney ordered him to move directly towards the main army, rather that make an obvious flanking maneuver. Ney was to swing to the left, across the Spree, and into a flanking position on the allied right only at the last possible movement.

On 7 May, the XII Corps (Oudinot) had deployed as ordered by Napoleon. The 29th (Bavarian) Division (Raglovich) was in Bischofswerda, the 14th Division (Lorencz) was in Thumitz, and the 13th Division (Pacthod) was in Rothnauslitz. However, because of the position of the XI Corps, the 13th Division found itself obliged to move forward slightly, to improve communications with the XI Corps (Macdonald).[8]

Mortier's Imperial Guard marched with the intent of reaching Bautzen on 19 May. Mortier and Latour-Maubourg were moved forward from Bischofswerda on 18 May. Simultaneously Oudinot was to move to the right of Macdonald, and in conjunction with Latour-Maubourg, sweep the forests to the right, driving out any allied detachments that might be there. Bertrand was to establish communications with Lauriston and Ney at Hoyerswerda, whom Napoleon expected to be there on 19 May. Beaumont was ordered to remain at Moritzburg.[9]

On 18 May, Napoleon issued orders that Mortier and Latour-Maubourg were to move on Bischofswerda. Oudinot was directed to move his entire corps into the front line, and occupy Neukirch and the positions on the right of the main French position, in such a manner as to clear that area of allied patrols. Latour-Maubourg's cavalry was to perform a similar task, sweeping the allied cavalry patrols from between Neustädt and Neukirch. This was a reordering of the effort to secure the southern flank to the Bohemian border of Austria. The Imperial Guard, with the reserve artillery, was to leave Dresden and move towards Bautzen, down the main route. Barrois' 2nd Young Guard Division was now with the Imperial Guard.[10]

Ney issued orders on 18 May, that the next day's march were to position the V Corps on the right and the III Corps on the left of the Zerna-Neudorf line, facing south. Lauriston was to maintain communications with the main army based on Ney's erroneous assumption that the allies had been in position west of the Spree and that Napoleon was facing them with his left on Kloster Marienstern. This resulted from a not unreasonable reading of the very unclear instructions issued by Berthier that did not clearly state the position of the allies. It was not until noon on 19 May, that Ney received the orders issued at 10:00 A.M. on 18 May that he realized the true position of the allies on the east bank of the Spree.

On the morning of 19 May, the main army was positioned such that the Imperial Headquarters and the Imperial Guard were in Klein Förstchen, the Young Guard and I Cavalry Corps were around Gödau. Bertrand's IV Corps (less Peyri's 15th Division, which was on the lines of communication with Lauriston in Königswartha), was in Gross-Welkau, the VI Corps (Marmont) was between the IV Corps (Bertrand) and the Dresden road, the XI Corps (Macdonald) was south of the Dresden road, in line with the VI Corps, and the XII Corps (Oudinot) was to the right of the XI Corps with an advanced force in Guschwitz. One of the brigades from Lorencz's 14th Division, was detached from the XII Corps to sweep the country to the right and rear of the army.

Lauriston's V Corps was marching towards Zerna. The III Corps (Ney) was moving towards Hoyerswerda, the VII Corps (Reynier), II Corps (Victor), and 2nd Cavalry Corps were behind the III Corps, also en route to Hoyerswerda.

As Lauriston marched towards the battle a courier, Major Grouchy, son of the future marshal, brought news of a hostile force advancing from Bautzen. Lauriston reacted by stopping the V Corps in Wittichenau and Maukendorf, sending word to Ney and awaiting new orders.

Ney arrived in Hoyerswerda at about 11 A.M. on 19 May, and received the clear orders of 18 May. Once again he changed his orders. The V Corps was to move through Mortke on Opitz and Lippitsch along the road to Klix and Brösa. The III Corps was ordered to dispatch Souham's 8th Division and Kellerman's cavalry brigade, as an advanced guard which would occupy Neudorf. The remaining four divisions were to take up positions in Niesendorf and Königswartha.

Because of his halt, Lauriston was still not clear of Hoyerswerda, which forced the III Corps to wait until he cleared the village, before it could move on Königswartha. This was because the terrain between the Black Elster and the Spree, is very marshy and passable only along two narrow roads during the spring and fall.[11]

THE ALLIED CAMP

The allies were not idle while the French army maneuvered against them, but they were not maneuvering their armies in a strategic endeavor to improve their situation. Instead, they chose to prepare field fortifications in and around Bautzen, improving the tactical strength of their position. They maintained a screen of cossacks and cavalry that scoured the country around their positions and kept their commanders apprised of the French maneuvers near Bautzen, hence the many French efforts to sweep their front clear of such patrols. They also engaged in a number of small forays against the French advanced posts. Some of these attacks were but a few hundred horsemen attacking an infantry picket, while others consisted of as many as two battalions, fifteen squadrons, and a battery, such as the attack against General Puthod's forces in Techritz on 18 May.[12]

On 18 May, the allies attacked the French near Neukirch. This force, consisting of a battalion of infantry, about 600 horse and three guns, took the French under Général de division Lorencz under fire. As Général Gruyer pushed against the left of Neukirch, the allies were forced to withdraw for fear of being cut off. Though the French had not changed their cannon from the travel mode into the firing mode,[13] when they found the allied cavalry passing in front of their guns at a very short range the French hurriedly fired their cannon, killing 40 allied cavalry.

The allied withdrawal continued until they reached Diehmen just before nightfall. The French lead elements had pierced the outskirts of Diehmen and echeloned the 2nd Brigade near Tröbigau.

The allied cavalry charged the 52nd Line Infantry Regiment twice, but it had formed square and held fast. The French infantry of the 52nd and 137th Regiments, actually reformed into column, and advanced at the "pas de charge" against the allied cavalry.[14] The cavalry, faced with this startling and unusual situation, withdrew. When night finally fell, the allies slipped out of contact with the French and the skirmish was over.

THE ALLIED STRATEGIC VIEW

On the strategic board Napoleon's dispositions had convinced the allies that the French intended to attack them frontally from across the Spree. They had learned from a captured dispatch that Lauriston was moving up and would be in Hoyerswerda on 18 May, but the direction of his march did not indicate a threat to their flank. They grew to believe that Lauriston was a day's march ahead of Ney, and that a swift allied maneuver might enable them to cut Lauriston off from the main French army.

Wittgenstein directed Barclay de Tolly to execute this maneuver, when he heard the sounds of an allied attack on the front of the main French army. He knew the frontal attack would prevent the French from interfering with the allied maneuver.

Barclay was given his own Russians, and Yorck's Prussians for this maneuver. His force totaled about 24,000 men. On the morning of 19 May, Tschaplitz, commanding Barclay's advanced guard, crossed the Spree at Nieder Gurig, and moved towards Johnsdorf, situated on the wooded heights that overlooked the French left.

THE SKIRMISH BY WEISSIG

Langeron and Raevsky crossed at Klix and Königswartha and moved towards Johnsdorf via Milkel and Opitz. Yorck crossed the Spree further north at Brösa, Guttau, Lomischau and Lieske. Tschlapitz's line of march led him to within 1 1/4 miles of Bertrand's outposts at Lubachau. The French observed his march, but made no effort to interfere with it because Peyri's Italian 15th Division was already moving on Königswartha to link up with Lauriston.

The Prussian forces in Barclay's corps were greatly weakened. The two musketeer battalions of the 1st East Prussian regiment totaled 980 men, slightly over the strength of a normal battalion.[15] The

YORCK

regiment's fusilier battalion had been combined with that of the Leib-Regiment. This combined battalion was under the command of a captain and contained 473 men.[16] Barclay commanded Steinmetz's 1st Prussian Brigade, Horn's 2nd Prussian Brigade, and Corswandt's reserve cavalry.

THE BATTLE OF KÖNIGSWARTHA

Peyri's 15th Division had bivouacked in Königswartha at noon on 18 May, and made no effort to ensure its security. The outposts were badly placed, and no effort was made at a reconnaissance of the surrounding terrain. Barclay joined Tschaplitz at 1:00 P.M., and observed the Italian's lack of attention. Peyri had 14 battalions, 10 guns, and 150 cavalry with his force. He posted four battalions in the castle's court and posted five before it, with the rest behind the village in reserve. His front was covered with woods.[17]

Assuming that Peyri was Lauriston's advanced guard, Barclay struck. Generalmajor Rudsewitch attacked the weak Italian outposts from the direction of Johnsdorf with a force of Russian jagers and swiftly threw the Italians back into the main village. Fortunately for the Italians, the thick woods slowed the Russian envelopment and gave them time to react. It was, however, to be insufficient time to prevent disaster.

The main allied columns moved into position, and the 18th Division of Langeron's corps, under the command of Generalmajor Scherbatov, formed the lead elements of the attack. He deployed his division so that its right wing was opposite the castle and its left wing was in the forest.[18] The 9th Division (Insov) formed behind them and supported the assault.[19]

The Russian assault threw the Italians back into the village, and a bloody street battle began. However the superior numbers of the Russians quickly told, and the Italians were pushed back.

When the Prussians arrived the Russians had already engaged the Italians for two hours and had thoroughly defeated them. The Prussians were too late to engage the Italians, and Barclay pursued the routed Peyri, until 5:00 P.M. Peyri lost 2,860 men, hors de combat, and 750 prisoners.

PRUSSIANS SKIRMISH IN THE WOODS

The losses also included Generals Martel and Balathier who were mortally wounded, two to ten guns (depending on whose report is read), and three caissons.[20]

Yorck's route was longer, and his movements were not coordinated with the rest of the force. At 3:00 P.M. he encountered the head of Lauriston's Corps in Hermsdorf. Combat quickly ensued and as it began in earnest, Yorck received Barclay's order to move to Johnsdorf where he was to act as a reserve.

Yorck would have been justified in ignoring this order in view of his circumstances, but he chose to obey those orders and began to evacuate his positions. As fate would have it, a second set of orders arrived from Barclay, indicating that Barclay had learned that Peyri was not part of Lauriston's Corps, and that Yorck was to hold Weissig.

When the Italians found the pressure slacking, they reformed themselves under the command of General Kellerman who had ridden up upon hearing the battle. Kellerman led them forward and reoccupied Königswartha. Yorck did his best to obey this last order, but, even with reinforcements coming from Barclay, he was unable to regain his earlier positions. Late in the evening, after three more hours of battle, the French occupied Weissig and Yorck retired on Klix, where he joined the rest of Barclay's forces.[21] Both Barclay and Yorck were to rejoin the main army on 20 May. Yorck had lost about 1,100 men and Barclay another 900 during the foray.

After reaching Klix General Yorck sent his advanced guard, consisting of the two squadrons of the Combined Silesian Hussar Regiment, the Combined Fusilier Battalion, the Leib Infantry and 1st East Prussian Infantry Regiments down the road to Wartha and Weissig. Once there he began to deploy his forces, because he learned that another French force was closing in on his position.[22] Yorck's advanced guard ran headlong into Général de division Maison's 16th Division. [23]

The terrain, where Yorck encountered Maison, is very broken and wooded. In addition, the Spree and some of its major tributaries ran through the immediate vicinity. Yorck crossed over the Schwarzen Wasser near Steinitz and where the village of Weissig lies. Here he deployed his skirmishers and posted a battery in the village of Weissig.

Lauriston found the Spree crossed by many bridges and fordable in many places. In fact, the river represented so little of a military obstacle that he was obliged to destroy many of the bridges as to assure his flanks were protected. He was also obliged to detach two battalions to assure the safe passage of his grand park and equipage.

When he arrived before Steinitz, about 3:00 P.M. on 19 May, he encountered Yorck's force of Prussian infantry (the combined fusilier battalion and the two musketeer battalions of the 1st East Prussian Infantry Regiment), and cavalry, supported by four horse guns. Four companies of voltiguers from Maison's 16th Division and a battery of six guns were sent through the heavy woods surrounding the enemy position in an effort to flank the Prussian position.[24]

The Prussians had deployed the two musketeer battalions of the 1st East Prussian Regiment, in and behind the woods that ran from Eich-Berg to Weissig. The 1st Battalion formed the first line and the 2nd Battalion stood about a musket's shot behind it. A Prussian foot battery with four guns was posted to the right of Eichberg, between the two wooded copses. The 1st Combined Fusilier Battalion was in the edge of the woods which lined the Spremberg-Bautzen road. Horn's brigade was posted in the woods to the south of Weissig.[25]

The 1st Combined Fusilier Battalion and the skirmisher züge of the two musketeer battalions of the 1st East Prussian Infantry, were struck by the French 154th Line[26] as it passed through the woods and driven back. The 134th and 155th French Line struck the 1/1st East Prussian Infantry. A fire fight erupted, punctuated with bayonet, but the Prussians were unable to withstand the weight of the French attack. There were 8,000 Frenchmen attacking about 1,300 Prussians.

The Prussians withdrew when they realized the threat to their flanks and moved towards Weissig, where their main force (Horn's brigade) lay concealed. The 151st and 153rd Infantry Regiments of Maison's 16th Division, pushed through the woods vigorously and cleared out what resistance they encountered. Lagrange's 18th Division advanced, sending three battalions of the 154th Line Regiment to the village of Klein-Steinitz on the right flank. The Prussians sought to seize this village and threaten the French flank.

As the Prussians arrived at Klein-Steinitz, the three battalions of the 154th Line Regiment pushed into the woods around the village. General Lafitte, of Rochambeau's division, led the 154th. Two further French battalions (one from the 149th and one from the 150th Regiments), were placed behind the 154th as a reserve. At the same time the 134th and 155th Regiments (Lagrange's 18th Division), struck through the middle of the woods at the hill on which the Prussians stood. Lafitte's maneuver took the Prussians in the flank, and forced them to withdraw with heavy losses. [27]

The Prussians countered by moving up ten battalions from Horn's brigade, a Russian half 12pdr battery, and a cavalry force consisting of the 2nd Silesian Hussars, the Prussian Lithuanian Dragoon Regiment, two squadrons of the 1st West Prussian Dragoons, and Horse Battery #2. The Lithuanian Dragoons, in zug column, attacked the 154th, going to the charge at a range of 250 paces, but made little impact on it.[28] The Prussian cavalry withdrew to the edge of the woods, where the French took them under cannister fire and savaged them.

At 6:00 P.M., the Prussians received reinforcements in the form of four Russian grenadier regiments (Ekaterinoslav, Arakcheyev, St. Petersburg and Tauride).[29] Lauriston met them with General Rochambeau and three battalions of the 135th Line Regiment. The 135th was pushed back, and the 2/134th Line Regiment, which had stood on the far bank of the Spree, was brought up to support its fellows. Despite counter attacks by allied cavalry, its attack was successful and drove the allies back.[30]

The French advance became general, and the 151st, 153rd, 135th and 134th Line Regiments advanced to cries of "Vive l'Emperor!" and moved to seize positions around Eich-Berg. The Prussians responded by sending the 5th Prussian Combined Infantry Regiment to reinforce their right and extend this wing to the woods already being held by the Rudolphi Fusilier Battalion. About the same time, the Russian Ekaterinoslav Grenadier Regiment, the Prussian Leib-Regiment, and half of Lieutenant Lang's horse battery counterattacked the masses of French infantry, moving from Weissig towards Eich-Berg in an effort to stall their advance. This assault was followed by a second wave, consisting of the 2nd West Prussian and the Lithuanian Dragoons, who drove the French back into the forest. It is reputed that a park of 60 allied guns was behind the allied lines and in serious danger of being taken by the French attack, and that is what prompted the counter-attack. [31]

Under the cover of this attack, Steinmetz reorganized his forces and went over to the attack himself. The Ekaterinoslav Grenadiers fell back and took up a position behind his left wing. The French stood waiting for this new attack with a full regiment, but it was insufficient to hold the attack of the 5th Prussian Combined Infantry Regiment, the Russian Grenadiers, and the Rudolphi Fusilier Battalion. [32]

The French responded to this thrust with a general assault, consisting of the 135th, 151st, 153rd, and 155th Regiments. This force moved against the Prussian center and left wing.

To cover his flank Horn had detached the skirmishers of the 5th Prussian Combined Infantry Regiment and the jäger detachment of the 1/Leib Regiment. They joined the Combined Fusilier Battalion just as it was being struck by a French column. The French column was forced to withdraw and the Prussians pursued it up to the edge of the woods. A renewed attack by the French from Neu-Steinitz struck and drove back the Prussians to their original positions.

The last Prussian attack came 10:00 P.M. that evening, when the Prussians organized a new attack with both infantry and cavalry. The cavalry was lead by Generalmajor Corswandt, and consisted of the Lithuanian Dragoons, 1st West Prussian Dragoons, and two squadrons of the Silesian Hussar Regiment. This attack was driven back by cannister fire at little loss to the French. The Prussians remaining on the battlefield formed in "battalionsmassen" as night fell. To their left, Yorck posted the Russian grenadiers and the cavalry was posted in the middle as a reserve.

The losses of the V Corps during the battles around Eich-Berg on 19 May 1813 were:[33]

	Killed		Wounded		Prisoners	
	Officers	Men	Officers	Men	Officers	Men
16th Division: Maison						
151st	4	36	6	156	1	—
153rd	48	10	163	—	—	—
Artillery	1	8	—	—	—	—
17th Division (detached)						
18th Division: Lagrange						
134th	2	49	3	201	80	—
154th	1	32	19	393	79	—
155th	3	25	7	270	24	—
19th Division: Rochambeau						
135th	2	10	7	145	—	—
149th	—	—	—	—	—	—
150th	—	—	—	—	—	—
3rd Light Cavalry Division: Chastel						
1st Chasseurs	3	7	—	—	—	—
2nd Chasseurs	—	1	—	—	—	—
3rd Chasseurs	—	—	5	—	—	—
9th Chasseurs	—	—	1	—	—	—
19th Chasseurs	—	—	2	—	—	—
2nd & 3rd Italian Chasseurs	—	—	3	—	—	—

The Prussians had suffered as well, but not as heavily. Yorck led 5,670 onto the battlefield. Their casualties, according to zur Lippe-Weissenfeld, totaled 7 staff officers, 45 subalterns, 917 men hors de combat. In separate reports, Plotho and Wagner give the Prussian losses at 77 officers and 1,806 NCO's and men.

The French records show 1,807 dead, wounded, and captured, despite the Prussian claims of 4,683 French casualties.[34] In a less jingoistic claim, Wagner reports the French losses at 300 dead and 1,400 wounded, which adds further credibility to his claim of Prussian casualties.

RESULTS OF THE ALLIED MANEUVER

It had been the best of luck for the allies that they had escaped so lightly. They had dispatched a quarter of their force (24,000 men), to engage Lauriston's 19,000 men, and had passed across the front of Bertrand's IV Corps. Bertrand must be censured for taking no action, and Napoleon did so shortly afterwards, but even Napoleon took no notice of the sound of guns in his rear, so Napoleon also deserves a share of the blame for having taken no action himself. He could have easily spared Bertrand for such a maneuver and still retained 72,000 men to face the 86,000 allies across the Spree.

The allies were fortunate to have engaged the lax Italians alone and were considerably the better for that engagement. The chances they took in face of the potential of Ney's entire force being present more than outweighed what they hoped to gain. However, despite the risk, they gained significantly more than they had hoped to gain. Their attack on Peyri convinced Ney that he faced an attack in the near future, and he prepared to receive that attack in Buchwalde.[35]

[1] Foucart, Bautzen, pg 233.

[2] Bonaparte, Correspondance, #20012.

[3] Foucart, Bautzen, pg 238.

[4] Foucart, Bautzen, pg 238.

[5] The Napoleon Dragoon Regiment was formed from Italians and belonged to the army of the Kingdom of Northern Italy.

[6] Petre, Napoleon's Last Campaign, pg 107.

[7] Foucart, Bautzen, pg 232.

[8] Foucart, Bautzen, pg 235.

[9] Bonaparte, Correspondance, #20020.

[10] Foucart, Bautzen, pgs 245–246, 248.

[11] Petre, Napoleon's Last Campaign, pg 111.

[12] Foucart, Bautzen, pg 260.

[13] Foucart, Bautzen, pg 270.

[14] von der Oelsnitz, Ersten Infanterie, pg 686.

[15] von Salisch, Siebenten Infanterie, pg 115.

[16] Wagner, Recueil des Plans, Vol II, pg 7.

[17] Wagner, Recueil des Plans, Vol II, pg 7.

[18] Plotho, Krieg in Deutschland, Vol I, pg 149.

[19] Wagner, Recueil des Plans, Vol II, pg 7.

[20] Foucart, Bautzen, pg 278.

[21] Plotho, Krieg in Deutschland, Vol I, pg 150.

[22] Wagner, Recueil des Plans, Vol II, pg 8.

[23] Schmitt, 151e Regiment d'Infanterie, pg 46.

[24] von der Oelsnitz, Ersten Infanterie, pg 688.

[25] Part of Lagrange's 18th Division.

[26] Wagner, Recueil des Plans, Vol II, pg 10.

[27] zur Lippe-Weissenfeld, 6. Husaren, pg 114.

[28] Plotho, Krieg in Deutschland, Vol I, pg 151.

[29] Schmitt, 151e Regiment d'Infanterie, pg 47.

[30] Wagner, Recueil des Plans, Vol II, pgs 10–11.

[31] von Salisch, Siebenten Infanterie, pg 116.

[32] Foucart, Bautzen, pg 308.

[33] zur Lippe-Weissenfeld, 6. Husaren, pg 115.

[34] Petre, Napoleon's Last Campaign, pg 114.

TSAR ALEXANDER I

The Battle of Bautzen
The First Day 20 May 1813

The city of Bautzen was situated on the right bank of the Spree River. It contained 7,000 to 8,000 inhabitants and was surrounded by a crenelated wall. The Spree flowed at the foot of the walls of the city, but was not particularly deep or wide, and presented no major military obstacle. The deep, narrow gorge of the Spree, to the west of Bautzen, was not assailable, but many roads lead to Bautzen and its suburbs, crossing the Spree and clearly indicating the fords that were practicable for artillery. To the north of Bautzen, one ford was near the village of Ohna, on the road from Teichnitz, and two others were located at the Ohna mill and the Schleifmühl mill. The latter two were not usable by infantry. The right bank for two miles north of Ohna was commanded by the left or western bank, and was generally bordered by meadows. On the right or eastern bank, there were numerous shallow ponds used to breed carp. These ponds were filled by means of branches of the Spree and represented a serious military obstacle. Further north, the Spree was fordable most places in ordinary weather, but there were some deep spots; one lies where the road from Nieder Gurig to Bautzen crosses above Nieder Gurig and extends south.

However, to the south of the Bautzen, there were many fords that were practicable for infantry, having less than two feet of water. The valley in which the Spree ran, to the south, was steep sided and averaged 150 feet deep. The command varied from side to side. To the extreme south, the battle field includes the wooded heights of Drohmberg and Schmoritzberg, the last ridges of the Lusatian mountain.

Knowing the weakness of this position, the allies had built two batteries to defend the approaches to the city. They were built to the left of the city where the river was most fordable. One had twelve guns and the other eight.

The French thought that another battery had been established to the right of the village behind a number of houses because of the fresh earth that was observed, but no finished work had been observed by 17 May. That flank of the city was only secured by the steep banks of the Spree, and a number of streams that entered the Spree.[1] In fact, many earth works had been raised behind Bautzen.

The space located between the Spree and the villages of Doberschütz, Rieschen, Litten, and Kreckwitz was a rolling plateau with no noteworthy features. North-west of Kreckwitz was a series of hills known as the Kreckwitz heights. North of these mounds, the terrain was generally flat with a few knolls. The largest of those knolls was between Malschwitz and Galina, and on top of this low ridge, near Galina, was the Galina windmill. This terrain was filled with carp ponds.

Parallel to the Spree, about two miles east, runs the Blöser-Wasser. It runs from Blösa, past Purschwitz and Klein Bautzen to join the Löbauer Wasser near Gottamelda. This stream was unexceptional and, of itself, no military obstacle, but its marshy bed was both an obstacle and provided excellent protection for the plains east of it. The road to Gorlitz via Würschen and the road to Zittau by Hochkirch ran across the Blöser-Wasser.[2]

The initial allied plan had been to defend the banks of the Spree, but this was abandoned because the east bank did not always command the western bank, the river was too fordable, and the line was longer than their forces allowed them to defend.

Instead, the allies chose to position themselves behind the Blöser-Wasser, and only fight an advanced guard action between the Spree and the Blöser-Wasser. The allied position was such that their left was supported by the wooded mountains and the steep banks of the Spree. Their center was behind Bautzen. The city itself was surrounded by a chain of redoubts. The allied right was supported on some hills at the mouth of the Spree, near the village of Nimschütz. These hills were fortified with a series of redoubts. The principal redoubts were positioned as follows:

1. One on the left, on the height northeast of Mehlteuer,
2. One on a height behind Rabitz
3. Three between Bautzen-Hochkirch road at Jenkwitz, and Baschütz.
4. Three between Baschütz and the Bautzen-Weissenberg road.
5. Three between the Bautzen-Weissenberg road and Litten.[3]

In addition, there were numerous smaller works along this line, and the village on the Kreckwitz heights were fortified and had abattis set up. The fortifications were so extensive that the French engineers later destroyed no less than 78 redoubts, batteries, and epaulements on the allied positions.[4]

The allied positions stood within six miles of the Austrian frontier, and therefore should not have been possible to turn the southern flank. The position was strong if attacked frontally from the west, but very vulnerable to a turning maneuver from the north. Behind the main line, about 18,000 feet was a second allied line. It too supported its left on the mountains to the south, about 12,000 paces behind the first line, and anchored on the village of Hochkirch. Hochkirch and Würschen, separated by a distance of five kilometers, were both fortified, and formed the heart of the allied position.[5]

The center of the second line was held in three fortified villages. Three quarters of the center of this position was covered by swamps and difficult terrain.[6] The allied force holding these positions consisted of the following:

Russians	Infantry	Cavalry	Cossacks	Engineers and Artillery	Guns
Miloradovich	8,000	3,400	1,750	650	54
Gortschakov	10,500	2,000	450	750	66
Constantine	11,300	5,350	—	3,250	252
Barclay	9,150	1,800	—	1,420	84
Kleist*	1,400	420	550	180	16
Prussians					
Blücher	17,040	4,710	—	1,550	90
Yorck	4,120	1,210	—	340	36
Kleist**	2,300	330	—	300	24
	63,810	*19,220*	*2,750*	*8,440*	*622*

* Russians assigned to Kleist.
** Prussians assigned to Kleist.

THE WALLS OF BAUTZEN

The allied battle plan was issued on 19 May. If Miloradovich found the French crossing with a superior force above and below Bautzen, he was to fall back on the heights between Auritz and Klein Jenkwitz.

If the French attacked the main allied position, a number of options were established. Should the French advance against the allied right wing, the army was to reinforce that flank by a "flank march." If the allied center was attacked, Barclay and Kleist were to attack the French left flank. If the allied left was attacked, Barclay and the center were to swing forward and drive the French against the mountains. If both flanks were simultaneously attacked, the allies planned to strengthen their right and drive forward. Then they would swing left, and drive the French south into the mountains. Unfortunately for the allies, no thought was given to what to do, if Napoleon did not attack the main position or in case of a French attack from the northern flank.[7]

THE ALLIED DISPOSITIONS

The allies had a number of small "streifkorps" detached to operate on the French lines of advance. These consisted of the three corps of Colonels Davidov, Mandatov, and Captain Giesmar. Five further cossack regiments under Generalmajor Karpov II, four under Generalmajor Illowaisky IV, and five cossack and a bashkir regiment under Generalmajor Kiassarov were detached as well.[8]

The first line, or Advanced Guard Corps, held the allied positions closest to the French. This force was under the overall command of General of Infantry Count Miloradovich. These forces stood on the right bank of the Spree, left of the city of Bautzen.

On the extreme right of the Advanced Guard Corps, stood the cavalry force of Generalmajor Lanskoi (advanced guard of the right wing). It was posted by Mühlfehl, where it was to maintain a watch on all of the French movements on that flank. On the right wing of this force was the Streifkorps of Colonel Prendel, then came Generalmajor Paradowski with the Alexandria and White Russia Hussar Regiments, the Lithuania Chasseur à Cheval Regiment, and Horse Battery #2, and finally four cossack regiments under Generalmajor Illowaisky XII.

To the left of Lanskoi, stood Generallieutenant Tschaplitz's advanced guard of the 3rd Army of the West. Generallieutenant Tschaplitz stood by Klix, occupying the bank of the Spree, and the villages of Nieder Gurig and Malschwitz. Tschaplitz commanded two brigades, one under Colonel Kaslowsky, containing the Olivopol Hussar Regiment and the Jitomir Uhlan Regiment. The other was under Generalmajor Rudsevitch, and contained the 12th and 22nd Jager Regiments. Light Battery #34 was posted to Rudsevitch's left and further to the left was Generalmajor Grekov VIII's three cossack regiments. To the right of the city of Bautzen, stood the corps of Generallieutenant Kleist. This was a combined Russo-Prussian force. Rüdinger formed Kleist's right, with the four squadrons of the Grodno Hussar Regiment, the Fus/Colberg Infantry Regiment, and two guns posted in Nieder Gurig.[9] Kleist's middle was formed by Generalmajor Vlastov with Horse Battery #23 and the 23rd and 24th Jager Regiments, the 25th and 26th Jager Regiments under Generalmajor Roth, and finally Oberstlieutenant Steinmetz's Prussian brigade (1/,2/,Fus/Colburg Infantry Regiment). Kleist's left was formed by Major von Thumen's brigade (two squadrons each from 1st and 2nd Silesian Hussar Regiments and Prussian Horse Battery #3), and three cossack regiments under Generalmajor Radinov II. The assignments of his other guns is not known, but sources indicate Kleist had from 39 to 40 guns with him.[10]

Miloradovich commanded the left wing directly. His right was formed by Generalmajor Knorring's cavalry brigade (Soum Hussars, Tartar Uhlan Regiment, and the Converged Dragoon Regiment). Generallieutenant Prinz Eugene von Wurttemberg's 2nd Corps infantry formed the middle.

Wurttemberg's forces occupied the city of Bautzen. Two battalions of the Revel Infantry Regiment and the 20th Jager Regiment were in the city of Bautzen. These three battalions were very under strength.[11] The Ortenburg fortress was garrisoned by two battalions of the Tschernigov and Murmon Infantry Regiments, the battalion of the 21st Jagers, and four guns from Wolff's brigade.[12] The city walls were lined with sharpshooters, and several parts of the wall were further reinforced with a palisade.[13] Two batteries were posted to the right of the city and one foot battery and a horse battery were posted to the left of the city.[14]

The rest of the 2nd Corps was formed in two lines, with its left on Bautzen and its right supported by the village of Oehne. Two batteries posted on its right, covered its front. A few cossack regiments and some cavalry, provided communications with Kleist's corps.

The middle was formed by the corps artillery under Generalmajor Nikitin (Heavy Battery #1, Light Battery #33, Horse Battery #7). The left was the 4th Division of Generalmajor Pischnitzki. Colonel Ivanov's brigade formed the right (4th and 34th Jager Regiment, and the battalion of the Tobolsk Infantry Regiment). The left was formed by Colonel Treffurt's brigade (Krementsoug, Volhynie, and Riajsk). The extreme left was formed by the cavalry brigade of Generalmajor Pantschoulidzev I, (Tchernigov Chasseur à Cheval Regiment, New Russia Dragoon Regiment, and Lithuanian Uhlan Regiment.)

The extreme left of the Advanced Guard Corps was formed by Generalmajor Emmanuel's cavalry force. Emmanuel was positioned in the mountains to the south. His assigned the task of observing any enemy movements against this flank. He commanded the Kiev and Kharkov Dragoon Regiments, six guns from Horse Battery #4, two cossack regiments, and the Orlov Streifkorps.

General of Infantry Barclay de Tolly's forces also formed part of the first line of battle. His forces extended from Klein Sauberwitz to Malschwitz. He formed his troops in two lines. The first line was the corps of General Langeron. Langeron's right was formed by the cavalry brigade of Generalmajor Umanetz (Kinbourn Dragoon and Sieversk Chasseur Regiments), Light Battery #35 and the 18th Division of Generalmajor Scherbatov (Vladimir, Dnieper, Kostroma, and Tambov Infantry Regiments, and 28th and 32nd Jager Regiments).

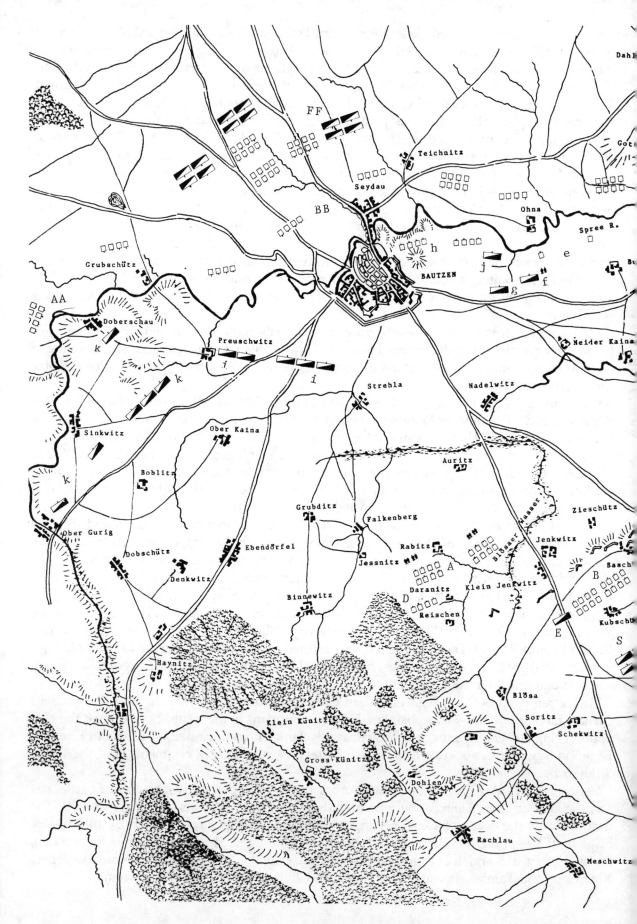

FF

BB

Teichnitz

Seydau

Ohna

Spree R.

Grubschütz

h

j

f

e

g

AA

Doberschau

k

Preuschwitz

i

i

Neider Kaina

k

Strehla

Nadelwitz

k

Sinkwitz

Ober Kaina

Boblitz

Auritz

Ober Gurig

Grubditz

Zieschütz

Dobschütz

Ebendörfel

Falkenberg

Jenkwitz

Denkwitz

Rabitz

A

Basch

Binnewitz

Jessnitz

B

Daranitz

Klein Jenkwitz

D

E

Kubsch

Reischen

S

Haynitz

Blösa

Soritz

Klein Künitz

Schekwitz

Gross Künitz

Dohlen

Rachlau

Meschwitz

212

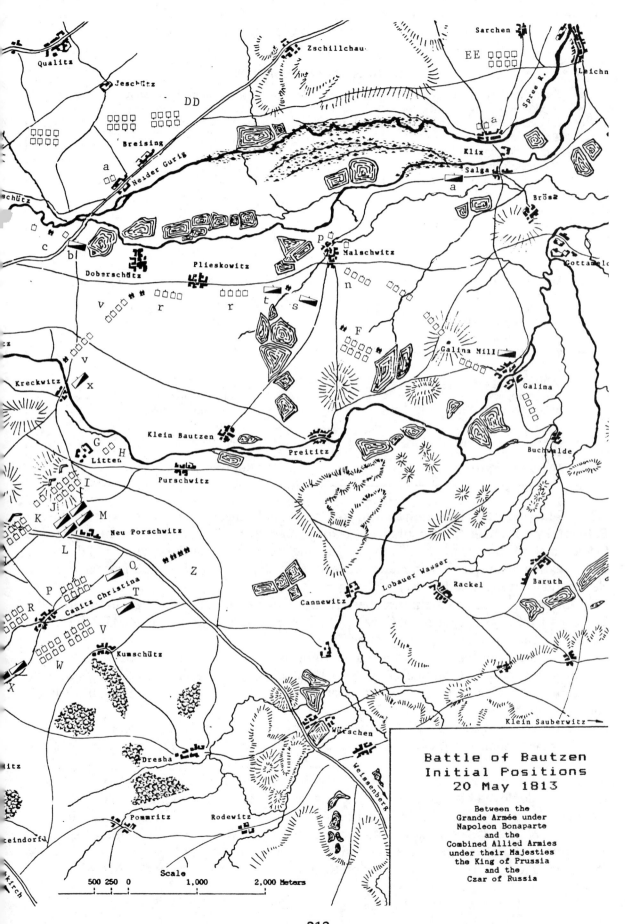

Battle of Bautzen
Initial Positions
20 May 1813

Between the
Grande Armée under
Napoleon Bonaparte
and the
Combined Allied Armies
under their Majesties
the King of Prussia
and the
Czar of Russia

Scale

500 250 0   1,000   2,000 Meters

BATTLE OF BAUTZEN
20 MAY 1813
BEGINNING DISPOSITIONS

a	Tshlaplitz's Advanced Guard		D	Englehardt's 8th Division
b	Grodno Hussar Regiment		E	Lissanevitsch's Division
c	Russian Horse Battery #23, 23rd & 24th Jager		F	Sass, Reserve of the 3rd Army of the West
	Regiments		G	Yorck's Corps
d	25th & 26th Jager Regiments		H	Roder's Brigade
e	Steinmetz's Brigade		I	Katzler's Brigade
f	1st & 2nd Silesian Hussar Regiments & 3rd		J	Prussian Guard Infantry Brigade
	Prussian Horse Battery		K	Natzmer's Brigade
g	Radinov II's Cossacks		L	Hobe's Brigade
h	Wurttemburg's 2nd Corps		M	Dolff's Reserve Cavalry
i	Knorring's Brigade		N	Markov's Corps
j	Pautschulid I's Brigade		O	Tscailkov's Guard Light Cavalry Division
k	Emanuel's Corps		P	Sulima's 1st Grenadier Division
l	Umanetz's Brigade		R	Zwielenief's 2nd Grenadier Division
m	Schervatov's 18th Division		S	Duca's 2nd Cuirassier Division
n	Insov's 9th Division		T	Gallizin's Guard Heavy Cavalry Division
p	10th & 38th Jager Regiments		V	1st Guard Infantry Division
r	Zeithen's Brigade		W	1st Guard Infantry Division
s	1st & 2nd Silesian Hussar Regiments		X	1st Cuirassier Division
	(Blucher)		Z	Jachwill's Artillery Reserve
t	Schmiedburg's Brigade			
v	Klux's Brigade		AA	Oudinot's Corps
x	Mutius' Brigade		BB	MacDonald's Corps
			CC	Marmont's Corps
A	Gortschakov's Corps		DD	Bertrand's Corps
B	Berg's Corps		EE	Lauriston's Corps
C	Uvaroff's Brigade		FF	Reserve Cavalry

The right was formed by the 9th Division of Generalmajor Insov. On his left was Generalmajor Poltaratzky's brigade (Nacheburg and Iakout Infantry Regiment), and on his right was Generalmajor Udom I's brigade (10th and 38th Jager Regiment), in the village of Malschwitz. On his extreme left was Generalmajor Pahlen II's cavalry brigade (Tver and Dorpat Dragoon Regiments) and Light Battery #28.

To Kleist's right, by Krekwitz and Plieskowitz, in the center of the allied position, stood the 2nd Prussian Corps of General of Cavalry Blücher. Blücher's right was formed by the Upper Silesian Brigade under Generalmajor von Ziethen.

Ziethen deployed his force from left to right as follows: Major von Blücher's brigade (the 2/,4/1st and 3/,4/2nd Silesian Hussar Regiments), Major von Schmiedburg's brigade (1/,2/Silesian Uhlan Regiment and Prussian Horse Battery #9 von Tuschen). Oberst Pirch commanded the Silesian Grenadier Battalion, 1/,3/,Fus/1st Silesian Infantry Regiment, 6pdr Foot Battery 8, 1/,3/2nd Silesian Infantry Regiment, the Silesian Schützen Battalion, 3rd Res/,5th Res/Leib Infantry Regiment, 6pdr Foot Battery #13, and Russian 12pdr Position Batteries #14 and #33.

Blücher's left wing was formed by the Lower Silesian Brigade under the command of Oberst Klüx. Klüx deployed his forces as follows: The infantry of Major von Jagow - West Prussian Grenadier Battalion, 2/,3/,Fus/1st West Prussian Infantry Regiment, 3rd Reserve/Leib Infantry Regiment, 2/,3/2nd West Prussian Infantry Regiment, 2nd Reserve/Leib Infantry Regiment, and 6pdr Foot Battery #9. He supported his infantry with Oberst von Mutius's cavalry (Neumärk and 1st West Prussian Dragoon Regiment, and Horse Battery #7 "Richter"). [15]

The second line started on the left, behind Miloradovich. The Russian forces of Generallieutenant Gortschakov II were posted here. In his second line of battle were the forces of Generallieutenant Markov. The third line was under Generallieutenant Berg. Their left flank was behind Klein-Jenkwitz, and the right flank stood near Baschütz. Both villages were occupied strongly.[16]

Berg's right was formed by Colonel Uvarov's brigade (Loubny Hussar Regiment, Moscow and Mitau Dragoon Regiments and Horse Battery #3). The right flank infantry was formed by the 5th Division of Generalmajor Lukov.

Lukov deployed his forces with Generalmajor Prince of Siberia's brigade on his right (Perm and Mohilev Infantry Regiments, and Position Battery #5), Generalmajor Kasatschkovsky's brigade in the middle (Kalouga and Sieversk Infantry Regiments, and Grand Duchess Cathrine Battalion), two musketeer regiments (Tenguinsk and Estonia) under Generalmajor Helfreich (14th Division), a brigade, detached from the 7th Division, formed with the Sophia and Pskov Infantry Regiments and the 11th Jager Regiment, Colonel Schindschin's brigade (Archangle,Schusselburg, and Old Ingremannland Infantry Regiments), two regiments (Kaporsk and 37th Jagers) under Colonel Stegemann, Position Battery #7, and Generalmajor Lissanevitch's brigade (Akhtyrsk Hussar Regiment, Tchougouiev Uhlan Regiment, and Kargopol Dragoon Regiment).

To the right of Gortschakov was the Prussian Corps of Generallieutenant Yorck. His right wing was under Generalmajor Corswandt. He deployed his forces with the two squadrons of the 1st West Prussian Dragoon Regiment and 6pdr Horse Battery #2 on the right. His center was the brigade under Oberst von Zielinsky (Fus/2nd, 1/,2/1st East Prussian Infantry Regiments, 1/,2/Leib Infantry Regiment, Combined Fusilier Battalion formed from the 1st East Prussian and Leib Infantry Regiments, and 6pdr Foot Batteries #1 and #2.

The left was formed by Horn's Brigade (6pdr Foot Battery #3, 1/1st and 2/2nd West Prussian Infantry Regiment, 2/1st and 2/2nd Silesian Infantry Regiments, the combined Fusilier Battalion of the 5th and 6th Infantry Regiments, 3pdr Foot Battery #1. The extreme left, under Major Schmalensee, was formed by the Horse Battery #1 and four squadrons of the Lithuanian Dragoon Regiment and two squadrons of the Brandenburg Dragoon Regiment.

Upon the beginning of the cannonade, Yorck moved his force from the position of Gottamelda, left to Preititz and Klein-Bautzen, towards Purschwitz.

The second line of battle stood behind the first. Acting as the general reserve, Generallieutenant Sass's forces stood behind General Barclay's corps, in the middle of the line. Generallieutenant Sass commanded the Reserve of the 3rd Army of the West. He deployed his forces as follows (right to left): Colonel Tern's brigade (Vitebsk and Kozlov Infantry Regiment), and 12pdr Position Batteries #15 and #18, Colonel Suthov's brigade (Kourin and Kolyvan Infantry Regiments, 7th Jager Regiment), Heavy Battery #34, and Light Battery #29. [17]

On Yorck's right, stood the Brandenburg Brigade of Generalmajor Röder. First came Oberstlieutenant Katzler's brigade (West Prussian Uhlan Regiment, and Horse Battery #8), Major von Alvensleben's Guard Brigade (1/,2/,Fus/Garde zu Fuss, Normal Infantry Battalion, Guard Foot Battery #4 "von Lehmann"), Major von Natzmer's brigade (Leib Grenadier Battalion, 1st East Prussian Grenadier Battalion, and 3/ and 1st Reserve/Leib Infantry Regiment) and finally Major Hobe's brigade (Brandenburg Hussar Regiment, 2nd Leib Hussar Regiment, and Guard Horse Battery #4 von Willmann).

The Guard Freiwilliger Jäger Battalion of Major von Wedell was posted in the village of Doberschütz, and the Guard Jäger Battalion of Major von Röder was in the village of Plieskowitz.[18] The Prussian reserve cavalry brigade of Oberst Dolffs stood in the second line. They were deployed with Oberstlieutenant von Werder's brigade on the right (Garde du Corps, Guard Light Cavalry Regiment, and Guard Horse Battery #4), and Oberst von Jürgass' brigade on the left (East Prussian, Silesian and Brandenburg Cuirassier Regiment, and Horse Battery #10 von Schaffer).

The left wing of the second line was formed by the forces of Generallieutenant Markov. Generalmajor Karpenkov's brigade (Light Battery #13 and the 1st and 33rd Jager Regiment) formed Markov's left. Next was Generalmajor Bistram's brigade (Podolsk and Jeletz Infantry

Mass de manoeuvre	Divisions	Effective Force
III Corps (Ney)	8th Souham	30,000
	9th Delmas	
	10th Albert	
	11th Ricard	
	39th Marchand	
V Corps (Lauriston)	16th Maison	27,000
	17th Puthod	
	18th Lagrange	
	19th Rochambeau	
VII Corps (Reynier)	32nd Durutte	9,500
	25th Sahr (Saxons)	
II Corps (Victor)	1st Philippon	13,000
	4th Dubreton	
I Cavalry Corps	Chastel	1,800
II Cavalry Corps (Sébastiani)	(not yet joined)	3,000
Main Body		
IV Corps (Bertrand)	12th Morand	25,000
	15th Peyri (Italian)	
	38th Franquemont (Württemberg)	
VI Corps (Marmont)	20th Compans	22,000
	21st Bonnet	
	22nd Friederichs	

Mass de manoeuvre	Divisions	Effective Force
XI Corps (Macdonald)	31st Fressinet	17,000
	35th Gérard	
	36th Charpentier	
XII Corps (Oudinot)	13th Pacthod	24,000
	14th Lorencz	
	29th Raglovich (Bavarians)	
Imperial Guard	Curial (Old Guard)	19,000
	Dumoustier (1st Young Guard)	
	Barrois (2nd Young Guard)	
Guard Cavalry	Lefebvre-Desnouëttes	4,000
	d'Ornano	
I Cavalry Corps (Latour-Maubourg)	Bruyère (Light Cavalry)	
	9 French Regiments	1,200
	1 Italian Regiment &	
	2 Saxon Regiments	2,400
	Bordesoulle (heavy cavalry)	
	7 French Regiments	1,200
	2 Saxon Regiments	1,200
	Doumerc (heavy cavalry)	
	7 French Regiments	1,200
	1 Italian Dragoon Regt	1,000
Total French Forces		203,500

FRENCH FORCES AT BAUTZEN[20]

Regiment), Generalmajor Turtscheninov's brigade (Olonetz and Staroskol Infantry Regiment), Colonel Scherbatov's brigade (Riazan and Brest Infantry Regiments) and on the right Colonel Kern's brigade (Belosersk Infantry Regiment and 45th Jager Regiment). Both Generalmajor Röder and the reserve cavalry brigade of Oberst von Dolffs, stood the foot of the Spitzberg, in a second line behind General Blücher's corps.

A third line was formed with the Russian Reserve Corps under the Grand Duke Constantine. It was posted centered on Canitz Christina. The first line was under Generallieutenant Raevsky. On Raevsky's right flank was Generalmajor Tschailikov's brigade (Guard Dragoon, Guard Uhlan Regiment, and Guard Hussar Regiments). To its left was the 1st Grenadier Division of Generalmajor Sulima.

Sulima deployed his division (left to right) the Heavy Battery #3 on the right, then the Count Arakcheyev, Ekaterino-slav, Tauride and St. Petersburg Grenadier Regiments, followed by the Converged Grenadiers of 5th and 14th Divisions, and two light batteries on the left.

Next was the 2nd Grenadier Division under Generalmajor Zwielenief. He deployed his division (right to left) Kiev, Moscow, Astrakhan, Fangoria, Little Russia and Siberian Grenadier Regiments and Heavy Battery #32 on his left.

To the left of the 2nd Grenadier Division was Generalmajor Duca's 2nd Cuirassier Division. He deployed his forces with Generalmajor Leontiev's brigade on his right (Gluchov and Pskof Cuirassier Regiments), Generalmajor Gudovitch's brigade in the center (Military Order and

Starodoub Cuirassier Regiments) and Colonel Massalov's brigade on the left (Little Russian and Novgorod Cuirassier Regiment).

Generallieutenant Count Gallizin V's forces formed the second line. On the right stood the Chevalier Guard, Horse Guard and Leibgarde Cuirassier Regiments under Generalmajor Arsenieff, and the Guard Horse Battery #1.

The center was formed by the Guard Corps under Generallieutenant Lavrov. The 1st Guard Division, under Generalmajor Baron Rosen, (Guard Position Battery #1, Preobragenski, Semenovski, Ismailov, and Guard Jager Regiments, and Guard Light Battery #1 stood on the right. The 2nd Guard Division, under Generalmajor Udom II (Lithuanian, Finland Guard Regiments and Guard Light Battery #2) formed the center and Generalmajor Scheltuchin II's brigade (Pavlov and Leib Grenadier Regiments) formed the right.

On the right of Scheltuchin stood Guard Heavy Battery #2, Guard Horse Battery #2, and the other brigade of the 1st Cuirassier Division under Generalmajor Rosen (Astrakhan, Empress, and Ekaterinoslav Cuirassier Regiments).

An artillery reserve was commanded by Generallieutenant Jachwill, and consisted of four position batteries, five light batteries, and four horse batteries. These were divided into two forces commanded by Generalmajors Euler and Merlin.[19]

Though several cossack detachments were deployed on the hills and valleys on the left flank, as far as the Bohemian border, five further cossack regiments were posted behind Klein-Burschwitz, in a line behind the entire battlefield. They were assigned the duties of military police, that is catching deserters and guarding the allied train.

The French Dispositions

The French army was positioned with Oudinot's XII Corps to the south, supported by the mountains, on the left bank of the Spree, and separated from the enemy only by the valley of the Spree. Macdonald's XI Corps sat before Bautzen, straddling the road to Dresden. Marmont's

VI Corps was to the left of Bautzen, centered on the village of Nimschütz. Bertrand's IV Corps stood on the left of Marmont's corps, positioned to descend from Jeschütz on the allied right. Marmont's corps was a half hour march from the city of Bautzen. He was to follow Bertrand over the Spree.

At 8:00 A.M., Napoleon ordered Oudinot to cross the Spree and to attack the mountains which supported the allied left. Macdonald was to throw a bridge across the Spree between Bautzen and the mountains, and attack the allied center. Soult was to advance a half league north of Bautzen with the IV Corps and part of the cavalry, and distract the allied right, while Ney, with Reynier and Lauriston, was to cross the Spree and turn the allied right.

The Assault on the Center

The artillery cannonade began at noon. Macdonald had no need to place a pontoon bridge across the Spree because he found

Marshal Marmont

an intact stone bridge, which his corps rapidly crossed. At the sound of the beginning of the cannonade, the Czar and the King of Prussia left their headquarters and moved to a position between Neider Kaina and Burk, to the right of the city of Bautzen, so they could watch the progress of the battle. Napoleon was on the Schmochtizer heights controlling the French operations.[21]

Macdonald's forces also crossed the Spree at a ford near the powder mill. The 31st Division was on the right, the 35th Division was on the left, and the 36th Division was in reserve.[22] As they crossed, they were struck by the Volhynie Infantry Regiment in a bayonet attack led by Colonel Kurnossov and momentarily slowed.[23]

The pressure against Wurttemberg's Russians was so great that he abandoned his efforts to defend the Spree against Macdonald's forces. Wurttemberg executed a conversion to the rear and refused his right, supporting his left on the city of Bautzen.[24] He moved a further four guns to the right flank of his corps. He took a strong position on the heights between Jenkwitz and Auritz, where St. Priest joined him with the 22nd Division. Miloradovich had sent him orders not to evacuate Bautzen.

Macdonald's advance was cautious. Wurttemberg detached the four jager regiments from the 2nd Corps, and sent them forward to defend the river and the ground before Auritz, supported by a heavy cannonade. St. Priest was deployed behind the villages of Falkenberg and Jessnitz, under heavy pressure from Macdonald. Both held their positions until Bautzen was turned and captured.[25]

THE ASSAULT IN THE NORTH

Marmont and Bertrand seized four bridges under the cover of heavy artillery and the VI Corps (Marmont) began its assault on Kleist's forces north of the city of Bautzen. Marmont's first units across the Spree crossed at Nimschütz, Nieder-Gürig, and Briesing. The 23rd Line Regiment, Morand's 12th Division, found itself on a hill on the right bank. It was only able to maintain its position by virtue of the fire of a battery of 22 guns (20 French 12pdrs and 2 Württemberg Howitzers) established on the Gottesberg heights on the left bank of the Spree.[26]

Despite that one tense situation, Marmont's other forces quickly occupied Rattwitz. After a lengthy cannonade and numerous allied counter-attacks, Général de division Compans leading the 20th Division, swung south, and advanced into Bautzen from behind. It was about 3:00 P.M.[27] The Russian battery which defended the city was taken at the "pas de charge," and the ramparts were scaled. All the Russians found in the city were killed or taken prisoner.[28] It was a long, hard fought battle, and it was not until 6:00 P.M., that Compan's 20th Division was well into the city.

The battle in the suburbs had been hand to hand, house to house combat, of the bloodiest sort. Men fought their way through kitchens and over garden walls. The Russians supported their positions with detachments of artillery that worked to deadly effect on their French assailants.

The Russians in the city, under Wurttemberg, held out until General Emmanuel's forces were driven back. They then found themselves faced with being surrounded by the advancing French. At 7:00 P.M. Wurttemberg evacuated the city.

MARMONT AND MACDONALD SHIFT NORTH

Kleist's force of 5,000 men, stood on the heights of Burg from 12:00 noon until late in the evening, in an effort to hold the French from encircling Bautzen from the north. The IV and part of the VI Corps struck him. His position was tenuous until he received reinforcements of Russian artillery and five Prussian battalions from Blücher's corps.

Kleist had stopped the French and forced them to send their next attack through Nieder-Gürig, further to the north. This assault struck Ziethen, who was supported by a large force of Prussian and Russian artillery.

It was at 8:00 P.M., that Bonnet's 21st Division advanced out of Bautzen to seize control of the heights Nieder-Kaina. Bonnet's 21st Division attacked Kleist, who had moved to reinforce the line, and was moving towards Kaina and Busankwitz. With his northern flank turned, Kleist held out until 8:30 P.M., and then withdrew behind the guns at Litten.

As Kleist was thrown back into the entrenched positions in the second allied line, the French began a general advance. General Bonnet's forces drove onward against the last elements of Emmanuel's forces, which were defending the heights on the northern flank. Seeing this assault, Prince Eugene von Wurttemberg sent the 4th, 20th, and 21st Jager Regiments under the command of Colonel Michaud, Wing Adjutant to the Czar, to support Emmanuel.[29] As the battle expanded, further reinforcements in the form of the Guard Jager Regiment and the Finland Guard Infantry Regiment were thrown into the battle. Despite these reinforcements, General Bonnet occupied Nieder-Kaina and Basankwitz. He then marched onto the plateau, which made him master of the allied positions.

The allied reaction was swift. Blücher dispatched his reserve cavalry in an effort to push Bonnet back. Bonnet quickly formed his units into squares, and resisted all of Blücher's assaults, holding his position on the plateau. As this happened, the XI Corps and Compans' 20th Division, VI Corps, carried Bautzen and began moving on Blöser-Wasser. By 6:00 P.M., the XI Corps sat on the heights between Strehla and Nadelwitz, facing Auritz.[30]

BERTRAND'S MOVEMENTS

Bertrand was ordered to occupy the plateau on the left bank of the Spree with the IV Corps and to move to the assistance of General Lauriston as soon as he heard gunfire. Once the battle began, Bertrand moved forward, forcing the Spree. General Morand had formed his 12th division into three columns. The center, commanded by General Hulot (3 battalions of light infantry, 3/3rd Légère, 4/8th Légère, & 2nd Provisional Croatian Regiment), was directed against Nieder-Gürig. The left, under General Bellair (13th Line Regiment - 5 battalions), moved through the village of Breising. General Sicard, commanding the third column (23rd Line Regiment - 4 battalions), supported the movements of the center, and moved onto the Doberschütz plateau, where he engaged in heavy combat with the allies.[31]

The 38th (Württemberg) Division seized a hill on the right, and placed 12 guns there supported by the 9th and 1/7th Württemberg Infantry Regiments.[32] This artillery inflicted heavy casualties on the allied cavalry, attempting to attack the French. The 15th (Italian) Division occupied a position in the rear and acted as a reserve. General Briche's cavalry (consisting solely of the 2nd Neapolitan Chasseur à Cheval Regiment with two squadrons) covered the French left and established contact with Ney.[33]

Bertrand's attack went poorly. The 1/10th Württemberg Infantry Regiment struck directly at Nieder-Gürig, where Rüdiger had posted the Grodno Hussars and the Fus/2nd East Prussian Infantry Regiment. The brigade of Général de brigade Sicard (2nd Provisional Croatian Regiment and 23rd Line Regiment) moved against it in a flanking maneuver.[34]

The allied position was quickly reinforced by the arrival of the 3rd and Fusilier Battalions of the 1st Silesian Regiment (Ziethen's Brigade). Rüdiger lead the Grodno Hussars forward driving the Württembergers attack back.

The Württembergers reformed their attack, with Sicard reforming and moving forward from the Kieferberg (Pine Hill). The 1/10th Württemberg Regiment, supported by the 1/2nd and 1/9th Württemberg Regiments pushed again in to Neider-Gürig.

However, when Napoleon learned that communications with Hoyerswerda were broken, he ordered Soult, with Morand's 12th Division, the 38th (Württemberg) Division of General Bertrand, Bruyère's 1st Light Cavalry Division, and Bordesoulle's 1st Heavy Cavalry Division (Latour-Maubourg's I Cavalry Corps), to re-establish communications with the French left and

NAPOLEON MAKING HIS PLANS FOR 21 MAY

facilitate the junction. Bertrand's attack stalled as he shifted his attention, and Marmont ordered the 22nd Division to occupy the positions that Bertrand abandoned.

THE SOUTHERN FLANK OF THE BATTLE

The French XII Corps (Oudinot) advanced without significant enemy contact. Oudinot found no bridge, and after placing his three pontoon bridges, forced his way across Spree. He advanced with Raglovich's 29th (Bavarian) Division on the left of the 14th Division, and the 3rd Cuirassier Division, under Doumerc, in support.

Oudinot encountered only a few skirmishers as he crossed the Spree. These were quickly pushed back, as Pacthod's 13th Division crossed two fords and the small bridges near the village of Sinkwitz. His forces had completed their passage of the Spree by 1:00 P.M. Pacthod's right moved onto a high plateau crowned with pines, and defended by a single Russian battalion in a strengthened position.[35]

The Russian battalion was chased out of its position, but the Russian General St. Priest quickly reacted, sending a combined force of infantry and cavalry to face Pacthod. The 4/1st Légère Regiment and the 3/,4/7th Line Regiment (1st Brigade, 13th Division), defended their positions bravely, pushing the allies back with a heavy loss. When this attack ceased, Pacthod advanced his two remaining regiments. These Russians were, no doubt, the first of the three jager regiments under Michaud, part of Prinz Eugene von Wurttemberg's command.[36]

The vigorous resistance by the Russians delayed Pacthod. A brigade of Lorencz's 14th Division, moved to form on Pacthod's right, while the Bavarians moved on Denkwitz, where they formed on the right of the 14th Division.[37]

220

When he reached Boblitz, Pacthod again encountered heavy resistance, but the voltigeur and carabinier companies of the 4/1st Légère Regiment drove them back. Despite the strength of their positions, and a vigorous defense of the mountain heights above Binnewitz, Pacthod drove the Russians back towards Hochkirch. The Russians had cut down many of the trees around Hochkirch, to give their artillery a clear field of fire as well as to build an abattis to increase the obstacles that the French would have to overcome.[38]

General Lorencz's 14th Division, with the 29th (Bavarian) Division of Raglovich in support, moved to the right towards the mountain chain and Hochkirch eleven kilometers south of Bautzen. Here he encountered an allied force seeking to maneuver against the French flank. The allies were forced back and the French occupied Denkwitz that evening.

Oudinot had taken his designated objective, the mountains, at 7:00 P.M., and had thrown the allies back to their second line. He spent the night in Ebendörfel. The head of the XII Corps was five kilometers east of the Spree. His divisions were echeloned with the left in advance. The echelon of the right, Lorencz's 14th Division (a single brigade), was two kilometers behind the echelon of the left (Pacthod's 13th Division), and Raglovich's Bavarians were in the second line in Brugditz, supporting Pacthod. The corps had a front of 2,000 meters, and a depth of 2,000 to 2,500 meters, and directly threatened Hochkirch, which was on the allied line of retreat.

During the course of the battle to drive Oudinot back, Wittgenstein had dispatched a brigade of Russian Guards (Pavlov and Leib Grenadiers),[39] drawn from the general reserve, south to help Miloradovich counter attack Oudinot's troops in Binnewitz and Tronberg. This small struggle was to have a significant impact on the next day's battle, because the departure of this single brigade from the general reserve, would prove to be the significant weakening of the overall allied position.[40]

NEY'S FLANKING MANEUVER

During the morning of 20 May, Maréchal Ney ignored Barclay's maneuvers of the previous day, and advised Lauriston that the III Corps would march on Königswartha. Ney's advanced guard moved along the road to Mörtcke, so as to cover the junction of the III Corps with the V Corps. In Wartha they encountered Peyri's battered 15th Division, and departed with Peyri following behind them. Behind Peyri came the main body of the III Corps.[41]

Ney's column arrived in Königswartha at 9 A.M., and found only a few allied wounded in the village. Once there, Ney dispatched a courier to Lauriston advising him that the III Corps would change its direction to the left and move on Klix. The 2nd brigade of the advanced guard was to push on Neudorfel, in an effort to contact the enemy. It would later follow the corps' flanking movement to the right.

When Ney arrived in Klein-Opitz, a small force of cossacks were encountered and pushed to the right. Ney encountered columns of cavalry along the Spree. Initially, it was assumed that this was Lauriston's corps, but in fact it was the enemy and the V Corps was not pursuing them.

In Klein-Opitz, a detachment of two légère battalions was established to provide a flank guard, while the main body moved along the road to Droben. As they cleared Klein-Opitz, a few cannon shot were fired to disperse the cossacks. At the same time, a powerful cannonade was heard from the direction of Bautzen. Ney's corps picked up its pace.

Ney was still concerned about not contacting Lauriston's V Corps, and dispatched a small force of 50 hussars and 300 voltigeurs, to move in the direction of Milkel in an effort to locate Lauriston. This force encountered only swamps and partisans.

When Ney arrived at Brehmen, he found his corps on a plateau with a magnificent view of the battlefield. The allies had a force near Zyllichau, and large masses around Scklir and Klix. The 9th Division (Delmas) was posted on a ridge at Brehmen, and began to cannonade everything that appeared from the direction of Zyllichau.

The 19th Provisional Regiment moved to Scklir, where it took up positions. The 8th Division (Souham) then passed through the village, and briefly cannonaded an enemy force between Scklir and Klix, that was under pressure from Lauriston. Ney observed about 2,000 cavalry formed between Särchen and Leichnam.

The 10th Division (Girard) advanced from the windmill by Scklir, as the 8th Division (Souham) advanced into Scklir, to assure the passage of the corps over the Spree. The 11th Division (Ricard) acted as a reserve, remaining by the Scklir windmill. At 7:30 P.M. night began to fall. Despite that, the Comte de Valmy was ordered to lead an assault on Klix and to seize control of it, with the advanced guard and the 8th Division.

Klix was strongly held with large numbers of infantry and several batteries. The 19th Provisional Regiment seized a position in a copse of woods, on the left flank of 2,000 allied cavalry near Saehrigen, as they were fired on by the 10th Division's (Girard) artillery. Klix was quickly taken with a strong bayonet charge. The allies counter attacked, but it was beaten back. The French slept in the fields around Klix that night, their infantry formed in squares by division. After dark the 39th Division (Marchand) arrived at Scklir and established itself.[42]

END OF THE FIRST DAY

The battle had raged until 10:00 P.M. After the roar of cannon and the crackle of musketry was done, both armies, illuminated by the flames leaping from the burning village of Ritschen, broke off combat and settled into their bivouacs for the night.

According to Prussian sources the allied losses for the day were 900 Russian hors de combat. A further 1,000 were lost in Kleist's corps. The French reputedly lost 3,000 dead and 7,000 wounded. Barclay de Tolly's corps had not been engaged and remained fresh for the next day's battle.[43]

The French army had seized Bautzen. Macdonald and Oudinot had moved their XII and XI Corps, into positions between Bautzen and the allied second line. The XII Corps was situated such that the 29th (Bavarian) Division was in Ebendörfel, Lorencz's 14th Division was in Tronberg, and Pacthod's 13th Division was in Binnewitz. The XI Corps was deployed with Gérard (35th Division), Charpentier (36th Division) and Fressinet (31st Division) established along the Strehla heights, facing Auritz.

Marmont's VI Corps was deployed such that Compans (20th Division), Friederichs (22nd Division) and Bonnet (21st Division) were aligned on the road from Bautzen to Hochkirch, to the right of Burk. A regiment of each of the three divisions occupied Nadelwitz, Nieder-Kaina, and Basankwitz. Bertrand's IV Corps was in Nieder-Gürig, on the left bank of the Spree, with Ney's forces (III and V Corps). Morand's 12th Division occupied the Nimschütz heights with five battalions and Nieder-Gürig with three battalions. The rest of his forces were between Nimschütz and Nieder-Gürig. The 38th (Württemberg) Division was between Kronfortschen and Nimschütz, with a detachment in Nimschütz. The 15th (Italian) Division was in Jeschütz. The Guard, Latour-Maubourg's cavalry reserve, which now included the 1st and 3rd Württemberg Cavalry Regiments[44] and the general headquarters were established in Bautzen.

Ney's forces stood on the northern most flank between Klix and Hornsdorf. His advanced guard, formed by Souham's 8th Division, III Corps, was in Klix, after having ejected Tschaplitz's forces from the village. Puthod's 17th Division and Lauriston's Corps were between Wartha and Hoyerswerda. The VII Corps (Reynier) was in Hoyerswerda. The II Corps (Victor) and Sébastiani's II Reserve Cavalry Corps were in Döbern.[45]

The Czar retired to his camp in Klein-Burschwitz, and the King of Prussia to his in Würschen. Napoleon camped on the field of battle, surrounded by his guard.

1 Foucart, Bautzen, pg 237.

2 Camon, Guerre Napoléonienne, Vol IV, pg 411.

3 Petre, Napoleon's Last Campaign In Germany, pg 118.

4 Foucart, Bautzen, pg 293.

5 Camon, Guerre Napoléonienne, Vol IV, pg 411.

6 Foucart, Bautzen, pgs 276–277.

7 Petre, Napoleon's Last Campaign In Germany, pg 120.

8 Sporschil, Grosse Chronik, Vol I, pg 208.

9 Wagner, Recueil des Plans, Vol II, pg 15.

10 Friederich, Befreiungskriege, pg 274.

11 Preussischen Grossen Generalstab, Kriegsgeschichtlich Einzelschriften, pg 42.

12 Fabry, Prince de Wurtemberg, pg 66.

13 Friederich, Befreiungskriege, pg 274.

14 Wagner, Recueil des Plans, Vol II, pg 15.

15 Sporschil, Grosse Chronik, Vol I, pg 208, & von Conrady, Sechsten Infanterie, pg 173.

16 Plotho, Krieg in Deutschland, Vol I, pg 156.

17 Sporschil, Grosse Chronik, Vol I, pg 209.

18 Plotho, Krieg in Deutschland, Vol I, pg 156.

19 Sporschil, Grosse Chronik, Vol I, pg 210.

20 Camon, Guerre Napoléonienne, Vol IV, pgs 415–416.

21 Sporschil, Grosse Chronik Vol I, pg 216.

22 Wagner, Recueil des Plans, Vol II, pg 17.

23 Fabry, Prince de Wurttemberg, pg 67.

24 This means that Wurttemberg pulled his line back to a new position, secured his left flank against the city of Bautzen and bending the right wing of his battle line back at an angle so that it bent away from the French.

25 Fabry, Prince de Wurttemberg, pg 68.

26 Clément, Campagne de 1813, pg 221.

27 Rehtwisch, Bautzen, pg 67.

28 Foucart, Bautzen, pg 298.

29 Plotho, Krieg in Deutschland, pg 162.

30 Clément, Campagne de 1813, pg 220.

31 Foucart, Bautzen, pg 301.

32 Rossler, Tagbücher, pg 313.

33 Camon, Guerre Napoléonienne, Vol IV, pg 425.

34 Wagner, Recueil des Plans, Vol II, pg 18.

35 Clément, Campagne de 1813, pg 219.

36 Sporschil, Grosse Chronik, Vol I, pg 218.

37 Clément, Campagne de 1813, pg 219.

38 Foucart, Bautzen, pg 296.

39 Wagner, Recueil des Plans, Vol II, pg 15.

40 Clément, Campagne de 1813, pg 223.

41 Fabry, Opérations des IIe & Ve Corps, pg 23.

42 Fabry, Opérations des IIe & Ve Corps, pg 25.

43 Sporschil, Grosse Chronik, Vol I, pg 218.

44 Rossler, Tagbücher, pg 312.

45 Clément, Campagne de 1813, pgs 221–222.

Bautzen, The Second Day
21 May 1813

At 5:00 A.M. on the morning of 21 May, Napoleon moved to the heights a mile and a half from Bautzen. The battle erupted shortly afterwards when Oudinot began a heavy fusilade on the Russian left. The Russians, who sensed the importance of that position, had placed a major portion of their army on their left to prevent it from being flanked.

Overall, Napoleon's plans were simple. He wished to continue his overt attempt to turn the allied left with Oudinot while his center remained stationary, holding the allies in place. As this happened, Ney and Lauriston were to attempt a sweeping flanking maneuver from the north, and turn Barclay's right flank.[1] Once Ney and Lauriston had moved well into the allied rear, specifically around Preititz and Blücher's rear, Napoleon intended to push Bertrand's corps across the Spree, and into Blücher's western front, cutting him off from the rest of the allied army and destroying him in detail. Ney and Lauriston were to continue their flanking maneuver and cut off the retreat of as much of the allied army as possible, once Blücher had been crushed.

Napoleon's initial orders were for the IV, VI, and XI Corps, his center, to remain immobile until ordered to advance. Napoleon ordered Oudinot (XII Corps) and part of Macdonald's XI Corps to engage the Russian left around Klein-Künitz, to force the allies to heavily reinforce their left from their general reserve. This attack was to pin Miloradovich for what he anticipated would be the final stroke at about noon or 1:00 P.M. The honor of executing the coup de grace was to fall to Bertrand.

Support for that blow was to come from Ney, who would fall on the extreme right of the allied line, move through Klix, on the Spree, and advance on Weissenberg and Hochkirch in an effort to take the allies in the flank and rear. Napoleon's orders to Ney read, "The intention of the Emperor is that you always follow the movements of the enemy. His Majesty has advised your staff officer of the enemy's position, which is protected by redoubts that he has constructed. The intention of the Emperor is that you be in the village of Preititz at 11:00 A.M. We shall attack the enemy at all points. Direct Lauriston to march on your left to be in position to turn the enemy if your movement obliges him to abandon his position."[2]

The Imperial Guard and the French cavalry reserve remained masked by a ridge, but were posted so that they could strike quickly to the right or left, depending on how the battle progressed. This reserve stood in the Basankwitz valley and consisted of one Old Guard and two Young Guard divisions, the 3rd Light and 3rd Cuirassier Divisions, the Guard Cavalry Divisions, the Guard artillery (48 foot guns and 18 horse guns), and the two horse batteries of the 1st Cavalry Corps. The allies did not know the position of this reserve.

THE ALLIED POSITIONS

During the night, the mountainous positions between Reischen and Kunitz were occupied by the 1st and 4th Corps, as well as the 1st Grenadier Division. This wing was under the command of General Prince Gortschakov. The cavalry of General Emmanuel was reinforced by the Guard Light Cavalry Division, under the command of General Tschailikov, as well as the cavalry under the command of General Lissanevitch. Emmanuel deployed his forces below Binnewitz and Falkenberg, near Gross Künitz. Knorring's cavalry was posted to Prince Eugene von Wurttemberg's right. Millesimo's detachment (the Loubny Hussar Regiment) moved into a reserve position by Kubschütz. The Russian Guard, less one brigade, moved into a position by

Jenkwitz, in support of Gortschakov, and the 2nd Grenadier Division and the cuirassiers formed the main reserve by Neu-Purschwitz. Prince Eugene von Wurttemberg was ordered to move the 2nd Corps from Auritz to the heights about Reischen. Wurttemberg placed the 2nd Corps to the right and rear of Reischen. The 3rd Division was to the left and the 4th Division was to the right.

St. Priest was to continue holding his positions at Falkenberg and Jessnitz, until the beginning of the enemy attack. Then he was to occupy the villages of Reischen and Daranitz.[3] Berg had moved his corps to Prince Eugene von Wurttemberg's right, and extended the Russian line to the Bautzen-Hochkirch road. To the north of Berg was Constantine's Corps. Constantine deployed his main line behind Baschütz, but detached smaller forces of infantry and artillery between the villages of Zieschütz, Jenkwitz, and Baschütz. The grenadier divisions, under Raevsky, were formed on the left and the Russian Guard on the right of Baschütz. Two battalions of the Finland Guard Infantry Regiment were posted in Bauschütz. The Guard Marine Equipage Battalion acted as the Czar's headquarters guard.

Nine heavy batteries formed the front of Constantine's forces, and the cuirassier reserve stood to the rear, but close enough to be called when needed. Behind the entire army was posted a screen of cossacks, whose function was to act as military police and stop any "unauthorized individual withdrawals," i.e. desertions.[4]

Yorck deployed his Prussians between Kreckwitz, Purschwitz, and Litten, with the bulk of his forces between Litten and Purschwitz. Three entrenched batteries formed his front. The center battery contained half of 12pdr Battery #3 and half of 6pdr Foot Battery #1. The remainder of 6pdr Foot Battery #1 stood between the middle and the left earth work. The other two were manned with Russian batteries. His two fusilier battalions were posted immediately behind the batteries. The Fus/2nd East Prussian Regiment was posted in Litten. Horse Battery #1 and the 2nd Leib Hussars were posted before Litten. A second horse battery and the 2nd Silesian Hussar Regiment were posted behind Litten to act as a reserve.

Steinmetz's Brigade stood to the right of Litten and Horn's brigade stood to its left. Both brigades were in column, behind the fusiliers. The cavalry was held in reserve behind the infantry with the Prussians in the first line and three Russian cuirassier regiments under Uvarov in the second line. The reserve horse artillery was posted, such that it could maneuver between the entrenched artillery before Yorck's position.[5]

Kleist was holding a position around Purschwitz, and was being held as a reserve force. The Colberg Infantry Regiment was to the right of Purschwitz, the Russian jagers to the left and the Grodno Hussars were in reserve. The church was occupied by the East Prussian Jägers.

Blücher's forces were behind the ponds around Doberschütz and Plieskowitz, facing Bertrand's forces. The Russians under Barclay de Tolly, were rather widely spread from Malschwitz and Galina on a row of heights. The terrain to his front and flank was broken by ponds, making communications with Blücher difficult.[6]

Because of the importance of Blücher's position, he was reinforced on 21 May with two Russian 12pdr Position Batteries (24 guns) and two Russian 6pdr Batteries (24 guns). Each gun was provisioned with 80 to 120 rounds of ammunition. The colonel commanding these guns was advised that more ammunition was available and would be sent when necessary. Of the 92 guns at Blücher's disposal, only 24 Russian 12pdrs and 32 Prussian 6pdrs were positioned on the heights, where they could engage the French. The remainder of the artillery, including five Prussian horse batteries, was held in a general reserve, sheltered behind the heights.[7]

Ziethen's right wing was anchored in Pleiskowitz. The Prussian Guard Fusilier Battalion, under Major Röder, Captain Zastrow's sharpshooters, and two other companies of the 3/Leib Infantry, as well as two companies from the Silesian Grenadier Battalion were posted in Plieskowitz.[8] Next to Röder, were the combined Silesian Hussar Regiment, and the Neumärk Dragoon Regiment whose job was to maintain contact with Barclay's corps.[9]

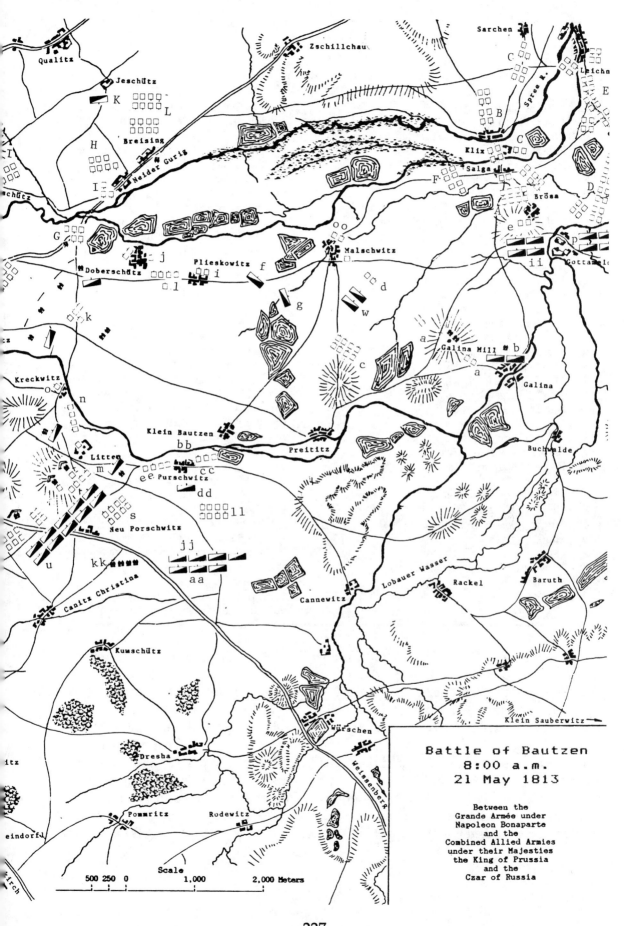

Qualitz

Jeschütz K

L

Breising

H

Neider Gurig

I

I

G

Doberschütz

j

l

Plieskowitz i f

k

Kreckwitz o

n

Klein Bautzen

bb

Litten m

Purschwitz ee cc

dd

s

Neu Porschwitz

ll

u jj

kk aa

Canitz Christina

Kumschütz

Dresha

Pommritz Rodewitz

Zschillchau

Sarchen

C

Leichn

B

E

Klix

C

Salga

F

A

e

D

Brösa

P

ii

Gottamel

oo

Malschwitz

d

w

g

a

Galina Mill b

a

c

Galina

Buchwalde

Preititz

Lobauer Wasser

Rackel

Baruth

Cannewitz

Klein Sauberwitz

Würschen

Weissenberg

**Battle of Bautzen
8:00 a.m.
21 May 1813**

Between the
Grande Armée under
Napoleon Bonaparte
and the
Combined Allied Armies
under their Majesties
the King of Prussia
and the
Czar of Russia

Scale

500 250 0   1,000   2,000 Meters

BATTLE OF BAUTZEN
8 A.M.
21 MAY 1813

A	10th Division (Albert)	**i**	Prussian Guard Fusilier Battalion, 2 Cos Silesian Grenadier Battalion & 3/Leib Infantry Regiment
B	11th Division (Ricard)	**j**	1/, 3/, Fus/ 1st Silesian Infantry Regiment & 2 Cos Silesian Grenadier Battalion
C	39th Division (Marchand's Badeners & Hessians)	**k**	Klüx's Brigade
D	8th Division (Souham)	**l**	Zeithen's Brigade
E	9th Division (Delmas)	**m**	Horn's Brigade
F	16th Division (Maison)	**n**	Zielinsky's Brigade (Steinmetz)
G	Sichard's Brigade, 12th Division (Morand)	**o**	2nd Res Bn/Leib Regiment & 3rd Res Bn/1st West Prussian Regiment (Klüx's Brigade)
H	Bellair's Brigade, 12th Division (Morand)	**p**	Lanskoi's Advanced Guard
I	38th Division (Franquemont's Württembergers)	**r**	Russian Guard Infantry
J	2nd Neapolitan Chasseur à Cheval Regiment	**s**	2nd Grenadier Division
K	Jell's Württemburg Cavalry Brigade	**t**	1st Grenadier Division
L	15th Division (Peyri's Italians)	**u**	1st & 2nd Russian Cuirassier Divisions
M	Imperial Guard Infantry	**w**	Dorpat & Tver Dragoon Regiments
N	Imperial Guard Cavalry	**x**	Berg's Corps
O	Cavalry Reserve (Latour-Maubourg)	**y**	St. Priest's Corps
P	1st Division (Compans)	**z**	Russian Guard Light Cavalry, Emmanuel's, & Lissanevitch's Cavalry Brigades
R	2nd Division (Bonnet)	**aa**	Uvarov's Cavalry Brigade
S	3rd Division (Friederich)	**bb**	Kleist's Advanced Guard
T	31st Division (Philipon)	**cc**	Colberg Infantry Regiment
V	35th Division (Gérard)	**dd**	Grodno Hussar Regiment
W	36th Division (Charpentier)	**ee**	23rd, 24th, 25th, & 26th Jager Regiments
X	13th Division (Pacthod)	**ff**	3rd Division (Schachafskoi)
Y	14th Division (Lorencz)	**gg**	4th Division (Pischnitzky)
Z	Bavarian Division (Raglovich)	**hh**	Loubny Hussar Regiment
AA	Reizet's Dragoon Brigade	**ii**	Tschlapitz's Advanced Guard
		jj	Dolff's Reserve Cavalry Brigade
a	18th Division (Schervatov)	**jj**	Russian Reserve Artillery (Jachwill)
b	Umanet's Cavalry Brigade	**ll**	Brandenburg Brigade
c	3rd Army of the West Reserve (Sass)	**mm**	Markov's Corps
d	9th Division (Insov)	**nn**	Knorring's Cavalry Brigade
e	28th & 32nd Jager Regiments	**oo**	7th, 10th, & 38th Jager Regiments
f	1st & 2nd Silesian Hussar Regiments		
g	Schmiedburg's Cavalry Brigade		

In the village of Doberschütz, stood the lst Silesian Regiment and two companies of the Silesian Grenadier Battalion under the orders of Major von Streit.

The 2nd Reserve Battalion/Leib Regiment, which was commanded by Major von Othengraven, stood in Kreckwitz. The 3rd Reserve Battalion/lst West Prussian Regiment stood behind the village in support. The Fusilier Battalion/lst West Prussian Regiment was deployed in companies to cover the guns, leaving Klüx with only four formed battalions. They were deployed with three battalions in the first line, and the grenadier battalion in the second line as a reserve. The Brandenburg Dragoons covered a battery by the Spree, and the Silesian Uhlans stood on the left wing. The Guard Freiwilliger Jägers, under von Wedel, were posted in Purschwitz.[10]

The allied positions were such, that the greatest concentration of forces were directly east of Bautzen. As the allied line stretched north, it rapidly tapered out, growing thinner and thinner.

THE FRENCH POSITIONS

Oudinot's corps faced Miloradovich's corps to the south. He strung his forces out across the mountainous countryside, between Klein Kunitz and Grubditz. To his left was Macdonald's XI Corps.

Macdonald's XI Corps extended from Falkenberg to a position facing Auritz, with a major portion of his forces posted behind the main line at Strehla. The Imperial Guard Infantry was deployed just to the east of Bautzen. Latour-Maubourg's I Cavalry Corps had its wing near Strehla. The Guard cavalry stood behind Latour-Maubourg's cavalry towards to Bautzen.

Marmont's VI Corps was behind Nieder Kaina and extended north. Sicard's brigade stood on the left bank of the Spree on a small knoll by the river known as Kieferberg. He was formed in square, to prevent the allied cavalry from throwing him back across the river. The 38th (Württemberg) Division stood with five battalions on the Gottesberg, and three in Neider-Gürig. Morand's 12th Division stood behind Neider-Gürig. Peyri's Italian 15th Division was by Breising. The two Württemberg cavalry regiments were near Jeschütz, and the Neapolitans were near Nimschütz. Ney's III and V Corps were poised on the western bank of the Spree, to the west of Klix.

NEY'S MOVEMENTS

Klix was occupied by Souham's 8th Division. And the North At 4:00 A.M., Maison's 16th Division, V Corps, moved through Klix and settled into Salga. Here Maison and a brigade of cavalry, formed into line and deployed behind a ravine. Maison's orders were to move from Klix towards Brösa and Gottamelda. From there it was to move in the direction of Baruth. The V Corps's orders were to coordinate its movements with those of Ney.

Ney's first act was to have the destroyed bridge at Klix rebuilt by the Spanish Sappers assigned to his corps. Despite the fire of a Russian battery assigned to Tschlapitz's advanced guard, the bridge was rebuilt and Maison's 16th Division advanced across the bridge. Maison's first brigade led the way, supported by the second brigade. Maison was supported by Ney's light cavalry brigade formed of the 10th Hussar Regiment and the Baden Dragoon Regiment.

When Maison had cleared the bridge, the divisions of Souham (8th) and Delmas (9th) crossed in column and deployed in echelon to the right. Albert's (10th) and Ricard's (11th) Divisions followed behind them. Two battalions of Marchand's 39th Division remained in Klix to watch the bridge, while the rest of the division remained by Särchen.

As soon as Maison closed on Salga, he came under the fire of a battery that Tschaplitz had established near Salga, and Maison was obliged to deploy a

NEY

229

brigade before Klix, and place his second brigade behind it. He then pushed the 28th and 32nd Jagers towards what remained of Tschlapitz's advanced guard, which were deployed in the small woods to the right of Klix.[11] The Russians were quickly forced back, being unable to withstand the force of an entire division. However, as they withdrew, they passed through Lomischau and behind Brösa, which they set on fire to cover their withdrawal.

Upon learning of Maison's encounter with Tschaplitz, Ney approved of Maison's actions. He then ordered Lagrange and Rochambeau to move their divisions towards Leichnam and cross the Spree.

When Maison had cleared the way, the rest of the corps began to move forward, and Ney directed Maison to move obliquely towards Malschwitz. He then directed divisions of Souham (8th Division) and Delmas (9th Division) to advance, and prepare to assault Barclay's positions on the windmill heights and around the village of Galina.

After crossing the Spree by Leichnam, Lauriston was ordered to move to Drehsa and Gottamelda. From there he was to move on Baruth with the 39th Division (Hessian and Baden troops), as well as the divisions of Albert (10th) and Ricard (11th). From there he was to begin an even wider sweep, aimed at passing Barclay's right flank.

Facing this maneuver of Lauriston was Lanskoi's cavalry, which was attempting to cover a massive stretch of front with a limited force of cavalry. Barclay saw both Ney and Lauriston's movements from the Galina heights, and realized his forces were tremendously out numbered. He called for reinforcements. Barclay had established a 24 gun battery (two 12pdr position batteries), on the windmill heights above Galina. On the left in Malschwitz, Barclay posted the 7th, 10th, and 38th Jager Regiments. The rest of his infantry was deployed between Galina and Malschwitz. His cavalry (Tver Dragoons and Dorpat Chasseurs à Cheval) were posted behind his line.

Unfortunately for the allies, all that remained uncommitted in the reserve as a result of the previous day's battle was 5,000 infantry, and the Czar Alexander did not judge it appropriate to dispatch that force towards Galina because he was transfixed by the actions of Oudinot against his southern flank. Instead of reinforcements, Barclay received an order to hold firm.[12] Indeed, he was told to hold Preititz and Klein Bautzen to the "last extremity." Barclay then contacted Blücher, who was lightly engaged on his left, asking him to guard the allied line of retreat through Würschen and Hochkirch while he engaged Ney's forces.

The French attack on the Galina heights was led by Delmas (9th Division) with Generals Albert (10th Division) and Souham (8th Division) standing on his left supporting his advance. The V Corps had occupied Gottamelda and was marching on Buchwald, while Maison's 16th Division was preparing to assault Malschwitz. However, after a brief cannonade and prior to the main attack, Barclay withdrew his forces on Preititz and sent a detachment to reinforce Lanskoi in Baruth. He realized that he was facing four divisions, far more than he could hope to hold with his few battalions.

BLÜCHER

230

LAURISTON

As Ney took Galina, about 9:30, he received Napoleon's order to be in Preititz at 11:00 A.M. He had already sent Souham's 8th Division against the village, but he saw the strong forces that Kleist had posted about the village. Ney also learned that Maison was heavily engaged around Malschwitz. He feared becoming too deeply entangled in this mass of allied forces and hesitated to push his attack with all his strength.

Souham's 8th Division continued to advance on Preititz with Delmas' 9th Division some distance to his rear. Albert's (10th) and Ricard's (11th) divisions were stopped in Galina, and Marchand (39th Division) was stopped in Klix. The result was that Souham's single division found itself isolated from its comrades, precisely at the moment when Blücher was responding to Barclay's call for assistance. Barclay left four jager battalions and two squadrons to hold Souham, while he rallied the rest of his forces around Rackel. By 10:00, Souham had taken possession of Preititz.[13]

Though word of the pending capture of Preititz and Baruth reached the Czar, he still refused to release any forces from his reserve. His attention was still locked on the south. However, Blücher was no longer being heavily attacked, so he began to send all available troops to assist Barclay. Kleist's detachment and Röder's Brandenburg Brigade were the first forces sent to aid Barclay's position around Preititz.

Preititz quickly became the target of a major force of Prussians. Shortly before 11:00 A.M., Röder's artillery and cavalry, which could only pass over the stream by the bridge at Klein-Bautzen, pushed forward to contest the French seizure of Preititz. The rest of the Brandenburg Brigade advanced in two lines. The first line consisted of four infantry battalions (probably the Leib Infantry Regiment and the Silesian Grenadier Battalion) and some artillery support under Major Tippelskirch. The second line consisted of the 1/,2/Garde zu Fuss, the Normal Infanterie-bataillon, two squadrons of the West Prussian Uhlans, and a force of artillery under the command of Major Alvensleben. They marched in column on Preititz, behind a screen of sharpshooters, and had a squadron of uhlans on each flank.

Also facing the French under Ney to the north, the Prussian Guard Horse Battery #4 and Horse Battery #10 withdrew under the cover of the East Prussian and Silesian Cuirassier Regiments to the heights between Pliskowitz and Preititz, where the reserve of Russian light batteries stood.[14]

The force of the French assault on Turtschaninov, caused Ziethen to send word that he too required reinforcements. This resulted in the gradual deployment, during the course of the battle, of two Russian 6pdr batteries (24 guns) and two Prussian horse batteries (16 guns) from the reserve cavalry to assist him.[15]

The Brandenburg Brigade struck the French in Preititz. The French were formed in three columns, each led by a six gun battery. About 11:30 P.M., Ney advanced out of Pretitz to engage the allies on the open plain. Delmas' 9th Division passed to the right of the village in column by divisions. Ricard's 11th Division was deployed behind Delmas in echelon. At the same time, he sent several messengers to Reynier and Lauriston to accelerate their movements.[16]

The ensuing artillery duel resulted in several French guns being dismounted. In the third column, Souham's division, the lead elements had only three guns with them. These guns were

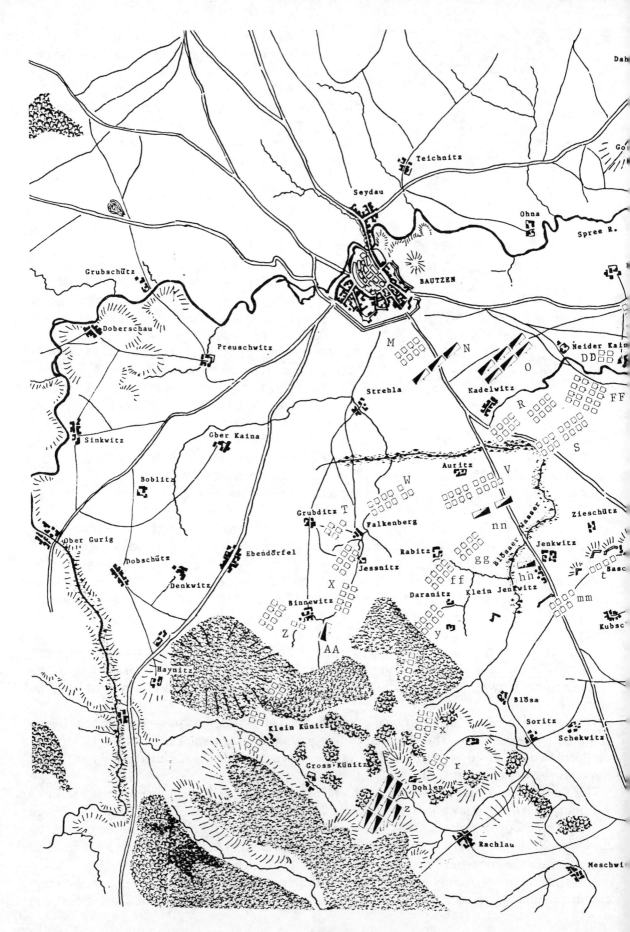

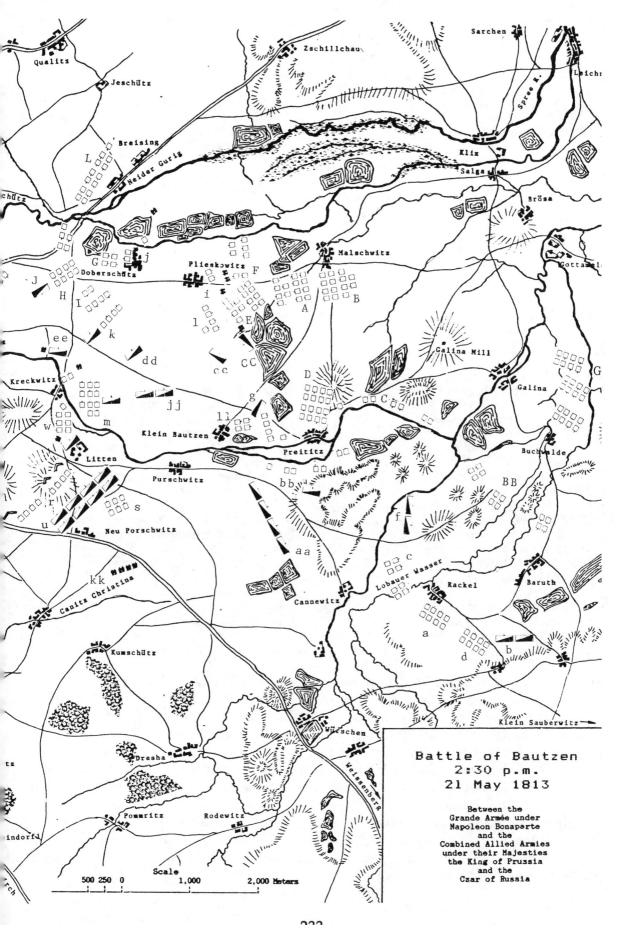

Qualitz

Jeschütz

Breising

Nieder Gurig

L

...chütz

G

Doberschütz

j

Plieskowitz

F

Malschwitz

Gottamel...

J

H

I

i

A

B

Brösa

Klix

Salga

Sarchen

Leicht...

Spree R.

Galina Mill

Galina

G

1

E

ee

k

dd

CC

cc

D

C

Buchwalde

Kreckwitz

jj

g

C

m

w

li

Klein Bautzen

Preititz

BB

Litten

Purschwitz

bb

f

r

s

Lobauer Wasser

Rackel

Baruth

u

Neu Porschwitz

aa

c

kk

Canitz Christina

Cannewitz

a

d

b

Kumschütz

Klein Sauberwitz

Dresha

Würschen

Weissenberg

Pommritz

Rodewitz

...indorf...

...tz

...rch

Battle of Bautzen
2:30 p.m.
21 May 1813

Between the
Grande Armée under
Napoleon Bonaparte
and the
Combined Allied Armies
under their Majesties
the King of Prussia
and the
Czar of Russia

Scale

500 250 0   1,000   2,000 Meters

233

A	10th Division (Albert)	d	9th Division (Insov)
B	11th Division (Ricard)	f	2nd Silesian Hussars, Neumark Dragoons & Freiwilliger Jägers
C	39th Division (Marchand's Badeners & Hessians)	g	Schmiedburg's Cavalry Brigade
D	8th Division (Souham)	i	Prussian Guard Fusilier Battalion, 2 Cos Silesian Grenadier Battalion & 3/Leib Infantry Regiment
E	9th Division (Delmas)		
F	16th Division (Maison)	j	1/, 3/, Fus/ 1st Silesian Infantry Regiment & 2 Cos Silesian Grenadier Battalion
G	Sichard's Brigade, 12th Division (Morand)		
H	Bellair's Brigade, 12th Division (Morand)	k	Klüx's Brigade
I	38th Division (Franquemont's Württembergers)	l	Zeithen's Brigade
J	Briche's Cavalry (2nd Neapolitan Chasseur à Cheval Regiment & Jell's Württemberg Cavalry Brigade)	m	Yorck's Brigade
		r	Russian Guard Infantry
		s	2nd Grenadier Division
L	15th Division (Peyri's Italians)	t	1st Grenadier Division
M	Imperial Guard Infantry	u	1st & 2nd Russian Cuirassier Divisions
N	Imperial Guard Cavalry	w	Guard Jager Regiment, Pernau & Kexholm Grenadiers, & Gluckov Cuirassiers
O	Cavalry Reserve (Latour-Maubourg)		
P	1st Division (Compans)	x	Berg's Corps
R	2nd Division (Bonnet)	y	St. Priest's Corps
S	3rd Division (Friederich)	z	Russian Guard Light Cavalry, Emmanuel's, & Lissanevitch's Cavalry Brigades
T	31st Division (Philipon)		
V	35th Division (Gérard)	aa	Uvarov's Cavalry Brigade
W	36th Division (Charpentier)	bb	Kleist's Advanced Guard
X	13th Division (Pacthod)	cc	1st & 2nd Silesian Hussar Regiment
Y	14th Division (Lorencz)	dd	Prussian Guard Light Cavalry & Brandenburg Cuirassier Regiments
Z	Bavarian Division (Raglovich)		
AA	Reizet's Dragoon Brigade	ee	2nd Leib Hussar Regiment & Horse Battery #1
BB	18th Division (Lagrange)		
CC	10th Hussars & Baden Dragoons	ff	3rd Division (Schachafskoi)
DD	Brigade of Young Guard Infantry	gg	4th Division (Pischnitzky)
EE	Guard Artillery (Desvaux)	hh	Loubny Hussar Regiment
FF	1st & 2nd Young Guard Infantry Divisions (Dumoustier & Barrois)	jj	Dolff's Reserve Cavalry Brigade
		kk	Russian Reserve Artillery (Jachwill)
GG	VII Corps (Reynier)	ll	Brandenburg Brigade
		mm	Markov's Corps
a	18th Division (Schervatov)	nn	Knorring's Cavalry Brigade
b	Umanet's Cavalry Brigade		
c	3rd Army of the West Reserve (Sass)		

instantly turned on the Prussian skirmishers covering the Brandenburg Brigade. Röder ordered his uhlans to strike the French skirmishers covering Souham's front in the flank, which they did, driving them back on the massed French infantry. This assault continued and the Brandenburg Uhlans, supported by Russian dragoons broke the initial French assault. They were followed by a bayonet attack against the front of Preititz, executed by the three battalions of the Brandenburg Brigade (1/,2/Garde zu Fuss and the Normal Infanterie-bataillon), while Tippelskirch led his four battalions and artillery around the left of Preititz, forcing Souham's 8th Division out of the village.

Souham reformed his division and thrust forward again, recapturing the village. Blücher's forces continued to arrive, in an effort to recapture Preititz. Three battalions of the Colberg Regiment, a number of Russian Jagers, Light Battery #23, and the Grodno Hussars took up positions on the right bank of the stream.

It was now the Prussian turn to advance. The Colberg Infantry Regiment, covered by the two companies of East Prussian Jägers, struck the village with its two musketeer battalions to the right and the fusilier battalion to the left. Half of Prussian Horse Battery #3 advanced in support, showering the French with cannister fire. The attack, however, was stopped short and the Brandenburg Brigade withdrew to the Kreckwitz Height to support Klüx.

Delmas, having held his position, was deployed along the stream and Marchand's 39th Division joined him to hold it. Delmas formed the 9th Division behind them, to form a reserve. Albert's 10th Division, formed in "brigade mass," now took the lead, with Ricard's 11th Division behind it in support. The Prussian Horse Battery #3, which stood on the heights to their left, took them under flank fire and forced them back. The French strongly garrisoned Preititz and it was to remain in their hands for the moment.

THE ALLIED EXTREME NORTHERN FLANK

Lauriston had begun the morning by moving his forces through Leichnam, over the Spree, and striking south eastward. He maintained his general position to the north of Ney's forces, and moved through Brösa formed in columns. Maison had earlier brushed aside Tschlapitz's advanced guard, it now stood before Lauriston, and he continued pushing it to the east. Lauriston continued his corps' movement and passed through Gottamelda with Lagrange leading the advance. About 11:30 A.M., Tschaplitz withdrew from Gottamelda and his troops set it afire to cover their retreat.[17] Once Gottamelda was cleared, Napoleon ordered Lauriston to advance on Klein-Bautzen and to attack it.[18]

Lauriston then deployed some of his forces to the right, facing Barclay's forces on the Galina ridge, while continuing his advance towards Buchwalde. He began an artillery bombardment on Barclay's forces along the Galina line. A bloody infantry battle ensued. Covered by several battalions deployed as skirmishers, Lauriston began the classic French sidestepping maneuver. Lauriston's corps was formed by Lagrange's 18th Division with ten battalions and Rochambeau's 19th Division, which had only eight of his original twelve battalions. Puthod's 17th Division had only just arrived from Hoyerswerda and advanced to join the main body. As they moved ever eastward, skirting Barclay's position, Ney's forces were driving towards Preititz, cutting behind Barclay and making his position most tenuous.

Cannon fire erupted along the entire front of Lauriston's and Barclay de Tolly's lines. Lauriston maneuvered Lagrange's 18th Division, 22 cannons, and his light cavalry brigade through Buchwald, and over the Lobauer-Wasser (River) and drove Rochambeau's 19th Division towards Rackel in an effort to turn Barclay's right flank.

Barclay responded to this and Ney's movement on Preititz by withdrawing and redeploying his forces to cover the line between Preititz and Rakel.

Lagrange's 18th Division now swung south and struck Kleist in the right flank. Kleist was behind the Lobauer-Wasser, facing Preititz. The Neumärk Dragoons, supported by the two squadrons of the lst Silesian Hussars, the jägers of the 2nd Silesian Hussars, and a squadron of Freiwilliger jägers, moved to defend Kleist's exposed flank. This force encountered Lauriston's light cavalry brigade, and though the French assault was slowed, Kleist's forces were forced to withdraw.[19]

Three hours after the battle had began, the two Monarchs began to realize the importance of Ney's move on Preititz and the movement of Lauriston's corps on their flank. In response, they ordered the Russian cavalry and its artillery reserve under Uvarov forward to support Kleist around Preititz, but the die was cast and the movement did little to stop the flood of French infantry towards their rear.

THE WURTTEMBERGERS ATTACK
KNÖTEL

MARMONT'S ORDERS

Marmont occupied a position in front of Bautzen, before the center of the main allied position. At 8:00 A.M., he received orders that his function that day was to assault the enemy redoubts. He was to compress his VI Corps to the right, while a brigade of Young Guard Infantry and a half battery from Barrois' 2nd Young Guard Division was detached to plug the gap, which existed between the IV (Bertrand) and VI Corps. However, prior to his assault, he was to engage the allied batteries with his artillery, and, by demonstrations before the allied center, hold the allies in place. When Napoleon heard the sounds of Ney's engagement around Preititz, he ordered Marmont to attack.

Facing this assault was Yorck's corps. Near Litten, Yorck had an advanced guard of three batteries, some infantry, and some cavalry. Two of the batteries were formed with Russian guns and a third, the middle battery, was formed with half of the Prussian 6pdr Battery #1, under Captain von Heut, and half of the Prussian 12pdr Battery #3 under Captain Rosinsky. Behind them were the converged Silesian Hussars, a horse battery, and the Fus/2nd West Prussian Infantry Regiment. His artillery steadily returned the French fire, resisting the French advance.

The brigades of Horn (Yorck's Corps) and Steinmetz (part of Kleist's Advanced Guard), stood in two closed columns behind Yorck's advanced guard. The reserve cavalry of General von Corswandt's brigade stood further back by Neu-Porschwitz.[20]

Around 11:00 A.M., the French had closed with the Prussians around Nieder-Kaina and Basankwitz, and a skirmish battle began in preparation for the main assault.

The French massed their artillery and began bombarding the Prussian positions around Baschütz. The pressure was so great, that Czar Alexander was obliged to dispatch Russian artillery from the reserves to stem the assault.

Despite the stubborn defense of Nieder-Kaina, Marmont advanced across the Blöser-Wasser, between Nieder-Kaina and Nadelwitz. His corps then moved a mile and a half, where he began

MORAND'S DIVISION REPELLING ALLIED CAVALRY

an assault on the Yorck's entrenchments around Kreckwitz and Litten. His assault was supported by a tremendous artillery barrage, and locked the allied center strongly in place.

MAISON'S CAPTURE OF PLIESKOWITZ

Maison's assault on Plieskowitz was led by two battalions and started about 1:00 P.M. The 151st Infantry and a battalion of the 153rd Infantry struck the Prussian flank. Major Röder, seeing this, drew all of his forces into Plieskowitz, and joined them with his Russian jagers in an effort to hold that key position as long as possible.

Major Röder held his position in Plieskowitz as long as he could, but the arrival of two Morand's French battalions from the direction of Neider-Gürig, proved too much and he withdrew. Maison pushed beyond Plieskowitz and established his batteries between Malschwitz and Preititz about 2:00 P.M., driving Ziethen's flank back and taking it under heavy artillery fire.[21]

The fall of Plieskowitz to Maison's 16th Division, allowed the French to push between Blücher's and Barclay's corps. Maison's 16th Division assumed a strong position, providing a link to Morand's 12th Division, and completing the juncture between Ney and the main French army. This juncture was one of the critical points of the battle.

SOULT'S ASSAULT: THE MASTER STROKE

When Napoleon heard Ney's guns engaging the allies at Preititz, he ordered elements of the Guard to march obliquely to the left, and take positions around Burk. They remained there until about 1:00 P.M., when Maréchal Soult began his attack. Soult had led Bertrand's IV Corps across

237

the Spree without attracting the notice of Blücher. Much of the corps artillery stood on the left bank of the Spree, and it prepared the way for the infantry's assault. They formed the battery on Gottesberg, which contained 22 12pdr cannons and 2 howitzers. This powerful battery glared down on its victims and would sledgehammer a hole in the allied lines before too long. Morand's 12th Division continued to occupy Nieder-Gürig with three battalions, and five further battalions were deployed in Briesnig. Only four battalions remained on the right bank, established on a ridge.

The allies understood the risks they were facing with Ney's advance towards Preititz, but in reviewing the situation on the battlefield, they felt that their best option was to delay Ney and to engage Soult. To do this, they had shifted Ziethen and Klüx's forces towards Soult.

The IV Corps' Assault

Facing Bertrand were Blücher's forces, which stood on a number of hills known as the Kreckwitz Heights. These hills overlooked the Spree and the French position. Blücher's positions were entrenched and defended by a large quantity of artillery. Around 8:00 A.M., two Russian 12pdr Position Batteries and two Russian 6pdr Light Batteries moved up to support the Prussian position. The two 12pdr batteries took up positions on the right of the Kreckwitz heights. The two 6pdr batteries stood in reserve, but were later moved forward, with one going to Malschwitz and the other to Preititz.[22] In addition, Prussian light infantry, Prussian Guard Horse Battery #4, and two squadrons of the Garde du Corps, stood near the bank to defend against an assault. To the left was a large plain on which the allies had deployed a major cavalry force.

To support the French attack, there was the 24 gun battery on the Gottesberg, another twelve French guns were posted on a hill on the left bank, and Major Coston established two batteries (15 guns each) to cover the assault. This would position 66 French guns so that their fire would cross on the main allied position and pulverize it. If that weren't enough artillery, yet another French battery was established in front of Basankwitz, to Blücher's south, where it would rake the Prussians.

The immediate area along the Spree, where Bertrand intended to cross, was covered by three batteries, Prussian Horse Battery #7 and two Russian, assigned to Klüx's brigade. This artillery had engaged the French artillery on the Gottesberg all morning, as well firing on the infantry by the bridge at Nieder-Gürig.[23] However, the fight became one sided once all the French guns began firing. The intensity of the French artillery fire and the expenditure of all the ammunition allocated to the two Russian batteries obliged all three batteries to withdraw to new positions. The fire was intense enough that Prussian Horse Battery #7 lost four guns dismounted in this exchange. This gave the opening that Soult needed to establish his bridgehead and move Bertrand across the Spree; the artillery ceased its fire.

Bertrand's IV Corps began its passage over the Spree before 1:00 P.M., when Colonel Izoard, commander of the IV Corps engineers, erected a bridge over the Spree between Nimschütz and Nieder-Gürig. Bertrand quickly advanced 20,000 men, 30 guns, and a 1,000 man cavalry brigade consisting of the 1st and 3rd Württemberg Cavalry Regiments and the 2nd Neapolitian Chasseurs à Cheval,[24] over the bridge and into a position where they could move against the allies. Bertrand's artillery was posted on a small ridge on the right bank of the Spree, but was carefully warned not to fire until the assault had begun.

Bertrand chose initially to pound Blücher's main position with his artillery to soften it up before following up with his principal attack. At 2:00 P.M., when the order from Napoleon came, Bertrand launched his main assault. General Hulot seconded the principal attack, by passing over an arm of the Spree and driving towards the village of Doberschütz. To cover the flank, a battery stood on the approaches to the village of Breising.

The allied position stood 1,000 to 1,200 paces from the French line. It was on a hill and manned with 12 heavy guns and a large force of infantry. Behind this hill, about 800 paces, stood two more hills which were also defended by forces of artillery and infantary. This first hill was the strong point of Klüx's right flank. The battery on that hill was also placed where it could observe and fire on the entire Grande Armée deployed before it.[25]

The main assault was led by the 38th (Württemberg) Division. Franquemont formed his battalions into columns of companies, the 3rd Brigade in the lead, and advanced onto the plateau. Morand's 12th Division advanced behind him in support formed in two great squares. Briche's 1,000 cavalry moved in echelon on the right, to contain any enemy cavalry counterattack and to support a battery of 18 guns established by the advancing columns. The 24 guns on the Gottesberg roared with renewed vigor, showering the Prussian line with shot and shell.

Facing this assault were the Prussians of Klüx's brigade, supported by the two Russian 12pdr position batteries, who had engaged the French earlier.[26] One was now posted near Krekwitz and the other near Nieder-Gürig. Klüx's main forces consisted of four battalions and an uhlan regiment, which would have quickly been overrun but for the swift arrival of the Prussian Guard Light Cavalry Regiment and the Brandenburg Cuirassier Regiment.

As the assault closed, Klüx deployed his fusilier battalions into skirmish order. The brigade's Russian batteries deployed at a gallop to face the attacking columns of Württemberg infantry. A battery in Basankwitz quickly moved to the heights to the left of the Württemberg assault, deployed, and began to fire onto them. Prussian Horse Battery #1, covered by Yorck's flankers from the 2nd Leib Hussar Regiment, posted itself near Kreckwitz and began to strike the Württemberger's flank.[27] The Prussian fusilier companies formed on either side of the Russian batteries and poured heavy fire into the advancing Württembergers. This fire into the Württemberg flank forced them to swing their assault sharply to the right. This turn was to lead the division into greater danger as it then moved towards Kreckwitz where another heavy battery waited for it.[28]

The 2/Prinz Wilhelm (2nd) Infantry Regiment, with only three of the normal four companies present,[29] advanced at the "duplirschritt [quick pace or 'pas de charge']," against the Prussian artillery in Kreckwitz. Major Orthograven's reserve battalion supported the battery.

The Prussian 2nd Reserve/Leib Infantry Regiment, under Major Orthograven, counterattacked with bayonets and momentarily stalled the attack, taking many prisoners from the Württemberg 2/Prinz Wilhelm Infantry Regiment.[30] As this attack pulled back, Major Röder and his 3/2nd Silesian Regiment arrived to reinforce the position. The Württemberger losses were heavy, both due to the counter-attack and due to the artillery. The regimental colonel and major were wounded, casualties high, and most of the survivors of the 2/Prinz Wilhelm Regiment were captured. The regimental standard, however, escaped with the colonel.[31]

Despite the losses to the 2/Prinz Wilhelm, the remainder of the brigade closed to within 200 paces of the artillery, braving its intense fire, and with a great yell lunged forward to put its tormentors to the bayonet. The Prussian artillerists, unwilling to face the enraged Württembergers, limbered up their guns and withdrew.

It was about 2:30 P.M. as both brigades moved onto the heights and began to engage the Prussians with small arms fire. They were quickly reinforced by the Württemberg foot and horse artillery as well as a French artillery battery. Twice more the Prussians strove to retake the position and the two antagonists often came within 60 to 80 paces of one another as they exchanged fire, but the Württembergers held fast.[32]

Klüx responded by counter-attacking the Württembergers again. Two allied columns surged forward to strike the Württembergers. One column from was from Yorck's corps. It consisted of the Fus/2nd East Prussian Infantry and a horse battery. The composition of the other column is unknown. A violent firefight began in which General Franquemont was wounded and General Neusser was knocked from his horse, but he was not seriously wounded. Despite the fall, Neusser rose to respond to a Prussian battery which was striking the flank of the Württemberg attack. However, as he deployed the 1/Prinz Wilhelm (2nd) Regiment to face it, he was seriously wounded and obliged to pass command to Generalmajor Stockmeyer.

General Sicard, with a square of the 23rd Line Regiment, advanced, skirting the ponds to their left, and moved towards Doberschütz to turn the Prussian position. He moved his forces onto the second hill.

One of Neusser's regiments moved on Plieskowitz to assist Maison's attack on Malschwitz, and three other battalions, under General Hulot, moved on Doberschütz to improve the situation for the movement of Morand's 12th Division from Nieder-Gürig. General Hulot crossed the Spree, took Doberschütz and the hill below the village, making the French masters of the high ground on that front. At the same time, with the heights captured, the 24 guns of Major Coston's battery moved to the crest of the hill and began to pound the allied columns.

Despite the arrival of the 3/2nd Silesian Regiment reinforcement, their position was being turned by Sicard and the outnumbered Prussians were forced to withdraw, surrendering the heights to the Württembergers.

Because the ridges that had once formed the Prussian first line were now under French control and allowed them to dominate the rest of the field, a second major allied assault was sent forward. The guns in the second line began a heavy cannonade. Three powerful Prussian columns advanced against the French right and at the center on the main ridge. These assaults were unsuccessful. The renewed Prussian attack was broken by the combined fire of the Italian and Württemberg artillery, as Klüx tried to push the Württembergers back into the Spree. The 23rd Line Regiment counterattacked and drove as far as the base of one of the ridges before it was called back. In the counter-attack General Sicard was mortally wounded.

Once in control of Doberschütz, the IV Corps quickly moved to make its junction with Ney (Maison's 16th Division), which once completed, would provide the French with complete control of the right bank of the Spree. Morand's thrust continued and he gained ground steadily as he moved towards Pleiskowitz. The attack went well until a regiment of Morand's 12th Division arrived before the village of Plieskowitz. It was attacked by allied cavalry and obliged to form square. Once the allied attack was defeated, the advance was resumed.

About 2:30 P.M., the Württemberg attack had forced the Prussians from the heights to the north of Kreckwitz. A battalion of Württembergers moved into Kreckwitz, just as Maison's forces carried Malschwitz and Plieskowitz.

With Morand and Maison's divisions having touched, the 23rd Infantry Regiment (French) and the 38th (Württemberg) Division, then moved against the second allied line. The initial Württemberg assault had been so hot that it was necessary to replenish their ammunition supplies. General von Stockmeyer, who took Generalmajor Neusser's command after he was wounded, lead his division forward.

The Prussians refused to face this renewed assault and withdrew without firing more than a few shots. They fell back to their third line and took up defensive positions around Litten.[33]

THE GUARD STRIKES

The allied movement to face Soult's advance was what Napoleon had awaited. In the span of 20 minutes, he directed the Imperial Guard, Latour-Maubourg's two cavalry divisions (3rd Light & 3rd Cuirassier), and a large force of artillery to a position on the right flank of the allied forces, that had moved from what had become the Russian center.

As Morand's 12th Division and the 38th (Württemberg) Division seized the hills which formed the Prussian main position and General Sicard was mortally wounded, General Desvaux was establishing the Imperial Guard artillery by Basankwitz. They opened a violent cannonade on the massed Prussians around Kreckwitz. A brigade of Young Guard infantry was posted in Basankwitz to support them. At the same time, Generals Dulauloy and Drouot advanced rapidly with the 60 guns of the artillery reserve.

Blücher, reacting to the Württemberg assault on Kreckwitz, moved Ziethen's forces forward and placed them into line. Ziethen advanced, overrunning Kreckwitz, and pushed the French out. Blücher also tried to recall Kleist's forces from the battles around Preititz, but they were too heavily engaged to withdraw. Blücher then called for reinforcements from the general reserves and received the same negative response Barclay had received earlier.

Meanwhile, Mortier advanced the Young Guard divisions of Dumoustier and Barrois, cutting the road from Würschen to Bautzen. Barrois advanced his three remaining regiments in echelon to repulse any potential cavalry attacks. He directed the fire of six guns on a village (probably Kreckwitz) to his left. He attacked the village with a strong force of skirmishers and two formed pelotons. The village was quickly taken.

Blücher began to see that his situation was quickly becoming critical. He was under a heavy frontal assault from Soult, but at the same time Ney was turning his right and threatening his rear while the Young Guard was moving towards Litten in an effort to cut him off from the allied center. Blücher then determined that it was absolutely necessary for him to begin a hasty withdrawal before he was completely enveloped by the advancing French infantry.

Yorck shifted to the north, across the Blöser-Wasser, to support Blücher, and General Yermolov moved to fill his positions around Litten with the Pernau and Kexholm Grenadier Regiments, the Guard Jager Regiment, the Guard Marine Equipage Battalion, the Gluchov Cuirassier Regiment, and a horse battery.

It was 3:00 P.M., and though there was still no assurance of victory and the battle raged over a five mile front, Napoleon issued his victory announcement. The allies were now dancing to his tune.

As Yorck and Yermolov were shifting to cover Blücher's retreat, the French were bringing further forces across the Spree, in the form of the 13th Line Regiment (12th Division of Morand) and the 15th (Italian) Division.

Yermolov's Russians took up positions on the right of the Prussians to support as Yorck struck at the Krekwitz heights. A 12pdr position battery supported the attack by Yorck's 1/5th Combined Infantry and the combined fusilier battalions of the 5th and 6th Combined Infantry Regiments. The attack was unsuccessful.

The Württembergers advanced again at the geschwindschritt, pushing Klüx's Prussians (Blücher's Corps) back. They continued pushing forward and began to maneuver against the flank of the Brandenburg Brigade. The Brandenburg Brigade quickly withdrew, when it found its position turned by the Württemberg advance. Once the Prussians were cleared from this area, the heights were crowned with the IV Corps artillery and the twelve Imperial Guard guns brought forward by General Desvaux. Here they took the entrenched allied batteries, stretching from Litten to Baschütz and Jenkwitz under a raking fire.

It was about 4:30 P.M., as Klüx withdrew from Kreckwitz and led his brigade (Blücher's Corps) back through Purschwitz, to the Weissenberg road. Once in Purschwitz the skirmishers of the 3rd Reserve/1st West Prussian Infantry Regiment, deployed at the edge of the village to delay the French advance. The allies made no further attempts to retake their earlier positions. The Prussian artillery deployed and Yorck engaged in a fighting withdrawal as he led his men back through Litten.

Röder and his Brandenburg Brigade, having been turned by the Württembergers, withdrew towards the east. The 2nd Reserve Battalion/Leib Regiment moved to Purschwitz, while the Freiwilliger Jäger Battalion von Wedell and the skirmishers of the lst Guard Battalion moved into Klein Bautzen, to hold those positions, while the main body of the brigade moved through them. Ziethen withdrew his forces from Doberschütz, and moved towards Purschwitz.

Horn's brigade had suffered heavy casualties prior to this battle. Because of the casualties in its engagement at Hoyerswerda, he had combined the lst and 2nd Battalions of the Prussian 5th Combined Infantry Regiment into a single combined battalion, under the command of Major Löbell. As Horn moved to Purschwitz, Löbell moved his battalion into Litten in an effort to try to hold the line against the advancing French columns.

Löbell had barely arrived when the French Young Guard began to press against Litten and forced him to withdraw. Uvarov's cavalry moved forward and covered the withdrawal of Löbell's tiny command from the field.[34]

To cover the withdrawal, the entrenched artillery in the allied center began to bombard the advancing Young Guard columns. The artillery in the allied center was seconded by the Russian Guard who, standing behind it, had orders not to allow it to abandon its position. The Russian cuirassier corps and all its supporting horse batteries demonstrated against the advancing French, and the French I Cavalry Corps responded to this maneuver. In addition, the French and Württemberg artillery on the Kreckwitz heights took advantage of the opportunity to wreak havoc on the Russian cavaliers as they maneuvered before them.

Behind the retreating Prussians, a small rear guard formed by Prussian Horse Battery #9 and Foot Battery #11, under the command of Major Braun, was covered by a force of Prussian cavalry. He engaged the French until he was so seriously threatened, that he began to withdraw. As he was limbering his guns, a force of about 50 Württemberg cavalry entered the battery in an effort to cut it off. They were quickly driven off by the Neumärk Dragoons and Silesian Hussars.

Major Braun's force covered Blücher's corps as it marched 1,200 paces behind Purschwitz and reorganized itself in the best possible order to face the next assault.[35]

At the same time as the Prussians were withdrawing, the allied batteries in the center, near Baschütz and Jenkwitz, continued to fire. General Yermolov held his positions around Litten with the two Russian Guard divisions and a grenadier brigade.[36]

Barrois, advancing with the Young Guard, directed the fire of ten guns on Uvarov's cavalry which was in front of and to the right of three redoubts that he found before him.

As allied artillery in those redoubts returned fire, Barrois noted that, despite the youth of his troops, they stood as firm as veterans. When the order to assault the redoubts came he formed his columns into a "bataillon carré", supported them with a battery advancing on their left, and supported their right with another strong artillery battery. He quickly overran the redoubts to the south of Litten and consolidated his position.

To Barrois' left, and behind the Württembergers, the 13th Line Regiment (12th Division of Morand) and the 15th (Italian) Division, had advanced onto the main ridge and down the road to Würschen. The IV Corps took positions at Drehsa and sent patrols towards Hochkirch to determine if the village was held.[37]

THE SECOND PHASE OF NEY'S ASSAULT

As Marmont began his assault on the allies around Basankwitz, and as Bertrand's forces began their assault between Nimschütz and Nieder-Gürig, Ney's forces were spread between Malschwitz and Preititz. Ney waited until both Marmont and Bertrand's assaults were well under way before he began his second assault on the allies. He had established a large battery between these two towns that began to cannonade Blücher's forces with bloody results. Blücher renewed his assaults on Ney's position and brought up his entire reserve. He threw the Brandenburg Brigade into Purschwitz to support his desperately pressed line.

The allies had found themselves obliged to strip their right flank to face Soult's attack. Maréchal Ney profited by this shift of forces to resume his attack. Ney seized Preititz and advanced beyond it towards Würschen. Ney no longer required Lauriston around Preititz, and was able to detach Puthod's 17th Division, V Corps, for other duties. Lauriston took Buchwald with Lagrange's 18th Division and drove Rochambeau's 19th Division towards Baruth. The VII Corps, under Reynier, crossed the Spree at Klix and began advancing on the allies.[38]

On the north, Ney organized the divisions of Delmas (9th), Albert (10th), and Ricard (11th), supported by his light cavalry, into a massive pile driver aimed at the hills between Doberschütz and Klein-Bautzen. He placed a battery of sixteen 12pdr guns on the flanks of this column that tore apart the Prussians that stood before him. Ney's maneuver, timed with the assault of the Imperial Guard, was more than the allies could handle.[39]

When the allies saw that their right flank had been turned, they began to withdraw from the battlefield, ceding it to Napoleon. This withdrawal soon lost much of its cohesion and some units broke and fled. Unfortunately, the French did not act and allowed the allies to escape.

Ney was in a position to strike at the flank of Blücher's retreating columns of infantry, but for some unknown reason he did not choose to advance beyond the Blöser-Wasser. It is possible that he was concerned about the masses of allied cavalry that he saw on the far bank and the lack of French cavalry was playing on his mind. Crossing a stream in the face of strong enemy cavalry, could have been a disaster if luck was against him and there was a force of Russian cuirassiers that had moved to a position, where they could strike him. As Ney only had 600 cavalry, it is reasonable to assume that this might have been the principal reason for his hesitation. There was also some confusion that appears to have gotten into the French ranks, when the III and IV Corps touched.

Order was restored to the French ranks by 5:00 P.M. and the advance was resumed. Albert's 10th Division led the renewed advance with the other divisions behind it. At 7:00 P.M., Ney, Reynier, and Lauriston arrived in Würschen. At the same time, the IV Corps arrived in Purschwitz and the Young Guard arrived in Litten. Oudinot received orders to advance on the Cunewald and Hochkirch, as well as into the entrenched villages and redoubts, that the allies were obliged to evacuate the day before. He was to take a position on the left flank of the withdrawing allies. Macdonald pushed hard on the enemy's left and inflicted serious casualties on them.

THE SOUTHERN FLANK

At 6:00 A.M., Oudinot began his advance covered by heavy artillery fire on both flanks aimed at the Russian lines. Pacthod's 13th Division moved Reischen, while Lorenzc's 14th Division moved against Klein-Künitz and Pielitz. The 29th (Bavarian) Division remained in mass near Binnewitz, with the 31st Division (Philipon) to the west.

At the same time, the XI Corps formed its two remaining divisions en echelon with the right advanced a few hundred paces, so as to maintain contact with the Oudinot's XII Corps and to cover his movement. The 35th Division (Gérard) was in Falkenberg and the 36th Division (Charpentier) was in Strehla.

The passage over the Spree went without mishap. As the XII Corps passed over, a brigade of 3,000 to 4,000 Neapolitan infantry moved onto a ridge on the eastern bank of the Spree. As it took up its position a single Russian cannon fired on them, its shot passing 100 feet over their heads. Overcome with surprise, and though not a man was touched, the entire brigade dropped to its knees in panic. The laughter of the corps staff immediately behind them so embarassed the Neapolitans that they leaped to their feet and flung themselves against a Russian advanced guard that stood before them.[40]

Around 8:00 A.M., Oudinot's forces had seized Mehltheuer, a small village between Binnewitz and Döhlen, and passed beyond it to Pielitz, while another column had passed nearly into Gross-Künitz. A Russian counter-attack, supported by a dragoon regiment, struck back as the French advanced on Pielitz. The French were driven back with the loss of one gun and 145 prisoners.

In the woods to the east, Lorencz's battalions detached their skirmishers to screen his advance. The woods were so dense that he was obliged to leave his guns behind him. Pacthod's also sent his skirmishers forward and was supported by the Bavarian Light Infantry Battalion "Fortis" in Binnewitz, with the 2/3rd Bavarian Infantry Regiment behind Binnewitz as a reserve.

Pacthod's 13th Division advanced into Rieschen, where it repulsed several attacks by the Russian Guard and the 3rd and 8th Russian Divisions. The 8th Division under Colonel von Rören held the position with the Tschernigov and Riajsk Infantry Regiments until relieved by the entire 3rd Division under Schachafskoi.

To the west, Macdonald sent battalions from the 31st Division (Philipon) to support the 35th Division (Gérard). One such detachment was attacked by the 3rd Ukrainian Cossack Regiment and two squadrons of the Tartar Uhlan Regiment, who quickly overran and broke it, capturing a cannon.[41]

By 11:00 A.M., Oudinot had advanced about 6,000 yards from his morning position, and engaged in a heavy a cannonade with the Russian redoubts and entrenchments before him.

As the Russian assaults increased in intensity, General Lorencz was sent forward in an effort to stop a Russian flanking movement. He advanced and occupied Pielitz and Döhlen. From there he moved on Rachlau.[42] The Russians were turned back, but they obtained significant advantages from the woods and abattis they had erected in that area. The Russians counterattacked again and again, but despite the Russian strength, the French 52nd and 137th Line Regiments were able to hold their positions.

Though the combat was bloody, it had the effect Napoleon desired. The force of the French attack to the south convinced Czar Alexander that this was the principal French attack, and he ordered Wittgenstein to dispatch a second Guard brigade from the reserve. The allied reserve now consisted solely of 8,000 cavalry and 120 guns.[43]

Because of the heavy combat, Lorencz's 14th Division was fatigued and began running short of ammunition. He was supported by the 29th (Bavarian) Division of General Raglovich, but despite this, they were both slowly pushed back from the plateau they had held for 18 hours. The arrival of a twelve gun Russian battery made the situation untenable, and finally forced the French off the plateau.

Lorencz's 14th Division withdrew in battalion squares and became Oudinot's reserve. Oudinot supported Lorencz with Reizet's brigade of dragoons and his corps artillery. Oudinot re-established his forces in Binnewitz and Tronberg. He still maintained the Bavarians as his principal reserve and engaged them as little as possible. Though Oudinot pleaded with Napoleon for reinforcements, Napoleon assured him that they would not be needed and sent none. At 3:00 P.M., he advised Oudinot that the battle was won.

Macdonald, to Oudinot's north, noticed a large allied force (Miloradovich) advancing on Oudinot. He felt that Oudinot's withdrawal would compromise his flank, and detached General Gérard's 35th Division to support Oudinot's XII Corps. Gérard was echeloned behind and to the left of the XII Corps. He was followed by a brigade, probably from Philipon's 31st Division, which also was in echelon to his left. This force advanced on Grubtitz and Binnewitz. According to Lejeune, Oudinot's chief of staff, the successes on the left flank rescued the XII Corps from a "critical position."

This assault forced the Russian attack to stall, and the XII Corps took advantage of the lull in the battle to reorganize itself. With the support of Gérard's fresh division and news of the success on the left, the fatigued soldiers of Oudinot's three divisions once again advanced and succeeded in recapturing the woods for the sixth time.[44] During this assault, Lorencz was wounded and General Brun took command of the 14th Division. The Bavarians supported the renewed advance, as did the Neapolitans under Baron d'Ambrosio.

MACDONALD'S ATTACK, WURTTEMBERG'S DEFENSE

At 6:00 A.M., Macdonald's attack became general and began pushing Prince Eugene von Wurttemberg's Russians back in several places. Wurttemberg's cavalry advanced guard withdrew behind his right, and General Millesimo moved towards Wurttemberg's left. Macdonald uncovered a 30 gun battery near Rabitz and began to cannonade Lieutenant Colonel Sievers' forces which occupied Rabitz.

The French repeatedly attacked Daranitz and Reischen, which were defended by the Russian 8th Division. The French slowly gained the upper hand and the Russians were about to withdraw from Reischen when the timely arrival of the Tschernigov Infantry Regiment allowed them to stabilize their hold on the village.

The French responded by passing around Prince Eugene von Wurttemberg's left and pushing back part of St.-Priest's forces in the woods. Wurttemberg responded by moving a battery to that flank which fired cannister on the French attack. Millesimo then advanced to Wurttemberg's left and deployed his horse artillery to engage the French.

About the same time, Schachafskoi attacked the French with the Russian 3rd Division, supported by St.-Priest's forces, and pushed the French back beyond Jessnitz. Reischen itself was attacked by the French, lost in a counterattack by the Russians, and retaken several times.

At 11:00 A.M., as Prince Eugene von Wurttemberg occupied himself with these movements, he suddenly saw the 4th Division (Pischnitzki), on his right retreat precipitously. The retreat was so fast that it was impossible for him to stop it or to determine its causes. His conclusion was that it was ordered to abandon its positions.

As St. Priest, who commanded the 2nd Line of Gortschakov's Corps, and Schachafskoi (3rd Division, Wurttemberg's Corps) had abandoned the defense of Reischen, Prince Eugene von Wurttemberg moved quickly to contact Miloradovich, whom he found near Blösa. Miloradovich was stunned by the news and reacted by ordering two batteries to move forward and fill their positions. The French apparently did not take advantage of the situation. When the two new Russian batteries arrived, the French artillery turned on them, but their assaults against Reischen ceased. St. Priest rallied his forces, launched an assault, and reoccupied Daranitz.

Despite that success, things were not going well for the allied left wing. A dragoon officer arrived by Sievers' battery, one of those sent by Miloradovich to fill the gap in the line. The officer cried out, "The Emperor is pleased with you, that is enough." The casualties suffered by this battery were terrible. Sievers and most of his officers were wounded, several guns were dismounted, and the ammunition supply was dwindling. Several men begged the dragoon officer permission to withdraw. The 4th Division had earlier withdrawn because of casualties and only its skirmishers covered the battery. They were unable to hold back the French, and the dragoon officer apparently authorized the withdrawal. The French began to move through the gap in the Russian lines.

Prince Eugene von Wurttemberg received word from Gortschakov, that he was heavily engaged on the heights and requested assistance. Wurttemberg detached Wolff with the Mourmansk Infantry Regiment and the 2nd Jagers to move to his assistance.

Prince Eugene von Wurttemberg also shifted the Revel, Riajsk, and Tobolsk Infantry with the 4th and 21st Jagers, south to join him as well if their assistance became necessary. As this force took up its positions, the French had already been pushed back into the plains near Binnewitz.

Prince Eugene von Wurttemberg returned to Reischen from his conference with Miloradovich, just as Macdonald renewed his attacks. He directed St. Priest and Schachafskoi to advance to Daranitz. A few French columns were attempting to push between his forces and those of Prince Gortschakov. Lieutenant Colonel Wolff maneuvered against their flank and forced them to withdraw. By 2:00 P.M., the French assaults on the allied left had been repulsed and the French had retired as far as Ebendörfel, ceding most of the day's battlefield to the allies.

About 3:30 P.M., Miloradovich received the order to withdraw. He delayed his withdrawal until about 4:30 P.M. in order to allow Gortschakov sufficient time to withdraw.[46]

THE ALLIED WITHDRAWAL

As the victorious French began to push through the northern flank, Yorck and Blücher formed their forces into a column between Kreckwitz and Neu-Porschwitz. These columns then passed over the Blöser-Wasser and moved on Würschen.

As the Brandenburg Brigade of General von Ziethen and that of Oberst von Klüx began to form for the withdrawal, Ney struck out from Preititz and obliged them to detach the two Guard infantry battalions and a line battalion to stem Ney's assault. The Prussian Guard Jäger Battalion took up positions in Klein-Bautzen and Neu-Porschwitz to cover the withdrawal.[47]

The brigades of Steinmetz and Horn joined with Blücher's column, and all three began to withdraw under the cover of the three heavy batteries in the allied center. These batteries were covered by three Russian regiments of the 2nd Guard Infantry Division, as well as the weakened battalions of the Kexholm and Pernau Infantry Regiments. A further support behind this force in the village of Litten was formed by the 1/5th Combined Prussian Infantry Regiment, detached from Yorck's Corps. Once Blücher and Yorck were on the heights behind Neu-Porschwitz and on the road to Weissenberg, this artillery and the Russian Guard joined the withdrawal.

Kleist was given command of a rearguard withdrawing through Purschwitz. It was formed with a force under Oberst von Katzler, who commanded a large force of light cavalry, Prussian Horse Batteries #2 and #3, and Horn's Brigade. As Kleist withdrew from Purschwitz, it was in flames.

To cover the withdrawal of the rest of the army, Kleist moved his force quickly to the heights before Würschen. Horn's Brigade took up a position on the heights to the right of the road. Katzler moved to a position on the left of the road, facing the French. He was shortly joined by the Colberg Regiment.

General Lauriston moved against this position with Puthod's 17th Division as well as with the VII Corps. The 134th and 135th Infantry Regiments assumed a position near Rackel, to threaten Kleist's right flank, while Puthod advanced. Ney sent Reynier's Saxons to the right, in the direction of Dresha. Around 7:00 P.M., Lauriston and Reynier advanced against Würschen.

As Kleist's Corps and the Prussian Reserve Cavalry, under Dolffs, withdrew from Würschen, Ney responded by sending artillery and skirmishers into Klein-Bautzen and Neu-Porschwitz to engage them. They were held at bay, however, by a Prussian horse battery which showered them with shot and shell.

As the Russians began to withdraw, Miloradovich passed through the defiles around Blösa and Pielitz. Napoleon responded to Miloradovich's movement by sending Latour-Maubourg's I Cavalry Corps against Kubschütz, which lay in the center of what had been Constantine's positions that morning. The French cavalry moved so quickly that only two Ukrainian Cossack Regiments, under the command of Count Obolenski, were there to counter them. However, they were quickly supported by several battalions from the 2nd Corps, the Loubny Hussars, and three horse batteries under Colonel Nikitin, which had been dispatched there to cover the Russian withdrawal. They stopped the French long enough for the Russian army to effect its withdrawal.

St. Priest remained in Steindörfel with three jager regiments, two Ukrainian Cossack Regiments, and the three horse batteries mentioned earlier, where they acted as a rear guard. The second allied column was formed by the Russians in the center and the left flank under the command of Miloradovich. They withdrew through Hochkirch, Lobau, and on towards Reichenbach. Barclay de Tolly formed the third column and moved through Baruth and to the east.

THE RESULTS OF THE BATTLE

The French had fought the battle with their infantry. Much of this was because they lacked sufficient cavalry to fight as they had historically fought, and what cavalry they had was not of very high quality. Napoleon had, in fact, only engaged some of the Guard light cavalry, lst Light, 3rd Light, and the 3rd Cuirassier Divisions in the battle, choosing to hold most of the heavy cavalry he had in reserve for future battles.[48] The lst Cuirassier Division had limited its actions to maneuvering before the allies and engaging them with its horse artillery.[49]

On the allied part, they did not choose to use their superior strength of cavalry to their advantage, and were content to let their infantry bear the brunt of the battle. The Russian 2nd Corps suffered between 1,600 and 1,700 casualties. Plotho reports that the total allied casualties were 5,000 Russians and 3,000 Prussians hors de combat. Wagner lists the losses for the Russians at 203 officers and 3,523 men killed and wounded. He lists a further two guns and 850 Russian soldiers being captured by the French. However, he gives the total losses for the Prussians and Russians at 12,000 to 13,000 men.[50] Plotho states that Yorck's Corps alone lost 249 dead, 1,473 wounded, and 252 prisoners.[51] In view of the intensity of the fighting, it is probably that Wagner's figures are more to be trusted than Plotho's.

Wagner and other sources state that Generals Ostermann-Tolstoy and Sibrsky were severely wounded, Yermolov and Tchoglikov were lightly wounded and Generallieutenant Jachwill, the artillery commander, suffered a concussion.

The French are estimated to have suffered 18,000 wounded and 6,000 to 8,000 dead. The Württembergers alone lost 111 dead, 788 wounded, 109 missing and 203 prisoners to the allies. Their total losses were 1,211 men.[52] Generals Franquemont, Neusser, Sicard, and Lorencz were wounded.

OBSERVATIONS ON BAUTZEN

Bautzen was a battle of opportunities missed and thrown away. Napoleon expressed his views on the battle in later years, as recorded by General Jomini. He said, "Ney crossed the Spree at Klix, placing Maison's division in flankers behind the ponds by Malschwitz, while pushing the two other divisions of Lauriston towards Gottamelda, and conducting all of the III Corps against the Galina windmill (Windmuhlenberg). These forces then moved on the clock towers of Hochkirch, and the VII Corps, one hour behind them, served as a reserve. Lauriston marched on Baruth and Belgern in the same direction.

"This maneuver was perfect, its result should have been incalculable, however, several unfortunate circumstances arose that minimized its success. I had waited a bit to give Ney the instructions on the role he was to play in the battle. These instructions were, unfortunately, insufficient, because I restricted myself to sending him a penciled note at 8:00 A.M. with the laconic order to be in Preititz at 11:00 A.M. and to attack the right of the enemy."

"The officer who carried this note made a long detour by Klix in the hope of finding the marshal there. He arrived at 10:00 on the heights of Galina where Ney had seized much earlier than I had anticipated."

"At that point all went well, because the direction assigned to our right hand columns on the towers of Hochkirch fit within the spectrum of the orders to move on Preititz."

"It was only 10:00 A.M. Preititz was only 1,600 to 1,800 yards from the heights of Galina. Ney did not wish to accelerate his attack one hour (Ney had interpreted his orders to be in Preititz at exactly 11:00 A.M.). He awaited Reynier's corps and lost three quarters of an hour reforming his troops. Finally he pushed Souham's single division into Preititz, leaving three divisions a half league away and his fourth division a full league away."

"Souham penetrated without support into the village at the same time Blücher detached Kleist to reinforce Barclay. Souham found himself between the two corps and suffered greatly for no purpose. His division scattered. Ney supported him from a distance and intermittently with his reserve batteries and Delma's division."

"Finally, about 1:00 pm., when he learned that Reynier's columns were behind Klix, Ney ordered his three divisions forward against Preititz."

"Lauriston, who had forded (the Spree) near Gottamelda, at the head of two infantry divisions against the feeble detachment of 3,000 men under the command of General Tschlapitz, announced that he had superior forces before him and refused to advance beyond the terrain that separated himself from Baruth."

"We had lost men and precious time to no avail. If Ney had advanced aggressively, as he had at Friedland, he would have arrived at noon in the rear of the allied positions, on the road to Würschen between Belgern and Purschwitz. One cannot calculate the tremendous results that would have followed this maneuver resembling the maneuver Blücher executed against us at Waterloo."

"Except, success was the difference. It was time, towards 1:00 P.M., to once again achieve great results. Unfortunately Ney did not appreciate his position. As he penetrated Preititz, Blücher, who found himself attacked in the rear, moved a few battalions to the heights of Klein-Bautzen with about 20 guns. These cannons struck the flanks of Ney's columns, distracting him from his advance on Hochkirch which had been indicated to him in the morning as his line of advance. Instead of placing himself astride the road to Würschen, he turned to the right to strike at the hills behind Klein-Bautzen. It is true that those heights dominated all of the battlefield, but it was completely the opposite direction that he should have pursued to cut the allies' line of retreat. In addition, the appearance of about twenty enemy squadrons on the plain, between Preititz and Purschwitz contributed to his choice of this false movement. Ney had only six weak squadrons of cavalry and feared to hazard the plain with Blücher on the heights to his rear."

In retrospect, Napoleon's evaluation of what Ney did and what he should have done is probably correct. However, in the heat of battle and with the sure knowledge that the loss of the battle could have been his fault if he had gotten himself overextended and cut off, Ney cannot be too hastily criticized. His initial movement into Preititz was certainly tentative. He does appear to have lost his old fire. Napoleon should share the blame, as his instructions were vague and a miserably incomplete transmission of his intentions and desires.

It is certain that if Ney had more fully understood what Napoleon expected of him and had acted more aggressively, the allied army would have been surrounded and crushed. Little more than a stream of rabble fleeing eastwards towards Russia would have survived.

On the allied side, it seems incomprehensible how, with their superiority of cavalry and their earlier strikes against the Italian division to the north, that they did not realize that there was a major French force advancing against their right wing. They stood entranced by the French army facing them across the Spree and the knowledge that Napoleon was with them.

The allied concept of fighting the battle of Bautzen was an 18th Century fixed piece battle, where the enemy marched up before their prepared positions and attacked them frontally. This displays their total failure to learn anything after 21 years of warfare.

If Napoleon's failure to clearly transmit his objectives and instructions to his subordinates cost him a major victory, it was the Czar's meddling and the allies lack of a modern, functioning general staff that nearly brought disaster down upon their heads. The Russians and Prussians showed themselves able to operate and fight tenaciously on ground they selected, to fight well on a brigade and corps level, but they continued to show that they had still failed to learn how to maneuver and fight armies. Indeed, despite the fact that they had been fighting Napoleon, and knew of his talent for maneuvering, they chose to back themselves into a corner, dig in, and wait for several days while Napoleon, almost at his leisure, maneuvered against them.

1 Foucart, Bautzen, pg 315.

2 Clément, Campagne de 1813, pg 225.

3 Fabry, Prince de Wurtemberg, pg 69.

4 Wagner, Recueil des Plans, Vol II, pg 25.

5 Wagner, Recueil des Plans, Vol II, pg 23.

6 Friederich, Die Befreiungskriege, pg 288.

7 Prussischen Grossen Generalstab, Kriegsgeschichtlich Einzelschriften, pg 43.

8 Sporschil, Die Grosse Chronik, Vol I, pg 223, & Wagner, Recueil des Plans, Vol II, pg 22.

9 Plotho, Krieg in Deutschland, Vol I, pg 165.

10 Wagner, Recueil des Plans, Vol II, pg 23.

11 Wagner, Recueil des Plans, Vol II, pg 22.

12 Clément, Campagne de 1813, pg 230.

13 Clément, Campagne de 1813, pg 231.

14 Wagner, Recueil des Plans, Vol III, pg 33.

15 Prussischen Grossen Geneneralstab, Kriegsgeschichtlich Einzelschriften, pg 43

16 Camon, Guerre Napoléonienne, pg 427.

17 de Lagarenne, 1er Régiment de Chasseurs, pg 174.

18 Sporschil, Grosse Chronik, Vol I, pg 224.

19 zur Lippe–Weissenfeld, 6. Husaren, pg 118.

20 Plotho, Krieg in Deutschland, Vol I, pg 167.

21 Wagner, Recueil des Plans, Vol II, pg 38.

22 Wagner, Recueil des Plans, Vol II, pg 30.

23 von Conrady, Sechsten Infanterie, pg 174.

24 Rossler, Tagbücher, pg 314.

25 Rossler, Tagbücher, pgs 314–315.

26 Plotho, Krieg in Deutschland, Vol I, pg 167.

27 Wagner, Recueil des Plans, Vol II, pg 39.

28 Rossler, Tagbücher, pg 315.

29 The fourth company of the Prinz Wilhelm Regiment had been detached to watch the divisional train.

30 Plotho, Krieg in Deutschland, Vol I, pg 168.

31 Rossler, Tagbücher, pg 315.

32 Rossler, Tagbücher, pgs 316–317.

33 Rossler, Tagbücher, pg 317.

34 Lewinski & Brauchitsch, Grenadier–Regiments Nr. 7., pg 86.

35 Preussischen Grossen Generalstab, Kriegsgeschichtlich Einzelschriften, pg 45.

36 Fabry, Prince de Wurtemberg, pg 73.

37 Foucart, Bautzen, pg 328.

38 Clément, Campagne de 1813, pg 234.

39 Camon, Guerre Napoléonienne, pg 429.

40 Lejeune, Memoirs , pgs 271–272.

41 Wagner, Recueil des Plans, Vol II, pg 27.

42 Clément, Campagne de 1813, pg 226.

43 Clément, Campagne de 1813, pg 226.

44 Foucart, Bautzen, pg 318.

45 Fabry, Prince de Wurtemberg, pg 70.

46 Fabry, Prince de Wurtemberg, pg 71.

47 Plotho, Krieg in Deutschland, Vol I, pgs 169–170.

48 de Martimprey, 8e Régiment de Cuirassiers, pg 161.

49 de Place, 12e Cuirassiers, pg 107.

50 Wagner, Recueil des Plans, Vol II, pgs 45–46.

51 Plotho, Krieg in Deutschland, Vol I, Appendices, pg 128.

52 Rossler, Tagbücher, pg 318.

The Aftermath of Bautzen
and the Path to Armistice
22 May — 1 June 1813

The allies resumed their retreat from Bautzen early in the morning of 22 May, and the two columns of weary soldiers moved steadily on Reichenbach. Their retreat continued on to Görlitz, but their rearguard remained in Reichenbach, eventually found by Reynier.[1]

At 7:00 A.M., Reynier's VII Corps and the 1st Cavalry Corps under Latour-Maubourg had begun their movement on Reichenbach. Lauriston's V Corps was on their left. The Imperial Guard and the VI Corps (Marmont) followed Reynier. The XI and IV Corps moved on Löbau, while Ney moved the III Corps to Weissenberg and Oudinot held the XII Corps in Bautzen to recover from its casualties during the battle of Bautzen.[2]

BATTLE OF REICHENBACH

At 10:00 A.M., Napoleon, in company with Reynier and the VII Corps, arrived before Reichenbach, where he contacted Wurttemberg's Russian 2nd Corps. Wurttemberg had once again been chosen to act as the Russian rearguard and was standing on the heights to the east of the town waiting for the French to close. Schachafskoi's division was placed on a very pronounced ridge with the Russian cavalry posted on his left and on the main road in a valley by Reichenbach. The line of the stream was occupied by the 21st and 34th Jager Regiments. The rest of the corps was formed in two lines in battalion columns, formed on the center.[3]

It was Wurttemberg's intention to cover the withdrawal of Miloradovich as long as possible, but he did not have a single gun at his disposal to do this as they had already been sent to the rear. As he saw the advancing forces, Wurttemberg quickly sent word to Miloradovich of his plight, advising him to hasten his march as well as to send artillery support.

While the French engaged the allied rearguard, Miloradovich, the Russian Guard, and a large artillery reserve moved steadily towards Mengelsdorf. Miloradovich was well aware of the danger of the French threat to the Reichenbach-Görlitz Road, and moved as quickly possible while Wurttemberg held the French at bay.

Miloradovich dispatched two jager battalions to a position south of Reichenbach, as well as a battery of 18 cannon under Yermolov.[4]

Reynier deployed to assault Wurttemberg frontally, while Lauriston maneuvered to turn his left flank. The Reichenbach valley was quickly filled with French and Saxon skirmishers, who engaged the skirmishers of the 21st and 34th Jagers. The Saxon infantry of the VII Corps advanced in column. The VII Corps artillery deployed and began to cover the Saxon advance.

Because of the terrible battle of the previous two days, the French and Saxons maneuvered cautiously. They were fatigued by their efforts and did not feel ready to engage in another major battle so soon. They were also uncertain if the rest of the allied army was deployed, ready for a general battle, or hidden from their view. Napoleon, anxious to come to grips with the Russians, sent the Polish and Dutch Guard Lancer Regiments, under the command of Général Lefebvre-Desnouëttes, across the brook flowing past Reichenbach above the village, so as to cut Wurttemberg's potential lines of retreat.[5]

A detachment of the 21st Jagers, on Wurttemberg's left, delayed the Saxon advance, until it was attacked and scattered by the 1,500 French Guard light cavalry, that pushed up to the outskirts of Reichenbach. Wurttemberg remarked at the appearance of the French cavalry, calling it a "new spectacle," as it had been a long time since he'd seen a force of French cavalry.[6]

As the jagers were being ridden down, Wurttemberg received reinforcements in the form of Sacharzewski's horse battery, and a little later, six 12pdr guns. Miloradovich had begun to hasten his withdrawal, but detached the 5th Division, 1st Corps, on the road between Reichenbach and Markersdorf, as a reserve for Wurttemberg.

Wurttemberg placed his newly received artillery on his left flank, to cover it against the French cavalry attacks. He then formed his infantry into "masses," and the Tobolsk and Riajsk Infantry Regiments were advanced to the side of Reichenbach to support the jagers occupying the village and its outskirts. Behind the French cavalry, Wurttemberg saw several strong columns of French and Saxon infantry.

Sensing that the attack was aimed at his left, Wurttemberg dispatched most of his cavalry to that flank. This force consisted of General Grengross's Dragoon Brigade, Knorring's Corps, Millesimo's, and Prince Troubetzkoi's forces, a total of about 7,000 men. This was countered by the appearance of Général Latour-Maubourg, with his 1,400 French and Saxon cuirassiers.[7] At 10:00 A.M., the French screened their attack with their cavalry, which also menaced Wurttemberg's first line. Wurttemberg responded by directing the fire of his artillery, now risen to 18 guns (a horse battery and 6 guns of a 12pdr position battery). The French Guard cavalry quickly swerved and moved to strike him in the rear, while other forces advanced against his front.

The advance of the Saxons was successful, and the battalion of the Saxon Leib-Grenadier-Garde Regiment seized the town. Behind the Saxons was a column of French infantry.

General Gerngross arrived at this time with two squadrons of dragoons. Wurttemberg directed him to attack the French Guard cavalry, which he did, taking them in the flank and forcing them to withdraw. General Millesimo then followed Gerngross with the rest of the dragoon brigade and a few hussars, throwing back the Saxon line. They handled the Saxon brigade of von Thümmel severely, but the rest infantry of the VII Corps had formed square and withstood the assault handily.

Latour-Maubourg brought the 1st Cavalry Corps into the battle. The French and Saxon heavy cavalry responded to the Russian attack and struck, driving the Russian cavalry of Gerngross and Millesimo behind the main Russian line.[8]

TROUBETZKOI

The French Guard cavalry returned at a trot and once again began to maneuver to take Wurttemberg in the flank. The Russian General Knorring arrived with the Tartar Uhlan Regiment and the Ukraine Dragoons in such a manner as to be able to strike at the French Guard cavalry's flank, again forcing the French to withdraw. Knorring then withdrew his forces, joined them with Millesimo's, and executed an attack against the Saxon infantry's flank, forcing them once again to pull back. At this time Latour-Maubourg began feeding in forces from his cavalry corps. They struck at Knorring and Millesimo, driving them back behind the Russian lines once again.

The French and Russians advanced once again to engage one another. A major cavalry battle occurred on the Russian flank and a total of between 10,000 and 13,000 cavalry were engaged. During this battle, Prince Troubetzkoi arrived with the Ukrainian brigade of Prince Obolenski, and a few other regiments.

FRENCH FORCES
BATTLE OF REICHENBACH
22 MAY 1813

Imperial Guard: Berg Lancers
    1st Guard Lancer Regt.
    2nd Guard Lancer Regt.
    Chasseurs à Cheval de la Garde
    Mamelouks
    Gendarmes d'élite
    Light Artillery
VII Corps: Général de division Reynier
32nd Division: Général de division Durutte
1st Brigade:
    ?/,4/35th Légère Regt. (2)
    3/,4/36th Légère Regt. (2)
    3/,4/131st Line Regt. (2)
    3/,4/132nd Line Regt. (2)
2nd Brigade:
    3/,4/133rd Line Regt. (2)
    1/,2/,3/Würzburg Infantry Regt. (3)
Royal Saxon Corps: Général of Cavalry Zeschau
1st Division: Brigadier-Oberst von Brause
    1st Light Regt. Lecoq (1 bn)
    1/Guard Grenadier Regt. (1)
    Prinz Frederich Infantry Regt. (1)
    von Steindel Infantry Regt. (1)
    Jägers (1 coy)
2nd Division: Générallieutenant von Sahr
    von Anger Grenadier Battalion (1)
    Prinz Anton Infantry Regt. (1)
    von Löw Infantry Regt. (1)
Artillery: 2 Foot batteries (6 guns each)
    1 Horse Battery (8 guns)
    1 Sapper Company
    French Artillery (12 guns)

1st Cavalry Corps: Général de division Latour-Maubourg
1st Light Cavalry Division: Général de division Bruyère
Brigade: Général de brigade Bessières
    7th Hussar Regt. *
    9th Chevauléger Regt.

    8th Hussar Regt.
    16th Chasseur à Cheval Regt.
    7th Chevauléger Regt.
Brigade: Général de brigade Cambraceres
    1st Chevauléger Regt.
    3rd Chevauléger Regt.
    5th Chevauléger Regt.
    8th Chevauléger Regt.

3rd Light Cavalry Division: Général de division Chastel
1st Brigade: Général de brigade Van Merlen
    6th Chasseur à Cheval Regt.
    25th Chasseur à Cheval Regt.
    6th Hussar Regt.
    8th Chasseur à Cheval Regt.
    Portuguese Legion Chasseur à Cheval Regt.
2nd Brigade: Général de brigade Richter
    9th Chasseur à ChevalRegt.
    19th Chasseur à Cheval Regt.
    2nd Italian Chasseur à ChevalRegt.
    3rd Italian Chasseur à Cheval Regt.
    1st Chasseur à Cheval Regt.
    2nd Chasseur à Cheval Regt.
    3rd Chasseur à Cheval Regt.
1st Cuirassier Division: Général de division Bordesoulle
1st Brigade: Général de brigade Berkheim
    2nd Cuirassier Regt.
    3rd Cuirassier Regt.
    6th Cuirassier Regt.
2nd Brigade: Général de brigade Quinette
    9th Cuirassier Regt.
    11th Cuirassier Regt.
    12th Cuirassier Regt.
3rd Brigade: Général Lessing
    Saxon Leib Cuirassier Regt. (4)
    Zastrow Cuirassier Regt. (4)
Corps Artillery:
    2 French Horse Batteries (12 guns)
    4/1st Italian Horse Artillery (6 guns)
    3rd Saxon Horse Battery (6 guns)

*Note: The French cavalry Regt.s listed here had little more than a company apiece.

Wurttemberg took this reinforcement and threw it once again into the French flank in an effort to break the assault. He threw the rest of his cavalry into their front, and his 18 guns continued to fire into the French cavalry during all the entire battle. Wurttemberg reported that the 2nd (Dutch) Imperial Guard Lancer Regiment lost 200 prisoners to the Russians in this battle.[9] The official French reports show the figure to be far fewer.

During the continuing cavalry battle, Wurttemberg sent the 4th and 20th Jagers into a small woods on his left flank. They were to threaten the flank of the Saxon infantry assault. As the cavalry battle ebbed, the Russian artillery then turned its attention on this area of the battlefield in an effort to support the two jager regiments.

The French cavalry began another assault aimed at the Russian jagers. This time the French attack was stopped short by the timely appearance of a Russian cuirassier division and yet another horse battery. They delayed the French long enough for the four threatened jager regiments to form square.

The Russian forces had been reinforced by the cavalry corps of Uvarov and the division of Pahlen, giving the allies a great superiority in cavalry. Unfortunately for the Russians, this

RUSSIAN FORCES
BATTLE OF REICHENBACH
22 MAY 1813

Corps: Generallieutenant Prince Eugene of Wurttemburg
Cavalry: Generalmajor Knorring
    Soum Hussar Regt. (2)
    Tartar Uhlan Regt. (4)
    Converged Dragoon Regt. (2)
3rd Division: Generalmajor Count Schachafskoi
Brigade: Colonel Baron Wolff
    Mourmansk Infantry Regt. (1)
    Revel Infantry Regt. (1)
    Tchernigov Infantry Regt. (1)
Brigade: Colonel Kapustin
    20th Jager Regt. (1)
    21st Jager Regt. (1)
4th Division: Generalmajor Pischnitzky
Brigade: Colonel Treffurt
    Tobolsk Infantry Regt. (1)
    Volhynie Infantry Regt. (1)
    Riajsk Infantry Regt. (1)
Brigade: Colonel Iwanov
    4th Jager Regt. (1)
    34th Jager Regt. (1)
    Tobolsk Infantry Regt. (1)
Artillery: Generalmajor Nikitin
    Heavy Artillery Battery #1
    Light Artillery Battery #33
    Horse Artillery Battery #7
Cavalry: Generalmajor Pantschulid I
    Tchernigov Chasseur à Cheval Regt. (3)
    New Russia Dragoon Regt. (2)
    Lithuanian Uhlan Regt. (2)
Reinforcements:
Artillery: unknown Position Battery (6 guns)
    unknown Light Battery (12 guns)

Brigade: Generalmajor Millesimo
    Kiev Dragoon Regt. (3)
    Karkov Dragoon Regt. (3)
    Horse Artillery Battery #4
Cossacks: Generalmajor Count Obolensky
    3rd Ukranian Cossack Regt. (4)
Brigade: Generalmajor Pahlen II
    Tver Dragoon Regt. (2)
    Dorpat Dragoon Regt. (2)
Brigade: Colonel Uvarov
    Loubny Hussar Regt. (2)
    Horse Battery #3
Brigade: Generalmajor Gengross
    Mitau Dragoon Regt. (2)
    Moscow Dragoon Regt. (2)

Reserve:
5th Division: Generalmajor Lukov
Brigade: Generalmajor Prince of Siberia
    Perm Infantry Regt. (1)
    Mohilev Infantry Regt. (1)
Brigade: Generalmajor Kasatschkovsky
    Kalouga Infantry Regt. (1)
    Sievesk Infantry Regt. (1)
    Grand Duchess Catherine Battalion
    2nd Cuirassier Division: Generalmajor Duca
Brigade: Generalmajor Leontiev
    Gluchov Cuirassier Regt. (3)
    Pskof Cuirassier Regt. (3)
Brigade: Generalmajor Gudowitsch
    Military Order Cuirassier Regt. (3)
    Starodoub Cuirassier Regt. (3)
Brigade: Colonel Massalov
    Little Russian Cuirassier Regt. (3)
    Novgorod Cuirassier Regt. (3)
Artillery:
    Unidentified Horse Battery

Unidentified Formations:
    Mellentin's Infantry

---

superiority was negated by the tremendously powerful French artillery forces which had been deployed and were beginning to pound any Russian force that appeared in their sights.

Napoleon, seeing that his attempts to turn the Russian left had not succeeded, turned his attention to their center. The VII Corps reformed itself on the Töpferberge heights, where it was supported by French artillery. The Saxon line was formed between the villages of Dobschütz and Mengelsdorf.[10] Under this artillery support, the Saxon corps prepared another assault on the Russian lines about 4:00 P.M.. The Saxon Guard Battalion advanced on the left flank of the Saxon attack, formed so as to defend that flank from cavalry attack.

In reacting to this assault, Wurttemberg drew the 4th, 20th, 21st and 34th Jagers back onto the Tobolsk and Riajsk Infantry regiments. At the same time, Wurttemberg was becoming aware of the flanking maneuver of Lauriston. Wurttemberg then began to withdraw his forces to a position between Markersdorf and Holtendorf, where his reserve, the 5th Division, was posted. His cavalry withdrew on his extreme left through Markersdorf and Paulsdorf, as far as Friedersdorf.

As Wurttemberg joined the 5th Division, he detached a brigade in the small woods on his right, and deployed the 2nd Corps in two lines between those woods and some brush on his left, where he deployed the 4th and 20th Jagers. His horse artillery was deployed before his line and the half position battery was drawn behind Markersdorf with Scharzewski's battery.

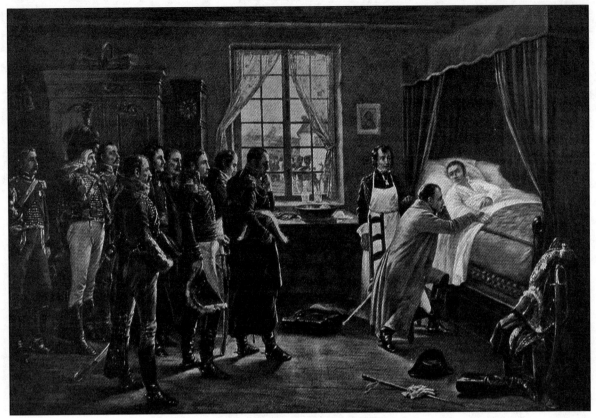

THE DEATH OF DUROC

The French closed this position and engaged both wings simultaneously in a lively fire right which lasted about an hour. At that time, Wurttemberg broke off the battle and withdrew by way of Markersdorf towards Miloradovich's position. Schachrzewski's battery continued to fire until the last of the jagers had cleared the field and then withdrew itself.

The village of Neider Markersdorf was occupied by the 21st and 34th Jagers, a brigade of the 1st Corps, as well as the 4th and 20th Jagers. They too shortly found themselves engaged by French skirmishers who, by night fall, had succeeded in seizing part of the village. Once in Görlitz, Wurttemberg's forces passed over the river and burnt the bridge.[11] Having deployed for the battle, it now took the French an hour to untangle their forces and reorganize to renew the pursuit.

As the Russians had burnt the bridge over the Neisse, a crossing had to be found. The Saxon pontooneers were sent to bridge the river, and struggled under enemy fire to place a pontoon bridge over the Neisse. By noon on 23 May, the French lead elements had crossed over to the eastern bank. Latour-Maubourg's 1st Cavalry Corps and the IV Corps resumed the pursuit.

THE DEATH OF DUROC

Napoleon had been close to the battle during its course and as Wurttemberg began his withdrawal, about 3:00 p.m., one cannon shot had passed quite close to him. That shot struck and killed General of Engineers Kirgener and mortally wounded Grand Marshal of the Palace Duroc, who died twelve hours later. Duroc's loss struck Napoleon as hard as the loss of Lannes had during the battle at Essling. Another shot had killed General Bruyère. Even Mortier had a close call with the shot that killed Kirgener and Duroc, though he was spared any wounds.[12]

Reynier requested an opportunity for his fatigued men to rest, after Reichenbach. They had marched furiously in an effort to reach Bautzen in time for the battles of 20/21 May, and Reynier was losing stragglers. Napoleon refused the request and premptorily ordered him to move to Görlitz.

The day's battle had inflicted a number of casualties on the French. The Berg lancers, the 1st and 2nd Guard Lancers, the Chasseurs à Cheval de la Garde and the Mamelukes, the Gendarmerie d'élite and the Guard light artillery were engaged, losing one officer killed, two captured and six wounded, 33 enlisted killed or captured and 179 wounded. The 32nd Division and the Saxon Division lost one officer and 64 enlisted killed, and 15 officers and 364 enlisted wounded. During the battle the French artillery fired 6,292 round shot and 6,323 howitzer shells.[13] Official French records indicate the following casualties:

	Killed	Wounded	Captured
Guard Cavalry			
Officers	1	6	2
Enlisted	33	179	*
VII Corps			
Officers	1	15	—
Enlisted	64	364	*
I Cavalry Corps			
Officers	—	7	—
Enlisted	67	122	67
3rd Light Cavalry Division			
Officers	1	—	—

*Figures for captured included in killed.[14]

That night the V, VI, and VII Corps and the Guard camped about Markersdorf, while the IV and XI Corps were south of Reichenbach. The III Corps was in Weissenberg, while the II Corps and Sébastiani's cavalry were behind Baruth.

SKIRMISH AT LEOPOLDSHAYNE

After the rearguard action at Reichenbach, the Russian 2nd Corps moved to a position between Holtendorf and Pfaffendorf. The 20th Jagers were left in Neider-Markersdorf, to occupy the Saxons as they attempted to throw their pontoon bridge over the river. The 4th and 34th Jagers were placed in Pfaffendorf. The 21st Jagers and the Revel Infantry Regiment were placed into Holtendorf.

Though Miloradovich was pleased with the action around Reichenbach, he did not remain with Wurttemberg. He did, however, attach Pantschoulidzev's dragoon division to Wurttemberg's rearguard force.

The night was not a calm one. The fear of the French cavalry appears to have returned to the Russians, and during the night a false alarm was raised with the cries of "Cavalry!" The advanced posts began to fire blindly into the night and the skirmishers of the Revel Infantry Regiment fired on a Prussian corps. This latter incident brought the entire corps to arms. Not being able to sleep, at 2:00 A.M. Wurttemberg brought his rearguard to its feet and resumed his withdrawal. The infantry moved through Görlitz, and moved towards Leopoldshayne on the main road from Lauban. Generallieutenant Pahlen strung his cavalry in a chain of advanced posts and left a force of cavalry to observe the burnt bridges over the Neisse.

When daybreak of the 23rd arrived, it was the beginning of what would be a long day for Wurttemberg's skirmishers. Pahlen's cavalry withdrew from the Neisse and fell back on Ober-Lichtenberg. As they withdrew, the French attacked the woods and village of Leopoldshayn, where Wurttemberg had posted his infantry. A firefight began at 10:00 A.M., and lasted until 5:00 P.M., when the 2nd Corps placed itself on the heights of Lichtenberg. A Württemberg column, consisting of the 6th and 2/7th Württemberg Infantry Regiments,[15] attempted to pass the Russians right by moving through Hennersdorf and Stangenhain. However, it was attacked by a partisan cavalry detachment under Colonel Löwenstern near Troitschendorf, and they stopped their flanking maneuver there.

Macdonald's forces held the Russians frontally, and Bertrand, upon hearing the sound of Macdonald's guns, swung towards them in time to appear on the Russian right, forcing them to withdraw before they were cut off.

The rearguard action broke off quickly and night fell. The Russians once again slipped away, while the French collapsed around their campfires after yet another arduous day of a fighting advance.

Nightfall found Lauriston's V Corps across the Neisse, on the road to Waldau and Bunzlau. Its advance guard had fought almost constantly since it passed through Stutzenham. Marmont and the VI Corps were in Hermsdorf. Macdonald's XI Corps was in Schönberg. Bertrand's IV Corps, which had moved to the sound of Reynier's guns, found its advanced guard in Troitschendorf and its main body between the XI and VI Corps. The Imperial Guard was in Görlitz, Ney's III Corps was in Weissenberg and Oudinot's XII Corps was in Bautzen, recovering from the effects of that battle.[16]

On 24 May, as the march resumed, Napoleon placed the V, VI, and VII Corps under the command of Maréchal Ney and directed them to move down the road to Buntzlau. The Guard was to follow. The IV and XI Corps were to move on Lauban in a manner so as to be able to act in conjunction with Ney, if the occasion should arise. The II Corps (Victor) and Sébastiani's reserve cavalry were to move on Rothenberg and to follow the allies towards to east, while maintaining contact with the main army. The III Corps was to march on Görlitz. The XII Corps was ordered to Hoyerswerda so as to protect the main body against any possibility of Bülow's descending against their flank and rear.

On 25 May, Napoleon thought the allies had stopped to the west of Liegnitz and prescribed that the V Corps was to move from Buntzlau to Kreibau, the VII Corps was to move its advance guard to Modelsdorf and its main body to Mittlau. The VI Corps was to cross the Bober at Oltendorf and to push its advanced guard to Gross-Hartmansdorf while leaving its main body in Alt-Jaschwitz. The IV and XI Corps were to move as close as possible to Löwenberg.

Unfortunately, a number of broken bridges prevented these orders from arriving in time for them to be executed. As a result, by days' end, the V Corps and the cavalry reserve remained echeloned between Wolfshain and Scheibendorf, the VII Corps was in Neu-Jaschwitz, and the VI Corps was echeloned from Alt-Jaschwitz and Oltendorf.

The right hand column, the XI Corps, moved through Lauban, and encountered a strong Russian rearguard at Kanzendorf. The attack began at 10:00 a.m., but Macdonald feared he was engaging significantly superior forces and acted with considerable caution against it. The engagement ended at 10:00 P.M.. The IV Corps, marching to the sound of his guns, moved towards the south, but arrived to late too engage in the battle.

The Guard and III Corps arrived in Buntzlau, except for Marchand's Division, which remained in Görlitz. The II Corps had moved from Kohlfurt to Thommendorf.[17]

THE FRENCH MARCH EAST CONTINUES

By the end of the 25th, the French were located such that the V Corps and the I Cavalry Corps were between Wolfshain, Thomaswalde, and Martinswalde. The VII Corps was in Neu-Jaschwitz, the VI Corps was in Alt-Jaschwitz and Ottendorf, the XI and IV Corps were in Stekicht and Wenig Rächnitz respectively, the Guard and III Corps were near Bunzlau, and the II Corps was on the left in Thommendorf.[18]

In the allied camp anger mounted and tempers flared. Wittgenstein's position with the Czar had become impossible. The Czar passed orders directly to Wittgenstein's subordinate commanders, as well as took council from others without talking to Wittgenstein. Wittgenstein offered his resignation and it was accepted. Barclay de Tolly was appointed in his place, in as much as he was the only commander available who was acceptable to the Prussians. Unfortunately for the Czar, Barclay's opinions were nearly identical with Wittgenstein's. He knew that the allied army was slowly melting away and now totaled only 80,000 men. It was demoralized by a string of defeats and continuous retreat. He wished to withdraw to Poland, recover his strength, and reorganize the army.

To the Prussians, this plan of the Russians to withdraw to Poland would leave their country naked to Napoleon's mercies. It would also strip the Prussian army of its recruiting grounds and principal source of supplies and material.

A compromise was struck between the Russian and Prussian commanders, and the retreat moved south-east towards Schweidnitz. This kept the allies in Silesia and in contact with Austria, whose intervention was being urgently courted by their respective ambassadors.

This compromise had its disadvantages, in as much as it gave Napoleon the opportunity to outflank their right, to cut their line of retreat on Warsaw, and the chance to once again crush them up against the Austrian frontier.[19]

SKIRMISH AT SEIFERSDORF

Macdonald's advanced guard continued to pursue the Russians, and on 25 May it passed through Seifersdorf. At 4:00 p.m., it encountered a few thousand cossacks supported by Count Pahlen's division, which moved out of a nearby woods and pushed into the village of Seifersdorf. They were not observed until their attack was well developed and they penetrated into the village, cutting Macdonald's column in two. The 1st Chevauléger-lancier Regiment, in march column, was just advancing into the village when it came into contact with the cossacks. It formed into a dense column (serrée) by half squadrons and pushed through the village while simultaneously detaching an adjutant to the next regiment advising it of the cossack occupation of Seifersdorf.

This regiment, a regiment of Württemberg cavalry, also formed a dense column of half squadrons and attempted to push through the village, but fell back in great disorder. The cossacks pursued it wildly, only to pull up short when they encountered another regiment formed and ready to deal with them. The Württembergers reformed and counter charged their tormentors, driving them through the streets of Seifersdorf until they were stopped by the Russian infantry and their regimental commander was struck down by a musket ball.

The remainder of the French force pulled up and began a flanking maneuver around the village, but Pahlen resumed his withdrawal towards Löwenberg.[20]

TROUBLE IN THE FRENCH CAMP

On 26 May, a clash of personalities between Ney and Marmont erupted. It was to have serious consequences. Marmont, anxious to be away from Ney, who had been placed over him, persuaded himself that the allies had only a rearguard on the Bunzlau-Liegnitz road and that the bulk of their forces were retreating on Löwenberg and Goldberg. He had been ordered by Ney to march on Ottendorf, but with his perception of the situation demanded permission to move on Löwenberg. Ney refused and Marmont was obliged to continue towards Ottendorf.

At this point Napoleon intervened, accepting Marmont's reports as truth, and ordered Ney, with the V and VII Corps to move on Hainau, while Marmont was to move with his corps and Latour-Maubourg, in conjunction with Macdonald and Bertrand, to turn the right flank of the allies supposed to be on the southern road. The III Corps was to move to a position 2½ miles from Bunzlau, under the orders of Ney. There was a report that the enemy had disappeared northwards, so Victor, with the II Corps, was to advance to the north towards Sprottau and follow anything that might be moving towards Berlin. Victor soon found this report to be false.

At 3:00 p.m., Maison's 16th Division, leading the V Corps, moved through Hainau. It had only 4,000 men as it moved to the heights east of Michelsdorf, just beyond Hainau on the road to Liegnitz. The countryside was open and rolling, well suited for cavalry action. Any enemy force could easily hide itself behind some knoll a short distance from the road without being observed.

Maison was marching carelessly and failed to take proper steps to protect himself from surprise. His flank guards consisted solely of about 50 troopers, who were most disinterested in the task before them. Chastel's 3rd Light Cavalry Division, which should have been with Maison, had stopped short of Hainau, believing the day's march was complete. All that remained was for the allies to act. They soon did.[21]

As Maison halted his six battalions and three batteries beyond Michelsdorf, the Baumandsdorf mill on his right burst into flames. It was the signal for Ziethen's attack. A Prussian horse battery opened fire on the heights only 400 yards from Maison's division. At the same time, 3,000 Prussian cavalry under Dolffs, 22 squadrons, supported by three horse batteries from the Prussian cavalry reserve, surged out of a valley by Baudmansdorf. They galloped over and down a hill into the mass of disorganized French. Before the French could reorganize their units the Prussian cavalry were amongst them, slashing right and left at the helpless Frenchmen.

The Prussians had carefully planned this attack. It was executed as they had hoped, but, if it had failed, the cavalry was to pull back towards Pohlsdorf, where Oberst Pirch had established his cavalry in the defiles, on both wings of the allied position. In addition Major Lange with the Fusilier/1st Silesian Infantry Regiment, half the Silesian Schützen Battalion and the detached sharpshooters from the battalions of Sacken[22] and Offenay (3/1st Silesian Infantry Regiment) were posted with the rearguard to stop the French. In addition a force of several battalions was stationed to check what might pass through the rearguard. This consisted of the battalions of Majors Offenay (3/1st Silesian), Koschisky (1/1st Silesian), Reichenbach (2/2nd Silesian), Sacken and Bülow (3rd Res/Leib), which were posted in the first rank and a second rank was formed with the Silesian Grenadier Battalion and the battalion of Major Bentheim (3rd Res/1st Silesian).[23]

When Dolffs launched his attack, the first line was formed by the Prussian Guard Light Cavalry Regiment, the Silesian Uhlans, and the Silesian Cuirassiers. The East Prussian Cuirassiers formed the second line and the third was formed by the Garde du Corps and the Brandenburg Cuirassier regiments. Between the last two regiments of cavalry were the horse batteries.[24]

The Prussian Guard Light Cavalry Regiment drove towards the French right flank, with the Silesian Uhlans and the Silesian Cuirassier Regiment. The Silesian Cuirassiers crushed one partially formed French square, and the East Prussian Cuirassiers moved between Michelsdorf and Hainau, crushing all formed bodies of French infantry they found between the two villages.

The 16th Division broke and fled in a bloody rout to Michelsdorf, where they encountered two organized and fresh French battalions of the 148th Infantry Regiment. This new force stopped the Prussian assault and recaptured six guns that had temporarily been lost to the Prussians.

Puthod's 17th Division and the 3rd Light Cavalry Division arrived at the double and put an end to the battle. The engagement had lasted only a few minutes, yet it had cost Maison heavily in dead, wounded, prisoners, and equipment. It was fortunate that the assault had been so close to Michelsdorf, for if he had been farther from shelter his division would probably have ceased to exist. It had been Ziethen's intention to let them advance farther, but word had reached him that Reynier's corps was closing and he feared if he waited too long the chance would be lost. Again, the sources provide mixed results. Prussian sources state that they lost 86 men, including 16 officers,[25] while French sources indicate about 300 Prussians and Oberst Dolffs were hors de combat.[26] Whichever is correct, the Prussians were the clear winners of this engagement.

	Killed		Wounded		Prisoners	
	Officers	Men	Officers	Men	Officers	Men
16th Division (Maison)						
151st	—	44	—	173	—	399
153rd	4	55	3	252	—	30
Total	4	99	3	425	0	429
17th Division						
146th	—	—	—	—	—	—
147th	1	2	2	8	—	—
148th	—	—	1	7	—	15
18th Division						
19th Division						
Artillery	1	54	5	142	—	43
Engineers	—	3	—	39	—	19
3rd Light Cavalry Division						
6th Chasseurs	—	1	—	2	—	2
25th Chasseurs	—	3	1	27	—	5
6th Hussars	—	—	—	—	—	1
8th Chasseurs	—	—	—	—	—	—
Portuguese	—	1	—	1	—	3
9th Chasseurs	—	—	—	1	—	—
19th Chasseurs	—	—	—	—	—	—
2nd & 3rd Italian	—	1	—	10	—	2
1st Chasseurs	—	—	—	—	—	—
2nd Chasseurs	—	—	—	—	—	—
3rd Chasseurs	—	—	—	—	—	—
	10	*263*	*15*	*1,099*	*0*	*948*

FRENCH CASUALTIES AT HAINAU ON 26 MAY 1813[27]

On the French right, Marmont, Bertrand, and Macdonald had been delayed for one reason or another and did not close with the Russian rearguard at Pilgramsdorf until nightfall too late for another engagement. The allies main army had safely crossed the Katzbach and stood with its right flank on Liegnitz and its left at Goldberg.

THE PURSUIT RESUMES

On 27 May, Lauriston moved to Gross Rechern, east of Liegnitz, with Reynier on his right. The Imperial Headquarters and Guard were moved to Liegnitz, the III Corps to Hainau, and Marchand's 38th Division was in Bunzlau.

Marmont moved to Kröitzsch in an effort to cut the road between Goldberg and Liegnitz, while the IV and XI Corps continued towards Goldberg. Between Pilgramsdorf and Goldberg, Macdonald encountered a strong Russian rearguard. He directed a division of French cavalry from Latour-Maubourg's corps against the allied cavalry, but it behaved very poorly[28] and lost the engagement.

When the French infantry moved forward, the Russians withdrew and Macdonald moved through Goldberg to a position between the Liegnitz and Jauer roads, on Marmont's right. Bertrand had been obliged to stop in Griersdorf because Marmont crossed his front. Victor moved into Sprottau and cut off a Russian artillery convoy.

On the 27th, the allies began withdrawing towards Schweidnitz. Their right hand column moved into Mertschütz, and its rearguard was posted in Kloster-Wahlstädt. Their left column marched from Goldberg to Jauer and left its rearguard posted in Hermannsdorf. On the 28th, the French left remained stationary, while on the right, Marmont moved across the Katzbach and drove back a strong force of allied forces.

Macdonald reached Jauer and Bertrand occupied Hermannsdorf. Victor, on the far left, marched from Sprottau to Primkenau where he was able to break the siege of Glogau. The allies arrived in Striegau.

On 29 May, the III Corps moved into Liegnitz, leaving Marchand in Hainau. The V and VIII Corps, followed by the Guard, moved towards Neukirch, but Napoleon directed the VII Corps to stop in Kloster-Wahlstädt.

Ney had ordered Reynier to keep abreast of Lauriston but the order was countered by Berthier. When Reynier did not do so, Ney demanded an accounting. Ney's tender sensibilities were wounded by Berthier's oversight in not communicating it to him. In a fit of childish rage, unfortunately common amongst Napoleon's prima donna marshalate, Ney requested to be relieved of his command of the advanced guard, pleading his wounds. He was, however, persuaded to reconsider and eventually he withdrew his request.[29]

At the same time, the allies reached Schweidnitz but found that it was not a suitable position as the fortifications that had been destroyed in 1807 were still not repaired.

On 30 May, Lauriston remained stationary so Reynier could close up with his flank. The Guard and Imperial Headquarters were Neukirch. The VI Corps and Latour-Maubourg moved into Eisendorf and Ober Moys. The IV and XI Corps moved only a short distance east of Jauer because Macdonald had heard that the main allied army was retiring on Schweidnitz. Victor advanced into Randten.

On 31 May, Lauriston advanced to within three miles of Breslau, driving before him Schuler's detachment of 5,800 infantry, 2,750 cavalry and twelve guns. Schuler had been blockading Glogau with his force of second rate troops, and now that Lauriston was threatening him, he endeavored in vain to cover Breslau.[30]

The VII Corps moved into Arnoldsmühl, the III Corps moved into Neukirch. The VI Corps remained in Eisendorf, while the IV and XI Corps did not stir. At 6:00 P.M., Lauriston advanced into Neukirch and attempted to cross the Lohe River. The bridge was defended by three Prussian reserve battalions and a battery of eight guns. This tiny force of Prussians held the bridge until 10:00 P.M.[31]

Napoleon was now convinced that the allies were withdrawing on Schweidnitz and arranged his army such that the V Corps was in Kryptau and Mochbern, facing south. A detachment was posted to Breslau, and a division in Purschwitz. Chastel's cavalry was moved to Hartlieb. The VII Corps moved to Purschwitz. The III Corps moved south of Neukirch, with Marchand at Liegnitz. The VI Corps and two divisions of cavalry were in Eisendorf and Noys. The IV and XI Corps were around Jauer. Victor was ordered to prepare to march back on Sagan, to support Oudinot at Hoyerswerda, in a movement on Berlin.

THE SKIRMISH BY GROSS ROSEN

As Macdonald's corps moved down the road to Herzogswaldau, the 38th (Württemberg) Division marched towards the villages of Prosen and Gross Rosen. The French 12th (Morand) and Italian 15th (Peyri) Divisions followed behind and to the left. As the Württembergers advanced they found themselves subjected to a swarming attack by hundreds of cossacks. The Württemberg cavalry, however, easily chased them off.

As the 38th (Württemberg) Division reached the heights above Herzogswaldau they found themselves greeted by heavy artillery fire from two batteries. In addition, the allies had assumed a position with their infantry behind Herzogswaldau and Gross Rosen as well as with strong forces in both villages. The 38th Division halted and began to deploy for the attack.[32]

Around 4:00 p.m. General Bertrand ordered General von Stockmeyer to take the light infantry brigade, under Oberst von Spitzemberg, and advance into the woods before Gross Rosen as well as to take the village of Gross Rosen.

The 9th and 10th Württemberg Infantry Regiments[33] drove into the woods where they engaged the Russian and Prussian skirmishers. As they came out the far side of the woods Oberst von Spitzemberg was struck from his horse by a cannon ball and killed. The Russian and Prussian light infantry counter attacked and pushed the Württembergers, who were short of ammunition, back. To support them, the 7th Württemberg Infantry Regiment advanced into the woods, clearing them and taking the village of Gross Rosen. To support this advance the 2/1st and two companies of the 2nd Württemberg Infantry Regiments were sent into the woods.

The Russians and Prussians did not leave the Württemberg possession of Gross Rosen uncontested and a savage battle began. The 7th Württemberg Regiment, the 2/Prinz Paul Regiment and von Wickede's battery fired off most of their munitions holding the village. Eventually the village was set afire and the Württembergers were unable to hold it. At 11:00 P.M. the battle broke off. The 38th Division withdrew to positions around Jauer around, arriving 1:00 A.M.

THE CAMPAIGN COMES TO A HALT

From 2 to 4 June, when the armistice was signed, the French made no movement of importance. In contrast, the allies made hasty maneuvers because, if Napoleon were to close his left on Breslau, they would have been in great danger of being cut off from the Oder. The allies immediately began to move eastwards so as to reach the Oder between Ohlau and Brieg. The river was quickly bridged, and during the next two days the Russo-Prussian army moved to the

PRUSSIAN CAVALRY AT HAINAU

line of Strehlen-Nimptsch. Schuler's detachment and the head of Sacken's Corps, now arriving from Poland, were on the right bank of the Oder.

To Blücher and Yorck, this maneuver smacked of the earlier Russian plan to withdraw into Poland, and they wrote to the King of Prussia, proposing that if the Russians did move across the Oder, the Prussians should detach themselves from the Russians, so as to operate independently. They would then withdraw along the Bohemian mountains, while the Silesian landwehr would assemble around Neisse and Glatz.

Bülow Behind the French Advance

Bülow had, after the battle at Halle, withdrawn his forces back and acted as a reserve corps covering the Saal, watching Victor's Corps and acting as a flank guard for the main allied army. After the battle at Halle, he found himself significantly reinforced in the form of three battalions of the 3rd East Prussian Infantry Regiment and the 2nd East Prussian Grenadier Battalion, a company of East Prussian Jägers, two companies of fusiliers from the 3rd East Prussian Infantry Regiment, four squadrons of the Königin Dragoons, two squadrons of the 2nd East Prussian Dragoons, three squadrons of the 1st Leib Hussar Regiment, and three batteries, a total of 4,500 men.[34] On 2 May, he had his forces before Oppen, which was occupied by the French.

The French had barricaded three gates, but not the Galgenthor, where they had posted three cannons and a howitzer. The Prussians struck this gate with two columns. On the right were the two fusilier companies and the jäger company. Behind them were three squadrons of hussars and a half foot battery. This force moved over the Saal from a position to the right of the heights of Hand and Giebichenstein.

On those heights stood the three battalions of the 3rd East Prussian Infantry Regiment, forming the middle column. They were supported by four cannons and two squadrons of the East Prussian Dragoons and were destined to strike the Galgenthor. The reserve was formed by the grenadier battalion, the four squadrons of the Königin Dragoons, and a half horse battery.

The French skirmishers engaged the right column with heavy fire and stopped its assault, but not before the suburbs were taken in a fearsome house to house battle. The fight forced back the 3/3rd East Prussian Infantry and their supporting force of West Prussian Dragoons. This force reformed and drove forward again, supported by the grenadier battalion. The Prussians rushed the gate, captured the guns and began another street to street fight with the French as they slowly took the entire town.

However, with the retreat of the allied armies from Lützen, Bülow found himself in a compromised position. He began to abandon what he had captured and take a stronger position.

Oudinot's March on Berlin

Oudinot had been left behind after the battle of Bautzen. His orders were to reorganize and prepare for a march on Berlin. However, he was only able to reach Hoyerswerda by 27 May.

Bülow, facing Oudinot's march, had collected 25,000 men, some of them landwehr and reserve infantry of little fighting value. This force consisted of General Oppen's 6th Brigade (Fusilier/3rd East Prussian Infantry Regiment, 1st & 3rd Lithuanian Fusilier Battalions,[35] the 1st Leib Hussar Regiment, and the Bichalow Cossack Regiment). The forces of Prinzen Ludwig von Hessen-Homburg consisted of the 2nd East Prussian Grenadier Battalion, 1/,2/,3/1st East Prussian Infantry, the 1/,2/3rd East Prussian Infantry, Rembow's 1st East Prussian Reserve Battalion, 2nd West Prussian Dragoons, a half 12pdr Battery #1, 6pdr Battery #5, and Horse Battery #6. The forces of General Thümen consisted of the 1/,2/,3/4th East Prussian Infantry, 3/3rd East Prussian Infantry, Herman's Battalion (4th Res/Leib), Kikebusch's 2nd East Prussian Reserve Battalion, and the 6pdr Foot Batteries #6 and #16. The forces of General Borstell forces consisted of the Pommeranian Grenadiers, 1/,2/Pommeranian Infantry Regiment, Fus/4th

East Prussian Infantry, Königin Dragoons, a half Horse Battery #10, 6pdr Foot Battery #10, and a cossack regiment. The Russians under General Harppe consisted of the Polish Uhlan and Niejinsk Chasseur Regiments, Navaginsk and Toula Infantry Regiments, and 12pdr Position Batteries #21 and #28. Oberst Boyen's forces consisted of 3rd Reserve/Colberg Infantry Regiment, 1st and 2nd Convalescent Battalions, two march battalions, a battalion of foreign volunteers,[36] 5/West Prussian Uhlan Regiment, the jäger squadron of the Prussian Lithuanian Dragoon Regiment, two march squadrons, a 1/2 6pdr Foot Battery #19. The forces under Major von Warwitz consisted of five squadrons and two battalions of Kurmark Landwehr detached near Wittenberg.[37]

Bülow moved towards Luckau, as soon as Napoleon had begun his concentration on Bautzen. Bülow led this force against Hoyerswerda, where he expected to find only a small detachment. To his surprise, he encountered the entire XII Corps and Beaumont's detachment.

BATTLE OF HOYERSWERDA

At day break of 28 May the two brigades of Borstell and Oppen moved from Laubusch towards Hoyerswerda. They moved in two columns, Oppen was on the left and Borstell's forces, under Oberst Krafft, were on the right. They were hoping to catch a French advanced guard, estimated to consist of 6,000 men, they thought was in Hoyerswerda.

Oppen's column struck down the left bank of the Elster, crossing at Narditz, where they hit the Bavarian advanced posts of General Raglovich and drove them back. A cannonade began and Oppen pushed three battalions and nine squadrons across the two dams in the city. The Bavarian infantry was quickly pushed back into the city. The French response was quick and four strong columns of infantry, under Maréchal Oudinot, moved out of Hoyerswerda to strike at the Prussians.

As Oppen struck at Narditz, Oberst Krafft's attack down the right bank of the Elster struck. The Prussian sharpshooters from Borstell's brigade occupied the villages of Bergen and Siedewinkel, as they moved forward. A strong French column moved from Hoyerswerda through the woods in an effort to turn Krafft's flank.

The initial course of the battle did not go well for the French. Oudinot found himself forced to take shelter inside an infantry square. However, a brigade of Hessian cavarly, under General Wolff, two French battalions, and an eight gun French 12pdr battery moved out to support Oudinot's forces. When the 12pdrs opened up on the allies, they quickly destroyed 8 to 10 of the allied guns and began breaking up their lines. The flow of the battle shifted against the allies.[38]

Being severely outnumbered by the forces immediately at hand, 12,000 to his 6,000, the battle quickly turned against Bülow and he withdrew as quickly as he could, using his light forces as a screen as he withdrew north. The French and Bavarians were not inclined to pursue and allowed the battle to break off.

On 29 May, Bülow pulled Thümen and Oppen back to Altdöbern, near Kahlau, and Borstell back to Cottbus. On 30 May, he collected his forces in Kahlau and formed them into two columns. One was under Prinz Ludwig von Hessen-Homburg and the second was under General Thümen. These two columns were then drawn to Cottbus, where Bülow had his headquarters.[39]

Then hearing that Victor was moving on Sagan, Bülow dispersed his troops along a front of over sixty miles in an attempt to cover Krossena and Berlin at the same time. Had Oudinot marched promptly on Luckau, he might well have destroyed Bülow's rag-tag forces in detail. However, he delayed until Bülow realized the folly of his actions and concentrated his troops by forced marches.

Oudinot did finally stir, but when he reached Luckau on 4 June, he found Bülow's entire force strongly positioned. Oudinot attempted to make up for his failure and rashly attacked, only to be bloodied himself, losing 2,000 men, and retreated to Uebigau.

Luckau lies on the Perste stream which ran through a deep ravine below the walls of Luckau. Its banks were marshy and make fording it difficult. The city's main entry required passage along the water course and over a single bridge that was so narrow that a man could touch each side of it at the same time. It was a strong position.

The Russo-Prussian forces disposed themselves so that the Russian brigade of General Harppe formed the right wing, (two squadrons of the Polish Uhlan Regiment, two squadrons of Niejinsk Chasseurs à Cheval, the Grekov #9 Cossack Regiment, the Tver Opolochenie Cossack Regiment, the Navaguinsk Infantry Regiment, and 12pdr Position Batteries #21 and #28). The two Russian batteries were posted on the windmill hill and were able to cover the entire front of the city. The village of Willmannsdorf was strongly held by the Russians and the cossacks were posted along the morass and the main road to Kirchhayne.

The middle was formed by Thümen's brigade (two battalions of the 4th East Prussian Infantry Regiment and 6pdr Foot Batteries #6 and #16). The infantry was posted north of the suburb, with part of it to the right in the village of Sando. The skirmishers were in the gardens before the city and along the length of the stream, while the batteries were on a rise behind their position.

The left wing was formed by Hessen-Homburg's brigade (2nd East Prussian Grenadier Battalion, three battalions of the 2nd East Prussian Infantry, two squadrons of the West Prussian Dragoons, half 12pdr Battery #1, 6pdr Foot Battery #5, and Horse Battery #6). Hessen-Homburg strung his forces out between the village of Wieringsdorf and Giesmannsdorf.

The 4th Reserve Battalion/Leib Infantry Regiment occupied Luckau proper, in the Kahlau suburb and its gardens there were three jäger companies, and to the right of the city on the Perste stood one Russian and four Prussian battalions.

The advanced guard under Oppen was posted between the villages of Kahnsdorf and Freszdorf. Obersten Boyen's forces were formed behind the right wing of General Borstell. The four brigades forming the allied position consisted of 16½ battalions, 10 squadrons, and 6½ batteries—a total of 15,800 men.[40]

When dawn broke, the French forces stood five miles from Kahlau, but the leading elements of their column did not arrive before Luckau until 10:00 am. Once it arrived, it began to cannonade the allied positions. By 11:00 a.m., the advanced forces of General Oppen were forced back across the Perste.

The French attack developed on the right bank of the Perste Stream. Their columns advanced, supported by artillery and covered by a screen of skirmishers. Their target was the jäger companies in the Kahlau suburb, the bridge behind them, and the Kahlau Gate. The Prussian jägers held them, while the schützen and 300 flankers from the 2nd East Prussian Grenadier Battalion moved through Zaucke village and took the French in the right flank. At the same time, a Prussian fusilier battalion, supported by a Russian battalion, advanced into the Kahlau suburbs, bayonets bristling, and drove the French troops out of the suburb and its gardens.

Oudinot observed this from the windmill hill between Kahnsdorf and Fressdorf. He directed fresh troops, heavily supported by artillery, into the suburb and towards the Kahlau Gate. However, the bridge to the gate was broken down by the Prussian troops present, and the houses in the village on the right side of the gate were filled with allied skirmishers. The street battle became intensive and eventually the suburb was set afire.

Oudinot began to shower the city with howitzer bombs in an effort to expand the fires and discomfort the allied garrison. General Oppen organized a force of ten squadrons of cavalry and cossacks and a horse battery. The burning suburb forced him to move through Wieringsdorf in a sweeping movement as they advanced against the French.[41]

They struck at the French right flank. The French responded by directing their own cavalry to counter them. Despite their efforts, the French cavalry was driven back and the Prussian cavalry closed on the French infantry columns attacking the city's suburbs. The French infantry recoiled, but not before the allies overran a battery and captured three guns. The French broke off the attack and withdrew. The losses in this engagement were reported at 1,900 killed, wounded, and prisoners for the French, 500 for the Prussians, and 210 for the Russians. Fortunately for Oudinot, Bülow's men were too fatigued to pursue him, and on 9 June, word of the armistice arrived halting all actions.

THE WAR IN THE FRENCH REAR

Davout had been joined by Vandamme, and now had 8,000 Danes at his disposal. Wallmoden, commanding the allies at Hamburg, had found himself unsupported by the Swedes in Mecklenburg and evacuated the city. It was occupied by Davout on 30 May. Lübeck fell to the French on 1 June, and the entire 32nd Military Division was in their hands when news of the armistice arrived.

On the French lines of communications, the cossacks and freikorps wrought considerable damage. On 25 May, Tschernigov's 1,200 cossacks and two guns destroyed a cavalry "regiment de marche," and on 30 May, they captured an artillery convoy escorted by 1,600 Westphalian troops. On the same day, they also chased four battalions, 4,000 men, and a force of 400 cavalry moving to rescue the convoy, back to their starting positions in Brunswick. The Westphalian General Ochs' forces suffered the loss of six officers, 1,000 men, 14 cannons, 80 powder wagons and 800 train horses. The Russians lost only 40 dead and wounded.[42]

The most serious such attack was on Leipzig itself. The city was filled with sick and wounded, it was a major park, and contained a cavalry "division de march" under the command of Arrighi. This "division" was completely untrained and useless for fighting.

Voronzov, the Russian general watching Magdeburg, had decided to strike Leipzig by surprise. He left 1,000 cavalry and 7,000 Prussian landwehr to watch Magdeburg, and crossed the Elbe near Dessau with 5,000 infantry and cavalry in the night of 5/6 June, where he met Tschernigov moving in from Bernberg with another 1,200 cavalry. The force marched hard, the infantry being transported in wagons. The allies advanced in two columns. Tschernigov's 1,200 cavalry formed the first column. The second column was under Count Voronzov (3,500 Russians and 1,200 Prussians). It consisted of a hussar regiment, an uhlan regiment, a cossack regiment, and two horse batteries under Count Orurk; a jager regiment, six grenadier battalions, and a musketeer battalion under Colonel Krassowsky and von Lützow's Freikorps. At dawn on 7 June, he reached Leipzig, quickly slaughtered the cavalry recruits and captured 17 officers and 550 men. His assault was stopped literally as he entered the city and received notice of the armistice.

Voronzov's assault on Leipzig was a continuation of the allies use of bands of cossacks and light troops operating in the French rear areas that had earlier lead to the capture of Hamburg. These actions drew major portions of the Grande Armée away from the main battlefields of Saxony and would continue to do so until the French were pushed back across the Rhine in November 1813. This was a problem that would plague Napoleon's efforts to establish a secure base upon which to operate in the 1813 Fall campaign. In addition to obliging Napoleon to dispatch large numbers of troops to guard his lines of supplies, successful cossack actions were to disrupt the French movement of troops and supplies to the front. They struck at the very fiber of French morale and caused both the French soldiers and their generals to constantly keep an eye on their back lest a cossack struck them from behind.

PRUSSIAN HUSSARS OVERRUN A FRENCH BATTERY AT LUCKAU
KNÖTEL

1 Friederich, Die Befreiungskriege, pgs 283–4.

2 Petre, Napoleon's Last Campaign in Germany, pg 142.

3 Fabry, Prince de Wurtemberg, pg 75.

4 Friederich, Die Befreiungskriege, pg 295.

5 Foucart, Bautzen, La Poursuite, pg 4.

6 Fabry, Prince de Wurtemberg, pg 75.

7 de Martimprey, 8e Régiment de Cuirassiers, pg 161.

8 Schuster & Francke, Geschichte der Sachsischen Armee, pg 352.

9 Fabry, Prince de Wurtemberg, pg 77.

10 Plotho, Krieg in Deutschland, Vol I, pg 175.

11 Fabry, Prince de Wurtemberg, pg 79.

12 Petre, Napoleon's Last Campaign In Germany, pg 143.

13 Foucart, Bautzen, La Poursuite, pg 5 & 7.

14 Foucart, Bautzen, La Poursuite, pg 5–9.

15 Plotho, Krieg in Deutschland, Vol I, pg 181.

16 Clément, G., Campagne de 1813, pg 248.

17 Clément, G., Campagne de 1813, pg 250.

18 Petre, Napoleon's Last Campaign inGermany, pg 145.

19 Petre, Napoleon's Last Campaign in Germany, pg 146.

20 Weil, La Cavalerie des Armées Alliés, pgs 54–55.

21 Clément, Campagne de 1813, pg 253.

22 This particular Sacken is not the Russian general, but a Prussian.

23 Plotho, Krieg in Deutschland, Vol I, pg 186.

24 Weil, La Cavalerie des armées alliés, pg 60.

25 Friederich, Die Befreiungskriege, pg 300.

26 Clément, Campagne de 1813, pg 254.

27 Foucart, Bautzen, La Poursuite, pgs 143–144.

28 The source document was not clear on what the French cavalry did. However, the term "behaved poorly" should be interpreted to mean that the French cavalry was shy, did not act aggressively and press its attacks, and generally had no stomach for the fight.

29 Petre, Napoleon's Last Campaign in Germany, pg 149.

30 Friederich, Die Befreiungskriege, pg 301.

31 Friederich, Die Befreiungskriege, pg 302.

32 Rossler, Tagbücher, pg 325.

33 The 9th and 10th Regiments were, despite their sequential numbering with the line infantry, the reorganized Württemberg light infantry.

34 Plotho, Krieg in Deutschland, Vol I, pg 211.

35 The identity of these two battalions is uncertain. They were, no doubt, new levies raised in those portions of old Lithuania that were part of Prussia and were probably landwehr.

36 Though not identified in the original source this is probably the Thüringian Battalion.

37 Sporschil, Grosse Chronik, Vol I, pgs 260–261.

38 Lejeune, Memoirs, pgs 275–276.

39 Sporschil, Grosse Chronik, Vol I, pg 263.

40 Sporschil, Grosse Chronik, Vol I, pgs 264–265.

41 Sporschil, Grosse Chronik, Vol I, pg 267.

42 Sporschil, Grosse Chronik, Vol I, pg 269.

The Armistice

When Napoleon had returned from Russia in December, he had begun attempts to get into contact with the Czar. He had desired to keep the negotiations between Russia and himself, but the arrival of Austria's emissaries, Count Stadion with the allies and Bubna with the French, had derailed this.

Stadion's instructions represented the aim of Austria, as those of armed neutrality and a durable peace, with the curtailment of French influence and possessions east of the Rhine. This included the returning of Poland to its position before the last peace of Vienna. Prussia was to receive back her territories lost in 1806, France was to renounce all claims on Germany, east of the Rhine. Holland was to be independent. The states of the Church were to be restored and all French garrisons were to be withdrawn from Italy. Austria was to be reinstated in all that she possessed in Italy, previous to the Peace of Lunéville signed in 1801. This would mean returning to Austria all that had been won at Ulm, Austerlitz, and Wagram. France was to renounce all claim to suzerainty in Germany or to special influence in the kingdom of Italy.

That was the maximum, to which it was hopeless to expect Napoleon to agree. As a minimum position, Austria proposed the surrender of Dalmatia and Illyria, the dissolution of the Grand Duchy of Warsaw, a new boundary between Austria and Bavaria settling the Tyrolian issue, the return of South Prussia to Prussia, the abandonment by Napoleon of his possessions on the right bank of the Rhine, and the dissolution of the Confederation of the Rhine. There was not much chance of Napoleon accepting those terms either, unless under extreme duress.

Stadion presented the allies with a memorandum, showing them when Austria would be in a position to join them, on the assumption that Napoleon rejected the Austrian terms. This led to the "Program of Würschen," in which the allies laid down their mutual aims. They were:[1]

1.) The restoration of Austria to her position previous to 1805,
2.) The restoration of Prussia to her possessions previous to 1806,
3.) The dissolution of the Confederation of the Rhine,
4.) The independence of Germany,
5.) The dissolution of the Grand Duchy of Warsaw,
6.) The independence of Holland,
7.) The restoration of the Bourbon dynasty in Spain, and
8.) The elimination of all French influence in Italy.

Noting that this was more than even the maximum that Austria had proposed, Stadion stated emphatically that his country would not fight for all this.

Meanwhile, Bubna, who had left Vienna after the news of Lützen and the withdrawal of the allied armies, carried a much softer message to Dresden. Nothing was said of the Austrian maximum. He pressed for the dissolution of the Grand Duchy of Warsaw, the return of Illyria and Dalmatia to Austria, and the surrender of the French possessions beyond the Rhine. The readjustment of the Austro-Bavarian frontier and the abandonment of the Confederation of the Rhine were only briefly mentioned as being desirable, and the independence of French influence in central Europe was mentioned as a conducive to a permanent peace. Despite this, Napoleon knew more about the Austrian aims from his ambassador in Vienna and from the King of Saxony.

The interviews between Bubna and Napoleon became stormy when Napoleon learned that if he was to negotiate for a peace or an armistice, he was expected to retire behind the Elbe and to comply with other similar conditions. He was not willing to accept.

The next step occurred on 17 May, when the battle of Bautzen was imminent. Napoleon sent Caulaincourt to endeavor again to negotiate separately with the Czar. His instructions were to establish personal communications with the Czar, who was known to have strong liking for Caulaincourt from his days as ambassador to St. Petersburg.

Caulaincourt was to represent to the Czar that it would be to his advantage to negotiate directly with Napoleon rather than use Austria as a mediator. Napoleon was to be represented as desirous of avoiding the impending bloodshed (Bautzen), whilst Austria was to be held up as having treated Russia badly and to be acting from selfish reasons. These were secret goals.[2]

Openly, Caulaincourt was to say that Napoleon was prepared to agree to the assembly of a Congress at Prague, or some other neutral site, for the settlement of terms of peace. Napoleon said that he was willing to conclude an armistice with the allies in order to allow time for such negotiations and to avoid bloodshed. Unfortunately for the French this mission failed as Caulaincourt was politely refused permission to pass through the allied lines.

However, the day after Bautzen, the allies suddenly saw the wisdom of opening negotiations, but they did so through Stadion, and not directly. As they often are, these negotiations were remarkably slow, probably, because the old men doing the negotiating were not themselves under the threat of cannon and bayonet.

Caulaincourt was told that anything less than two and a half months was insufficient for Napoleon to reorganize his cavalry, and was unacceptable. He was also given instructions to: 1.) have the demarcation line for the armistice established along the Oder, 2.) have the allies withdraw from the sieges of Danzig, Modlin and Zamosc, to open no work within cannon shot of them, and that the garrisons be furnished provisions every five days, 3.) that couriers be allowed to pass every eight days from those garrisons to him, and 4.) that the armistice last as long as negotiations were continuing; however, he would accept a three month armistice plus fifteen days notice before the resumption of hostilities.[3] Napoleon also stated that he wanted Breslau to be included within the French line of demarcation as well as a number of other lesser points.[4]

On 2 June, the plenipotentiaries of both armies negotiated a 36 hour suspension of arms. The allies, as much as Napoleon, had strong reasons to negotiate an armistice. The allies wanted to stop the French momentum after two major victories. They wanted to reinforce their shattered armies as well as to let their morale recover. In addition, they wanted to further their efforts to bring Austria into the war.[5]

With the suspension of arms in place, the negotiations for the armistice began. On 4 June, the negotiations came to a conclusion. In the end, Napoleon accepted a seven week armistice with only six days notice of termination. Breslau was placed in a neutral strip. The French line in Silesia was roughly that of the Katzbach to its junction with the Oder; the allied line was that of the Striegau-Wasser. The French were limited on the north, by the northern frontier of Saxony, from the Oder to Wittenberg on the Elbe. From Wittenberg downstream, they were confined to the left bank of the Elbe, except that they were to hold the islands in the river, and so much of the 32nd Military Division as might actually be in their possession at midnight on 8 June. Danzig, Mödlin, Zamosc, Stettin, and Küstrin were to be regularly supplied with provisions every five days by the besiegers, and, if Hamburg was only besieged by the French, the same provision was to hold.[6]

Acceptance of this armistice, indeed, agreeing to an armistice at all, was not an easy matter for Napoleon. However, his failure to crush the allies at Bautzen and subsequent failure to bring them to battle left him little choice.

The principal reasons given for his acceptance of the armistice were his need to organize his cavalry and the pending danger of Austria's entry into the war. Any further advance of his armies eastwards left Austria more and more of a threat to his lines of communication.

The question of cavalry has been downplayed by many critics, but it is certain that Napoleon realized that the battle of Lützen would have had quite a different outcome if he had the cavalry he had in 1806. He also sorely felt the unchecked stings by Tschernigov in his rear, and the disaster at Leipzig might have helped to drive the point home. No doubt Maison's drubbing at the hands of Ziethen also echoed in his mind.

On the other hand, Napoleon still had many advantages and much to gain from continuing the campaign. He was clearly in a position to strike hard against the allies. If he had continued to push and maneuvered once again as he had at Bautzen on 2 June, rather than remaining stationary, it is certain that he could have forced a serious action with the demoralized allied army, pinning them against the Austrian border to their south and the Oder to their rear. Instead he remained stationary and allowed them to scuttle quickly across the Oder to safety. What caused Napoleon to decide to stop his advance at this time will forever remain a mystery.

Thus ended the Spring Campaign of 1813. It was a hard fought campaign, executed by two armies trying to recover from the ravages of a cruel winter campaign, and a third army going through its birthing pains. It was not a campaign of strong, fresh armies marching off to war, but more a clumsy match between armies of new recruits, who learned their trade as they went to battle, leavened with a core of battle hardened and weary veterans of the snows of Russia.

It was a campaign of opportunities lost and thrown away. It was marked with petty quarrels and jealousies that cost the common men their lives, while the various grandees nursed their easily bruised egos. It was also a brilliant campaign built on an administrative miracle. A shattered army was resurrected after a catastrophe that would have utterly destroyed any other army of its day and, but for a few mischances and poor decisions, it could well have redeemed Napoleon's fortunes and prevented what was to become two more years of warfare.

As the 1813 spring campaign ended, so, too, did Napoleon's last chance for a military victory over his enemies. Though a diplomatic coup anytime after the armistice through his eventual banishment to St. Helena could have saved Napoleonic France and restored Napoleon to a stable throne, he would never again have so few and such weakened enemies before his legions. The chance to crush a weakened enemy would vanish over the summer as the allied armies rebuilt and were reinforced by the arrival of the massive Austrian armies.

Sweden also joined the allies. In return for his joining the alliance, Bernadotte's ego would demand and receive a major contingent of Prussian and Russian troops to command. However, he was never willing to commit the Swedish army for fear of weakening his control over the Swedish throne and seemed to prefer parading his entire Army of the North around Germany than engaging the French in serious combat.

The spring campaign was a prelude of a military symphony that would, after the prolonged and dramatic pause brought about by the signing of the armistice, once again rumble across the stage of Europe and come to a crashing climax in the fields around Leipzig.

[1]   Galli, L'Allemagne en 1813, pg 171.

[2]   Bonaparte, Correspondance, #20017.

[3]   Bonaparte, Correspondance, #20052.

[4]   Petre, Napoleon's Last Campaign in Germany, pg 156.

[5]   Galli, H., L'Allemagne en 1813, pg 144.

[6]   Fain, Mil Huit Cent Treize, pgs 483–489.

ARMISTICE OF PLESSWITZ
4 JUNE 1813

The Duc de Vicence, Grand Equerry of France, General de division, etc., etc., plenipotentiary named by His Majesty the Emperor of the French, King of Italy, Protector of the Confederation of the Rhine, Mediator of the Swiss Confederation, etc., and granted complete powers of His Serene Highness the Prince of Neufchatal, Lord High Constable and Major General of the Army.

The Count de Schouvaloff, Generallieutenant , aide de camp to His Majesty the Emperor of all the Russias, Grand Cross of the Order of Vladimir Second Class, etc., etc.;

And M. Kleist, Generallieutenant in the service of His Majesty the King of Prussia, Grand Cross of the Red Eagle of Prussia, etc., etc.;

Granted complete powers by His Excellency General of Infantry Barclay de Tolly, General in Chief of the Allied Armies; after having exchanged their respective powers at Gebersdorf on 20 May/1 June and signed a 36 hour suspension of hostilities, and having joined together in the village of Plesswitz, neutralized by this act, between the advanced posts of their respective armies to continue the negotiation for a complete suspension of hostilities between the belligerent troops, no matter where they should find themselves, have concluded the following articles:

Article 1. The hostilities shall cease on all points upon notification of the present armistice.

Article 2. The armistice shall continue from 8 July/20* July inclusive plus six days for the announcement of its expiration.

Article 3. Hostilities cannot, in consequence, recommence until six days after the denouncement of the armistice at the headquarters of the respective armies.

Article 4. The line of demarcation is between the belligerent armies and is fixed as follows:

In Silesia: The line of the French army shall move from the Bohemian border, passing by Seiffershau, Altranitz, following the course of the small river which passes into the Bober, not far from Bertelsdorf, and from the Bober to Lahn. From there to Neukirch, on the Katzback, by the line most direct, from where it follows the course of this river to the Oder.

The cities of Parchwihtz, Liegnitz, Goldberg and Lahn, on which ever bank they lie, and their suburbs shall be occupied by French forces.

The line of demarcation for the Allied Army shall move from the frontiers of Bohemia, pass by Dittersbach, Pfaffendorf, Landshut, follow the border to Rudelstdt, pass from there by Bolkenhayn, Striegau, follow the Striegauwasser to Canth, and join the Oder and pass by Bettlem, Oltaschin and Althoff.

The Allied Army may occupy the cities of Landshut, Rudelstdt, Bolkenhayn, Striegau and Canth, as well as their suburbs.

All the territory between the line of demarcation of the French armies and the Allied armies shall be neutral and may not be occupied by any troops, or by militias; this disposition applies, by consequence, to the city of Breslau.

From the mouth of the Katzbach, the line of demarcation follows the course of the Oder River to the frontier of Saxony, along the Saxon and Prussian border and joins the Elbe, leaving the Oder, not far from Muhlrose, and follows the Prussian frontier in such a manner that all of Saxony, the country of Dessau and the small states of the Princes of the Confederation of the Rhine, belong to the French Army, and its allies, and all of Prussia belongs to the Allied Army.

The Prussian enclaves in Saxony shall be considered as neutral and may not be occupied by any troops.

The Elbe, as far as its mouth, fixes and terminates the line of demarcation between the belligerent armies with the exception of the following points:

The French army shall control the islands and all that they occupy in the 32nd Military Division as of midnight on 27 May/8 June shall form for the 32nd Military division, this armistice demarcation, except the military modifications which the commanders may judge necessary. These modifications shall be made in concert with a staff officer of each army according to the principal of complete reciprocity.

Article 5. The cities of Danzig, Modlin, Zamosc, Stettin, and Custrin shall be reprovisioned every five days, according to the strength of their garrisons, by the efforts of the commander of the besieging forces.

A commissioner named by the commander of each city shall work with the commander of the besieging forces to assure that the exact quantity of provisions is provided.

Article 6. During the duration of the armistice, each city shall, from its walls at a distance of one French league be surrounded by a neutral zone. Magdeburg shall have, by consequence of its frontier, or one league, such a zone on the right bank of the Elbe.

Article 7. The commissioners named by each of the belligerents shall regulate the price of provisions which shall be furnished. The accounting shall, at the end of each month, be paid to the commissioners charged with maintaining the armistice at the paymaster of each army at that armies headquarters.

Article 9. Staff officers shall be named by both sides to rectify in concert the general line of demarcation those points which are not determined by the flow of water and on those which are not otherwise defined.

Article 10. All of the movements of troops shall be regulated in such a manner that each army shall occupy the new line by 31 May/12 June. All of the corps or parts of the allied army which may be across the Elbe or in Saxony shall return to Prussia.

Article 11. French and Allied officers shall be dispatched jointly to cease hostilities on all points. The respective commanders in chief shall grant them the necessary powers.

Article 12. Both belligerents shall name two General Commissioners to oversee the execution of the stipulations of the present armistice. They shall remain in the neutral zone in Neumark, to arbitrate differences which may arise.

The commissioners shall arrive there in 24 hours in order to expedite the officers and the orders which must be sent by virtue of the present armistice.

Made and decreed the present act in twelve articles and in duplicate, this day, month, and year below.

Signed: Caulaincourt, Duc de Vicence
Signed: Count de Schouvaloff
Signed: Von Kleist

Witnessed and approved:
Signed: Barclay de Tolly, Commanding General of the Allied Armies.

* This reflects the Russian and Gregorian calenders respectively.

273

Bibliography

d'Amonville, Cpt. Les Cuirassiers du Roy, Le 8e Cuirassiers, Journal Historique du Régiment 1638-1892, Lahure, Paris, 1892.

Anonymous, Historique du 2eme Regiment d'Artillerie, Librairie Dauphinoise, Grenoble, 1899.

Anonymous, Denkwürdigkeiten des Mecklenburg-Strelitzischen Husaren- Regiments in den Jahrewn des Befreiungskampfes 1813 bis 1815 C. Brünslow, Neubrandenburg, 1854.

Anonymous, Geschichte des Magdeburgischen Husaren-Regiments Nr. 10, A. Duncker, Berlin, 1863.

Anonymous, Campagne de Prince Eugène en Italie Pendant les Annees 1813 et 1814, Paris, 1817.

Anonymous, Historique du 127e Régiment d'Infanterie, P.& G.Girard, Valenciennes, 1897.

Anonymous, Historique du 3e Régiment de Cuirassiers, ci-devant du Commissaire Général 1645-1892, Boussod, Valadon & Cie, Paris, 1893.

Anonymous, Historique du 4e Régiment de Cuirassiers, 1643-1897, Lahure & Cie, Paris, 1893.

von Ardenne, Geschichte des Husaren-Regiments von Zieten (Brandenburgisches) Nr. 3 Mittler & Son, Berlin, 1905.

Arthur, R. A Legiao Portuguesa ao servico de Napoleo 1808-1813, Livraria Ferin, Lisbon, 1901.

d'Artois, P.H., Relation de la Defense de Danzig en 1813, Ladrange, Paris, 1820.

Atteridge, A.H., Joachim Murat, Brentano's, New York, 1911.

Arvers, P., Historique du 82e Régiment d'Infanterie de Ligne et du 7e Régiment d'Infanterie Légère, 1684-1876, Tyopgrahie Lahure, Paris, 1876.

Aubier, Lt., Un Régiment de Cavalerie Légère de 1793 à 1815 Berger-Levrault & Cie., Paris, 1888.

de Behaine, Cdt L., La Campagne de France, Napoleon et les Allies sur la Rhin, Perrin & Cie. Paris, 1913.

Beitzke, Dr. H., Geschichte der Deutschen Freiheitskriege in den Jahren 1813 und 1814, Duncker & Humblot, Berlin, 1864.

Belhomme, Lt. Col., Histoire de l'Infanterie en France, H. Charles-Lavauzelle, Paris.

Bigge, W., Geschichte des Infanterie-Regiments Kaiser Wilhelm (2. Grossherzoglich Hessisches) Nr. 116, Mittler & Son, Berlin, 1893.

Bleibtreu, C., Maschalle, Generale, Soldaten, Napoleons I, A. Schall, Berlin, unknown.

Blond, G., La Grande Armée, R. Laffont, Paris, 1979.

Bogdanovitch, M., Istoria Bojny 1813 Goda, Za Nezavisimost' Germanii po Dostobernym' Istochnikam' Sostabdena po Byso chayshchemy Pobeleniju, St. Petersburg, 1863

Bonin, U. von, Geschichte des Ingenieurkorps und der Pioniere in Preussen, LTR Verlag, Wiesbaden, 1981.

Bonaparte, N., Correspondance de Napoléon ler H. Plon, Paris, 1868.

Bonnières de Wierre, Cpt. A., Historique du 3e Régiment de Dragons, Bourgeois, Nantes, 1892.

Boppe, A., Les Espagnols dans la Grande Armée; Le Division Romana (1808-1809); Le Regiment Joseph Napoleon (1809-1813), Berger-Levrault & Cie., Paris, 1899.

Boppe, A., La Legion Portuguese (1808-1813), Berger-Levrault & Cie., Paris, 1897.

Bory, J.r. Régiments Suisses au Service de France, Collection "Le Shako", Freiburg, 1975.

Bouchard, S., Historique du 28e Regiment de Dragons,, Berger-Levrault & Cie., Paris, 1893.

Boucquoy, E.L., Les Gardes d'honneur du Premier Empire, A.Crépin-Leblond, Paris, 1908.

Boucquoy, E.L., La Garde Imperaile; Troupes a Pied, J.Grancher, Paris, 1977.

Boucquoy, E.L., La Garde Imperaile; Troupes a Cheval, J.Grancher, Paris, 1977.

Boucquoy, E.L., La cavalerie légère (les hussards, les chasseurs à cheval) J.Grancher, Paris, 1980.

Boucquoy, E.L., L'infanterie, J.Grancher, Paris, 1979.

Boucquoy, E.L., Les Cuirassiers, J.Grancher, Paris, 1978.

Boucquoy, E.L., Dragons et Guides d'Etat-major J.Grancher, Paris, 1980.

Breton de la Martinière, M, Campagnes de Buonaparte en 1812, 1813, et 1814 jusqu'a son Abdication, J..Dentu,Paris, 1814.

Brett-James, A., Europe Against Napoleon, McMillan, New York, 1970.

Burghersh, Memoir of the Operations of the Allied Operations under Prinz Schwarzenburg and Marschal Blucher During the Latter End of 1813 and the Year 1814, J.Murray, London, 1822.

Calmon-Maison, J.J.R Le Général Maison et le 1er Corps de la Grande Armée; Campagne de Belgique (decembre 1813- avril 1814), Paris, 1870.

Camon, Col., La guerre Napoléonienne, Les Batailles, Vol IV, Librairie Militaire R. Chapelot, Paris, 1910.

du Cassé, A., Mémoires et Correspondance Politique et Militaire du Prince Eugène, Michel Lévy Frères, Paris, 1859

Cathcart, G., Commentaires on the War in Russia and Germany in 1812 and 1813, J.Murray, London, 1850.

Chandler, D., Dictionary of the Napoleonic Wars, MacMillian, New York, 1979.

Chandler, D., The Campagins of Napoleon, MacMillian, New York, 1966.

Chandler, D., Napoleon's Marshals, MacMillian New York, 1987.

Charras, Lt. Col., Historie de la Guerre de 1813 en Allemagne, Paris, 1870.

Chlapowski, D., Memoirs of a Polish Lancer, Emperor's Press, 1992

Chuquet, A., Inédits Napoléoniens, Ancienne Librairie Fontemoing et Cie., Paris, 1914-1919

Chuquet, A., Ordres et Apostilles de Napoléon, Librarie Ancienne Honoré Champion, Paris, 1912,

Chavane, J., Historie du lle Cuirassiers, C.Charavay, Paris, 1889

Clément, G., Campagne de 1813, H. Charles-Lavauzelle, Paris, unknown.

Clerc, Historique du 79e Régiment d'Infanterie, Berger-Levrault & Cie, Paris, 1896.

von Conrady, C., Geschichte des Königlich Preussischen Sechsten Infanterie-Regiments von seiner Stiftung im Jahr 1773 zu Ende des Jahres 1865 C.Flemming, Glogau, 1857.

Corda, H., Le Regiment de la Fère et le 1er Régiment d'Artillerie, Berger-Levrault & Cie., Paris, 1906.

Cossè-Brissac, R., Historique du 7e Régiment de Dragoons 1673- 1909),Leroy, Paris, 1909.

Diamant-Berger, M., Le 19e Régiment du Chasseurs à Cheval 1792-1826, 1872-1919, Librairie Courtot, Paris, unknown.

Demmler, H., "Anteil der bayerischen Division Raglovich an der Frührjahrzuge 1813," Bayerische Kreigs und Herresgeschichte, Vol 16, Lindauerschen Buchhandlung, Munich, 1907.

Drexl, Dr. F., Die Befreiungskriege 1813-1815, F. Habbel, Regensberg, 1913.

Dupuy, Cmdt. R., Historique du 12e Régiment de Chasseurs de 1788 à 1891, E. Person, Paris, 1891.

Duroisel, Cpt. G., Historique du 93 Régiment d'Infanterie Ancien Enghien et 18e Légère, Ivonnet & Son, La Roche-sur-Yon, 1893.

von Eck, Geschichte des 2. Westfälischen Husaren-Regiments Nr. ll und seiner Stammtruppen von 1807-1893, H. Kusittich, Mainz, 1893.

d'Eckmuhl, Le Maréchal Davout, Prince d'Eckmuhl, Correspondence inedite 1790-1815, Perrin & Cie., Paris, 1887.

Esposito, Gen., A Military History and Atlas of the Napoleonic Wars, AMS Press, New York, 1978.

Fabry, G., Journal des Operations des III et V Corps en 1813, Librairie Militaire R. Chapelot et Cie, Paris, 1902.

Fabry, G., Journal des Campagnes du Prince du Wurtemberg, Librairie Militaire R. Chapelot et Cie, Paris, 1907.

Fain, Baron,Manuscript de Mil Huit Cent Treize, Delauny, Paris, 1824.

Fiffre, E., Histoire des Troupes Etrangeres au Service de France, Librairie Militaire, Paris, 1854.

Foucart, P.J., Bautzen (un bataille de deux jours) 20-21 mai 1813, Berger-Levrault & Cie., Paris, 1897

Friederich, E., Die Befreiungskriege 1813-1815, Ernst Siegfried Mittler & Sohn, Berlin, 1913.

Freiherr von Holz, Col. G., 1813-1815 Osterreich in den Befreiungskriegens, A.Edlingers, Vienna, 1912.

von Fritz Kersten & Ortenberg, G., Hessisches Militar zur Zeit des Deutschen Bundes, Deutschen Gesellschaft für erreskunde e. V., Beckum, 1984.

Galli, L'Allemagne en 1813, Garnier Freres, Paris, 1889.

General Staff of the French Army "Revue d'Histoire" La Campagne de 1813, No. 115

Giesse, K., Kassel-Moskau-Kustrin 1812-1813, Verlag der Dykschen Buchlandlung, Leipzig, 1912.

Gleich, Die ersten l00 Jahren des Uhlanen-Regiments König Wilhelm (2 Württemberger) Nr. 20, Uhland'schen Buchdruckerei, G.m.b.h., Stuttgart, unknown.

Grossen Generalstab Kreigsgeschichteliche Abteilung II Deutschland, Urkundlich Beitrage und Forschung zur Geschichte des Preussischen Herres: Die Gefechtsausbildung der Preussische Infanterie von 1806, LTR-Verlag, Weisbaden, 1982.

Grossen Generalstab Kreigsgeschichteliche Abteilung II Deutschland, Urkundlich Beitrage und Forschung zur Geschichte des Preussischen Herres: Der Preussische Kavallerdienst von 1806, LTR-Verlag, Weisbaden, 1984.

Grossen Generalstab Kreigsgeschichteliche Abteilung II Deutschland, Plane der Schlachten und Treffen welche von der preussischen Armee in den feldzügen der Jahre 1813, 14, und 15 geliesert worden, G.Reimer, Berlin, 1821

Grossen Generalstab Kreigsgeschichteliche Abteilung II Deutschland, Kreigsgeschichtliche Einzelschriften, Vol I, "Feldzug 1813, Bemerkungen über die Schlacht bei Gross-Görschen am 2 Mai 1813" E. S.Mittler & Sohn, Belrin, 1885

Guillon, E., Napoleon et la Suisse, 1803-1815, Librairie Plon, Paris, 1910.

Gumtau, C.F, Die Jäger und Schützen des Preussischen Heeres, E.S.Mittler, Berlin, 1835.

Guye, A., Le Bataillon de Neuchatel, dit les Canaris au service de Napoleon, A la Baconnière, Neuchatel, 1964.

Henderson, E., Blucher and the Uprising of Prussia against Napoleon 1806-1815, AMS Press, New York, 1978.

Heuman, Lt. Col., Historique du 148e Régiment d'Infanterie, H.Charles-Lavauzelle, Paris, unknown.

Holleben, Gen. Maj. von, Geschichte des Frühjahrsfeldzuges 1813 und Vorgeschichte, E.Siegfried Mittler & Sohn, Berlin, 1904.

Jacobi, B., Hannover's Theilnahme an der detuschen Erhebung im Frühjahre 1813 mit besonderer Rücksicht auf die Truppen-formationen an der Elbe, Hannover, Helwig'sche Hofbuchhandlung, 1863.

James, C., An Universal Military Dictionary in English and French in which are explained the Terms of the Principal Sciences that are Necessary for the Information of an Officer, T.Egerton, London, 1816.

Jasson, P.E., Leipzig, The Battle of the Nations, Almark Publishing Co, London, 1975.

Jerabek, R., Die Kampf in Sudkarnten 1813, Herresgeschichtiches Museum, Vienna, 1986.

Jomini, Gen. Baron, Historie Critique et Militaire des Campagnes de la Revolution Paisant suit au Traite des Grandes Operations militaires, Paris, 1816.

Jomini, Gen. Baron, The Art of War, Greenwood Press, Westport, Conn., unknown.

Jomini, Gen. Baron, Réplique du Colonel Jomini à Lord Londonderry (General Stuart) sur les evenemens de la Campagne de Dresde en 1813

Jomini, Gen. Baron, Traite des Grand Operations Militaires, Contenant l'Historie Critique des Campagnes de Frederic II, Comparéesa celles de l'Emperor Napoléon, Magimel, Paris, 1811

de Juzancourt, G. Historique du 7e Régiment du Cuirassiers (1659- 1886), Berger-Levrault & Cie., Paris, 1887.

de Juzancourt, G. Historique du l0e Régiment du Cuirassiers (1643-1891), Berger-Levrault & Cie., Paris, 1893.

Kircheisen, F., Napoleon I. und das Zeitalter der Befreiungskriege in Bildern, G.Müller, Munich, 1914.

Klessman, E., Die Befreiungskriege in Augenseugen berichten, Krag Rauch, Germany, 1967.

von Knobelsdorff-Brenkenhoff, B.,Breife aus den Befreiungskriegen, Ein Beitrag zur Situation von Truppe und Heimat in den Jahren 1813/14, Bonn, 1981.

Königlich Bayerischen Kriegsarchiv, Darstellungen aus der Bayerischen Kreigs- und Herresgeschichte J. Lindauersche, Buch handlung, Munich, 1904

Kraft, Die Württemberger in den Napoleonischen Kreigen, Stuttgart 1953.

Lachouque, H., The Anatomy of Glory, Brown University Press, Providence, R.I., 1962.

Lejeune, Baron, Memoirs of Baron Lejeune, Worley Publications, 1987.

Lesage, C., Napoleon ler, Greancier de la Prusse, Librairie Hachette, Paris, 1924.

Lewinski & Brauchitsch, Geschichte des Grenadier-Regiments König Wilhelm I (2. Westpreussischen) Nr. 7., C. Flemming, Glogau, 1897.

zur Lippe-Weissenfeld, E. Graf Geschichte des königlich Preussischen 6. Husaren-Regiments (ehedem 2. Sch lesischen, Königlichen Geheimen Ober-Hofbuchdruckerei, Berlin, 1860

Louvat, Cpt., Historique du 7eme Hussars, Pairault & Cie., Paris, 1887.

Lumbroso, A., Correspondance du Joachim Murat, Roux Frassati et Cie., Turin, 1899.

Lunsman, F., Die Armee des Königreichs Westfalen 1807-1813, C.Leddihn, Berlin, 1935.

Maag, Dr. A., Geschichte der Schweizer truppen in Franzosischen Dienst vom Ruckzug aus Russland bvis zum zweiten Pariser Freiden, E.Kuhn, Basel, 1894.

Madelin, L., Histoire du Consulate et de l'Empire, Librairie Hachette, Paris, 1950.

de Margon, Cmdt, Historique du 8e Régiment de Chasseurs de 1788 à 1888, Benvé-Lallemant, Verdun, 1889

de Martimprey, A., Historique du 8e Régiment de Cuirassiers d'apres les Archives du Corps, celles du Depot de Guerre, et autres Documents, Berger-Levrault, Paris, 1888

de Marmont, A.F.L.V, Memoires du Maréchal Marmont, Duc de Raguse, de 1792 à 1841, Perrotin, Paris, 1857

Martinet, M., Historique du 9e Régiment de Dragons, H.T.Hamel, Paris, 1883.

Martinien, A., Tableaux par corps et par batailles des Officieres Tues et Blesses pendant les Guerres de l'Empire (1805-1815) Editions Militaires Europeennes, Paris, 1984.

Mason, F., Cavaliers de Napoleon, Librairie Ollendorff, Paris, unknown.

Maude, F.N., 1813: The Leipzig Campaign, MacMillian, NY, 1908.

de Mazade, Ch., Correspondance du Maréchal Davout, Prince d'Eckmühl 1801-1815, Librairie Plon, Paris, 1885.

McQueen, J., The Campaigns of 1812, 1813, and 1814, E. Khull & Co., Glasgow, 1815.

Mollard, J., Historique du 63 Régiment d'Infanterie, Berger- Levrault & Cie, Paris, 1887.

Nafziger, G.F, The Russian Army, 1800-1815 RAFM, Cambridge, Ontario, 1983.

Nafziger, G.F., The Bavarian and Westphalian Armies, 1799-1815, RAFM, Cambridge, Ontario, 1981.

Nafziger, G.F., The Württemberg Army 1793-1815, Raider Games, Leeds, UK, 1987.

von der Oelsnitz, A.C., Geschichte des Königlich Preussischen Ersten Infanterie-Regiments seit seiner Stiftung im Jahr 1619 bis zur Gegenwart, E.C. Mittler & Son, Berlin, 1855.

Odeleben, O. von, Napoleons Feldzug in Sachsen im Jahr 1813, Anton Hain K.G., Meisenheim, 1970.

Ore, C., ler Régiment de Chasseurs 1651-1903, Laussedat, Chateaudun, 1903.

Paret, P., Yorck and the Era of Prussian Reform 1807-1815, Princton Univ. Press, Princton, N.J., 1966.

Parquin, Cpt, Souvenirs du Capitaine Parquin 1803-1814, Boussod, Valadon, & Cie., Paris, 1892.

Paulig,F.R., Geschichte der Befreiungskriege, Frederich Paulig, Frankfort, 1891.

Petre, F.L., Napoleon's Last Campaign in Germany - 1813, Hippocrene Books, N.Y., 1974.

Pfister, A., Aus dem Lager des Rheinsbundes 1812 und 1813, Deutsche Verlags-Anstalt, Leipzig, 1897.

Pflug-Harttung, 1813-1815, Illustriert Geschichte der Befreiungskriege, Union Deutsche Verlagsgeselleschaft, Germany 1913.

Phillippart, J., Napoleon's Campaign in Germany and France 1813- 1814, C.J.Barrington, London, 1814.

Memoires and Campaigns of Charles John, Prince Royal of Sweden, C.J.Barrington, London, 1814.

Pichard & Tuety, Unpublished Correspondance of Napoleon I, Duffield & Co., N.Y., 1913.

Pietsch, P.von, Die Formations - und Uniformierungs Geschichte des Preussischen Herres 1808-1914, Verlag H.Gerhard Schulz, Hamburg, 1963.

Pitot, Lt., Historique du 83e Régiment d'Infanterie 1684-1891, Private Publication, Toulouse, unknown.

de Place, R., Historique du 12e Cuirassiers (1668-1888), Lahure, Paris, 1889.

Plotho, C., Der Kreig in Deutschland und Frankreich in den Jahren 1813 und 1814, Carl Friedrich, Berlin, 1817.

Poniatowski, J., Correspondance du Prince Joseph Poniatowski avec la France, Poznan, 1929.

Reboul, F., Campagne de 1813, Les Preliminaires, Vol II, Le Commande ment du Prince Eugene, ler Periode de Posen a Berlin (16 Janvier - 28 Fevrier), Paris, 1912.

Rehtwisch, T., Grossgörschen 2 May 1813, Turm Verlag, Leipzig, 1912

Rehtwisch, T., Bautzen, 20. und 21. Mai 1813, Turm Verlag, Leipzig, 1912

Rothwiller, Baron, Historique du Deuxième Régiment de Cuirassiers ancien Royal de Cavalerie (1635-1876), Plon & Cie, Paris, 1877.

Roulin, Lt. Col., 125e Régiment d'Infanterie, George Jacob, Orléans, 1890.

Rousset, C., La Grande Armée de 1813, Librairie Académique Didier, Paris, 1892.

Rousset, M.C., Souvenirs du Marechal Macdonald, Duc de Tarente, Librairie Hachette & Cie., Paris, 1892.

Rossler, Tagbücher aus den zehen Feldzügen der Württemberger, unter der Regierung Königs Friderich, Ludwigsburg, Friedrich Nast, 1820.

Ruby, Col., & de Labeau, Cpt., Historique du 2me Régiment de Cuirassiers (1668-1942), Etablissements Moullot Fils Aine, Marseille, 1944.

von Ruesch, von Lossow, von Günther & von l'Estocq, Geschichte des königlichen Zweiten Ulanen-Regiments, A. Stein, Potsdam, 1858.

St. Cyr, G., Memoires du Maréchal Gouvion Saint-Cyr 1812-1813, Remanences, Paris, 1982.

von Salisch, G., Geschichte des Königlich Preussischen Siebenten Infanterie-Regiments von seiner Stiftung in Jahre 1797 bis zum lsten July 1854, C. Flemming, Glogau, 1854

Sauzey, Cpt., Les Allemands sous les Aigles Francaises Librairie Militaire R. Chapelot et Cie.

Sauzey, Cpt., Le Contingent Badois, 1904.

Sauzey, Cpt., Les Saxons dans nos rangs, 1907.

Sauzey, Cpt., Le Regiment des Duches de Saxe, 1908.

Sauzey, Cpt., Nos Allies les Bavarois, 1910.

Sauzey, Cpt., Les soldats de Hesse et Nassau, 1912.

Freiherr von Schauthroth, W.F., Im Rhinbund-Regiment der Herzoglich Sächsischen Kontingente Kobufg-Hildburghausen- Gotha-Weimar wahrend der feldzüge in Tirol, Spanien und Russland, 1809-1813, E.S.Mittler & Sohn, Berlin, 1905.

Schmidt, C., Le Grand-Duche de Berg (1806-1813); Etude sur la Domination Francaise en Allemagne sous Napoléon 1er, Paris, 1905.

Schmitt, Lt., 151e Régiment d'Infanterie, Paris, 1901.

Schuster, O. & Francke, F.A..Geschichte der Sachsischen Armee von deren errichtung bis auf die neuste Zeit, Leipzig, 1855.

Shanahan, W.O., Prussian Military Reforms 1786-1813, Columbia Univ. Press, N.Y., 1945.

von Sichart, A. und R., Geschichte der Königlich-Hannoverschen Armee, Han'sche Buchhandlung, Hanover & Leipzig, 1898.

Simond, E., Le 28e de Ligne, Historique du Régiment, Megard & Cie., Rouen, 1889.

Le Spectateur Militaire, "Premier Siège de Glogau, Mars 1813 à Juin 1813," Vol LX, H.Charles-Lavauzelle, Paris, 1905

Sporschil, J, Die Grosse Chronik, Geschichte des Kreiges des Verbundeten Europa's gegen Napoleon Bonaparte, in den Jahren 1813, 1814, und 1815, G. Westermann, Braunschweig, 1841.

Stiegler, E., Le Marechal Oudinot Duc de Reggio, Librairie Plon, Paris, 1894.

Strotha, von, Die Königlich Preussische Reitende Artillerie von Jahre 1759 bis 1816, LTR Verlag, Wiesbaden, 1981.

Suremain, Memoirs du Lieutenant General Suremain (1794-1815), Plon-Nourritt et Cie., Paris, 1902.

Suzanne, Histoire de la Cavalerie Francaise, C. Terana, Paris, 1984.

Ternaux-Compans, M., Le General Compans (1769-1845), Librairie Plon, Paris, 1912.

Thiry, Baron J., Lutzen et Bautzen, Editions Berger-Levrault, Paris, 1971.

Thomas, J., Un régiment Rhénan sous Napoléon Premier, H. Vaillant-Charmanne, Liege, 1928.

Tournes, R., La Campagne de Printemps en 1813, Lutzen, Charles-Lavauzelle & cie, Paris, 1931.

d'Ussel, V.J., La Defection de la Prusse, Libraire Plon, Paris, 1907.

de Vaudoncourt, Gen. G., Histoire des Campagnes d'Italie en 1813 et 1814, Avec un Atlas Militaire, T.Egerton, London, 1817.

de Vaudoncourt, Gen. G., Histoire Politique et Militaire du Prince Eugène Napoleon, Vice-roi d'Italie, Librairie Universelle de P. Mongie, Paris, 1828.

Viger, Count, Davout, Maréchal d'Empire, P. Ollendorff ed, Imprierie H. Bouilant, Paris, 1898.

Vogel, Theilnahme der König. Preuss. Artillerie an dem Kampf des Befreiungskriege, LTR Verlag, Weisbaden, 1981.

Voigtlander, L., Das Tagebuch des Johann Heinrich Lang aus Lubeck und die Feldzuge der Hanseaten in den Jahren 1813-1815, Verlag Schmidt-Romhild, Lubeck, 1980.

Voisin, Ch., Historique du 6e Hussards, G.Maleville, Libourne, 1888

Vollmer, U., Die Bewaffnung der Armeendes Königsreichs Württemberg und des Grossherzogtums Baden, Journal Verlag Schwend GmbH, Schwabisch Hall, 1981.

Wagner, A., Recueil des Plans de Combat et de Batailles livrees par l'Armèe Prussienne pendant les campagnes des Annes 1813, 1814, et 1815 avec des eclaircissements Historiquesa, G.Reimer, Berlin, 1821.

Weil, M.H, Campagne de 1813, La Cavalerie des armées alliés, Librairie Militai5re de L. Baudoin et Cie., Paris, 1886

Wilhelm, Duke of Brunswick, Geschichte des Magdeburgischen Husaren-Regiments, Nr. 10, A.Duncker, Berlin, 1863.

Zweguintov, L'Armee Russie, unpublished manuscript.

ORDERS OF BATTLE

How to Read the Orders of Battle

FORMATION SENIORITY

The unit closest to the left margin is the senior formation and all units listed immediately below it and indented are part of that command.

STRENGTHS

The French strength figures drawn from the archives are "men under arms," not the effective strength, which includes various categories of individuals not present, often including those in hospital etc. If strength figures drawn from other sources are "men under arms" or "effective strength" is not known.

If one number appears in parenthesis after the unit's name it is a total strength figure, which may or may not include the officers. If two appear they are the number of officers and men. If more than two figures are presented, there will be a footnote to explain the numbers. This footnote applies only to that particular order of battle and all similar numerical notations should be read in the same manner.

The following illustrates the general formation of the orders of battle and explains how to read them.

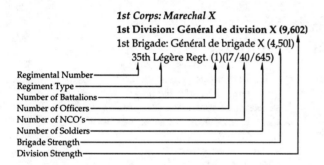

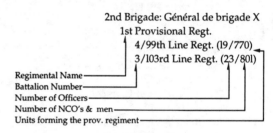

CAVALRY

Cavalry was organized with regiments and squadrons. Its notations are as follows:

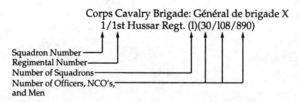

ARTILLERY

The artillery was organized by regiments and companies. Their notations are:

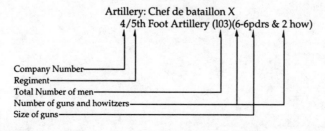

TRAIN AND SUPPORT UNITS

These formations were organized by battalion and company. Their notations are:

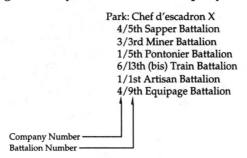

Park: Chef d'escadron X
4/5th Sapper Battalion
3/3rd Miner Battalion
1/5th Pontonier Battalion
6/l3th (bis) Train Battalion
1/1st Artisan Battalion
4/9th Equipage Battalion

Company Number
Battalion Number

OTHER

If there are several brigade commanders they will be listed after a single brigade listing, i.e.

Division: Général de division X
Brigades: Generaux de brigade A, B, & C

If it is known that General Max was replaced during the campaign by General Smith, but the organization of the unit was not altered, the succeeding general's name is listed as follows:

Division: Général de division Max (Smith)

If a regiment is not of the nationality indicated by the title of the OB, it will generally be identified by one of the following methods:

(1) Russian Corps: Generallieutenant Raevsky
(2) Division: Generallieutenant Wolfenstein
Brigade: Generalmajor Schmidt
1st Wurttemberg Infantry Regt.
2nd Rhinbund Regt. (Nassau)

GENERAL NOTES ON ARTILLERY

Where documents have indicated the actual numbers and types of guns in the various armies they are provided. There are, however, standard equipment allocations and these should be assumed unless otherwise noted.

The French divisional foot batteries were normally organized with six 6pdr cannon and two howitzers. The type of howitzer could and did vary, but the 24pdr was the most common. The corps reserve foot batteries were equipped with six 12pdrs and two 6" howitzers, though this too could vary. Horse batteries were equipped with four 6pdrs and two 24pdr howitzers. The Imperial Guard varied slightly from this and the howitzers were generally 5.7" howitzers.

The Russian position batteries were always equipped with four medium 12pdr guns, four short 12pdr guns, and four 20pdr licornes. The Cossacks, horse, and light batteries were always organized with eight 6pdr guns and four 10pdr licornes. The licorne was a cross between a cannon and a howitzer that was unique to the Russian army. Its barrel was longer than the typical howitzer, but much shorter than a cannon's barrel. It served the same function as a howitzer, firing explosive shells, but was significantly more accurate.

The Prussian batteries had six guns and two howitzers each. The light foot battery or a horse battery had six 6pdrs and two 7pdr howitzers, while the heavy foot battery had six 12pdrs and two 10pdr howitzers.

ARMY OF THE GRAND DUCHY OF WARSAW
1 JANUARY 1813

	Under Arms		In Hospital		Effective
	Off	Men	Off	Men	Men
Infantry					
1st Infantry Regiment	15	683	-	40	738
2nd Infantry Regiment	28	404	-	58	490
3rd Infantry Regiment	26	336	-	49	411
6th Infantry Regiment	15	319	1	71	406
8th Infantry Regiment	22	604	-	2	628
12th Infantry Regiment	23	805	-	12	840
13th Infantry Regiment	54	2,249	5	243	2,551
14th Infantry Regiment	25	558	-	78	661
15th Infantry Regiment	32	496	-	67	595
16th Infantry Regiment	30	440	-	71	541
17th Infantry Regiment	26	644	-	119	799

	Under Arms		Horses		In Hospital		Effective	
	Off	Men	Off	Men	Off	Men	Men	Horse
Cavalry								
1st Regiment	14	236	39	180	2	14	266	219
2nd Regiment	16	465	20	451	-	3	484	471
3rd Regiment	20	719	50	544	-	22	761	594
4th Regiment	11	239	23	214	-	11	261	237
5th Regiment	12	422	28	307	-	20	454	335
6th Regiment	13	413	25	344	-	10	436	369
7th Regiment	23	377	58	257	-	16	416	315
8th Regiment	15	295	31	225	-	4	314	256
10th Regiment	9	159	29	48	-	18	186	77
11th Regiment	12	436	27	339	-	20	468	366
12th Regiment	25	427	50	390	1	18	481	440
13th Regiment	38	592	102	346	2	37	669	448
14th Regiment	5	76	7	24	-	4	84	31
15th Regiment	10	171	23	67	-	20	201	90
16th Regiment	32	447	48	358	-	7	516	406
Foot Artillery	45	342	107	155	1	13	401	262
Horse Artillery	18	60	30	15	-	-	78	45
Supplementary Artillery Bn	20	95	39	32	-	5	120	71
Pontoniers	5	27	10	-	-	-	32	10
Sapper Bn	10	231	20	56	-	9	251	76
Zamosc Garrison	87	2,505	-	223	4	675	3,271	223

(13th Infantry Regiment, levies, national guards, foot artillery, and depot)

	Under Arms		Horses		In Hospital		Effective	
Military Equipage Bn	13	112	176	91	-	40	165	108

Poniatowski Correspondance.

BAVARIAN VI CORPS
1 JANUARY 1813

1st Brigade:
  1st Light Infantry Battalion (4/102)
  3rd Light Infantry Battalion (8/128)
  6th Light Infantry Battalion (9/123)
  1/1st Combined (1st) Line Infantry Regiment (12/291)
  2/1st Combined (9th) Line Infantry Regiment (16/237)
  1/2nd Combined (4th) Line Infantry Regiment (17/333)
  2/2nd Combined (10th) Line Infantry Regiment (12/229)
  1/3rd Combined (9th) Line Infantry Regiment (21/273)

2/3rd Combined (Replacements for the 13th) Line Infantry Regiment (2/252)

2nd Brigade:
  2nd Light Infantry Battalion (11/93)
  4th Light Infantry Battalion (8/110)
  5th Light Infantry Battalion (7/102)
  1/1st Combined (2nd) Line Infantry Regiment (23/225)
  2/1st Combined (6th) Line Infantry Regiment (23/302)
  1/2nd Combined (3rd) Line Infantry Regiment (12/226)
  2/2nd Combined (7th) Line Infantry Regiment (15/214)
  1/3rd Combined (5th) Line Infantry Regiment (16/245)
  2/3rd Combined (11th) Line Infantry Regiment (15/83)

Cavalry:
  1/Combined (1st & 2nd) Chevauleger Regiment (3/95)
  2/Combined (3rd & 6th) Chevauleger Regiment (2/93)
  3/Combined (4th & 5th) Chevauleger Regiment (4/108)

Artillery:
  Hosstetten Battery (3/35)(4-6pdrs & 2 howitzers)
  Wagner Battery (3/4)(2-6pdrs & 2 howitzers)
  Dietrich Battery (3/11)(4-6pdrs & 2 howitzers)
  Roys Battery (2/15)(2-12pdrs & 2 howitzers)
  Train (3/35)

Königlich Bayerischen Kriegsarchiv, Darstellungen, pg. 81.

BAVARIAN REINFORCEMENT COLUMNS
4-13 JANUARY 1813

1st Bavarian Reinforcement Column: Rodt
  Staff (2/0)
  5th Line Regiment (2/254)
  7th Line Regiment (3/254)
  13th Line Regiment (2/254)
  4th Light Battalion (2/127)
  5th Light Battalion (1/127)
  6th Chevauleger Regiment (1/60)

2nd Bavarian Reinforcement Column: Haussman, later Rummel
  Staff (4/0)
  1st Line Regiment (2/254)
  3rd Line Regiment (3/254)
  4th Line Regiment (3/254)
  8th Line Regiment (2/254)
  1st Light Battalion (3/126)
  3rd Light Battalion (2/124)
  3rd Chevauleger Regiment (1/50)
  4th Chevauleger Regiment (1/60)
  5th Chevauleger Regiment (2/60)
  Artillery (1/41)

3rd Bavarian Reinforcement Column: Hoffnaasz
  Staff (2/0)
  2nd Line Regiment (3/254)
  6th Line Regiment (3/254)
  9th Line Regiment (4/254)
  10th Line Regiment (2/222)
  11th Line Regiment (3/252)
  2nd Light Battalion (1/127)
  6th Light Battalion (2/127)
  1st Chevauleger Regiment (1/50)
  2nd Chevauleger Regiment (1/50)

4th Bavarian Reinforcement Column: Belsen
  Staff (3/0)

1st Line Regiment (1/90)
4th Line Regiment (1/73)
5th Line Regiment (1/113)
7th Line Regiment (3/203)
8th Line Regiment (1/110)
1st Light Battalion (1/55)
3rd Light Battalion (2/158)
4th Light Battalion (2/142)
5th Light Battalion (2/177)

5th Bavarian Reinforcement Column:
  Staff (1/0)
  2nd Line Regiment (2/15l)
  3rd Line Regiment (3/3l6)
  6th Line Regiment (1/115)
  9th Line Regiment (3/238)
  l0th Line Regiment (2/138)
  llth Line Regiment (3/339)
  2nd Light Battalion (0/7)
  6th Light Battalion (1/29)

Königlich Bayerischen Kriegsarchiv, Darstellungen, pg. 81.

FRENCH 31ST DIVISION
5 JANUARY 1813

31st Division: Général de division De Lagrange (in Stettin)
1st Brigade: Général de brigade de la Bassée (in Stettin)
  10th Demi-brigade (in Stettin)
    Staff (1/0)
    4/27th Line Infantry Regiment (19/518)
    4/63rd Line Infantry Regiment (20/693)
    4/76th Line Infantry Regiment (20/452)
    4/96th Line Infantry Regiment (18/568)
  11th Demi-brigade (in Glogau)
    Staff (1/0)
    4/50th Line Infantry Regiment (19/547)
    4/27th Légère Infantry Regiment (17/716)
2nd Brigade: Général de brigade Schobert (in Stettin)
  12th Demi-brigade (in Stettin)
    Staff (1/0)
    4/124th Line Infantry Regiment (16/415)
    4/124th Line Infantry Regiment (5/210)(in Damm)
    3/123rd Line Infantry Regiment (14/658)
    4/125th Line Infantry Regiment (14/422)
    4/125th Line Infantry Regiment (5/215)
    (in Swinnemunde)
  13th Demi-brigade (in Magdeburg)
    Staff (1/0)
    4/5th Line Infantry Regiment (18/730)
    4/llth Line Infantry Regiment (20/626)
    4/79th Line Infantry Regiment (20/680)
Artillery:
  14/5th Foot Artillery
  18/8th Foot Artillery

Rebou1, Campagne de 1813, Vol II & Spectateur Mi1itaire,#118.

FRENCH IV CORPS
7 JANUARY 1813

Italian Royal Guard:
  Gardes d'Honneur (5 cos)(3/31)
  1/,2/Velites Royaux (24/31)
  1/,2/Chasseurs Royaux (23/41)

  1/,2/Grenadiers de la Garde (12/4)
  Marine Company (3/5)
13th Division:
  1/,2/8th Légère Regiment (17/131)
  1/,2/Provisional Croatian Regiment (30/193)
  1/,2/,3/,4/84th Line Regiment (38/67)
  1/,2/,3/,4/92nd Line Regiment (25/121)
  1/,2/,3/,4/106th Line Regiment (24/60)
14th Division:
  1/,2/18th Légère Regiment (20/125)
  1/,4/Joseph Napoleon (Spanish) Regiment (6/54)
  1/,2/,3/,4/9th Line Regiment (44/151)
  1/,2/,3/,4/35th Line Regiment (26/68)
  1/,2/,3/,4/53rd Line Regiment (18/34)
l5th Division:
  4/1st Italian Légère Regiment (5/11)
  1/,2/,3/Dalmatian Regiment (16/64)
  1/,2/,3/3rd Italian Légère Regiment (24/137)
  1/,2/,3/2nd Italian Line Regiment (13/50)
  1/,2/,3/3rd Italian Line Regiment (19/50)
Artillery:
  French (9/20)
  Italian (21/60)
Engineers:
  French (0/1)
  Italian (2/14)
Equipage:
  French (4/0)
  Italian (12/36)
Other:
  Imperial gendarmes (3/7)

Spectateur Military #108.

1ST CORPS D'OBSERVATION DE RHIN
TO BE FORMED IN MAINZ
7 JANUARY 1813

1st Division:
lst Brigade:
  2nd Provisional Regiment
    3/2nd Légère Regiment
    3/4th Légère Regiment
  14th Provisional Regiment
    4/34th Line Regiment
    3/40th Line Regiment
    1/,2/l34th Line Regiment
2nd Brigade:
  6th Provisional Regiment
    2/6th Légère Regiment
    3/25th Légère Regiment
  l8th Provisional Regiment
    3/50th Line Regiment
    4/65th Line Regiment
  l9th Provisional Regiment
    6/32nd Line Regiment
    3/58th Line Regiment
2nd Division:
lst Brigade:
  4th Provisional Regiment
    4/l2th Légère Regiment
    1/29th Légère Regiment
  llth Provisional Regiment
    4/lst Line Regiment
    2/62nd Line Regiment
  l3th Provisional Regiment

3/14th Line Regiment
3/16th Line Regiment
2nd Brigade:
8th Provisional Regiment
4/5th Légère Regiment
4/23rd Légère Regiment
16th Provisional Regiment
6/26th Line Regiment
6/82nd Line Regiment
17th Provisional Regiment
3/36th Line Regiment
4/43rd Line Regiment
3rd Division:
1st Brigade:
10th Provisional Regiment
3/16th Légère Regiment
1/28th Légère Regiment
20th Provisional Regiment
5/66th Line Regiment
3/122nd Line Regiment
21st Provisional Regiment
3/59th Line Regiment
4/69th Line Regiment
2nd Brigade:
24th Provisional Regiment
3/88th Line Regiment
3/103rd Line Regiment
25th Provisional Regiment
3/47th Line Regiment
3/86th Line Regiment
13th Line Regiment (2)
4th Division:
1st Brigade:
2/,3/32nd Légère Regiment
3/,4/15th Line Regiment
3/,4/70th Line Regiment
2nd Brigade:
34th Légère Regiment (2)
1/,3/,4/22nd Line Regiment
3/,4/121st Line Regiment
Artillery:
6 Foot Batteries (8 guns ea)
2 Reserve Foot Batteries (8 guns ea)
2 Horse Batteries (6 guns ea)

Bonaparte, Correspondance & Belhomme, l'Infanterie

FRENCH CORPS D'OBSERVATION DE L'ELBE
TO BE FORMED IN HAMBURG
7 JANUARY 1813

1st Division:
4th Brigade
50th, 51st, 52nd, 53rd & 54th National Guard Cohorts
10th Brigade:
18th, 19th, 55th, 56th, 57th & 58th National Guard Cohorts
2nd Division:
3rd Brigade:
3rd, 76th, 77th, 78th, 79th, & 88th National Guard Cohorts
11th Brigade:
4th, 20th, 21st, 22nd, 59th & 60th National Guard Cohorts
3rd Division:
5th Brigade:
47th, 48th, 49th, 79th, 80th, & 81st National Guard Cohorts
9th Brigade:
13th, 14th, 62nd, 68th, 69th, & 70th National Guard Cohorts

4th Division:
1st Brigade:
1st, 8th, 9th, 10th, 11th, & 12th National Guard Cohorts
6th Brigade:
44th, 45th, 46th, 64th, 65th, & 66th National Guard Cohorts
5th Division:
7th Brigade:
16th, 17th, 40th, 41st, 42nd, & 43rd National Guard Cohorts
12th Brigade:
6th, 23rd, 24th, 25th, 26th, & 27th National Guard Cohorts
Artillery:
8 Foot Batteries (8 guns ea)
2 Reserve Foot Companies (8 guns ea)
2 Horse Batteries (6 guns each)
Engineers:
6 Sapper Companies
Engineering Train

Bonaparte, Correspondance & Belhomme, l'Infanterie

SOUHAM'S DIVISION
14 JANUARY 1813

Division (Mainz): Général de division Souham
1/,2/22nd Line Regiment (2)
6th Provisional Regiment
2/6th Légère Regiment
3/25th Légère Regiment
10th Provisional Regiment
3/16th Légère Regiment
1/28th Légère Regiment
14th Provisional Regiment
4/34th Line Regiment
3/40th Line Regiment
21st Provisional Regiment
3/59th Line Regiment
4/69th Line Regiment
24th Provisional Regiment
3/88th Line Regiment
3/103rd Line Regiment
1/,2/,3/,4/10th Hussar Regiment
5/,6/Hussar Regiment (to be organized)

Bonaparte, Correspondance

FRENCH II RESERVE CAVALRY CORPS
15 JANUARY 1813

◊Numbers are officers, men, officers' horses and men's horses.
2nd Light Cavalry Division: Général de division Exelmans
7th Light Cavalry Brigade: Général de brigade Castex
11th Chasseur à Cheval Regiment (28/80/22/43)
12th Chasseur à Cheval Regiment (21/181/18/139)
8th Light Cavalry Brigade: Général de brigade Corbineau
5th Hussar Regiment (19/101/24/24/46)
9th Hussar Regiment (20/88/45/23)
2nd Cuirassier Division: Général de division Wathier
1st Brigade:
5th Cuirassier Regiment (24/82/0/5)
2nd Brigade:
8th Cuirassier Regiment (23/64/0/4)
3rd Brigade:
10th Cuirassier Regiment (25/79/0/35)
2nd Chevau-léger Regiment (25/176/0/51)
4th Cuirassier Division: Général de division de France

284

1st Brigade:
  1st Carabinier Regiment (26/123/0/7)
2nd Brigade:
  2nd Carabinier Regiment (20/99/0/44)
3rd Brigade:
  4th Cuirassier Regiment (21/70/65)
  4th Chevau-léger Regiment (19/107/0/126)
II Corps Light Cavalry: Général de division Pajol
5th Brigade:
  23rd Chasseur à Cheval Regiment (20/116/58/72)
  24th Chasseur à Cheval Regiment (13/73/29/34)
6th Brigade:
  7th Chasseur à Cheval Regiment (20/92/30/74)
  20th Chasseur à Cheval Regiment (20/103/50/83)
  8th Chevau-léger Regiment (6/11/28/11)
III Corps Light Cavalry:
9th Brigade:
  4th Chasseur à Cheval Regiment (30/75/65/11)
  11th Hussar Regiment (17/48/41/47)
  6th Chevau-léger Regiment (30/75/65/11)

Reboul, Campaigne de 1813, Vol II.

1st Young Guard Division
9 February 1813

1st Young Guard Division: Général de division Barrois
Brigade: Général de brigade Rothenberg
  Guard Fusilier Regiment (2)
  1/,2/2nd Voltigeur Regiment
  1/,2/2nd Tirailleur Regiment
Brigade: Général de brigade Tindal
  1/,2/6th (bis) Voltigeur Regiment
  1/,2/6th (bis) Tirailleur Regiment
  Pupilles de la Garde (2)
Artillery:
  4 Guard Foot Batteries
  Guard Sapper (1 company)
  Guard Marine (1 company)

Cavalry:
  Regiment de marche
  Grenadiers à Cheval (1 sqn)
  Guard Dragoons (1 sqn)
  Chasseurs à Cheval (2 sqns)
  2nd Lancer Regiment (1 sqn)
  2 Guard Horse Batteries

Bonaparte, Correspondance.

2nd Bavarian Brigade In Thorn
21 January - 8 June 1813

◊Numbers are officers, men, & horses.
20 January 1813
  Brigade Staff (4/?/?)
  2nd Jäger Battalion (14/169/8)
  4th Jäger Battalion (16/307/8)
  5th Jäger Battalion (11/325/8)
  1st Combined Regiment (44/916/25)
  2nd Combined Regiment (38/1,097/28)
  3rd Combined Regiment (34/1,069/25)

18 April 1813

Brigade Staff (4/-/-)
  2nd Jäger Battalion (14/128/8)
  4th Jäger Battalion (16/170/8)
  5th Jäger Battalion (11/200/8)
  1st Combined Regiment (43/723/25)
  2nd Combined Regiment (37/851/28)
  3rd Combined Regiment (34/871/25)

Departed Thorn on 8 June:
  Brigade Staff (4/-/-)
  2nd Jäger Battalion (12/80/6)
  4th Jäger Battalion (14/112/8)
  5th Jäger Battalion (9/97/8)
  1st Combined Regiment (35/422/25)
  2nd Combined Regiment (33/427/30)
  3rd Combined Regiment (31/476/24)

Königlich Bayernisch Kriegsarchiv, Darstellungen.

French Forces in Danzig
21 January 1813

X Corps:
  Commanding General: Général de division Count Rapp
  Aides de camp: Chef d'escadron Turkheim
                   Capitaine Marnier
  Chief of Staff: Général de brigade d'Hericourt

General Staff: (29/0)
  Gendarmerie: Lieutenant Andre (1/10)

Imperial Guard: Chef d'escadron Martin-Laforest
  Mixed Guard Force (7/321)

7th Division: Général de division Grandjean
  Division Staff (11/0)
1st Brigade: Général de brigade Bachelu
  1/,2/13th Bavarian Line Regiment (42/959)
  1/,2/1st Westphalian Line Regiment (46/888)
  1/,2/,3/,4/10th Polish Line Regiment (83/1,069)
2nd Brigade: Général de brigade Prince Radziwill
  1/,2/,3/,4/5th Polish Line Regiment (80/1,497)
  1/,2/,3/,4/11th Polish Line Regiment (70/1,680)
30th Division: Général de division Count Heudelet
  Division Staff (13/0)
1st Brigade: Général de brigade Breissan
  1st Provisional Demi-Brigade
    4/2nd Légère Regiment (22/748)
    4/4th Légère Regiment (18/577)
    4/17th Légère Regiment (21/618)
  6th Provisional Demi-Brigade
    4/16th Légère Regiment (20/416)
    4/21st Légère Regiment (18/671)
    4/28th Légère Regiment (17/606)
2nd Brigade: Général de brigade Husson
  7th Provisional Demi-Brigade
    4/8th Line Regiment (17/562)
    4/14th Line Regiment (18/597)
    4/94th Line Regiment (17/500)
  8th Provisional Demi-Brigade
    4/24th Line Regiment (22/503)
    4/45th Line Regiment (20/639)
    4/59th Line Regiment (19/500)
3rd Brigade: Général de brigade Gault
  9th Provisional Demi-Brigade
    4/54th Line Regiment (19/479)
    4/88th Line Regiment (21/395)

4/95th Line Regiment (21/402)
17th Provisional Demi-Brigade
  4/6th Légère Regiment (19/530)
  4/25th Légère Regiment (19/436)
  4/39th Line Regiment (19/704)
33rd Division: Lieutenant Général Destrées
Division Staff (8/0)
1st Brigade: Marechal de camp Pepe
  Neapolitan Royal Guard (1/58)
  1/,2/5th Neapolitan Line Regiment (33/1,055)
  1/,2/6th Neapolitan Line Regiment (35/1,059)
  1/,2/7th Neapolitan Line Regiment (21/861)
  (note, all elite companies were detached)
34th Division: Général de brigade Franceschi
Division Staff (7/0)
1st Brigade: Général de brigade Devilliers
  6/22nd Légère Regiment (12/152)
  4/3rd Line Regiment (6/73)
  4/29th Line Regiment (38/367)
  4/103rd Line Regiment (4/54)
  4/113rd Line Regiment (21/272)
  Frankfurt Regiment (28/181)
  4th Rhinbund (Saxon Ducal Houses) Regiment (27/280)
  5th Rhinbund (Lippe & Anhalt) Regiment (32/536)
  6th Rhinbund (Schwarzburg, Waldeck, Reuss) Regiment (22/368)
  Depot 44th Line Regiment (1/20)
  Depot Saxon von Rechten Regiment (1/13)
Cavalry Brigade: Général de brigade Cavaignac
Brigade Staff (9/0)
1st Provisional Cavalry Regiment
  2nd Dragoon Regiment (8/146)
  5th Dragoon Regiment (3/75)
  12th Dragoon Regiment (5/110)
  13th Dragoon Regiment (5/101)
2nd Provisional Cavalry Regiment
  14th Dragoon Regiment (3/59)
  17th Dragoon Regiment (5/87)
  19th Dragoon Regiment (6/92)
  20th Dragoon Regiment (9/130)
3rd Provisional Cavalry Regiment
  3rd, 6th, 8th Cuirassier Regiments (4/92)
  3rd, 7th, 11th, 19th, 23rd, 24th, 25th
  Chasseur à Cheval Regiments (7/190)
  7th, 8th Hussars, 28th Dragoons (7/105)
9th Chevauléger-lancier Regiment (Poles)(30/413)
Artillery: Général de brigade Lepin
  4/, 5/, 9/, 10/, 19/5th Foot Regiment (13/431)
  7/, 12/, 17/, 22/7th Foot Regiment (10/311)
  21/8th Foot Regiment (2/90)
  6/, 18/9th Foot Regiment (6/136)
  2/, 3/, 4/, 5/, 6/2nd Pontooneer Battalion
  6th Ouvrier Company (1/84)
  3rd Armorer Company (2/33)
  7th Principal Train Battalion
  11th Principal Train Battalion
  12th Principal Train Battalion
  1st (bis) Train Battalion
  9th (bis) Train Battalion
  11th (bis) Train Battalion (total train 2/229)
  2nd Bavarian Artillery Company (3/70)
  5th Wurttemberg Artillery Company (2/41)
  10th Saxon Artillery Company (4/89)
  6th & 16th Polish Foot Artillery Companies (6/170)
  1st Polish Horse Artillery Companies (4/131)
  Regimental Artillery, 29th Line and Regiments of 7th Division (11/321)
  Powder Technicians (0/3)
Engineers: Général de division Campredon

Engineering Staff (42/39)
2/1st Miner Battalion (4/95)
4/3rd Sapper Battalion (5/191)
Polish Sapper Battalion (3/68)
Spanish Pioneer Battalion (5/548)
Marine: Contre-amiral Dumanoir
Staff (6/0)
4th Equipage de Flotille (12/109)
17th Equipage de Flotille (11/198)
Danube Marine Artisian Battalion (6/51)
1st L'Escaut Marine Artisian Battalion (15/332)
Customs: Directeur Bonneville (13/155)

---

d'Artois, la Defense de Danzig.

FRENCH GRANDE ARMEE PROVISIONAL ORGANIZATION END OF JANUARY 1813

I Corps: 20 January
1st Provisional Battalion
1st division
  13th Légère Infantry Regiment (4/130)
  17th Line Infantry Regiment (3/79)
  30th Line Infantry Regiment (3/100)
2nd division
  15th Légère Infantry Regiment (4/90)
  33rd Line Infantry Regiment (4/80)
  48th Line Infantry Regiment (3/45)
2nd Provisional Battalion
3rd division
  7th Légère Infantry Regiment (6/282)
  12th Line Infantry Regiment (6/205)
  21st Line Infantry Regiment (6/116)
  127th Line Infantry Regiment (3/29)
3rd Provisional Battalion
5th division
  21st Line Infantry Regiment (7/103)
  57th Line Infantry Regiment (3/88)
  61st Line Infantry Regiment (7/86)
  111th Line Infantry Regiment (3/150)
Attached:
◊Numbers are: Staff, officers, non-commissioned officers, troops, and horses.
  Mobile Battery (5/4/14/71/0)
  1st Principal Train Battalion (0/3/6/29/0)
  8th Principal Train Battalion (0/1/4/30/73)
  1st Polish Train Battalion (0/2/1/28/46)
  Auxiliary Soldiers (0/0/0/40/41)
  10 6pdrs (60 horses)
  10 6pdr caissons (60 horses)
  4 12pdr caissons (24 horses)
  8 infantry caissons (40 horses)
  1 Wagon (4 horses)
Attached Cavalry:
  1st Chasseur à Cheval Regiment (37/136/0/35)
  2nd Chasseur à Cheval Regiment (42/94/10/28)
  3rd Chasseur à Cheval Regiment (unknown)
  9th Chevauléger Regiment (4/39/5/45)

II Corps:
  Organized in Custrin on 25 January 1813
1st Provisional Battalion
  26th Légère Infantry Regiment (6/257)
  19th Line Infantry Regiment (3/97)
  56th Line Infantry Regiment (3/121)

1st Swiss Infantry Regiment (2/63)
2nd Swiss Infantry Regiment (3/90)
2nd Provisional Battalion
    11th Légère Infantry Regiment (6/245)
    2nd Line Infantry Regiment (3/147)
    37th Line Infantry Regiment (3/152)
    3rd Provisional Croatian Infantry Regiment (3/107)
3rd Provisional Battalion
    3/128th Line Infantry Regiment (22/604)
Other: Independent organization in Custrin
    123rd & 124th Line Infantry Regiment (2 cos)
Corps Cavalry: Général de division Pajol 15 January
5th Brigade:
◊Numbers are officers, men, officer's horses, & troop horses.
    23rd Chasseur à Cheval Regiment (20/116/58/72)
    24th Chasseur à Cheval Regiment (13/73/29/34)
6th Brigade:
    7th Chasseur à Cheval Regiment (20/92/30/74)
    20th Chasseur à Cheval Regiment (20/103/50/83)
    8th Chevauléger Regiment (6/11/28/11)

III Corps:
    Organized in Custrin on 28 January 1813
1st Provisional Battalion (23/578)
    Staff (5/0)
    Grenadiers (3/87)
    1st Company (3/99)
    2nd Company (3/106)
    3rd Company (3/117)
    4th Company (3/96)
    Voltigeurs (3/73)
2nd (3/129th) Provisional Battalion (22/411)
    Staff (5/0)
    Grenadiers (2/59)
    1st Company (3/72)
    2nd Company (3/60)
    3rd Company (3/66)
    4th Company (3/67)
    Voltigeurs (3/87)
Corps Cavalry: 15 January
9th Brigade: General Walbanch
    11th Hussar Regiment (17/48/41/47)
    6th Chevauléger Regiment (22/64/60/23)
    4th Chasseur à Cheval Regiment (30/75/65/11)

IV Corps: 4 February
13th Division: Chef de bataillon Warthe
    8th Légère Infantry Regiment (2 cos)(6/193)
    Croatian Infantry Regiment (1)(4/190)
    84th Line Infantry Regiment (1)(4/97)
    92nd Line Infantry Regiment (1)(5/115)
    106th Line Infantry Regiment (1)(4/105)
14th Division: Chef de bataillon Farvant
    18th Légère Infantry Regiment (2)(7/253)
    Joseph Napoleon Infantry Regiment (1)(3/154)
    9th Line Infantry Regiment (1)(5/125)
    35th Line Infantry Regiment (1)(4/116)
    53rd Line Infantry Regiment (1)(4/59)
15th Division: Chef de bataillon Olivazzi
    Dalmatian Infantry Regiment (1)(3/45)
    3rd Italian Légère Infantry Regiment (1)(3/109)
    2nd Italian Line Infantry Regiment (1)(4/150)
    3rd Italian Line Infantry Regiment (1)(6/59)

IX Corps: Corps Cavalry: 21 January
    1st Berg Lancer Regiment (5/28/14/225)
    2nd Berg Lancer Regiment (captured)
    Saxon Prinz Clemens Uhlan Regiment (captured)
    Baden Hussar Regiment (unknown)

Hessian Chevauleger Regiment (unknown)

1st Reserve Cavalry Corps: 21 January 1813
1st Light Cavalry Division:
    9th Chevauléger Regiment (18/95/43/44)
    16th Chasseur à Cheval Regiment (23/184/26/69)
    7th Hussar Regiment (22/160/67/35)
    8th Hussar Regiment (27/120/57/49)
    Portuguese Legion Chasseur à Cheval Regt. (5/15/0/0)
1st Cuirassier Division:
    1st Chevauléger Regiment (30/94/43/25)
    2nd Cuirassier Regiment (19/74/26/5)
    3rd Cuirassier Regiment (23/148/28/17)
    9th Cuirassier Regiment (26/121/30/7)
5th Cuirassier Division:
    5th Chevauléger Regiment (21/139/48/62)
    6th Cuirassier Regiment (19/65/34/20)
    11th Cuirassier Regiment (23/83/18/5)
    12th Cuirassier Regiment (13/138/11/13)
    5th Horse Artillery Regiment (5/6/5/0)

2nd Reserve Cavalry Corps: 15 January 1813
2nd Light Cavalry Division: General de division Exelmans
7th Brigade: Général de brigade Castex
    11th Chasseur à Cheval Regiment (28/90/22/43)
    12th Chasseur à Cheval Regiment (21/181/18/139)
8th Brigade: Général de brigade Corbineau
    5th Hussar Regiment (19/101/24/46)
    9th Hussar Regiment (20/88/45/23)
2nd Cuirassier Division: Général de division Wathier
1st Brigade:
    5th Cuirassier Regiment (24/82/0/5)
2nd Brigade:
    8th Cuirassier Regiment (23/64/0/4)
3rd Brigade:
    10th Cuirassier Regiment (25/79/0/35)
    2nd Chevauléger Regiment (25/176/0/51)
4th Cuirassier Division: Général de division Defrance
1st Brigade
    1st Carabinier Regiment (26/123/0/7)
2nd Brigade:
    2nd Carabinier Regiment (20/99/0/44)
3rd Brigade:
    1st Cuirassier Regiment (21/70/0/65)
    4th Chevauléger Regiment Regiment (19/107/0/126)

Reboul, F., Campagne de 1813, Vol II & General Staff of the French Army, "Revue dHistoire," No. 115.

FRENCH CORPS D'OBSERVATION UNDER EUGÉNE
END OF JANUARY 1813

1st Division: Général de division Gérard
    3/3rd Line Infantry Regiment (11/416)
    3/105th Line Infantry Regiment (15/530)
    3/127th Line Infantry Regiment (12/520)
    1/,2/Neapolitan Elites (12 cos)(35/1,326) (detached from 5th, 6th & 7th Neapolitan Regts)
    Neapolitan Guard Marines (1 co)(3/116)
    Neapolitan Guard Artillery (6/58)
    Neapolitan Guard Train (0/29)
    Neapolitan Guard Ambulance Service (4/2)
    Artillery and Train (7 6pdrs & 1 howitzer)(2/107)
2nd Division: Général de division Girard
    1st Vistula Infantry Regiment (37/115)

2nd Vistula Infantry Regiment (38/113)
3rd Vistula Infantry Regiment (26/128)
4th Vistula Infantry Regiment (38/1,840)
4th Polish Line Infantry Regiment (42/185)
7th Polish Line Infantry Regiment (27/252)
9th Polish Line Infantry Regiment (37/267)
17th Lithuanian Lancer Regiment (22/559/695) (unfit for duty)
19th Lithuanian Lancer Regiment (37/566/719) (unfit for duty)
8/18th Foot Artillery (4 6pdrs) (5/31)
5/8th Principal Train Battalion (1/26)
Bavarian Division: Generalmajor Rechberg
1st Bavarian Jäger Battalion (8/190)
3rd Bavarian Jäger Battalion (9/310)
6th Bavarian Jäger Battalion (7/172)
1st Bavarian Combined Infantry Regiment (37/841)
2nd Bavarian Combined Infantry Regiment (31/805)
3rd Bavarian Combined Infantry Regiment (18/401)
4 6pdrs & 2 howitzers
Imperial Guard Division: Général de division Roguet
1/,2/2nd Voltigeur Regiment (916)
1/,2/2nd Tirailleur Regiment (885)
Fusilier Chasseur Regiment (126)
Fusilier Grenadier Regiment (118)
1/1st Guard Chasseur à Pied Regiment (415)
1/1st Guard Grenadier à Pied Regiment (408)
Velites of Florence (342)
Velites of Turin (461)
Hessian Battalion (1 6pdr gun)(208)
Italian Royal Guard (279)
Guard Artillery & Train (6-6pdrs & 2 howitzers)(265)
Guard Sappers (26)
Westphalian Division: (1,200)
2 Regiments de marche which became the 4th & 5th Westphalian Line Regiments
Cavalry: Major Lion
1st Guard Chevauléger-lancier (Polish) Regt. (125/125)
2nd Guard Chevauléger-lancier (Dutch) Regiment (31/29)
Guard Chasseur à Cheval Regiment (260/242)
Empress Dragoon Regiment (120/107)
Guard Grenadier à Cheval Regiment (127/116)
Florence Gardes d'honneur (76/73)
Turin Gardes d'honneur (85/82)
Detachment Italian Cavalry (under Palombini)(320/310)
Bavarian Cavalry (10/314/361)
Artillery:
Imperial Guard (6-6pdrs & 2 howitzers)
Bavarians (4-6pdrs & 2 howitzers)
Gérard's Division (7 6pdrs & 1 howitzer)
Girard's Division (4 6pdrs)
Hessian Battery (1 6pdr)
I Corps (1 12pdr, 1 6pdr, 3 3pdrs & 2 howitzers)
Headquarters Troops:
Imperial Gendarmes (no strength given)
Elite Company (4/45)
28th Chasseur à Cheval Regiment (8/9)

Reboul, F., Campagne de 1813, Vol II & General Staff of the French Army, "Revue dHistoire," No. 115.

FRENCH 35TH DIVISION
5 FEBRUARY 1813

Corps Commander: Général Count Grenier
Chief of Staff: Général de brigade Thomas

Cavalry:

4th Italian Chasseurs à Cheval (38/1,084)
Infantry:
1st Brigade: Général de brigade Fressinet
3/14th Légère Regiment (638)
4/14th Légère Regiment (605)
1/ & 2/22nd Légère Regiment (1,352)
3/ & 4/22nd Légère Regiment (1,290)
2nd Brigade: Général de brigade Senecal
3/6th Line Regiment (627)
4/6th Line Regiment (617)
1/,2/,3/,4/112th Line Regiment (4)(3,617)
3rd Brigade: Général de brigade Meunier
4/3rd Légère Regiment (768))
6/10th Line Regiment (1)(865)
6/20th Line Regiment (1)(854)
4/102th Line Regiment (686)
5th Illyrian/Swiss Battalion de Marche (721)
3/2nd Italian Légère Regiment (776)
4/2nd Italian Légère Regiment (760)
Regimental artillery 2nd Italian Légère Regiment (52)
4th Brigade: Général de Brigade Zucchi
1/5th Italian Line Regiment (900)
2/5th Italian Line Regiment (855)
3/5th Italian Line Regiment (869)
4/5th Italian Line Regiment (877)
Artillery:
3/1st Italian Horse Artillery
6/1st French Foot Artillery

Plotho, C., Der Krieg in Deutschland

NEW ORGANIZATION OF FRENCH
1ST & 2ND CAVALRY CORPS
4 FEBRUARY 1813

•Numbers are officers, men, & horses.
1st Cavalry Corps:
1st Light Cavalry Division: Général de division Bruyère
3rd Brigade:
7th Hussar Regiment (2 cos)(18/167/37)
9th Chevauléger Regiment (2 cos)(11/134/121)
4th Brigade:
16th Chasseur à Cheval Regiment (3 cos) (24/239/199)
8th Hussar Regiment (29/441/124)
Attached:
1st Chevauléger Regiment (2 cos)(17/204/119)
3rd Chevauléger Regiment
5th Chevauléger Regiment (1 co)(5/101/80)
8th Chevauléger Regiment
3rd Light Cavalry Division: Général de division Chastel
10th Brigade:
6th Chasseur à Cheval Regiment
25th Chasseur à Cheval Regiment
11th Brigade:
6th Hussar Regiment
8th Chasseur à Cheval Regiment
12th Brigade:
9th Chasseur à Cheval Regiment
19th Chasseur à Cheval Regiment
13th Brigade:
2nd Italian Chasseur à Cheval Regiment
3rd Italian Chasseur à Cheval Regiment
Attached:
1st Chasseur à Cheval Regiment (4 cos)(21/323/130)
2nd Chasseur à Cheval Regiment (1 co)(12/73/36)

3rd Chasseur à Cheval Regiment (2 cos)(12/145/106)
3rd Cuirassier Division: Général de division Doumerc
Brigade
    4th Cuirassier Regiment
    7th Cuirassier Regiment
    14th Cuirassier Regiment
Brigade:
    7th Dragoon Regiment
    23rd Dragoon Regiment
    28th Dragoon Regiment
    30th Dragoon Regiment
1st Cuirassier Division: Général de division Bordesoulle
Brigade:
    2nd Cuirassier Regiment (3 cos)(16/234/81)
    3rd Cuirassier Regiment (2 cos)(11/124/13)
    9th Cuirassier Regiment (3 cos)(16/289/13)
Brigade:
    6th Cuirassier Regiment (2 cos)(17/141/37)
    11th Cuirassier Regiment (3 cos)(17/240/131)
    12th Cuirassier Regiment (2 cos)(16/115/21)
Other:
    4/2nd Berg Lancer Regiment (2 cos)(8/243/263)

2nd Cavalry Corps:
2nd Light Cavalry Division: Général de division Pajol
7th Brigade:
    11th Chasseur à Cheval Regiment
    12th Chasseur à Cheval Regiment
8th Brigade:
    5th Hussar Regiment
    9th Hussar Regiment
Attached:
    2nd Chevauléger Regiment
    4th Chevauléger Regiment
4th Light Cavalry Division: Général de division Exelmans
Attached:
    4th Chasseur à Cheval Regiment (13/158/16/7)
    11th Hussar Regiment (19/157/26/67)
    6th Chevauléger Regiment(5/58/9/3)
6th Light Cavalry Brigade:
    7th Chasseur à Cheval Regiment (14/237/20/20)
    20th Chasseur à Cheval Regiment (16/218/18/17)
5th Brigade:
    23rd Chasseur à Cheval Regiment: (25/197/30/316)
    24th Chasseur à Cheval Regiment (17/169/24/154)
2nd Cuirassier Division: Général de division Wathier
Brigade:
    5th Cuirassier Regiment
    8th Cuirassier Regiment
    10th Cuirassier Regiment
Brigade:
    1st Cuirassier Regiment
    1st Carabinier Regiment
    2nd Carabinier Regiment

Reboul, F., Campagne de 1813, Vol II.

PRUSSIAN ARMY AT MOBILIZATION JANUARY 1813

Silesian Army Corps: General of Cavalry von Blücher
1st Brandenburg Brigade: Oberst von Röder
Infantry: Major von Tippelskirch
    1st Garde zu Fuss Regiment (3)(2,411)
    Normal Infantrie-Bataillon (801)
    Guard Jäger Battalion (801)

    Leib-Grenadier Battalion (805)
    East Prussian Grenadier Battalion (805)
    Depot/Leib Infantry Regiment (1)(801)
Cavalry: Major von Katzeler
    1/,2/Brandenburg Hussar Regiment (2)(300)
    1/,2/Brandenburg Uhlan Regiment (2)(300)
    1/,2/,3/,4/West Prussian Uhlan Regiment (4)(601)
Artillery:
    6pdr Horse Battery #8 (148)
    6pdr Foot Battery #4 (139)
    6pdr Foot Battery #9 (139)
Lower Silesian Brigade: Oberst von Klüx
Infantry: Major von Jagow
    West Prussian Grenadier Battalion (805)
    Fus/1st West Prussian Infantry Regiment (801)
    2/1st West Prussian Infantry Regiment (801)
    Depot/1st West Prussian Infantry Regiment (801)
    2/2nd West Prussian Infantry Regiment (801)
    Depot/2nd West Prussian Infantry Regiment (801)
Cavalry: Oberst von Mutins
    1/,2/,3/,4/Neumärk Dragoon Regiment (601)
    2/,4/1st West Prussian Dragoon Regiment (300)
Artillery:
    6pdr Horse Battery #7 (148)
    6pdr Foot Battery #7 (139)
    6pdr Foot Battery #8 (139)
Upper Silesian Brigade: Oberst von Zeithen
Infantry: Oberst von Pirch
    Silesian Grenadier Battalion (805)
    1/1st Silesian Infantry Regiment (801)
    Fus/1st Silesian Infantry Regiment (801)
    Depot/1st Silesian Infantry Regiment (801)
    1/2nd Silesian Infantry Regiment (801)
    Depot/2nd Silesian Infantry Regiment (801)
    Silesian Schützen Battalion (801)
Cavalry: Major Laroche von Starkenfels
    1/,2/Silesian Uhlan Regiment (2)(300)
    2/,4/1st Silesian Hussar Regiment (2)(300)
    3/,4/2nd Silesian Hussar Regiment (2)(300)
Artillery:
    6pr Horse Battery #9 (148)
    6pdr Foot Battery #11 (139)
    6pdr Foot Battery #13 (139)
Reserve Cavalry: Oberst von Dolffs
Guard Cavalry Brigade: Oberstleutnant von Werder
    1/,2/,3/,4/Garde du Corps (4)(601)
    1/,2/,3/,4/Guard Light Cavalry Regiment (4)(601)
    6pdr (Guard) Horse Battery #4 (148)
Cuirassier Brigade: Oberst von Jürgass
    1/,2/,3/,4/Silesian Cuirassier Regiment (4)(601)
    1/,2/,3/,4/East Prussian Cuirassier Regiment (4)(601)
    1/,2/,3/,4/Brandenburg Cuirassier Regiment (4)(601)
    6pdr Horse Battery #10 (148)
Reserve Artillery:
    6pdr Foot Battery #12 (139)
    1/2 l2pdr Foot Battery #3 (94)
    3 Park Columns (99)
    Field Pioneer Companies (2)(8l ea)

Army Corps: Generalleutnant von Yorck
1st Brigade: Oberst von Hünerbein
Infantry: Major von Steinmetz
    1st Combined Infantry Regiment (3)(2,403)
      2/,Fus/1st East Prussian Infantry Regiment
      1/2nd East Prussian Infantry Regiment
    2nd Combined Infantry Regiment (3)(2,403)
      1/3rd East Prussian Infantry Regiment
      1/,Fus/4th East Prussian Infantry Regiment
    3rd Combined Infantry Regiment

2/1st Pommeranian Infantry Regiment (801)
1/Colberg Infantry Regiment (801)
Fus/2nd East Prussian Infantry Regiment (801)
Cavalry:
1st Combined Hussar Regiment (4)(801) (only had 200 horses)
3/,4/1st Leib Hussar Regiment
2/,3/2nd Leib Hussar Regiment
Artillery:
6pdr Horse Battery #2 (148)
2 6pdr Foot Batteries #1 & #3 (139 ea)
2nd Brigade: Oberst von Horn
Infantry: Major von Zielinsky
4th (Leib) Infantry Regiment (3)(2,403)
5th Infantry Regiment (3)(2,403)
1/1st West Prussian Infantry Regiment
1/,Fus/2nd West Prussian Infantry Regiment
6th Infantry Regiment (3)(2,403)
2/1st Silesian Infantry Regiment
2/,Fus/2nd Silesian Infantry Regiment
East Prussian Jäger Battalion (801)
Cavalry:
2nd Combined Hussar Regiment (4)(801) (only had 200 horses)
3/,4/Brandenburg Hussar Regiment
1/,3/Pommernian Hussar Regiment
Artillery:
6pdr Horse Battery #3 (148)
2 6pdr Foot Batteries #2 & #6 (139 ea)
Reserve Cavalry: Generalmajor von Corswandt
1st Combined Dragoon Regiment (4)(801)
1/,3/Lithuanian Dragoon Regiment
1/,2/2nd West Prussian Dragoon Regiment
2nd Combined Dragoon Regiment (4)(801)
1/,3/Brandenburg Dragoon Regiment
1/,3/1st West Prussian Dragoon Regiment
Horse Battery #1 (148)
Reserve Artillery:
1/2 l2pdr Battery #3 (94)
5 Park Columns (165)
Handwerk Column (18)
3 Field Pioneer Companies (81 ea)

Pommeranian Brigade: Generalmajor von Borstell
Pommeranian Grenadier Battalion (805)
1/1st Pommeranian Infantry Regiment (801)
Depot/1st Pommeranian Infantry Regiment (801)
Fus/1st Pommeranian Infantry Regiment (801)
2/Colberg Infantry Regiment (801)
Depot/Colberg Infantry Regiment (801)
Fus/Colberg Infantry Regiment (801)
Cavalry:
1/,2/,3/,4/Königin Dragoon Regiment (4)(601)
2/,4/Brandenburg Dragoon Regiment (2)(300)
Artillery:
6pdr Horse Battery #5 (148)
2 6pdr Foot Batteries #5 & #10 (139 ea)
1 Field Pioneer Company (81)
East Prussian Brigade: Generalmajor von Bülow
2nd East Prussian Grenadier Battalion (805)
1/1st East Prussian Infantry Regiment (801)
Depot/1st East Prussian Infantry Regiment (801)
1/2nd East Prussian Infantry Regiment (801)
Depot/2nd East Prussian Infantry Regiment (801)
2/3rd East Prussian Infantry Regiment (801)
Depot/3rd East Prussian Infantry Regiment (801)
Fus/3rd East Prussian Infantry Regiment (801)
2/4th East Prussian Infantry Regiment (801)
Depot/4th East Prussian Infantry Regiment (801)

Cavalry:
1/,3/Lithuanian Dragoon Regiment (2)(300)
3/,4/West Prussian Dragoon Regiment (2)(300)
1/,2/1st Leib-Hussar Regiment (2)(300)
3/,4/2nd Leib-Hussar Regiment (2)(300)
Artillery:
Horse Battery #6 (148)
2 6pdr Foot Batteries #?, #16 (139 ea)
l2pdr Foot Battery #1 (139)
1 Field Pioneer Company (81)

Garrisons:
In Prussia:
Garrison Bn/1st East Prussian Infantry Regiment (801)
Garrison Bn/2nd East Prussian Infantry Regiment (801)
1st East Prussian Brigade Garrison Battalion (801)
Artillery Companyof East Prussian Brigade (200)
Det. Artillery Artisan (31)
Det. Prussian Pioneer Co. (23)
Graudenz Garrison
Garrison Bn/3rd East Prussian Infantry Regiment (801)
Garrison Bn/4th East Prussian Infantry Regiment (801)
2nd East Prussian Brigade Garrison Battalion (801)
1st West Prussian Brigade Garrison Battalion (801)
2nd West Prussian Brigade Garrison Battalion (801)
ArtilleryCompanyof East Prussian Brigade (200)
4 Krümper Foot Artillery Companies of the East Prussian Brigade (200 men ea)
Det. Artillery Artisans (24)
Mounted Artillery Depot (100)
Prussian Pioneer Company (123)
Det. Cavalry (108)
In Pommerania and the Mark:
Garrison Bn/1st Pommeranian Infantry Regiment (801)
Garrison Bn/Colberg Infantry Regiment (801)
Foot Artillery Company (200)
5 Krümper Foot Artillery Companies (200 ea)
Brandenburg Pioneer Company (123)
Depot/Königin Dragoon Regiment (150)
1/2 Depot/Brandenburg Dragoon Regiment (75)
1/2 Depot/Pommeranian Hussar Regiment (75)
In Field in Pommerania:
Reserve Bn/1st East Prussian Infantry Regiment (801)
Reserve Bn/2nd East Prussian Infantry Regiment (801)
Reserve Bn/3rd East Prussian Infantry Regiment (801)
Reserve Fusilier Bn/3rd East Prussian Infantry Regiment (801)
Reserve Bn/4th East Prussian Infantry Regiment (801)
Reserve Bn/1st Pommeranian Infantry Regiment (801)
Reserve Fusilier Bn/1st Pommeranian Infantry Regiment (801)
Reserve Bn/Colberg Infantry Regiment (801)
Reserve Fusilier Bn/Colberg Infantry Regiment (801)
Reserve Bn/2nd East Prussian Grenadier Battalion (801)
Reserve Bn/Pommeranian Grenadier Battalion (801)
2/,4/Pommeranian Hussar Regiment (2)(300)
6 Foot Artillery Companies (1,200)
In Silesia:
Garrison of Silberberg:
1st Lower Silesian Garrison Battalion (801)
Foot Artillery Company (200)
3 Krümper Foot Artillery Companies (200 ea)
Garrison of Schweidnitz:
Garrison Bn/1st West Prussian Infantry Regiment (801)
1/2 Depot/1st West Prussian Dragoon Regiment (750)
Garrison of Glatz:
Guard Garrison Company (200)
Garrison Bn/Leib Infantry Regiment (801)
2nd Brandenburg Brigade Garrison Battalion (801)

Foot Artillery Company (200)
5 Krümper Foot Artillery Companies (200 ea)
Pioneer Company (1)(123)
Garrison of Neise:
  1st Brandenburg Brigade Garrison Battalion (801)
  2nd Lower Silesian Brigade Garrison Battalion (801)
  Garrison Bn/1st Silesian Infantry Regiment (801)
  2 Foot Artillery Companies (200 ea)
  3 Krümper Foot Artillery Companies (200 ea)
  1 Pioneer Company (1)(123)
Garrison of Cosel:
  1st Upper Silesian Brigade Garrison Battalion (801)
  2nd Upper Silesian Brigade Garrison Battalion (801)
  1 Foot Artillery Company (200)
  5 Krümper Foot Artillery Companies (200 ea)
  1 Pioneer Company (123)

Other Forces:
1st Formation
  Reserve Bn/Garde zu Fuss (801)
  Reserve Bn/Leib Grenadier Battalion (801)
  Reserve Bn/1st East Prussian Grenadier Battalion (801)
  Reserve Bn/West Prussian Grenadier Battalion (801)
  Reserve Bn/Silesian Grenadier Battalion (801)
  Reserve Fus Bn/1st West Prussian Infantry Regiment (801)
  Reserve Bn/1st West Prussian Infantry Regiment (801)
  Reserve Bn/2nd West Prussian Infantry Regiment (801)
  Reserve Bn/1st Silesian Infantry Regiment (801)
  Reserve Fusilier Bn/1st Silesian Infantry Regiment (801)
  Reserve Bn/2nd Silesian Infantry Regiment (801)
2nd Formation
  1st Reserve Battalion
  2nd Reserve Battalion
  3rd Reserve Battalion
  4th Reserve Battalion
  5th Reserve Battalion
  6th Reserve Battalion
  7th Reserve Battalion
  8th Reserve Battalion
  9th Reserve Battalion
  l0th Reserve Battalion
  3/,4/Brandenburg Hussar Regiment (2)(300)
  3/,4/Brandenburg Uhlan Regiment (2)(300)
  3/,4/Silesian Uhlan Regiment (2)(300)
Depots:
  Depot Guard Jäger Battalion (110)
  Depot East Prussian Jäger Battalion (110)
  Depot Silesian Schützen Battalion (110)
  Depot Garde du Corps Regiment (150)
  Depot Guard Light Cavalry Regiment (150)
  Depot Silesian Cuirassier Regiment (150)
  Depot East Prussian Cuirassier Regiment (150)
  Depot Brandenburg Cuirassier Regiment (150)
  Depot Neumärk Dragoon Regiment (150)
  Depot West Prussian Uhlan Regiment (150)
  Depot Silesian Hussar Regiment (150)
  Depot Silesian Uhlan Regiment (150)
  Depot Brandenburg Uhlan Regiment (150)
  Depot Brandenburg Hussar Regiment (150)
  1/2 Depot 1st West Prussian Dragoon Regiment (75)

German General Staff, Das Preussische Heer im Jahre 1813

RUSSIAN ARMY
1 JANUARY 1813

RUSSIAN RIGHT WING OR 1ST MAIN COLUMN
Commander-in-Chief: General of Cavalry Count
Wittgenstein
  Chief of Staff: Generalmajor d'Auvray
  Quartermaster General: Generalmajor Diebitsch II
  General of the Day: Generalmajor Count Inge1strohm
  Chief of Secretariate: Colonel of the General Staff Teslev

Detachment: Generalmajor Schepelev (65/162/1,957)
  Converged Guard Cavalry Regiment
  Converged Dragoon Regiment
  Converged Hussar Regiment
  Tenguinsk Infantry Regiment
  Horse Artillery Battery #23 (6 guns)
Detachment: Generalmajor Baron Diebitsch II (45/102/1,654)
  Grodno Hussar Regiment
  Rodinov #2 Cossack Regiment
  Tscharninov Cossack Regiment
  23rd Jager Regiment (1)
  Horse Battery #1 (8 guns)
Advanced Guard: Generalmajor Kutusov (167/257/4,418)
Cavalry
  Isoum Hussar Regiment
  Finland Dragoon Regiment
  Kazan Dragoon Regiment
Cossacks
  Platov #4 Cossack Regiment
  Lotchilin Cossack Regiment
  Koschkin Cossack Regiment
  Illowaiski #10 Cossack Regiment
  Selivanov Cossack Regiment
  Gorin #1 Cossack Regiment
  Illowaiski #4 Cossack Regiment
Infantry: Colonel Baron Rosen
  Lithuanian Infantry regiment
  23rd Jager Regiment (1)
  24th Jager Regiment (1)
  1st Cohort St. Petersburg Militia
  9th Cohort St. Petersburg Militia
  Tver Militia
Artillery:
  Heavy Artillery Battery #28 (6 guns)
  Light Artillery Battery #11 (6 guns)
  Horse Artillery Battery #2 (2 guns)
I Corps: Generallieutenant Steingel (198/545/6,139)
Cavalry Brigade: Generalmajor Alexejev
  Mitau Dragoon Regiment
  Riga Dragoon Regiment (2)
14th Division: Generalmajor Helfreich
Brigade: Generalmajor Harpe
  Toula Infantry Regiment
  Navajinsk Infantry Regiment
Brigade: Generalmajor Roth
  Estonia Infantry Regiment
  26th Jager Regiment
21st Division: Colonel Turtschaninov
Brigade: Colonel Scheel I
  Narva Infantry Regiment
  Petrovsk Infantry Regiment
  2nd Jager Regiment
  3rd Jager Regiment (from 6th Division)
Artillery:
  Heavy Artillery Battery #6

Heavy Artillery Battery #21
Light Artillery Battery #28
Horse Artillery Battery #3
Militia:
2nd Cohort St. Petersburg Militia
7th Cohort St. Petersburg Militia
8th Cohort St. Petersburg Militia
7th Cohort Novgorod Militia
8th Cohort Novgorod Militia
II Corps: Generallieutenant von Berg (164/393/4,40l)
Attached: Iambourg Chasseur a Cheval Regiment
5th Division: Generalmajor Kastichkovsky
Brigade: Colonel Lukov
Perm Infantry Regiment
Sievesk Infantry Regiment
Brigade: Colonel Treskin
Kalouga Infantry Regiment
Azov Infantry Regiment (from 6th Division)
Brigade: Colonel Peiker (from 25th Division)
1st Marine Infantry Regiment
2nd Marine Infantry Regiment
St. Petersburg Mlitia (5 cohorts)
Novgorod Militia (2 cohorts)
Artillery:
Heavy Artillery Battery #5
Heavy Artillery Battery #14
Light Artillery Battery #27
Reserve Corps: Generalmajor Fock (207/374/5,184)
Brigade: Generalmajor Count Sibirsky
Converged Cuirassier Regiment
Mohilev Infantry Regiment (from 5th Division)
Nisov Infantry Regiment (from 6th Division)
Voronezh Infantry Regiment (from 25th Division)
1st Grenadier Division: (Depot or Reserve Bns)
Count Arakcheyev Grenadier Regiment (1)
Pavlov Grenadier Regiment (1)
Ekaterinoslav Grenadier Regiment (1)
Tauride Grenadier Regiment (1)
St. Petersburg Grenadier Regiment (1)
Converged Grenadiers:
Converged Grenadiers of the 5th Division (2)
Converged Grenadiers of the 14th Division (2)
Militia: Generalmajor Akltcheieff
4th Cohort St. Petersburg Militia
6th Cohort St. Petersburg Militia
16th Cohort St. Petersburg Militia
17th Cohort St. Petersburg Militia
18th Cohort St. Petersburg Militia
Artillery:
Heavy Artillery Battery #28 (4 guns)
Light Artillery Battery #11 (6 guns)
Horse Artillery Battery #1 (2 guns)
Horse Artillery Battery #23 (6 guns)
Detachment: Generalmajor Schwetschin (36/39/990)
5th Bashkir Regiment
Podolsk Infantry Regiment
3rd Cohort St. Petersburg Militia
Detachment: Colonel Nikolaev (74/236/2,678)
Riga Dragoon Regiment (1)
1st Guard Reserve Battalion
2nd Guard Reserve Battalion
Heavy Artillery Battery #50
Light Artillery Battery #35
Light Artillery Battery #49
1st Pioneer Regiment (2 cos)
Colonel Muller's Company
Captain Herda's Company
12th Cohort St. Petersburg Militia
2 Cohorts Novgorod Militia

Detached towards Wolinsk: (11/34/448)
Voronezh Infantry Regiment detachment
Novgorod Militia, 2 Sotnias
Detached to Keidani (41/131/1,107)
10th Cohort St. Petersburg Militia
llth Cohort St. Petersburg Militia
Heavy Artillery Battery #27 (6 guns)
Light Artillery Battery #9 (7 guns)
Light Artillery Battery #25
Detached towards Sebesche (12/54/641)
l Cohort Novgorod Militia
Detachment: Colonel Tschernov (11/25/331)
Riga Dragoon Regiment (1)
14th Cohort St. Petersburg Militia
Detachment to Georgenburg: (19/71/865)
13th Cohort St. Petersburg Militia
15th Cohort St. Petersburg Militia

2ND MAIN COLUMN: GENERAL OF CAVALRY AND ATAMAN COUNT PLATOV
Detachment: Generalmajor Ilowaisky XII
Ataman Don Cossack Regiment
Illowaiski #12 Cossack Regiment
Kutainikov #4 Cossack Regiment
Rebrikov Cossack Regiment
Semenschenko Cossack Regiment
Strawrapolsch Kalmuck Regiment
Bihalov #1 Cossack Regiment
Illowaiski #3 Cossack Regiment
Illowaiski #5 Cossack Regiment
Kutainikov #6 Cossack Regiment
Don Horse Battery #1
Don Horse Battery #2
Detachment: Generalmajor Tschernischef
Siraewa #3 Cossack Regiment
Grekov #18 Cossack Regiment
Vlassov #3 Cossack Regiment
Illowaiski #11 Cossack Regiment
Girova Cossack Regiment
Don Horse Battery (4 guns)
Detachment: Colonel Tettenborn
Denissov #7 Cossack Regiment
Grebzov Cossack Regiment
Sulima #9 Cossack Regiment
Komissarev Cossack Regiment
Detachment: Generalmajor Dornberg
Melnikov #4 Cossack Regiment
Andrev #2 Cossack Regiment
1st Bashkir Regiment
Detachment: Generallieutenant Martinov
Grekov #7 Cossack Regiment
Grekov #5 Cossack Regiment
Kharitonov #7 Don Cossack Regiment
Illowaiski #9 Cossack Regiment
Sharnusubov #8 Cossack Regiment
Sutischilin #2 Cossack Regiment
Semphiropolsch Tartar Regiment
Perkop Tartar Regiment

3RD MAIN COLUMN: VICE ADMIRAL TSCHITAGOV
Chief of Staff: General St. Sabanejev
Quartermaster General: Generalmajor Berg
General of the Day: Colonel and Wing Adjutant Oldekop

Advanced Guard: Generallieutenant Tschaplitz
Cavalry: Generalmajor Count Orurk
Pavlovgrad Hussar Regiment
Volhynie Uhlan Regiment

Olivopol Hussar Regiment
Jitomir Dragoon Regiment
Light Artillery Battery #29
Infantry: Generalmajor Voronzov
Brigade: Generalmajor Karnielov
  13th Jager Regiment
  14th Jager Regiment
Brigade: (from 18th Division)
  28th Jager Regiment
  32nd Jager Regiment
Artillery:
  Light Artillery Battery #26
Converged Grenadiers: Generalmajor Metscherinov
  9th Infantry Division (2)
  15th Infantry Division (2)
  18th Infantry Division (2)

I Corps: General of Infantry Count Langeron
9th Division: Generalmajor Insov
Brigade: Colonel Poltarazky
  Nacheburg Infantry Regiment
  Iakout Infantry Regiment
Brigade:
  Riajsk Infantry Regiment
  Apcheron Infantry Regiment
Brigade: Generalmajor Udom II
  10th Jager Regiment
  38th Jager Regiment
18th Division: Generalmajor Scherbatov
Brigade: General Bernodossov
  Vladimir Infantry Regiment
  Dnieper Infantry Regiment
Brigade:
  Kostroma Infantry Regiment
  Tambov Infantry Regiment
Brigade: (Detached to advanced guard)
  28th Jager Regiment
  32nd Jager Regiment
Artillery:
  Heavy Artillery Battery #12
  Heavy Artillery Battery #15
  Light Artillery Battery #34
  Light Artillery Battery #35

II Corps: Generallieutenant Voinov
Brigade: Generalmajor Rudisevitch
  7th Jager Regiment (from 8th Division)
  12th Jager Regiment (from 13th Division)
  22th Jager Regiment (from 13th Division)
15th Division: Generalmajor Nassimov
Brigade: Colonel Tern
  Kozlov Infantry Regiment
  Vitebsk Infantry Regiment
Brigade:
  Kolyvan Infantry Regiment
  Kourin Infantry Regiment
Artillery:
  Heavy Artillery Battery #18
  Heavy Artillery Battery #34
  Light Artillery Battery #25
Cavalry: Generallieutenant Sass
Brigade: Generalmajor Count Pahlen II
  Starodoub Cuirassier Regiment
  Dorpat Dragoon Regiment
  Sieversk Dragoon Regiment
  Kinbourn Dragoon Regiment
  Tver Dragoon Regiment
  Arasmass Dragoon Regiment
Cossacks: Generalmajor Grekov VIII
  Grekov #8 Cossack Regiment
  Kutainikov #8 Cossack Regiment

Isaeva #2 Cossack Regiment
Kirpeva Cossack Regiment

4TH MAIN COLUMN FIELD MARSHAL COUNT KUTUSOV
  Quartermaster General: Generalmajor Toll
  Commissariate General: Generalmajor Kankerin
  Commander of Artillery: Generallieutenant Yermolov
  Generalmajor Lowenstern
  Commander of Engineers: Generalmajor Cout Siewers
  Chief of Hospitals: Generalmajor Bellogradtzky

Main Army: General of Cavalry Tormassov
3rd Corps: Generallieutenant Konovitzin
1st (Grenadier) Division: Generallieutenant Stroganof
Brigade: Colonel Kniaschnin II
  Count Arakcheyev Grenadier Regiment
  Ekaterinoslav Grenadier Regiment
Brigade: Generalmajor Sulima
  Tauride Grenadier Regiment
  St. Petersburg Grenadier Regiment
Brigade: Generalmajor Scheltuchin II
  Leib Grenadier Regiment
  Pavlov Grenadier Regiment
**2nd (Grenadier) Division: Generallieutenant Prince Karl of
Mecklenburg-Schwerin**
Brigade: Generalmajor Zwieleniev
  Kiev Grenadier Regiment
  Moscow Grenadier Regiment
Brigade: Colonel Baron Damas
  Astrakhan Grenadier Regiment
  Fangoria Grenadier Regiment
Brigade: Colonel Hesse
  Little Russia Grenadier Regiment
  Siberia Grenadier Regiment
5th (Guard) Corps: Generallieutenant Lavrov
Brigade: Generalmajor Baron Rosen
  1/Preobragenski Guard Regiment
  2/Preobragenski Guard Regiment
  1/Semenovski Guard Regiment
  2/Semenovski Guard Regiment
Brigade: Generalmajor Krapovitzky
  1/Guard Jager Regiment
  2/Guard Jager Regiment
  1/Ismailov Guard Regiment
  2/Ismailov Guard Regiment
Brigade: Generalmajor Udom II
  1/Lithuanian Guard Regiment
  2/Lithuanian Guard Regiment
  1/Finland Guard Regiment
  2/Finland Guard Regiment
  Guard Marine Equipage Battalion
Artillery: Generalmajor Euler
  Guard Heavy Battery #1
  Guard Heavy Battery #2 (Count Arakcheyev Battery)
  Guard Light Battery #1
  Guard Light Battery #2
Cavalry Corps: Grand Duke Constantine
  Chief of Staff: Colonel Kurutta
  Quartermaster: Colonel Baron Crossard

1st Cuirassier Division: Generalmajor Depreradovitsch
Brigade: Generalmajor Schaevitch
  Chevalier Guard Regiment
  Horse Guard Regiment
  Emperor Cuirassier Regiment
Brigade: Generalmajor Baron Rosen
  Empress Cuirassier Regiment
  Astrakhan Cuirassier Regiment

2nd Cuirassier Division:Generallieutenant Duke Gallizin V
Brigade: Generalmajor Kretov
   Ekaterinoslav Cuirassier Regiment
   Military Order Cuirassier Regiment
   Gluchov Cuirassier Regiment
Brigade: Generalmajor Duka
   Little Russian Cuirassier Regiment
   Novgorod Cuirassier Regiment
Guard Light Cavalry Division: (Remained in Wilna)
Brigade:
   Guard Don Cossack Regiment
   Guard Black Sea Cossack Sotnia
Artillery:
   Guard Horse Artillery Battery #1
   Guard Horse Artillery Battery #2
Cossacks: Generalmajor Karpov II
   Karpov #2 Cossack Regiment
   Grekov #2 Cossack Regiment
   Jagodin Cossack Regiment
   2nd Bug Cossack Regiment
   Zoikelef Cossack Regiment
Russian Reserve Artillery:
   Heavy Artillery Battery #7
   Heavy Artillery Battery #30
   Heavy Artillery Battery #31
   Heavy Artillery Battery #32
   Heavy Artillery Battery #33
   Light Artillery Battery #5
   Light Artillery Battery #32
   Light Artillery Battery #36

5th Main Column: General of Infantry Miloradovitch
llth Division: Generalmajor Tschoglikov
Brigade: Colonel Turgenev
   Polotsk Infantry Regiment (3)
   Jeletz Infantry Regiment (2)
Brigade: Colonel Yemelianov
   Pernov Infantry Regiment (2)
   Kexholm Infantry Regiment (1)
Brigade: Generalmajor Karpentov
   1st Jager Regiment (2)
   33rd Jager Regiment
22nd Division: Generalmajor Tartschaninov
Brigade: Generalmajor Schapskoy
   Olonetz Infantry Regiment (2)
   Staroskol Infantry Regiment (3)
Brigade: Generalmajor Reppninsky II
   Kaporsk Infantry Regiment (2)(from 6th Division)
   43rd Jager Regiment (2)(from 16th Division)
Corps: Generallieutenant Duke Volchonsky
8th Division: Generalmajor Englehardt I
Brigade: Colonel Schindschin
   Archangle Infantry Regiment (2)
   Schusselburg Infantry Regiment (2)
Brigade: Colonel Stegemann
   Old Ingremannland Infantry Regiment (1 1/2)
   37th Jager Regiment (1)
17th Division:
Brigade: Colonel Kern
   Riazan Infantry Regiment (2)
   Bieloserk Infantry Regiment (2)
   Brest Infantry Regiment (2)
Cavalry: Generallieutenant and Adjutant Korff
4th Cavalry Division: Generallieutenant and Adjutant Wassilschikov
Brigade: Generalmajor Millesinov
   Akhtyrsk Hussar Regiment
   Loubny Hussar Regiment
Brigade: Generalmajor Pantschulidsev

   New Russia Dragoon Regiment
   Tchernigov Dragoon Regiment
Brigade: Generalmajor Emanuel
   Kiev Dragoon Regiment
   Moscow Dragoon Regiment
Cavalry Division: Generalmajor Lissanevitch
Brigade: Generalmajor Yussesovitch
   Tchougouiev Uhlan Regiment
   Karkov Dragoon Regiment
   Kargopol Dragoon Regiment
Cossack Regiments:
   3rd Ural Cossack Regiment
   Pantelev #2 Cossack Regiment
   1st Teptar Cossack Regiment
   Yachontov Volunteer Cossack Regiment
   Barbantchikov Cossack Regiment
   1st Bashkir Regiment
Artillery: Generalmajor Merlin
   Heavy Artillery Battery #2
   Light Artillery Battery #3
   Light Artillery Battery #14
   Light Artillery Battery #42
   Light Artillery Battery #44
   Light Artillery Battery #19
   Horse Artillery Battery #4
   Horse Artillery Battery #6
   Horse Artillery Battery #10
   Reserve Heavy Artillery Battery #30

Corps: Generallieutenant and Adjutant Winzingerode
Partisan Corps
   Colonel Duke Mandatof
   Colonel Davydov
   Colonel Predel
Advanced Guard: Generalmajor Landskoy
Brigade: Colonel Duke Vadbolsky
   Alexandria Hussar Regiment
   White Russia Hussar Regiment
   Soum Hussar Regiment
Brigade: Generalmajor Knorring
   Tartar Uhlan Regiment
   Lithuanian Uhlan Regiment (2)
   Finland Dragoon Regiment
Brigade: Generalmajor Count Witte
   1st Ukranian Cossack Regiment
   2nd Ukranian Cossack Regiment
Cossack Regiments:
   Grekov #3 Cossack Regiment
   Grekov #9 Cossack Regiment
   Grekov #21 Cossack Regiment
   Popov #13 Cossack Regiment
   Shurscherinov Cossack Regiment
   1st Bug Cossack Regiment
2nd Corps: Generallieutenant Prince Eugene of Wurttemburg
3rd Division: Generalmajor Duke Schachafskoi
   Mourmansk Infantry Regiment
   Revel Infantry Regiment
   Tchernigov Infantry Regiment
   20th Jager Regiment
   21st Jager Regiment
   Jager Regiment formed from POWs from Breslau
4th Division: Generalmajor Pischnitzky
   Tobolsk Infantry Regiment
   Volhynie Infantry Regiment
   Riajsk Infantry Regiment
   Krementchug Infantry Regiment
   4th Jager Regiment
Artillery

Heavy Artillery Battery #3
Light Artillery Battery #6
Light Artillery Battery #7
Light Artillery Battery #33
Horse Artillery Battery #7
Horse Artillery Battery #8

Corps: Generallieutenant Baron Sacken
Cavalry: Generalmajor Yurkovsky
Brigade: Generalmajor Hamper
  Smolensk Dragoon Regiment
  Vladimir Dragoon Regiment
Brigade: Colonel Duke Schevachov
  4th Ukranian Cossack Regiment
  Serpuchov Dragoon Regiment
Cossacks:
  Sharnusubov #4 Cossack Regiment
  Loukoffkin Cossack Regiment
  Zikilev Cossack Regiment
  Yesremov Cossack Regiment
  2nd Bashkir Regiment
  2nd Kalmuck Regiment
10th Division: General Lieven III
Brigade: Colonel & Flugel Adjutant Sass
  Bieloserk Infantry Regiment
  Jaroslav Infantry Regiment
  Crimea Infantry Regiment
Brigade: Colonel Achlestischef
  8th Jager Regiment
  39th Jager Regiment
16th Division: Generalmajor Bulatov
  Kamtchatka Infantry Regiment
  Okhotsk Infantry Regiment
  29th Jager Regiment
Artillery:
  Heavy Artillery Battery #10
  Heavy Artillery Battery #13
  Light Artillery Battery #24
  Horse Artillery Battery #18

VII Corps: General of Infantry Doctorov
12th Division: Generalmajor Duke Chovansky
Brigade:
  Smolensk Infantry Regiment
  Narva Infantry Regiment
Brigade:
  Alexopol Infantry Regiment
  New Ingremannland Infantry Regiment
Brigade: Generalmajor Pallitzin I
  6th Jager Regiment
  41st Jager Regiment
26th Division: Generalmajor Paskievitch
Brigade: Generalmajor Savayna
  Ladoga Infantry Regiment
  Nivegorod Infantry Regiment
Brigade:
  Poltava Infantry Regiment
  Orel Infantry Regiment
Brigade:
  5th Jager Regiment
  42nd Jager Regiment
Artillery:
  Heavy Artillery Battery #26
  Light Artillery Battery #18
  Light Artillery Battery #47
  Light Artillery Battery #48
Siege Force at Modlin
  Veliki-Loutzk Infantry Regiment
  Galitz Infantry Regiment
  Saratov Infantry Regiment
Cossack Regiments

Vlassov #2 Cossack Regiment
Andreinov #3 Cossack Regiment
Danilof #2 Cossack Regiment
Shamschev Cossack Regiment
4th Ural Cossack Regiment
Corps: Generallieutenant Radt
Siege of Zamozsk: Generalmajor Sbijevsky
  Pensa Infantry Regiment (from 13th Division)
  Mingrelia Infantry Regiment (from 16th Division)
  Neutchlot Infantry Regiment (from 16th Division)
  43rd Jager Regiment (from 16th Division)
Artillery
  Heavy Artillery Battery #11
  Heavy Artillery Battery #16
  Heavy Artillery Battery #22
  Light Artillery Battery #31
Cavalry
  Pereiaslav Dragoon Regiment (1)
  Tiraspol Dragoon Regiment (1)
  Tourtchaininov Cossack Regiment
  Platov #5 Cossack Regiment

Plotho, C., Der Krieg in Deutschland

PRUSSIAN ARMY
9 FEBRUARY 1813

1st Brandenburg Brigade:
Infantry:
  1/,2/,Fus/1st Garde zu Fuss Regiment (3)
  Normal Infantry Battalion (1)
  Leib-Grenadier Battalion
  Depot/Leib Infantry Regiment (1)
  Garrison/Leib Infantry Regiment (1)
  Guard Garrison Company
  1st Brandenburg Brigade Garrison Company
  2nd Brandenburg Brigade Garrison Company (in Glatz)
Cavalry:
  1/,2/,3/,4/,Depot/Garde du Corps Regiment (5)
  Guard Hussar Squadron
  Guard Uhlan Squadron
  Guard Dragoon Squadron
  1/,2/,3/,4/,Depot/Brandenburg Cuirassier Regiment (5)
  1/,2/Brandenburg Uhlan Regiment (2)
  1/,2/,Depot/Brandenburg Hussar Regiment (2 1/2)
  Depot/Silesian Uhlan Regiment
East & West Prussian Brigade:
  1st East Prussian Grenadier Battalion (1)
  Res. Bn. 1st East Prussian Grenadier Battalion (1)
  1/,2/,3/,4/,Depot/East Prussian Cuirassier Regiment (5)
  1/,2/,3/,4/,Depot/West Prussian Uhlan Regiment (5)
Lower Silesian Brigade:
Infantry:
  West Prussian Grenadier Battalion
  Res. Bn/West Prussian Grenadier Battalion
  2/1st West Prussian Infantry Regiment
  Reserve/1st West Prussian Infantry Regiment
  Garrison/1st West Prussian Infantry Regiment
  Depot/1st West Prussian Infantry Regiment
  Fus/1st West Prussian Infantry Regiment
  2/2nd West Prussian Infantry Regiment
  Reserve/2nd West Prussian Infantry Regiment
  Garrison/2nd West Prussian Infantry Regiment
  Depot/2nd West Prussian Infantry Regiment
  Depot/East Prussian Jäger Battalion
  1st Lower Silesian Garrison Company (in Silberberg)
  2nd Lower Silesian Garrison Company (in Silberberg)

Cavalry:
   1/,2/,3/,4/,Depot/Neumärk Dragoon Regiment (5)
   2/,4/,Depot/1st West Prussian Dragoon Regiment (2 1/2)
   2/,4/2nd Silesian Hussar Regiment (2)
Upper Silesian Brigade:
Infantry:
   Silesian Grenadier Battalion
   Res/Silesian Grenadier Battalion
   1/1st Silesian Infantry Regiment
   Res/1st Silesian Infantry Regiment
   Depot/1st Silesian Infantry Regiment
   Garrison/1st Silesian Infantry Regiment
   Fus/1st Silesian Infantry Regiment
   Res. Fus/1st Silesian Infantry Regiment
   Fus. Depot/1st Silesian Infantry Regiment
   Fus. Garrison/1st Silesian Infantry Regiment
   1/2nd Silesian Infantry Regiment
   Res/2nd Silesian Infantry Regiment
   Depot/2nd Silesian Infantry Regiment
   Garrison/2nd Silesian Infantry Regiment
   1st Upper Silesian Brigade Garrison Company (in Cosel)
   2nd Upper Silesian Brigade Garrison Company (in Cosel)
Cavalry:
   1/,2/,3/,4/,Depot/Silesian Cuirassier Regiment (5)
   1/,2/,3/,4/,Depot/Silesian Uhlan Regiment (5)
   1/,2/1st Silesian Hussar Regiment (2)
   Depot/1st Silesian Hussar Regiment
Artillery:
In Breslau:
   3 6pdr Foot Batteries
   1/2 12pdr Foot Battery
   3 6pdr Horse Batteries
   3 Park Columns
In Neise:
   4 6pdr Foot Batteries
   1 6pdr Horse (Reserve) Battery
   1 Reserve Park Column
In Neustadt:
   1 6pdr Horse (Reserve) Battery

German General Staff, Das Preussische Heer im Jahre 1813

PRUSSIAN ARMY
1 MARCH 1813

Silesian Corps: General of Cavalry von Blücher

Brandenburg Brigade: Oberst von Röder
Guard: Major von Tippelskirch
   1/,2/,Fus/, Normal/Guard Infantry Regiment (4)
   Leib Grenadier Battalion (1)
   1st East Prussian Grenadier Battalion (1)
   3/Leib Infantry Regiment (1)
   Guard Jäger Battalion (1)
Cavalry: Major Katzeler
   1/,2/Brandenburg Hussar Regiment (2)
   1/,2/Brandenburg Uhlan Regiment (2)
   1/,2/,3/,4/West Prussian Uhlan Regiment (4)
Artillery:
   6pdr Horse Battery No. 8 Konnemann
   Guard 6pdr Foot Battery No. 4 Lehmann
   6pdr Foot Battery No. 9 Gravenitz

Lower Silesian Brigade: Oberst von Klüx
Infantry: Major von Jagov
   West Prussian Grenadier Battalion (1)
   2/1st West Prussian Infantry Regiment (1)

   3/1st West Prussian Infantry Regiment (1)
   2/2nd West Prussian Infantry Regiment (1)
   3/2nd West Prussian Infantry Regiment (1)
   Fus/1st West Prussian Infantry Regiment (1)
Cavalry: Oberst von Mutius
   1/,2/,3/,4/Neumärk Dragoon Regiment (4)
   2/,4/1st West Prussian Dragoon Regiment (2)
Artillery:
   6pdr Horse Battery No. 7 Richter
   6pdr Foot Battery No. 7 Holzheimer
   6pdr Foot Battery No. 8 Schone

Upper Silesian Brigade: Oberst von Zeiten
Infantry: Oberst von Pirch
   1/1st Silesian Infantry Regiment (1)
   Silesian Grenadier Battalion
   3/1st Silesian Infantry Regiment (1)
   1/2nd Silesian Infantry Regiment (1)
   3/2nd Silesian Infantry Regiment (1)
   Fus/1st Silesian Infantry Regiment (1)
   Silesian Schützen Battalion (1)
Cavalry: Major Laroche-Starkenfels
   1/,2/Silesian Uhlan Regiment (2)
   2/,4/1st Silesian Hussar Regiment (2)
   3/,4/2nd Silesian Hussar Regiment (2)
Artillery:
   6pdr Horse Battery No. 9 Tuchsen
   6pdr Foot Battery No. ll Mandelslohe
   6pdr Foot Battery No. l3 Held

Cavalry Reserve: Oberst von Dolffs
Brigade: Oberstlieutenant von Werder
   1/,2/,3/,4/Guard du Corps (4)
   1/,2/,3/,4/Guard Light Cavalry (4)
   Guard Horse Battery No. 4 Willman
Brigade: Oberst von Jürgass
   1/,2/,3/,4/Silesian Cuirassier Regiment (4)
   1/,2/,3/,4/East Prussian Cuirassier Regiment (4)
   1/,2/,3/,4/Brandenburg Cuirassier Regiment (4)
   6pdr Horse Battery No. 10 Schaffer
Reserve Artillery:
   6pdr Foot Battery #l2
   1/2 l2pdr Foot Battery #3

II Corps: Generallieutenant von Yorck
Generallieutenant von Kleist
Brigade: Oberst von Hünerbein, Major von Steinmetz
   •1st Combined Infantry Regiment (3)
      2/,Fus/1st East Prussian Infantry Regiment
      1/2nd East Prussian Infantry Regiment
   •2nd Combined Infantry Regiment (3)
      1/3rd East Prussian Infantry Regiment
      1/,Fus/4th East Prussian Infantry Regiment
   •3rd Combined Infantry Regiment (3)
      1/Colberg Infantry Regiment
      2/,Fus/1st Pommeranian Infantry Regiment
   7th Fusilier Battalion (1)(Fus/2nd East Prussian IR)
   •1st Combined Hussar Regiment (4)
      3/,4/1st Leib Hussar Regiment
      2/,3/2nd Leib Hussar Regiment
   6pdr Foot Battery #l
   6pdr Foot Battery #3
   6pdr Horse Battery #2
Brigade: Oberst von Horn
   •1/,2/,Fus/4th (Leib) Infantry Regiment (3)
   •5th Combined Infantry Regiment (3)
      1/1st West Prussian Infantry Regiment
      1/,Fus/2nd West Prussian Infantry Regiment
   •6th Combined Infantry Regiment (3)

296

2/1st Silesian Infantry Regiment
2/,Fus/2nd Silesian Infantry Regiment
•2nd Combined Hussar Regiment (4)
3/,4/Brandenburg Hussar Regiment
1/,3/Pommeranian Hussar Regiment
6pdr Horse Battery #3
6pdr Foot Battery #2
6pdr Foot Battery #6
Cavalry Reserve: Generalmajor von Corswandt
•1st Combined Dragoon Regiment (4)
2/,4/Lithuanian Dragoon Regiment
1/,2/2nd West Prussian Dragoon Regiment
•2nd Combined Dragoon Regiment (4)
1/,3/1st West Prussian Dragoon Regiment
1/,3/Brandenburg Dragoon Regiment
6pdr Horse Battery #1
Artillery Reserve:
Major von Schmidt
1/2 12pdr Foot Battery #3
3pdr Foot Battery #1
5 Park Columns
1 Handwerker Column
Engineering Forces
3 Field Pioneer Companies
•These combined regiments are those that entered Russia
with Macdonald as part of the French X Corps

III Corps: Generalmajor von Bülow
Brigade: Generalmajor Prince von Hessen-Homburg
1/1st East Prussian Infantry Regiment
Depot (3rd)/1st East Prussian Infantry Regiment
2/2nd East Prussian Infantry Regiment
Depot (3rd)/2nd East Prussian Infantry Regiment
1/,3/Lithuanian Dragoon Regiment (2)
3/,4/2nd West Prussian Dragoon Regiment (2)
Brigade: Colonel von Thümen
2nd East Prussian Grenadier Battalion
2/3rd East Prussian Infantry Regiment
Depot (3rd)/3rd East Prussian Infantry Regiment
Fus/3rd East Prussian Infantry Regiment
2/4th East Prussian Infantry Regiment
Depot (3rd)/4th East Prussian Infantry Regiment
1/,2/1st Leib Hussars (2)
1/,4/2nd Leib Hussars (2)
Artillery
6pdr Horse Battery #6
6pdr Foot Battery #16
12pdr Foot Battery #1
Pioneer Company (1)

IV Corps: (Pommeranian Brigade) Generalmajor von Borstell
Infantry: Oberst von Krafft
Pommeranian Grenadier Battalion (1)
1/1st Pommeranian Infantry Regiment (1)
Depot (3rd)/1st Pommeranian Infantry Regiment (1)
Fus/1st Pommeranian Infantry Regiment (1)
2/Colberg Infantry Regiment (1)
Depot (3rd)/Colberg Infantry Regiment (1)
Fus/Colberg Infantry Regiment (1)
Cavalry:
1/,2/,3/,4/Königin Dragoon Regiment (4)
1/,2/,3/,4/Brandenburg Dragoon Regiment (4)
6pdr Horse Battery #5
6pdr Horse Battery #11
6pdr Foot Battery #10
6pdr Foot Battery #?
2 Park Columns
1 Field Pioneer Company

Holleben, Geschichte des Frühjahrsfeldzuges 1813 und seine Vorgeschichte.

FRENCH GRANDE ARMÉE
1 MARCH 1813

MAIN ARMY: PRINCE EUGENE BEAUHARNAIS
Danzig Garrison: Général de division Rapp
X Corps: Général de division Rapp

7th Division: Général de division Grandjean
(as of 7 January)
Brigade: Général de brigade Radzwill
1/,2/,3/,Art/5th Polish Infantry Regiment (63/1,731)
1/,2/,3/,Art/10th Polish Infantry Regiment (61/1,697)
1/,2/,3/,Art/11th Polish Infantry Regiment (62/1,435)
Brigade: Général de brigade Bachelu
1/,2/,Art./1st Westphalian Infantry Regiment (34/1,094)
1/,2/,Art./13th Bavarian Infantry Regiment (41/1,032)
33rd Division: Général de division Detrees(as of 3 January)
Brigade: Général de brigade Rosarollo
1/,2/5th Neapolitan Infantry Regiment (1,356)
1/,2/6th Neapolitan Infantry Regiment (1,290)
1/,2/7th Neapolitan Infantry Regiment (1,372)
30th Division: Général de division Heudelet
(As of 15 December 1812 & 7 January 1813)
Brigade: Général de brigade Husson
1st Provisional Demi-brigade
4/2nd Légère Regiment (21/791)
4/4th Légère Regiment (19/632)
4/17th Légère Regiment (18/649)
6th Provisional Demi-brigade
4/16th Légère Regiment (17/575)
4/21st Légère Regiment (16/673)
4/28th Légère Regiment (16/679)
7th Provisional Demi-brigade
4/8th Line Regiment (15/611)
4/14th Line Regiment (15/642)
4/94th Line Regiment (18/552)
Brigade: Général de brigade Grissand
8th Provisional Demi-brigade
4/54th Line Regiment (16/555)
4/88th Line Regiment (20/418)
4/95th Line Regiment (20/479)
9th Provisional Demi-brigade
4/24th Line Regiment (22/521)
4/45th Line Regiment (20/618)
4/59th Line Regiment (21/555)
17th Provisional Demi-brigade
4/6th Légère Regiment (20/575)
4/25th Légère Regiment (20/555)
4/39th Line Regiment (20/782)
34th Division: Général de division Franceschi
(As of 7 January 1813)
Brigade: Général de brigade Gault
3rd Line Regiment (1 co)(4/13)
1/29th Line Regiment (26/214)
Artillery Co./29th Line Regiment (2/54)
105th Line Regiment (1 co)(?)
113th Line Regiment (2 cos)(20/210)
1 Co., Prince Primate Regiment (5/34)
1 Co., 4th Rhinbund Regiment (14/90)
1 Co., 5th Rhinbund Regiment (22/159)
1 Co., 6th Rhinbund Regiment (12/281)
Artillery:

18/8th Foot Artillery (2/39)
5/8th Train Battalion (1/23)
Corps Artillery: Colonel Gusskel
7/7th Foot Artillery (3/90)
17/7th Foot Artillery (2/95)
18/9th Foot Artillery (2/90)
4/12th Principal Train Battalion (1/98)
5/8th Principal Train Battalion (1/23)
1/7th Sapper Battalion (2/92)
Cavalry: Général de brigade Cavagnac
◊Numbers are officers, men, and horses.
9th Polish Uhlan Regiment (7/314/330)
17th Polish Uhlans (1/30/31)
19th Polish Uhlans (3/62/62)
Provisional Cavalry Regiment (15/382/397)
1st Provisional Dragoon Regiment (20/494/514)
2nd Provisional Dragoon Regiment (24/443/461)
Naval Forces
1st Spanish Pioneers Battalion (0/407)
Guard Marines (1/1)
4th Equipage de Flotilla (10/95)
17th Equipage de Flotilla (12/217)
Bataillon du Danube (7/61)
Bataillon de l'Escaut (15/297)
Attached:
Imperial Gendarmerie (0/10/12)
Imperial Guard Depot (0/398)
Sapper Depot (0/168)
4/5th Foot Artillery (0/36)
5/5th Foot Artillery (0/27)
9/5th Foot Artillery (0/108)
19/5th Foot Artillery (0/112)
10/5th Foot Artillery (0/86)
18/9th Foot Artillery (0/90)
21/8th Foot Artillery (0/103)
Dets. 1/,3/,4/,6/5th Horse Artillery (0/24)
9/1st Pontooneer Battalion (0/31)
6th Artillery Artisan Company (82)
3rd Armorer Company (0/33)
5th Armorer Company (0/12)
Saltpeter and Powder Workers (0/11)
Artillery Depot (0/137)
Württemberg Artillery (0/28)
Bavarian Artillery (0/16)
Polish Artillery (0/118)
Hessian Artillery (0/54)
1/2nd Miner Battalion (0/11)
Engineering Workers Company (0/75)
Det. Engineering Train Company (0/41)
1st Equipage Train Worker Company (0/140)
2nd Equipage Train Worker Company (0/53)
Det. 20th Equipage Train Battalion (0/37)

Advanced Guard or XI Corps: Général de division Grenier (as of 20 February)
31st Division: Général de division Grandeau
10th Provisional Demi-brigade
4/27th Line Regiment (19/500)
4/63rd Line Regiment (20/649)
4/76th Line Regiment (19/449)
4/96th Line Regiment (17/665)
11th Provisional Demi-brigade
4/27th Légère Regiment (17/770)
4/50th Line Regiment (20/587)
12th Provisional Demi-brigade
4/123rd Line Regiment (16/677)
4/124th Line Regiment (21/671)
4/134th Line Regiment (19/644)
13th Provisional Demi-brigade

4/5th Line Regiment (21/739)
4/11th Line Regiment (19/555)
4/79th Line Regiment (21/675)
Artillery:
8/8th Foot Artillery (3/50)
20/8th Foot Artillery (2/105)
7/5th Sapper Battalion (2/78)
35th Division: Général de division Grenier
1st Brigade: Général de brigade Sénécal
3/,4/6th Line Regiment (27/1,510)
1/,2/,3/,4/112th Line Regiment (65/3,522) (Figures include artillery detachment)
2nd Brigade: Général de brigade Zucchi
3/,4/2nd Italian Légère Regiment (47/1,685) (Figures include artillery detachment)
1/,2/,3/,4/5th Italian Line Regiment (90/3,420) (Figures include artillery detachment)
Cavalry:
1/,2/,3/,4/4th Italian Chasseur à Cheval Regiment (40/1,025/1,093)
Artillery: (14/475)
1st Italian Foot Artillery (5/113)
Det/10th Italian Company Battalion (2/80)
3/Italian Horse Artillery (8/100)(6-6pdrs & 2 how)
Det/10th Italian Train Company (2/102)
9th Italian Sapper Company (2/68)
2nd Venetian Sailors (2/100)
36th Division: Général de division Charpentier
1st Brigade: Général de brigade Simmer
3/,4/14th Légère Regiment (30/1,001)
(Figures include artillery detachment)
1/,2/,3/,4/22nd Légère Regiment (79/2,623)
(Figures include artillery detachment)
2nd Brigade: Général de brigade Meunier
14th Provisional Demi-brigade
6/10th Line Regiment (15/850)
6/20th Line Regiment (16/868)
3/67th Line Regiment (18/884)
15th Provisional Demi-brigade
4/3rd Légère Regiment (18/767)
4/102nd Line Regiment (20/942)
Illyrians & Swiss (9/616)
Artillery:
19/2nd Foot Artillery (3/115)(6-6pdrs & 2 how)
2/12th Principal Train Battalion (2/150)
9th Italian Sapper Company (1/40)
Det/18th Equipage Battalion (2/98)
Cavalry: Général de Brigade Poinsot
1/Würzburg Chevauléger Regiment (13/155/197)
Division: Général de division Gérard (figures from 2/1/13)
3/3rd Line Regiment (8/290)
3/105th Line Regiment (15/488)
3/127th Line Regiment (13/467)
1/,2/Neapolitan Elite Regiment (25/1,318)
1st Chasseur à Cheval Regiment (1/31)
1st Neapolitan Marine Company (3/127)
1st Neapolitan Horse Battery (6/61)
13/5th Foot Artillery (2/27)
Det/Artillery Train (1/80)
VI Corps: General Rechberg
1st Bavarian Light Battalion (6/151)
3rd Bavarian Light Battalion (9/240)
6th Bavarian Light Battalion (7/136)
1st Bavarian Combined Line Regiment (37/684)
2nd Bavarian Combined Line Regiment (28/619)
3rd Bavarian Combined Line Regiment (17/274)
Combined Bavarian Chevauleger Regiment
1st Chevaulegers (2/53/54)
2nd Chevaulegers (1/45/46)

3rd Chevaulegers (2/50/55)
4th Chevaulegers (3/63/65)
5th Chevaulegers (2/74/75)
6th Chevaulegers (1/52/57)
Bavarian Artillery (4/51)
Bavarian Train (1/27)

VIII Corps: General Fullgraff
1/,2/4th Westphalian Regiment (25/561)
Det/4th Westphalian Regiment (6/544)(en route)
1/,2/5th Westphalian Regiment (22/578)
Det/5th Westphalian Regiment (6/544)(en route)
Westphalian Artillery (2/40)
Württemberg Battalion (6/50)
French Train & Artillery(7/69)

VII Corps: Général de division Reynier (as of 1 February)
21st (Saxon) Division: Generalleutnant Lecoq
Brigade: Generalmajor von Steindel
von Liebenau Grenadier Battalion (12/347)
1/,2/,Artillery Co./Prinz Friederich Infantry Regiment (23/557)
1/,2/,Artillery Co./Prinz Clement Infantry Regiment (29/810)
Brigade: Generalmajor von Nostitz
1/,2/,Artillery Co./Prinz Anton Infantry Regiment (27/756)
1/,2/1st Light Infantry Regiment (20/689)
Artillery:
1st Saxon Foot Battery (von Brause)(4/148)
Park Division (3/72)
22nd (Saxon) Division: Generalleutnant von Funck
Brigade: Generalmajor von Sahr
Eichelberg Grenadier Battalion (8/355)
1/,2/,Artillery Co./König Infantry Regiment (6/226)
1/,2/,Artillery Co./Niesemeuschel Infantry Regiment (16/643)
Brigade:
Spiegel Grenadier Battalion (10/281)
von Anger Grenadier Battalion (9/406)
1/,2/2nd Light Infantry Regiment (20/703)
Artillery:
3rd Foot Battery (6pdrs)(5/115)
Divisional Park (2/75)
32nd Division: Général de division Durutte
1st Brigade: Général de brigade Devaux
1/35th Légère Infantry Regiment (20/650)
2/35th Légère Infantry Regiment (19/494)
2/36th Légère Infantry Regiment (18/394)
3/36th Légère Infantry Regiment (19/425)
2nd Brigade: Général de brigade Jalras
2/131st Infantry Regiment (21/509)
3/131st Infantry Regiment (17/551)
2/Würzburg Infantry Regiment (13/321)
3/Würzburg Infantry Regiment (16/279)
4/Würzburg Infantry Regiment (15/351)
3rd Brigade: Général de brigade Jarry
2/132nd Infantry Regiment (15/412)
3/132nd Infantry Regiment (12/334)
1/133rd Infantry Regiment (23/361)
2/133rd Infantry Regiment (20/491)
3/133rd Infantry Regiment (16/348)
Cavalry:
Det/6th Polish Uhlan Regiment (0/3/3)
Det/11th Polish Uhlan Regiment (1/85/91)
Artillery:
22/1st Foot Artillery (2/77)
6/5th Foot Artillery (3/78)
17/5th Foot Artillery (0/6)
4/9th Foot Artillery (3/75)

Artillery Artisans (0/4)
Det/2nd Principal Train Battalion
Det/7th (bis) Train Battalion
2/,3/,4/9th (bis) Train Battalion
Det/11th Principal Train Battalion
Det/13th (bis) Train Battalion
Det/Italian Train
Total Train (2/185)
Corps Cavalry
23rd Brigade: Generalmajor Gablenz
1-8/Saxon Hussar Regiment (18/377/563)
1-4/Prinz Clemens Uhlan Regiment (Saxon) (8/168/228)
1-4/von Polenz Chevauleger Regiment (Saxon) (16/298/393)
Saxon Horse Artillery (4/140)
Artillery Park: Major Haussman
2nd Saxon Foot Artillery "Gau" (5/90)
4th Saxon Foot Artillery "Weiser" (4/91)
Saxon Artillery Reserve "Hauseman" (12/374)
1st Saxon Sapper Company (4/60)
1st Saxon Military Equipage Battalion (3/506)

V Corps, Lithuanian & Grand Duchy of Warsaw Troops (figures as of 1 February 1813)
1st Polish Infantry Regiment (22/572)
2nd Polish Infantry Regiment (37/518)
3rd Polish Infantry Regiment (27/600)
6th Polish Infantry Regiment (27/458)
8th Polish Infantry Regiment (24/552)
12th Polish Infantry Regiment (24/413)
1/,2/,3/13th Polish Infantry Regiment (54/2,248) (Zamosc garrison)
14th Polish Infantry Regiment (31/171)
15th Polish Infantry Regiment (36/381)
16th Polish Infantry Regiment (26/495)
17th Polish Infantry Regiment (34/419)
18th Polish Infantry Regiment (54/824)
19th Polish Infantry Regiment (22/22)
20th Polish Infantry Regiment (39/891)
21st Polish Infantry Regiment (23/575)
22nd Polish Infantry Regiment (12/53)
1st Polish Chasseur à Cheval Regiment (10/166/134)
2nd Polish Uhlan Regiment (13/280/252))
3rd Polish Uhlan Regiment (14/478/338)
4th Polish Chasseur à Cheval Regiment (8/172/129)
5th Polish Chasseur à Cheval Regiment (10/286/187)
7th Polish Uhlan Regiment (19/276/200)
6th Polish Uhlan Regiment (10/263/216)
8th Polish Uhlan Regiment (14/352/178)
10th Polish Hussar Regiment (17/360/202)
11th Polish Uhlan Regiment (9/276/204)
12th Polish Uhlan Regiment (21/307/275)
13th Polish Hussar Regiment (34/462/297)
14th Polish Cuirassier Regiment (11/216/130)
15th Polish Uhlan Regiment (19/367/238)
16th Polish Uhlan Regiment (29/347/263)
18th Polish Uhlan Regiment (26/153/141)
20th Polish Uhlan Regiment (21/125/200)
Polish Foot Artillery (32/416)
Polish Horse Artillery (11/59)
Polish Pontooneers (4/27)
Polish Supernumerary Artillery Battalion (18/80)
Polish Sapper Battalion (12/67)
I Corps: (Figures are as of 10 February 1813)
1st Division:
1/17th Line Regiment (3/137)(2 cos)(in Stettin)
1/17th Line Regiment (3/80)(ship's garrison) (in Stettin)
2/17th Line Regiment (19/50)(6 cos)(in Erfurt)
2/17th Line Regiment (0/581)(en route from depot) (in Stettin)

1/30th Line Regiment (3/116)(2 cos)(in Stettin)
1/30th Line Regiment (3/30)(ship's garrison) (in Stettin)
2/30th Line Regiment (19/721)(enroute Leipzig)
1/33rd Line Regiment (3/107)(2 cos)(in Stettin)
1/33rd Line Regiment (2/86)(ship's garrison) (in Stettin)
2/33rd Line Regiment (15/714)(enroute Leipzig)
1/48th Line Regiment (3/145)(2 cos)(in Thorn)
1/48th Line Regiment (3/20)(ship's garrison) (in Stettin)
2/48th Line Regiment (19/22)(battalion cadre) (in Erfurt)
2/48th Line Regiment (0/675)(en route from depot)
1/12th Line Regiment (4/127)(2 cos)(in Stettin)
2/12th Line Regiment (22/41)(battalion cadre) (in Erfurt)
2/12th Line Regiment (0/700)(en route from depot)
1/21st Line Regiment (3/112)(2 cos)(in Stettin)
1/21st Line Regiment (2/70)(ship's garrison) (in Stettin)
2/21st Line Regiment (19/61)(battalion cadre) (in Cassel)
2/21st Line Regiment (0/700)(en route from depot)
1/85th Line Regiment (3/127)(2 cos)(Thorn)
2/85th Line Regiment (21/730)(enroute Leipzig)
1/108th Line Regiment (3/160)(2 cos)(in Stettin)
1/108th Line Regiment (1/80)(ship's garrison) (in Stettin)
2/108th Line Regiment (23/53)(battalion cadre)(Erfurt)
2/108th Line Regiment (0/700)(en route from depot)
1/25th Line Regiment (3/121)(2 cos)(in Stettin)
1/25th Line Regiment (3/90)(ship's garrison) (in Stettin)
2/25th Line Regiment (21/56)(battalion cadre)(Erfurt)
2/25th Line Regiment (0/700)(en route from depot)
1/57th Line Regiment (3/109)(1 co)(in Stettin)
2/57th Line Regiment (20/717)(enroute Leipzig)
1/61st Line Regiment (4/89)(battalion cadre) (in Stettin)
1/61st Line Regiment (2/66)(ship's garrison) (in Stettin)
2/61st Line Regiment (21/723)(enroute Leipzig)
1/111th Line Regiment (3/107)(2 cos)(in Stettin)
2/111th Line Regiment (14/726)(enroute Leipzig)
1/7th Légère Regiment (6/169)(2 cos)(in Stettin)
2/7th Légère Regiment (18/81)(battalion cadre) (in Erfurt)
2/7th Légère Regiment (0/700)(en route from depot)
1/13th Légère Regiment (4/107)(1 co)(in Stettin)
2/13th Légère Regiment (20/61)(battalion cadre) (in Erfurt)
2/13th Légère Regiment (0/700) (en route from depot)
1/15th Légère Regiment (3/89)(1 co)(in Stettin)
2/15th Légère Regiment (17/55)(battalion cadre) (in Erfurt)
2/15th Légère Regiment (0/700) (en route from depot)
2/33rd Légère Regiment (12/46)(battalion cadre) (in Erfurt)
2/33rd Légère Regiment (0/250) (en route from depot)

II Corps: (Strengths as of 20 February 1813)
1/2nd Line Regiment (3/143)(2 cos)(Custrin)
1/2nd Line Regiment (2/90)(ship's garrison) (in Custrin)
2/2nd Line Regiment (23/61)(battalion cadre)(Erfurt)
2/2nd Line Regiment (0/612)(en route from depot)
1/19th Line Regiment (3/97)(2 cos)(Custrin)
1/19th Line Regiment (2/100)(ship's garrison) (in Custrin)
2/19th Line Regiment (19/72)(battalion cadre) (in Erfurt)
2/19th Line Regiment (0/700)(en route from depot)
1/37th Line Regiment (3/152)(2 cos)(Custrin)
1/37th Line Regiment (3/114)(ship's garrison) (in Custrin)
2/37th Line Regiment (20/58)(battalion cadre)(Erfurt)
2/37th Line Regiment (0/588)(en route from depot)
1/56th Line Regiment (3/121)(2 cos)(Custrin)
1/56th Line Regiment (2/103)(ship's garrison)(Custrin)
2/56th Line Regiment (15/45)(battalion cadre) (in Cassel)
2/56th Line Regiment (0/700)(en route from depot)
1/11th Légère Regiment (6/245)(2 cos)(in Custrin)
2/11th Légère Regiment (15/61)(battalion cadre) (in Cassel)
2/11th Légère Regiment (0/561) (en route from depot)

1/26th Légère Regiment (6/247)(2 cos)(Erfurt)
2/26th Légère Regiment (14/42)(battalion cadre) (in Erfurt)
2/26th Légère Regiment (0/700) (en route from depot)
1/24th Légère Regiment (15/76)(2 cos)(Spandau)
2/24th Légère Regiment (15/48)(battalion cadre) (in Erfurt)
2/24th Légère Regiment (0/700) (en route from depot)
1/4th Line Regiment (5/98)(2 cos)(in Spandau)
1/4th Line Regiment (3/90)(ship's garrison) (in Magdeburg)
2/4th Line Regiment (22/62)(battalion cadre) (in Erfurt)
2/4th Line Regiment (0/608)(en route from depot)
1/18th Line Regiment (4/62)(2 cos)(in Spandau)
1/18th Line Regiment (2/80)(ship's garrison) (in Spandau)
2/18th Line Regiment (17/735)(in Erfurt)
1/46th Line Regiment (5/98)(2 cos)(Spandau)
1/46th Line Regiment (3/50)(ship's garrison) (in Magdeburg)
2/46th Line Regiment (20/67)(battalion cadre) (in Erfurt)
2/46th Line Regiment (0/700)(en route from depot)
1/72nd Line Regiment (3/78)(2 cos)(Spandau)
1/72nd Line Regiment (1/80)(ship's garrison) (in Spandau)
2/72nd Line Regiment (21/31)(battalion cadre) (in Erfurt)
2/72nd Line Regiment (0/640)(en route from depot)
1/93rd Line Regiment (2/100)(2 cos)(in Spandau)
1/93rd Line Regiment (2/96)(ship's garrison) (in Spandau)
2/93rd Line Regiment (20/60)(battalion cadre) (in Erfurt)
2/93rd Line Regiment (0/592)(en route from depot)

IV Corps: (Strength as of 10 February 1813)
4th Division:
1/8th Légère Regiment (6/200)(2 cos)(Glogau)
1/18th Légère Regiment (7/225)(2 cos)(Glogau)
2/9th Line Regiment (5/109)(2 cos)(Glogau)
2/9th Line Regiment (3/116)(ship's garrison) (in Magdeburg)
2/9th Line Regiment (15/65)(cadres of 4 cos) (in Augsburg)
2/9th Line Regiment (0/473)(en route from depot)
2/35th Line Regiment (4/100)(2 cos)(Glogau)
2/35th Line Regiment (3/110)(ship's garrison) (in Magdeburg)
2/35th Line Regiment (15/65)(cadres of 4 cos) (in Augsburg)
2/35th Line Regiment (0/386)(en route from depot)
2/53rd Line Regiment (4/43)(2 cos)(Glogau)
2/53rd Line Regiment (3/146)(ship's garrison) (in Magdeburg)
2/53rd Line Regiment (15/65)(cadres of 4 cos) (in Augsburg)
2/53rd Line Regiment (0/700)(en route from depot)
2/84th Line Regiment (4/89)(2 cos)(in Glogau)
2/84th Line Regiment (15/65)(cadres of 4 cos) (in Augsburg)
2/84th Line Regiment (0/443)(en route from depot)
2/92nd Line Regiment (5/99)(2 cos)(Glogau)
2/92nd Line Regiment (15/65)(cadres of 4 cos) (in Augsburg)
2/92nd Line Regiment (0/482)(en route from depot
2/106th Line Regiment (4/91)(2 cos)(Glogau)
2/106th Line Regiment (3/130)(ship's garrison) (in Magdeburg)
2/106th Line Regiment (15/65)(cadres of 4 cos) (in Augsburg)
2/106th Line Regiment (0/607)(en route from depot)
1/Dalmatian Regiment (3/30)(1 co)(Glogau)
1/3rd Italian Légère Regiment (3/92)(1 co)(Glogau)
1/2nd Italian Line Regiment (4/134)(1 co)(Glogau)

1/3rd Italian Line Regiment (6/45)(1 co)(Glogau)
1/1st Provisional Croatian Regiment (24/1,258) (in Glogau)
2/123rd Line Regiment (21/60)(battalion cadre) (in Erfurt)
2/123rd Line Regiment (0/560)(en route from depot)
2/124th Line Regiment (21/62)(battalion cadre) (in Erfurt)
2/124th Line Regiment (0/340)(en route from depot)
2/127th Line Regiment (21/40)(battalion cadre) (in Erfurt)
2/127th Line Regiment (0/386)(en route from depot)
2/128th Line Regiment (20/41)(battalion cadre) (in Erfurt)
2/128th Line Regiment (0/580)(en route from depot)
2/129th Line Regiment (17/39)(battalion cadre) (in Erfurt)
2/129th Line Regiment (0/405)(en route from depot)

I Reserve Cavalry Corps Général de division Latour-Maubourg

1st Light Division: Général de division Bruyère
Brigade: Général de brigade Bessières
  7th Hussar Regiment (2 cos)(2/40/44)
  9th Chevaulèger-lancier Regiment (2 cos)(3/74/82)
  16th Chasseur à Cheval Regiment (3 cos)(4/81/91)
  8th Hussar Regiment (5 cos)(assigned, not present)
Brigade: Général de brigade Mouriez
  1st Chevaulèger-lancier Regiment (1 co)(2/49/54)
  3rd Chevaulèger-lancier Regiment (1 co)(4/93/102)
  5th Chevaulèger-lancier Regiment (1 co) (assigned, not present)
  8th Chevaulèger-lancier Regiment (1 co) (assigned, not present)

3rd Light Division: Général de division Chastel
Brigade: Général de brigade van Merlen
  6th Chasseur à Cheval Regiment (2 cos)(40/69/78)
  25th Chasseur à Cheval Regiment (2 cos)(4/70/79)
  8th Chasseur à Cheval Regiment (2 cos)(4/70/79)
  6th Hussar Regiment (1 co)(4/60/66)
Brigade: Général de brigade Richter
  9th Chasseur à Cheval Regiment (1 co)(2/18/22)
  19th Chasseur à Cheval Regiment (1 co)(3/32/39)
  1st Chasseur à Cheval Regiment (4 cos)(4/100/109)
  2nd Chasseur à Cheval Regiment (1 co)(2/40/44)
  3rd Chasseur à Cheval Regiment (2 cos) (assigned, not present)
  2nd Italian Chasseur à Cheval Regiment (assigned, not present)
  3rd Italian Chasseur à Cheval Regiment (assigned, not present)

1st Cuirassier Division: Général de division Bordesoulle
Brigade: Général de brigade Berckheim
  2nd Cuirassier Regiment (3 cos)(assigned, not present)
  3rd Cuirassier Regiment (2 cos)(assigned, not present)
  6th Cuirassier Regiment (3 cos)(3/48/56)
Brigade: Général de brigade Quinette
  9th Cuirassier Regiment (2 cos)(assigned, not present)
  11th Cuirassier Regiment (3 cos)(2/48/51)
  12th Cuirassier Regiment (2 cos)(assigned, not present)
3rd Cuirassier Division: Général de division Doumerc
Brigade: Général de brigade Chouard
  4th Cuirassier Regiment (2 cos)(3/45/52)
  7th Cuirassier Regiment (2 cos)(2/44/48)
  14th Cuirassier Regiment (1 co)(assigned, not present)
Brigade: Général de brigade Reisset
  7th Dragoon Regiment (1 co)(7/123/133)
  23rd Dragoon Regiment (2 cos)(4/56/65)
  28th Dragoon Regiment (2 cos)(5/76/88)
  30th Dragoon Regiment (1 co)(8/137/148)

II Reserve Cavalry Corps: Général de division Sèbastiani

2nd Division: Général de division Pajol
Brigade: Général de brigade Gérard

11th Chasseur à Cheval Regiment (1 co)(5/123/128)
12th Chasseur à Cheval Regiment (3 cos)(4/125/129)
5th Hussar Regiment (3 cos)(3/52/55)
Brigade: Général de brigade Subervie
  9th Hussar Regiment (3 cos)(11/266/277)
  2nd Chevauléger-lancier Regiment (2 cos)(0/46/46)
  4th Chevauléger-lancier Regiment (2 cos)(0/71/71)

4th Light Division: Général de division Excelmans
Brigade: Général de brigade Maurin
  6th Chevauléger-lancier Regiment (1 co)(assigned, not present)
  4th Chasseur à Cheval Regiment (3 cos)(4/141/145)
  7th Chasseur à Cheval Regiment (3 cos)(4/98/102)
Brigade: Général de brigade Jacquinot
  20th Chasseur à Cheval Regiment (3 cos)(9/214/223)
  23rd Chasseur à Cheval Regiment (4 cos)(4/150/154)
  24th Chasseur à Cheval Regiment (3 cos)(4/90/94)
  11th Hussar Regiment (1 co)(3/47/50)

2nd Cuirassier Division: Général de division Wathier St. Alphonse
Brigade: Général de brigade Noirot
  1st Carabinier Regiment (3 cos)(6/83/100)
  2nd Carabinier Regiment (2 cos)(3/40/45)
  1st Cuirassier Regiment (2 cos)(4/62/72)
Brigade: Général de brigade Doudenaerd
  5th Cuirassier Regiment (4 cos)(11/137/178)
  8th Cuirassier Regiment (2 cos)(7/63/79)
  10th Cuirassier Regiment (4 cos)(assigned, not present)

Imperial Guard: (Figures as of 1 February 1813)
Infantry:
  1/2nd Voltigeur Regiment (19/872)
  1/2nd Tirailleur Regiment (16/834)
  Chasseurs & Fusilier-Chasseur Battalion (23/456)
  Grenadier & Fusilier-Grenadier Battalion (22/381)
  Velites of Florence (17/322)
  Velites of Turin (15/436)
  Royal Italian Guard (27/273)
  Hessian Troops (30/291)
Cavalry:
  1st Chevaulèger-lanciers de la Garde (9/118/138)
  2nd Chevaulèger-lanciers de la Garde (2/27/31)
  Chasseurs à Cheval de la Garde (18/249/289)
  Grenadiers à Cheval de la Garde (11/111/140)
  Empress Dragoon Regiment (11/119/138)
  Gardes d'honneur de Florence (1 co)(3/62/79)
  Gardes d'honneur de Turin (1 co)(2/71/83)
  1st, 2nd, & 3rd Escadrons de Marche (9/295/305)
Other:
  Guard Artillery (4/68)
  Guard Artillery Train (1/61)
  Line Artillery Train (1/59)
  Guard Sappers & Sailors (2/46)

Garrisons: (strengths as of 15 February 1813)
Garrison of Magdeburg Général de division Haxo
  Imperial Gendarme Squadron (10/540/555)
  Artillery & Train reorganizing (83/967)
  Equipage Train reorganizing (109/1,302)
  13th Provisional Demi-brigade (44/1,252)
    4/11th Line Regiment
    4/79th Line Regiment
  1/,2/3rd Westphalian Line Regiment (31/1,596)
  3/4th Westphalian Line Regiment (20/363)
  Westphalian Gendarmes (1/5/6)
  4/4th Foot Artillery (2/67)
  5/4th Foot Artillery (2/71)
  10/6th Foot Artillery (2/99)
  1/9th Foot Artillery (3/105)
  5/9th Foot Artillery (3/114)

11th Artillery Artisan Company (1/55)
3/1st Miner Battalion (4/59)
Det/4th Sapper Battalion (0/16)
Garrison of Stettin: Général de brigade Bruny
5th Bataillon de marche (6/536)
2nd Compagnie de marche, 30th & 34th Divisions (4/212)
Convalescent Depot (16/377)
2/1st Foot Artillery (3/112)
4/,7/8th Foot Artillery (4/193)
20/9th Foot Artillery (1/57)
11/3rd Foot Artillery (2/32)
3/9th Foot Artillery (2/50)
Det/5th Armorer Company (1/20)
Det/1st Pontooneer Battalion (4/44)
Det/7th Artillery Artisan Company (0/22)
Det/1st Provisional Dragoon Regiment (0/22/26)
Artillery & Train (6/84)
2/3rd Sapper Battalion (3/68)
Det/6th Rhinbund Regiment (0/75)
10th Provisional Demi-Brigade (75/2,263)
12th Provisional Demi-Brigade (56/1,992)
Det/1st Division, I Corps (51/1,812)(see above)
Garrison of Custrin: Général de brigade (Fornier d'Albe)
13/3rd Foot Artillery (3/56)
1/3rd Foot Artillery (2/27)
14/7th Foot Artillery (2/97)
8/5th Sapper Battalion (3/58)
Det/5th Armorer Company (1/14)
Det/II Army Corps, 2nd Division (24/2,009)(see above)
Garrison of Glogau: Général de brigade Laplane
1/,2/1st Baden Line Regiment(22/1,000)
Detached personnel (1/93)
16/4th Foot Artillery (2/118)
2/6th Foot Artillery (2/111)
9th Saxon Foot Battery (4/128)
9/5th Sapper Battalion (3/40)
Det. 4th Division, IV Corps (79/1,515)(see above)
Garrison of Spandau: Général de brigade Barthelemy
Prussian Troops (9/179)
6/1st Artillery (1/87)
8/1st Artillery (3/107)
8/5th Artillery (1/83)
Det/14th Artillery Artisan Company (1/23)
Det. II Corps, 3rd Division (24/512)
Garrison of Berlin: Général de brigade Gifflenga
18th Equipage Battalion (6/280)
Cavalry Depot (60/1,512/894)
Artillery Detachments (16/270)
Sapper Detachments (2/68)
1st Brigade, 35th Division:
3/,4/6th Line Regiment (27/1,510)
1/,2/,3/,4/112th Line Regiment (65/3,522)
Garrison of Swedish Pommerania: Général de division Morand
1/Prinz (Saxon) Maximilian Regiment (13/513)
2/Prinz (Saxon) Maximilian Regiment (15/709)
3/8th Foot Artillery (3/100)
17/8th Foot Artillery (4/99)
15/9th Foot Artillery (2/66)
9th Saxon Foot Battery (4/158)
Garrison of Erfurth:
15/4th Foot Artillery(2/117)
Convalescent Depot (1/73)
II Corps (106/4,200)
Garrison of Modlin: Général de division Daendels
18th Polish Regiment (54/824)
19th Polish Regiment (22/22)
20th Polish Regiment (39/89)
21st Polish Regiment (23/575)

22nd Polish Regiment (12/53)
3rd Polish Regiment (unknown)
17th Polish Regiment (unknown)
Würzburg Regiment (1 bn)(unknown)
18/7th Foot Artillery (3/103)
Garrison of Thorn: Général de brigade Poitevin
Det/85th Line Regiment (10/111)
Det/108th Line Regiment (9/125)
2nd Bavarian Jäger Battalion (12/134)
4th Bavarian Jäger Battalion (15/276)
5th Bavarian Jäger Battalion (8/256)
1st Bavarian Line Regiment (34/744)
2nd Bavarian Line Regiment (34/938)
3rd Bavarian Line Regiment (29/936)
Sapper Detachment (3/16)
13/1st Foot Artillery (3/111)
3/5th Foot Artillery (3/36)
8th Polish Foot Artillery (3/62)
Bataillons de Marche
Bataillon de marche - Corps d'Observation d'Italie (In Bamberg)
7th Line Regiment (4/105)
10th Line Regiment (2/59)
13th Line Regiment (3/97)
20th Line Regiment (3/63)
42nd Line Regiment (2/75)
52nd Line Regiment (1/66)
67th Line Regiment (3/71)
101st Line Regiment (2/51)
102nd Line Regiment (2/70)
Bataillon de marche - 31st Division (in Magdeburg)
3rd Line Regiment (1/101)
5th Line Regiment (2/122)
11th Line Regiment (3/112)
24th Line Regiment (2/97)
59th Line Regiment (2/31)
79th Line Regiment (2/100)
81st Line Regiment (2/49)
105th Line Regiment (1/77)
112th Line Regiment (1/12)
Bataillon de marche - Corps d'Observation du Rhin (in Frankfurt)
1st Line Regiment (2/91)
14th Line Regiment (3/128)
16th Line Regiment (3/141)
47th Line Regiment (1/85)
62nd Line Regiment (2/76)
70th Line Regiment (2/84)
86th Line Regiment (1/110)
122nd Line Regiment (1/79)
Bataillon de marche - Corps d'Observation du Rhin (in Mainz)
Destined to be incorporated into the weakest units in this corps.
66th Line Regiment (2/123)
114th Line Regiment (0/10)
115th Line Regiment (1/81)
116th Line Regiment (2/105)
117th Line Regiment (1/40)
118th Line Regiment (1/7)
119th Line Regiment (0/12)
120th Line Regiment (0/13)
V Corps or Corps d'Observation de l'Elbe: (as of 2/20/13)
1st Division: Général de division Maison
Brigade: Général de brigade Avril
1/151st Line Regiment (22/657)
2/151st Line Regiment (17/634)
3/151st Line Regiment (17/652)

4/151st Line Regiment (19/587)
1/152nd Line Regiment (19/718)
2/152nd Line Regiment (21/739)
3/152nd Line Regiment (19/637)
4/152nd Line Regiment (18/680)
Brigade: Général de brigade Penne
1/153rd Line Regiment (19/707)
2/153rd Line Regiment (21/773)
3/153rd Line Regiment (22/675)
4/153rd Line Regiment (18/769)
Artillery: Chef de bataillon Chateaubrun
1/1st Foot Artillery (1/69)
3/1st Foot Artillery (3/95)
7/3rd Principal Train Battalion (2/148)
Det. 7/4th Principal Train Battalion (0/30)
1/6th Sapper Batalion (3/117)
1/2nd Military Equipage Train Battalion (3/124)

2nd Division: Général de division Puthod
Brigade Général de brigade Vachot
1/146th Line Regiment (22/398)
2/146th Line Regiment (21/774)
3/146th Line Regiment (23/777)
4/146th Line Regiment (19/670)
1/147th Line Regiment (20/720)
2/147th Line Regiment (21/784)
3/147th Line Regiment (18/797)
4/147th Line Regiment (18/544)
Brigade Général de brigade Pastol
1/148th Line Regiment (20/342)
2/148th Line Regiment (21/567)
3/148th Line Regiment (16/609)
4/148th Line Regiment (13/477)
Artillery: Chef de Bataillon Scheille
10/1st Foot Artillery (2/94)
5/2nd Foot Artillery (3/99)
7/9th Principal Train Battalion (2/148)
7/4th Principal Train Battalion (0/30)
2/6th Sapper Batalion (3/117)
2/2nd Military Equipage Train Battalion (3/127)

3rd Division: Général de division Lagrange
Brigade: Général de brigade Laurent
1/134th Line Regiment (10/629)
2/134th Line Regiment (11/679)
Det/79th Line Regiment (0/200)
Det/69th Line Regiment (0/200)
Det/76th Line Regiment (0/100) (det to be incorporated into 134th)
1/3rd Foreign Regiment (Irish Legion)(21/725)
2/3rd Foreign Regiment (Irish Legion)(25/800)
Brigade: Général de brigade Suden
1/154th Line Regiment (19/559)
2/154th Line Regiment (22/707)
3/154th Line Regiment (21/696)
4/154th Line Regiment (20/458)
1/155th Line Regiment (23/579)
2/155th Line Regiment (20/587)
3/155th Line Regiment (18/567)
4/155th Line Regiment (19/609)
Artillery: Chef de bataillon Farjon
15/1st Foot Artillery (2/91)
11/5th Foot Artillery (3/106)
7/2nd Principal Train Battalion (2/148)
Det. 7/4th Principal Train Battalion (0/30)
3/6th Sapper Battalion (3/117)
3/2nd Military Equipage Train Battalion (3/127)

4th Division: Général de division Rochambeau
Brigade: Général de brigade Lacroix
1/135th Line Regiment (19/588)
2/135th Line Regiment (19/741)

3/135th Line Regiment (18/633)
4/135th Line Regiment (20/566)
1/149th Line Regiment (24/527)
2/149th Line Regiment (20/632)
3/149th Line Regiment (20/694)
4/149th Line Regiment (15/742)
Brigade: Général de brigade Longchamp
1/150th Line Regiment (19/574)
2/150th Line Regiment (18/529)
3/150th Line Regiment (18/766)
4/150th Line Regiment (18/772)
Artillery: Chef de bataillon Richard
12/5th Foot Artillery (2/94)
14/9th Foot Artillery (1/105)
7/8th Principal Train Battalion (2/148)
Det. 7/4th Principal Train Battalion (0/30)
4/6th Sapper Battalion (3/117)
4/2nd Military Equipage Train Battalion (3/127)

Reserve and Park: Colonel Chauveau
12/1st Foot Artillery (2/116)
16/1st Foot Artillery (3/92)
17/1st Foot Artillery (2/101)
1/5th Foot Artillery (1/117)
17/5th Foot Artillery (2/95)
9/7th Foot Artillery (2/98)
15/7th Foot Artillery (3/100)
16/8th Foot Artillery (2/104)
Det. 7/4th Principal Train Battalion (1/30)
1/12th Principal Train Battalion (2/148)
7/14th Principal Train Battalion (1/99)
Det. 7/14th Principal Train Battalion (1/49)
7/3rd (bis) Train Battalion (2/148)
7/11th (bis) Train Battalion (2/148)
7/6th Principal Train Battalion (2/148)
1/11th Principal Train Battalion (2/148)
7/11th Principal Train Battalion (2/148)
7/12th Principal Train Battalion (2/148)
4/2nd Sapper Battalion (1/126)
8/4th Sapper Battalion (1/141)
5/2nd Military Equipage Battalion (3/127)

I Corps d'Observation du Rhin: (15 February 1813)
1st Division: Général de division Souham
Brigade: Général de brigade Chasseraux
6th Provisional Regiment
2/6th Légère Regiment (16/599)
Det/10th Légère Regiment (0/200)
(det to be incorporated into 6th)
3/25th Légère Regiment (13/598)
Det/10th Légère Regiment (0/150)
(det to be incorporated into 25th)
10th Provisional Regiment
3/16th Légère Regiment (11/484)
Det/27th Légère Regiment (0/300)
(det to be incorporated into 16th)
1/28th Légère Regiment (7/824)
14th Provisional Regiment
4/34th Line Regiment (7/676)
Det/100th Line Regiment (0/100)
(det to be incorporated into 34th)
3/40th Line Regiment (19/646)
Det/54th Line Regiment (0/100)
(det to be incorporated into 40th)
17th Provisional Regiment
4/43rd Line Regiment (15/225)
Det/8th Line Regiment (0/50)
Det/28th Line Regiment (0/200)
Det/55th Line Regiment (0/400)
(dets to be incorporated into 43rd Regt)
3/75th Line Regiment (17/558)

Det/94th Line Regiment (0/150)
(det to be incorporated into the 75th Line Regt)
Brigade: Général de brigade Goris
21st Provisional Line Regiment
3/59th Line Regiment (9/659)
Det/96th Line Regiment (0/200)
(det to be incorporated into 59th)
4/69th Line Regiment (19/800)
24th Provisional Line Regiment
3/88th Line Regiment (21/823)
3/103rd Line Regiment (9/752)
1/22nd Line Regiment (12/714)
3/22nd Line Regiment (18/722)
4/22nd Line Regiment (8/212)
5/22nd Line Regiment (7/214)
Detachments to be incorporated into 22nd
63rd Line Regiment (0/480)
64th Line Regiment (0/100)
76th Line Regiment (0/150)
94th Line Regiment (0/150)
18th Cohort (0/100)
19th Cohort (0/100)
13th Cohort (0/70)
14th Cohort (0/69)
Artillery:
21/1st Foot Artillery (3/97)(6-6pdrs & 2 how)
7/2nd Foot Artillery (3/93)(6-6pdrs & 2 how)
7/8th (bis) Train Battalion (2/148)
7/1st (bis) Train Battalion (1/30)
1/Spanish Sapper Battalion (3/187)
1/6th Military Equipage Battalion (3/124)
2nd Division: Général de division Brenier
Brigade: Général de brigade Desailly
2nd Provisional Légère Regiment
3/2nd Légère Regiment (17/634)
Det/28th Légère Regiment (0/100)
(det to be incorporated into 2nd)
3/4th Légère Regiment (17/605)
Det/28th Légère Regiment (0/100)
(det to be incorporated into 4th)
1/29th Légère Regiment (18/764)
2/29th Légère Regiment (not ready to depart)
1/136th Line Regiment (18/705)
2/136th Line Regiment (17/682)
3/136th Line Regiment (18/735)
4/136th Line Regiment (19/570)
Brigade: Général de brigade Godard
1/138th Line Regiment (16/448)
2/138th Line Regiment (19/552)
3/138th Line Regiment (21/555)
4/138th Line Regiment (16/480)
1/145th Line Regiment (20/521)
2/145th Line Regiment (19/559)
3/145th Line Regiment (17/435)
4/145th Line Regiment (20/522)
Artillery:
8/2nd Foot Artillery (2/91)(6-6pdrs & 2 how)
21/2nd Foot Artillery (1/107)(6-6pdrs & 2 how)
7/13th (bis) Train Battalion (2/148)
Det. 7/1st (bis) Train Battalion (0/30)
2/Spanish Sapper Battalion (3/187)
2/6th Military Equipage Battalion (3/124)
3rd Division: Général de division Girard
1st Brigade: Général de brigade Chemineau
4th Provisional Légère Regiment
4/5th Légère Regiment (16/668)
4/12th Légère Regiment (21/787)
1/139th Line Regiment (20/533)
2/139th Line Regiment (18/597)

3/139th Line Regiment (15/685)
4/139th Line Regiment (20/674)
2nd Brigade: Général de brigade Van Dedem
1/140th Line Regiment (20/656)
2/140th Line Regiment (17/532)
3/140th Line Regiment (16/695)
4/140th Line Regiment (14/735)
1/141st Line Regiment (19/565)
2/141st Line Regiment (16/530)
3/141st Line Regiment (20/465)
4/141st Line Regiment (19/510)
Artillery:
5/5th Foot Artillery (1/106)(6-6pdrs & 2 how)
15/5th Foot Artillery (3/96)(6-6pdrs & 2 how)
7/1st Principal Train Battalion (2/148)
7/1st (bis) Train Battalion (0/30)
3/Spanish Sapper Battalion (3/187)
3/6th Military Equipage Battalion (3/124)
4th Division: Général de division Ricard
1st Brigade: Général de brigade Tarayre
3/9th Légère Regiment (20/808)
4/9th Légère Regiment (8/118)
Det/17th Légère Regiment (0/400)
(det incorporated into 9th)
18th Provisional Line Regiment
3/50th Line Regiment (13/497)
Det/8th Line Regiment (0/150)
(det incorporated into 43rd)
3/65th Line Regiment (16/715)
19th Provisional Regiment
6/32nd Line Regiment (15/792)
Det/76th Line Regiment (0/100)
(det incorporated into 32nd)
2/58th Line Regiment (21/745)
2nd Brigade: Général de brigade Coutard
1/142nd Line Regiment (19/464)
2/142nd Line Regiment (15/570)
3/142nd Line Regiment (23/627)
4/142nd Line Regiment (20/610)
1/144th Line Regiment (17/619)
2/144th Line Regiment (9/558)
3/144th Line Regiment (15/504)
4/144th Line Regiment (12/501)
Artillery:
18/5th Foot Artillery (2/112)(6-6pdr & 2 how)
20/5th Foot Artillery (2/107)(6-6pdr & 2 how)
7/9th (bis) Train Battalion (2/148)
7/1st (bis) Train Battalion (0/30)
4/Spanish Sapper Battalion (3/187)
4/6th Military Equipage Battalion (3/124)
23rd Light Cavalry Brigade: Général de brigade Laboissière
1-6/10th Hussar Regiment (15/387/420)
Det/10th Hussar Regiment (0/110/110) (arrived 3/31/13)
1-6/10th Hussar Regiment (30/958/970)(on 4/25/13)
1-4/Hessian Chevauleger Regiment (30/470/570)
1-4/Baden Light Dragoon Regiment (30/470/570)
Reserve:
1/7th Foot Artillery (1/87)
6/7th Foot Artillery (1/92)
16/7th Foot Artillery (3/90)
22/7th Foot Artillery (3/108)
7/1st (bis) Train Battalion (0/30)
7/5th Principal Train Battalion (2/148)
3/10th Principal Train Battalion (2/148)
7/10th Principal Train Battalion (2/148)
Park:
10/8th Foot Artillery (3/81)
12/8th Foot Artillery (2/110)
16/9th Foot Artillery (3/90)

3/13th Foot Artillery (2/109)
5/5th (bis) Train Battalion (2/128)
6/5th (bis) Train Battalion (2/128)
7/5th (bis) Train Battalion (2/128)
1/10th (bis) Train Battalion (2/148)
2/10th (bis) Train Battalion (2/148)
7/10th (bis) Train Battalion (2/148)
5/,6/Spanish Sapper Battalion (4/236)
5/6th Military Equipage Battalion (3/124)

II Corps d'Observation du Rhin: (15 February 1813)
1st Division: Général de division Compans
1st Brigade: Général de brigade Cacault
  1/,2/,3/,4/,5/,6/1st Marine Artillery Regiment (19/1,072)
  Det/1st Marine Regiment (16/622)(arrived 3/20)
  Det/1st Marine Regiment (17/970)(arrived 3/22)
  Det/1st Marine Regiment (8/617)(arrived 3/24)
  Det/1st Marine Regiment (2/52)(arrived 3/24)
  1/,2/,3/3rd Marine Regiment (31/1,011)
  Det/3rd Marine Regiment (18/417)(arrived 3/20)
  Det/3rd Marine Regiment (1/47)(arrived 3/1)
  1/4th Marine Regiment (14/353)
2nd Brigade: Général de brigade Joubert
  25th Provisional Line Regiment
    3/47th Line Regiment (15/624)
    3/86th Line Regiment (15/779)
  20th Provisional Line Regiment
    5/66th Line Regiment (12/769)
    3/122nd Line Regiment (15/687)
    Det/72nd Line Regiment (0/100)
    (det to be incorporated into 122nd)
  2/32nd Légère Regiment (18/749)
  3/32nd Légère Regiment (12/750)
Artillery: Chef de bataillon Heckmann
  18/1st Foot Artillery (2/86)(6-6pdrs & 2 how)
  1/7th Foot Artillery (3/82)(6-6pdrs & 2 how)
  7/2nd (bis) Train Battalion (2/148)
  7/12th (bis) Train Battalion (0/30)
  Sapper Battalion (1 co)(2/118)
  1/15th Military Equipage Battalion (3/124)
2nd Division: Général de division Bonnet
1st Brigade: Général de brigade Grillot
  1/37th Légère Regiment (18/810)
  2/37th Légère Regiment (18/810)
  3/37th Légère Regiment (15/811)
  4/37th Légère Regiment (15/810)
  1/,2/,3/2nd Marine Regiment (36/1,277)
  4/,5/2nd Marine Regiment (23/1,091)
  6/,7/,8 /2nd Marine Regiment (35/1,603)
  2/,3/4th Marine Regiment (28/721)
  Det/4th Marine Regiment (4/207)(arrived 3/14)
Artillery: Chef de bataillon Terhost
  2/7th Foot Artillery (3/100)(6-6pdrs & 2 how)
  3/7th Foot Artillery (2/97)(6-6pdrs & 2 how)
  7/6th (bis) Train Battalion (2/148)
  Det. 7/12th (bis) Train Battalion (0/30)
  Sapper Battalion (1 co)(2/118)
  2/15th Military Equipage Battalion (3/124)
3rd Division: Général de division Friederichs
Brigade: Général de brigade Buquet
  11th Provisional Line Regiment
    4/1st Line Regiment (14/538)
    Det/79th Line Regiment (0/100)
    (det incorporated into 1st)
    2/62nd Line Regiment (7/443)
    Det/79th Line Regiment (0/100)
    (det incorporated into 62nd)
  13th Provisional Line Regiment
    3/14th Line Regiment (22/755)
    Det/76th Line Regiment (0/150)

    (det incorporated into 14th)
    4/16th Line Regiment (13/729)
  16th Provisional Line Regiment
    6/26th Line Regiment (16/507)
    Det/64th Line Regiment (0/200)
    (det incorporated into 26th)
    6/82nd Line Regiment (16/428)
    Det/27th Line Regiment (0/200)
    (det incorporated into 82nd)
  3/23rd Légère Regiment (6/567)
  4/23rd Légère Regiment (8/40)
    Det/10th Légère Regiment (0/300)
    Det/17th Légère Regiment (1/200)
    Det/21st Légère Regiment (1/300)
    (3 detachments incorporated into 23rd)
  3/121st Line Regiment (17/447)
  4/121st Line Regiment (8/256)
    Det/27th Line Regiment (0/350)
    Det/45th Line Regiment (0/300)
    (2 detachments incorporated into 121st)
  3/,4/44th Line Regiment
  (did not join, awaiting conscripts)
Artillery: Chef de bataillon Levis
  4/7th Foot Artillery (3/94)(6-6pdrs & 2 how)
  19/7th Foot Artillery (3/104)(6-6pdrs & 2 how)
  6/6th (bis) Train Battalion (2/148)
  7/12th (bis) Train Battalion (0/30)
  Sapper Battalion (1 co)(2/118)
  3/15th Military Equipage Battalion (3/124)
4th Division: Général de division Teste
•Most of these forces were not in Mainz until 6–10 April.
Brigade: Général de brigade Bartier
  3/15th Line Regiment (14/467)
  4/15th Line Regiment (16/254)
    Det/5th Line Regiment (0/500)
    Det/24th Line Regiment (0/100)
    Det/100th Line Regiment (0/100)
    (3 detachments incorporated into the 15th)
  3/36th Line Regiment (unfit for duty)
  4/36th Line Regiment (11/597)
  3/51st Line Regiment (unfit for duty)
  4/51st Line Regiment (8/312)
  3/,4/55th Line Regiment (awaiting conscripts)
    Det/95th Line Regiment (0/500)
    (detachment incorporated into the 95th)
Brigade: Général de brigade Camus
  3/70th Line Regiment (13/306)
  4/70th Line Regiment (11/234)
    Det/11th Line Regiment (0/400)
    Det/81st Line Regiment (0/300)
    (both detachments incorporated into 70th)
  27th Provisional Regiment
    4/131st Line Regiment (15/720)
    4/132nd Line Regiment (20/774)
  28th Provisional Regiment
    4/35th Légère Regiment (proposed, not yet assigned)
    4/36th Légère Regiment (20/819)
  2/113th Line Regiment (13/760)(in Paris)
  6/113th Line Regiment (unfit for duty)
Corps Reserve Artillery: Chef de bataillon Klie
  21/7th Foot Artillery (2/109)(6-6pdrs & 2 how)
  13/8th Foot Artillery (2/112)(6-6pdrs & 2 how)
  5/6th (bis) Train Battalion (2/148)
  7/12th (bis) Train Battalion (1/30)
  Sapper Battalion (1 co)(2/118)
  4/15th Military Equipage Train Battalion (3/124)
Park: Colonel Levavasseur
  14/8th Foot Artillery (2/89)
  15/8th Foot Artillery (2/79)

7/9th Foot Artillery (2/97)
8/9th Foot Artillery (2/89)
11/9th Foot Artillery (2/95)
21/9th Foot Artillery (1/97)
22/9th Foot Artillery (1/87)
22/5th Foot Artillery (1/89)
7/4th (bis) Train Battalion (2/128)
7/7th Principal Train Battalion (2/118)
6/2nd Sapper Battalion (3/140)
9/4th Sapper Battalion (3/137)
5/15th Military Equipage Train Battalion (3/124)

Corps d'Observation d'Italie: Général de division Comte Bertrand (10 February 1813)

1st Division: Général de division Pactod
Brigade: Général de brigade Pouchin
    1/2nd Provisional Croatian Regiment (20/820)
    2/2nd Provisional Croatian Regiment (20/820)
    1/23rd Line Regiment (12/545)
    2/23rd Line Regiment (12/531)
    4/23rd Line Regiment (12/567)
    6/23rd Line Regiment (14/601)
    Det/23rd Line Regiment (0/702)(new conscripts)
Brigade: Général de brigade Decouz
    3rd Provisional Regiment
        3/3rd Légère Regiment (21/522)
        Det/8th Légère Regiment (0/200) (detachment incorporated into 3rd)
        4/8th Légère Regiment (14/757)
    1/13th Line Regiment (20/869)
    2/13th Line Regiment (17/789)
    3/13th Line Regiment (18/829)
    4/13th Line Regiment (19/867)
    6/13th Line Regiment (18/869)
Artillery: Chef de bataillon Berre
    18/4th Foot Artillery (1/91)(6-6pdrs & 2 how)
    25/4th Foot Artillery (2/89)(6-6pdrs & 2 how)
    1/7th (bis) Train Battalion (2/118)
    7/7th (bis) Train Battalion (1/30)
    8/1st Sapper Battalion (2/50)
    7/9th Military Equipage Train Battalion (3/124)
2nd Division: Général de division Ledru
Brigade: Général de brigade Pourailly
    Cadre 3/1st Légère Regiment (awaiting conscripts)
    4/1st Légère Regiment (18/564)
    Det/22nd Légère Regiment (0/408)
    1/4th Neapolitan Légère Regiment (22/704)
    2/4th Neapolitan Légère Regiment (20/682)
    3/4th Neapolitan Légère Regiment (20/656)
    3/,4/7th Line Regiment (35/1,166)
    Det/106th Line Regiment (0/200)
Brigade: Général de brigade Gruyer
    23rd Provisional Regiment
        Det. 7/6th Line Regiment (8/489) (arrived 3/1)
        Det. 7/6th Line Regiment (7/462) (arrived 3/12)
        4/67th Line Regiment (15/797)
    12th Provisional Regiment
        4/10th Line Regiment (12/502)
        Det/60th Line Regiment (0/238) (detachment incorporated into 10th)
        4/42nd Line Regiment (10/599)
    2/,3/,4/101st Line Regiment (24/1,039)
    Det/9th Line Regiment (0/300)
    Det/53rd Line Regiment (0/300)
    Det/84th Line Regiment (0/300)
    Det/92nd Line Regiment (0/300)
Artillery: Chef de bataillon Rapallo
    2/4th Foot Artillery (2/93)(6-6pdrs & 2 how)
    20/4th Foot Artillery (2/101)(6-6pdrs & 2 how)

2/7th (bis) Train Battalion (2/118)
7/7th (bis) Train Battalion (0/30)
Det. 8/1st Sapper Battalion (1/50)
2/9th Military Equipage Train Battalion (3/124)
3rd Division: Général de division Merle
Brigade: Général de brigade Leclerc de Essarts
    3/52nd Line Regiment (7/689)
    4/52nd Line Regiment (5/685)
    5th Provisional Regiment
        7/14th Légère Regiment (8/353)
        7/14th Légère Regiment (8/442)(arrived 3/3)
        6/18th Légère Regiment (9/458)
        Det/14th Légère Regiment (0/100) (incorporated into 18th)
Brigade: Général de brigade Ficatier
    1/137th Line Regiment (10/718)
    2/137th Line Regiment (23/558)
    3/137th Line Regiment (23/732)
    4/137th Line Regiment (21/623)
    1/156th Line Regiment (21/741)
    2/156th Line Regiment (20/671)
    3/156th Line Regiment (22/683)
    4/156th Line Regiment (20/687)
Artillery: Chef de bataillon Boyer
    24/2nd Foot Artillery (1/97)(6-6pdrs & 2 how)
    26/2nd Foot Artillery (2/89)(6-6pdrs & 2 how)
    3/7th (bis) Train Battalion (2/118)
    7/7th (bis) Train Battalion (0/30)
    Det. 8/1st Sapper Battalion (1/50)
    9/9th Military Equipage Train Battalion (3/124)
4th Division: Général de division Peyri
Brigade: Général de brigade Renard
    3/,4/1st Italian Line Regiment (33/1,783)
    1 (bis)/,2 (bis)/,3/,4/,Artillery Co./
    4th Italian Line Regiment (68/3,600)
    Milan Battalion (18/980)
Brigade: Général de brigade Martel
    3/,4/6th Italian Line Regiment (33/1,839)
    1/,2 (bis)/, 3 (bis)/, 4 (bis)/,Artillery Co./
    7th Italian Line Regiment (68/3,558)
Artillery:
    1st & 13th Italian Foot Batteries (6/244)
    4th Italian Horse Battery (2/98)
    5th, 6th, 6th (bis) Italian Train Cos (6/443)
    8th Italian Sapper Company (2/118)
    3rd Italian Naval Artisans (2/104)
    2nd Italian Naval Company (3/107)
    5th Italian Transport Company (2/103)
    Italian Ambulance (3/141)
Light Cavalry Division: Général de division Fresia
1st Brigade: Général de brigade Briche
    1/,2/,3/,4/Napoleon Dragoon Regiment (40/1,060/1,008)
    1/,2/,3/,4/1st Italian Chasseur à Cheval Regiment (40/1,060/1,008)
    •The strengths for the Napoleon Dragoons and the 1st Italian Chasseurs are "hoped for" strengths, not actual field returns.
2nd Brigade: Général de brigade Stedman
    1/,2/,3/,4/13th Hussar Regiment (forming)
    1/,2/,3/,4/14th Hussar Regiment (forming)
3rd Brigade: Général de brigade Balabio
    1/2nd Neapolitan Chasseur à Cheval Regiment (13/240/249)
    3/,4/2nd Neapolitan Chasseur à Cheval Regiment (forming)
    2/2nd Neapolitan Chasseur à Cheval Regiment (9/231/245)
    1/,2/,3/,4/,5/,6/19th Chasseur à Cheval Regiment (forming)

Reserve & Park: Colonel Menoire
1/2nd Foot Artillery (2/118)
3/2nd Foot Artillery (2/115)
4/7th (bis) Train Battalion (2/118)
5/7th (bis) Train Battalion (2/118)
6/7th (bis) Train Battalion (2/118)
Det. 7/7th (bis) Train Battalion (0/30)
Det. 13th Artillery Artisan Company (1/29)

1st Young Guard Division: Général de division Barrois (15 February 1815)
•Units arriving in Mainz between 8 and 12 March.
Brigade: Général de brigade Tindal
2/2nd Voltigeur Regiment (17/618)
2/2nd Tirailleur Regiment (13/614)
1/,2/6th (bis) Voltigeur Regiment (25/1,447)
1/,2/6th (bis) Tirailleur Regiment (26/1,250)
1/,2/(bis) Fusilier Regiment (34/1,218)
1/Pupille Regiment (17/884)
7/Pupille Regiment (16/883)
Guard Chasseur à Cheval Regiment (2 sqns)(7/350/515)
Guard Dragoon Regiment (1 sqn)(5/142/266)
Guard Grenadier à Cheval Regiment (1 sqn)(2/119/231)
2nd Guard Chevauléger Regiment (1 sqn)(4/150/258)
Guard Marines & Sappers (1 co)(2/65)
Guard Military Equipage (2/131)
Guard Workers (1/93)
Artillery:
1st Column:
Old Guard Foot Artillery (2/100)
Young Guard Foot Artillery (6/266)
Guard Train (6/318)
2nd Column: (total 14/770)
Guard Foot Artillery
Guard Horse Artillery
Guard Train
Imperial Guard Detachments In Mainz: (31 March 1813)
Chasseurs à Pied
Grenadiers à Pied
Young Guard Infantry
   Total Infantry (33/800)
2nd Chevaulégers
Chasseurs à Cheval
Dragoons
Grenadiers à Cheval
   Total Cavalry (30/938/1,068)
1st Guard Foot Battery
2nd Guard Horse Battery
Total Artillery (16/492)
   Military Equipage
Ambulance
   Equipage & Ambulance (10/195)

Most of these forces were not in Mainz until 6–10 April.

PRUSSIAN ARMY
1 APRIL 1813

1st Corps: *General der Kavallerie von Blücher*
Chief of staff: Generallieutenant von Scharnhorst
Quartermaster General: Generalmajor von Gneisenau
Adjutant to C-in-C: Major Graf von Gloz

Brandenburg Brigade: Generalmajor and Generaladjudant von Röder
Brigade: Colonel von Tippelskirch
1/Garde zu Fuss (805)

2/Garde zu Fuss (805)
3/Garde zu Fuss (805)
Normal Infanterie Battalion (805)
von Wedell Freiwilliger Jäger Battalion (500)
Garde Jäger Battalion (805)
Leib Grenadier Battalion (805)
1st East Prussian Grenadier Battalion (805)
3/Leib Infantry Regiment (805)
Brigade: Oberst von Katzeler
1/,2/,Brandenburg Hussars (2)(300)
1/,2/,Brandenburg Uhlans (2)(300)
1/,2/,3/,4/West Prussian Uhlans (4)(60l)
Artillery:
Guard Foot Battery #4 (278)
6pdr Foot Battery #9 Von Grevenitz (148)
6pdr Horse Battery #8
Lower Silesian Brigade: Oberst und Flugeladjudant von Klüx
Brigade: Major von Jagow
2/1st West Prussian Infantry Regiment (805)
3/1st West Prussian Infantry Regiment (805)
Fus/1st West Prussian Infantry Regiment (805)
2/2nd West Prussian Infantry Regiment (805)
3/2nd West Prussian Infantry Regiment (805)
Brigade: Oberst von Mutius
1/,2/,3/,4/Neumärk Dragoons (4)(60l)
2/,4/1st West Prussian Dragoons (2)(300)
Artillery:
6pdr Foot Battery #7 (278)
6pdr Horse Battery #7 (148)
Upper Silesian Brigade: Generalmajor von Ziethen
Brigade: Oberst von Pirch I
Silesian Grenadier Battalion (805)
1/1st Silesian Infantry Regiment (805)
3/1st Silesian Infantry Regiment (805)
Fus/1st Silesian Infantry Regiment (805)
1/2nd Silesian Infantry Regiment (805)
3/2nd Silesian Infantry Regiment (805)
Silesian Schützen Battalion (805)
Brigade: Major Laroche von Starkenfels
1/,2/Silesian Uhlan Regiment (2)(300)
Combined Silesian Hussar Regiment (4)(60l)
   2/,4/1st Silesian Hussar Regiment
   3/,4/2nd Silesian Hussar Regiment
Artillery:
6pdr Foot Battery #8 (278)
6pdr Foot Battery #13 von Held (278)
6pdr Horse Battery #9 von Tuchsen (148)
Reserve Cavalry Brigade: Oberst von Dolffs
Brigade: Oberst von Werder
1/,2/,3/,4/Garde du Corps (4)(750)
Guard Volunteer Cossack Squadron (1)
1/,2/,3/,4/Guard Light Cavalry Regiment (4)(600)
Guard Volunteer Jäger Squadrons (2)(300)
Guard 6pdr Horse Battery #4 von Willmann (148)
Brigade: Oberst von Jürgass
1/,2/,3/,4/Silesian Cuirassier Regiment (4)(60l)
1/,2/,3/,4/East Prussian Cuirassier Regiment (4)(60l)
1/,2/,3/,4/Brandenburg Cuirassier Regiment (4)(60l)
6pdr Horse Battery #10 (148)
Reserve Artillery:
6pdr Foot Battery #11 (139)
1/2 l2pdr Battery #3 (94)
Park Column (99)
Pioneer Company (162)

Army Corps: *Generallieutenant von Yorck*
Chief of Staff: Oberst von Rauch
Quartermaster General: Oberst Valentini

Adjutant to C-in-C: Rittmeister Graf Brandenburg

Infantry: Generallieutenant von Kleist
Division: Generalmajor von Hünerbein
Brigade: Oberst von Steinmetz
  1/1st East Prussian Infantry Regiment
  2/1st East Prussian Infantry Regiment
  Fus/1st East Prussian Infantry Regiment
  1/2nd Pommeranian (Colberg) Infantry Regiment
  2/2nd Pommeranian (Colberg) Infantry Regiment
  Fus/2nd Pommeranian (Colberg) Infantry Regiment
  Fus/2nd East Prussian Infantry Regiment
  East Prussian Jäger Battalion
Brigade: Oberst von Horn
  4th Combined Infantry Regiment
    1/,2/,Fus/Leib Infantry Regiment
  5th Combined Infantry Regiment
    1/1st West Prussian Infantry Regiment
    2/,Fus/2nd West Prussian Infantry Regiment
  6th Combined Infantry Regiment
    2/1st Silesian Infantry Regiment
    2/,Fus/2nd Silesian Infantry Regiment
Cavalry Brigade: Generalmajor von Corswandt
  1/,2/,3/,4/Lithuanian Dragoon Regiment (4)
  2nd Combined Dragoon Regiment
    1/,3/1st West Prussian Dragoons (2)
    1/,3/Brandenburg Dragoons (2)
    2/,3/2nd Leib Hussars
  3rd Combined Hussar Regiment
    2/,3/1st Silesian Hussars (2)
    1/,3/2nd Silesian Hussars (2)
Artillery: Oberst von Schmidt
  1/2 12pdr Foot Battery #3
  6pdr Foot Battery #1
  6pdr Foot Battery #2
  6pdr Foot Battery #3
  6pdr Foot Battery #6
  6pdr Horse Battery #1
  6pdr Horse Battery #2
  6pdr Horse Battery #3
  3 Pioneer Companies
  Park column
  Handwerkskolonne

East and West Prussian Reserve Corps:
Generallieutenant von Bülow
1st Brigade: Generalmajor Prince Ludwig von Hessen-Homburg
  2nd East Prussian Grenadier Battalion (805)
  3/1st East Prussian Infantry Regiment (805)
  1/2nd East Prussian Infantry Regiment (805)
  2/2nd East Prussian Infantry Regiment (805)
  1/3rd East Prussian Infantry Regiment (805)
  2/3rd East Prussian Infantry Regiment (805)
  3/3rd East Prussian Infantry Regiment (805)
  Fus/3rd East Prussian Infantry Regiment (805)
  East Prussian Jäger Battalion (2 cos)
2nd Brigade: Major von Clausewitz
  1/4th East Prussian Infantry Regiment (805)
  2/4th East Prussian Infantry Regiment (805)
  3/4th East Prussian Infantry Regiment (805)
  6pdr Foot Battery #6 von Ludwig
Cavalry Brigade: Generalmajor von Oppen
  1/,2/,3/,4/1st Leib Hussar Regiment (4)
  1/,2/,3/,4/2nd West Prussian Dragoon Regiment (4)
Artillery: Major von Holzendorf
  1/2 12pdr Foot Battery #1 von Witte
  6pdr Foot Battery #5 von Glasenapp
  6pdr Horse Battery #6 von Steinwehr

Pioneer Company von Zavarovsky
Munitions Column

Pommeranian Division: Generalmajor and generaladjudant von Borstel
Brigade: Major von Zastrow
  Pommeranian Grenadier Battalion (805)
  1/1st Pommeranian Infantry Regiment (805)
  2/1st Pommeranian Infantry Regiment (805)
  Fus/4th East Prussian Infantry Regiment (805)
  1/,2/,3/,4/Königins Dragoon Regiment (4)
Brigade: Major Rohde
  6pr Foot Battery #10 Lt. Von Magenhoefer
  Horse Battery #11 Lt. von Borchard
  Pioneer Co. #4 Cpt von Rohwedel

Plotho, Der Krieg in Deutschland und Frankreich in den Jahren 1813 und 1814.

GRANDE ARMÉE
15 APRIL 1813

COMMANDER-IN-CHIEF: EMPEROR NAPOLEON I
Aides-de-Camp to the Emperor
  Général de division Comte Lemarois
  Général de division Duc de Plaisance Lebrun
  Général de division Comte de Lobau
  Général de division Comte Durosnel
  Général de division Comte Dejean
  Général de division Comte Hogendorp
  Général de brigade Comte Gueheneuc
  Général de brigade Baron Corbineau
  Général de brigade Flahault
  Colonel of Engineers Barnard
Staff
  1st Chamberlain - Comte de Turenne
  Prefect of the Palace - Baron Beausset
  Sergeant-major of the Palace - Canouville
  Secretary to the Cabinet - Baron Fain
  Secretary to the Cabinet - Baron Mounier
  Secretary Intrepreter - Lelorgne d'Ideville

General Staff
  Adjutant General: Alexandre Berthier, Prince of Neuchatel and Wagram

1st Staff of the General Staff
  Adjudant Commandant - Baron Pernet
  Colonel Baron Bongars
  Chef d'escadron Baron Anatole de Montesquiou
  Chef d'escadron Courbon
  Capitaine Beaufremont
  Capitaine Cardon

2nd Staff of the General Staff
  Chief of Staff to Adjutant General: Général de division Count Monthion
  Lieutenant aide de camp - Couthan
  Général de brigade - Guilleminot
  Lieutenant aide de camp - Devitherne

Inspector General of Baggagemasters of the Army: Colonel Lassan
Baggagemaster of the Principal General Quarters: Chef de bataillon Margerin
Baggagemaster of the Lesser General Quarters:

Lieutenant Coignet
Commander of the Gendarmerie, Grand Provost: Général de brigade Lauer
Chief of the Geographical Engineers: Colonel Bonne

General Staff of Artillery
Commander-in-Chief of Artillery: Général de division Sorbier
2nd in Command: Général de division Pernety
Chief of Staff: Général de brigade Nourry
Artillery Park
Director of the Park - Général de brigade Neigre

Pontooneer Train
Commander of the Equipage - Général de division Danthouard

General Staff of Engineers
Commander-in-Chief: Général Rogniat
Chief of Staff: Colonel Montfort

General Staff of Military Equipage
Inspector General of Military Equipage:
Général de brigade Picard

General Administration of the Army
Director of the Administration of the Army: Count Daru
Director General: Count Dumas

ARMÉE DE L'ELBE

I Corps: Maréchal Davout
1st Division: Général de division Philippon
Brigade: Général de brigade Pouchelon
  29th Provisional Regiment
    2/7th Légère Regiment (15/674)
    2/13th Légère Regiment (21/681)
  30th Provisional Regiment
    2/15th Légère Regiment (18/650)
    2/33rd Légère Regiment (12/263)
  31st Provisional Regiment
    2/17th Line Regiment (18/501)
    2/30th Line Regiment (17/729)
  32nd Provisional Regiment
    2/33rd Line Regiment (16/670)
    2/48th Line Regiment (18/537)
  33rd Provisional Regiment
    2/12th Line Regiment (18/527)
    2/21st Line Regiment (20/684)
  34th Provisional Regiment
    2/85th Line Regiment (21/714)
    2/108th Line Regiment (18/709)
  35th Provisional Regiment
    2/25th Line Regiment (17/682)
    2/57th Line Regiment (20/702)
  36th Provisional Regiment
    2/61st Line Regiment (23/669)
    2/111th Line Regiment (20/649)
Artillery:
  7/2nd Foot Artillery (2/100)(6-6pdrs & 2 how)
2nd Division: Général de division Dumonceau
Brigade: Général de brigade Delaage
  29th (bis) Provisional Regiment
    4/7th Légère Regiment (14/784)
    4/13th Légère Regiment (16/716)
  30th (bis) Provisional Regiment
    4/15th Légère Regiment (15/406)
    Det 4/15th Légère Regiment (7/271) (arrived 5/10/13)
    4/33rd Légère Regiment (recruiting suspended)

  31st (bis) Provisional Regiment
    4/17th Line Regiment (12/480)
    Det. 4/17th Line Regiment (7/274) (arrived 5/12/13)
    4/30th Line Regiment (17/521)
    Det. 4/30th Line Regiment (6/274) (arrived 5/3/13)
  32nd (bis) Provisional Regiment
    4/33rd Line Regiment (12/486)
    Det. 4/33rd Line Regiment (6/274) (arrived 5/2/13)
    4/48th Line Regiment (14/489)
    Det. 4/48th Line Regiment (6/274) (arrived 5/3/13)
  33rd (bis) Provisional Regiment
    4/12th Line Regiment (8/480)
    Det. 4/12th Line Regiment (5/271) (arrived 5/2/13)
    4/21st Line Regiment (10/471)
    Det. 4/21st Line Regiment (6/274) (arrived 5/2/13)
  34th (bis) Provisional Regiment
    4/85th Line Regiment (16/506)
    Det. 4/85th Line Regiment (5/258) (arrived 5/2/13)
    4/108th Line Regiment (10/683)
    Det. 4/108th Line Regiment (2/60) (arrived 5/2/13)
  35th (bis) Provisional Regiment
    4/25th Line Regiment (12/722)
    4/57th Line Regiment (10/517)
    Det. 4/57th Line Regiment (6/274) (arrived 5/2/13)
  36th (bis) Provisional Regiment
    4/61st Line Regiment (14/521)
    Det. 4/61st Line Regiment (3/274) (arrived 5/2/13)
    4/111th Line Regiment (16/470)
Artillery:
  5/5th Foot Artillery (1/72)(6-6pdrs & 2 how)
    Det/Train (1/49)
3rd Division: Général de division Thiebault
Brigade: Général de brigade Gengoult
  1/13th Légère Regiment (9/383)
  1/13th Légère Regiment (11/437)•(depot outfitting)
  1/17th Line Regiment (7/241)
  1/17th Line Regiment (11/581)•(depot outfitting)
  1/25th Line Regiment (6/202)
  1/25th Line Regiment (12/620)•(depot outfitting)
  1/48th Line Regiment (3/101)
  1/48th Line Regiment (11/395) (arrived 5/10/13)
  1/48th Line Regiment (4/326)•(depot outfitting)
  1/108th Line Regiment (5/273)
  1/108th Line Regiment (5/275) (arrived 5/10/13)
  1/108th Line Regiment (6/276)•(depot outfitting)
  1/7th Légère Regiment (6/288)
  1/7th Légère Regiment (12/584)•
  1/15th Légère Regiment (20/820)•
  1/12th Line Regiment (20/820)•
  1/21st Line Regiment (20/820)•
  1/30th Line Regiment (20/820)•
  1/33rd Line Regiment (20/820)•
  1/57th Line Regiment (5/274)
  1/57th Line Regiment (15/546)•(depot outfitting)
  1/61st Line Regiment (6/274)
  1/61st Line Regiment (12/548)•(depot outfitting)
  1/85th Line Regiment (14/546)
  1/85th Line Regiment (6/274)•(depot outfitting)
  1/111th Line Regiment (20/820)•
3rd (bis) Division: Général de division Loison
  1st Provisional Demi-brigade
    3/7th Légère Regiment (20/820)†
    3/13th Légère Regiment (20/820)†
    3/15th Légère Regiment (20/820)†
    3/33rd Légère Regiment (recruiting suspended)
  6th Provisional Demi-brigade
    3/12th Line Regiment (20/820)†
    3/21st Line Regiment (20/820)†
    3/17th Line Regiment (20/820)†

7th Provisional Demi-brigade
  3/25th Line Regiment (20/820)†
  3/30th Line Regiment (20/820)†
  3/33rd Line Regiment (20/820)†
8th Provisional Demi-brigade
  3/48th Line Regiment (20/820)†
  3/57th Line Regiment (20/820)†
  3/108th Line Regiment (20/820)†
9th Provisional Demi-brigade
  3/61st Line Regiment (20/820)†
  3/65th Line Regiment (20/820)†
  3/111th Line Regiment (20/820)†
I Corps Cavalry Brigade:
◊Numbers are officers, men, and horses.
  28th Chasseur à Cheval Regiment (4/95/108)
  17th Polish (Lithuanian) Uhlan Regiment (18/250/300)

II Corps: Maréchal Victor (State as of 4/15/13)
4th Division: Général de division Dubreton
1st Brigade: Général de brigade Ferrière
  37th Provisional Line Regiment
    2/24th Légère Regiment (16/650)
    2/26th Légère Regiment (15/620)
  38th Provisional Line Regiment
    2/11th Légère Regiment (18/690)
    2/2nd Line Regiment (23/627)
  39th Provisional Line Regiment
    2/19th Line Regiment (19/695)
    2/37th Line Regiment (20/681)
2nd Brigade: Général de brigade Brun
  40th Provisional Line Regiment
    2/4th Line Regiment (18/660)
    2/56th Line Regiment (18/689)
  41st Provisional Line Regiment
    2/18th Line Regiment (14/701)
    2/46th Line Regiment (18/727)
  42nd Provisional Line Regiment
    2/72nd Line Regiment (18/680)
    2/93rd Line Regiment (18/660)
Artillery:
  11/4th Foot Artillery (2/88)(6-6pdrs & 2 how)

Note:
The II Corps was to consist of the 4th, 5th and 6th
Divisions, but the 5th was with Davout in the 32nd
Military Division and the 6th was still forming in
Wesel. The corps had no staff or services. Victor
had the 1st Division, I Corps under his orders.

5th Division: Général de division Dufour (state as of 4/15/13)
Brigade: Général de brigade Brun
  37th (bis) Provisional Légère Regiment
    4/26th Légère Regiment (11/550)
    Det. 4/26th Légère Regiment (6/237) (arrived 5/12/13)
    4/24th Légère Regiment (14/744)
  38th (bis) Provisional Légère Regiment
    4/11th Légère Regiment (20/819)
    4/2nd Line Regiment (14/479)
    Det. 4/2nd Line Regiment (6/292) (arrived 5/1/13)
  39th (bis) Provisional Line Regiment
    4/19th Line Regiment (7/341)
    Det. 4/19th Line Regiment (5/420) (arrived 5/11/13)
    4/37th Line Regiment (15/486)
  40th (bis) Provisional Line Regiment
    4/56th Line Regiment (9/334)
    Det. 4/56th Line Regiment (4/269) (arrived 5/7/13)
    4/4th Line Regiment (5/346)
    Det. 4/4th Line Regiment (2/141) (arrived 5/7/13)

    Det. 4/4th Line Regiment (3/147) (arrived 5/27/13)
  41st (bis) Provisional Line Regiment
    4/18th Line Regiment (5/454)
    Det. 4/18th Line Regiment (2/272) (arrived 5/9/13)
    4/46th Line Regiment (6/397)
    Det. 4/46th Line Regiment (4/262) (arrived 5/9/13)
  42nd (bis) Provisional Line Regiment
    4/72nd Line Regiment (18/804)
    4/93rd Line Regiment (11/605)
Artillery: Capitaine Ferrary
  12/2nd Foot Artillery (2/59)(6-6pdrs & 2 how)
  Det/Artillery Train (3/56)
6th Division: Général de division Vial
Brigade: Général de brigade Baville
  1/19th Line Regiment (8/197)(arrived 5/2/13)
  1/19th Line Regiment (4/151)(arrived 5/18/13)
  1/19th Line Regiment (6/474)•
  1/46th Line Regiment (8/418)(arrived 5/14/13)
  1/46th Line Regiment (10/404)•
  1/72nd Line Regiment (18/822)
Brigade:
  1/24th Légère Regiment (8/371)
  Det. 1/24th Légère Regiment (10/441) (arrived 5/20/13)
  1/26th Légère Regiment (20/820)
  1/37th Line Regiment (6/252)
  1/37th Line Regiment (12/570)•
  1/56th Line Regiment (20/820)
  1/4th Line Regiment (20/820)
  1/18th Line Regiment (4/275)
  1/18th Line Regiment (12/549)•
  1/93rd Line Regiment (17/258)
  1/93rd Line Regiment (11/564)•
  1/2nd Line Regiment (3/108)
  1/2nd Line Regiment (15/714)•
  1/11th Légère Regiment (20/820) (the conscripts
    for this battalion from Corsica had stopped
    arriving)
6th (bis) Division:
  2nd Provisional Demi-brigade‡
    3/11th Légère Regiment (20/820)
    3/24th Légère Regiment (20/820)
    3/26th Légère Regiment (20/820)
  10th Provisional Demi-brigade‡
    3/2nd Line Regiment (20/820)
    3/19th Line Regiment (20/820)
    3/37th Line Regiment (20/820)
  11th Provisional Demi-brigade‡
    3/56th Line Regiment (20/820)
    3/72nd Line Regiment (20/820)
    3/46th Line Regiment (20/820)
  12th Provisional Demi-brigade‡
    3/4th Line Regiment (20/820)
    3/18th Line Regiment (20/820)
    3/93rd Line Regiment (20/820)
Artillery:
  20/2nd Foot Artillery (2/88)(6-6pdrs & 2 how)

V Corps: Général de division Lauriston
16th Division: Général de division Maison
1st Brigade: Général de brigade Avril
  1/151st Line Regiment (38/240)
  2/151st Line Regiment (19/555)
  3/151st Line Regiment (19/575)
  4/151st Line Regiment (17/476)
2nd Brigade: Général de brigade Fezensac
  1/152nd Line Regiment (20/578)
  2/152nd Line Regiment (20/648)
  3/152nd Line Regiment (21/505)
  4/152nd Line Regiment (surrendered Lüneburg)

3rd Brigade: Général de brigade Penne
  1/153rd Line Regiment (32/730)
  2/153rd Line Regiment (20/685)
  3/153rd Line Regiment (19/656)
  4/153rd Line Regiment (15/715)
  Artillery:
    1/1st Foot Artillery (2/87)(6-6pdrs & 2 how)
    3/1st Foot Artillery (3/96)(6-6pdrs & 2 how)
    Det. 7/1st (bis) Train Battalion (0/32)
    7/2nd Principal Train Battalion (1/102)
    Det. 1/12th Principal Train Battalion (0/63)
    1/6th Sapper Battalion (6/108)
    1/2nd Military Equipage Train Battalion (3/127)
17th Division: Général de division Puthod
Brigade: Général de brigade Vachot
  1/146th Line Regiment (29/687)
  2/146th Line Regiment (14/503)
  3/146th Line Regiment (17/706)
  4/146th Line Regiment (17/640)
  1/147th Line Regiment (20/696)
  2/147th Line Regiment (13/680)
  3/147th Line Regiment (14/659)
  4/147th Line Regiment (14/650)
Brigade: Général de brigade Pastol
  1/148th Line Regiment (22/420)
  2/148th Line Regiment (16/623)
  3/148th Line Regiment (14/720)
  4/148th Line Regiment (14/420)
  Artillery:
    1/5th Foot Artillery (1/78)(6-6pdrs & 2 how)
    11/5th Foot Artillery (3/103)(6-6pdrs & 2 how)
    Det. 7/11th & 1/11th Principal Train Battalion (1/140)
    2/6th Sapper Battalion (3/114)
    2/2nd Military Equipage Train Battalion (3/127)
18th Division: Général de division Lagrange
1st Brigade: Général de brigade Charrière
  1/134th Line Regiment (25/802)
  2/134th Line Regiment (25/797)
  1/154th Line Regiment (21/405)
  2/154th Line Regiment (16/366)
  3/154th Line Regiment (19/644)
  4/154th Line Regiment (17/632)
2nd Brigade: Général de brigade Suden
  1/155th Line Regiment (31/558)
  2/155th Line Regiment (16/388)
  3/155th Line Regiment (16/456)
  4/155th Line Regiment (16/578)
  1/3rd Foreign Regiment (Irish Legion)(24/600)
  2/3rd Foreign Regiment (Irish Legion)(21/604)
  Artillery:
    10/1st Foot Artillery (3/100)(6-6pdrs & 2 how)
    12/1st Foot Artillery (2/96)(6-6pdrs & 2 how)
    4/8th (bis) Train Battalion (1/105)
    Det. 4/1st (bis) Train Battalion (0/32)
    3/6th Sapper Battalion (3/103)
    3/2nd Military Equipage Train Battalion (3/127)
19th Division: Général de division Rochambeau
1st Brigade: Général de brigade Longchamp
  1/135th Line Regiment (27/552)
  2/135th Line Regiment (16/703)
  3/135th Line Regiment (15/604)
  4/135th Line Regiment (12/585)
2nd Brigade: Général de brigade Lacrois
  1/149th Line Regiment (39/486)
  2/149th Line Regiment (15/581)
  3/149th Line Regiment (14/644)
  4/149th Line Regiment (13/714)
3rd Brigade: Général de brigade Lafitte
  1/150th Line Regiment (31/637)

  2/150th Line Regiment (14/609)
  3/150th Line Regiment (13/728)
  4/150th Line Regiment (16/755)
  Artillery:
    12/5th Foot Artillery (2/100)(6-6pdrs & 2 how)
    17/5th Foot Artillery (2/97)(6-6pdrs & 2 how)
    4/4th Principal Train Battalion (1/123)
    Det. 1/12th Principal Train Battalion (1/68)
    4/6th Sapper Battalion (3/107)
    4/2nd Military Equipage Train Battalion (3/127)
Reserve & Park: Colonel Levasseur
  15/1st Foot Artillery (3/99)
  16/1st Foot Artillery (3/95)
  17/1st Foot Artillery (1/92)
  2/5th Horse Artillery (3/81)
  7/6th Horse Artillery (3/81)
  Det. 7/1st (bis) Train Battalion (0/62)
  Det. 7/2nd (bis) Train Battalion (0/20)
  Det. 1/12th (bis) Train Battalion (0/30)
  Det. 1/11th (bis) Train Battalion (0/34)
  Det. 4/4th Principal Train Battalion (0/12)
  Det. 4/8th (bis) Train Battalion (0/24)
  7/3rd Principal Train Battalion (1/130)
  7/9th Principal Train Battalion (1/126)
  4/9th (bis) Train Battalion (1/134)
  Det. 4/11th (bis) Train Battalion (0/77)
  Det. 4/14th Principal Train Battalion (1/72)
  4/2nd Sapper Battalion (3/121)
  5/2nd Military Equipage Train Battalion (3/127)
Troops en route to V Corps:
  135th Line Regiment (1/143)
  155th Line Regiment (2/204)
  149th Line Regiment (2/272)
  151st Line Regiment (1/103)

VII Corps: Général de division Reynier (State as of 4/1/13)

32nd Division: Général Durutte
1st Brigade: Général de brigade Devaux
  1/35th Légère Regiment (11/28)(en route to Verona)
  1/35th Légère Regiment (0/720)(in Verona)
  2/35th Légère Regiment (15/144)(in Gera)
  3/35th Légère Regiment (20/820) (en route Ratisbonne)
  4/35th Légère Regiment (20/822)(in Antibes)
  2/36th Légère Regiment (21/230)(in Gera)
  3/36th Légère Regiment (11/37)(en route to Verona)
  3/36th Légère Regiment (0/720)(in Verona)
  4/36th Légère Regiment (18/626)(provisionally assigned to 21st Division, VI Corps)
2nd Brigade: Général de brigade Jarry
  2/131st Line Regiment (14/267)(in Gera)
  3/131st Line Regiment (14/54)(en route to Verona)
  3/131st Line Regiment (0/720)(in Verona)
  4/131st Line Regiment (16/763)(provisionally assigned to 21st Division, VI Corps)
  2/132nd Line Regiment (11/90)(in Gera)
  3/132nd Line Regiment (10/23)(en route to Verona)
  3/132nd Line Regiment (0/720)(in Verona)
  4/132nd Line Regiment 17/647)(provisionally assigned to 21st Division, VI Corps)
3rd Brigade: Général de brigade Brayer
  1/133rd Line Regiment (in Modlin garrison)
  2/133rd Line Regiment (20/131)(in Gera)
  3/133rd Line Regiment (14/36)(en route to Verona)
  3/133rd Line Regiment (0/720)(in Verona)
  4/133rd Line Regiment (18/820)(provisionally assigned to 21st Division, VI Corps)
  2/Würzburg Regiment (18/703)(provisionally assigned to 21st Division, VI Corps)

3/Würzburg Regiment (17/702)(provisionally assigned to 21st Division, VI Corps)
4/Würzburg Regiment (in Modlin garrison)
Artillery:
22/1st Foot Artillery (2/14)
6/5th Foot Artillery (3/34)
4/9th Foot Artillery (3/19)
2/,3/,4/9th (bis) Train Battalion (2/104)
Note: On 1 May this division was reinforced by the 3,648 men who marched with Bonnet's division of the VI Corps, the 4/36th Légère, 4/131st, 4/132nd, 4/133rd Line and 2/,3/Würzburg.

VIII (Polish) Corps:
No state received by archives.
Dombrowski's Corps: Général de division Dombrowski
2nd Polish Line Regiment (58/733)
14th Polish Line Regiment (56/641)
2nd Polish Uhlan Regiment (49/1,050/907)
4th Polish Chasseur à Cheval Regiment (48/1,050/705)
Polish Horse Battery (5/87)(6 guns)
Polish Train (1/32)

XI Corps: Maréchal Macdonald (State as of 4/15/13)
31st Division: Général de division Ledru
Brigadiers: Généraux de brigade Labassée, Schobert, Bardet and Fressinet
10th Provisional Demi-brigade (91/2,316)
  4/27th Line Regiment
  4/63rd Line Regiment
  4/76th Line Regiment
  4/96th Line Regiment
11th Provisional Demi-brigade
  4/27th Légère Regiment (19/682)
  4/50th Line Regiment (20/524)
12th Provisional Demi-brigade (49/1,950)
  3/123rd Line Regiment
  4/124th Line Regiment
  4/134th Line Regiment
13th Provisional Demi-brigade
  4/5th Line Regiment (19/691)
  4/11th Line Regiment (20/639)
  4/79th Line Regiment (20/690)
  3/3rd Line Regiment (11/352)
  3/105th Line Regiment (17/282)
  3/127th Line Regiment (11/187)
  1/,2/Neapolitan Elite Regiment (31/625)
  Neapolitan Marines (1 co)(2/60)
`Artillery:
  16/5th Foot Artillery (3/114)(6-6pdrs & 2 how)
  1st Neapolitan Horse Battery (5/54)
  Det/8th Principal Train Batatlion (1/86)
  Det/12th Principal Train Batatlion (1/39)
35th Division: Général de division Gerard
1st Brigade: Général de brigade Sénécal
  3/6th Line Regiment (26/642)
  4/6th Line Regiment (14/661)
  Artillery Co./6th Line Regiment (2/55)
  1/112th Line Regiment (27/701)
  2/112th Line Regiment (15/648)
  3/112th Line Regiment (17/721)
  4/112th Line Regiment (17/755)
  Artillery Co./112th Line Regiment (3/60)
2nd Brigade: Général de brigade Zucchi
  3/2nd Italian Légère Regiment (25/612)
  4/2nd Italian Légère Regiment (17/648)
  Artillery Co./2nd Italian Légère Regiment (2/55)
  1/5th Italian Line Regiment (35/758)
  2/5th Italian Line Regiment (17/717)

3/5th Italian Line Regiment (18/704)
4/5th Italian Line Regiment (18/707)
Artillery Co./5th Italian Line Regiment (2/56)
Cavalry:
1/4th Italian Chasseur à Cheval Regiment (16/285/319)
1/Würzburg Jäger zu Pferd Regiment (8/131/158)
Artillery: Chef de bataillon Pron
6/1st Foot Artillery (3/91)
20/5th Foot Artillery (3/104)
3rd Italian Horse Battery (4/92)
19th Italian Train Company (4/188)
9th Italian Sapper Company (3/62)
36th Division: Général de division Charpentier
1st Brigade: Général de brigade Simmer
  3/14th Légère Regiment (26/646)
  4/14th Légère Regiment (18/678)
  Artillery Co./14th Légère Regiment (2/60)
  1/22nd Légère Regiment (29/654)
  2/22nd Légère Regiment (17/663)
  3/22nd Légère Regiment (16/634)
  4/22nd Légère Regiment (17/675)
  Artillery Co./22nd Légère Regiment (2/60)
2nd Brigade: Général de brigade Meunier
  14th Provisional Demi-brigade
    6/10th Line Regiment (23/737)
    6/20th Line Regiment (16/763)
    3/67th Line Regiment (16/787)
  15th Provisional Demi-brigade
    4/3rd Légère Regiment (22/679)
    4/102nd Line Regiment (16/766)
    Artillery Co./102nd Line Regiment (2/60)
Artillery:
  5/1st Foot Artillery (2/77)(6-6pdrs& 2 how)
  19/2nd Foot Artillery (3/93)(6-6pdrs& 2 how)
  Det/7th Principal Train Battalion (1/95)
  2/12th Principal Train Battalion (1/134)
Reserve & Park:
  3rd Italian Pontooneer Company (2/50)
  7/5th Sapper Battalion (3/64)
  1/7th Sapper Battalion (3/47)
  2/7th Sapper Battalion (3/47)
  Det/12th Military Equipage Battalion (7/179)
Troops en route to XI Corps:
  50th Line Regiment (2/276)(arrived 5/3/13)(in Mainz)
  27th Légère Regiment (1/64)(arrived 5/3/13)(in Mainz)
  27th Légère Regiment (1/143)(arrived 5/13/13)(in Mainz)
  50th Line Regiment (1/131)(arrived 5/25/13)(in Mainz)
37th Division: Generallieutenant Hammerstein
Brigade: (Forming. strengths are goals, not actual)
  1/,2/2nd Westphalian Line Regiment (30/1,650)(in Cassel)
  1/,2/3rd Westphalian Line Regiment (30/1,650)(Magdeburg)
  Det. 4th Westphalian Line Regiment (6/544) (en route to Custrin)
  Det. 5th Westphalian Line Regiment (6/544) (en route to Custrin)
  1/,2/1st Westphalian Line Regiment (in Danzig)(no return)
  1/,2/4th Westphalian Line Regiment (Custrin)(no return)
  1/,2/5th Westphalian Line Regiment (Custrin)(no return)
  2nd Westphalian Light Battalion (20/820)(in Cassel)
  4th Westphalian Light Battalion (20/820)(in Cassel)
Cavalry Brigade: (60/1,440)
  1/,2/,3/,4/Westphalian Chevauleger-lancier de la Garde Regiment
  1/,2/,3/1st & 1/,2/,3/2nd Westphalian Hussar Regiments
Artillery:
  2 Batteries (10/410)
40th Division Général de brigade Bronikowski (State as of

312

4/15/13)
  1st Vistula Regiment (25/162)(in Spandau)
  2nd Vistula Regiment (28/126)(in Spandau)
  3rd Vistula Regiment (23/152)(in Spandau)
  Det/4th Vistula Regiment (3/352)(in Spandau)
  4th Vistula Regiment (48/967)(in Wittemberg)
  4th Polish Line Regiment (3/352)(in Spandau)
  Det/4th Polish Line Regiment (8/131)(in Magdeburg)
  7th Polish Line Regiment (24/206)(in Spandau)
  Det/7th Polish Line Regiment (10/103) (in Magdeburg)
  9th Polish Line Regiment (33/362)(in Spandau)
  Det/9th Polish Line Regiment (8/118) (in Halberstadt)

I Cavalry Corps: Général de division Latour-Maubourg
1st Light Division: Général de division Bruyère
1st Brigade: Général de brigade Bessières
  7th Hussar Regiment (7/109/125)#
  9th Chevauléger-lancier Regiment (1/19/21)
  8th Hussar Regiment (6/61/69)
  16th Chasseur à Cheval Regiment (7/124/138)
2nd Brigade: Général de brigade Cambracéres
  1st Chevauléger-lancier Regiment (4/133/142)
  3rd Chevauléger-lancier Regiment (2/66/72)
  5th Chevauléger-lancier Regiment (2/23/28)
  8th Chevauléger-lancier Regiment (unknown)
3rd Light Division: Général de division Chastel
1st Brigade: Général de brigade Van Merlen
  1st Chasseur à Cheval Regiment (7/153/165)
  25th Chasseur à Cheval Regiment (4/104/113)
  6th Hussar Regiment (6/180/197)
  8th Chasseur à Cheval Regiment (5/90/94)
2nd Brigade: Général de brigade Vallin
  9th Chasseur à Cheval Regiment (3/64/70)
  19th Chasseur à Cheval Regiment (4/122/130)
  2nd & 3rd Italian Chasseur à Cheval Regiments (7/96/107)
  1st Chasseur à Cheval Regiment (6/149/163)
  2nd Chasseur à Cheval Regiment (2/94/98)
  3rd Chasseur à Cheval Regiment (1/53/55)
1st Cuirassier Division: Général de division Bordesoulle
1st Brigade: Général de brigade Berkheim
  2nd Cuirassier Regiment (6/150/167)
  3rd Cuirassier Regiment (4/113/126)
  6th Cuirassier Regiment (7/103/115)
2nd Brigade: Général de brigade Quinette
  9th Cuirassier Regiment (4/184/194)
  11th Cuirassier Regiment (5/138/146)
  12th Cuirassier Regiment (8/83/90)
3rd Cuirassier Division: Général de division Doumerc
1st Brigade: Général de brigade Daudenaerde
  4th Cuirassier Regiment (3/44/52)
  7th Cuirassier Regiment (3/58/64)
  14th Cuirassier Regiment (1/23/26)
2nd Brigade: Général de brigade Reiset
  7th Dragoon Regiment (unknown)
  23rd Dragoon Regiment (unknown)
  28th Dragoon Regiment (unknown)
  30th Dragoon Regiment (unknown)
  Provisional Dragoon Regiment (unknown)
Artillery:
  3/1st Horse Artillery (3/81)(4-6pdrs & 2 how)
  1/6th Horse Artillery (3/87)(4-6pdrs & 2 how)
  Det/1st (bis) Train Battalion (1/60)
  Det/8th (bis) Train Battalion (1/53)

II Cavalry Corps: Général de division Sébastiani
2nd Light Cavalry Division: Général de division Roussel d'Hurbal

Brigade: Général de brigade Gérard
  11th Chasseur à Cheval Regiment (8/142/150)
  12th Chasseur à Cheval Regiment (7/215/223)
  5th Hussar Regiment (6/145/158)
Brigade: Général de brigade Montbrun
  9th Hussar Regiment (10/364/384)
  2nd Chevauléger-lancier Regiment (4/118/126)
  4th Chevauléger-lancier Regiment (7/89/104)
4th Light Cavalry Division: Général de division Exelmans
Brigade: Général de brigade Maurin
  6th Chevauléger-lancier Regiment (0/27/27)
  4th Chasseur à Cheval Regiment (9/168/165)
  7th Chasseur à Cheval Regiment (13/182/217)
Brigade: Général de brigade Beurmann
  20th Chasseur à Cheval Regiment (10/275/300)
  11th Hussar Regiment (5/111/122)
  23rd Chasseur à Cheval Regiment (11/294/312)
  24th Chasseur à Cheval Regiment (9/199/217)#
2nd Cuirassier Division: Général de division Wathier
Brigade: Général de brigade Bouvier des Eclats
  1st Carabinier Regiment (7/113/126)
  2nd Carabinier Regiment (6/97/109)
  1st Cuirassier Regiment (6/107/131)
Brigade: Général de brigade Poinsot
  5th Cuirassier Regiment (14/234/282)
  9th Cuirassier Regiment (6/104/120)
  10th Cuirassier Regiment (7/127/143)
Corps Artillery:
  7/1st Horse Artillery (3/78)(4-6pdrs & 2 how)
  Det/11th (bis) Train Battalion (1/45)

ARMÉE DE MEIN
  Commanding General: Maréchal Soult
  Commander of Infantry: Maréchal Mortier
  Commander of Cavalry: Maréchal Bessieres
  Commander of Artillery: Général Comte Dulauloy
  Commander of Engineers: Général Kirgener

III Corps: Maréchal Ney
8th Division: Général de division Souham
1st Brigade: Général de brigade Chemineau
  6th Provisional Légère Regiment
    2/6th Légère Regiment (17/892)
    3/25th Légère Regiment (19/770)
  10th Provisional Légère Regiment
    3/16th Légère Regiment (16/731)
    1/28th Légère Regiment (20/820)
  14th Provisional Line Regiment
    4/34th Line Regiment (19/777)
    3/40th Line Regiment (20/781)
  19th Provisional Line Regiment
    6/32nd Line Regiment (17/673)
    2/58th Line Regiment (20/585)
2nd Brigade: Général de brigade Chasseraux
  21st Provisional Line Regiment
    3/59th Line Regiment (10/760)
    4/69th Line Regiment (22/812)
  24th Provisional Line Regiment
    3/88th Line Regiment (20/758)
    3/103rd Line Regiment (14/797)
  1/22nd Line Regiment (24/797)
  3/22nd Line Regiment (20/781)
  4/22nd Line Regiment (19/743)
  6/22nd Line Regiment (16/767)
  Provisional Regiment
    2/127th Line Regiment (18/337)
    2/128th Line Regiment (24/562)
    2/129th Line Regiment (17/314)
Artillery: Chef de bataillon Leclerc

9/2nd Foot Artillery (2/72)(6-6pdrs & 2 how)
10/2nd Foot Artillery (2/78)(6-6pdrs & 2 how)
Det. 4/3rd (bis) Train Battalion (1/95)
Det. 4/8th Principal Train Battalion (0/87)
1/Spanish Sapper Battalion (3/184)
1/6th Equipage Train (2/117)

9th Division: Général de division Brenier
1st Brigade: Général de brigade Grillot
  2nd Provisional Légère Regiment
    3/2nd Légère Regiment (18/582)
    3/4th Légère Regiment (17/595)
  1/29th Légère Regiment (19/659)
  2/29th Légère Regiment (16/924)(Erfurt 19 May)
  1/136th Line Regiment (27/720)
  2/136th Line Regiment (16/663)
  3/136th Line Regiment (17/704)
  4/136th Line Regiment (17/622)
2nd Brigade: Général de brigade Godard
  1/138th Line Regiment (26/453)
  2/138th Line Regiment (18/549)
  3/138th Line Regiment (20/584)
  4/138th Line Regiment (22/493)
  1/145th Line Regiment (29/500)
  2/145th Line Regiment (24/529)
  3/145th Line Regiment (18/406)
  4/145th Line Regiment (21/490)
Artillery: Chef de bataillon Charvet
  2/9th Foot Artillery (2/82)(6-6pdrs & 2 how)
  11/9th Foot Artillery (2/81)(6-6pdrs & 2 how)
  Det. 4/3rd (bis) Principal Train Battalion (0/42)
  Det. 4/12th Principal Train Battalion (0/9)
  4/6th Principal Train Battalion (1/135)
  2/Spanish Sapper Battalion (2/163)
  2/6th Military Equipage Battalion (2/127)

10th Division: Général de division Girard
1st Brigade: Général de brigade Goris
  4th Provisional Légère Regiment
    4/5th Légère Regiment (17/604)
    4/12th Légère Regiment (21/408)
  1/139th Line Regiment (28/647)
  2/139th Line Regiment (24/631)
  3/139th Line Regiment (23/510)
  4/139th Line Regiment (23/565)
2nd Brigade: Général de brigade Van Dedem
  1/140th Line Regiment (30/637)
  2/140th Line Regiment (17/585)
  3/140th Line Regiment (15/659)
  4/140th Line Regiment (16/656)
  1/141st Line Regiment (21/450)
  2/141st Line Regiment (22/507)
  3/141st Line Regiment (17/476)
  4/141st Line Regiment (19/490)
Artillery: Chef de bataillon Tripp
  3/7th Foot Artillery (3/81)(6-6pdrs & 2 how)
  4/7th Foot Artillery (2/89)(6-6pdrs & 2 how)
  4/1st Principal Train Battalion (1/136)
  Det. 7/11th Principal Train Battalion (1/52)
  3/Spanish Sapper Battalion (3/178)
  3/6th Military Equipage Battalion (3/127)

11th Division: Général de division Ricard
1st Brigade: Général de brigade Tarayre
  3/,4/9th Légère Regiment (27/1,218)
  17th Provisional Line Regiment (33/1,376)
    4/43rd Line Regiment
    3/75th Line Regiment
  18th Provisional Line Regiment (29/1,139)
    3/50th Line Regiment
    3/65th Line Regiment
2nd Brigade: Général de brigade Bertrand

1/,2/,3/,4/142nd Line Regiment (89/2,008)
1/,2/,3/,4/144th Line Regiment (94/1,940)
Artillery: Chef de bataillon Ricard
  18/1st Foot Artillery (6-6pdr & 2 how)(1/86)
  19/7th Foot Artillery (6-6pdr & 2 how)(1/87)
  Det. 7/11th Principal Train Battalion (0/44)
  Det. 7/12th Principal Train Battalion (0/18)
  4/13th (bis) Train Battalion (1/132)
  4/Spanish Sapper Battalion (2/181)
  4/6th Military Equipage Battalion ((3/127)

Detachment 38th Division: Général de division Marchand
  1/7th Württemberg Line Regiment (19/567)
  2/7th Württemberg Line Regiment (16/564)

39th Division: Général de division Marchand
Brigade: Generalmajor Stockhorn
  1/1st Baden Line Regiment (15/595)
  2/1st Baden Line Regiment (14/664)
  1/3rd Baden Line Regiment (15/829)
  2/3rd Baden Line Regiment (14/829)
2nd Brigade: Generalmajor Prinz Emil von Hessen
  1/1st Hessian Light Regiment (9/657)
  2/1st Hessian Light Regiment (10/658)
  1/2nd Hessian Line Regiment (22/624)
  2/2nd Hessian Line Regiment (15/618)
  1/,2/Guard Infantry Regiment (20/1,250)
Brigade:
  1/Frankfurt "Zweyer" Regiment ((16/676)
Artillery:
  Baden Foot Battery (2/67)(4 guns)
  Baden Artillery Train (1/60)
  Hessian Foot Battery (1/119))(3 guns)

III Corps Light Cavalry Division: Général de division Kellerman
23rd Light Cavalry Brigade: Général de brigade Laboissière
  1-3/10th Hussar Regiment (32/685/765)
  4/10th Hussar Regiment (10/309/325)(arrived 4/28/13)
  5/10th Hussar Regiment (2/118/122)(arrived 5/1/13)
  5/10th Hussar Regiment (4/126/135) (arrived 5/13/13)
  6/10th Hussar Regiment (10/240/255) (arrived 5/15/13)
  1/,2/,3/,4/Hessian Light Dragoon Regiment (30/470/530)
  1/,2/,3/Baden Dragoon Regiment (26/474/530)
24th (Württemberg) Light Cavalry Brigade:
  (strengths are ordered strength, not actual.)
  Leib-Kavallerie Regiment #2 (4)(30/470/530)
  Prinz Herzog Louis Jäger zu Pferd Regiment #3 (4)(30/470/530)
  König Jäger Regiment #4 (4)(30/470/530)
  Prinz Adam Jäger Regiment #1 (4)(30/470/530)

Reserve and Park: Major Tamissier
  6/3rd Foot Artillery (2/84)
  23/3rd Foot Artillery (2/82)
  24/3rd Foot Artillery (2/82)
  7/9th Foot Artillery (2/79)
  8/9th Foot Artillery (2/88)
  17/9th Foot Artillery (1/80)
  1/3rd Horse Artillery (2/76)
  3/4th Horse Artillery (2/76)
  Det. 4/6th (bis) Train Battalion (1/72)
  Det. 4/6th (bis) Train Battalion (0/63)
  3/10th Principal Train Battalion (1/95)
  Det. 4/3rd Principal Train Battalion (0/5)
  5/9th Principal Train Battalion (1/106)
  2/2nd Sapper Battalion (3/141)
  3/5th Sapper Battalion (2/143)
  5th Engineering Train Company (2/103)
  5/6th Military Equipage Train Battalion (3/127)
Troops en route to III Corps:
  1st Bataillon de marche

Det/6th Légère Regiment (2/223)
Det/65th Line Regiment (2/64)
Miscellaneous infantry (2/372)
138th Line Regiment (0/228)
140th Line Regiment (0/485)
144th Line Regiment (0/116)
145th Line Regiment (3/592)
142nd Line Regiment (2/337)(arrived 5/29/13)(Mainz)
16th Légère Regiment (4/170)(arrived 5/17/13)(Mainz)
145th Line Regiment (1/97) (arrived 5/25/13)(Mainz)
58th Line Regiment (2/131)(arrived 5/25/13)(Mainz)
88th Line Regiment (0/48) (arrived 5/25/13)(Mainz)
40th Line Regiment (1/52) (arrived 5/17/13)(Eisenach)
69th Line Regiment (2/117)(arrived 5/17/13)(Eisenach)
103rd Line Regiment (1/40)(Mainz)
9th Légère Regiment (1/50)(Mainz)
75th Line Regiment (1/71) (arrived 5/22/13)(Mainz)
6th Légère Regiment (4/238)(arrived 5/27/13)(Mainz)
2nd Légère Regiment (3/137)(arrived 5/16/13)(Mainz)
4th Légère Regiment (2/125)(arrived 5/15/13)(Mainz)
16th Légère Regiment (1/69) (arrived 5/17/13)(Mainz)
25th Légère Regiment (1/36) (arrived 5/17/13)(Eisenach)
59th Line Regiment (3/392)(arrived 4/29/13)(Mainz)
65th Line Regiment (0/31) (arrived 5/20/13)(Mainz)
29th Légère Regiment (0/107)(arrived 5/5/13)(Mainz)
6th Légère Regiment (1/40) (arrived 5/5/13)(Mainz)
28th Légère Regiment (2/153)(arrived 5/1/13)(Mainz)
48th Line Regiment (1/55) (arrived 5/29/13)(Mainz)

IV Corps: Général de division Comte Bertrand
12th Division: Général de division Morand
1st Brigade: Général de brigade Bellair
1/13th Line Regiment (35/777)
2/13th Line Regiment (16/758)
3/13th Line Regiment (17/765)
4/13th Line Regiment (17/739)
6/13th Line Regiment (18/739)
Artillery Det./13th Line Regiment (2/66)(2-3pdrs)
3rd Provisional Line Regiment
3/3rd Légère Regiment (21/640)
4/8th Line Regiment (15/661)
2nd Brigade: Général de brigade Nagel
2nd Provisional Croatian Regiment
2/3rd Croatian Regiment (27/794)
1/4th Croatian Regiment (18/839)
1/23rd Line Regiment (23/753)
2/23rd Line Regiment (9/777)
4/23rd Line Regiment (10/764)
6/23rd Line Regiment (10/776)
Artillery Det./23rd Line Regiment (1/65)(2-3pdrs)
Artillery:
1/2nd Foot Artillery (2/88)(6-6pdrs & 2 how)
3/2nd Foot Artillery (3/87)(6-6pdrs & 2 how)
1/7th (bis) Train Battalion (1/117)
2/7th (bis) Train Battalion (0/49)
1/9th Military Equipage Company (2/127)
15th Division: Général de division Peyri
1st Brigade: Général de brigade Martel
3/1st Italian Line Regiment (26/735)
4/1st Italian Line Regiment (18/808)
Artillery Det./1st Italian Line Regiment (1/13) (2-3pdrs)
1/4th Italian Line Regiment (19/619)
2/4th Italian Line Regiment (17/545)
3/4th Italian Line Regiment (19/627)
4/4th Italian Line Regiment (17/633)
Artillery Det./4th Italian Line Regiment (3/64) (2-3pdrs)
2nd Brigade: Général de brigade St. Andrea
2/1st Italian Légère Regiment (25/820)
3/1st Italian Légère Regiment (15/820)

4/1st Italian Légère Regiment (15/820) (regiment in Augsburg 6/1/13)
Artillery Det./1st Italian Légère Regiment (2/78) (2-3pdrs)
3/6th Italian Line Regiment (24/805)
4/6th Italian Line Regiment (18/797)
Artillery Det./6th Italian Line Regiment (3/67) (2-3pdrs)
1/Milan Guard Battalion (21/805)
1/7th Italian Line Regiment (30/716)
2/7th Italian Line Regiment (16/612)
3/7th Italian Line Regiment (14/654)
4/7th Italian Line Regiment (17/658)
Artillery Det./7th Italian Line Regiment (1/27) (2-3pdrs)
Artillery: (20 guns)
1st Italian Foot Artillery Company (4/117)
13th Italian Foot Artillery Company (5/107)
5th Italian Train Company (3/140)
6th Italian Train Company (2/141)
8th Italian Sapper Company (3/115)
3rd Italian Naval Artisan Company (2/95)
2nd Italian Sailor Company (3/109)
5th Italian Military Equipage Company (2/126)
Cavalry Division: Général de division Fresia
Brigade: Général de brigade Briche
1/19th Chasseur à Cheval Regiment (en route & organizing)
2/19th Chasseur à Cheval Regiment (8/250) (arrived Augsburg 10 June)
3/19th Chasseur à Cheval Regiment (4/246/254) (en route, arrived Augsburg 4/23)
4/19th Chasseur à Cheval Regiment (4/256/260) (arrived Augsburg 17 May)
5/19th Chasseur à Cheval Regiment (8/242/260) (to depart 1 June, equipping)
6/19th Chasseur à Cheval Regiment (8/242/260) (to depart 10 June, organizing)
Croatian Hussar Regiment (50/1,450/1,500) (assigned, organizing, and never arrived)
Brigade: Général de brigade Stedmann
1/13th Hussar Regiment (8/207)(in Florence 3 June)
2/13th Hussar Regiment (8/248)(departed 5 June)
3/13th Hussar Regiment (8/200)(Augsburg 20 June)
4/13th Hussar Regiment (6/200)(Augsburg 30 June)
1/14th Hussar Regiment (10/235/256)(Augsburg 4 June)
2/14th Hussar Regiment (5/225/220)(Augsburg 4 June)
3/14th Hussar Regiment (8/209)(Augsburg 24 June)
4/14th Hussar Regiment (7/206)(Augsburg 24 June)
1/,2/,3/,4/2nd Italian Chasseur à Cheval Regiment (30/870/950)(Augsburg 6/1)
Brigade: Général de brigade Jacquet
1/Napoleon Dragoon Regiment (11/234/253)
2/Napoleon Dragoon Regiment (6/216/238)
3/Napoleon Dragoon Regiment (6/219/237)
4/Napoleon Dragoon Regiment (5/216/235)
1/1st Italian Chasseur à Cheval Regiment (17/233/276)
2/1st Italian Chasseur à Cheval Regiment (5/180/196)
3/1st Italian Chasseur à Cheval Regiment (7/228/240)
4/1st Italian Chasseur à Cheval Regiment (5/217/224)
1/2nd Neapolitan Chasseur à Cheval Regiment (13/247/276)
2/2nd Neapolitan Chasseur à Cheval Regiment (7/244/258)(arrived Augsburg 9 June)
3/2nd Neapolitan Chasseur à Cheval Regiment (8/222/236)(arrived Augsburg 9 June)
4/2nd Neapolitan Chasseur à Cheval Regiment (6/212/225)
Artillery: Chef de bataillon Pont
8/4th Horse Artillery (5/79)(4-6pdrs & 2 How)
Det. 5/7th (bis) Train Battalion (1/49)
4th Italian Horse Artillery (0/100)

6th Italian Train Company (1/147)
Corps Artillery: Colonel Menoire
26/2nd Foot Artillery (3/81)
Det. 2/7th (bis) Train Battalion (1/24)
6/7th (bis) Train Battalion (1/26)
7/7th (bis) Train Battalion (1/129)
7th (bis) Train Battalion (0/300)
13th Artillery Artisan Company (1/29)
2/1st Sapper Battalion (2/148)
8/1st Sapper Battalion (1/115)
3/3rd Sapper Battalion (2/148)
Det/Engineering Equipage Train (1/33)
2/9th Military Equipage Battalion (2/127)
3/9th Military Equipage Battalion (2/118)
4/9th Military Equipage Battalion (2/115)
5/9th Military Equipage Battalion (2/125)
6/9th Military Equipage Battalion (2/107)
Troops en route to IV Corps:
  Ship's garrison, 13th Line Regiment (0/90)
  Troops from Italian depots (0/914)(Augsburg May 17)
  Bataillon de marche (Augsburg May 14)
    23rd Line Regiment (1/27)
    3rd Légère Regiment (0/56)
    8th Légère Regiment (0/5)
  Det/13th Line Regiment (2/180)
  Italian Bataillon de marche
    2nd Légère Regiment (3/144)
    1st Line Regiment (3/148)
    4th Line Regiment (3/201)
    5th Line Regiment (2/196)
    6th Line Regiment (1/95)
    7th Line Regiment (2/201)

VI Corps: Maréchal Marmont
20th Division: Général de division Compans
1st Brigade: Général de brigade Cacault
  1/,2/,3/,4/1st Marine Artillery Regiment (79/3,269)
  Cadre 5/1st Marine Artillery Regiment (16/110)
  Cadre 6/1st Marine Artillery Regiment (16/106) (both
  cadres in Mainz)
  1/,2/,3rd Marine Artillery Regiment (27/1,367)
  Cadre/3rd Marine Artillery Regiment (9/106) (in Mainz)
2nd Brigade: Général de brigade Joubert
  25th Provisional Line Regiment
    3/47th Line Regiment (15/680)
    4/86th Line Regiment (9/487)
    Det. 4/86th Line Regiment (6/214) (arrived in Mainz 6/
    1/13)
  20th Provisional Line Regiment
    5/66th Line Regiment (11/710)
    Det. 5/66th Line Regiment (1/37) (arrived Mainz 5/20/
    13)
    3/122nd Line Regiment (12/541)
    Det. 3/122nd Line Regiment (3/124) (arrived in Mainz
    on 6/7/13)
    2/32nd Légère Regiment (18/524)
    3/32nd Légère Regiment (11/670)
Artillery: Chef de bataillon Grosjean
  1/4th Foot Artillery (6-6pdrs & 2 how)(2/61)
  10/4th Foot Artillery (6-6pdrs & 2 how)(2/113)
  1/10th (bis) Train Battalion (1/85)
  6/2nd Sapper Battalion (2/108)
  1/15th Equipage Battalion (3/127)
21st Division: Général de division Bonnet
1st Brigade: Général de brigade Desailly
  1/,2/,3/,4/,5/,6/2nd Marine Artillery Regiment (91/
  3,169)
  Cadre 7/2nd Marine Artillery Regiment (15/107)
  Cadre 8/2nd Marine Artillery Regiment (13/110) (both

  cadres were in Mainz organizing)
  1/,2/4th Marine Artillery Regiment (33/1,400)
  3/4th Marine Artillery Regiment (10/730) (arrived 5/17/
  13)
2nd Brigade: Général de brigade Beaudouin
  1/37th Légère Regiment (15/801)
  2/37th Légère Regiment (14/807)
  3/37th Légère Regiment (15/789)
  4/37th Légère Regiment (16/797)
  1/Joseph Napoleon Regiment (14/754)
Provisional Brigade: Général de brigade Brayer
  4/36th Légère Regiment (18/626)
  4/131st Line Regiment (18/763)
  4/132nd Line Regiment (17/647)
  4/133rd Line Regiment (18/820)
  2/,3/Würzburg Regiment (35/1,405)
Artillery: Chef de bataillon Malavillers
  14/4th Foot Artillery (6-6pdrs & 2 how)(2/83)
  21/7th Foot Artillery (6-6pdrs & 2 how)(2/90)
  4/4th (bis) Train Battalion (1/108)
  7/12th Principal Train Battalion (1/85)
  9/4th Sapper Battalion (2/108)
  2/15th Equipage Train Battalion (3/127)
22nd Division: Général de division Friederichs
Brigade: Généraux de brigade Ficatier & Buquet
  3/23rd Légère Regiment (12/621)
  4/23rd Légère Regiment (9/657)
  11th Provisional Line Regiment
    4/1st Line Regiment (12/532)
    2/62nd Line Regiment (8/467)
  13th Provisional Line Regiment
    3/14th Line Regiment (18/709)
    4/16th Line Regiment (13/687)
  16th Provisional Line Regiment
    6/26th Line Regiment (18/592)
    6/82nd Line Regiment (12/536)
  3/121st Line Regiment (14/607)
  Det. 3/121st Line Regiment (3/100)(arrived 6/1/
  13)(Mainz)
  4/121st Line Regiment (10/561)
  Det. 4/121st Line Regiment (3/110)(arrived 6/1/
  13)(Mainz)
  3/15th Line Regiment (17/506)
  4/15th Line Regiment (8/542)
  Det. 15th Line Regiment (6/110)(arrived 5/28/13)(Mainz)
  Det. 5th Line Regiment (0/380) (dets of 5th incorporated
  into 15th Line
  on 21 April)
  3/70th Line Regiment (15/558)
  4/70th Line Regiment (10/468)
  Det. 11th Line Regiment (0/100)(incorporated into 70th
  Line on 4/21/13)
Artillery: Chef de bataillon Lebaut
  5/9th Foot Artillery (2/82)(6-6pdrs & 2 how)
  22/9th Foot Artillery (3/79)(6-6pdrs & 2 how)
  Det. 4/8th Principal Train Battalion (1/58)
  Det. 5/6th (bis) Train Battalion (2/88)
  Det. 4/11th (bis) Train Battalion (0/48)
  2/4th Sapper Battalion (3/127)
  3/15th Military Equipage Train Battalion (3/127)
23rd Division: Général de division Teste
Brigade: Général de brigade Bartier
  3/36th Line Regiment (20/820)(depart Calais 5/30)
  4/36th Line Regiment (11/540)
  3/,4/44th Line Regiment (40/1,640) (depart Valenciennes
  June)
  3/51st Line Regiment (20/820)(depart Lille 5/25)
  4/51st Line Regiment (8/652)
Brigade: Général de brigade Camus

3/,4/55th Line Regiment (40/1,640)(departed Dunkirk in June)
27th Provisional Regiment
    2/8th Légère Regiment (17/671)(Mainz 4/28)
    2/18th Légère Regiment (15/727)(Mainz 5/11)
Artillery: Chef de bataillon Terhost
    14/9th Foot Artillery (1/73)(6-6pdrs & 2 How)
    21/9th Foot Artillery (2/88)(6-6pdrs & 2 How)
    4/2nd (bis) Train Battalion (2/116)
    Det. 4/14th Principal Train Battalion (0/50)
    4/7th Sapper Battalion (3/147)
    4/15th Military Equipage Battalion (3/127)
Corps Cavalry Brigade:
    1/,2/7th Chevauléger-lancier Regiment (15/517/556)
    3/,4/7th Chevauléger-lancier Regiment (15/485/515)
Corps Reserve Artillery Park: Colonel Montgenet
    5/2nd Foot Artillery (2/79)
    21/5th Foot Artillery (2/88)
    18/5th Foot Artillery (1/80)
    10/8th Foot Artillery (2/75)
    12/8th Foot Artillery (2/83)
    16/8th Foot Artillery (2/71)
    1/1st Horse Artillery (2/67)
    5/1st Horse Artillery (2/79)
    Det. 5/3rd (bis) Train Battalion (0/69)
    Det. 5/3rd (bis) Train Battalion (1/64)
    5/10th (bis) Train Battalion (1/105)
    6/6th (bis) Train Battalion (1/111)
    3/7th Sapper Battalion (3/150)
    2/5th Sapper Battalion (3/147)
    5/15th Military Equipage Train Battalion (3/127)
Troops en route to VI Corps:
    1st Line Regiment (0/43)(arrived 5/25/13)
    14th Line Regiment (0/99)(arrived 5/14/13)
    14th Line Regiment (1/99)(arrived 5/17/13)
    15th Line Regiment (0/286)
    16th Line Regiment (3/106)(arrived 5/25/13)
    24th Line Regiment (2/125)(arrived 5/16/13)
    24th Line Regiment (1/64) (arrived 5/17/13)
    24th Line Regiment (3/180)(arrived 5/17/13)
    26th Line Regiment (2/108)(arrived 6/19/13)
    39th Line Regiment (1/68)(arrived 4/30/13)
    47th Line Regiment (1/101)(arrived 6/25/13)
    58th Line Regiment (1/70)(arrived 4/30/13)
    62nd Line Regiment (1/130)(arrived 5/25/13)
    63rd Line Regiment (1/77)(arrived 5/5/13)
    70th Line Regiment (0/77)
    70th Line Regiment (2/92)
    82nd Line Regiment (1/67)(arrived 6/22/13)
    86th Line Regiment (2/89)
    96th Line Regiment (2/305)(arrived 5/9/13)
    1st Marine Regiment (4/626)(arrived 6/11/13)
    2nd Marine Regiment (0/12)
    2nd Marine Regiment (0/92)
    2nd Marine Regiment (9/1,000)(arrived 5/28/13)
    4th Marine Regiment (1/219)(arrived 5/17/13)
    17th Légère Regiment (0/43)(arrived 5/5/13)
    17th Légère Regiment (1/89)(arrived 4/30/13)
    23rd Légère Regiment (1/44)
    23rd Légère Regiment (0/34)(arrived 5/23/13)
    32nd Légère Regiment (2/225)(arrived 5/25/13)

IX Corps:
28th Division:
    Listed but no state received: organization unknown.
29th Division: Générallieutenant Raglovich
Brigade: Generalmajor Beckers
    1st Light Batalion (7/636)
    2/Prinz Carl #3 Bavarian Infantry Regiment (16/537)

    Res/13th Bavarian Infantry Regiment (12/584)
    1/Isenburg #4 Bavarian Infantry Regiment (13/817)
    2/Herzog Pius #8 Bavarian Infantry Regiment (15/705)
Brigade: Généralmajor Maillot
    2nd Light Batalion (7/594)
    2/Presing #5 Bavarian Infantry Regiment (13/611)
    2/7th Bavarian Infantry Regiment (19/733)
    2/#9 Bavarian Infantry Regiment (17/790)
    2/Junker #10 Bavarian Infantry Regiment (6/843)
Cavalry: Oberst Seyssal
    1st Combined Bavarian Chevauleger Regt. (9/244/262)
    2nd Combined Bavarian Chevauleger Regt. (8/220/235)
    3rd Combined Bavarian Chevauleger Regt. (8/243/265)
Artillery:
    1st Bavarian Foot Battery (4/142)
    2nd Bavarian Foot Battery (4/133)
    Bavarian Reserve Foot Battery (2/104)
    Bavarian Train Company (unknown)

XII Corps: Maréchal Oudinot
13th Division: Général de division Pacthod
Brigade: Général de brigade Pourailly
    4/1st Légère Regiment (18/836)
    3/7th Line Regiment (17/609)
    4/7th Line Regiment (14/509)
    12th Provisional Regiment
        4/10th Line Regiment (10/609)
        4/42nd Line Regiment (15/570)
    23rd Provisional Regiment
        7/6th Line Regiment (15/719)
        4/67th Line Regiment (13/728)
Brigade: Général de brigade Gruyer
    1/4th Neapolitan Légère Regiment (29/629)
    2/4th Neapolitan Légère Regiment (13/641)
    3/4th Neapolitan Légère Regiment (16/518)
    2/101st Line Regiment (20/689)
    3/101st Line Regiment (16/629)
    4/101st Line Regiment (18/528)
Artillery:
    18/4th Foot Artillery (2/87)(6-6pdrs & 2 how)
    20/4th Foot Artillery (2/80)(6-6pdrs & 2 how)
    Det. 2/7th (bis) Train Battalion (1/98)
    3/7th (bis) Train Battalion (2/76)
Engineers:
    4/2nd Sapper Battalion (4/132)
    2/9th Military Equipage Battalion (1/58)
14th Division: Général de division Lorencz
1st Brigade: Général de brigade Leclerc
    3/52nd Line Regiment (18/720)
    4/52nd Line Regiment (17/587)
    1/137th Line Regiment (18/729)
    2/137th Line Regiment (12/740)
    3/137th Line Regiment (15/789)
    4/137th Line Regiment (15/774)
Brigade: Général de brigade d'Henin
    5th Provisional Regiment
        7/14th Légère Regiment (16/480)
        6/18th Légère Regiment (15/399)
    1/156th Line Regiment (20/727)
    2/156th Line Regiment (20/736)
    3/156th Line Regiment (19/648)
    4/156th Line Regiment (15/671)
    2/Illyrian Regiment (22/674)
Artillery: Chef de bataillon Boyer
    2/4th Foot Artillery (2/110)
    25/4th Foot Artillery (1/77)
    Det. 2/7th Principal Train Battalion (1/27)
    4/7th (bis) Train Battalion (1/123)
    4/6th Sapper Battalion (4/132)

3/9th Equipage Battalion (1/76)
XII Corps Artillery Reserve
24/2nd Foot Artillery (2/86)
Det. 2/7th (bis) Train Battalion (0/27)
Det. 5/7th (bis) Train Battalion (1/69)
3/3rd Sapper Battalion (2/137)
7/3rd Sapper Battalion (3/134)
4/9th Equipage Train Battalion (2/87)
Troops en route to XII Corps:
2/53rd Line Regiment (0/600)
2/106th Line Regiment (0/590)
2/92nd Line Regiment (0/450)
2/84th Line Regiment (0/450)
7th Line Regiment (0/100)
10th Line Regiment (0/50)
42nd Line Regiment (0/70)
52nd Line Regiment (0/60)
67th Line Regiment (0/70)
101st Line Regiment (0/50)
Italians en route (0/2,000)(Augsburg 5/17)
137th Line Regiment (1/30)(Augsburg 5/17)
156th Line Regiment (1/70)(Augsburg 5/17)
4th Neapolitan Légère Regiment (1/28)(Augsburg 5/17)
Bataillons de marche coming from Verona (Augsburg 5/17)
101st Line Regiment (2/76)
42nd Line Regiment (0/27)
156th Line Regiment (3/257)
1st Légère Regiment (0/35)
6th Line Regiment (1/46)
10th Line Regiment (0/41)
7th Line Regiment (0/38)
67th Line Regiment (1/38)
52nd Line Regiment (0/27)
137th Line Regiment (2/53)
14th Légère Regiment (0/50)
18th Légère Regiment (0/30)

I Cavalry Corps: (state as of 1 May 1813)
1st Division de Marche: Général de division Milhaud
Brigade: Général de brigade Lallemand
1st Regiment de Marche (forming in Gotha)
6th Hussar Regiment (2/96/100)
7th Hussar Regiment (3/125/130)
8th Hussar Regiment (8/241/257)
6th Chasseur à cheval Regiment (3/125/131)
9th Chasseur à cheval Regiment (2/206/210)
16th Chasseur à cheval Regiment (3/120/126)
25th Chasseur à cheval Regiment (6/222/233)
2nd Regiment de Marche (forming in Hanau)
1st Chevauléger-lancier Regiment (3/125/130)
3rd Chevauléger-lancier Regiment (4/125/133)
5th Chevauléger-lancier Regiment (8/173/188)
8th Chevauléger-lancier Regiment (not ready to depart)
1st Chasseur à cheval Regiment (3/104/108)
2nd Chasseur à cheval Regiment (5/160/170)
3rd Chasseur à cheval Regiment (3/125/131)
8th Chasseur à cheval Regiment (4/126/134)
Brigade: Général de brigade Noirot
3rd Regiment de Marche (forming in Gotha)
2nd Cuirassier Regiment (4/100/108)
3rd Cuirassier Regiment (4/100/108)
6th Cuirassier Regiment (4/100/108)
9th Cuirassier Regiment (6/186/198)
11th Cuirassier Regiment (4/100/108)
12th Cuirassier Regiment (3/99/107)
4th Regiment de Marche (forming in Gotha)
4th Cuirassier Regiment (4/100/108)
7th Cuirassier Regiment (4/100/108)
14th Cuirassier Regiment (4/100/108)

7th Dragoon Regiment (2/91/95)
23rd Dragoon Regiment (4/98/106)
28th Dragoon Regiment (4/100/108)
30th Dragoon Regiment (2/50/56)
2nd Division de Marche Général de division Pajol
(Units arrived between 5/15/13 and 6/1/13)
1st Brigade: Général de brigade Thiry
5th Regiment de marche
6th Hussar Regiment (3/117/123)
7th Hussar Regiment (2/125/130)
8th Hussar Regiment (3/122/128)
6th Chasseur à Cheval Regiment (1/125/127)
9th Chasseur à Cheval Regiment (1/50/52)
16th Chasseur à Cheval Regiment (4/126/134)
25th Chasseur à Cheval Regiment (4/125/134)
6th Regiment de marche
1st Chevauléger-lancier Regiment (4/127/138)
3rd Chevauléger-lancier Regiment (3/120/125)
5th Chevauléger-lancier Regiment (3/122/128)
8th Chevauléger-lancier Regiment (not ready to depart)
1st Chasseur à Cheval Regiment (3/122/128)
2nd Chasseur à Cheval Regiment (3/120/126)
3rd Chasseur à Cheval Regiment (4/125/130)
8th Chasseur à Cheval Regiment (5/146/156)
2nd Brigade: Général de brigade Queunot
7th Regiment de Marche
2nd Cuirassier Regiment (3/92/98)
3rd Cuirassier Regiment (3/94/99)
6th Cuirassier Regiment (3/100/105)
9th Cuirassier Regiment (3/98/104)
11th Cuirassier Regiment (3/95/100)
12th Cuirassier Regiment (3/92/98)
8th Regiment de Marche
4th Cuirassier Regiment (3/98/104)
7th Cuirassier Regiment (4/80/89)
14th Cuirassier Regiment (3/86/92)
7th Dragoon Regiment (8/51/69)
23rd Dragoon Regiment (1/16/18)
28th Dragoon Regiment (2/98/102)
30th Dragoon Regiment (3/71/77)

II Cavalry Corps: (state as of 1 May 1813)
1st Division de Marche: Général de division St.-Germain
Brigade: Général de brigade d'Haugeranville
1st Regiment de Marche (forming in Gotha)
5th Hussar Regiment (3/125/132)
9th Hussar Regiment (6/250/262)
11th Chasseur à cheval Regiment (8/245/261)
12th Chasseur à cheval Regiment (7/247/265)
4th Chevauléger-lancier Regiment (4/120/128)
2nd Regiment de Marche (forming in Gotha)
4th Chasseur à cheval Regiment (3/122/128)
7th Chasseur à cheval Regiment (2/125/129)
20th Chasseur à cheval Regiment (7/300/315)
23rd Chasseur à cheval Regiment (3/108/114)
11th Hussar Regiment (3/125/131)
Brigade: Général de brigade Domanget
3rd Regiment de Marche (still not formed)
2nd Chevauléger-lancier Regiment (4/122/131)
6th Chevauléger-lancier Regiment (5/125/135)
24th Chasseur à cheval Regiment (4/124/138)
4th Regiment de Marche (493)(forming in Gotha)
5th Cuirassier Regiment (2/100/104)
8th Cuirassier Regiment (4/100/108)
10th Cuirassier Regiment (3/100/106)
1st Carabinier Regiment (4/100/109)
2nd Carabinier Regiment (4/100/109)
1st Cuirassier Regiment (5/101/111)
2nd Division de Marche (Units arrived between 5/15/13 and

1st Brigade: Général de brigade Piquet
  5th Regiment de marche
    5th Hussar Regiment (3/122/128)
    9th Hussar Regiment (3/124/130)
    11th Chasseur à Cheval Regiment (3/122/128)
    12th Chasseur à Cheval Regiment (3/120/126)
    4th Chevauléger-lancier Regiment (6/109/129)
  6th Regiment de marche
    4th Chasseur à Cheval Regiment (3/107/112)
    7th Chasseur à Cheval Regiment (2/101/105)
    20th Chasseur à Cheval Regiment (4/125/135)
    23rd Chasseur à Cheval Regiment (2/128/134)
    11th Hussar Regiment (2/123/130)
2nd Brigade: Général de brigade Paultre
  7th Regiment de marche
    2nd Chevauléger-lancier Regiment (4/123/131)
    6th Chevauléger-lancier Regiment (5/125/135)
    24th Chasseur à Cheval Regiment (4/121/135)
  8th Regiment de marche
    5th Cuirassier Regiment (3/120/120)
    8th Cuirassier Regiment (4/60/68)
    10th Cuirassier Regiment (3/120/125)
    1st Carabinier Regiment (2/97/101)
    2nd Carabinier Regiment (2/95/99)
    1st Cuirassier Regiment (3/100/106)

III Cavalry Corps: Général de division Arrighi

1st Division de marche: Général de division de Lorge
(Units arrived between 9 and 25 May)
Brigade: Général de brigade Lamotte
  1st Regiment de marche
    10th Chasseur à cheval Regiment (3/125/131)
    13th Chasseur à cheval Regiment (8/250/266)
    14th Chasseur à cheval Regiment (3/250/256)
    26th Chasseur à cheval Regiment (4/246/254)
    28th Chasseur à cheval Regiment (4/100/109)
    31st Chasseur à cheval Regiment (4/125/134)
  2nd Regiment de marche
    1st Hussar Regiment (2/100/104)
    2nd Hussar Regiment (1/100/102)
    3rd Hussar Regiment (1/126/128)
    4th Hussar Regiment (1/125/127)
    12th Hussar Regiment (1/125/127)
Brigade: Général de brigade Avice
  3rd Regiment de marche
    2nd Dragoon Regiment (2/100/104)
    5th Dragoon Regiment (1/124/126)
    12th Dragoon Regiment (1/100/102)
    13th Dragoon Regiment (1/100/105)
    14th Dragoon Regiment (2/100/104)
    17th Dragoon Regiment (1/90/92)
  4th Regiment de marche
    6th Dragoon Regiment (1/100/102)
    11th Dragoon Regiment (2/100/104)
    21st Dragoon Regiment (1/75/77)
    19th Dragoon Regiment (5/200/210)
    20th Dragoon Regiment (6/194/204)

Imperial Guard

Old Guard Division: Général de division Roguet
1st Brigade: Général de brigade Rottembourg
  1/2nd Voltigeur Regiment (17/437)
  1/2nd Tirailleur Regiment (11/474)
  1/1st Chasseurs à Pied Regiment (15/496)
  1/1st Grenadiers à Pied Regiment (17/412)
2nd Brigade:
  Velites of Turin (15/293)
  Velites of Florence (17/197)
  Italian Royal Guard (26/173)

  Hessian Troops (12/104)
Cavalry:
  Turin Gardes d'Honneur (2/65)
  Tuscan Gardes d'Honneur (3/49)
  Italian Gardes d'Honneur (1/22)
  Det/Italian Guard Dragoon Regiment (1/28)
  Det/Italian Queen's Dragoon Regiment (1/39)
Artillery:
  21/7th Foot Artillery (3/100)(6-6pdrs & 2 how)
  3/5th Foot Artillery (4/85)(6-6pdrs & 2 how)
  Det/1st (bis) Train Battalion (0/5)
  Det/3rd (bis) Train Battalion (1/97)
  Det/11th (bis) Train Battalion (0/33)
Engineers:
  Imperial Guard Sappers (1/25)
2nd Guard Division: Général de division Barrois
Brigade: Général de brigade Tindal
  2/2nd Voltigeur Regiment (17/618)
  2/2nd Tirailleur Regiment (13/614)
  1/,2/6th (bis) Voltigeur Regiment (25/1,447)
  1/,2/6th (bis) Tirailleur Regiment (26/1,250)
  Fusilier (bis) Regiment (34/1,218)
    1/Fusilier Grenadier Regiment
    1/Fusilier Chasseur Regiment
  1/Pupilles Regiment (17/784)
  7/Pupilles Regiment (16/823)
  Chasseur à Cheval Regiment (7/350/515)
  Empress Dragoon Regiment (5/142/264)
  Grenadier à Cheval Regiment (2/119/229)
  2nd Guard Chevauléger-lancier Regiment (4/150/258)
  Sailors and Sappers (2/65)
  Military Equipage (1 co)(2/131)
  Guard Worker Company (1/93)
  1st Artilery and Train Column (14/684)
  2nd Artilery and Train Column (14/770)
3rd Division: Général de division Laborde
  Forming in Frankfurt, no units yet assigned.
4th Division:
  Forming in Paris, no units yet assigned.
Guard en route from France
1st Column:
  Chasseurs à pied
  Grenadiers à pied
  Young Guard
    Total - 33/800
  2nd Guard Chevauléger-lancier Regiment
  Chasseurs à cheval
  Grenadiers à cheval
  Dragoons
    Total - 30/938/1,068
  Guard Foot Battery
  2 Guard Horse Batteries
    Total Artillery - 16/492
  Guard Equipage & Ambulances (10/195)
2nd Column:
  Flanqueur Regiment (1 bn)(20/776)
  1/,2/1st Voltigeur Regiment (36/1,528)
  1/,2/,1st Tirailleur Regiment (37/1,500)
  2nd Guard Chevauléger-lancier Regiment (6/123/125)
  Chasseur à Cheval Regiment (5/111/139)
  Empress Dragoon Regiment (6/98/112)
  Grenadier à Cheval Regiment (10/194/110)
  Guard Foot Battery (6/230)
3rd Column
  Flanqueur Regiment (1)(14/770)
  1/,2/7th Voltigeur Regiment (30/1,507)
  1/,2/3rd Voltigeur Regiment (28/1,524)
  1/,2/,3rd Tirailleur Regiment (34/1,385)
  2/Fusilier Chasseur & 2/Fusilier Grenadier (30/1,525)

Mixed Bataillon de marche (5/755)
Guard Cavalry (26/651/733)
Imperial Gendarmes (2/192/244)
1st Old Guard Battery (1/224)
Unidentified artillery battery (2/153)

Vandamme's Command: Général de division Vandamme
Brigadiers: Generaux de brigade Osten, de Fezensac and Colonel Prince von Reuss
  1/152nd Line Regiment (20/578)
  2/152nd Line Regiment (20/648)
  3/152nd Line Regiment (21/535)
  1st Bataillon de marche (9/547)
    8th Line Regiment
    54th Line Regiment
    59th Line Regiment
    88th Line Regiment
    94th Line Regiment
    95th Line Regiment
  2nd Bataillon de marche (9/423)
    27th Line Regiment
    45th Line Regiment
    39th Line Regiment
    88th Line Regiment
  3rd Bataillon de marche (11/377)
    2nd Légère Regiment
    4th Légère Regiment
    21st Légère Regiment
    25th Légère Regiment
    27th Légère Regiment
  4th Bataillon de marche (6/770)
    14th Line Regiment
    24th Line Regiment
    54th Line Regiment
    63rd Line Regiment
    94th Line Regiment
    95th Line Regiment
  Det/5th Equipage de Flotilla (13/436)
  Battalion of Foot Custom's Officers (33/426)
  Mounted Custom's Officers (2/23/25)
  Foot Gendarmes (0/31)
  Mounted Gendarmes (2/36/40)
  Det. 4/19th Dragoon Regiment
  Det. 4/20th Dragoon Regiment
    Total dragoons (1/12/14)
  15/9th Foot Artillery (3/96)
  Artillery Train (0/30)
5th Division: Général de division Dufour
Brigade: Général de brigade Brun
  37th (bis) Provisional Regiment
    4/26th Légère Regiment (11/550)
    Det/26th Légère Regiment (6/237) (arrived 5/12/13)
    4/24th Légère Regiment (14/744)
  38th (bis) Provisional Regiment
    4/11th Line Regiment (20/819)
    4/2nd Line Regiment (14/479)
    Det/4th Line Regiment (6/292) (arrived 5/1/13)
  39th (bis) Provisional Regiment
    4/19th Line Regiment (7/341)
    Det/19th Line Regiment (5/420) (arrived 5/11/13)
    4/37th Line Regiment (15/486)
  40th (bis) Provisional Regiment
    4/56th Line Regiment (9/334)
    Det/56th Line Regiment (4/269) (arrived 5/7/13)
    4/4th Line Regiment (5/346)
    Det/4th Line Regiment (2/141) (arrived 5/8/13)
    Det/4th Line Regiment (3/147) (arrived 5/27)
  41st (bis) Provisional Regiment

4/18th Line Regiment (5/454)
Det/18th Line Regiment (2/272)
4/46th Line Regiment (6/397)
Det/46th Line Regiment (4/262)
42nd (bis) Provisional Regiment
  4/72nd Line Regiment (18/804)
  4/93rd Line Regiment (11/605)
Artillery: Capitaine Ferrary
  12/2nd Foot Battery (2/59)
  Det/Artillery Train (3/56)
50th Division: Général de division Carra St.-Cyr
  (unit destined for Hamburg)
  6/3rd Line Regiment (4/736)
  Det. 6/3rd Line Regiment (1/194)(arrived 5/3/13)
  3/29th Line Regiment (20/817)
  4/29th Line Regiment (10/587)
  Det. 4/29th Line Regiment (4/235)(arrived 6/9/13)
  6/105th Line Regiment (6/458)
  Det. 6/105th Line Regiment (2/102)(arrived 5/9/13)

X Corps: Général de division Rapp (Garrison of Danzig)
  (State is of 3/1/13, but is repeated in 4/15/13 state)
7th Division: Général de division Grandjean
Brigade: Général de brigade Radzwill
  1/,2/,3/,Art/5th Polish Infantry Regiment (63/1,731)
  1/,2/,3/,Art/10th Polish Infantry Regiment (61/1,697)
  1/,2/,3/,Art/11th Polish Infantry Regiment (62/1,435)
Brigade: Général de brigade Bachelu
  1/,2/,Art./1st Westphalian Infantry Regiment (34/1,094)
  1/,2/,Art./13th Bavarian Infantry Regiment (41/1,032)
33rd Division: Général de division Detrees
Brigade: Général de brigade Rosarollo
  1/,2/5th Neapolitan Infantry Regiment (41/1,315)
  1/,2/6th Neapolitan Infantry Regiment (32/1,258)
  1/,2/7th Neapolitan Infantry Regiment (27/1,345)
30th Division: Général de division Heudlet
Brigade: Général de brigade Breissand
  6th Provisional Demi-brigade
    4/16th Légère Regiment (17/575)
    4/21st Légère Regiment (16/673)
    4/28th Légère Regiment (16/679)
  7th Provisional Demi-brigade
    4/8th Line Regiment (15/611)
    4/14th Line Regiment (15/642)
    4/94th Line Regiment (18/552)
  8th Provisional Demi-brigade
    4/54th Line Regiment (16/555)
    4/88th Line Regiment (20/418)
    4/95th Line Regiment (20/479)
Brigade: Général de brigade Husson
  1st Provisional Demi-brigade
    4/2nd Légère Regiment (21/791)
    4/4th Légère Regiment (19/632)
    4/17th Légère Regiment (18/649)
  9th Provisional Demi-brigade
    4/24th Line Regiment (22/521)
    4/45th Line Regiment (20/618)
    4/59th Line Regiment (23/555)
  17th Provisional Demi-brigade
    4/6th Légère Regiment (20/575)
    4/25th Légère Regiment (20/555)
    4/39th Légère Regiment (20/782)
34th Division: Général de division Franceschi
Brigade: Général de brigade Gault
  3rd Line Regiment (1 co)(4/13)
  1/29th Line Regiment (26/214)
  Artillery Co./29th Line Regiment (2/54)
  105th Line Regiment (1 co)(?)

113th Line Regiment (2 cos)(20/210)
1 Co., Prince Primate Regiment (5/34)
1 Co., 4th Rhinbund Regiment (14/90)
1 Co., 5th Rhinbund Regiment (22/159)
1 Co., 6th Rhinbund Regiment (12/281)
Artillery:
18/8th Foot Artillery (2/39)
5/8th Train Battalion (1/23)
Corps Artillery: Colonel Gusskel
7/7th Foot Artillery (3/90)
17/7th Foot Artillery (2/95)
18/9th Foot Artillery (2/90)
4/12th Principal Train Battalion (1/98)
5/8th Principal Train Battalion (1/23)
1/7th Sapper Battalion (2/92)
Cavalry: Général Cavagnac
9th Polish Uhlan Regiment (8/30/330)
17th Polish Uhlans (1/30/31)
19th Polish Uhlans (3/62/65)
Provisional Cavalry Regiment (15/382/397)
1st Provisional Dragoon Regiment (20/494/514)
    4/2nd Dragoon Regiment (5/125/130)
    4/5th Dragoon Regiment (4/129/133)
    4/12th Dragoon Regiment (6/139/143)
    4/13th Dragoon Regiment (5/103/108)
2nd Provisional Dragoon Regiment (24/443/461)
    4/14th Dragoon Regiment (4/87/90)
    4/17th Dragoon Regiment (6/123/123)
    4/19th Dragoon Regiment (7/105/113)
    4/20th Dragoon Regiment (7/128/130)
Naval Forces
1st Spanish Pioneer Battalion (6/407)
Guard Marines (1/1)
4th Equipage de Flotilla (10/95)
17th Equipage de Flotilla (12/217)
Bataillon du Danube (7/61)
Bataillon de l'Escaut (15/297)
Attached:
Imperial Gendarmerie (0/10/12)
Imperial Guard Depot (10/398)
Sapper Depot (4/164)
4/5th Foot Artillery (0/36)
5/5th Foot Artillery (0/27)
9/5th Foot Artillery (1/107)
10/5th Foot Artillery (2/110)
19/5th Foot Artillery (2/86)
12/7th Foot Artillery (3/100)
22/7th Foot Artillery (3/56)
21/8th Foot Artillery (2/92)
6/9th Foot Artillery (3/94)
Dets. 1/,3/,4/,6/5th Horse Artillery (0/24)
9/1st Pontooneer Battalion (0/31)
6th Artillery Artisan Company (82)
3rd Armorer Company (0/33)
5th Armorer Company (0/12)
Saltpeter and Powder Workers (0/11)
Train & Artillery Depot (2/135)
Württemberg Artillery (0/28)
Bavarian Artillery (0/160)
Polish Artillery (2/118)
Hessian Artillery (0/54)
1/2nd Miner Battalion (0/11)
1st Engineering Workers Company (1/74)
Det. Engineering Train Company (1/41)
1st Equipage Train Worker Company (1/139)
2nd Equipage Train Worker Company (1/52)
Det. 20th Equipage Train Battalion (1/36)

Garrison of Modlin: Général de division Daendels

(as of 2/15/13)
18th Polish Regiment (54/824)
19th Polish Regiment (22/22)
20th Polish Regiment (39/891)
21st Polish Regiment (23/575)
22nd Polish Regiment (12/53)
3rd Polish Regiment (unknown)
17th Polish Regiment (unknown)
1/Niesmeuschel (Saxon) Regiment (12/414)
4/Würzburg Regiment (17/361)
1/133rd Line Regiment (17/402)
18/7th Foot Artillery (3/103)
2/5th Foot Artillery (1/23)
8/9th Foot Artillery (0/7)

Garrison of Stettin: Général de brigade Grandeau
(as of 3/10/13)
31st Division: Général de division Grandeau
Brigade: Général de brigade Dufresse
10th Provisional Demi-brigade (91/2,316)
    4/27th Line Regiment
    4/63rd Line Regiment
    4/76th Line Regiment
    4/96th Line Regiment
12th Provisional Demi-brigade (49/1,950)
    4/123rd Line Regiment
    4/124th Line Regiment
    4/134th Line Regiment
Miscellaneous Detachments (91/2,133)
    5/17th Line Regiment (2 cos)
    5/30th Line Regiment (2 cos)
    5/33rd Line Regiment (2 cos)
    5/48th Line Regiment (2 cos)
    5/12th Line Regiment (2 cos)
    5/21st Line Regiment (2 cos)
    5/108th Line Regiment (3 cos)
    5/25th Line Regiment (2 cos)
    5/57th Line Regiment (2 cos)
    5/61st Line Regiment (2 cos)
    5/111th Line Regiment (2 cos)
    5/7th Légère Regiment (2 cos)
    5/13th Légère Regiment (2 cos)
    5/15th Légère Regiment (2 cos)
5th Provisional Battalion de Marche (6/460)
2nd Compagnie de marche, 31st & 32nd Divisions (3/253)
6th Rhinbund Regiment (0/77)
1st Provisional Dragoon Regiment (0/22/26)
2/1st Foot Artillery (3/112)
11/3rd Foot Artillery (2/51)
7/6th Foot Artillery (2/112)
7/8th Foot Artillery (3/97)
8/8th Foot Artillery (3/53)
3/9th Foot Artillery (2/63)
Artillery Train (6/84)
2/3rd Sapper Battalion (3/71)
1/1st Pontooneer Battalion (4/44)
Det/1st & 5th Armorer Companies (0/33)
Det/7th Artillery Artisan Company (0/8)
Det/18th Military Equipage Train Battalion (0/21)

Garrison of Custrin: Général de brigade Fornier d'Albe
(as of 3/10/13)
1/,2/4th & 1/,2/5th Westphalian Line Regiments (47/953)
3/128th Line Regiment (21/507)
Miscellaneous Detachments (79/2,121)
    5/2nd Line Regiment (2 cos)
    5/19th Line Regiment (2 cos)
    5/37th Line Regiment (2 cos)
    5/56th Line Regiment (2 cos)

5/11th Légère Regiment (2 cos)
5/26th Légère Regiment (2 cos)
1/3rd Foot Artillery (3/27)
13/3rd Foot Artillery (3/56)
14/7th Foot Artillery (2/87)
20/9th Foot Artillery (1/57)
Det/5th Armorer Company (1/14)
8/5th Sapper Battalion (2/66)

Garrison of Glogau: Général de brigade Laplane
(as of 3/10/13)
Miscellaneous detachments (57/1,626)
   1/8th Légère Regiment (2 cos)
   1/18th Légère Regiment(2 cos)
   2/9th Line Regiment (1 co)
   2/35th Line Regiment (1 co)
   2/53rd Line Regiment (1 co)
   2/84th Line Regiment (1 co)
   2/106th Line Regiment(1 co)
   1/Dalmatian Regiment (1 co)
   1/3rd Italian Légère Regiment (1 co)
   1/2nd Italian Line Regiment (1 co)
   1/3rd Italian Line Regiment (1 co)
1st Provisional Croatian Regiment (37/963)
1/,2/1st Baden Line Regiment (41/981)
5/3rd Foot Artillery (2/85)
16/4th Foot Artillery (2/118)
2/6th Foot Artillery (2/109)
4/8th Foot Artillery (1/90)
9th Saxon Foot Battery (3/132)
Individuals of various diverse corps (2/148)
9/5th Sapper Battalion (1/40)
Posen Provost Guard (10/173/180)•
Portuguese Legion (2/158)

Garrison of Spandau: Général de brigade Bruny
Miscellaneous Detachments (45/1,228)
   3/129th Line Regiment (6 cos)
   5/24th Légère Regiment (2 cos)
   5/4th Line Regiment (1 co)
   5/18th Line Regiment (2 cos)
   5/46th Line Regiment (1 co)
   5/72nd Line Regiment (2 cos)
   5/93rd Line Regiment (2 cos)
1/Vistula Legion (25/162)
2/Vistula Legion (28/126)
3/Vistula Legion (23/152)
4/Vistula Legion (3/352)
4th Polish Infantry Regiment (40/184)
7th Polish Infantry Regiment (24/206)
9th Polish Infantry Regiment (33/362)
Depot/5th Italian Line Regiment (6/107)
8/1st Foot Artillery (3/107)
8/5th Foot Artillery (1/83)
Det/14th Artillery Artisan Company (1/22)
Det/Artillery Train (1/111)

Garrison of Magdeburg Général de division Haxo
(State as of 4/15/13)
1st Magdeburg Citadel Garrison Battalion (11/525)
   2/9th Line Regiment (2 cos)
   2/35th Line Regiment (2 cos)
   2/53rd Line Regiment (2 cos)
   2/106th Line Regiment (2 cos)
2nd Magdeburg Citadel Garrison Battalion (6/223)
   Det/24th Line Regiment
   Det/59th Line Regiment
   Det/81st Line Regiment
21/1st Foot Artillery (2/67)
4/4th Foot Artillery (2/70)

5/4th Foot Artillery (2/55)
10/6th Foot Artillery (2/100)
1/9th Foot Artillery (3/101)
16/9th Foot Artillery (3/103)
Det/1st & 5th Armorer Companies (2/19)
Det/11th Artillery Artisan Company (1/54)
Italian Naval Artisans (2/45)
Det/4th Sapper Battalion (1/15)
3/1st Miner Battalion (1/54)
8/4th Sapper Battalion (3/135)
Imperial Gendarmes (1/9/11)
29th Provisional Regiment
   2/7th Légère Regiment (15/674)
   2/13th Légère Regiment (21/681)
32nd Provisional Regiment
   2/33rd Line Regiment (16/670)
   2/48th Line Regiment (18/537)
36th Provisional Regiment
   2/61st Line Regiment (23/669)
   2/111th Line Regiment (20/649)
37th Provisional Regiment
   2/24th Légère Regiment (15/620)
   2/26th Légère Regiment (16/650)
38th Provisional Regiment
   2/2nd Line Regiment (13/627)
1/,2/3rd Westphalian Line Regiment (30/1,650)

Garrison of Erfurt: Général de brigade Doucet
2/123rd Line Regiment (18/577)
2/124th Line Regiment (21/359)
3/134th Line Regiment (10/303)
6/134th Line Regiment (5/409)
2/1st Provisional Croatian Regiment (1 co)(3/117)
Det/29th Line Regiment (2/35)
15/4th Foot Artillery (3/115)

Garrison of Wittemberg: Général de division Lapoype
Généraux de brigade Bardet & Bronikowski
1/,2/4th Vistula Regiment (48/967)
3/3rd Line Regiment (11/352)
4/11th Line Regiment (20/639)
3/105th Line Regiment (17/282)
3/127th Line Regiment (11/187)
6/7th Foot Artillery (2/68)
16/7th Foot Artillery (2/59)
1/7th Sapper Battalion (3/47)

Cavalry Depots in Hanover and Brunswick
Hanoverian Depot
   1st Carabinier Regiment (4/80/86)
   2nd Carabinier Regiment (3/102/74)
   1st Cuirassier Regiment (3/45/48)
   2nd Cuirassier Regiment (2/48/43)
   3rd Cuirassier Regiment (3/84/13)
   4th Cuirassier Regiment (3/161/63)
   5th Cuirassier Regiment (1/57/140)
   6th Cuirassier Regiment (1/19/0)
   7th Cuirassier Regiment (0/27/4)
   8th Cuirassier Regiment (1/108/27)
   9th Cuirassier Regiment (0/22/13)
   10th Cuirassier Regiment (2/103/29)
   11th Cuirassier Regiment (1/55/40)
   12th Cuirassier Regiment (6/158/73)
   14th Cuirassier Regiment (0/18/0)
   1st Chevauléger-lancier Regiment (1/17/0)
   2nd Chevauléger-lancier Regiment (5/85/75)
   3rd Chevauléger-lancier Regiment (0/44/47)
   4th Chevauléger-lancier Regiment (5/9/144)
   5th Chevauléger-lancier Regiment (2/53/62)
   6th Chevauléger-lancier Regiment (6/96/81)
   8th Chevauléger-lancier Regiment (2/65/64)

9th Chevauléger-lancier Regiment (21/534/729)(Hamlin)
2nd Dragoon Regiment (1/36/32)
5th Dragoon Regiment (4/39/16)
7th Dragoon Regiment (1/29/19)
12th Dragoon Regiment (0/25/3)
13th Dragoon Regiment (3/32/20)
14th Dragoon Regiment (0/28/10)
17th Dragoon Regiment (1/30/13)
19th Dragoon Regiment (0/27/5)
20th Dragoon Regiment (0/25/6)
23rd Dragoon Regiment (1/41/19)
28th Dragoon Regiment (1/44/21)
30th Dragoon Regiment (0/23/3)
1st Chasseur à Cheval Regiment (0/2/0)
2nd Chasseur à Cheval Regiment (0/5/4)
3rd Chasseur à Cheval Regiment (0/12/8)
4th Chasseur à Cheval Regiment (0/32/5)
6th Chasseur à Cheval Regiment (0/11/1)
7th Chasseur à Cheval Regiment (9/63/58)
8th Chasseur à Cheval Regiment (0/23/4)
9th Chasseur à Cheval Regiment (1/23/1)
11th Chasseur à Cheval Regiment (1/5/13)
12th Chasseur à Cheval Regiment (6/70/40)
16th Chasseur à Cheval Regiment (2/73/68)
19th Chasseur à Cheval Regiment (0/21/27)
20th Chasseur à Cheval Regiment (2/43/38)
23rd Chasseur à Cheval Regiment (11/121/162)
24th Chasseur à Cheval Regiment (3/76/100)
25th Chasseur à Cheval Regiment (2/54/39)
28th Chasseur à Cheval Regiment (5/31/42)
Portuguese Chasseur à Cheval Regiment (8/57/33)
4th Italian Chasseur à Cheval Regiment (1/25/4)
5th Hussar Regiment (8/129/123)
6th Hussar Regiment (0/24/8)
7th Hussar Regiment (3/23/25)
8th Hussar Regiment (0/5/4)
9th Hussar Regiment (1/135/86)
11th Hussar Regiment (5/37/60)
17th Polish (Lithuanian) Uhlan Regiment (47/290/333)
Artillery Train (18/271)
Military Equipage Train (8/339)
Horse Artillery (11/88)
Brunswick Depot
2nd Cuirassier Regiment (3/56/47)
3rd Cuirassier Regiment (6/91/57)
4th Cuirassier Regiment (12/107/98)
6th Cuirassier Regiment (6/48/32)
7th Cuirassier Regiment (14/233/140)
9th Cuirassier Regiment (9/107/78)
11th Cuirassier Regiment (7/80/36)
12th Cuirassier Regiment (6/52/18)
14th Cuirassier Regiment (6/132/94)
1st Chevauléger-lancier Regiment (7/81/104)
3rd Chevauléger-lancier Regiment (4/23/48)
5th Chevauléger-lancier Regiment (6/95/65)
7th Chevauléger-lancier Regiment (2/33/42)
8th Chevauléger-lancier Regiment (21/315/417)
7th Dragoon Regiment (4/73/90)
23rd Dragoon Regiment (8/136/170)
28th Dragoon Regiment (4/56/55)
30th Dragoon Regiment (5/73/76)
1st Chasseur à cheval Regiment (5/89/91)
2nd Chasseur à cheval Regiment (8/79/44)
3rd Chasseur à cheval Regiment (5/74/70)
6th Chasseur à cheval Regiment (5/66/86)
8th Chasseur à cheval Regiment (4/73/85)
9th Chasseur à cheval Regiment (4/45/44)
16th Chasseur à cheval Regiment (11/109/59)
19th Chasseur à cheval Regiment (2/39/47)

25th Chasseur à cheval Regiment (5/84/88)
Portuguese Chasseur à cheval Regiment (2/10/9)
2nd Italian Chasseur à cheval Regiment
3rd Italian Chasseur à cheval Regiment
Total Italian chasseurs (12/135/153)
6th Hussar Regiment (1/52/64)
7th Hussar Regiment (4/54/12)
8th Hussar Regiment (9/103/106)

Corps d'Observation de Mainz:
(This formation was a proposed formation and all figures are projected, not actual strengths.)
42nd Division: Général de division Molitor
Brigade: Général de brigade Gency
  3rd Provisional Demi-brigade
    3/10th Légère Regiment (20/820)
    4/10th Légère Regiment (20/820)
    3/21st Légère Regiment (20/820)
  4th Provisional Demi-brigade
    6/9th Légère Regiment (20/820)
    3/27th Légère Regiment (20/820)
    6/28th Légère Regiment (20/820)
Brigade: Général de brigade Rostollant
  16th Provisional Demi-brigade
    3/39th Line Regiment (20/820)
    4/40th Line Regiment (20/820)
    3/96th Line Regiment (20/820)
  17th Provisional Demi-brigade
    3/43rd Line Regiment (20/820)
    3/65th Line Regiment (20/820)
    4/65th Line Regiment (20/820)
    2/123rd Line Regiment (in Erfurt)
    1/,4/123rd Line Regiment (recruiting suspended)
Artillery:
  2 Foot Companies (4/240)
  2 Train Companies (4/180)
  1 Military Equipage Company (2/127)
43rd Division: Général de division Gilly
Brigade: Général de brigade Nalèche
  3/29th Légère Regiment (20/820)
  4/29th Légère Regiment (20/820)
  19th Provisional Demi-brigade
    3/100th Line Regiment (20/820)
    4/100th Line Regiment (20/820)
    4/103rd Line Regiment (20/820)
Brigade: Général de brigade Lauberdière
  20th Provisional Demi-brigade
    3/8th Line Regiment (20/820)
    3/45th Line Regiment (20/820)
    3/54th Line Regiment (20/820)
  21st Demi-brigade provisoire
    3/24th Line Regiment (20/820)
    3/94th Line Regiment (20/820)
    3/95th Line Regiment (20/820)
    2/124th Line Regiment (in Erfurth)
    1/,3/124th Line Regiment (recruiting suspended)
Artillery:
  2 Foot Companies (4/240)
  2 Train Companies (4/180)
  1 Military Equipage Company (2/127)
44th Division: Général de division Frère
Brigade: Général de brigade H.Boyer
  1/8th Légère Regiment (20/820)
  3/8th Légère Regiment (20/820)
  26th Provisional Demi-brigade
    3/5th Line Regiment (20/820)
    3/11th Line Regiment (20/820)
    4/60th Line Regiment (20/820)
  27th Provisional Demi-brigade

3/79th Line Regiment (20/820)
6/81st Line Regiment (20/820)
4/32nd Légère Regiment (20/820)
Brigade: Général de brigade Paillard
  35th Provisional Demi-brigade
    3/27th Line Regiment (20/820)
    3/64th Line Regiment (20/820)
    4/64th Line Regiment (20/820)
  1/127th Line Regiment (recruiting suspended)
  2/127th Line Regiment (in 8th Division/III Corps)
Artillery:
  2 Foot Companies (4/240)
  2 Train Companies (4/180)
  1 Military Equipage Company (2/127)
45th Division: Général de division Razout
Brigade: Général de brigade Verger Desbarreaux
  1/113th Line Regiment (20/820)
  2/113th Line Regiment (20/820)
  3/,4/113th Line Regiment (recruiting suspended)
  18th Provisional Demi-brigade
    3/34th Line Regiment (20/820)
    3/69th Line Regiment (20/820)
    3/76th Line Regiment (20/820)
Brigade: Général de brigade Pageot
  22nd Provisional Demi-brigade
    4/32nd Line Regiment (20/820)
    4/58th Line Regiment (20/820)
    3/12th Légère Regiment (20/820)
  1/18th Légère Regiment (20/820)
  1/128th Line Regiment (recruiting suspended)
  2/128th Line Regiment (in 8th Division/III Corps)
  1/129th Line Regiment (recruiting suspended)
  2/129th Line Regiment (in 8th Division/III Corps)
Artillery:
  2 Foot Companies (4/240)
  2 Train Companies (4/180)
  1 Military Equipage Company (2/127)
Battalions proposed by Napoleon to replace the 14 battalions
of the Corps d'Observation de Mainz when recruiting was
suspended
These battalions were to be formed by conscripts of the Class
of 1814 originally intended for the guard and it had been
proposed to Napoleon that they be sent to the line.
  2/4th Légère Regiment (20/820)
  2/59th Line Regiment (20/820)
  2/51st Line Regiment (20/820)
  2/75th Line Regiment (20/820)
  2/50th Line Regiment (20/820)
  2/28th Line Regiment (20/820)
  4/28th Line Regiment (20/820)
Reserve Park Artillery:
  2 Foot Companies (4/240)
  2 Horse Companies (4/240)
  4 Train Companies (8/360)
  2 Military Equipage Companies (4/254)
  2 French Sapper Companies (2/240)

Corps d'Observation de l'Adige:
  (This formation was a proposed formation and all figures
are projected, not actual strengths.)
46th Division: Général de division Sémélé
Brigade: Général de brigade Cailler
  1/,2/,3/,4/9th Line Regiment (20/820 ea)
  Artillery Co./9th Line Regiment (2/68)
  1/,2/3rd Provisional Croatian Regiment (20/820ea)
Brigade: Général de brigade Campy
  1/,2/,3/,4/35th Line Regiment (20/820 ea)
  Artillery Co./35th Line Regiment (2/68)
  6/112th Line Regiment (20/820)

Brigade:
  1/,2/,3/,4/53rd Line Regiment (20/820 ea)
  Artillery Co./53rd Line Regiment (2/68)
  8/6th Line Regiment (20/820)
Artillery:
  4/2nd Foot Artillery (2/98)
  6/2nd Foot Artillery (2/98)
  2 train companies (4/180)
  1 military equipage company (2/127)
47th Division: Général de division Verdier
Brigade: Général de brigade Lasalcette
  1/,2/,3/,4/84th Line Regiment (20/820 ea)
  Artillery Co./84th Line Regiment (2/68)
  1/,2/Bns d'élite, 1st Foreign Regiment (15/585 ea)
•The "élite" battalions were battalions formed of converged
elite companies from the parent regiments indicated in the
new units title.
  Artillery Co/1st Foreign Regiment (2/68)
Brigade: Général de brigade Launay
  1/,2/,3/,4/92nd Line Regiment (20/820 ea)
  Artillery Co./92nd Line Regiment (2/68)
  8/14th Légère Regiment (20/820)
Brigade:
  28th Provisional Demi-brigade
    6/7th Line Regiment (20/820)
    6/52nd Line Regiment (20/820)
    6/67th Line Regiment (20/820)
  1/Elite (2nd Foreign) Regiment (15/585)
  2/Elite (2nd Foreign) Regiment (15/585)
  Artillery Co., 2nd Foreign Regiment (2/68)
Artillery:
  17/2nd Foot Artillery (2/98)
  23/2nd Foot Artillery (2/98)
  2 Train companies (4/180)
  1 Military equipage company (2/127)
48th Division: Général de division Broussier
Brigade: Général de brigade Castella de Bertins
  1/,2/,3/,4/106th Line Regiment (20/820 ea)
  Artillery Co./106h Line Regiment (2/68)
Brigade: Général de brigade Cambelle
  29th Provisional Demi-brigade
    3/42nd Line Regiment (20/820)
    6/42nd Line Regiment (20/820)
    6/101st Line Regiment (20/820)
  30th Provisional Demi-brigade
    4/20th Line Regiment (20/820)
    3/102nd Line Regiment (20/820)
    6/102nd Line Regiment (20/820)
Brigade:
  1/,2/,3/1st Neapolitan Line Regiment (20/820 ea)
  1/,2/,3/1st Neapolitan Line Regiment (20/820 ea)
Artillery:
  25/2nd Foot Artillery (2/98)
  9/4th Foot Artillery (2/98)
  2 Train companies (4/180)
  1 Military equipage company (2/127)
49th Division:
Brigade:
  1/,2/,3/,4/2nd Italian Line Regiment (20/820 ea)
  1/,2/Dalmatian Regiment (20/820 ea)
Brigade:
  1/,2/3rd Italian Légère Regiment (20/820 ea)
  4/4th Italian Légère Regiment (20/820)
  2/,3/6th Italian Line Regiment (20/820 ea)
Brigade:
  1/,2,3/,4/3rd Italian Line Regiment (20/820 ea)
  2/2nd Italian Légère Regiment (20/820)
Artillery:
  Italian Foot Artillery (108)

Italian Foot Artillery (108)
2 Italian train companies (4/180)
1 Italian military equipage company (2/127)
51st Division: Général de division Marcognet
Brigade: Général de brigade Pamplona
1/,2/4th Provisional Croatian Regiment (20/820 ea)
Fusilier Cos, 1/,2/,3/,4/,6/1st Foreign Regt (15/585 ea)
Brigade: Général de brigade Dupeyroux
Fusilier Cos, 1/,3/,4/2nd Foreign Regiment (15/585 ea)
25th Provisional Demi-brigade
2/1st Line Regiment (20/820)
3/16th Line Regiment (20/820)
4/62nd Line Regiment (20/820)
Brigade:
23rd Provisional Demi-brigade
6/47th Line Regiment (20/820)
6/70th Line Regiment (20/820)
6/86th Line Regiment (20/820)
24th Provisional Demi-brigade
6/15th Line Regiment (20/820)
6/121st Line Regiment (20/820)
6/122nd Line Regiment (20/820)
Artillery
19/4th Foot Artillery (2/98)
24/4th Foot Artillery (2/98)
2 Train companies (4/180)
1 Military equipage company (2/127)
52nd Division:
Brigade:
3/1st Italian Line Regiment (20/820)
3/4th Italian Line Regiment (20/820)
3/7th Italian Line Regiment (20/820)
2 (bis)/1st Italian Légère Regiment (20/820)
3/2nd Italian Légère Regiment (20/820)
3/,4/Dalmatian Regiment (20/820 ea)
Brigade:
Regiment to be designated (3)(50,2,460)
1/,2/,3/3rd Neapolitan Regiment (20/820 ea)
Brigade:
1/,2/,3/4th Neapolitan Regiment (20/820 ea)
1/,2/,3/,4/Neapolitan Légère Regiment (20/820 ea)
Artillery:
2 Italian Foot Artillery Batteries (108 ea)
2 Italian train companies (108)
1 Italian military equipage company (2/127)
Corps Cavalry:
1/Queen's Dragoon Regiment (15/245/270)
2/Queen's Dragoon Regiment (8/242/250)
3/Queen's Dragoon Regiment (8/242/250)
4/Queen's Dragoon Regiment (8/242/250)
1/3rd Italian Chasseur à cheval Regiment (15/245/270)
2/3rd Italian Chasseur à cheval Regiment (8/242/250)
3/3rd Italian Chasseur à cheval Regiment (8/242/250)
4/3rd Italian Chasseur à cheval Regiment (8/242/250)
1/1st Neapolitan Chasseur à cheval Regt. (15/245/270)
2/1st Neapolitan Chasseur à cheval Regiment (8/242/250)
3/1st Neapolitan Chasseur à cheval Regiment (8/242/250)
1/3rd Neapolitan Chasseur à cheval Regt. (15/245/270)
2/3rd Neapolitan Chasseur à cheval Regt. (8/242/250)
3/3rd Neapolitan Chasseur à cheval Regt. (8/242/250)
5/13th Hussar Regiment (8/242/250)
5/14th Hussar Regiment (8/242/250)
7/19th Chasseur à cheval Regiment (8/242/250)
cavalry regiment to be designated (1)(8/242/250)
Reserve and Park Artillery:
2 French Foot Artillery Companies (4/196)
2 French Artillery Train Companies (4/180)
4/4th Horse Artillery (2/88)
5/4th Horse Artillery (2/88)

6/4th Horse Artillery (2/88)
3 French Artillery Train Companies (6/270)
1 Italian Horse Artillery Company (2/80)
1 Italian Artillery Train Company (2/90)
1 Italian Sapper Company (2/118)
1 French Sapper Company (2/118)
2 French military equipage train companies (4/254)

• Awaiting armament, clothing, or other equipment
before being able to depart to the regiment.
† These battalions were to be completed with drafts from
the Class of 1814 and sent to Utrecht.
‡ These battalions were to be completed with drafts from
the Class of 1814 and sent to Mainz.

RUSSO-PRUSSIAN ORDER OF BATTLE BATTLE OF LÜTZEN 2 MAY 1813

RUSSIAN COMMANDER: GENERAL OF CAVALRY WITTGENSTEIN
Advanced Guard and Streifkorps
Brigade: Colonel Davidov
Davydov Streifkorps (4)
Brigade: Colonel Mandatov
Mandatov Streifkorps (4)
Brigade: Generalmajor Karpov II
Karpov #2 Don Cossack Regiment
Grekov #2 Don Cossack Regiment (2)
Jagodin #2Don Cossack Regiment (2)
Zikelev Don Cossack Regiment (2)
2nd Bug Cossack Regiment (2)
Brigade: Generalmajor Ilowaisky IV
Grekov #3 Don Cossack Regiment (2)
Grekov #9 Don Cossack Regiment (2)
Semenschenkov Don Cossack Regiment
Brigade: Generalmajor Ilowaisky X
Platov #4 Don Cossack Regiment (2)
Lotschilin #1 Don Cossack Regiment (2)
Koschkin Don Cossack Regiment
Illowaiski #10 Don Cossack Regiment (2)
Gorin #1 Don Cossack Regiment (2)
5th Bashkir Regiment (2)
Other:
2nd Bug Cossack Regiment
Staropol Kalmuck Regiment

1ST LINE: GENERAL OF CAVALRY BLÜCHER
Right Wing or Upper Silesian Brigade: Generalmajor von Zeithen
Cavalry: Major Laroche von Starkenfeld
Brigade: Major von Blücher
2/,4/1st Silesian Hussar Regiment (2)
3/,4/2nd Silesian Hussar Regiment (2)
Brigade: Major von Schmiedburg
1/,2/Silesian Uhlan Regiment (2)
Prussian Horse Battery #9 von Tuschen
Infantry: Oberst von Pirch
Brigade: Major von Carnall
Silesian Grenadier Battalion (1)
1/1st Silesian Infantry Regiment
3/1st Silesian Infantry Regiment
Artillery:
Russian Position Battery #1
6pdr Foot Battery #11 von Mandelsohe
Brigade: Oberst von Losthin

1/2nd Silesian Infantry Regiment
3/2nd Silesian Infantry Regiment
Fus/1st Silesian Infantry Regiment
Silesian Schützen Battalion
Artillery:
6pdr Foot Battery #13 von Held
1/2 12pdr Foot Battery #3 (4 guns)
Russian Position Battery #33

Left Wing or Lower Silesian Brigade: Oberst and Wing Adjutant von Klüx
Cavalry Brigade: Oberst von Mutius
1/,2/,3/,4/Neumark Dragoon Regiment (4)
2/,4/1st West Prussian Dragoon Regiment (2)
Prussian Horse Battery #7 Richter
Infantry: Major von Jagow
Brigade:
West Prussian Grenadier Battalion
2/1st West Prussian Infantry Regiment
3/1st West Prussian Infantry Regiment
Brigade: Major von Anhalt
2/2nd West Prussian Infantry Regiment
3/2nd West Prussian Infantry Regiment
6pdr Foot Battery #7
Russian Position Battery #14
Fus/1st West Prussian Infantry Regiment
Reserve of the 1st Line or Brandenburg Brigade: Generalmajor von Röder
Brigade: Oberstlieutenant Katzler
1/,2/,3/,4/West Prussian Uhlan Regiment (4)
1/,2/Brandenburg Hussar Regiment (2)
Horse Battery #8
Infantry: Oberstlieutenant von Tippelskirch
Brigade: Major von Albensleben
Guard Jäger Battalion (1)
1/Guard Infantry Regiment
2/Guard Infantry Regiment
Fus/Guard Infantry Regiment
Normal Infantry Battalion
Guard 6pdr Foot Battery #4 von Lehmann
6pdr Foot Battery #9 von Grevenitz
Brigade: Major von Natzmer
Leib Grenadier Battalion
1st East Prussian Grenadier Battalion
3/Leib Infantry Regiment
Guard Freiwilliger Jager Battalion von Wedell

2ND LINE: GENERALLIEUTENANT VON YORCK
Right Wing: Generalmajor Berg
Brigade: Generalmajor Alexeiev
Mitau Dragoon Regiment
Position Battery #5
5th Division: Generalmajor Lukov
Brigade: Generalmajor Mesenzov
Perm Infantry Regiment (1)
Sievesk Infantry Regiment (1)
Grandduchess Catherine Battalion
Brigade: Generalmajor Prince of Siberia
Kalouga Infantry Regiment (1)
Mohilev Infantry Regiment (1)
14th Division: Generalmajor Lalin
Brigade: Generalmajor Helfreich
Tenguinsk Infantry Regiment (1)
Estonia Infantry Regiment (1)
Light Battery #27
Left Wing: Generalmajor von Hünerbein
Brigade:
1st Combined Infantry Regiment

2/1st East Prussian Infantry Regiment
Fus/1st East Prussian Infantry Regiment
1/2nd East Prussian Infantry Regiment
Fus/Leib Infantry Regiment
1/,2/,3/,4/Lithuanian Dragoon Regiment (4)
1/2 6pdr Foot Battery #3
6pdr Foot Battery #1
Brigade: Oberst Horn
5th Combined Infantry Regiment
1/1st West Prussian Infantry Regiment
2/,Fus/2nd West Prussian Infantry Regiment
East Prussian Jäger Battalion (2 cos) (Detached to Kleist)
6th Combined Infantry Regiment
2/1st Silesian Infantry Regiment
2/2nd Silesian Infantry Regiment
Fus/2nd Silesian Infantry Regiment
2nd Combined Dragoon Regiment
1/,2/1st West Prussian Dragoon Regiment (2)
1/,3/Brandenburg Dragoon Regiment (2)
Artillery:
1/2 12pdr Battery #3 Roszynsky (4 guns)
6pdr Foot Battery #2
Reserve of Right Wing of 2nd Line: Generalmajor Kasatschkosky
Ataman Cossack Regiment
Don Cossack Battery #1
Brigade Colonel Brischinsky
Converged Grenadiers of 5th Division (2)
Converged Grenadiers of 14th Division (2)
Brigade:
Reserve Grenadier Battalions of 1st Division (5)
Reserve of the Left Wing of the 2nd Line: Oberstleutnant von Steinmetz
1/,2/,3/,4/2nd Leib Hussar Regiment (4)
6pdr Horse Battery #2
1/Colberg Infantry Regiment
2/Colberg Infantry Regiment
Fus/Colberg Infantry Regiment
3pdr Foot Battery #1

1st Reserve: Generallieutenant Baron von Winzingerode
Prussian Reserve Cavalry Brigade: Oberst von Dolffs
Brigade: Oberstlieutenant von Werder
1/,2/,3/,4/Garde du Corps Regiment (4 + 1 Freiwilligerjäger Squadron)
1/,2/,3/,4/Guard Light Cavalry Regiment (4 + 2 Freiwilligerjäger Squadrons)
Guard Horse Battery #4 von Willmann
Brigade: Oberst von Jürgass
1/,2/,3/,4/East Prussian Cuirassier Regiment (4)
1/,2/,3/,4/Silesian Cuirassier Regiment (4)
1/,2/,3/,4/Brandenburg Cuirassier Regiment (4)
Horse Battery #10 von Schöffer
Attached from Steinmetz:
Horse Battery #3
Cavalry Reserve: Generalmajor Count Trubetzkoy
Hussar Division: Generalmajor Lanskoi
Brigade: Generalmjor Paradovsky
Alexandria Hussar Regiment (3)
White Russia Hussar Regiment (3)
Soum Hussar Regiment (2)
Lithuanian Chasseur à Cheval Regiment (3)
Cavalry: Generalmajor Knorring
Lithuanian Uhlan Regiment (2)
Tartar Uhlan Regiment (4)
Converged Dragoon Regiment (2)
Horse Artillery Reserve: Generalmajor Nikitin
Horse Battery #1 (2 guns)

Horse Battery #3 (11 guns)
Horse Battery #7 (12 guns)
Horse Battery #8 (12 guns)
Horse Battery #2
Cossack Regiments: Generalmajor Ilowaisky XII
   Ilowaisky #12 Don Cossack Regiment
   Kutainikov #4 Don Cossack Regiment
   Sementshenko Don Cossack Regiment
   Grekov #3 Don Cossack Regiment
   Grekov #21 Don Cossack Regiment

2nd Corps: Generalleutnant Prinz Eugene von Wurttemberg
Brigade:
   1st Ukrainian Cossack Regiment
   Light Battery #6
3rd Division: Generalmajor Count Schachafskoi
Brigade: Colonel Schilvinsky
   Mourmansk Infantry Regiment (1)
   Revel Infantry Regiment (1)
   Tchernigov Infantry Regiment (1)
Brigade: Colonel Kapustin
   20th Jager Regiment (1)
   21st Jager Regiment (1)
   Light Artillery Battery #7
4th Division: Generalmajor St. Priest
Brigade: Colonel Treffurt
   Tobolsk Infantry Regiment (1)
   Volhynie Infantry Regiment (1)
   Krementsoug Infantry Regiment (1)
Brigade: Colonel Ivanov
   4th Jager Regiment (1)
   34th Jager Regiment (1)
Artillery:
   Light Battery #33
   Attached:
   3rd Ukrainian Cossack Regiment

RESERVE ARMY: GENERAL OF CAVALRY TORMASSOV
1st Line: Generalleutnant Konovnizin
Guard Light Cavalry Division: Generalmajor Schaevitch
Brigade: Generalmajor Tschailkov
   Guard Uhlan Regiment (4)
   Guard Hussar Regiment (4)
   Horse Battery #4
Brigade: Generalmajor Tichischerin
   Guard Dragoon Regiment
   Guard Cossack Regiment
   Guard Black Sea Cossack Sotnia
1st Grenadier Division: Generalmajor Sulima
Brigade: Colonel Kniaschnin II
   Count Arakcheyev Grenadier Regiment (2)
   Ekaterinoslav Grenadier Regiment (2)
Brigade: Colonel Acht
   Tauride Grenadier Regiment (2)
   St. Petersburg Grenadier Regiment (2)
   Position Battery #30
   Light Battery #14
2nd Division: Generalmajor Zwielenief
Brigade: Colonel Pissareff
   Kiev Grenadier Regiment (2)
   Moscow Grenadier Regiment (2)
Brigade: Colonel Golowin
   Astrakhan Grenadier Regiment (2)
   Fangoria Grenadier Regiment (2)
Brigade: Colonel Hesse
   Little Russia Grenadier Regiment (2)
   Siberian Grenadier Regiment (2)
Artillery:
   Position Battery #32

2nd Line: Generalleutnant Gallizin V
1st Cuirassier Division: Generalmajor Depreradovich
Brigade: Generalmajor Arenief
   Chevalier Garde Regiment
   Horse Guard Regiment
Brigade: Generalmajor Rosen
   Emperor (Leib Garde) Cuirassier Regiment
   Empress Cuirassier Regiment (3)
Brigade: Generalmajir Kretov
   Astrakhan Cuirassier Regiment (3)
   Ekatrinoslav Cuirassier Regiment (3)
Artillery:
   Guard Horse Battery #1
1st Guard Division: Generalmajor Baron Rosen
Brigade: Generalmajor Potemkin
   1/Preobragenski Guard Regiment
   2/Preobragenski Guard Regiment
   1/Semenovski Guard Regiment
   2/Semenovski Guard Regiment
Brigade: Generalmajor Krapovitzky
   1/Guard Jager Regiment
   2/Guard Jager Regiment
   1/Ismailov Guard Regiment
   2/Ismailov Guard Regiment
Artillery:
   Guard Light Battery #1
   Guard Position Battery #1
2nd Guard Division: Generalmajor Udom II
Brigade: Colonel Krischanovsky
   1/Lithuanian Guard Regiment
   2/Lithuanian Guard Regiment
   1/Finland Guard Regiment
   2/Finland Guard Regiment
Brigade: Generalmajor Scheltuchin II
   1/,2/Pavlov Grenadier Regiment (2)
   1/,2/Leib Grenadier Regiment (2)
Artillery:
   Guard Light Battery #2
   Guard Position Battery #2
2nd Cuirassier Division: Generalmajor Duca
Brigade: Generalmajor Leontiev
   Gluchov Cuirassier Regiment (3)
   Pskof Cuirassier Regiment (3)
Brigade: Generalmajor Gudowitsch
   Military Order Cuirassier Regiment (3)
   Starodoub Cuirassier Regiment (3)
Brigade: Colonel Massalov
   Little Russian Cuirassier Regiment (3)
   Novgorod Cuirassier Regiment (3)
   Guard Horse Battery #2
Artillery Reserve: Generalmajor Euler
   Position Battery #7
   Position Battery #31
   Light Battery #5
   Light Battery #28
   Light Battery #32
   Light Battery #36

Plotho, C., Der Krieg in Deutschland

FRENCH ORDER OF BATTLE
LÜTZEN 2 MAY 1813

COMMANDER: EMPEROR NAPOLEON I
Imperial Guard: Maréchal Mortier
(Strength Figures as of 25 April 1813)

Old Guard Division: Général de division Roguet
Velites of Turin (15/301)
Velites of Florence (16/173)
1/1st Grenadier à Pied Regiment (15/421)
1/1st Chasseur à Pied Regiment (17/495)
1/2nd Grenadier à Pied Regiment (15/569)
1/2nd Chasseur à Pied Regiment (18/689)
3rd Old Guard Foot Battery (6-6pdrs & 2-5.7" howitzers)

1st Young Guard Division: Général de division Dumoustier
1st Brigade: Général de brigade Berthezène
1/Fusilier Chasseur Regiment (14/637)
1/Fusilier Grenadier Regiment (15/528)
1/6th Tirailleur Regiment (14/521)
2/6th Tirailleur Regiment (14/597)
1/7th Tirailleur Regiment (17/710)
2/7th Tirailleur Regiment (14/712)
2nd Brigade: Général de brigade Lanusse
1/1st Tirailleur Regiment (15/680)
2/1st Tirailleur Regiment (8/690)
1/2nd Tirailleur Regiment (11/458)
2/2nd Tirailleur Reigment (16/650)
3rd Brigade: Général de brigade Tindal
1/1st Voltigeur Regiment (15/529)
2/1st Voltigeur Regiment (12/684)
1/2nd Voltigeur Regiment (17/449)
2/2nd Voltigeur Regiment (16/668)
1/6th Tirailleur Regiment (14/521)
2/6th Tirailleur Regiment (14/597)
Artillery:
2nd Old Guard Foot Battery (6-12pdrs & 2 5.7" howitzers)
1st Young Guard Foot Battery (6-6pdrs & 2-5.7" howitzers)
2nd Young Guard Foot Battery (6-6pdrs & 2-5.7" howitzers)

Guard Cavalry: Maréchal Bessières (2,800)
Division: Général de division Walther
1st Brigade: Général de Ornano
◊Numbers are officers, men and horses.
Guard Chasseur à Cheval Regiment (28/707/813)
Chevau-Léger de Berg (18/487/551)
2nd Guard Lancer Regiment (26/664/750)
Gendarmes d'élite (11/287/336)
2nd Brigade: Général Letort
1st Guard Lancer Regiment (42/496/510)
Guard Dragoon Regiment (27/630/769)
Guard Grenadier à Cheval Regiment (21/485/583)
Guard Artillery: Général de brigade Dulaloy (later Drouot)
1st Old Guard Foot Battery (6 12pdrs & 2-6" howitzers)
4th Old Guard Foot Battery (6 12pdrs & 2-6" howitzers)
5th Old Guard Foot Battery (6 12pdrs & 2-6" howitzers)
1st Guard Horse Battery (4 6pdrs & 2-5.7" howitzers)
2nd Guard Horse Battery (4 6pdrs & 2-5.7" howitzers)
Total Young Guard Foot Artillery (10/542)
Total Old Guard Foot Artillery (15/617)
Total Old Guard Horse Artillery (14/287)
Troops à la suite
Italian Royal Guard (27/179)
Gardes d'honneur of Turin (2/58/81)
Gardes d'honneur of Florence (3/40/60)
Gardes d'honneur of Italy (1/19/23)
Italian Guard Dragoons (4/58/71)
Queen's (Italian) Dragoons (9/88/128)
Hessian Infantry (4/82)

III Corps: Marechal Ney
(Strength figures as of 25 April)
8th Division: Général de division Souham (12,227)
1st Brigade: Général de brigade Chasseraux
6th Provisional Légère Regiment

2/6th Légère Regiment (17/652)
3/25th Légère Regiment (19/667)
10th Provisional Légère Regiment
3/16th Légère Regiment (16/691)
1/28th Légère Regiment (20/750)
14th Provisional Line Regiment
4/34th Line Regiment (19/700)
3/40th Line Regiment (20/710)
19th Provisional Line Regiment
6/32nd Line Regiment (16/520)
3/58th Line Regiment (20/515)
2nd Brigade: Général de brigade Chemineau
21st Provisional Line Regiment
3/59th Line Regiment (9/689)
4/69th Line Regiment (22/702)
24th Provisional Line Regiment
3/88th Line Regiment (18/689)
3/103rd Line Regiment (15/705)
1/22nd Line Regiment (24/701)
3/22nd Line Regiment (20/700)
4/22nd Line Regiment (19/670)
6/22nd Line Regiment (16/687)
Artillery:
9/2nd Foot Artillery (2/67)(6-6pdrs & 2-5.7" howitzers)
10/2nd Foot Artillery (2/59)(6-6pdrs & 2-5.7" howitzers)
4/3rd (bis) Train Battalion (1/95)
4/8th Principal Train Battalion (0/80)
1/Spanish Sapper Battalion (3/169)
1/6th Equipage Battalion (2/117)

9th Division: Général de division Brenier
1st Brigade: Général de brigade Anthing
2nd Provisional Légère Regiment
3/2nd Légère Regiment (17/482)
3/4th Légère Regiment (17/495)
1/29th Légère Regiment (19/539)
2/29th Légère Regiment (15/829)
1/136th Line Regiment (27/680)
2/136th Line Regiment (15/620)
3/136th Line Regiment (10/680)
4/136th Line Regiment (12/592)
2nd Brigade: Général de brigade Grillot
1/138th Line Regiment (20/450)
2/138th Line Regiment (18/529)
3/138th Line Regiment (18/507)
4/138th Line Regiment (20/480)
1/145th Line Regiment (24/460)
2/145th Line Regiment (20/489)
3/145th Line Regiment (18/405)
4/145th Line Regiment (15/429)
Artillery: Chef de bataillon Charvet
2/9th Foot Artillery (2/70)(6-6pdrs & 2-5.7" howitzers)
11/9th Foot Artillery (2/6)(6-6pdrs & 2-5.7" howitzers)
Det. 4/3rd (bis) Principal Train Battalion (0/40)
Det. 4/12th Principal Train Battalion (0/9)
Det. 4/6th Principal Train Battalion (1/118)
2/Spanish Sapper Battalion (2/140)
2/6th Military Equipage Battalion (2/120)
10th Division: Général de division Girard
1st Brigade: Général de brigade Goris
4th Provisional Légère Regiment
4/5th Légère Regiment (17/604)
4/12th Légère Regiment (21/408)
1/139th Line Regiment (24/617)
2/139th Line Regiment (20/607)
3/139th Line Regiment (21/529)
4/139th Line Regiment (21/507)
2nd Brigade: Général de brigade Van Dedem
1/140th Line Regiment (30/529)
2/140th Line Regiment (16/507)

3/140th Line Regiment (15/606)
4/140th Line Regiment (15/589)
1/141st Line Regiment (24/410)
2/141st Line Regiment (20/467)
3/141st Line Regiment (16/420)
4/141st Line Regiment (18/417)
Artillery: Chef de bataillon Tripp
   3/7th Foot Artillery (2/76) (6-6pdrs & 2-5.7" howitzers)
   4/7th Foot Artillery (2/75)(6-6pdrs & 2-5.7" howitzers)
   4/1st Principal Train Battalion (1/129)
   7/11th Principal Train Battalion (1/49)
   3/Spanish Sapper Battalion (3/150)
   3/6th Military Equipage Battalion (2/117)

11th Division: Général de division Ricard
1st Brigade: Général de brigade Tarayre
   3/9th Légère Regiment (14/627)
   4/9th Légère Regiment (13/547)
   17th Provisional Line Regiment
      4/43rd Line Regiment (16/629)
      3/75th Line Regiment (17/571)
   18th Provisional Line Regiment
      3/50th Line Regiment (15/571)
      4/65th Line Regiment 14/489)
2nd Brigade: Général de brigade Dumoulin
   1/142nd Line Regiment (29/520)
   2/142nd Line Regiment (20/467)
   3/142nd Line Regiment (20/481)
   4/142nd Line Regiment (18/499)
   1/144th Line Regiment (24/487)
   2/144th Line Regiment (20/529)
   3/144th Line Regiment (17/517)
   4/144th Line Regiment (20/417)
Artillery:
   18/1st Foot Artillery (1/86)(6-6pdr & 2-5.7" howitzers)
   19/7th Foot Artillery (1/87)(6-6pdr & 2-5.7" howitzers)
   Det. 7/11th Principal Train Battalion (0/40)
   Det. 7/12th Principal Train Battalion (0/17)
   Det. 4/13th (bis) Train Battalion (1/130)
   4/Spanish Sapper Battalion (2/150)
   4/6th Military Equipage Battalion (2/115)
39th Division: Général de division Marchand
1st Brigade: Généralmajor Stockhorn
   2/1st Baden Line Regiment (14/664)
   1/3rd Baden Line Regiment (15/729)
   2/3rd Baden Line Regiment (14/709)
2nd Brigade: Généralmajor Prinz Emil von Hessen
   1/1st Hessian Light Regiment (9/567)
   2/1st Hessian Light Regiment (10/589)
   1/2nd Hessian Line Regiment (22/620)
   2/2nd Hessian Line Regiment (15/617)
   1/Hessian Leib-Garde Infantry Regiment (16/620)
   2/Hessian Leib-Garde Infantry Regiment (14/607)
Brigade:
   2/Frankfurt "Zweyer" Regiment (16/660)
Artillery:
   1st Baden Foot Battery (2/60)(4 guns)
   1st Baden Artillery Train Company (1/60)
   1/2 Hessian Foot Battery (1/115)(3 guns)
Cavalry Brigade: Général de brigade Laboissière
   1/10th Hussar Regiment (16/207/250)
   2/10th Hussar Regiment (8/216/226)
   3/10th Hussar Regiment (7/198/212)
   4/10th Hussar Regiment (8/269/283)
   1/,2/,3/Baden Dragoon Regiment (26/474/530)
24th Light Cavalry Brigade: Generalmajor von Jett
•The return shows strengths for the 2nd Chevauleger
Regiment, but it was disbanded in January 1813.
   1/,2/,3/Hessian Chevauleger Regiment (29/461/486)
   1/,2/,3/2nd Württemberg Chevauleger Regiment (28/

469/500)
   1/,2/,3/4th Württemberg Jager zu Pferd Regiment (25/
475/500)
Reserve and Park: Major Tamissier
   6/3rd Foot Artillery (2/68)
   23/3rd Foot Artillery (2/57)
   24/3rd Foot Artillery (2/80)
   8/4th Foot Artillery (2/79)
   7/9th Foot Artillery (2/87)
   8/9th Foot Artillery (2/87)
   17/9th Foot Artillery (2/69)
   1/3rd Horse Artillery (2/68)
   3/4th Horse Artillery (2/79)
   Det. 4/6th (bis) Train Battalion (1/71)
   Det. 4/6th (bis) Train Battalion (0/63)
   Det. 3/10th Principal Train Battalion (1/95)
   Det. 4/3rd Principal Train Battalion (0/5)
   Det. 5/9th Principal Train Battalion (1/105)
   Det. 3/1st Principal Train Battalion (0/57)
   Det. 2/1st Principal Train Battalion (1/68)
   7/10th Principal Train Battalion (1/131)
   6/1st Principal Train Battalion (1/120)
   Det. 4/5th Principal Train Battalion (1/29)
   Det. 4/8th Principal Train Battalion (0/18)
   5/5th (bis) Train Battalion (1/140)
   4/9th (bis) Train Battalion (0/38)
   2/2nd Sapper Battalion (3/128)
   3/5th Sapper Battalion (2/140)
   5th Engineering Train Company (2/143)
   5/6th Military Equipage Train Battalion (2/115)

VI Corps: Maréchal Marmont
(Strengths as of 25 April 1813)
20th Division: Général de division Compans
1st Brigade: Général de brigade Calcault
   1/1st Marine Artillery Regiment (20/609)
   2/1st Marine Artillery Regiment (15/617)
   3/1st Marine Artillery Regiment (18/605)
   4/1st Marine Artillery Regiment (17/661)
   1/3rd Marine Artillery Regiment (15/710)
   2/3rd Marine Artillery Regiment (12/625)
   3/3rd Marine Artillery Regiment (16/758)
2nd Brigade: Général de brigade Joubert
   25th Provisional Line Regiment
      3/47th Line Regiment (15/607)
      3/86th Line Regiment (9/485)
   20th Provisional Line Regiment
      5/66th Line Regiment (12/745)
      3/122nd Line Regiment (12/527)
   2/32nd Légère Regiment (16/519)
   3/32nd Légère Regiment (12/589)
Artillery: Chef de bataillon Grosjean
   1/4th Foot Artillery (2/61)(6-6pdrs & 2-5.7" howitzers)
   10/4th Foot Artillery (2/115) (6-6pdrs & 2-5.7" howitzers)
   Det. 4/5th (bis) Train Battalion (1/100)
   1/10th (bis) Train Battalion (1/85)
   6/2nd Sapper Battalion (2/110)
   1/15th Military Equipage Battalion (3/127)
21st Division: Général de division Bonnet
1st Brigade: Général de brigade Buquet
   1/2nd Marine Artillery Regiment (20/529)
   2/2nd Marine Artillery Regiment (15/467)
   3/2nd Marine Artillery Regiment (15/429)
   4/2nd Marine Artillery Regiment (16/427)
   5/2nd Marine Artillery Regiment (12/460)
   6/2nd Marine Artillery Regiment (13/489)
   1/4th Marine Artillery Regiment (15/710)
   2/4th Marine Artillery Regiment (16/687)
   3/4th Marine Artillery Regiment (10/715)

2nd Brigade: Général de brigade Jamin
  1/37th Légère Regiment (15/760)
  2/37th Légère Regiment (15/795)
  3/37th Légère Regiment (15/780)
  4/37th Légère Regiment (16/766)
  1/Joseph Napoleon Regiment (14/689)
Artillery: Chef de bataillon Malavillers
  14/4th Foot Artillery (2/85)(6-6pdrs & 2-5.7" howitzers)
  21/7th Foot Artillery (2/87)(6-6pdrs & 2-5.7" howitzers)
  Det. 4/4th (bis) Train Battalion (1/108)
  Det. 7/12th Principal Train Battalion (1/85)
  9/4th Sapper Battalion (2/110)
  2/15th Equipage Train Battalion (2/125)
22nd Division: Général de division Friederichs
Brigade: Généraux de brigade Ficatier & Buquet
  3/23rd Légère Regiment (12/589)
  4/23rd Légère Regiment (9/597)
  11th Provisional Line Regiment
    4/1st Line Regiment (12/469
    2/62nd Line Regiment (8/450)
  13th Provisional Line Regiment
    3/14th Line Regiment (18/785)
    4/16th Line Regiment (12/629)
  16th Provisional Line Regiment
    6/26th Line Regiment (15/560)
    6/82nd Line Regiment (12/517)
  3/121st Line Regiment (14/587)
  4/121st Line Regiment (10/529)
  3/15th Line Regiment (16/689)
  4/15th Line Regiment (12/595)
  3/70th Line Regiment (10/515)
  4/70th Line Regiment (10/549)
Artillery: Chef de bataillon Lehaut
  5/9th Foot Artillery (2/80)(6-6pdrs & 2-5.7" howitzers)
  22/9th Foot Artillery (2/69) (6-6pdrs & 2-5.7" howitzers)
  Det. 4/8th Principal Train Battalion (1/58)
  Det. 5/6th (bis) Train Battalion (2/80)
  Det. 4/11th (bis) Train Battalion (0/49)
  2/4th Sapper Battalion (3/110)
  3/15th Military Equipage Battalion (2/115)
29th Light Cavalry Brigade: Général de brigade Beaumont
  1/7th Chevauléger-lancier Regiment (10/256/285)
  2/7th Chevauléger-lancier Regiment (7/256/265)
Corps Reserve Artillery: Colonel Montgenet
  5/2nd Foot Artillery (2/76)
  21/2nd Foot Artillery (2/80)
  18/5th Foot Artillery (1/80)
  25/5th Foot Artillery (2/89)
  10/8th Foot Artillery (2/76)
  12/8th Foot Artillery (2/75)
  16/8th Foot Artillery (2/81)
  1/1st Horse Artillery (2/76)
  5/1st Horse Artillery (2/76)
  Det. 5/3rd (bis) Train Battalion (0/69)
  Det. 5/3rd (bis) Train Battalion (1/64)
  Det. 2/10th (bis) Train Battalion (1/105)
  Det. 6/6th (bis) Train Battalion (1/110)
  7/6th (bis) Train Battalion (2/151)
  Det. 4/4th (bis) Train Battalion (1/32)
  4/10th (bis) Train Battalion (2/108)
  Det. 4/12th (bis) Train Battalion (0/59)
  Det. 6/6th (bis) Train Battalion (0/16)
  Det. 4/8th Principal Train Battalion (1/86)
  Det. 4/9th Principal Train Battalion (1/99)
  2/6th Principal Train Battalion (1/120)
  3/7th Sapper Battalion (3/135)
  2/5th Sapper Battalion (3/129)
  5/15th Military Equipage Battalion (3/120)

IV Corps: *Général de division Bertrand*
(Strengths as of 25 April)
12th Division: Général de division Morand
1st Brigade: Général de brigade Bellair
  1/13th Line Regiment (35/777)
  2/13th Line Regiment (16/758)
  3/13th Line Regiment (17/765)
  4/13th Line Regiment (17/739)
  6/13th Line Regiment (18/739)
  Artillery Det./13th Line Regiment (2/66)(2-3pdrs)
  3rd Provisional Line Regiment
    3/3rd Légère Regiment (21/640)
    4/8th Légère Regiment (15/661)
2nd Brigade: Général de brigade Nagel
  2nd Provisional Croatian Regiment
    2/3rd Croatian Regiment (27/794)
    1/4th Croatian Regiment (18/839)
  1/23rd Line Regiment (23/753)
  2/23rd Line Regiment (9/777)
  4/23rd Line Regiment (10/764)
  6/23rd Line Regiment (10/776)
  Artillery Det./23rd Line Regiment (1/65)(2-3pdrs)
Artillery: Major Pingenot
  1/2nd Foot Artillery (2/88) (6-6pdrs & 2-24pdr howitzers)
  3/2nd Foot Artillery (3/87) (6-6pdrs & 2-24pdr howitzers)
  Det. 1/7th (bis) Train Battalion (1/117)
  Det. 2/7th (bis) Train Battalion (0/49)
  Det. 1/9th Military Equipage Battalion (1/117)
15th Division: Général de division Peyri
1st Brigade: Général de brigade Martel
  3/1st Italian Line Regiment (26/735)
  4/1st Italian Line Regiment (18/803)
  Artillery Det./1st Italian Line Regiment (1/13) (2-3pdrs)
  1/4th Italian Line Regiment (19/619)
  2/4th Italian Line Regiment (17/545)
  3/4th Italian Line Regiment (19/627)
  4/4th Italian Line Regiment (17/633)
  Artillery Det./4th Italian Line Regiment (3/64) (2-3pdrs)
2nd Brigade: Général de brigade St. Andrea
  3/6th Italian Line Regiment (24/805)
  4/6th Italian Line Regiment (18/797)
  Artillery Det./6th Italian Line Regiment (3/67) (2-3pdrs)
3rd Brigade: Général de brigade Moroni
  1/Milan Guard Battalion (21/805)
  1/7th Italian Line Regiment (30/716)
  2/7th Italian Line Regiment (16/612)
  3/7th Italian Line Regiment (14/654)
  4/7th Italian Line Regiment (17/658)
  Artillery Det./7th Italian Line Regiment (1/27) (2-3pdrs)
Artillery: Chef de bataillon Gorio
  1st Italian Foot Artillery Company (5/115) (6-6pdrs & 2 howitzers)
  13th Italian Foot Artillery Company (4/110) (6-6pdrs & 2 howitzers)
  5th Italian Train Company (3/140)
  6th Italian Train Company (2/141)
  3rd Italian Sapper Company (3/115)
  3rd Italian Naval Artisan Company (3/109)
  2nd Italian Sailor Company (2/95)
  5th Italian Military Equipage Company (2/126)
38th Division: Generallieutenant Franquemont
Brigade: Generalmajor Stockmayer
  1/9th Württemberg Light Regiment (13/675)
  1/10th Württemberg Light Regiment (13/654)
  1/7th Württemberg Line Regiment (9/275)
  2/7th Württemberg Line Regiment (11/409)
Brigade: Generalmajor Neuffer
  1/1st Württemberg Line Regiment (14/546)
  2/1st Württemberg Line Regiment (14/562)

330

1/2nd Württemberg Line Regiment (14/621)
2/2nd Württemberg Line Regiment (14/583)
Artillery:
1st Württemberg Foot Battery "Toikede" (3/113) (4-6pdrs
& 2 howitzers)
1st Württemberg Horse Battery "Burgi" (3/138) (4-6pdrs &
2 howitzers)
Cavalry Division: Général de division Fresia
Brigade: Général de brigade Briche
1/2nd Neapolitan Chasseur à Cheval Regt. (13/247/276)
2/2nd Neapolitan Chasseur à Cheval Regt. (7/248/258)
Artillery: Chef de bataillon Ions
8/4th Horse Artillery (5/79)(4-6pdrs & 2-24pdr howitzers)
Det. 5/7th (bis) Train Battalion (1/49)
Corps Artillery: Colonel Ménoire
26/2nd Foot Artillery (3/81) (4-6pdrs & 2-24pdr
howitzers)
Det. 2/7th (bis) Train Battalion (0/6)
6/7th (bis) Train Battalion (2/148)
7/7th (bis) Train Battalion (2/187)
Det. 13th Artillery Artisan Company (1/29)
2/1st Sapper Battalion (2/148)
8/1st Sapper Battalion (2/148)
3/3rd Sapper Battalion (transferred to XII Corps)
Det/Engineering Equipage Train (1/33)
2/9th Military Equipage Battalion (2/127)
3/9th Military Equipage Battalion (2/118)
4/9th Military Equipage Battalion (2/115)
5/9th Military Equipage Battalion (2/119)
6/9th Military Equipage Battalion (2/125)

XII Corps Maréchal Oudinot
(Strengths as of 25 April 1813)
13th Division: Général de division Pacthod
Brigade: Général de brigade Pourailly
4/1st Légère Regiment (18/836)
3/7th Line Regiment (17/609)
4/7th Line Regiment (14/589)
12th Provisional Regiment
4/10th Line Regiment (10/709)
4/42nd Line Regiment (15/670)
23rd Provisional Regiment
7/6th Line Regiment (15/819)
4/67th Line Regiment (13/828)
Brigade: Général de brigade Gruyer
1/4th Neapolitan Légère Regiment (29/629)
2/4th Neapolitan Légère Regiment (13/641)
3/4th Neapolitan Légère Regiment (16/518)
2/101st Line Regiment (20/689)
3/101st Line Regiment (16/629)
4/101st Line Regiment (18/528)
Artillery: Chef de bataillon Rapallo
18/4th Foot Artillery (2/87 (6-6pdrs & 2-24pdr howitzers)
20/4th Foot Artillery (2/80) (6-6pdrs & 2-24pdr howitzers)
Det. 2/7th (bis) Train Battalion (1/58)
3/7th (bis) Train Battalion (2/76)
1/17th Military Equipage Battalion (2/147)
14th Division: Général de division Lorencz
1st Brigade: Général de brigade Leclerc
3/52nd Line Regiment (18/720)
4/52nd Line Regiment (17/587)
1/137th Line Regiment (18/729)
2/137th Line Regiment (12/740)
3/137th Line Regiment (15/789)
4/137th Line Regiment (15/774)
Brigade: Général de brigade d'Henin
5th Provisional Regiment
7/14th Légère Regiment (16/580)
6/18th Légère Regiment (15/520)

1/156th Line Regiment (20/727)
2/156th Line Regiment (20/736)
3/156th Line Regiment (19/748)
4/156th Line Regiment (15/771)
2/Illyrian Regiment (22/674)
Artillery: Chef de bataillon Boyer
2/4th Foot Artillery (2/110) (6-6pdrs & 2-24pdr howitzers)
25/4th Foot Artillery (1/77) (6-6pdrs & 2-24pdr howitzers)
Det. 2/7th (bis) Train Battalion (1/30)
4/7th (bis) Train Battalion (1/90)
2/17th Equipage Battalion (2/147)
XII Corps Artillery Reserve:
24/2nd Foot Artillery (2/86)(6-12pdrs & 2-6" howitzers)
Det. 2/7th (bis) Train Battalion (0/20)
5/7th (bis) Train Battalion (2/99)
3/3rd Sapper Battalion (2/137)(in Augsburg 4 June)
7/3rd Sapper Battalion (3/134)(in Augsburg 4 June)
3/17th Equipage Train Battalion (2/147)
4/17th Equipage Train Battalion (2/145)
5/17th Equipage Train Battalion (2/147)
6/17th Equipage Train Battalion (2/137)

ARMÉE DE L'ELBE: PRINCE EUGÈNE
V Corps: Général de division Lauriston (strength as of 1 May)
16th Division: Général de division Maison
1st Brigade: Général de brigade Avril
1/151st Line Regiment (34/433)
2/151st Line Regiment (18/461)
3/151st Line Regiment (19/454)
4/151st Line Regiment (19/450)
2nd Brigade: Général de brigade Montesquou Fezensac
1/152nd Line Regiment (20/578)
2/152nd Line Regiment (20/648)
3/152nd Line Regiment (21/535)
3rd Brigade: Général de brigade Penne
1/153rd Line Regiment (31/725)
2/153rd Line Regiment (21/641)
3/153rd Line Regiment (17/620)
4/153rd Line Regiment (15/648)
Artillery: Vozguet
1/1st Foot Artillery (2/90) (6-6pdrs & 2 24pdr howitzers)
3/1st Foot Artillery (2/96) (6-6pdrs & 2 24pdr howitzers)
Det. 7/1st (bis) Train Battalion (0/64)
Det. 7/2nd Principal Train Battalion (1/60)
Det. 1/12th Principal Train Battalion (1/76)
1/6th Sapper Battalion (3/104)
1/2nd Military Equipage Battalion (3/127)
17th Division: Général de division Puthod
1st Brigade: Général de brigade Gachod
1/146th Line Regiment (32/561)
2/146th Line Regiment (13/445)
3/146th Line Regiment (16/655)
4/146th Line Regiment (19/549)
1/147th Line Regiment (34/675)
2/147th Line Regiment (13/602)
3/147th Line Regiment (14/643)
4/147th Line Regiment (13/611)
2nd Brigade: Général de brigade Pastol
1/148th Line Regiment (22/420)
2/148th Line Regiment (16/623)
3/148th Line Regiment (12/720)
4/148th Line Regiment (14/420)
Artillery: Chef de bataillon Bonafos
1/5th Foot Artillery (1/99)(6-6pdrs & 2-5.7" howitzers)
11/5th Foot Artillery (3/103) (6-6pdrs & 2-5.7" howitzers)
7/11th Principal Train Battalion (1/160)
2/6th Sapper Battalion (3/112)

2/2nd Military Equipage Battalion (3/127)

18th Division: Général de division Lagrange
1st Brigade: Général de brigade Charrière
  1/134th Line Regiment (23/753)
  2/134th Line Regiment (23/749)
  1/154th Line Regiment (25/390)
  2/154th Line Regiment (17/385)
  3/154th Line Regiment (21/625)
  4/154th Line Regiment (20/601)
2nd Brigade: Général de brigade Suden
  1/155th Line Regiment (35/547)
  2/155th Line Regiment (17/362)
  3/155th Line Regiment (15/433)
  4/155th Line Regiment (15/534)
  1/3rd Foreign Regiment (Irish Legion)(27/496)
  2/3rd Foreign Regiment (Irish Legion)(22/476)
Artillery: Chef de bataillon Chateaubrun
  10/1st Foot Artillery (2/96) (6-6pdrs & 2 2-24pdr howitzers)
  12/1st Foot Artillery (2/94) (6-6pdrs & 2 2-24pdr howitzers)
  4/8th (bis) Train Battalion (1/64)
  7/1st (bis) Train Battalion (0/64)
  3/6th Sapper Battalion (3/101)
  3/2nd Military Equipage Battalion (3/127)

19th Division: Général de division Rochambeau
1st Brigade: Général de brigade Lacrois
  1/135th Line Regiment (31/530)
  2/135th Line Regiment (15/681)
  3/135th Line Regiment (16/587)
  4/135th Line Regiment (13/579)
2nd Brigade: Général de brigade Lafitte
  1/149th Line Regiment (40/492)
  2/149th Line Regiment (14/597)
  3/149th Line Regiment (14/636)
  4/149th Line Regiment (13/696)
3rd Brigade: Général de brigade Harlet
  1/150th Line Regiment (21/617)
  2/150th Line Regiment (17/578)
  3/150th Line Regiment (18/716)
  4/150th Line Regiment (20/744)
Artillery: Chef de bataillon Richard
  12/5th Foot Artillery (2/94) (6-6pdrs & 2-24pdr howitzers)
  17/5th Foot Artillery (2/94) (6-6pdrs & 2-24pdr howitzers)
  4/4th Principal Train Battalion (1/71)
  1/12th Principal Train Battalion (1/76)
  4/6th Sapper Battalion (3/102)
  4/2nd Military Equipage Train Battalion (3/127)

Corps Reserve: Général de brigade de Camas
  15/1st Foot Artillery (3/93) (6-12pdrs & 2 5.7" howitzers)
  16/1st Foot Artillery (3/94) (6-12pdrs & 2 5.7" howitzers)
  2/5th Horse Artillery (2/83) (4-6pdrs & 2-24pdr howitzers)
  7/6th Horse Artillery (2/81) (4-6pdrs & 2-24pdr howitzers)
  Det. 3/3dr Principal Train Battalion (1/125)
  Det. 4/11th (bis) Train Battalion (0/77)
  4/2nd Sapper Battalion (3/118)
  5/2nd Military Equipage Battalion (3/127)
Artillery Park: Colonel Levasseur
  17/1st Foot Artillery (1/91)
  Det. 7/1st (bis) Train Battalion (0/64)
  Det. 7/2nd Principal Train Batalion (0/60)
  Det. 1/12th Principal Train Batalion (0/75)
  Det. 7/11th Principal Train Batalion (1/24)
  Det. 4/8th (bis) Train Batalion (0/65)
  Det. 4/4th Principal Train Battalion (0/60)
  Det. 7/9th Principal Train Battalion (1/123)
  Det. 4/9th (bis) Train Battalion (1/133)

Det. 4/14th Principal Train Battalion (1/73)

XI Corps: Maréchal Macdonald
(strength as of 1 May)
31st Division: Général de division Fressinet (92/2,496)
  11th Provisional Demi-brigade
    4/27th Légère Regiment
    4/50th Line Regiment
  13th Provisional Demi-brigade
    4/5th Line Regiment
    4/11th Line Regiment
    4/79th Line Regiment (19/733)
  Neapolitan Elite Regiment (1)
  Neapolitan Marines (1 co)
Artillery: Chef de bataillion Pariset
  16/5th Foot Artillery Company (6-6pdrs & 2-5.7" howitzers)
  1st Neapolitan Horse Battery (4-6pdrs & 2-24pdr howitzers)
  Det/8th Principal Train Battalion
  Det/12th Principal Train Battalion
  Det/14th Principal Train Battalion
35th Division: Général de division Gérard (197/5,926)
1st Brigade: Général de brigade Senecal
  3/,4/,7/6th Line Regiment
  1/,2/,3/,4/112th Line Regiment
2nd Brigade: Général de brigade Zucchi
  3/,4/2nd Italian Légère Regiment
  1/,2/,3/,4/5th Italian Line Regiment
Cavalry: (2/443)
  1/4th Italian Chasseur à Cheval Regiment
  1/Würzburg Jäger zu Pferd Regiment
Artillery:
  6/1st Foot Artillery Company (6-6pdrs & 2-5.7" howitzers)
  20/5th Foot Artillery Company (6-6pdrs & 2-5.7" howitzers)
  3rd Italian Horse Battery (4-6pdrs & 2-24pdr howitzers)
  Det. 1/11th (bis) Train Battalion
  10th Italian Train Company
  9th Italian Sapper Company
36th Division: Général de division Charpentier (193/5,944)
1st Brigade: Général de brigade Simmer
  3/,4/14th Légère Regiment (46/1,384)
  1/,2/,3/,4/22nd Légère Regiment
2nd Brigade: Général de brigade Meunier
  14th Provisional Demi-brigade
    3/67th Line Regiment
    6/10th Line Regiment
    6/20th Line Regiment
  15th Provisional Demi-brigade
    4/3rd Légère Regiment
    4/102nd Line Regiment
Artillery: Chef de brigade Dérivaux
  5/1st Foot Artillery Company (6-6pdrs & 2-5.7" howitzers)
  19/2nd Foot Artillery Company (6-6pdrs & 2-5.7" howitzers)
  Det. 1/7th Principal Train Battalion
  Det. 2/12th Principal Train Battalion
Reserve & Park: Major Gargant
  3rd Italian Pontooneer Company
  7/5th Sapper Battalion
  1/7th Sapper Battalion
  2/7th Sapper Battalion
  Det/12th Equipage Train Battalion

I Cavalry Corps: Général de division Latour-Maubourg
(strength as of 1 May)
1st Light Cavalry Division: Général de division Bruyère

(34/519/81/514 horses)
1st Brigade: Général de brigade Bessières
•Figures are officers, men, officers horses and enlisted horses.
   1/,2/,3/7th Hussar Regiment (7/106/18/107)
   1/,2/,3/8th Hussar Regiment (6/93/12/94)
   7th Chevauléger-lancier Regiment (3/24/7/23)
•The records in the army archives indicate that the 7th Chevauléger Regiment was present, but those of the National Archives indicate it was absent.
   1/,2/,3/9th Chevauléger-lancier Regiment (2/17/6/16)
   1/,2/,3/16th Chasseur à Cheval Regiment (6/114/14/113)
2nd Brigade: Général de brigade Cambraceres
   1/,2/,3/1st Chevauléger-lancier Regiment (5/92/11/91)
   1/,2/,3/3rd Chevauléger-lancier Regiment (3/56/6/55)
   1/,2/,3/5th Chevauléger-lancier Regiment (2/17/7/15)
   1/,2/,3/8th Chevauléger-lancier Regiment (24/276/364)
3rd Light Cavalry Division: Général de division Chastel (Chastel was absent) (35/871/70/876)
1st Brigade: Général de brigade Van Merlen
   1/,2/,3/6th Chasseur à Cheval Regiment (6/141/11/140)
   1/,2/,3/25th Chasseur à Cheval Regiment (3/55/7/55)
   1/,2/,3/6th Hussar Regiment (6/178/14/179)
   1/,2/,3/8th Chasseur à Cheval Regiment (4/78/9/78)
   Portuguese Legion Chasseur à Cheval Regt. (3/68/6/68)
2nd Brigade: Général de brigade Richter (absent)
   1/,2/,3/9th Chasseur à Cheval Regiment (-/detached)
   1/,7/19th Chasseur à Cheval Regiment (-/detached)
   1/,2/,3/1st Chasseur à Cheval Regiment (4/138/149)
   1/,2/,3/2nd Chasseur à Cheval Regiment (2/81/85)
1st Cuirassier Division: Général de division Bordesoulle (31/723)
1st Brigade: Général de brigade Berkheim
   1/,2/,3/2nd Cuirassier Regiment (6/145/19/144)
   1/,2/,3/3rd Cuirassier Regiment (5/105/12/106)
   1/,2/,3/6th Cuirassier Regiment (6/96/12/95)
2nd Brigade: Général de brigade Quinette
   1/,2/,3/9th Cuirassier Regiment (5/167/10/168)
   1/,2/,3/11th Cuirassier Regiment (6/129/13/136)
   1/,2/,3/12th Cuirassier Regiment (3/81/7/81)
3rd Cuirassier Division: Général de division Doumerc (34/612)
1st Brigade: Général de brigade Chouard
   1/,2/,3/4th Cuirassier Regiment (3/41/7/42)
   1/,2/,3/7th Cuirassier Regiment (3/53/7/52)
   1/,2/,3/14th Cuirassier Regiment (1/22/2/22)
2nd Brigade: Général de brigade Reizet
   1/,2/,3/7th Dragoon Regiment (6/113/13/113)
   1/,2/,3/23rd Dragoon Regiment (6/119/14/119)
   1/,2/,3/28th Dragoon Regiment (5/114/14/113)
   1/,2/,3/30th Dragoon Regiment (8/126/11/127)
   Provisional Dragoon Regiment (2/24/4/24)
Corps Artillery:
   3/1st Horse Artillery (3/76) (4-6pdrs & 2 24pdr howitzers)
   1/6th Horse Artillery (3/81) (4-6pdrs & 2 24pdr howtzers)
   1/1st (bis) Train Battalion (1/51)
   1/8th (bis) Train Battalion (1/52)
•Figures are officers, men and horses.

DUMOUSTIER'S 1ST YOUNG GUARD DIVISION
4 MAY 1813

1st Brigade:
   Combined Regiment (26/1,092)
   1/Fusilier-Grenadier Regiment

   1/Fusilier-Chasseur Regiment
   2nd Tirailleur Regiment (16/816)
   2nd Old Guard Foot Battery (2/99)
   Guard Train Battalion (1 co)(1/91)
2nd Brigade: Général de brigade Lanusse
   1/,2/1st Voltigeur Regiment (21/997)
   1/,2/2nd Voltigeur Regiment (24/701)
   1/,2/6th Voltigeur Regiment (28,1050)
   1st Young Guard Foot Battery (2/133)
   Guard Train Battalion (1 co)(1/112)
3rd Brigade: Général de brigade Tindal
   1/,2/1st Tirailleur Regiment (20/1,025)
   1/,2/6th Tirailleur Regiment (23/992)
   1/,2/7th Tirailleur Regiment (26/1,042)
   2nd Young Guard Foot Battery (2/125)
   Guard Train Battalion (1 co)(0/103)
Artillery Reserve:
   1st Old Guard Foot Battery (4/107)
   Guard Train Battalion (1 co)(1/111)
   Administration:
   Equipage Train (4/352)
   Ouvriers d'Administration (2/80)

5 MAY 1813

1st Brigade:
   1/Fusilier-Chasseur Regiment (12/598)
   1/Fusilier-Grenadier Regiment (14/499)
   1/,2/2nd Tirailleur Regiment (19/318)
2nd Brigade:
   1/,2/1st Voltigeur Regiment (25/990)
   1/,2/2nd Voltigeur Regiment (24/705)
   1/,2/6th Voltigeur Regiment (28/1,053)
3rd Brigade:
   1/,2/1st Tirailleur Regiment (27/1,031)
   1/,2/6th Tirailleur Regiment (24/922)
   1/,2/7th Tirailleur Regiment (26/1,048)
Guard Artillery:
   2nd Old Guard Artillery Company (3/97)
   1st Young Guard Artillery Company (3/105)
   2nd Young Guard Artillery Company (2/137)
   Artillery Artisans (0/7)
   Artillery Train (3/259)

French Archives, Carton C2–537

RUSSO-PRUSSIAN ORDER OF BATTLE
BATTLE OF BAUTZEN
20 & 21 MAY 1813

RUSSIAN COMMANDER: GENERAL OF CAVALRY WITTGENSTEIN

Streif Corps
Brigade: Colonel Davydov (not present in battle)
   Davydov Streifkorps (4)
Brigade: Colonel Mandatov (not present in battle)
   Mandatov Streifkorps (4)
Brigade: Generalmajor Karpov II (not present in battle)
   Karpov #2 Don Cossack Regiment
   Grekov #2 Don Cossack Regiment (2)
   Jagodin #2 Don Cossack Regiment (2)
   Zikelev Don Cossack Regiment (2)
   2nd Bug Cossack Regiment (2)
Brigade: Generalmajor Illowaisky IV (not present at battle)
   Grekov #3 Don Cossack Regiment (2)

Grekov #9 Don Cossack Regiment (2)
Grekov #21 Don Cossack Regiment (2)
Sutsherinov Don Cossack Regiment (2)
Brigade: Generalmajor Ilowaisky X
Platov #4 Don Cossack Regiment (2)
Lotschilin #1 Don Cossack Regiment (2)
Koschkin Don Cossack Regiment
Illowaiski #10 Don Cossack Regiment (2)
Gorin #1 Don Cossack Regiment (2)
5th Bashkir Regiment (2)
Brigade: Generalmajor Kaissrov (not present in battle)
Pantelev #2 Don Cossack Regiment (2)
Barbantchikov #2 Don Cossack Regiment (2)
1st Teptar Cossack Regiment (2)
1st Bashkir Regiment (2)
3rd Ural Cossack Regiment (2)
Jachontov Opolochenie Cossacks Regiment (2)
Brigade: Captain Baron Giesmar (not present in battle)
Giesmar Streifkorps (4)
Advanced Guard of the Right Wing: Generalmajor Lanskoy
Brigade:
Streifkorps Prendel (4)
Brigade: Generalmjor Paradovsky
Alexandria Hussar Regiment (3)
White Russia Hussar Regiment (3)
Lithuania Chasseur à Cheval Regiment (3)
Horse Artillery Battery #2
Brigade: Generalmajor Ilowaisky XII
Ataman Don Cossacks
Illowaiski #12 Don Cossack Regiment
Kutainikov #4 Don Cossack Regiment
Semenschenkov Don Cossack Regiment
**Advanced Guard of the 3rd Army of the West:
Generallieutenant Tschaplitz**
Brigade: Colonel Koslovsky
Olivopol Hussar Regiment (2)(17/364)
Jitomir Uhlan Regiment (2)(10/142)
Brigade: Generalmajor Rudsevitsch
12th Jager Regiment (2)(28/772)
22nd Jager Regiment (2)(24/538)
Brigade: Generalmajor Grekov VIII
Grekov #8 Don Cossack Regiment (2)(13/350)
Kutainikov Don Cossack Regiment (2)(13/313)
Isaeva #2 Don Cossack Regiment (2)(9/240)
Artillery:
Light Artillery Battery #34 (5/164)
Prussian Advanced Guard: Generallieutenant von Kleist
Brigade: Generalmajor Rudiger
Grodno Hussar Regiment (4)
Brigade: Generalmajor Vlastov
23rd Jager Regiment (1)
24th Jager Regiment (1)
Brigade: Generalmajor Roth
25th Jager Regiment
26th Jager Regiment
Artillery:
Russian Horse Artillery Battery #23
Brigade: Oberstleutnant von Steinmetz
1/Colberg Infantry Regiment
2/Colberg Infantry Regiment
Fus/Colberg Infantry Regiment
Brigade: Major von Thumen
1/,3/1st Silesian Hussar Regiment (2)
1/,2/2nd Silesian Hussar Regiment (2)
Prussian Horse Battery #3
Brigade: Generalmajor Radionov II
Illowaiski #4 Don Cossack Regiment (2)
Radinov #2 Don Cossack Regiment (2)
Selivanov #2 Don Cossack Regiment (2)

*Advanced Guard of the Left Wing: General of Infantry
Count Miloradovich*
*2nd Corps: Generallieutenant Prince Eugene of
Wurttemburg*
Cavalry: Generalmajor Knorring
Soum Hussar Regiment (2)
Tartar Uhlan Regiment (4)
Converged Dragoon Regiment (2)
3rd Division: Generalmajor Count Schachafskoi
Brigade: Colonel Schilvinsky
Mourmansk Infantry Regiment (1)
Revel Infantry Regiment (1)
Tchernigov Infantry Regiment (1)
Brigade: Colonel Kapustin
20th Jager Regiment (1)
21st Jager Regiment (1)
Artillery: Generalmajor Nikitin
Heavy Artillery Battery #1
Light Artillery Battery #33
Horse Artillery Battery #7
4th Division: Generalmajor Pischnitzky
Brigade: Colonel Treffurt
Krementsoug Infantry Regiment (1)
Volhynie Infantry Regiment (1)
Riajsk Infantry Regiment (1)
Brigade: Colonel Ivanov
4th Jager Regiment (1)
34th Jager Regiment (1)
Tobolsk Infantry Regiment (1)
Cavalry: Generalmajor Pantschulid I
Tchernigov Chasseur à Cheval Regiment (3)
New Russia Dragoon Regiment (2)
Lithuanian Uhlan Regiment (2)
Corps: Generalmajor Emmanuel
Brigade: Generalmajor Millesimo
Kiev Dragoon Regiment (3)
Kharkov Dragoon Regiment (3)
Horse Artillery Battery #4
Brigade:
Rebrikov #3 Cossack Regiment (2)
Stavropol Kalmuck Regiment (2)
Orlov Streifkorps (4)

*3rd Army of the West: General of Infantry Barclay de
Tolly*
**Right wing: Generalmajor Count Scherbatov (18th
Division)**
Brigade: Generalmajor Umanetz
Kinbourn Dragoon Regiment (2)(18/239)
Sieversk Chasseur Regiment (2)(11/274)
Light Artillery Battery #35 (6/135)
Brigade: Generalmajor Bernodossov
Vladimir Infantry Regiment (1)(21/502)
Dnieper Infantry Regiment (1)(23/488)
Brigade: Colonel Heidenreich
Kostroma Infantry Regiment (1)(28/482)
Tambov Infantry Regiment (1)(22/520)
Brigade: Generalmajor Karnielov
28th Jager Regiment (1)(12/527)
32nd Jager Regiment (1)(24/532)
Left Wing: Generalmajor Insov (9th Division)
Brigade: Generalmajor Poltaratzky
Nacheburg Infantry Regiment (1)(22/613)
Iakout Infantry Regiment (1)(20/514)
Brigade: Generalmajor Udom I
10th Jager Regiment (1)(15/374)
38th Jager Regiment (1)(18/401)

Artillery:
Light Artillery Battery #28
Brigade: Generalmajor Pahlen II
Tver Dragoon Regiment (2)(12/312)
Dorpat Dragoon Regiment (2)(9/252)

Prussian Army: General of Cavalry Blücher
Upper Silesian Brigade: Generalmajor von Zeithen
Cavalry: Major Laroche von Starkenfeld
Brigade: Major von Blücher
2/,4/1st Silesian Hussar Regiment (2)
3/,4/2nd Silesian Hussar Regiment (2)
Brigade: Major von Schmiedburg
1/,2/Silesian Uhlan Regiment (2)
Prussian Horse Battery #9 von Tuschen
Infantry: Oberst von Pirch
Brigade: Major von Carnall
Silesian Grenadier Battalion (1)
1/1st Silesian Infantry Regiment
3/1st Silesian Infantry Regiment
Fus/1st Silesian Infantry Regiment
Artillery:
6pdr Foot Battery #8 von Mandelsohe
Brigade: Oberst von Losthin
1/2nd Silesian Infantry Regiment
3/2nd Silesian Infantry Regiment
Silesian Schützen Battalion
3rd Res Bn/Leib Infantry Regiment
5th Res Bn/Leib Infantry Regiment
Artillery:
6pdr Foot Battery #13 von Held
Artillery:
Russian Position Battery #14
Russian Position Battery #33
Lower Silesian Brigade: Oberst and Wing Adjutant von Klüx
Cavalry: Oberst von Mutius
Brigade: Major von Bork
1/,2/,3/,4/Neumärk Dragoon Regiment (4)
2/,4/1st West Prussian Dragoon Regiment (2)
Prussian Horse Battery #7 Richter
Infantry: Major von Jagov
Brigade: Major von Anhalt
West Prussian Grenadier Battalion
2/1st West Prussian Infantry Regiment
3/1st West Prussian Infantry Regiment
Fus/1st West Prussian Infantry Regiment
3rd Res Bn/Leib Infantry Regt
2/2nd West Prussian Infantry Regiment
3/3rd West Prussian Infantry Regiment
2nd Res Bn/Leib Infantry Regiment
6pdr Foot Battery #9
Prussian Corps: Generallieutenant von Yorck
Right Wing: Generalmajor Corswandt
Brigade: Oberstlieutenant von Wuthernov
1/,3/1st West Prussian Dragoon Regiment (2)
6pdr Horse Battery #2
Brigade: Oberst von Zielinsky
Fus/2nd East Prussian Infantry Regiment
1/1st East Prussian Infantry Regiment
2/1st East Prussian Infantry Regiment
1/Leib Infantry Regiment
2/Leib Infantry Regiment
Combined Fusiliers of the 1st East Prussian & Leib
Infantry Regiments (1)
6pdr Foot Battery #1
6pdr Foot Battery #2
Brigade: Oberst von Horn
1/1st West Prussian Infantry Regiment

2/2nd West Prussian Infantry Regiment
2/1st Silesian Infantry Regiment
2/2nd Silesian Infantry Regiment
Combined Fusiliers of the 5th & 6th Combined Infantry
Regiments
Fus/2nd West Prussian Infantry Regiment
Fus/2nd Silesian Infantry Regiment
Prussian 6pdr Foot Battery #3
Prussian 3pdr Foot Battery #1
Prussian 6pdr Horse Battery #1
Attached:
1/,2/,3/,4/Lithuanian Dragoon Regiment (4)
1/,3/Brandenburg Dragoon Regiment (2)
2nd Line Battle Corps: Generallieutenant Gortschakov II
Corps: Generallieutenant Berg
Cavalry Brigade: Colonel Uvaroff
Loubny Hussar Regiment (2)
Moscow Dragoon Regiment (2)
Mitau Dragoon Regiment (2)
Horse Battery #3
Brigade: Generalmajor Lissanevitsch
Akhtyrsk Hussar Regiment (2)
Tchougouiev Uhlans (2)
Kargopol Dragoon Regiment (2)
1st Line: Generallieutenant Berg
5th Division: Generalmajor Lukov
Brigade: Generalmajor Prince of Siberia
Perm Infantry Regiment (1)
Mohilev Infantry Regiment (1)
Position Battery #5
Brigade: Generalmajor Kasatschkovsky
Kalouga Infantry Regiment (1)
Sievesk Infantry Regiment (1)
Grand Duchess Catherine Battalion
14th Division: Generalmajor Lalin
Brigade: Generalmajor Helfreich
Tenguinsk Infantry Regiment (1)
Estonia Infantry Regiment (1)
2nd Line: Generallieutenant St. Priest
7th Division: Generalmajor Tallisin III
Brigade:
Sophia Infantry Regiment (1)
Pskof Infantry Regiment (1)
llth Jager Regiment (1)
8th Division: Generalmajor Engelhardt I
Brigade: Colonel Schindschin
Archangle Infantry Regiment (1)
Schusselburg Infantry Regiment (1)
Old Ingremannland Infantry Regiment (1)
Brigade: Colonel Stegeman
Kaporsk Infantry Regiment (1)
37th Jager Regiment (1)
Heavy Artillery Battery #7

2ND LINE OF BATTLE
Reserve of the 3rd Army of the West: Generallieutenant Baron Sass
Artillery: Generalmajor Wassilizky
Heavy Artillery Battery #15 (8/203)
Heavy Artillery Battery #18 (8/236)
Brigade: Colonel Tern
Vitebsk Infantry Regiment (1)(13/552)
Kozlov Infantry Regiment (1)(16/476)
Brigade: Colonel Suthov
Kourin Infantry Regiment (1)
Kolyvan Infantry Regiment (1)(20/475)
7th Jager Regiment (1)

Artillery:
    Heavy Artillery Battery #34 (8/241)
    Light Artillery Battery #29 (7/138)
    Pioneer Company Cpt. Kanatchkov (2/l19)
Brigade:
    Arasmass Uhlan Regiment (5/134)
    Kirev Cossack Regiment (7/279)

Brandenburg Reserve: Generalmajor von Röder
Brigade: Oberstlieutenant Katzler
    1/,2/,3/,4/West Prussian Uhlan Regiment (4)
    1/,2/Brandenburg Uhlan Regiment (2)(not in battle)
    Horse Battery #8
Division: Oberstlieutenant von Tippelskirch
Brigade: Major von Albensleben
    Guard Jäger (1)
    1/Guard Infantry Regiment
    2/Guard Infantry Regiment
    Fus/Guard Infantry Regiment
    Normal Infantry Battalion
    Guard Foot Battery #4 von Lehmann
Brigade: Major von Natzmer
    Leib Grenadier Battalion
    1st East Prussian Grenadier Battalion
    3/Leib Infantry Regiment
    1st Res Bn/Leib Infantry Regiment
    Guard Freiwilliger Jäger Battalion von Wedell
Brigade: Major Hobe
    1/,2/Brandenburg Hussar Regiment (2)
    1/,2/,3/,4/2nd Leib Hussar Regiment (4)
Prussian Reserve Cavalry Division: Oberst von Dolffs
Brigade: Oberstlieutenant von Werder
    1/,2/,3/,4/Garde du Corp Regiment (4 + 1 Jäger
    Squadron)
    1/,2/,3/,4/Guard Light Cavalry Regiment (4 + 2 Jäger
    Squadrons)
    Guard Horse Battery #4 von Willmann
Brigade: Oberst von Jürgass
    1/,2/,3/,4/East Prussian Cuirassier Regiment (4)
    1/,2/,3/,4/Silesian Cuirassier Regiment (4)
    1/,2/,3/,4/Brandenburg Cuirassier Regiment (4)
    Horse Battery #10 von Schäffer

Russian 2nd Line: Generallieutenant Markov
Brigade: Generalmajor Karpenkov
    1st Jager Regiment (1)
    33rd Jager Regiment (1)
    Light Battery #13
Brigade: Generalmajor Bistram
    Podolsk Infantry Regiment (1)
    Jeletz Infantry Regiment (1)
Brigade: Colonel Schertov
    Riazan Infantry Regiment (1)
    Brest Infantry Regiment (1)
22nd Division: (Unknown)
Brigade: Generalmajor Turtschaninov
    Olonetz Infantry Regiment (1)
    Staroskol Infantry Regiment (1)
Brigade: Colonel Kern
    Belosersk Infantry Regiment (1)
    45th Jager Regiment (1)
    Light Artillery Battery #27

3RD LINE:
RUSSIAN MAIN RESERVE: GRAND DUKE CONSTANTINE
1st Line: Generallieutenant Raevsky
Guard Light Cavalry Division: Generalmajor Schaevitch
Brigade: Generalmajor Tschailkov
    Guard Dragoon Regiment (4)
    Guard Uhlan Regiment (4)

Guard Hussar Regiment (4)
1st Grenadier Division: Generalmajor Sulima
Brigade: Colonel Kniaschnin II
    Count Arakcheyev Grenadier Regiment (2)
    Ekaterinoslav Grenadier Regiment (2)
Brigade: Colonel Acht
    Tauride Grenadier Regiment (2)
    St. Petersburg Grenadier Regiment (2)
Brigade: Generalmajor Tschoglikov
    Pernau Infantry Regiment (2)
    Kexholm Infantry Regiment (2)
Brigade: Colonel Brischinsky
    Converged Grenadiers of 5th Division (2)
    Converged Grenadiers of 14th Division (2)
Artillery:
    Position Battery #3
    Light Artillery Battery #14
    Light Artillery Battery #36
2nd Division: Generalmajor Zwielenief
Brigade: Colonel Pissareff
    Kiev Grenadier Regiment (2)
    Moscow Grenadier Regiment (2)
Brigade: Colonel Golowin
    Astrakhan Grenadier Regiment (2)
    Fangoria Grenadier Regiment (2)
Brigade: Colonel Hesse
    Little Russia Grenadier Regiment (2)
    Siberian Grenadier Regiment (2)
Artillery:
    Heavy Artillery Battery #32
2nd Cuirassier Division: Generalmajor Duca
Brigade: Generalmajor Leontiev
    Gluchov Cuirassier Regiment (3)
    Pskof Cuirassier Regiment (3)
Brigade: Generalmajor Gudowitsch
    Military Order Cuirassier Regiment (3)
    Starodoub Cuirassier Regiment (3)
Brigade: Colonel Massalov
    Little Russian Cuirassier Regiment (3)
    Novgorod Cuirassier Regiment (3)

2nd Line: Generallieutenant Count Gallizin V
Guard Corps: Generallieutenant Lavrov
1st Cuirassier Division: Generalmajor Depreradovich
Brigade: Generalmajor Arenief
    Chevalier Garde Regiment
    Horse Guard Regiment
    Emperor Cuirassier Regiment
    Guard Horse Battery #1
Brigade: Generalmajor Rosen
    Astrakhan Cuirassier Regiment (3)
    Empress Cuirassier Regiment (3)
    Ekatrinoslav Cuirassier Regiment (3)
    Guard Horse Battery #2
1st Guard Division: Generalmajor Baron Rosen
Brigade: Generalmajor Potemkin
    1/Preobragenski Guard Regiment
    2/Preobragenski Guard Regiment
    1/Semenovski Guard Regiment
    2/Semenovski Guard Regiment
    Guard Heavy Battery #1
Brigade: Generalmajor Krapovitzky
    1/Guard Jager Regiment
    2/Guard Jager Regiment
    1/Ismailov Guard Regiment
    2/Ismailov Guard Regiment
    Guard Marine Equipage Battalion (at HQ)
    Guard Light Battery #1
    Guard Light Battery #2

2nd Guard Division: Generalmajor Yermolov
Brigade: Colonel Krischanovsky
  1/Lithuanian Guard Regiment
  2/Lithuanian Guard Regiment
  1/Finland Guard Regiment
  2/Finland Guard Regiment
Brigade: Generalmajor Scheltuchin II
  Pavlov Grenadier Regiment (2)
  Leib Grenadier Regiment (2)
  Guard Heavy Battery #2
Reserve Artillery: Generalleutnant Prince Jachwill
Brigade: Generalmajor Euler
  Position Battery #2
  Position Battery #?
  Position Battery #30
  Position Battery #31
  Light Battery #19
Brigade:
  Light Battery #5
  Light Battery #7
  Light Battery #32
  Light Battery #42
Brigade: Generalmajor Merlin
  Horse Battery #1
  Horse Battery #6
  Horse Battery #8
  Horse Battery #10

Plotho, Der Krieg in Deutschland und Frankreich in den Jahren 1813 und 1814. & Sporschild, Die grosse Chronik. & Bogdanovich, M.I., Istorich Voin 1813 Goda Za Nezavicimost Germanii Po Dostovern'm' Istochnikam'

GRANDE ARMÉE
BATTLE OF BAUTZEN 20/21 MAY 1813

Commander-in-Chief: Emperor Napoleon I

Imperial Guard:
1st Division: Général de division Roguet
Brigade: Général de brigade Decouz
  1/,2/1st Grenadiers à Pied Regiment
  1/,2/2nd Grenadiers à Pied Regiment
  1/,2/1st Chasseurs à Pied Regiment
  1/,2/2nd Chasseurs à Pied Regiment
  Vélites of Turin
  Vélites of Florence
1st Young Guard Division: Général de division Dumoustier
Brigade: General de brigade Mouton-Duvernet
•Strength figures as of 5 May 1813.
  1/Fusilier-Grenadier Regiment (14/499)
  2/Fusiliers-Grenadier Regiment
  1/Fusilier-Chasseur Regiment (12/598)
  2/Fusilier-Chasseur Regiment
Brigade: Général de brigade Tindel
  1/,2/1st Voltigeur Regiment (25/990)
  1/,2/2nd Voltigeur Regiment (24/705)
Brigade: Général de brigade Lanusse
  1/,2/3rd Voltigeur Regiment
  1/,2/6th Voltigeur Regiment (28/1,053)
  1/,2/7th Voltigeur Regiment
2nd Young Guard Division: Général de division Barrois
Brigade: Général de brigade Rottembourg
  1/,2/1st Tirailleur Regiment (27/1,031)
  1/,2/2nd Tirailleur Regiment

Brigade: Général de brigade Berthezène
  1/,2/3rd Tirailleur Regiment
  1/,2/6th Tirailleur Regiment (24/922)
  1/,2/7th Tirailleur Regiment (26/1,048)
Artillery: Général Devaux
  1st Old Guard Artillery Battery (6-6pdrs & 2-5.7" howitzers)
  2nd Old Guard Artillery Battery (6-12pdrs & 2-6" howitzers)
  3rd Old Guard Artillery Battery (6-12pdrs & 2-6" howitzers)
  4th Old Guard Artillery Battery (6-6pdrs & 2-6" howitzers)
  1st Young Guard Artillery Battery (6-6pdrs & 2-5.7" howitzers)
  2nd Young Guard Artillery Battery (6-6pdrs & 2-5.7"howitzers)
  1st Old Guard Horse Artillery Battery (4-6pdrs & 2-5.7"howitzers)
  2nd Old Guard Horse Artillery Battery (4-6pdrs & 2-5.7"howitzers)
  Engineers: Sappers/Marines (3 coys)
  Equipage: Compagnies de Train d'Equipage
1st Cavalry Division: Général de division Lefebvre-Desnoettes
  Berg Chevauxléger-lanciers (500)
  1st Chevauléger-lanciers de la Garde
  2nd Chevauléger-lanciers de la Garde (1,500 men in 1st & 2nd Lancers)
2nd Cavalry Division: Général de division d'Ornano
  Chasseurs à Cheval de la Garde (1,500)
  Grenadiers à Cheval de la Garde (1,200)
  Empress Dragoons (1,200)
  Gendarmes d'Elite (500)

II Corps: Maréchal Victor
  (Strengths as of 15 May 1813)
4th Division: Général de division Dubreton
Brigade: Général de brigade Ferrière
  37th Provisional Line Regiment
    2/24th Légère Regiment (15/616)
    2/26th Légère Regiment (16/660)
  38th Provisional Line Regiment
    2/11th Légère Regiment (18/720)
    2/2nd Line Regiment (23/647)
  39th Provisional Line Regiment
    2/19th Line Regiment (19/730)
    2/37th Line Regiment (20/661)
Brigade: Général de brigade Brun
  40th Provisional Line Regiment
    2/4th Line Regiment (18/647)
    2/56th Line Regiment (18/710)
  41st Provisional Line Regiment
    2/18th Line Regiment (14/696)
    2/46th Line Regiment (15/736)
  42nd Provisional Line Regiment
    2/72nd Line Regiment (18/653)
    2/93rd Line Regiment (16/680)
Artillery:
  11/4th Foot Artillery (2/90)(6-6pdrs & 2-24pdr howitzers)
  14/8th Foot Artillery (4/68)(6-6pdrs & 2-24pdr howitzers)

III Corps: Maréchal Ney
8th Division: Général de division Souham
Brigade: Général de brigade Chasseraux
  6th Provisional Légère Regiment
    2/6th Légère Regiment
    3/25th Légère Regiment
  10th Provisional Légère Regiment
    3/16th Légère Regiment

1/28th Légère Regiment
14th Provisional Line Regiment
4/34th Line Regiment
3/40th Line Regiment
19th Provisional Line Regiment
6/32nd Line Regiment
3/58th Line Regiment
Brigade: Général de brigade Chemineau
21st Provisional Line Regiment
3/59th Line Regiment
4/69th Line Regiment
24th Provisional Line Regiment
3/88th Line Regiment
3/103rd Line Regiment
1/,3/,4/,6/22nd Line Regiment
Artillery:
9/2nd Foot Artillery (6-6pdrs & 2-24pdr howitzers)
10/2nd Foot Artillery (6-6pdrs & 2-24pdr howitzers)
3rd (bis) Train Battalion (2 cos)
8th Principal Train Battalion (2 cos)
Engineers: Spanish Sappers (1 coy)

9th Division: Général de division Delmas
Brigade: Général de brigade Anthing
2nd Provisional Légère Regiment
3/2nd Légère Regiment
3/4th Légère Regiment
1/29th Légère Regiment
1/,2/,3/,4/136th Line Regiment
Brigade:
1/,2/,3/,4/138th Line Regiment
1/,2/,3/,4/145th Line Regiment
Artillery:
1/9th Foot Artillery (6-6pdrs & 2-24pdr howitzers)
11/9th Foot Artillery (6-6pdrs & 2-24pdr howitzers)
4/3rd (bis) Train Battalion
4/6th Principal Train Battalion
4/12th Principal Train Battalion
Engineers: Spanish Sappers (1 coy)

10th Division: Général de division Albert
Brigade: Général de brigade Goris
4th Provisional Légère Regiment
4/5th Légère Regiment
4/12th Légère Regiment
1/,2/,3/,4/139th Line Regiment
Brigade: Général de brigade van Dedem
1/,2/,3/,4/140th Line Regiment
1/,2/,3/,4/141th Line Regiment
Artillery:
3/7th Foot Artillery (6-6pdrs & 2-24pdr howitzers)
4/7th Foot Artillery (6-6pdrs & 2-24pdr howitzers)
4/, & Det.7/1st Principal Train Battalion
11th Principal Train Battalion
Engineers: Spanish Sappers (1 coy)

11th Division: Général de division Ricard
Brigade: Général de brigade Tarayre
3/,4/9th Légère Regiment
17th Provisional Line Regiment
4/43rd Line Regiment
3/75th Line Regiment
18th Provisional Line Regiment
3/50th Line Regiment
4/65th Line Regiment
Brigade: Général de brigade Dumoulin
1/,2/,3/,4/142nd Line Regiment
1/,2/,3/,4/144th Line Regiment
Artillery:
18/1st Foot Artillery (6-6pdrs & 2-24pdr howitzers)
19/7th Foot Artillery (6-6pdrs & 2-24pdr howitzers)
Det. 7/11th Principal Train Battalion

Det. 7/12th Principal Train Battalion
4/13th (bis) Train Battalion
Engineers: Spanish Sappers (1 coy)
39th Division: Général de division Marchand
Brigade: Generalmajor Stockhorn
1/,2/3rd Baden Line Regiment
1/1st Baden Line Regiment
Brigade: Generalmajor Prince Emile de Hesse
1/,2/1st Hessian Fusilier Regiment
1/,2/2nd Hessian (Leib) du Corps Regiment
1/,2/Hessian Leib-Garde Regiment
Artillery:
1st Baden Foot Battery (3-6pdrs & 1-24pdr howitzer)
1st Baden Train Company
1/2 Hessian Foot Battery (2-6pdrs & 1-24pdr howitzer)
Brigade:
1/,2/,3/10th Hussar Regiment
1/,2/,3/,4/Baden Dragoon Regiment

IV Corps: Général de division Comte Bertrand
(Strengths as of 10 May 1813)
12th Division: Général de division Morand
Brigade: Général de brigade Belair
1/13th Line Regiment (27/791)
2/13th Line Regiment (15/758)
3/13th Line Regiment (16/753)
4/13th Line Regiment (15/747)
6/13th Line Regiment (18/758)
Artillery Det./13th Line Regiment (2/44)(2-3pdrs)
3rd Provisional Line Regiment
3/3rd Légère Regiment (20/597)
4/8th Légère Regiment (21/666)
Brigade: Général de brigade Sicard
2nd Provisional Croatian Regiment
2/3rd Croatian Regiment (21/510)
1/4th Croatian Regiment (17/402)
1/23rd Line Regiment (29/738)
2/23rd Line Regiment (13/764)
4/23rd Line Regiment (14/730)
6/23rd Line Regiment (13/745)
Artillery Det./23rd Line Regiment (2/64)(2-3pdrs)
Artillery: Major Pingenot
1/2nd Foot Artillery (2/82)(6-6pdrs & 2-24pdr howitzers)
3/2nd Foot Artillery (3/80)(6-6pdrs & 2-24pdr howitzers)
Det. 1/7th (bis) Train Battalion (1/99)
Det. 2/7th (bis) Train Battalion (0/27)
Det. 1/9th Military Equipage Battalion (1/119)
15th Division: Général de division Peyri
Brigade: Général de brigade Martel
3/1st Italian Line Regiment (27/718)
4/1st Italian Line Regiment (17/772)
Artillery Det./1st Italian Line Regiment (1/13) (2-3pdrs)
1/4th Italian Line Regiment (25/584)
2/4th Italian Line Regiment (15/512)
3/4th Italian Line Regiment (16/588)
4/4th Italian Line Regiment (16/598)
Artillery Det./4th Italian Line Regiment (3/63) (2-3pdrs)
2nd Brigade: Général de brigade St. Andrea
3/6th Italian Line Regiment (25/700)
4/6th Italian Line Regiment (20/688)
Artillery Det./6th Italian Line Regiment (3/67) (2-3pdrs)
3rd Brigade: Général de brigade Moroni
1/Milan Guard Battalion (20/754)
1/7th Italian Line Regiment (30/670)
2/7th Italian Line Regiment (16/589)
3/7th Italian Line Regiment (13/634)
4/7th Italian Line Regiment (17/629)
Artillery Det./7th Italian Line Regiment (1/30) (2-3pdrs)
Artillery: Chef de bataillon Gorio

1st Italian Foot Artillery Company (3/106) (6-6pdrs & 2-24pdr howitzers)
13th Italian Foot Artillery Company (4/107) (6-6pdrs & 2-24pdr howitzers)
5th Italian Train Company (3/142)
6th Italian Train Company (3/136)
3rd Italian Sapper Company (3/90)
3rd Italian Naval Artisan Company (1/27)
2nd Italian Sailor Company (3/107)
Italian Military Equipage Company (2/137)
Cavalry Brigade: Général de brigade Briche
   1/2nd Neapolitan Chasseur à Cheval Regiment (12/182/205)
   2/2nd Neapolitan Chasseur à Cheval Regiment (6/185/188)

38th Division: Generallieutenant Franquemont
•The strength figures of this state are suspect, as they are the same strengths reported by the National Archives for 25 April.
Brigade: Generalmajor Stockmayer
   1/9th Württemberg Light Regiment (13/675)
   1/10th Württemberg Light Regiment (13/654)
   1/7th Württemberg Line Regiment (9/275)
   2/7th Württemberg Line Regiment (11/409)
Brigade: Generalmajor Neuffer
   1/1st Württemberg Line Regiment (14/546)
   2/1st Württemberg Line Regiment (14/562)
   1/2nd Württemberg Line Regiment (14/621)
   2/2nd Württemberg Line Regiment (14/583)
Artillery:
   1st Württemberg Foot Battery "Toikede" (3/113)
   1st Württemberg Horse Battery (6 guns) (4-6pdrs & 2-7pdr howitzers)

24th Light Cavalry Brigade: Generalmajor Jett
   1/,2/,3/4/1st Württemberg Chevaulegers "Prince Adam" (18/507/500)
   1/,2/,3/4/3rd Württemberg Chevaulegers "Duke Louis" (19/482/496)
   1st Württemberg Horse Battery "Burgi" (3/138) (4-6pdrs & 2 7pdr howitzers)

Corps Artillery: Colonel Ménoire
   24/2nd Foot Artillery (2/86) (4-6pdrs & 2-24pdr howitzers)
   Det. 2/7th (bis) Train Battalion (0/6)
   6/7th (bis) Train Battalion (2/128)
   7/7th (bis) Train Battalion (2/129)
   Det. 13th Artillery Artisan Company (1/29)
   2/1st Sapper Battalion (2/140)
   8/1st Sapper Battalion (3/114)
   Det/Engineering Equipage Train (1/24)
   2/9th Military Equipage Battalion (2/127)
   3/9th Military Equipage Battalion (2/118)
   4/9th Military Equipage Battalion (2/105)
   5/9th Military Equipage Battalion (2/109)
   6/9th Military Equipage Battalion (2/125)

V Corps: *Général de division Lauriston*
(strengths as of 15 May)
16th Division: Général de division Maison
Brigade: Général de brigade Avril
   1/151st Line Regiment (35/394)
   2/151st Line Regiment (17/396)
   3/151st Line Regiment (19/418)
   4/151st Line Regiment (18/414)
Brigade: Général de brigade Penne
   1/153rd Line Regiment (32/715)
   2/153rd Line Regiment (20/627)
   3/153rd Line Regiment (17/601)
Artillery:

   1/1st Foot Artillery (2/85) (6-6pdrs & 2-24pdr howitzers)
   3/1st Foot Artillery (2/96) (6-6pdrs & 2-24pdr howitzers)
   7/11th Principal Train Battalion (1/174)
   Engineers: (1 coy)
   Equipage: (1 coy)
17th Division: Général de division Puthod
Brigade: Général de brigade Vachot
   1/146th Line Regiment (32/561)
   2/146th Line Regiment (13/466)
   3/146th Line Regiment (16/682)
   4/146th Line Regiment (19/599)
   1/147th Line Regiment (33/670)
   2/147th Line Regiment (16/600)
   3/147th Line Regiment (14/639)
   4/147th Line Regiment (13/587)
Brigade: Général de brigade Pastol
   1/148th Line Regiment (24/409)
   2/148th Line Regiment (18/518)
   3/148th Line Regiment (18/657)
   4/148th Line Regiment (16/402)
Artillery: Bonneftos
   1/5th Foot Artillery (1/99) (6-6pdrs & 2-24pdr howitzers)
   11/5th Foot Artillery (3/103) (6-6pdrs & 2-24pdr howitzers)
   3/3rd Principal Train Battalion (1/122)
   Det. 1/12th Principal Train Battalion (1.50)
   2/2nd Military Equipage Battalion (3/127)
18th Division: Général de division Lagrange
Brigade: Général de brigade Charrière
   1/134th Line Regiment (23/725)
   2/134th Line Regiment (21/727)
   1/154th Line Regiment (26/367)
   2/154th Line Regiment (18/391)
   3/154th Line Regiment (21/588)
   4/154th Line Regiment (20/571)
Brigade: Général de brigade Suden
   1/155th Line Regiment (35/546)
   2/155th Line Regiment (17/349)
   3/155th Line Regiment (15/433)
   4/155th Line Regiment (15/485)
   1/3rd Foreign Regiment (Irish Legion)(25/538)
   2/3rd Foreign Regiment (Irish Legion)(20/434)
Artillery: Chef de bataillon Chateaubrun
•Prior to the battle, 2–6pdrs & 1 howitzer were captured by allies. Which batteries lost them is not known.
   10/1st Foot Artillery (2/96) (6-6pdrs & 2-24pdr howitzers)
   12/1st Foot Artillery (2/95) (6-6pdrs & 2-24pdr howitzers)
   4/4th Principal Train Battalion (1/122)
   Det. 1/12th Principal Train Battalion (0/56)
   3/2nd Military Equipage Battalion (2/127)
19th Division: Général de division Rochambeau
Brigade: Général de brigade Lacrois
   1/135th Line Regiment (27/436)
   2/135th Line Regiment (14/507)
   3/135th Line Regiment (8/335)
   4/135th Line Regiment (11/512)
Brigade: Général de brigade Lafitte
   1/149th Line Regiment (40/696)
   2/149th Line Regiment (14/574)
   3/149th Line Regiment (14/600)
   4/149th Line Regiment (12/635)
Brigade: Général de brigade Harlet
   1/150th Line Regiment (21/620)
   2/150th Line Regiment (17/559)
   3/150th Line Regiment (18/708)
   4/150th Line Regiment (20/720)
Artillery: Chef de bataillon Richard
   12/5th Foot Artillery (2/92) (4-6pdrs & 1-24pdr howitzer)
   17/5th Foot Artillery (1/56) (6-6pdrs & 2-24pdr howitzers)

7/9th Principal Train Battalion (1/122)
Det. 4/14th Principal Train Battalion (1/72)
4/2nd Military Equipage Train Battalion (2/127)
Corps Artillery Reserve: Général de brigade de Camas
15/1st Foot Artillery (3/91)
16/1st Foot Artillery (3/94)
17/1st Foot Artillery (1/93) (12-12pdrs & 4-6" howitzers)
2/5th Horse Artillery (3/80)(4-6pdrs & 2-6" howitzers)
7/6th Horse Artillery (2/81)(4-6pdrs & 2-6" howitzers)
Det. 7/1st (bis) Train Battalion (0/127)
Det. 7/11th Principal Train Batalion (1/174)
Det. 4/8th (bis) Train Batalion (1/128)
Det. 4/11th (bis) Train Battalion (0/70)
1/6th Sapper Battalion (6/99)
2/6th Sapper Battalion (3/105)
3/6th Sapper Battalion (3/102)
5/2nd Military Equipage Battalion (2/127)

VI Corps: Maréchal Marmont
20th Division: Général de division Compans
Brigade: Général de brigade Cacault
1/,2/,3/,4/1st Marine Artillery Regiment
1/,2/3rd Marine Artillery Regiment
Brigade: Général de brigade Joubert
25th Provisional Regiment
3/47th Line Regiment
3/86th Line Regiment
20th Provisional Regiment
5/66th Line Regiment
3/122nd Line Regiment
2/,3/32nd Légère Regiment
Artillery:
16/5th Foot Artillery Company (6-6pdrs & 2-24pdr howitzers)
10/8th Foot Artillery Company (6-6pdrs & 2-24pdr howitzers)
Detachment 7/4th (bis) Train Battalion
Detachment 4/1st (bis) Train Battalion
21st Division: Général de division Bonet
Brigade: Général de brigade Buquet
1/,2/,3/,4/,5/,6/2nd Marine Artillery Regiment (6)
1/,2/4th Marine Artillery Regiment
Brigade: Général de brigade Jamin
1/,2/,3/37th Légère Regiment
1/Joseph Napoleon Regiment
Provisional Brigade:
4/36th Légère Regiment (18/829)
4/131st Line Regiment (16/760)
4/132nd Regiment (17/647)
4/133rd Regiment (18/810)
2/Würzburg Infantry Regiment (18/710)
Artillery:
10/4th Foot Artillery Company (6-6pdrs & 2-24pdr howitzers)
18/5th Foot Artillery Company (6-6pdrs & 2-24pdr howitzers)
Detachment 1/10th (bis) Train Battalion
Detachment 1/8th Principal Train Battalion
Detachment 2/8th Principal Train Battalion
22nd Division: Général de division Friederichs
Brigades: Generaux de brigade Ficatier, Cohorn
3/,4/23rd Légère Regiment
11th Provisional Regiment
4/1st Line Regiment
2/62nd Line Regiment
13th Provisional Regiment
3/14th Line Regiment
4/16th Line Regiment
16th Provisional Regiment

6/26th Line Regiment
6/82nd Line Regiment
3/,4/121st Line Regiment
3/,4/15th Line Regiment
3/,4/70th Line Regiment
Artillery:
14/4th Foot Artillery Company (6-6pdrs & 2-24pdr howitzers)
22/9th Foot Artillery Company (6-6pdrs & 2-24pdr howitzers)
Detachment 3/8th Principal Train Battalion
Detachment 2/10th (bis) Train Battalion

VII Corps: Général de division Reynier
Division: Général de division Durutte
(strengths as of 15 May, forces shown as "en route")
Brigade: Général de brigade Devaux
2/35th Légère Regiment (15/970)
4/35th Légère Regiment (19/707)
4/36th Légère Regiment (18/829)
Brigade: Général de brigade Jarry
3/131st Line Regiment (14/829)
4/131st Line Regiment (16/760)
3/132nd Line Regiment (15/860)
4/132nd Line Regiment (17/647)
Brigade: Général de brigade Brayer
3/133rd Line Regiment (14/849)
4/133rd Line Regiment (18/810)
2/Würzburg Regiment (18/710)
3/Würzburg Regiment (17/700)
Artillery:
22/1st Foot Artillery (2/36)
6/5th Foot Artillery (3/60)
4/9th Foot Artillery (3/24)
2/,3/,4/9th (bis) Train Battalion (2/105)
Royal Saxon Corps: General der Kavallerie Zeschau
1st Division: Brigadier-Oberst von Brause
1st Light Regiment Lecoq (1 bn)
1/Guard Grenadier Regiment (1)
Prinz Frederich Infantry Regiment (1)
von Steindel Infantry Regiment (1)
Jägers (1 coy)
2nd Division: Générallieutenant von Sahr
von Anger Grenadier Battalion (1)
Prinz Anton Infantry Regiment (1)
von Löw Infantry Regiment (1)
Artillery:
2 Foot batteries (6 guns ea)
1 Horse Battery (8 guns)
1 Sapper Company
French Artillery (12 guns)

XI Corps: Maréchal Macdonald
(strengths as of 15 May)
31st Division: Général de division Ledru
11th Provisional Demi-brigade
4/27th Légère Regiment (12/312)
4/50th Line Regiment (10/419)
13th Provisional Demi-brigade
4/5th Line Regiment (16/424)
4/79th Line Regiment (12/357)
Brigade: Général de brigade Bardet
1/Neapolitian Elite Regiment (20/261)
2/Neapolitian Elite Regiment (13/398)
Artillery:
16/5th Foot Artillery Company (3/93) (6-6pdrs & 2-24pdr howitzers)
Neapolitan Horse Battery (5/39) (4-6pdrs & 2-24pdr howitzers)

Det. 8th Principal Train Battalion (0/82)
Det. 12th Principal Train Battalion (1/28)
Det. 14th Principal Train Battalion (0/13)
35th Division: Général de division Gérard
Brigade: Général de brigade Senecal
3/6th Line Regiment (13/408)
4/6th Line Regiment (10/447)
Artillery Det./6th Line Regiment (2/60)
1/112th Line Regiment (24/562)
2/112th Line Regiment (12/494)
3/112th Line Regiment (15/514)
4/112th Line Regiment (17/524)
Artillery Det. /112th Line Regiment (2/50)
Brigade: Général de brigade Zucchi
3/2nd Italian Légère Regiment (18/284)
4/2nd Italian Légère Regiment (11/308)
Artillery Det./2nd Italian Légère Regiment (2/47)
1/5th Italian Line Regiment (30/594)
2/5th Italian Line Regiment (12/523)
3/5th Italian Line Regiment (14/547)
4/5th Italian Line Regiment (13/545)
Artillery Det./5th Italian Line Regiment (2/79)
Cavalry Brigade:
1/4th Italian Chasseur à Cheval Regt. (17/230) (18/234 horses)
1/Würzburg Jäger zu Pferd (9/203)(20/219 horses)
Artillery:
6/1st Foot Artillery Company (2/84) (6-6pdrs & 2-24pdr howitzers)
20/5th Foot Artillery Company (3/96) (6-6pdrs & 2-24pdr howitzers)
3rd Italian Horse Battery (7/74) (4-6pdrs & 2-24pdr howitzers)
Det. 1/11th (bis) Train Battalion (?)
10th Italian Train Company (4/181)
9th Italian Sappers (3/42)
36th Division: Général de division Charpentier
Brigade: Général de brigade Simmer
3/14th Légère Regiment (28/454)
4/14th Légère Regiment (14/633)
Artillery Det. /14th Légère Regiment (1/58)
1/22nd Légère Regiment (33/554)
2/22nd Légère Regiment (13/487)
3/22nd Légère Regiment (16/493)
4/22nd Légère Regiment (16/546)
Artillery Det. 22nd Légère Regiment (1/56)
Brigade: Général de brigade Meunier
14th Provisional Demi-Brigade
6/10th Line Regiment (9/362)
6/20th Line Regiment (11/419)
3/67th Line Regiment (15/537)
15th Provisional Demi-Brigade
4/3rd Légère Regiment (17/500)
4/102nd Line Regiment (10/432)
Artillery Det./102nd Line Regiment (1/53)
Artillery: Chef de brigade Dérivaux
5/1st Foot Artillery Company (3/59) (6-6pdrs & 2-24pdr howitzers)
19/2nd Foot Artillery Company (3/87) (6-6pdrs & 2-24pdr howitzers)
Det. 1/7th Principal Train Battalion (1/55)
Det. 2/12th Principal Train Battalion (1/145)
7/5th Sapper Battalion (2/51)
1/7th Sapper Battalion (3/47)
2/7th Sapper Battalion (3/45)
Det/12th Equipage Train Battalion (7/260)

XII Corps: Maréchal Oudinot
13th Division: Général de division Pacthod

Brigade: Général de brigade Pourailly
4/1st Légère Regiment
3/,4/7th Line Regiment
12th Provisional Line Regiment
4/10th Line Regiment
4/42nd Line Regiment
23rd Provisional Line Regiment
7/6th Line Regiment
4/67th Line Regiment
Brigade: Général de brigade Gruger
1/,2/1st Neapolitian Légère Regiment
2/,3/,4/101st Line Regiment
Artillery: Chef de bataillon Rapallo
18/4th Foot Artillery (6-6pdrs & 2-24pdr howitzers)
20/4th Foot Artillery (6-6pdrs & 2-24pdr howitzers)
Det. 2/7th (bis) Train Battalion
3/7th (bis) Train Battalion
1/17th Military Equipage Battalion
14th Division: Général de division Lorencz
1st Brigade: Général de brigade Leclerc
3/,4/52nd Line Regiment
1/,2/,3/,4/137th Line Regiment
Brigade: Général de brigade d'Henin
1/,2/,3/,4/156th Line Regiment
Artillery: Chef de bataillon Boyer
2/4th Foot Artillery (6-6pdrs & 2-24pdr howitzers)
25/4th Foot Artillery (6-6pdrs & 2-24pdr howitzers)
Det. 2/7th Principal Train Battalion
4/7th (bis) Train Battalion
2/17th Equipage Battalion
29th (Bavarian) Division: Generallieutenant Raglovich
(Strength as of 25 April 1813)
1st Brigade: Generalmajor Becker
1st Light Battalion (7/534)
2/Prinz Carl #3 Bavarian Infantry Regiment (16/537)
Res/13th Bavarian Infantry Regiment (12/579)
1/Isenburg #4 Bavarian Infantry Regiment (13/789)
2/Herzog Pius #8 Bavarian Infantry Regiment (15/769)
Brigade: Oberst Maillot de la Traille
2nd Light Battalion (7/590)
2/Preysing #5 Bavarian Infantry Regiment (13/610)
7th Bavarian Infantry Regiment (18/715)
2/#9 Bavarian Infantry Regiment (17/769)
2/Junker #10 Bavarian Infantry Regiment (6/817)
Artillery: Major Marabini
1st Bavarian Foot Battery (4/142) (6-6pdrs & 2-7pdr howitzers)
2nd Bavarian Foot Battery (4/133) (6-6pdrs & 2-7pdr howitzers)
Bavarian Reserve Foot Battery (2/104) (6-12pdrs & 2-7pdr howitzers)
Bavarian Train Company
Corps Cavalry: Général de division Beaumont
29th Light Cavalry Brigade: Général Wolff
1/,2/Westphalian Chevauleger-lancier Regiment
1/,2/,3/Hessian Chevauleger Regiment
Light Cavalry Brigade: Oberst von Syssel
Cobmined Bavarian Chevaulegers (16/394)
Corps Artillery Reserve:
24/2nd Foot Artillery (6-12pdrs & 2-5.7" howitzers)
Det. 2/7th (bis) Train Battalion
5/7th (bis) Train Battalion
3/3rd Sapper Battalion
7/3rd Sapper Battalion
3/17th Equipage Train Battalion
4/17th Equipage Train Battalion
5/17th Equipage Train Battalion
6/17th Equipage Train Battalion

I Cavalry Corps: Général de division Latour-Maubourg

(Strengths as of 15 May 1813)

1st Light Cavalry Division: Général de division Bruyère
Brigade: Général de brigade Bessières
◊Numbers are officers, enlisted men, officers' horses, and enlisted's horses.

7th Hussar Regiment (7/106/18/107)
9th Chevauléger Regiment (2/17/6/16)
8th Hussar Regiment (6/93/12/94)
16th Chasseur à Cheval Regiment (6/114/14/113)
7th Chevauléger Regiment (3/24/7/23)

Brigade: Général de brigade Cambraceres
1st Chevauléger Regiment (5/92/11/91)
3rd Chevauléger Regiment (3/56/6/55)
5th Chevauléger Regiment (2/17/7/15)
8th Chevauléger Regiment (20/240/43/241)

Brigade: Général de brigade Jacquet
1/1st Italian Chasseur à Cheval Regiment (7/188/13/189)
2/1st Italian Chasseur à Cheval Regiment (4/140/8/143)
3/1st Italian Chasseur à Cheval Regiment (7/180/16/182)
4/1st Italian Chasseur à Cheval Regiment (5/173/11/174)
Saxon Hussar Regiment (10/362/10/368)
Saxon Chevauleger Regiment (8/356/8/356)

3rd Light Cavalry Division: Général de division Chastel
1st Brigade: Général de brigade Vallin
6th Chasseur à Cheval Regiment (9/255/17/252)
25th Chasseur à Cheval Regiment (7/183/9/181)
6th Hussar Regiment (8/223/17/223)
8th Chasseur à Cheval Regiment (7/177/15/178)
Portuguese Legion Chasseur à Cheval Regt. (3/68/6/68)

2nd Brigade: Général de brigade Guyon
9th Chasseur à Cheval Regiment (4/110/9/109)
19th Chasseur à Cheval Regiment (0/5/0/6)
2nd Italian Chasseur à Cheval Regiment
3rd Italian Chasseur à Cheval Regiment
    Italian combined strength - (8/147/14/146 horses)
1st Chasseur à Cheval Regiment (5/167/10/170)
2nd Chasseur à Cheval Regiment (2/88/4/88)
3rd Chasseur à Cheval Regiment (2/69/4/72)

1st Cuirassier Division: Général de division Bordesoulle
1st Brigade: Général de brigade Berkheim
2nd Cuirassier Regiment (13/197/30/200)
3rd Cuirassier Regiment (12/187/28/188)
6th Cuirassier Regiment (5/90/10/90)

2nd Brigade: Général de brigade Quinette
9th Cuirassier Regiment (16/241/45/240)
llth Cuirassier Regiment (14/185/35/194)
12th Cuirassier Regiment (11/154/36/153)

3rd Brigade: Général de brigade Lessing
Saxon Leib Cuirassier Regiment (23/603/69/601)
Zastrow Cuirassier Regiment (17/389/52/406)

3rd Cuirassier Division: Général de division Doumerc
Brigade: Général de brigade d'Oudenarde
4th Cuirassier Regiment (8/113/19/113)
7th Cuirassier Regiment (4/68/9/66)
14th Cuirassier Regiment (1/35)2/35)
7th Dragoon Regiment (8/121/8/121)

Brigade: Général de brigade Reizet
23rd Dragoon Regiment (9/159/20/161)
28th Dragoon Regiment (7/128/18/128)
30th Dragoon Regiment (14/147/27/147)
Provisional Dragoon Regiment (4/65/9/67)
Staff/Italian Napoleon Dragoon Regiment (7/8/20/8)
1/Italian Napoleon Dragoon Regiment (5/195/12/195)
2/Italian Napoleon Dragoon Regiment (5/193/10/194)
3/Italian Napoleon Dragoon Regiment (6/203/14/201)
4/Italian Napoleon Dragoon Regiment (4/200/9/201)

Corps Artillery:

1/1st Horse Artillery (1/59)
1/1st (bis) Train Battalion (1/39)
1/6th Horse Artillery (3/81)
1/8th (bis) Train Battalion (1/52)
4th Italian Horse Artillery (3/97)
6th Italian Train Company (2/96)
3rd Saxon Horse Battery (4/91)
12-6pdrs & 6-24pdr howitzers
•The number of guns probably does not include Saxon guns. They should have consisted of 4–6pdrs and two howitzers.

H. Lachouque, The Anatomy of Glory. & Foucart, Bautzen (un bataille de deux jours) 20–21 Mai 1813 & Fabry, G., Journal des Operations des IIIe & Ve Corps en 1813, & French Army Archives, Château Vincennes V, VII, XI Corps Strength figures – Carton C2–540, 541, 543, 544. Guard Strength figures – Carton C2–537 & French National Archives II, IV, VII Corps Strengths – Carton AFVI*–1340

FRENCH III CORPS CASUALTIES AT THE BATTLE OF BAUTZEN 20/21 MAY 1813

III Corps:: Marechal Ney
8th Division: Général de division Souham
lst Brigade: Général de brigade Chasseraux
6th Provisional Légère Regiment
◊Numbers are officers dead, enlisted dead, officers wounded, enlisted wounded, officers captured, enlisted captured.
2/6th Légère Regiment (0/7/4/134/0/0)
3/25th Légère Regiment (1/8/1/103/0/0)
10th Provisional Légère Regiment
3/16th Légère Regiment (0/3/3/119/0/0)
1/28th Légère Regiment (0/6/4/190/0/0)
14th Provisional Line Regiment (1/90/10/300/0/30)
4/34th Line Regiment
3/40th Line Regiment
19th Provisional Line Regiment
6/32nd Line Regiment (1/14/1/120/0/0)
3/58th Line Regiment (0/8/2/75/0/0)

2nd Brigade:
21st Provisional Line Regiment (0/118/9/386/0/0)
3/59th Line Regiment
4/69th Line Regiment
24th Provisional Line Regiment (2/51/5/117/2/205)
3/88th Line Regiment
3/103rd Line Regiment
1/,3/,4/,6/22nd Line Regiment (6/102/13/628/0/135)

9th Division: Général de division Delmas
lst Brigade: Général de brigade Anthing
2nd Provisional Légère Regiment (1/16/7/265/2/1)
3/2nd Légère Regiment
3/4th Légère Regiment
1/29th Légère Regiment (0/0/9/0/1/497)
135th Line Regiment (2/22/11/466/1/0)

2nd Brigade:
138th Line Regiment (2/69/9/335/0/76)
145th Line Regiment (0/26/9/277/0/135)

10th Division: Général de division Albert
lst Brigade: Général de brigade Goris
4th Provisional Légère Regiment (0/37/4/271/0/0)
4/5th Légère Regiment
4/12th Légère Regiment
139th Line Regiment (0/1/4/39/0/3)

2nd Brigade: Général de brigade Van Dedem

140th Line Regiment (0/8/2/25/0/35)
141st Line Regiment (0/9/2/30/0/33)
llth Division: Général de division Ricard
lst Brigade: Général de brigade Tarayre
  3/,4/9th Légère Regiment (0/16/13/2520/147)
  17th Provisional Line Regiment (0/11/0/106/0/16)
    4/43rd Line Regiment
    3/75th Line Regiment
  18th Provisional Line Regiment (1/14/4/122/0/47)
    3/50th Line Regiment
    4/65th Line Regiment
2nd Brigade: Général de brigade Dumoulin
  142nd Line Regiment (1/23/3/205/0/175)
  144th Line Regiment (1/16/2/145/0/85)
39th Division: Général de division Marchand
Brigade: Généralmajor Stockhorn
  3rd Baden Line Regiment (unknown)
  lst Baden Line Regiment (unknown)
2nd Brigade: Généralmajor Prinz Emil von Hessen
  Hessian Fusilier Regiment (unknown)
  Hessian (Leib) du Corps Regiment (unknown)
  Hessian Leib-Garde Infantry Regiment
Cavalry Brigade: Général de brigade Laboissière
  10th Hussar Regiment (0/6/1/12/0/12)
  Baden Dragoon Regiment (0/1/1/1/0/0)
Corps Engineers:
  1/Spanish Sapper Battalion (9/4/0/6/0/15)
  2/Spanish Sapper Battalion (0/1/0/1/0/36)
  3/Spanish Sapper Battalion (unknown)
  4/Spanish Sapper Battalion (0/3/0/0/0/8)
  2/2nd French Sapper Battalion (0/0/0/1/0/0)
  3/5th French Sapper Battalion (0/0/0/0/0/0)
Artillery (3/21/8/117/0/19)

French Archives

Prusso-Russian Army 5 June 1813

Commander-in-Chief: General of Infantry
Barclay de Tolly
  Chief of Staff: Generallieutenant Sabaneiev
  General Quartermaster: Generalmajor Baron Diebitsch II
  General of the Day: Generalmajor Oldekop

Army of the Left Wing: General of Cavalry
Count Wittgenstein
Light Troops: Generalmajor Emanuel
Brigade: Generalmajor Illowaiski X
  Illowaiski #10 Don Cossack Regiment
  Koschkin Cossack Regiment
Brigade: Generalmajor Karov
  Gorin #1 Cossack Regiment
Brigade:
  Stavrapol Kalmuck Regiment
  Grekov #2 Cossack Regiment
  Karpov #2 Cossack Regiment
Brigade: Illowaiski X
  Illowaiski #4 Don Cossack Regiment
  Rabinov #2 Cossack Regiment
  Jagodin Cossack Regiment
Advanced Guard: Generalmajor Roth
Brigade: Generalmajor Vlassov
  23rd Jager Regiment
  24th Jager Regiment
Brigade:
  25th Jager Regiment

26th Jager Regiment
Other Forces:
  Kiev Dragoon Regiment
  New Russia Dragoon Regiment
  7th Jager Regiment
  30th Jager Regiment
  Tomsk Infantry Regiment
  Position Battery #34 (4 guns)
Corps: Generallieutenant Count St. Priest
8th Division: Generalmajor Urussov
  Schusselburg Infantry Regiment
  Archangle Infantry Regiment
  Old Ingermannland Infantry Regiment
  37th Jager Regiment
17th Division: Generalmajor Pillar
  Riazan Infantry Regiment
  Bieloserk Infantry Regiment
  Wilmanstrand Infantry Regiment
  Brest Infantry Regiment
  18th Jager Regiment
22nd Division: Generalmajor Turtshaninov
  Viatka Infantry Regiment
  Olonetz Infantry Regiment
  Staroskol Infantry Regiment
  45th Jager Regiment
  19th Jager Regiment
  Position Battery #32
  Horse Battery #6
1st Corps: Generallieutenant Count Gortchakov
5th Division: Generalmajor Lukov
  Perm Infantry Regiment
  Sievesk Infantry Regiment
  Mohilev Infantry Regiment
  Kalouga Infantry Regiment
  Grandduchess Catherine Battalion
llth Division: Generalmajor Count Urussov
  Polotsk Infantry Regiment
  Jeletz Infantry Regiment
  Rilsk Infantry Regiment
  Ekaterinburg Infantry Regiment
  1st Jager Regiment
  33rd Jager Regiment
  Kaporsk Infantry Regiment
14th Division: Generalmajor Helfreich
  Tenguinsk Infantry Regiment
  Estonia Infantry Regiment
  Position Battery #5
  Light Battery #27
2nd Corps: Generallieutenant Prince Wurttemberg
3rd Division: Generalmajor Count Schachafskoy
Brigade: Colonel Shilvinski
  Mourmansk Infantry Regiment
  Tchernigov Infantry Regiment
Brigade: Colonel Kapustin
  20th Jager Regiment
  21st Jager Regiment
4th Division: Generalmajor Pishinsky
Brigade: Colonel Treffurt
  Tobolsk Infantry Regiment
  Volhynie Infantry Regiment
  Krementchug Infantry Regiment
Brigade: Colonel Iavanov
  4th Jager Regiment
  34th Jager Regiment
7th Division: Generalmajor Tallisin
Brigade: Colonel Dietrich
  Pskof Infantry Regiment
  Sofia Infantry Regiment
  llth Jager Regiment

Artillery:
   Position Battery #3
   Light Battery #7
   Light Battery #13
Cavalry Corps: Generallieutenant Count Pahlen I
Brigade: Generalmajor Pantschulidfev
   Tchernigov Chasseur à Cheval Regiment
   Finland Dragoon Regiment
   Kargopol Dragoon Regiment
   Akhtyrsk Hussar Regiment
   Converged Light Cavalry Regiment
Brigade: Generalmajor Jusefovitch
   Loubny Hussar Regiment
   Karkov Dragoon Regiment
   Brigade: Generalmajor Rudinger
   Grodno Hussar Regiment
   1st Ukranian Cossack Regiment
   3rd Ukranian Cossack Regiment
Brigade: Generalmajor Gengross
   Mitau Dragoon Regiment
   Moscow Dragoon Regiment
Assigned to Headquarters:
   2nd Bug Cossack Regiment
   Command of Platov #4 Cossack Regiment
   Command of Jachontov Cossack Regiment
   Olonetz Opolochenie Battalion
   Vologna Opolochenie Battalion
   Ingremannland Dragoon Regiment
Corps: General of Infantry Count Langeron
Advanced Guard: Generalmajor Rudsevitch
Brigade: Illowaiski XII
   Illowaiski #12 Don Cossack Regiment
   Rebrejev #3 Cossack Regiment
   Grekov #8 Don Cossack Regiment
   Teptar Cossack Regiment
Brigade: Generalmajor Grekov VIII
   Kutainiov #8 Cossack Regiment
   Selivanov #2 Don Cossack Regiment
   Jsaev Cossack Regiment
   Zikelev Cossack Regiment
Brigade: Generalmajor Berdaev
   Tver Dragoon Regiment
   10th Jager Regiment
   38th Jager Regiment
   Horse Battery #2 (6 guns)
Reserve:
   Dorpat Dragoon Regiment
   12th Jager Regiment
   22nd Jager Regiment
   Light Battery #24 (6 guns)
   Light Battery #34
Corps: Generalmajor Udom
7th Division:
Brigade: Colonel Poltaratzky
   Nacheburg Infantry Regiment
   Riajsk Infantry Regiment
   Iakout Infantry Regiment
Brigade: Major Grimbladt
   10th Jager Regiment
   38th Jager Regiment
15th Division: Generalmajor Rudsevitch
Brigade: Colonel Tern
   Vitebsk Infantry Regiment
   Kozlov Infantry Regiment
Brigade: Lt. Colonel Anesur
   Kolyvan Infantry Regiment
   Kourin Infantry Regiment
Brigade: Major Kitaev
   12th Jager Regiment

   22nd Jager Regiment
Artillery:
   Light Battery #29
   Position Battery #34
   Position Battery #18
Corps: Generlmajor Count Scherbatov
7th Division:
Brigade: Colonel Anugstov
   Moscow Infantry Regiment
   Libau Infantry Regiment
   30th Jager Regiment
18th Division: Generalmajor Bernodassov
Brigade:
   Vladimir Infantry Regiment
   Dnieper Infantry Regiment
Brigade: Colonel Hendrich
   Kostroma Infantry Regiment
   Tambov Infantry Regiment
Brigade: Generalmajor Karnielov
   28th Jager Regiment
   32nd Jager Regiment
Artillery:
   Light Battery #15
   Light Battery #28
   Position Battery #35
Cavalry Corps: Generalmajor Count Pahlen II
Division: Generalmajor Liffanevitch
Brigade: Generalmajor Knorring
   Tchougouiev Uhlan Regiment
   Tartar Uhlan Regiment
   Lithuania Uhlan Regiment
   Jitomir Uhlan Regiment
Brigade:
   Olivopol Hussar Regiment
   Kinbourn Dragoon Regiment
   Sieversk Dragoon Regiment
   Lithuanian Chasseur à Cheval Regiment
   Horse Battery #8

ROYAL PRUSSIAN MAIN ARMY: GENERAL OF CAVALRY BLÜCHER
Advanced Guard: Generalmajor von Corswandt
   1/,2/,3/,4/Brandenburg Hussar Regiment (4)
   Brandenburg Hussar Regiment Freiwilliger Jager Det.
   2/1st East Prussian Infantry Regiment
   3/1st West Prussian Infantry Regiment
   Fus/2nd Silesian Infantry Regiment
   2nd Reserve/Leib Infantry Regiment
   1/,2/,3/,4/Neumärk Dragoon Regiment (4)
   Neumark Dragoon Regiment Freiwilliger Jager Det.
   Horse Battery #7 von Richter

1st Army Corps: Generallieutenant von Yorck
1st Brigade: Prince Karl von Mecklenburg-Strelitz
   1/1st East Prussian Infantry Regiment
   Fus/1st East Prussian Infantry Regiment
   Res/1st East Prussian Infantry Regiment
   1/, 2/, Fus/Colberg Infantry Regiment
   East Prussian Jäger Battalion (2 cos)
   3rd Battalion Trebnitz-Oels Landwehr
   Nimptsch-Schweidnitzer Landwehr Battalion
   1/,2/,3/,4/2nd Leib Hussar Regiment (4)
   2/1st East Prussian Infantry Regiment
2nd Brigade: Oberst von Horn
   3/, 4/Guard Jäger Battalion
   1/, 2/, Fus/Leib Infantry Regiment
   1st Res/Leib Infantry Regiment
   2nd Res/Leib Infantry Regiment (with advanced guard)

5th Res/Leib Infantry Regimenta
Ohlau Landwehr Battalion
Strehlen and Reichenbach Landwehr Battalion
Brandenburg Hussar Regiment (4)
Reserve Cavalry Brigade: Generalmajor von Corswandt
   1/,2/,3/,4/1st West Prussian Dragoon Regiment (4)
   1/,2/,3/,4/Lithuanian Dragoon Regiment (4)
   1/,2/,3/,4/West Prussian Uhlan Regiment (4)
   1/,3/Brandenburg Dragoon Regiment (2)
Artillery: Major von Fiebig
   Horse Battery #1 von Zinken
   Horse Battery #2 von Borowsky
   Horse Battery #3 Fischer
   6pdr Foot Battery #1 Heut
   6pdr Foot Battery #2 Lange
   6pdr Foot Battery #3 von Neander
   3pdr Foot Battery #1 Hertig
   1/2 12pdr Foot Battery #3 von Roszynski
   Park Columns (3)

Corps: Generallieutenant von Kleist

1st Brigade: Oberst und Flugel Adjutant Klüx
   1/,2/,3/,Fus/1st West Prussian Regiment
   1/,2/,3/,Fus/2nd West Prussian Regiment (3rd Bn
   detached to advanced guard)
   Silesian Schützen Battalion (2 cos)
   1/,2/,3/,4/2nd Silesian Hussar Regiment (4)
   1/,2/,3/,4/Brandenburg Uhlan Regiment (4)
   `6pdr Foot Battery #7
   6pdr Foot Battery #8
2nd Brigade: Generalmajor von Zeithen
   1/,2/,3/,Fus/1st Silesian Regiment
   1/,2/,3/,Fus/2nd Silesian Regiment
   Silesian Schützen Battalion (2 cos)
   1/,2/,3/,4/1st Silesian Hussar Regiment (4)
   1/,2/,3/,4/Silesian Uhlan Regiment (4)
   Provision Column
   6pdr Foot Battery #11
   6pdr Foot Battery #13 von Held
Reserve Infantry Brigade: Oberstlieutenant von Tippelskirch
   1/, 2/, Fus/Garde zu Fuss Regiment
   Normal Infantry Battalion
   1/,2/Guard Jäger Battalion
   Leib Grenadier Battalion
   West Prussian Grenadier Battalion
   Silesian Grenadier Battalion
   1st East Prussian Grenadier Battalion
   Guard 6pdr Foot Battery #4
   6pdr Foot Battery #9
   Silesian National Hussar Regiment
Reserve Cavalry Brigade: Generalmajor von Röder
   1/,2/,3/,4/Garde du Corps Regiment (+ Jäger Sqn)
   1/,2/,3/,4/Guard Light Cavalry Regiment (+2 Jäger Sqns)
   1/,2/,3/,4/East Prussian Cuirassier Regiment
   1/,2/,3/,4/Silesian Cuirassier Regiment
   1/,2/,3/,4/Brandenburg Cuirassier Regiment
   1/,2/,3/,4/Neumärk Dragoon Regiment
   Guard Horse Battery #4 von Willmann
   Horse Battery #10 Schaffer
   Provision Column
   Horse Depot
Artillery Reserve:
   Horse Battery #7 von Richter
   Horse Battery #8
   Horse Battery #9 von Tuchsen
   1/2 12pdr Foot Battery #3 von Schlemmer
   Park Column #7

Park Column #8
Park Column #9
Artisan Column

RESERVE ARMY: GRAND DUKE CONSTANTINE

3rd (or Grenadier) Corps: Generallieutenant Raevsky

1st Grenadier Division: Generalmajor Tchoglikov
Brigade: Colonel Kniachnin II
   Count Arakcheyev Grenadier Regiment
   Ekaterinoslav Grenadier Regiment
Brigade: Generalmajor Sulima
   Tauride Grenadier Regiment
   St. Petersburg Grenadier Regiment
Brigade: Colonel Jemelianov
   Pernau Infantry Regiment
   Kexholm Infantry Regiment
2nd Grenadier Division: Generalmajor Zwieleniev
Brigade: Colonel Pissarev
   Kiev Grenadier Regiment
   Moscow Grenadier Regiment
Brigade: Colonel Golovin
   Astrakhan Grenadier Regiment
   Fangoria Grenadier Regiment
Brigade: Colonel Hesse
   Siberia Grenadier Regiment
   Little Russia Grenadier Regiment
Artillery:
   Position Battery #33
   Position Battery #3
   Light Battery #14
   Light Battery #36

5th (or Guard) Corps: Generallieutenant Lavarov

1st Guard Infantry Division: Generalmajor Rosen
Brigade: Generalmajor Potemkin
   Preobragenski Guard Infantry Regiment
   Semenovski Guard Infantry Regiment
Brigade: Generalmajor Krapovitzky
   Ismailov Guard Infantry Regiment
   Guard Jager Infantry Regiment
   Guard Marine Equipage Battalion
2nd Guard Infantry Division: Generallieutenant Yermolov
Brigade: Generalmajor Udom II
   Finland Guard Infantry Regiment
   Lithuania Guard Infantry Regiment
Brigade: Generalmajor Scheltuchin II
   Leib-Guard Grenadier Regiment
   Pavlov Guard Grenadier Regiment
Artillery:
   Guard Position Battery #1
   Guard Position Battery #2
   Guard Light Battery #1
   Guard Light Battery #2
   Guard Marine Equipage Battery (2 guns)
1st Cuirassier Division: Generalmajor Depreradovitch
Brigade: Generalmajor Arseniev
   Chevalier Garde Regiment
   Horse Guard Regiment
Brigade: Generalmajor Baron Rosen
   Guard (formerly Emperor) Cuirassier Regiment
   Empress Cuirassier Regiment
2nd Cuirassier Division: Generalmajor Chretov
Brigade: Generalmajor Karatieov
   Astrakhan Cuirassier
   Ekaterinoslav Cuirassier
Brigade: Generalmajor Leontiev
   Gluchov Cuirassier
   Pskof Cuirassier
3rd Cuirassier Division: Generalmajor Duka

Brigade: Generalmajor Count Gudovitch
   Military Order Cuirassier
   Starodoub Cuirassier
Brigade:
   Little Russia Cuirassier
   Novgorod Cuirassier
Guard Light Cavalry Division: Generalmajor Chavitch
Brigade: Generalmajor Tchailikov
   Guard Hussar Regiment
   Guard Uhlan Regiment
Artillery: Generalmajor Kosen
   Guard Horse Battery #1
   Guard Horse Battery #2
Artillery Reserve:
   Position Battery #2
   Position Battery #7
   Position Battery #14
   Position Battery #30
   Light Battery #3
   Horse Battery #1
   Horse Battery #2
   Horse Battery #4
   Horse Battery #10
   Horse Battery #23

Corps of Generallieutenant Baron Sacken
Advanced Guard: Generalmajor Jurkovsky
Forward Posts: Generalmajor Lukovkin
   Don Cossack Regiment
   2nd Bashkir Regiment
   2nd Kalmuk Regiment
Brigade:
   St. Petersburg Opolochenie Cossack Regiment
   8th Jager Regiment
   39th Jager Regiment
   Light Battery #32
Brigade: Generalmajor Semenschenko
   Semenschenko Cossack Regiment
   Tcharnusubov IV Cossack Regiment
Brigade:
   4th Ukrainian Cossack Regiment
   Marioupol Hussar Regiment
   Horse Battery #18 (4 guns)
Corps: Generalmajor Count Lieven III
10th Division: Colonel Sass
   Jaroslav Infantry Regiment
   Kursk Infantry Regiment
   Crimea Infantry Regiment
   Bieloserk Infantry Regiment
16th Division: Generalmajor Bulatov
   Okhotsk Infantry Regiment
   Kamtchatka Infantry Regiment
   29th Jager Regiment
Artillery:
   Position Battery #10
   Position Battery #13
Corps: Generallieutenant Neverovski
27th Division: Colonel Stavitsky
   Odessa Infantry Regiment
   Tarnopol Infantry Regiment
   Vilna Infantry Regiment
   Simbrisk Infantry Regiment
   49th Jager Regiment
   50th Jager Regiment
   Position Battery #28
Cavalry: Generalmajor Lanskoy
   White Russia Hussar Regiment
   Alexandria Hussar Regiment
   Prendel Streifkorps

   Vladimir Uhlan Regiment
   Serpuchov Uhlan
   Smolensk Dragoon Regiment
   Kourland Dragoon Regiment
   Horse Battery #18
Prussian Corps: Generalmajor Schüler von Senden
Cavalry:
   Brandenburg Uhlan Regiment (4)
   Brandenburg Dragoon Regiment (2)
   Silesian Landjager (240 men)
   6pdr Foot Battery
Infantry:
   1 Res/, 2nd Res/1st West Prussian Infantry Regiment
   1 Res/, 2nd Res/2nd West Prussian Infantry Regiment
   1 Res/, 2nd Res/1st Silesian Infantry Regiment
   1 Res/, 2nd Res/2nd Silesian Infantry Regiment
   Thuringian Battalion
   1 Pioneer Company
Corps: Generallieutenant Baron Winzingerode
Advanced Posts: Generalmajor Illowaiski IV
   Rebrejev #2 Cossack Regiment
   Grekov Don Cossack Regiment
   1st Bug Cossack Regiment
   3rd Ural Cossack Regiment
Advanced Guard:
   Barbantchikov #2 Cossack Regiment
   Illowaiski #4 Don Cossack Regiment
   Pantelev Cossack Regiment
   4th Jager Regiment
   Light Battery #42

Corps in Lissa
   Elisabethgrad Hussar Regiment
   St. Petersburg Dragoon Regiment
Detachment from 24th Division: Generalmajor Lichatcheff
   Bourtirki Infantry Regiment
   Chirvan Infantry Regiment
   Oufa Infantry Regiment
   Position Battery #31
   Light Battery #42
Detachment : Oberst von Dobschutz
   5 Battalions of Lower Silesian Landwehr
Brigade: Oberst von Ploetz
   1st Silesian Landwehr Regiment (5)
Blockade Corps of Kustrin
   6 Battalions
   12 Guns
   2 Cossack Regiments

Corps: Generallieutenant von Bülow
Advanced Guard: Generalmajor von Borstell
Right Wing: Major von Cardell
   Cossack Regiment (1)
   Fus/1st Pommeranian Infantry Regiment
   3/Pommeranian Hussar Regiment
Center: Generalmajor von Thümen
   Cossack Regiment (2)
   2/1st Pommeranian Infantry Regiment
   1/Pommeranian Hussar Regiment
Left Wing: Major von Raden
   Cossack Regiment (2)
   Reserve Fusilier Battalion (1 co)
   4/Pommeranian Hussar Regiment
Detachment: Major von Mirbach
   Cossack Regiment (3)
   Reserve Fusilier Battalion (2 cos)
   Freiwilliger Jägers of Pommeranian Hussar Regiment

Index

L

M

N

R

S